**fourth
edition**

THERAPEUTIC PSYCHOLOGY

Fundamentals of Counseling and Psychotherapy

LAWRENCE M. BRAMMER
University of Washington

EVERETT L. SHOSTROM
Insitute of Actualizing Therapy

PRENTICE-HALL, INC., Englewood Cliffs, New Jersey   07632

Library of Congress Cataloging in Publication Data

BRAMMER, LAWRENCE M.
    Therapeutic psychology.

    Bibliography
    Includes index.
    1. Psychotherapy.   2. Counseling.
3. Self-actualization (Psychology)   I. Shostrom,
Everett L.   II. Title. [DNLM:
1. Counseling.   2. Psychotherapy. WM 420
B815t]
RC480.5.B7 1982   616.89'14   81-17804
ISBN 0-13-914614-8   AACR2

Editorial supervision and text design: Serena Hoffman
Cover: Wanda Lubelska Design
Manufacturing buyer: Edmund W. Leone

PRINTED IN THE UNITED STATES OF AMERICA

10   9   8   7   6

ISBN 0-13-914614-8

PRENTICE-HALL INTERNATIONAL, INC., *London*
PRENTICE-HALL OF AUSTRALIA PTY. LIMITED, *Sydney*
PRENTICE-HALL OF CANADA, LTD., *Toronto*
PRENTICE-HALL OF INDIA PRIVATE LIMITED, *New Delhi*
PRENTICE-HALL OF JAPAN, INC., *Tokyo*
PRENTICE-HALL OF SOUTHEAST ASIA PTE. LTD., *Singapore*
WHITEHALL BOOKS LIMITED, *Wellington, New Zealand*

Contents

PART II: TECHNIQUES

PART III: SPECIAL AREAS OF APPLICATION

12   Counseling and Psychotherapy with Couples and Families   347

Preface

The specialties of counseling and clinical psychology have been growing closer together. The authors of this text—one from university teaching and counseling and the other from private clinical practice—have worked together to produce this fourth edition. We have each contributed from our unique experience to this common approach to counseling and psychotherapy. This fourth edition attempts to reassess the current status, trends, and problems in research and practice of general counseling and psychotherapy with mildly disturbed people.

Professional acceptance of early editions of *Therapeutic Psychology* have convinced us that our developmental and creative synthesis approach to counseling issues is productive of research, discussion, and improved practice. The aims of this edition are to update the findings and expand such topics as counseling theory, values, and professional issues. Helping people to help themselves is a continuous theme. Our actualizing counseling point of view is evaluated in detail. It is presented as an illustrative model in our creative synthesis approach, which attempts to go beyond popular eclecticism.

People everywhere are concerned not only with living more comfortably with their life problems, but also with improving their human effectiveness and reaching their true potential. This demand puts counseling in a framework much broader than traditional solving of personal problems or planning educational and vocational futures. People want help with a broad range of philosophical concerns about the meaning and purpose of life, as well as with problem-solving skills. Mastery of their environment is important, but looking inward toward self-understanding and development is of increasing concern. Counseling and psychotherapy must meet these challenges.

The authors wish to thank their students and colleagues who have contributed criticisms and suggestions for this revision. We are grateful for the criticism provided by the following reviewers: Jerry L. Davis, University of Wisconsin at Milwaukee; Bianca Bernstein, Wayne State University; and Elizabeth Reynolds Welfel, Boston College. We are also grateful to the large number of dedicated people in research and practice of counseling and psychotherapy who put their findings and thoughts on the pages of technical journals and papers. We wish to acknowledge with special gratitude the generous permission of Robert Knapp, President of Educational and Industrial Testing Service, to quote extensively from *Actualizing Therapy*. George Lockwood has been particularly helpful in developing the ideas in several chapters on actualizing theory and testing. We also thank Ms. Sharon Roberts for her careful preparation of the manuscript.

LAWRENCE M. BRAMMER
EVERETT L. SHOSTROM

I

FOUNDATIONS

1

Professional Counseling and Psychotherapy

INTRODUCTION

The helping functions of counseling and psychotherapy offer great challenges, rewards, and opportunities to persons interested in helping their fellow human beings. Help is defined as providing conditions for people to fulfill their needs for security, love and respect, self-esteem, decisive action, and self-actualizing growth; help also means providing resources and skills that enable people to help themselves. Professional helpers offer their services under the specified conditions described in this book.

Professionals not only avoid deluding themselves that they can be all things to all people, but they are also aware of their limitations and needs to be helpful. They can see when help becomes control, and when they need clients to fulfill their own needs for love, power, or prestige. Counselors need rewards for their efforts, however; seeing clients become self-sufficient, realize their hidden potentials, and function at higher levels of effective living are such rewards.

In addition to describing the fundamental techniques of counseling and psychotherapy, this volume presents historical foundations, personality theory, professional issues, and special adaptations necessary for the practice of counseling and psychotherapy in various settings: schools, colleges, agencies, churches, industries, and clinical practice.

Chapter 1 covers origins of the counseling and psychotherapeutic emphases in psychology, present status and trends, and pressing professional problems in practice. Since counselors and psychotherapists are concerned with facilitating personality changes in their clients, an introductory discussion of the significance of theory, varied approaches, and brief descriptions of views on the nature and functioning of personality are included in Chapter 2. Principles of personality growth with the special problems of each stage from birth to old age are discussed in Chapter 3, and an overview of the nature of the counseling and psychotherapeutic processes is presented in Chapter 4.

The principal purposes of Part I are to promote broad understandings of professional problems and to prepare the reader with personality theory and concepts about the development of human personality for the technique discussions in Parts II and III. Part I contains four unique key terms. The first, and the title of this book, *therapeutic psychology,* encompasses much of the accumulated wisdom of the helping professions. *Creative synthesis* is our term for efforts to develop a comprehensive dynamic outlook on personality structure and change as a basis for counseling practice. *Multidimensional* refers to the varied modalities of theory underlying the helping process—philosophical, structural, functional, developmental, and research. *Actualizing counseling and psychotherapy* is our illustrative understanding and action approach described in Chapter 3.

Part II includes the "how to do it" aspect of counseling and psychotherapy. Beginning with Chapter 5 on preparing a client for the counseling experience, important points of technique are described in Chapters 6 through 8. These chapters are concerned with the nature of the counseling relationship, how it is established and maintained, and which factors create problems for the counselor. In Chapters 9 through 11, important techniques of interpretation, appraisal, information giving, and group methods are described and illustrated. A basic assumption underlying Part II is that psychotherapeutic attitudes and skills are learned, not endowed. Hence, effective counseling methods can be acquired with conscientious study, practice, and evaluation. It is intended that readers, whatever their professional setting, will be able to choose those techniques which have particular application to their specialties and institutional roles.

Part III covers applications of techniques to problems of intimate partnerships, family life, religion, intellectual functioning, and choice of future life style. The purpose of Part III is to present some of the problems and methods, unique materials, and adaptations of general theory and technique required in several counseling specializations.

The overview of this volume will help the reader to understand the title of the book, *Therapeutic Psychology.* Much material has been included that is not technique, but rather knowledge and values considered necessary to the professional background of a counselor or psychotherapist. Although we do not assume that this material represents *all* that should be known for competence in this field, we hope that the student in training and the practitioner already at work will find this volume a useful description of how counseling skill is developed and applied.

THERAPEUTIC PSYCHOLOGY

Therapeutic psychology represents a body of knowledge that gathers its data from a number of related professions. All embody the helping function. In psychology, the clinical specialty, with its traditional emphasis on diagnostic evaluation, concentrates more on psychotherapy and counseling. Counseling psychology incorporates traditional counseling and assessment in education, industry, mental health, and rehabilitation with newer emphases on achieving self-actualization and improving human effectiveness. School psychology is a third division of applied psychology where counseling and psychotherapy are being utilized increasingly. Psychiatry has contributed greatly to the concepts and techniques currently employed in the helping process. The field of social work has also given us a rich heritage of casework and interviewing skills. Pastoral counseling by ministers is one of the traditional helping areas which has contributed much to therapeutic psychology in the realm of values clarification and choosing life styles. Community psychology is a growing field which also applies counseling and psychotherapy methods to varied institutional settings such as clinics, prisons, homes for the elderly, and drug treatment centers.

The establishment of a formal area of therapeutic psychology that incorporates contributions from many helping professions is a natural phenomenon. For many years psychology has collaborated with other professions in contributing its unique approaches to understanding human behavior. In order to succeed in counseling and psychotherapeutic efforts, it is necessary that counseling and clinical psychologists recognize and utilize the understandings of all the established helping professions in addition to capitalizing on the unique findings of their own science. Figure 1 illustrates the unique contributions as well as the interrelationship among disciplines which contribute to the viewpoints of this volume.

The study of therapeutic psychology, then, has four broad purposes: (1) to create an appreciation of the scope and depth of learning necessary for competency as a skilled counselor and psychotherapist; (2) to develop an understanding of relevant knowledge from behavioral sciences; (3) to develop competencies for the various specialties in counseling and psychotherapy; and (4) to understand research results and needs.

Since therapeutic psychology embraces both counseling and psychotherapy, it is necessary to comment on the similarities and differences. The authors of this book are a counseling psychologist with experience in college, school, and agency settings and a clinical psychologist experienced in community agency and private-practice settings. We bring to-

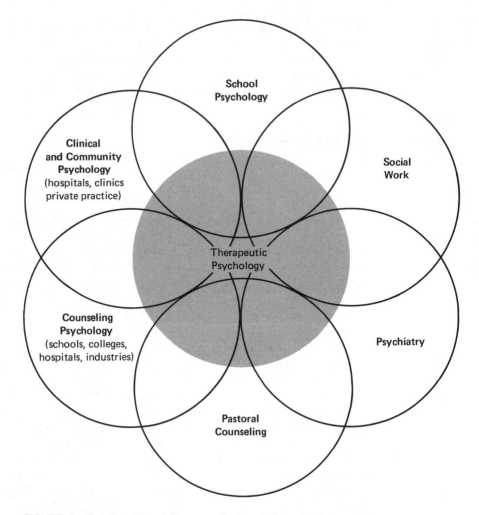

FIGURE 1. Relationship of Therapeutic Psychology to Selected Helping Professions

gether viewpoints from our respective areas of experience to create a body of knowledge which overlaps and contributes to both counseling and psychotherapy. The result, entitled *Therapeutic Psychology,* may be defined as the body of understandings, values, research, and skills common to both counseling and psychotherapy. The substance of therapeutic psychology comes from several helping professions and is rooted in applied behavioral sciences.

Figure 2 illustrates the scope of therapeutic psychology. Counseling and psychotherapy are viewed as overlapping areas of professional competence. Historically, counseling has been characterized by the following words: educational, vocational, supportive, situational, problem solving, conscious awareness, normal, present time, and short term. Psychotherapy has been described with terms such as supportive (in a crisis setting), recon-

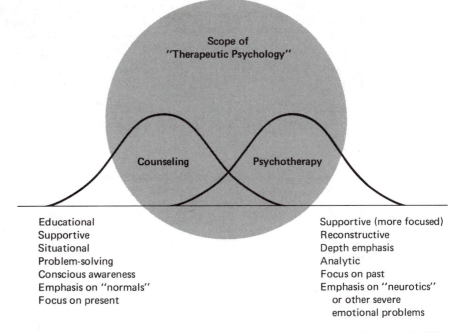

Scope of
"Therapeutic Psychology"

Counseling   Psychotherapy

Educational   Supportive (more focused)
Supportive   Reconstructive
Situational   Depth emphasis
Problem-solving   Analytic
Conscious awareness   Focus on past
Emphasis on "normals"   Emphasis on "neurotics"
Focus on present   or other severe
                                 emotional problems

FIGURE 2. *The Scope of Counseling and Psychotherapy within the Framework of Therapeutic Psychology*

structive, depth emphasis, analytical, focus on the past, emphasis on "neurotics" or other severe emotional problems, and long term. In current usage, however, counseling and psychotherapy are used interchangeably. In the remainder of this volume we will use either term to encompass the other, unless otherwise stated.

We believe that most professionals would endorse the two lists in Figure 2 that characterize the extreme ends of the counseling-psychotherapeutic continuum. An exception is the trend toward work with psychotic people on an out-patient basis in community clinics. Therapists in Veterans Administration Centers or mental hygiene clinics, for example, would call this psychotherapy, but they would also emphasize its supportive rather than personality-change features. Most people probably would not call this intensive type of activity counseling, however.

Blos (1946) and Pepinsky and Pepinsky (1954) state that counseling deals with relatively nonembedded problem cases, that is, with those persons who have not developed rigid neurotic patterns, but are primarily victims of pressures from the outside environment. Thorne (1950), a psychologist and a psychiatrist, describes counseling as a type of psychotherapy adaptable to problems of normal people. Robinson (1950) contributes a useful concept to the definition of counseling, which he describes as aiding normal people to achieve higher level adjustment skills. These changes are manifested as increased maturity, independence, personal integration, and responsibility. The phrase *increasing human effectiveness* is used frequently to describe the goal of counseling (Brayfield 1961; Blocher 1966; Gordon 1971). Ivey and Simek-Downing (1980) summarize the main goals of counseling as helping the person to develop "intentionality" and "cultural expertise." This means that the client has a sense of purpose and the capability to generate a flexible and active approach to problems. Clients must learn to communicate well within their own cultures and to act on the existing possibilities. This description of counseling goals implies that counselors must have these qualities also, especially the ability to communicate well across diverse cultural groups to help clients who are from cultures different from their own.

Although attempts to formulate precise inclusive definitions of *counseling* have been difficult, Gustad (1957) marshaled the historical definitions into three categories: *participants,* generally two in number and with specified professional roles or affiliations, such as teachers, ministers, or psychologists; *goals,* in terms of improved adjustment or higher functioning; and definitions stressing *learning outcomes,* such as improved social skills.

Gustad, from his survey, suggested a composite definition of *counseling* which includes three key elements:

Counseling is a learning-oriented process, carried on in a simple, one-to-one social environment, in which a counselor, professionally competent in relevant psychological skills and knowledge, seeks to assist the client by methods appropriate to the latter's needs . . . to learn more about himself, to learn how to put such understanding into effect in relation to more clearly perceived, realistically defined goals to the end that the client may become a happier and more productive member of his society. (1957, p. 17)

Counseling, therefore, stresses more rational planning, problem solving, decision making, intentionality, prevention of severe adjustment problems, and support for situational pressures arising in the everyday lives of normal people. Counseling, consequently, is shorter in duration than psychotherapy and is defined by what professional counselors do—their roles and matching competencies.

Psychotherapy, in contrast, is defined as more inclusive reeducation of the individual. The basic aims of psychotherapy are to gain perceptual clarity and change, to integrate insights into everyday behavior, and to cope with intense feelings originating in past hurtful experiences. Existing defenses are modified so that readjustment is obtained. Thus psychotherapy emphasizes intensity and length of involvement and is more concerned with alleviating severe problems in living.

To many clinicians distinctions between psychotherapy and counseling appear to be primarily quantitative rather than qualitative in nature. We have chosen for the purposes of this book to use the terms counselor, psychotherapist, clinician, psychological counselor, psychotherapeutic counselor, and psychologist interchangeably in the broad areas of overlap. Yet we recognize that there are some differences in usage of the terms.

Wherever possible, distinctions will be made in those areas judged to be primarily the concern of either counseling or psychotherapy.

Another approach to differentiating forms of therapeutic help is to look at traditional professional roles and responsibilities. Figure 3 shows the great overlap that exists between psychology and psychiatry, as well as some of the unique functions of medical therapists on the extreme left and of psychologists and counselors on the extreme right. The reeducative or psychotherapeutic functions shared by both groups are listed in the middle with factors to be considered in determining responsibility for psychotherapy.

There are psychiatrists who claim that all psychotherapy is medicine and would crowd counselors and clinical psychologists to the extreme right of Figure 3. Some psychologists and educators would do the same for physicians. We feel there are logical and practical reasons for sharing responsibility in psychotherapy, especially in the growing emphasis upon holistic health and the prevention of disease through life styles. The answer, in our opinion, lies in making carefully defined distinctions around the

Psychiatry and Neurology (Medicine)		Counseling-Clinical (Psychology)
Treatment of severe neuroses or psychoses, involving, for example:	*Psychotherapy or re-education*	*Planning and problem solution, involving, for example:*
	Criteria applied to determine the locus of responsibility in a medical or psychological therapist	
Psychosurgery		Diagnostic and predictive psychological tests
Electro-shock		Informational resources
Narcosynthesis	*Therapist factors:*	Interpretation of data
Tranquilizers		
Sedatives	Amount of training in psychotherapy	*Learning difficulties, involving:*
Hormones	Experience in psychotherapy	
Insulin shock	Diagnostic skill and knowledge of psychotherapy	Remedial techniques
Vitamins		Diagnostic psychological tests
	Amount of therapeutic responsibility delegated by the institution	
	Type of institutional setting (hospital or school)	*Feeling problems, including:*
	Legal restrictions	Working through situational anxiety, hostility, ambivalence, and their nonincapacitating, nonimbedded symptoms
	Patient or client factors:	Case studies and descriptions of personality functioning through use of psychometric tests
	Depth of involvement in the personality	
	Rigidity of defense structure	
	Strength of the ego and other personality resources	
	Somatic involvement	
	Incapacitating nature of the symptoms	
	Nature of the therapeutic goal	

FIGURE 3. *Therapy Continuum between Medicine and Psychology*

middle transitional area of Figure 3. The criteria of depth, training, experience, responsibility, and institutional setting should determine who does psychotherapy and to what degree.

This introductory chapter deals with seven trends in the practice of therapeutic psychology: (1) insistence on accountability and competency; (2) professionalization and deprofessionalization; (3) dual emphases on the personal characteristics of the counselor combined with helping skills; (4) use of behavioral science data and research methods in the solution of human problems; (5) use of group counseling and contributions from the human potential movement; (6) the emergence of unifying constructs to reconcile conflicting viewpoints and to explain the process of change; and (7) broadening goals and wider applications of counseling, especially in self-help and peer-help programs.

TREND I: ACCOUNTABILITY AND COMPETENCY

The prevalence of the term *accountability* is indicative of the concern of professional helpers, their clients, and their agencies about responsibility and productivity. Counselors recognize the necessity to strive for improved competency, evaluation of expected outcomes, and cost effectiveness. When agencies tighten their budgets on human services, we are pressed harder than ever to show that our efforts help clients and agencies reach their goals efficiently as well as effectively. Increasingly, counselor training programs are incorporating a competency approach. This emphasis on counselor performance is characterized by describing counselor behavior in terms of specific competencies, assessing candidates before training to establish baseline achievement, prescribing training events to achieve minimum performance on prescribed competencies, and assessing results at the end of training to ascertain achievement of minimum performance.

Therapeutic psychology has its roots in many disciplines. The following historical sketch covers the development of therapeutic psychology as a responsible service and illustrates how each field is related to therapeutic psychology.

*Counseling
Psychology*

Counseling psychology is a synthesis of many related trends found in the guidance, mental hygiene, psychometrics, social casework, and psychotherapy movements. A counseling psychologist assumes that it is *people,* not problems, that need help through counseling. Fractionation of the personality into problem areas, such as vocational, marital, or reading, is largely a phenomenon of the past. Holistic is the current password.

Counseling psychology is at a point comparable to that of medicine at the turn of the century. Sir William Osler at that time took the medical "tower of Babel" and formulated an eclectic system of scientific medical practice from the many diffuse and conflicting therapies. *Counseling psychologist* has been an occupational title of the Veterans Administration for many years (Moore and Bouthilet 1952; Super 1955). Private and collegiate counseling centers have counseling psychologists on their staffs. Some schools and rehabilitation centers use this title also. Yamamoto (1963) surveyed the characteristics of over one thousand members of the Division on Counseling Psychology of the American Psychological Association. The results suggested that counseling psychology had grown into a psychological specialty with unique roles and functions.

Counseling psychology seems to be moving closer to clinical psychology as this latter specialty concerns itself more with personal assets and less with behavior pathology. Training programs often use the title *professional-scientific* to blur the distinctions further. A new professional emphasis, such as community counselor or psychologist, may absorb both clinical and counseling psychology.

On the other hand, there are indications that counseling psychology is alive and well with its own specialized standards (APA 1978) and strong task groups to redefine counseling psychology (APA, Division 17, 1980). The outlook generally appears optimistic about the continuing need for counseling psychologists. Their flexible open approach to meeting client needs in a variety of settings, and their emphasis upon improving client functioning and personal decision-making skills, are needed in the current climate of preoccupation with mental illness and irresponsible behavior. Primary prevention of mental health problems is a key function of the counseling psychologist. Kagan called the counseling psychologist "mental health's primary care worker" (Kagan 1977). Current American and Canadian health policy, as reflected through government agencies, stresses the prevention of mental and physical illness. Counseling psychologists are in the front of this crusade for promotion of healthful living.

The vitality of a profession must be judged also on how it deals with issues of social justice and equality. The Division of Counseling Psychology as well as the American Psychological Association have had active task groups working on women's issues and minority concerns. Position papers such as "Cross-Cultural Counseling Competencies" (Sue 1981) and the comprehensive study by Hill, Tanney, Leonard, and Reiss (1977) of counselor reactions to age and types of problems of female clients are examples of such research.

Counseling psychologists have taken a strong lead in developing counseling programs for women. Three special issues of *The Counseling Psychologist* (1973, 1976, 1979) have been devoted exclusively to counseling women. The APA Division 17 Committee on Women developed a set of thirteen basic "Principles Concerning the Counseling and Therapy of Women" (1979) that were endorsed by the entire membership of counseling psychologists. A task force of the same committee produced a special report on "Models of Training Counselors of Women" (Johnson and Richardson 1981). This report deals with the special problems created when the majority of consumers of counseling and therapy services are women and the majority of service providers are men. The report points up the need to reduce male bias and raise the consciousness of male counselors about the special concerns of women.

Largely as a result of a conference of psychologists at Northwestern

University in 1951, the American Psychological Association (APA) changed the designation of Division 17 from Counseling and Guidance to Counseling Psychology in recognition of the growing discreteness of the counseling branch of psychology (Super 1955). Similarly, the American Board of Examiners in Professional Psychology conducts certification proceedings for counseling psychologists as one of its four areas of specialization.

The 1964 Greyston Conference (1964) of psychologists interested in counselor education reconsidered the status and future preparation of counseling psychologists. The consensus of the conferees was that counseling psychology is one significant answer to the increasing social need for varied counseling services.

The Vail Conference, held in 1974, sought to examine the current trends and futures of applied psychology (1975). A key conclusion was the need for counselors and psychotherapists to be more aware of racial-cultural differences between practitioners and clients and the necessity to develop more practitioners from minority groups. A second element in changing roles was the need for counselors to become aware not only of social problems and injustices, but also skilled in community change and client advocacy. It appears that counseling psychology is moving more toward the concept of community psychology with its dual focus on facilitating human development and community change to make human potentials more realizable.

Hence, a growing body of terminology and usage supports the contention that counseling psychology is a full professional endeavor, but that it must revise roles constantly and encourage competencies in community change. The APA's Division on Counseling Psychology is working continuously on defining counseling psychology and roles for counseling psychologists (APA, Division 17, 1980). Fretz and Whiteley (1980) have documented this process and predict a productive future for counseling psychology.

Other occupational designations for counselors have been made. It is quite apparent that the term *counselor* must be preceded by an adjective to be meaningful, since so many persons with differing skill levels claim to do "counseling." Other terms have been suggested to describe the psychological counseling function—general clinical counselor (Hahn 1950), psychological counselor (Bordin 1955; Tyler 1969), psychotherapeutic counselor (Porter 1950), community counselor (Lewis and Lewis 1976), and psychosocial educator (Ivey 1977). Employment Service Counselor is another type of counseling psychologist serving persons in the throes of career or job changes.

*Clinical
Psychology*

Clinical psychology grew largely out of intelligence testing efforts from 1912 to 1930. Clinical psychology and counseling psychology have much in common, since both use case study methods, evaluation instruments, and psychotherapeutic interviewing techniques. There are, nevertheless, significant historical and functional distinctions. After studying historical differentiations between counseling and clinical psychology at length, Gustad (1953) concluded that counseling and clinical psychology are essentially the same general endeavor, but that they have differing emphases. This is also the view of contemporary psychologists.

Clinical psychologists' skills in assisting with diagnostic evaluation of psychotic people and their consequent unique role on a clinical or hospital team is another major distinction. As Super (1955) has pointed out, counseling is more concerned with the *hygiology* than the *psychopathology* of behavior. Hygiology is the study of problems in normal people and the prevention of serious emotional difficulties. Clinical psychologists, on the other hand, are found mainly in hospitals and clinics where severe behavior disorders are treated.

Institutional settings for counseling or therapy determine other distinctions between counselors and clinicians. As Williamson (1947) has suggested, therapeutic counseling takes its place naturally in the educational setting where the school assumes its societal function of learning and personality development. Clinical psychologists, however, are found in hospitals, clinics, and, increasingly, in private practice. Some counseling psychologists are found in hospitals and many are in private practice (Moore and Bouthilet 1952); but educational settings attract counseling psychologists interested primarily in maturational problems of school- and college-age youth. On the other hand, clinical psychologists in private or agency practice work with marital, rehabilitation, geriatric, and parental problems of essentially normal people in nonschool relationships.

Clinical psychology has had its periodic training and role-definition conferences similar to those of counseling psychology. Boulder, Miami, Chicago, and Vail have been locations for crucial conferences of leaders in the education of clinicians. These conferences have reflected a growing shift from almost exclusive concern about responsibility to the individual client to a much more widespread concern about responsibility to the broader community and public interest. Clinical psychology has specialty standards comparable to those of counseling psychology and credentialing programs for practitioners similar to those of counseling psychologists.

Psychiatry, a third psychotherapeutic counseling specialty, is difficult to distinguish functionally from other counseling specialties. The obvious distinction is one of differential training—the psychiatrist having an M.D. degree and the psychologist generally having a Ph.D. Medical therapies used in the treatment of severe emotional conditions contribute other clear distinctions. Prescription of drugs, for example, can be done only by psychiatrists.

Counselors and psychotherapists cannot escape the reality of medical responsibility. The physician has legal responsibility for care, having life or death implications for the individual. From one point of view, this concept embraces all of life's activities. From another view, the psychiatrically trained physician's responsibility covers psychotherapy mainly to the point where the problem becomes one of ignorance or learning rather than one of illness. Mowrer offers a useful distinction between the psychologist's and the psychiatrist's view of psychotherapy:

Personality disorders are from one point of view no more disease than ignorance is a disease. Both prominently involve the phenomenon of learning. And if, as educators, we have any business working with the ignorant mind, we also have a right and an obligation to be interested in the confused, disordered mind. (1951, p. 21)

Fine distinctions between ignorance and illness, however, become very vague in practice. Szasz (1960) has created considerable controversy with his emphasis upon severe emotional problems as disorders of learning and perception rather than illness in the traditional medical meaning. Szasz, a physician, certainly recognizes that there are brain diseases which affect behavior profoundly. He objects to the mental illness idea that all disorders of thought and feeling are related to some neurological defect. Problems of living, from this viewpoint, are reduced to a biochemical process which will be discovered ultimately. Such difficulties in everyday living, or differences in belief or value causing personal problems, are then by definition "mental illnesses" because they differ little from analogous bodily disease. Szasz argues that this view is erroneous because it confuses a *defect* correlated with a lesion in the central nervous system with a *belief,* a learned behavior. Szasz also emphasizes the role of social value norms in making judgments about who is deviant or "sick."

Finally, the concept of *personal responsibility* for one's behavior enters this controversy. If people believe they cannot function because they are "sick," they relieve themselves of responsibility for their behavior. If they believe, on the other hand, that their beliefs and choices determine their behavior, then they carry the awesome burden of responsibility for their actions. The relationship of personal attitudes to physical illness, while controversial, is illustrative of the role of personal responsibility. The Simontons (1978), for example, cite the role of psychological methods in the treatment and prevention of cancer. Cousins's personal document on how he took responsibility for dealing successfully with his illness, diagnosed as terminal, is indicative of the power of psychological methods (1979). This issue of personal responsibility is critical in dealing with criminal behavior also.

Perls (1969), also a psychiatrist, expresses his disillusionment with the medical model of sickness or wellness. Perls emphasizes the person who has experienced problems of living and uses self-defeating manipulative patterns. Similarly, Glasser (1965), who is also medically trained, stresses the therapist's role of teaching clients more responsible and self-fulfilling behavior. He emphasizes how this learning approach is incompatible with a conventional conception of mental illness.

Psychotherapeutic counseling involves helping the individual whose learning is incomplete or who has more or less conscious conflicts that have as their accompaniment so-called normal anxiety. This, of course, places a severe burden on the counselor to distinguish "normal" from "pathological," but this recognition of pathology and therapeutic limitations has become part of the psychologist's professional training. It is important for any professional group to realize that it cannot be all things to all people and to practice only in its areas of demonstrated competence.

Psychiatric
Social Work

Psychiatric social work, a fourth counseling specialty, also is difficult to distinguish from psychology in terms of psychotherapeutic function. Many practitioners of this professional group, especially those in private practice, feel they are doing psychotherapy in the formal sense. One principal difference, however, is the training route. Social workers generally complete a two-year graduate program, including a year of supervised agency work, leading to a master's degree in social work. Clinical social workers function, as do clinical psychologists, on health-care teams, although many go into private practice. In clinics they specialize in the intake process, deal with other agencies, work with families, and collect psychiatric histories. Social workers, by tradition and training, have had responsibilities in family counseling services, although they perform counseling roles in many types of community agencies.

School
Counseling

A fifth counseling specialty, educational counseling, differs from other specialties largely on the basis of breadth of training and experience required. School counselors deal with a wide variety of educational problems close to the areas of teaching and administration, in addition to working with the personal counseling problems of children and adolescents.

Levels of service is a significant concept in school counseling. Three general counseling levels are identifiable on the basis of differences in training, competence, and counseling time. These are functional levels, not status differentials. On the first level is the educational counselor whose professional roots are mostly in teaching and who may be doing part-time counseling largely of the educational planning type. This counselor primarily gives information and suggestions. The counselors on this level are frequently called "advisers."

At the second level is the counselor whose professional affiliation is primarily in education and who generally has a masters degree or special training in counseling. This counselor deals with the majority of school counseling problems, ranging from giving simple information on college requirements, through vocational planning and social conduct, to dealing with the more emotionally involved problems concerned with maturation. School counselors suffer from a severe identity problem, since the historical educational guidance model does not meet their needs. Since school counseling deals with the kinds of developmental problems described under counseling psychology, it appears that this model holds hope for the school counseling specialist. The American School Counselors' Association, a component of the American Personnel and Guidance Association, developed a statement on policy and guidelines for implementation of this policy on roles and functions of school counselors (1963).

The counselor on the third level is the counseling or clinical psychologist, described earlier in this chapter. School or college counselors on this level generally have experience in educational positions; but their primary graduate professional education has been psychology, psychiatric social work, or medicine.

Psychosocial Nursing

Psychosocial nursing, sometimes designated psychiatric nursing, is a health-care specialty with a strong clinical counseling component. Special areas of counseling focus are death and dying, stress management, life-style change, family counseling, and geriatrics. While working mainly in health-care agencies, many persons trained in this specialty go into private counseling practice.

Pastoral Psychology

Ministers have been counseling for years. Not until recently, however, has there been an emphasis on clinical training for the clergy to do psychological counseling. Increasingly, seminarians are taking clinical internships in counseling agencies. Many churches offer extensive counseling on marriage, divorce, widowhood, drug abuse, and family problems in line with their traditional community helping services. The American Association of Pastoral Counseling has procedures for certifying individuals on the basis of their clinical and behavioral science education plus supervised clinical training leading to fellow and diplomate status. In addition, the association has an accrediting process for preparation programs. In Chapter 14 we describe more completely some of the specialized concerns with which all secular and religious counselors must come to grips as they deal with clients on moral and spiritual value problems.

Marriage and Family Counseling

While general counseling and clinical psychologists work with couples and families extensively, a specialty has emerged with is own professional organizations, journals, and state licensing, as in California. Family counselors come from many of the human service professions mentioned in these pages. In addition to their basic professional affiliation these counselors often belong to the American Association for Marriage and Family Therapy. This association has an elaborate process for certifying individuals for clinical membership and an accrediting procedure for preparation programs. More of their functions will be described in Chapter 12.

Rehabilitation and Employment Counselors

With considerable national emphasis on solutions to problems of handicapped and underprivileged citizens, counseling has become a central helping function. Vocational rehabilitation counselors, working in state rehabilitation offices, hospitals, and private agencies with the physically and emotionally handicapped, have had their functions increased by law to include mentally, socially, and economically handicapped clients. Rehabilitation counseling services may become the wave of the future for massive nonschool counseling services, since 10 percent of the American population is handicapped in some way.

In similar fashion, recent labor and economic opportunity legislation has created expanded roles for employment counselors, who traditionally have been concerned primarily with placement problems. With fast-changing economic conditions, many persons need counseling connected with retraining and upgrading of job skills, and planning for retirement. Inflationary pressures mean people will be working well beyond usual retirement age and often in new careers. Agencies such as state employment services, government service programs, halfway houses, drug and alcohol treatment centers, and crisis clinics employ counselors to perform a wide range of counseling tasks.

TREND II: PROFESSIONALIZATION AND DEPROFESSIONALIZATION

The current professional scene contains many paradoxes. One relating to professionalization is the widespread effort to train various kinds of helpers in more specialized services, for which increasingly larger fees are charged. One consequence is the growing dependence on experts. Another is the formalizing of the helping process, even in law, so that helping and being helped, instead of being normal human functions, are ritualized into elaborate specialties. While few persons deny the need for behavior change specialists, many feel society has gone too far in formalizing the helping function and take the view that we should deprofessionalize counseling and give psychology away. We believe that a key function of professional counselors and psychotherapists is to serve as trainers of others in helping skills, such that a vast multiplier effect is put into motion to make helping skills widely available in the population.

As indicated earlier, many professional groups use counseling and psychotherapeutic techniques. Conflicts among psychologists who view themselves as *either* scientists *or* professional practitioners have been strong for forty years. Pepinsky and Pepinsky (1954) face this conflict neatly in their concept of the "scientist-practitioner," in which the counselor or psychotherapist is a scientist primarily, using the methods of hypothetico-deductive thinking, and a practitioner secondarily. This view is stressed because of the undeveloped state of psychological knowledge and its application to counseling.

The following important characteristics of a profession are discussed below: (1) socially useful services which individuals cannot render to themselves; (2) skills and procedures; (3) sequences and standards of training (including selection procedures); (4) professional societies and journals dedicated to advancement of the profession and its basic scientific foundations; (5) planned research programs; (6) certification and licensing; (7) a code of ethics; (8) working relationships with other professions; and (9) professional freedom.

The development of these characteristics is made from the viewpoint of the psychological practitioner. Variations will be found in the psychotherapeutic training of psychiatrists, social workers, and clergymen. The following material on training, certification, publications, and organizations is cited to illustrate the broad developments in the psychological fields. These developments are also included as a sobering reminder that reading this book and special skills training will not make a psychotherapist or counselor out of the reader. Extensive background and professional development are needed for such a complex human service.

Socially Useful
Services

The first and most important value of psychotherapeutic counseling is its usefulness in helping *individuals* with problems. The military forces utilized psychological personnel extensively during World War II. The programs of the Veterans Administration are testimony to public acceptance of counseling over the past thirty years. Public marriage and mental hygiene clinics and rehabilitation centers, as well as school and college counseling centers, are further evidence that not only are such services requested, but also that clients are satisfied that the services are effective in helping them achieve their goals. Growth centers emerging from the human potential movement utilize many counseling styles and methods.

Another socially useful service which psychotherapeutic counseling performs is that of *discovering and developing human talent.* There is talent in all segments of our social structure. Finding the talented and appraising educational need and opportunity have been special functions of counselors. Likewise, the efforts of counselors to conserve human talent and to prevent emotional breakdowns have been extended to all age levels. Efforts have not been limited to potential delinquents and drug abusers. Many leaders in the helping professions are asking why youth must break down emotionally before they receive help, and why our society is more willing to support jails and hospitals than schools and counseling. These preventive and personal development services need more attention now that the focus appears to be moving away from "salvage" services for the pathological client.

A third value of psychotherapeutic counseling, and another example of the concept for conserving human talent, is that of *national survival.* Counseling is very much concerned with social values and environmental issues. Political and economic crises throughout the world make it imperative that we find talented youth, encourage them to make the most of their potentialities, and help them over the rough spots in achieving high-level productive and personal adjustment skills without sacrificing values of freedom of choice and responsibility.

Being an agent of community change is perceived by a growing number of counselors as a key value of counseling. Clients are encouraged to better their circumstances and to fight injustice. Counselors even see themselves as advocates until clients are able to act for themselves. Some advocates of this broader community counseling role emphasize the active involvement of the counselor in local community change processes (Lewis and Lewis 1976). A movement entitled "radical counseling" has advocated changing systems and institutions rather than trying so hard to change individuals.

Assisting the individual to achieve his or her dream of *social advancement* is a fifth value of psychotherapeutic counseling. Although many persons find themselves hemmed in by circumstances of history and birth, such as race or poverty, our American democratic social organization and expanding economy still provide means for social mobility. Psychotherapeutic counseling services are ideally suited to help the individual acquire a knowledge of needs and goals as well as to plan for opportunities.

With automation and economic abundance reducing work opportunities for many citizens, counseling offers much hope for the future. We must face the possibility that large segments of our population will not be able to find productive work, which has been the mainstay in developing personal worth and a sense of identity. A new approach to leisure, service, and personal growth must be found to take the place of previous dependence on work. Counseling programs hold great promise for this task of reorienting our attitudes toward work, leisure, and retraining for new careers.

The demand for counseling services in all areas has far outstripped the supply. Since facilities in counselor education cannot cope with this demand, a number of short courses to develop counselors and counselor aides have been organized, largely by government agencies. How to meet social demands for counseling services in high professional levels is one of the greatest problems facing the helping professions.

Skills and Procedures

One of our assumptions is that there is an identifiable body of fairly valid techniques and procedures for counseling and psychotherapy. The major portion of this book is devoted to substantiating this assertion, and to describing these techniques and procedures for different settings.

Training Sequences and Standards for Psychological Services

Two organizations interested in counselor and psychotherapist training are the American Psychological Association and the American Personnel and Guidance Association. The American Psychological Association, the Association for Counselor Education and Supervision, and the American College Personnel Association have published recommended training standards for counseling psychology, clinical psychology, school counseling, and college personnel work. These training programs are superimposed generally on a basic background of behavioral sciences and general education. Early graduate years contain further basic training in general psychology, experimental methods, statistics, measurement, human development, physiological and social psychology, personality theory, and behavior pathology. Advanced training leading to the doctoral degree should contain, according to the APA Committee on Accreditation (1979), additional work in appraisal, internship, professional issues, and research.

The American Psychological Association has published a list of generic standards for the providers of psychological services (APA 1975). From these basic statements, specialty standards, as mentioned earlier, have been developed in counseling, clinical, and school psychology. These documents provide general principles, definitions of providers, accountability principles, and guidelines for practice. Standards statements supplement previously published APA ethics statements and are used by APA Committees on program accreditation, service agencies, and third-party insurers.

The counselor educator division of the American Personnel and Guidance Association has developed a statement of standards for counselor education over the last twenty years, and, most recently, it has developed and applied accreditation procedures for accrediting masters and doctoral programs in counselor education under these standards (APGA 1978). Since mental health and rehabilitation counselors come under the APGA division umbrella, these standards apply to a wide range of training programs for these counseling psychologists. Similarly, the American Association for Marriage and Family Counselors has an elaborate credentialing process for individuals and training programs.

The American Psychological Association and the Association for Counselor Education and Supervision stress the need for predoctoral internship training to give supervised experience in counseling and clinical psychology as well as to enable the student to synthesize many fragments of information from previous graduate work. Internships are demanded for psychologists in doctoral programs approved by the APA Committee on Accreditation. There is a need for more postgraduate continuing education in counseling to update practices. Most states have a continuing education requirement as part of their licensing renewal programs for psychologists.

Competency-based programs, as described earlier under accountability, are becoming the norm in counselor training. Specified counselor behaviors in a competency program, especially when tied to client outcomes, clarify expectations and role definitions of counselors. One consequence is a strong emphasis on skills training to meet competency requirements, yet we know that counseling competence requires refined judgments on ethical, case management, and intervention issues. It is doubtful at this stage whether a strictly skills development approach is adequate for development of helping professionals.

The practice of training and of utilizing paraprofessionals has become widespread. These persons function at prescribed helping tasks under the supervision of professionals who monitor their client work and provide training. Usually, the paraprofessional has competencies in basic helping skills, but does not have experience or training in complex case management skills, research competence to answer basic questions of practice, or theoretical background to conceptualize client problems.

In addition to didactic course work and practice with clients, counselors must confront themselves in order to become more aware of their strengths and weaknesses. Individual therapy is not practical for most counselors. As a result, sensitivity, or encounter, groups are fulfilling this need for self-confrontation in many training programs.

Professional Societies and Publications

Another criterion of a profession is the existence of societies and publications dedicated to improving the science and practice of the profession. In psychology, for example, the American Psychological Association is one group the object of which is "to advance psychology as a science, as a profession, and as a means of promoting human welfare" (1954). The American Personnel and Guidance Association is another professional association dedicated to the improvement of counseling services, particularly in educational and rehabilitation institutions.

The vigor of professional journals is a further criterion of a profession's growth. Some of the representative publications of help to counselors and psychotherapists are the *Journal of Counseling Psychology*, the *Journal of Clinical and Consulting Psychology*, the *Personnel and Guidance Journal*, *American Psychologist*, *The School Counselor*, *The Counseling Psychologist*, *Psychotherapy: Theory, Research and Practice*, the *Journal of Marriage and Family Counseling*, and the *Journal of Applied Behavioral Science*.

Research Orientation

In a profession and science as young as psychology, research plays a significant part in discovering new procedures, validating current techniques, and resolving contradictions and theoretical confusion. A large portion of the graduate program is directed to research techniques so that the practitioner has a research orientation in whatever professional activity he or she performs. In addition, there is a strong social obligation to validate constantly the psychological services offered to the public.

It should be emphasized that the frontiers of knowledge in the field of psychological services are pushed back through an interaction of both practice and pure research in human sciences. One endeavor helps the other in reciprocal fashion. An example is outcome assessment in group approaches to counseling and psychotherapy.

Certification and Licensing

With the prevalence of incompetent practitioners in the field of counseling and psychotherapy, it is imperative that the public as well as the profession be protected. Although a certificate or license does not guarantee competence, it informs the public that the practitioner has been exposed to several years of training and supervision in the techniques he or she espouses.

As we have become more professionalized, we have expressed our concerns for protecting the public and the practitioners through an elaborate credentialing or certification process. Students of therapeutic psychology must be prepared to cope with this development regardless of their anticipated practice setting. Students wishing to go beyond this overview of credentialing are urged to read Fretz and Mills's *Licensing and Certification of Psychologists and Counselors* (1980).

A certificate is a document attesting achievement granted by a public or private group. It is solicited voluntarily by the individual. An example is the postdoctoral certificate or diploma granted by the American Board of Professional Psychology. Diplomas are issued by this board in four areas: clinical, industrial, counseling, and school psychology. The written examination covers basic professional knowledge in the candidate's specialty. The oral examination includes questions on client relationships, professional issues, and a field situation where candidates under observation perform services in their specialties. The American Association of Marriage and Family Counselors' certificate is another example of efforts to certify professional competence.

Almost all state boards of education maintain counselor certification as part of their credentialing programs. Most states now require demonstration of specific competencies as a condition of certification to do counseling in schools.

Actual licensing of psychologists poses a somewhat different problem from certification. Licenses to practice psychology are issued by state governments and usually are restricted to persons with doctorates. A license gives a psychologist a legal right to engage in psychological practice. A licensing law forbids certain practices, generally defines what a psychologist is, and describes psychological practice. Psychology certification and registration laws, which frequently describe practice, tend to restrict the use of the title *psychologist* only. Some states license counselors with masters degrees, but they cannot legally call themselves psychologists. Registers are additional means of recognizing practitioners and documenting their credentials to practice. Registers of psychologists list those who have state licenses. Additional registers for mental health practitioners and general counselors are in the planning stage at this writing. Licensing and certification which protect the public are further marks of a profession.

Code of Ethics

The opening statement in the APA *Ethical Standards of Psychologists* is, "Psychologists respect the dignity and worth of the individual and honor the preservation and protection of fundamental human rights" (1979, p. 1). Psychotherapeutic counseling, being a welfare service, is faced with ethical practice problems. Until codes were formulated, there were few guides for determining unethical practices. The presence of a well-defined code and tradition of ethical practice is a distinguishing mark of a profession.

The APA code of ethics is under continuous revision. The latest published version at this writing is the 1979 revision. The Committee on Ethical Practices of the American Personnel and Guidance Association has published a similar revised code aimed largely at educational settings (1981). While some of the code principles reflect timeless human values, these codes reflect professional and social values of the surrounding culture, hence their continuous revision.

The influence of values on the perception of people and the value context of psychology itself are important ethical topics (Corey, Corey, and Callanan 1979). Goals (such as "adjustment"), value conflicts, social forces, parochialism, and professional vanity are further examples of ethical issues. Ethical problems are covered at several points in this book because we feel so strongly that professional counselors need to give much thought to ethics.

Working Relationships with Other Professions

Each profession must recognize its limitations and the role of other professional groups in rounding out its knowledge and skills. One mark of the psychology profession is its willingness to collaborate with other professional disciplines in working for the client's best interests.

Professional Freedom

The American Psychological Association (1954) lists as one of the characteristics of a "good" profession the freedom to accept its responsibilities and to carry them out in ways dictated by its own wisdom. The profession willingly faces all evidence of social need for services and its own competence to fulfill these needs. The profession must not be swayed by attempts to restrict its activities which demonstrably fulfill its social function and advance human values. We feel that counseling and psychotherapy are well along in attempts to fulfill this professional principle.

TREND III: PERSONALITY FACTORS AND SKILLS TRAINING

For several decades counseling literature focused on the person of the counselor as the key variable in the change process. Recently, more emphasis has been placed on behavior change and general helping skills. Current research and practice efforts appear bent on discovering the best mix of these two key approaches on attitudes and skills. Figure 4 is a representation

Personal Factors in the Counselor	+	Counseling Skills	=	Growth-Producing Conditions	→	Desired Outcomes
Traits		For understanding		Trust		For the client
Attitudes		For support		Openness		For the counselor
Values		For action		Honesty		For the agency
						For society

FIGURE 4. The Helping Process. Adapted from L. M. Brammer, *The Helping Relationship: Process and Skills* (64, p. 4).

of how we see these key relationships in a helping paradigm. The combination of personal factors and skills produces growth conditions which lead to desired outcomes for the client, agency, society, and counselor.

Most literature on counseling and psychotherapy of the past thirty years has emphasized techniques and skills—tests, records, surveys, sociometrics—as if these were central. Shoben estimates that the amount of space in early counseling texts devoted to the "modification of client behavior through face-to-face contacts" (1955, p. 259) was only 8 percent of the total. One explanatory hypothesis regarding this deficit would be that so little was known about this important face-to-face relationship and the related personality factors that writers fell back on the traditional test and records diagnostic approach to counseling and psychotherapeutic problems. Now we estimate that counseling books include at least a third of their space on counselor helping skills and attitudes.

TREND IV: BEHAVIORAL SCIENCE AND RESEARCH METHODS

Although interest in personality factors in counseling relationships has increased, it has not appeared to overshadow or diminish the studies on the use of data in counseling. Efforts to develop new predictive and diagnostic tests, as well as to improve old instruments, have kept a steady pace of development. Interest in projective techniques is an evolving facet of this work. The use of computers has revolutionized research on counseling problems and offers great hope for automating some of the prediction and planning aspects of counseling. More detailed results on counseling implications of tests are summarized in Chapter 10.

Information from the fields of anthropology, computer technology, developmental psychology, gerontology, economics, rehabilitation, and sociology is appearing in forms useful to counselors and psychotherapists. The vast resources of the Federal Bureau of Labor Statistics, for example, are producing more useful materials to aid the counselor with career planning problems. Comparative culture studies on sexual behaviors, childrearing methods, and personality determinants are further examples. The cultural context of counseling was given considerable emphasis by Wrenn (1958) early in the development of counseling as a profession and reemphasized by Ivey and Simek-Downing (1980), so that counselors can be more effective with clients from cultures different from their own.

TREND V: GROUP THERAPY AND THE HUMAN POTENTIAL MOVEMENT

The human potential movement includes many human growth emphases which are related to counseling and therapy. At the center of this movement has been the small-group method applied in settings as diverse as management development, drug treatment, and family therapy (Corey 1981). The human potential movement includes a variety of sensory awareness methods to make one conscious of the body. Skills training for special needs such as assertiveness, sexual functioning, leadership, parenting, and conflict management has been a part also. Awareness training to broaden one's perception of the world and to achieve greater personal tranquillity is included in this movement to enhance the potential of every human being. In this sense the various liberation movements are included. While all of these facets relate to counseling and supplement the one-on-one focus of counseling and psychotherapy, only group counseling will be emphasized in Chapter 11.

The rapid increases in group approaches have come about partly as a result of limited access to costly individual counseling, but also because of increasing confidence of practitioners in the efficacy of group work. There is a growing recognition that people need other people for help through everyday problems, and that this help can come from peers as well as professional experts. One serious limitation is the lack of valid knowledge about the optimum conditions for personal growth through groups and the relative permanence of growth-enhancing or growth-retarding changes effected through the group process. Participants characteristically experience much enthusiasm after a group experience. As in all learning experiences, the crucial questions are what is the transfer value to everyday life, and do learnings from the group result in effective changes in behavior over time?

Groups often function as means to behavior change without individual counseling. At other times they function as adjunctive experiences to individual counseling. In any case, it behooves persons interested in individual counseling to know these group developments, since it is becoming increasingly apparent that skills and time for individual counseling are becoming very dear, and the counselor is looked upon as a change facilitator in family, community, and work groups.

This trend is supported by a vast body of research and descriptive literature on group methods in solving human problems. In addition to the long established models for group therapy with adults and multiple counseling groups for school-age clients, family therapy structures varying from several families meeting with one or more therapists at once to intensive weekend work with a single family unit have appeared. Increasing group work in prisons, with drug users such as Synanon, with elderly adults, and group self-help methods with alcoholics attest to the vigor of this trend.

TREND VI: UNIFIED THEORETICAL CONSTRUCTS

Out of concern for the divorce of science from practice, much thought has been devoted to integrating psychotherapeutic counseling practice with personality and learning data. Instead of thinking about the counseling process as a collection of cookbook recipes or miscellaneous techniques culled from experience, psychotherapeutic counseling may be viewed as the application of systematic and unified theory and principles to specialized learning situations in the interview. Some current and historical views on personality development, structure, and function, and their applications to counseling and psychotherapy, are presented in Chapters 2 and 3.

Throughout this book, we have attempted to bridge the gap between systematic theory and loose practice. This ideal is difficult to realize, however. Part of the problem lies in terminology and translation of terms such as transference and resistance into a meaningful theoretical framework. Counselors must strive constantly, nevertheless, to analyze what they are doing and to know what is happening in their counseling interviews. Theory often supplies the needed conceptual tools, though it is recognized that the need for technique often surpasses available verified knowledge and conceptual developments.

Counselors' awareness of their social responsibility and the welfare of their clients forces them to maintain a healthy balance between skepticism and confidence in their methods. As Shoben so aptly said, "When the chips are down, as they generally are in professional practice, skepticism about one's own resources is a luxury that few can afford" (1955, p. 252). Hahn and McLean's early comments apply to the contemporary counselor also. The counselor's humility of self-recognized ignorance is therefore of continuing importance. It must be a rational humility, however, an objective admission of limitation in the face of infinite complexity. It must never develop into an emotional sense of inferiority which leads to self-recrimination, depression, or overtimidity about undertaking responsibility for new cases. When this happens, the counselor himself is ready for psychotherapy (1950, p. 37). Rogers (1955) has stated the mixed feelings of counselors when they perceive themselves as subjective, sensitive therapists and tough-minded scientists combined.

Counseling has evolved as a significant counselor role. As a consultant, the counselor provides specialized information and facilitates client change through indirect methods, thus keeping the responsibility for change firmly with the client. The consultant role is involved in work with such groups as families and organizations that are concerned with teamwork, communications, and conflict management. Some counselors perceive their primary helping role as that of a consultant whose clients maintain the initiative and use the counselor as a specialist to help meet their personal growth goals.

Thoreson (1969) speaks of the counselor as an "applied behavioral scientist" who systematically undertakes to promote specific changes in client behavior which are related to the goals set mutually by client and counselor. A growing number of counselors stress additional roles, including community change facilitator, client advocate, skills trainer, and organizational consultant.

Rotter (1954) summarizes the principal values of theories in clinical work as follows: as bases for construction of new instruments and methods and of testing old ones; as tools for evaluating counseling techniques where experimental evidence is lacking; as encouragment for consistency of terminology and assumption; as evaluation devices for new ideas or unusual problems in practice; and as aids to help clinicians recognize and resolve apparent contradictions and inconsistencies in experiments, concepts, or practice.

Attempts to unify constructs have served to diminish the "school" emphasis in psychotherapeutic counseling. Wherever a parochial or segmental approach to counseling is promulgated, a "school" of counseling tends to spring up. This is not to discourage individual practitioner-scientists from launching into creative thinking or theory. Rogers comments that one of the critical problems of practicing psychologists today is the climate in the profession which discourages theory construction. Rogers goes on to postulate that this lack of theorizing rests in a "real fear of grappling with the new and unconventional" (1955, p. 247). There are encouraging signs, however, that we are moving toward more unity in theoretical views of counseling, even though practices vary widely.

TREND VII: GOALS, VALUES, AND SELF-HELP

Another prominent trend discernible in psychotherapeutic counseling discussions is that of increasing clarification of the goals and purposes of counseling. There has been a pronounced movement from preoccupation with process to a focus on outcomes. This trend naturally takes a tack into the realm of values and concern about what outcomes are desirable. This topic of goals and values is treated at several points in this volume—under ethical problems in Chapter 6, within the context of goals of psychotherapeutic counseling in Chapter 4, under relationship problems in Chapter 6, and in the discussion of values in Chapter 15.

The change in emphasis from the solution of immediate manifest problems the client may have, such as choosing a career goal, or relieving momentary situational anxiety, to more long-range goals is very apparent. An example of a long-range, generalized goal is the reinforcement of the self-directive capacities of the client which make him better able to solve his problems in the future without help. Self-help is a strong social trend with groups forming daily to cope with some special need, such as grieving, readjustment after divorce, single parenting, family abuse, and recovering from alcoholism. One key counseling goal is to help clients learn skills which will enable them to cope with future problems by themselves. Self-help approaches give deprived groups new ways of dealing with their problems and reaching out to others for mutual help.

Counselors with concerns about values tend to become involved in social issues such as racial injustice, peace and war, status of women, protection of the environment, nuclear energy, reduction of poverty, and protection of children.

SUMMARY

This introductory statement has included a survey of the trends contributing to professionalization of therapeutic psychology. The field of therapeutic psychology has many historical antecedents in clinical psychology, counseling psychology, psychiatry, social work, school psychology, and pastoral psychology. With this rich background, the profession is facing and mastering many problems of responsibility, interprofessional relationships, training, selection, scientific societies, research, certification, licensing, ethics, and freedom. Counseling and psychotherapy overlap on many topics, although they are unique entities. Psychotherapists generally aim at personality reorganization at relatively deep levels of personality, whereas the counselor is more concerned with the dénouement of incomplete maturing or learning processes.

2

Theoretical Foundations of Therapeutic Psychology

Practitioners must develop their own theories and styles of counseling and psychotherapy. To give precision, coherence, and promise to their counseling and psychotherapy techniques, they must become familiar with certain aspects of personality and learning theory, as well as with highlights of specific theories about helping. One of our basic assumptions is that counseling or therapy becomes an impulsive application of "cookbook" recipes to human problems unless the clinician has a firm foundation in the current thinking and research of other practitioners and has a consistent set of assumptions about personality structure and function. Psychological counselors must know their medium, just as mechanics must know the intricacies of a vehicle, or as surgeons must know anatomy and physiology.

This chapter contains, therefore, a discussion of the significance of theory, an overview of various approaches to counseling from the stand-point of Western views of personality and learning theory, and an attempted integration of various historical and contemporary theories as a basis for the consistent application of techniques. The principal purposes in present-ing the following materials are to provide the student with concepts from various personality theories which have useful implications for counseling, and to encourage development of a personal theory of counseling using a creative synthesis approach.

THE SIGNIFICANCE OF THEORY

One model of a psychotherapeutic counselor proposed in Chapter 1 was as scientist-practitioner. The premise of this model is that the counselor can be both subject and object; that is, he or she can be an objective observer, hence, critical of what goes on, yet can be a participant in the counseling process at the same time. The essences of scientific method used by this model counselor are observation, inference, and verification. Counseling practice involves the application of principles deduced from generalizations, or theories, as well as from specific experiences. One foundation of the scientific practice of psychotherapy and counseling, therefore, is theory. By *counseling theory* we mean a structure of hypotheses and generalizations based on counseling experience and experimental studies. Generally theory includes four elements: goals and values, assumptions, strategies, and expected outcomes. Since these elements change, one's theories are in a constant state of development.

When speaking of the counselor as a scientist, two related meanings should be distinguished. In the first meaning the counselor acts as a careful observer of the process. The counselor describes accurately what behavior is seen and may go to the second stage of making inferences about the meaning of the observations. In this descriptive sense everyone can be a scientist. The second is the scientific attitude that the counselor assumes so the he or she can verify the rough hypotheses and improve services. This second view of a counselor as scientist applies the scientific process to the work. It requires control of extraneous variables and manipulation of experimental variables according to the established rules of scientific practice. This is rarely possible in a counseling situation, unless a deliberate study is designed to test certain hypotheses about counseling. Therefore, the scientific approach to counseling in the latter sense remains, admittedly, an ideal.

Although counselors are interested in the applications of scientific attitudes and methods to improve practice, they are also interested in behavioral science as a science. That is, they are interested broadly in the greater understanding of human behavior, whether or not it leads to any practical results in counseling.

Theory helps to explain what happens in a counseling relationship and assists the counselor in predicting, evaluating, and improving results. Theory provides a framework for making systematic observations about counseling. Theorizing encourages the coherence of ideas about counseling and the production of new ideas. Hence, counseling theory can be very practical by helping to make sense out of the counselor's observations. What behaviors exemplify the scientific attitude? A counselor or psychotherapist who proceeds through daily tasks without asking the following questions is not likely to progress in therapeutic effectiveness, nor is he or she likely to contribute new ideas to the profession. The scientific attitude leads to questions such as: What is happening here? What is my model? What are my assumptions? What accounts for this event? What will happen if I try this? Unscientific counselors who do not ask themselves these vital questions are likely to develop dangerous feelings of smugness about their counseling methods.

Clinicians, acting as scientists, start with a question or problem; then they *observe* what happens in the interaction between themselves and their clients. They examine the data and formulate hypotheses about what is happening. These hypotheses are the *inferences* based on the observations and require further testing. Sets of refined hypotheses are generally referred to as theories. From these theories, counselors attempt to explain or predict further events in counseling. They must check constantly the validity of the new theories against the reality of their observations so as to bring the two closer together. The refined theories are then used to make more precise explanations and predictions of counseling events.

To illustrate this process, let us take a simplified example of the phenomenon of defense. A counselor observes that when he "pushes" a client too hard with questions or interpretations the client gets angry, stops talking, or even leaves counseling. He observes the various conditions under which the client behaves in this negative fashion and speculates why this might be so. The clinician observes similar cases and notes a pattern and a consistency. He hypothesizes that clients become negativistic or "defensive" when they are threatened, or perceive the counselor as a source of frustration and even psychological danger. The counselor may postulate an "unconscious" or a "self" in his client with feelings or attitudes which are inconsistent with the client's conscious feelings or attitudes. The therapist or counselor, perhaps, may be "pushing" the client too fast, so of course he checks his hypothesis about threat and defense with further observations until he has refined the concepts and generalizations to the point where they are useful in predicting what will happen to a client under threat. The counselor is then in a better position to evaluate both his hypotheses and his techniques.

The "miniature" theories, or confirmed hypotheses, are combined with much other data and hypotheses into more consistent and larger theories about personality structure and function in general. The broader theory is then used in a deductive fashion to produce more hypotheses to be tested experimentally or through counseling experience.

Although the preceding section expresses the ideal of the scientific clinician's approach, the novelty of the scientific approach for many practicing counselors makes it difficult to use in practice. In addition, there is still no compelling evidence that counseling effectiveness in producing certain outcomes definitely depends upon the extent and explicitness of one's theoretical foundations, nor that one particular theory of personality or psychotherapy is superior to another. The important question is: What theories work best with which clients, in what settings, and with what expected outcomes?

Much work has been done in the last few years in the area of systematic theory construction by psychologists having the temperament and ability to do so. A really satisfactory general counseling and psychotherapeutic theory, however, is not yet available. Because counselors attempt to explain what they see with their unique and limited perception, there are still a number of "schools" of counseling or therapy. A National Institute of Mental Health survey revealed over 130 different therapeutic approaches in the United States alone (1975). This multiplicity of theories is a healthy state of affairs in a young profession; but, ultimately, it is expected that a unified theory of behavior and of counseling practice will evolve. In the meantime, counselors must examine the thinking of others as well as work on the formulation of their own hypotheses about the structure and function of the human personality and the counseling process, as in the creative synthesis below. Even though most counselors cannot be creative theoreticians, they can develop an attitude of careful critical observation of everyday practice and an understanding of formal experimental approaches to counseling problems. They can also strive to be open to new ideas for expanding their own theory, which they must realize is in a state of infancy.

In assessing the current state of psychotherapeutic theory, Goldfried (1980) cited the growing discontent among therapists with their own orientation and their need for rapprochement among major theorists. He viewed the "rigid molds" therapists put themselves in as developing into a major crisis in psychotherapy. A likely outcome of this crisis of confidence in the efficacy of "my school" is a humble facing of limitations and a willingness to broaden awareness of other possibilities, including a major perceptual shift. Mahoney (1979) surveyed leading behavior therapists on their satisfaction with their present understanding of behavior. On a seven-point scale the average rating was less than two (the low end of the scale).

There has been a proliferation of writings recently advocating the very kind of synthesis we have been exploring for the last twelve years. We agree with Goldfried that the search for common ground should take place at the strategy level, rather than at the levels of basic assumptions or preferred methodology. On these there is likely to be continued disagreement. Strategies of therapy, however, are in an intermediate position between basic assumptions and specific methods. Goldfried suggests that an example of such a clinical strategy common to all approaches is to have the client engage early in new corrective experiences, trying new methods of behaving. Pressures from insurance companies and government agencies are reinforcing this effort to determine the most efficient and effective strategies to effect change within each major therapy approach.

One further point should be made. Black (1952), in one of the earliest comparative studies of psychotherapeutic approaches, found that follow-up research data indicated that all "schools" get positive results. Black predicted correctly that the ultimate resolution of theoretical differences would come about through critical analysis of the process itself, rather than through the promotion of a parochial or "school" point of view. Black found that, although differing in assumptions, all approaches stressed the significance of a working relationship, acceptance of the client, need for support, professional status of the counselor, and some types of limits. Fiedler (1950), using Q sort methods, in another early landmark study, found that, in spite of varying theoretical and methodological views among therapists, there was much agreement on their conceptions of the ideal therapeutic relationship. Gonyea's (1963) later study of the "ideal" therapeutic relationship and counseling outcomes used Fiedler's Q sort criteria of the ideal relationship. His study suggested that, while relationship quality is related to experience, positive outcomes and quality of relationship are not correlated for less-experienced counselors. In other words, counseling effectiveness improves with experience, but not simply because of improved relationship quality. This confusion about the significance of relationship points up the need for more information on the qualities of experienced therapists who produce more positive outcomes. Counselors must recognize that practitioners of different "schools" may not agree on theory points, such as the degree of rational analysis needed, even though they might agree on the importance of the relationship. The oft-quoted Fiedler relationship studies sometimes imply that all differences diminish with experience.

A word of caution is important here. While the early studies of Fiedler and similar studies by others suggested that younger counselors adhered to well-defined orientations and that experienced counselors moved to more general orientations and were more effective, more carefully conducted replication research of the last decade has produced different conclusions. Sundland (1977) reviewed the literature thoroughly and indicated that counselor theoretical orientations do influence greatly counselor attitudes, beliefs, and behaviors. Peterson and Bradley (1980) confirmed this statement with a study of four counseling orientations. They did not find an experience difference, however, and they seriously challenged the earlier studies that indicated that experience was a significant variable. They also found that the three main groups of theorists did not respond similarly to the Rogerian client-centered concepts, as had been stated in earlier studies.

A more recent national study by Larson (1980) of four large categories of psychotherapists found that the majority of therapists had multiple allegiances to schools of therapy. A majority also did not believe one-school therapies were most effective. Yet, these same therapists *in their practices* adhered to a primary school allegiance. Larson concluded that therapists in his study were caught between an eclectic desire to be open to all approaches, but were pulled by the advantages of financial and social support to one school.

Adopting an Approach

Counselors and psychotherapists can take one of three positions: identify with one of the theories already published and tested in practice, develop an eclectic position, or strive for a personalized creative synthesis of theory

Established Single Theory	Eclectic Approaches	Creative Synthesis
	Main Characteristic	
Integrated set of assumptions related directly to strategy and method	Strategies and methods from several approaches applied selectively to clients	Application of broad and varied strategies and methods related to a synthesized theory evolved and "owned" by the practitioner
	Examples	
Freud's Psychoanalytic Theory	Thorne's Integrative Psychology	Assagioli's Psychosynthesis
Rogers' Client-Centered Theory	Lazarus's Structural Eclecticism	Shostrom's Actualizing Therapy
	Advantages	
Ready-made system of assumptions and concepts	Collection of various methods	Continues synthesizing, extending, and amplifying personal system
Extensive experience and data base	Flexibility of choice on methods	Discourages competition
Consistency of theory and method	Wide agency application of methods	Fosters therapist's identity with own views
	Limitations	
Tendency toward restricted view of data	Encourages uncritical picking and choosing	A continuous lifelong task
Often a closed system	Deemphasizes integrative theorizing	Tends to be idealistic
Encourages hero worship	Tends toward faddism	Futuristic—ahead of its time
Fosters competition and divisiveness	Additive collection of what works for now	Requires continuous creativity
	Imitative, and tends toward limited creativiity	Requires trust in self
		Risky—requires standing on one's own
	Illustrative Comments by Practitioners	
"Client-centered theory speaks to me."	"I use what works."	"I'm constantly reevaluating my ideas."
"Ellis is my hero."	"I'm flexible."	"I develop my own theory to fit me."
"I dig Freud."	"I try many methods."	"I try to keep open and take some risks."
"I am analytic."	"I like TA methods but not the basic assumption."	"I trust my own observations and judgments."
"I stick with the tried and true."	"Everyone says something important."	

FIGURE 5. *Comparison of Basic Approaches to Theory Building*

and practice. These positions will be explored in the following sections and are summarized in Figure 5.

The Single Theory The case for a single theoretical approach is argued in terms of having a ready-made set of assumptions, concepts, and related strategies which have been proven useful over a long period. Research productivity flowing from a single theory is offered as another advantage. While numerous practitioners state their allegiance to a single approach such as analytic, behavioral, or client-centered, their actual practice, as indicated later in this chapter, is not so parochial. They tend to move beyond their favorite theory quickly. Having an allegiance to a single-theory group has the personal advantage of a solid professional identity and often substantial status.

The single-theory approach tends to promote the "great man" myth—a view that the original formulator was a genius of some kind with special gifts. While some persons, such as Freud, had special conceptualizing abilities, they were seeing events in terms of their unique life experiences and times. A highly elaborated system, such as analytic, tends over the years to become a closed system, and adherents tend to act more like disciples or hero worshippers than creative clinicians.

Eclectic Views   In one sense all theories are eclectic; but we restrict the definition to the process of selecting concepts, methods, and strategies from a variety of current theories which work. Some persons who take this position decline to theorize altogether, claiming that it is premature to identify too closely to a set of concepts or experimentally verified principles, or just that specific theorizing is not useful. The early "technical eclecticism" of Lazarus (1967) is an example. Later Lazarus developed a refined approach of his own called multimodal behavior therapy (1976). This is a broad application of methods in an equally wide theoretical framework. While Lazarus's basic approach is behavioral in the traditional sense, he employs numerous cognitive and affective processes. He explores systematically modalities of behavior, affect, sensation, imagery, cognition, interpersonal relationships, and biochemical factors.

Eclectic counselors prefer a kind of empirical principle of what works for them is valid. Some eclectic counselors choose this position out of inertia or feelings of defeatism to avoid the rigorous thinking necessary in developing a unique position. Their practice is based upon an additive process of picking and choosing among many theories, often relying on a superficial knowledge of them to suit their needs of the moment. Thus, a kind of faddism tends to develop which changes tomorrow when a more attractive method comes along. The principal limitations of the eclectic position are that it often attempts to equate opposite views, gloss over irreconcilable differences, or ignore larger philosophical issues.

To be fair to many persons who label themselves systematic eclectics, it must be stated that such persons struggle to integrate, to be consistent, to validate, and to create a unique personalized theory position. This approaches a different stage, however, which we have described in the next section as creative synthesizing. We feel this effort goes beyond what is currently regarded as eclecticism. Eclectic practitioners attempt to be flexible and open to new ideas and to apply methods as client needs demand. Eclecticism has become a popular position, as indicated in a survey by Garfield and Kurtz (1975). They surveyed 733 doctoral level clinical psychologists, of whom 211 were basically in teaching and research. The remaining 522 were practitioners or supervisors. Of the total group of 733, 64 percent identified their position as eclectic. Undoubtedly, many of this group saw themselves in terms of what we will describe as creative synthesizers. In his eclectic approach to psychotherapy Garfield (1979) describes theories in terms of the interaction effect of therapist and client. He approaches the question of what is effective with this client in this context, at this time, and with this therapist orientation.

The Creative Synthesis Approach

It is our view that each counselor and psychotherapist must ultimately develop a point of view which is uniquely his or her own. Freud was not a Freudian, Jung not a Jungian, and Rogers not a Rogerian. Each of them was himself most fully and completely, while building upon the wisdom of the past. Each practitioner must feel that his or her counseling practice reflects such individuality. This is the reason why no one text or school is fully adequate, and why we try to exemplify an approach which we have termed "creative synthesizing." This approach is not an arrogant attempt to put down predecessors. Ideas are rarely developed in solitary efforts. Usually, they are the results of many years of cumulative cross-fertilization of numerous minds. Isaac Newton is alleged to have said on this point, "If I have seen further, it is because I have stood on the shoulders of giants."

The "creative" element comes in when the counselor not only puts together concepts and practices from other theories in new ways, but also transforms them into ideas and methods which have continuing relevance for himself. As each new gestalt emerges, it becomes more than the sum of its parts. Each new gestalt goes a step beyond; it expands, modifies, and amplifies. Synergy is involved in that summated systems create a new whole which exceeds the power of the individual systems.

The "synthesis" element comes into the theory-building process as counselors strive to integrate in incremental fashion what appear to be separate ideas and uncoordinated methods. They synthesize dynamic and structural elements to form a basic personality model; they describe strategies and methods which follow from their assumptions and values. This could include culling relevant methods from psychoanalytic practices, cognitive strategies, existential viewpoints, and behavioral methods which are supported by the basic assumptions of the theorizer. In this process one must be careful about excessive conceptualizing beyond known empirical data. It is easy to get caught up in attractive metaphors which can go well beyond explanatory functions and inject a note of mysticism. Therefore, the criteria which must be applied to such synthesizing processes are that they must be simple, based on data, consistent, open to criticism and change, and useful to explain and predict behavior.

The growing and evolving qualities of the creative synthesis approach are illustrated by the abstractions in Figure 6. Large segments, such as cognition, feeling, action, or body strategies are integrated and then expanded with mini-segments to include concepts and methods flowing from the basic assumptions.

A number of people have attempted this difficult type of synthesis. Assagioli (1965) with his psychosynthesis, Gendlin (1978) with his synthesis

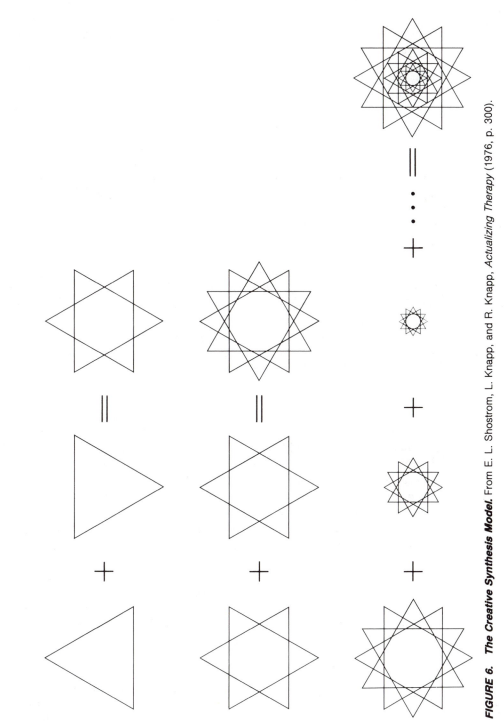

FIGURE 6. The Creative Synthesis Model. From E. L. Shostrom, L. Knapp, and R. Knapp, *Actualizing Therapy* (1976, p. 300).

views, Perls (1969) with his Gestalt synthesis, and Schutz's work (1971) with group process are some examples of efforts to integrate a wide range of psychological ideas, research findings, and methods into a broad and consistent point of view.

Our actualizing counseling and psychotherapy model is another effort at creative synthesizing. It will be described in the next chapter and will be used as an illustrative model in the remainder of the book.

STEPS IN PERSONAL THEORY BUILDING. Developing one's own view is a very demanding lifelong task. In addition to knowing current theories of personality structure and behavior change, counselors must know their own assumptions about the nature of man and the process of knowing, their own values and views of the good life, and their models of the mature well-functioning person. This goal is accomplished through self-study of client-counselor relationships and personal therapeutic experiences resulting in increased self-understanding. These understandings and assumptions are then related to one's goals for counseling, which in turn are matched with strategies and methods to reach those goals most effectively. One borrows from other theorists in the sense that one stands on their shoulders to reach higher levels of understanding and effectiveness in practice. Then, one synthesizes these pieces incrementally into a unified system which is comfortable and effective in a particular setting. Finally, one tests the theory in practice and formulates hypotheses which can be tested experimentally. The results then are incorporated into one's system, or one revises the system.

Parametric and Factor Analysis Clinicians seem to go through a process of professional growth toward a unique style with definable parameters. We define *therapeutic parameters* as the common factors of systematic counseling and psychotherapy adopted by a particular therapist. The resulting combination of parameters would be descriptive of his or her unique style or approach to counseling and psychotherapy. The technique of parametric analysis suggests that growing practitioners commit themselves to unique combinations of therapeutic parameters and apply them flexibly to the *emerging* therapeutic situation. Several investigators have verified this assertion. Larson's study (1980) included a factor analysis of therapist responses to a questionnaire on therapy styles and attitudes. He found six style variables that discriminated among his four therapy school groups. Sundland (1977) found similar results with the same questionnaire. In spite of their declared allegiance to a school or method, the experienced counselors in these two studies met changing therapeutic demands with flexibility of response.

THERAPEUTIC RATING FORM. Shostrom's Therapeutic Rating Form with ten parameters is an example of an instrument to rate therapists on the degree to which their approaches manifest these parameters. Albert Einstein is alleged to have said, "Never *ask* anyone what he does; follow him around and *see* what he does"; so it seems that the therapist may perform differently from what he *says* he does, that is, use different parameters.

Caring (C). It is the therapist's attitude of loving regard for the individual, whether expressed by unconditional warmth or aggressive critical caring.

Ego-strengthening (E). It is helping individuals to develop their thinking, feeling, and perceptive ability so that they can cope with life more effectively.

Encountering (N). It is providing the experience of active encounter between person and therapist—each of whom is being and expressing his or her real feelings.

Feeling (F). It is helping individuals to experience, in a psychologically safe relationship, feelings which they have heretofore found too threatening to experience freely.

Interpersonal Analyzing (I). It is the analyzing by the therapist of the person's perceptions or manipulations of the therapeutic relationship, and therefore of other interpersonal relationships in life.

Pattern Analyzing (P). It is the analyzing of unworkable patterns of functioning and assisting in the development of adaptive patterns of functioning for the individual.

Reinforcing (R). The therapist rewards behavior that is growth-enhancing as well as socially adaptive, and punishes behavior that is negative or self-defeating.

Self-disclosing (S). It is the exposing by the therapist of his or her own adaptive and defensive patterns of living which encourages the person to do the same thing.

Value Reorienting (V). It is the reevaluation by the therapist of the person's loosely formulated value orientations (assumptions about self and others, for example) which enables patients to commit themselves to examined and operational values.

Reexperiencing (X). The therapist assists patients in reexperiencing past influential learnings, and assists them in desensitizing the pathological effects of these learnings on present functioning.

A study by Shostrom and Riley (1968) confirms our general hypothesis that counselors tend to adopt a creative synthesizing approach. Each of the therapists in the study utilized all of the parameters to some degree in his work as judged by forty raters. The therapists rated were Carl Rogers, Fritz Perls, and Albert Ellis as they performed in the film "Three Approaches to Psychotherapy." Even Carl Rogers, whom many feel is the most parochial, included many parameters in his work. This study revealed the following:

1. Rogers scored highest on the parameters of *Caring* and *Feeling*.
2. Perls scored highest on *Encountering, Feeling* and *Interpersonal Analyzing*.
3. Ellis scored highest on *Value Reorienting* and *Pattern Analyzing*.

Thus it is possible for a supervisor of students in counseling or psychotherapy to describe a pattern of parameters which would give a clear picture of his or her particular style.

Major Theory Groups

The following section contains a summary of the major theories of personality with implications for counseling theory and practice. It offers the student a basis for establishing his or her own theoretical position.

This selection of theories reflects an arbitrary choice of basically Western views which emphasize individuality and personal worth. Eastern traditions and native American cultures focus more on people as extensions of nature and on subordination of the individual to the family group. They strive more than westerners, therefore, to blend with nature and return to simple natural states as a counterbalance for the complex demands of technological civilizations and supremacy of the individual.

Two historical bases for Western psychological counseling theory can be traced. One, the behavioristic approach, stresses relearning more adaptive problem-solving modes of response to life's demands through use of rewards, punishments, and information. The focus of effort is on the conditions which promote behavior change. Consider, for example, a client who has difficulty concentrating on his studies. The counselor makes a rational diagnosis to determine if the client is in the right field, if his study skills are adequate, if he possesses sufficient ability to do the work, and so on. Learning conditions are created wherein the client can acquire better work habits, more information, further appraisal of the realism of his goals, or more counseling on personal problems. Reinforcement of adaptive responses is a key element.

A related view stressing behavior change comes from the phenomenological tradition, with its emphasis upon perception and Gestalt principles. The principal focus is upon the client's perception of his world at this moment in time and how this perceptual matrix can be altered. The basic assumption is that the person's perception of himself and his world is the key determiner of behavior. Historical and depth factors are minimized.

Another view, depending largely on psychoanalytic principles, stresses the more underlying emotional, so-called dynamic, aspects of personality. Hence, although not overlooking cognitive considerations, the dynamic approach stresses attempts to elicit feelings about the problem and to understand the unconscious bases for behaving. Thus, through removing emotional obstacles to learning or "lifting of repression," the client is enabled to use more rational approaches to problem solving. For example, if a client has difficulty concentrating on her studies and also appears to resent her parents forcing her to go to school, it may be hypothesized that she unconsciously resists her parents by "inability" to study.

A "third force" in psychology, evolved in recent years, is labeled broadly existential or humanistic. It is partly a protest against the limitations and claims of psychoanalytic and behavioristic views of man. Briefly, it is a way of construing man's existence largely in nonbehavioral terms such as states of being and becoming. It lacks an elaborate rationale and methodology, yet it is having a profound impact on therapeutic psychology theory and practice. The existential viewpoint has been especially influential on persons subscribing to the Gestalt and self-theory approaches, although there are also views labeled *existential analysis.* The existential view emphasizes the search for meaning and authenticity in man's present circumstances. May (1953), Maslow (1970), Rogers (1961), and Bugental (1965) have written extensively on the problem of becoming an authentic person. Such persons are open and honest with themselves and others so that who they really are can be perceived clearly by others. Their observable behavior is consistent with their feelings.

To achieve the counseling goals of authenticity and meaningful existence, the existentialist counselor helps the client to become aware of and to confront the paradoxes in his or her existence, such as freedom-determinism and rationality-irrationality. He or she is encouraged to confront conditions which lead to loss of personal significance, confused identity, and anxiety resulting from threat to cherished values. The emphasis is upon the special personal meaning of these feelings rather than on causes or rational interpretations in light of some theory. Some writers, notably May (1967), assert that existential approaches do not constitute a distinctive "school" but a set of attitudes and assumptions about people and their condition which supplement traditional theories. As in all approaches, there are the dangers of using existentialism as a new type of intellectualization to avoid the experiencing of feelings—or its opposite, using existentialism as a kind of antiintellectualism rather than as a supplement to scientific ways of viewing man.

The categories for theorists in the following sections are often arbitrary and based upon historical oversimplifications. With the decreasing emphasis upon distinctive parochial views, there is a greater blending of ideas and integration of theories. The following overview, furthermore, includes the views of those writers who have been practitioners rather than primarily personality and learning theorists.

DYNAMICALLY ORIENTED THEORIES

Psychoanalytic Approaches
The psychoanalytic approach stresses the importance of the client's life history (psychosexual development), the influence of genetic impulses (instincts), a life energy (libido), the influence of early experiences on later personality of the individual, and the irrationality and unconscious sources of much of human behavior. The psychoanalytic concepts of levels of awareness are significant contributions. The conscious level consists of those ideas of which the individual is aware at the moment. The preconscious contains those ideas of which the individual is not aware at the moment but which can be recalled. The unconscious level consists of those memories and ideas which the individual has forgotten. Freud conceived the uncon-

scious as making up the bulk of the personality and of having a powerful influence on behavior.

A significant psychotherapeutic issue raised by the psychoanalytic approach is this: Do we need a "depth" approach that postulates that the origin and solution of human problems lie deep within the personality, or do the explanation and solution lie more within the perceptual organization of the individual? Psychoanalytic counselors emphasize the importance of having a concept of depth in personality and postulate a series of structural elements known as Freud's "iceberg" concept, which are illustrated in Figure 7. The largest element is the *id*, which has the characteristics of being unconscious, irrational, unorganized, pleasure-oriented, primitive, the source of *libido* or life force and energy, and the source of drives and basic wishes for life and death.

Another element of structure is the *ego*, which functions as a controlling, reality-oriented, mastery mechanism. The ego functions also as a mediating element among superego, id, and reality demands. One of the principal functions of the ego is that of controlling the id and keeping impulses and feelings, such as anxiety, out of consciousness. Ego control is accomplished through the mechanism of "defense," of which the main type is "repression." The id impulse, thwarted in direct expression, penetrates the ego barrier in a disguised and usually safer derivative form.

Although the early psychoanalytic theorists placed great emphasis upon repression of anxiety and the consequent symptoms, more recent classical or "orthodox" psychoanalytic therapists have been giving greater attention to ego psychology which emphasizes the adaptive mastery functions of personality.

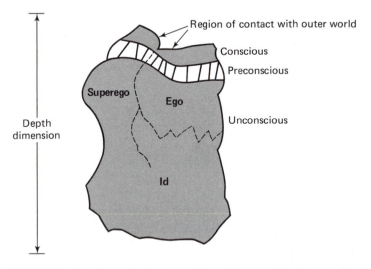

FIGURE 7. Psychoanalytic Conception of Personality Structure. J. F. Brown, *Psychodynamics of Abnormal Behavior* (New York: McGraw, 1940); adapted from W. Healy, A. Bronner, and A. Bowers, *The Structure and Meaning of Psychoanalysis* (New York: Knopf, 1930).

The *superego* is another Freudian concept which functions as a controlling agent in the personality. It is conceived generally as parental moral attitudes and social mores learned in early years, which become an important structural and functional part of personality in later years. In many ways, the concept is similar to the popular term "conscience."

Later students of Freud, such as Jung and Rank, not only modified, but also abandoned many of his basic postulates. Adler, a colleague of Freud, emphasized the goal-directedness or purposiveness of human beings more than did Freud, who saw clients more as blind victims of their impulses operating in a rather mechanical deterministic fashion. Adler felt that power and status motives were more significant for behavior than the broadly sexual motives of Freud. Adler saw superiority attitudes as compensations for perceived weakness or the "inferiority complex." Related to Adler's drive for mastery is his notion of the "masculine protest" of some women who envied the status and power of men.

Adler emphasized also the "social interest" or current "life style," as well as the biological determinants of behavior. One of the Adlerian therapist's devices to gain clues to his or her client's life style is to ask for "first recollections." This approach gives the therapist an idea of the experiences on which the client's style of life is based.

Adler is well known for his concept of the *ego ideal* or the person's model of the kind of person he would like to be, a prelude to the now popular concept of *self-image*. Helping the client become more aware of his unique life style, ideals, and self-images is one of the major goals of counseling. Adlerian concepts form the basis of a currently popular form of family counseling.

Jung stressed the uniqueness of human motives and the striving toward individuation. Jung postulated a broad *collective unconscious,* consisting of inherited *archetypes,* which are collections of primordial universal motives and human images. His second structural element is the *personal unconscious,* which contains forgotten and repressed material. The *conscious* is the external awareness level concerned with problems of everyday living. The *persona* is a type of mask hiding the deeper personality characteristics from others. Jung felt that the persona was an important and healthy element of personality, except where it tended to dominate the "real" personality or to blind the person to what Jung called his "shadow." The shadow part of the personal unconscious is considered to be impulsive and generally not consciously nor socially acceptable. In addition to the persona and shadow, there are other examples of archetypes—*animus* (masculine aspect of women), *anima* (feminine element in men), and *self* (the achievement of oneness and unity).

Jung emphasized that the psychotherapist must help the individual get something in place of his neuroses and "build" an individual self. Hence, he placed high value on religion and the integration of religion and psychology. Jung's descriptions of the paradoxes in human personality, such as the mixed feminine and masculine components, are often useful concepts in the interpretation phase of psychotherapy. Both Jung and Adler stressed the value of the direct, face-to-face contact of the psychotherapist with the client, as contrasted with the less direct, couch-centered treatment of the Freudians.

Rank contributed much to psychoanalytic theory by his emphasis upon the traumatic events of birth and separation from the mother. These ideas were expanded to include the security-seeking efforts of people. Rank pointed out many implications from the growth and development as a child for development of independence and security as an adult, thus offering counseling theory a significant and meaningful developmental point of view. One implication, for example, is the importance of "limits." According to this concept, the client is helped to gain a feeling of security by setting limits to his behavior, such as making him stay within the time and place of the interview. With children, especially, this is a significant part of the therapeutic process.

Rank's central concept is the *will,* which is a guiding, integrating, and instinct-inhibiting force. He views resistance as the operation of the will in maintaining the integrity of the personality. Rank's ahistorical views placed considerable emphasis upon the positive motivations of the client and his present feelings, rather than upon the therapist and his interpretations of the past.

Rank's major contributions to counseling were his insistence on viewing the client as a person, and his casting of the psychotherapist into a more personalized role. Rank believed stongly in "ethical self-determination," implying that the counselor should be careful not to force values on the client. Rank's view sharpens another significant issue in counseling: Where should the content of the process come from, primarily—the client's field of awareness or the counselor's?

Rank's theories have influenced several American psychotherapeutic writers. In addition to Carl Rogers in the adult psychotherapy field, Jesse Taft in social work and F. H. Allen in child psychotherapy have extended Rank's special adaptations of psychoanalytic theory. Rank's will is interpreted as a positive growth force. The conflict between dependence and independence needs is seen as a tendency to regress to earlier dependent relationships when the demands of life become too overpowering. Allen perceives that the basic adjustment difficulties of clients result from excessive demands being made upon them before they have the resources to cope with them. Rank's insistence upon the therapeutic power of the relationship itself has led naturally to a strong emphasis being placed on the attitudes held by the counselor and the importance of having clients assume their own psychotherapeutic responsibility.

IMPLICATIONS FOR COUNSELING AND PSYCHOTHERAPY. A significant implication for counseling is Freud's theory of defense mechanisms. Psychoanalysis has made us more aware of the unconscious bases of behavior, with the result that counselors are less concerned with the symptoms (defenses) and more concerned with the origins of the defensive behaviors. One therapeutic task is to help clients become more aware of their style of handling unconscious wishes and anxieties and to find more socially approved, as well as personally satisfying, ways of resolving tensions. Analytic counselors, furthermore, see this task as making the "unconscious more conscious," that is, of helping clients to know and utilize in a mature way their psychic energies and to become more aware of distorted behaviors that result from threatening unconscious impulses. Helping clients to become more aware of their unconscious feelings tends to result in more spontaneity, rationality, and other values implicit in the mature personality.

Psychoanalytic therapists use techniques such as abreaction of feelings, free association, and interpretation of resistance, dreams, and transference material. The assumptions, style, and length (usually two to five years) of psychoanalytic therapy make it of limited utility in psychotherapeutic counseling. A prominent feature of psychoanalytic technique is to encourage regression to promote exploration of early experiences. The therapist can help clients work through experiences which otherwise might have been beyond their awareness. An example is the transference event where clients see in the therapist characteristics from important persons in their past. Therapists interpret these transference relationships to enhance client awareness.

Counseling and brief psychotherapy, in contrast, are not as concerned with attempting *major* personality transformations through detailed interpretation of early and persistent unconscious conflicts as is psychoanalysis. Psychotherapy is concerned more with conflicts and feelings which are already in, or dimly in, present awareness and with helping the client to develop resources for handling them. In other words, the psychotherapist concentrates more on the "here and now," whereas the psychoanalyst is concerned with lifting repressions of deeply unconscious material. The analytic method of free association has applications in everyday counseling to help clients let thoughts and feelings flow freely to enhance awareness. The relevance of analytic techniques to psychotherapeutic counseling is treated in later chapters on relationship techniques.

One key implication of a deterministic system like Freud's, in which one has a blocked urge, then repression, then the neurotic symptom, is that individuals tend to deemphasize their personal responsibility for their behavior: "It is not I who is at fault; it is my frustrated id impulses which are causing me trouble." For example, "My hunger stole the fruit, not I." Psychotherapeutic counselors operate on the assumption that the client must, sooner or later, accept personal responsibility for his behavior. Existential therapists, for example, place great stress on the client feeling a sense of "ownership" of himself.

Jung's and Adler's amplification of psychoanalytic theory includes more of the social determinants, such as cooperativeness, and the purposive character of behavior. Rank, as well, stresses the person's integrating powers and the necessity for understanding the client's feelings and potentialities. This concept paved the way for later therapists such as Sullivan, Horney, Taft, Allen, and Rogers to develop theoretical positions of even greater value to psychological counselors.

RECENT POSITIONS.   Sullivan is known for his theory of interpersonal relationships, including the interaction between personality development and culture. According to the interpersonal theory, people appear quite different, both to themselves and to others, depending upon the particular personalities with whom they are interacting at the moment. The practical import of this view is that the individual can be understood only within the context of his or her friendships (real or imaginary), and broader social groups.

Sullivan postulates two basic goals of human behavior—physical satisfactions (food, drink, rest, sex) and security (defined as a state of pleasantness or euphoria resulting from fulfilled social expectations). Children, in the process of acculturation, frequently find themselves in conflict between need satisfaction and security. As parents use prohibitions and disapprovals in the acculturation process, children begin to feel anxiety as a result of their inability to fulfill these expectations. They develop increased muscle tension. They exclude from consciousness selected phases of experience which have proved anxiety-provoking. Their attempts to resolve these tensions through activity do not result in complete relief, since anxiety reduction does not tend to follow release patterns of other physiological tensions.

If children can obtain both satisfaction and security, they gain a sense of mastery or power; hence, they begin to experience a higher evaluation of themselves. This self-regarding attitude is thus determined by the attitude of others toward them. Self-attitudes, in addition, seem to determine the attitudes which they have toward others.

It is important to realize, therefore, that much anxiety originates in an interpersonal context. If considerable anxiety has been generated during the acculturation process, then useful learning, awareness, and capacity for insight will be greatly reduced. Sullivan speaks of this process as "selective inattention." When other persons in the interpersonal situation mention words or feelings which provoke anxiety in one's self, the evaluation of others tends to change in a negative direction; hence, individuals are alienated from one another. It helps, therefore, to understand that aggressive clients respond in this manner largely because they have been rebuffed in their bids for affection and understanding. Through their inability to receive as well as to give affection, they maintain hostile attitudes even toward those who attempt to satisfy their needs.

Sullivan traces self-development through a series of stages from preverbal infancy through adult maturity. The principal implications for counselors are the necessity to provide security relationships, to accept emotional outbursts which are indicative of tension buildups, and to organize learning situations which result in enhancement of self-regarding attitudes of worth and confidence. Therapists and counselors must realize that affectional growth may be poorly developed owing to disturbances in interpersonal relationships and, as a result, the client needs a treatment environment where he can develop self-esteem and confidence adequate to any situation. He needs an opportunity to develop the ability to love another person whose welfare is as significant as his own.

The counselor must be cautious, however, in interpreting the explanations of personality dynamics to the individual. Counselors must recognize also that they too have developed through the same social processes as their clients and that the present counseling relationship is changing them further through what Sullivan describes as his "participant-observer" status. This topic will be treated in Chapter 8 under *countertransference*.

In summary, the principal implication of Sullivan's theory for therapists and counselors is that the individual can be understood mainly in light of his or her interpersonal history. The quality of the client's interpersonal relationships must be examined, in particular, as a key to the client's understanding of his or her attitudes. The counselor must realize that the client's responses to the counselor are affected by these past relationships and that feelings expressed are displacements of feelings from previous personal relationships. Sullivan's ideas are related to the current emphasis in counseling known as the "communications approach."

Karen Horney (1937), who may be classified among the so-called neo-Freudians, differs from the earlier psychoanalysts in that she too stresses the cultural determinants of behavior and emphasizes that maladaptive behaviors arise largely from disturbances in human relationships. Horney, while remaining in the general framework of psychoanalytic theory, shifted the stress from early childhood experiences and repression of biological drives to presently existing character structure and conflicts. She does this, however, without negating the significance of early experience in personality formation. Horney feels that the totality of early childhood experiences and conflict forms a unique character structure which predisposes the person to later neurotic difficulties. This view differs somewhat from the earlier Freudian idea that adult conflicts and neuroses are essentially repetitions of isolated childhood experiences.

An example of the cultural origin of personal problems is the American emphasis on competition, which appears to produce considerable frustration and hostility. Our hostilities are projected to others who are then viewed as competitors. This creates anxiety about the potential danger of others and fear of retaliation for having hostilities of our own. This situation results in a need for security which is satisfied partially through love relationships. Since deeply satisfying affectional relationships are infrequent for many persons in our society, we are subjected to further frustration.

Horney stresses the competing and contradictory demands of our culture upon the person as one source of tensions. Examples are the conflicts between stimulation of demand for material goods and the limited means for satisfying them, independence and free choice as opposed to the limitations imposed by birth and social circumstances, brotherhood and love for your neighbor against competition and "eye for an eye and a tooth for a tooth."

The conflicts in the culture are often internalized and express themselves in various forms of aggressiveness and yielding, personal power and helplessness, self-aggrandizement and self-sacrifice, trust of people and fear of them. An implication here for psychological counseling is that these conflicts, faced by all people in our society, become accentuated or reappear as unintegrated childhood conflicts, causing feelings of distress. Individuals may then develop defense mechanisms annoying to themselves or others. The awareness of these conflicts, or the associated anxiety, drives people to seek psychological counseling. An example is the person with a self-effacement defense, so common in our middle-class culture. He feels it is important to "be nice to everyone, so they will be nice to me and will love me." He finds, however, that other people often dislike him anyway; so he is baffled, concludes that he is fighting a losing battle, and becomes even less assertive.

Another useful distinction that Horney makes is between "normal" anxiety, which is fear of concrete events such as accident and death, and "neurotic" or "basic" anxiety, which is fear that arises in early relationships when the person faces a potentially hostile world and which leads to neurotic defenses. One of the psychological counselor's tasks is to help individuals to recognize their basic anxieties and to help them build more satisfying ways of handling them.

Closely related to Horney's concept of basic anxiety is "basic hostility." Horney postulates that much neurotic anxiety stems from the presence of repressed hostility which has been projected to others. The perception of the world as a hostile place generates anxiety and further repression of hostility, and so begins the "vicious circle."

Of further interest to counselors is Horney's concept of the *basic conflict,* which exists largely at an unconscious level. This conflict concerns the feelings of dependence and affection which one has for parents versus feelings of hostility toward them for having to be dependent. The conflict may not be recognized at the conscious level because one cannot easily alienate one's self from those on whom one depends. The more normal individual moves freely between the opposing tendencies of independence and dependence, whereas the more neurotic people are more compulsive about their behavior and experience their independence-dependence feelings as being in direct conflict with one another. This condition has the effect of limiting spontaneity and of giving the victim a feeling of helplessness, indecision, and fatigue. One of the therapist's tasks, according to Horney, is to make the client aware of his or her basic conflicts and his or her attempts to solve the conflict by moving toward, against, or away from people.

One of Horney's (1950) formulations of interest to therapists is her description of the basic types of personalities that come for psychotherapy: (1) *Expansive types* give an impression of glorified self-regard, exhibit an arrogant and contemptuous demeanor, and seem to feel that they can impress and fool others into believing they are someone they are not. This type of client is difficult to involve in a therapeutic relationship initially, but later, when their defenses are reduced, they become involved quite easily. (2) *Self-effacing types* tend to subordinate themselves to others, to be dependent upon others, and to seek protection and affection. They are characterized by a strong feeling of failure, inferiority, and self-hate. They exhibit a demeanor of passivity and obsequiousness. They generally become involved easily in a counseling relationship. (3) *Resigned types* put on an air of disinterest, reflecting retreat from inner feelings and from the rigors of life. They take on more of a detached observer role in life's activities. They lack a strong achievement drive and avoid serious effort. This type of client maintains an emotional distance from others and avoids pressures to get involved in any kind of close human relationship. This avoidance behavior makes involvement in a counseling relationship very difficult.

Additional utilitarian concepts for counselors are Horney's "alienation from self" and the "tyranny of the shoulds" (1950). The former term refers to common client conditions involving fear of losing identity, hazy thoughts and feelings, and feelings of remoteness from one's thoughts and feelings. Horney's "tyranny of the shoulds" refers to the strong tendency in many clients to strive compulsively to be their ideal selves without due regard for reality conditions in their lives. Such clients, for example, operate on the assumption that nothing is or should be impossible for them.

Erich Fromm (1941, 1947), like Sullivan and Horney, is concerned with the social influences on behavior. He, too, stresses the client's individuality, goal-directedness, and productive possibilities.

Fromm was one of the first to use the term *self-realization* in a therapeutic context, viewing growth as an unfolding process of man's psychological powers. He places the responsibility for many personal conflicts on the economic structure and guilt formation. More broadly, Fromm conceives that the main problems of modern man center around ethical conflicts and relatedness, particularly in regard to loving and being loved. An example would be the social emphasis upon unselfishness versus social competitiveness and self-interest, both of which involve problems of relatedness and ethics. The relatedness of people to their world, particularly to other people, is an unending human problem. The counselor helps clients on these matters through improving their ability to lead creative lives and to relate to their worlds. The unifying "glue" in Fromm's discussion of human relationships is mature love, which will be elaborated upon in later chapters of this book.

Alexander and French (1946), though adhering closely to more classical Freudian assumptions and techniques, have modified the practice of psychoanalytic therapy so as to reduce the time required to achieve results. The amount of time that should be spent on a client is one of the key issues of professional counseling. Alexander and French have reduced the time required for therapy by selecting carefully therapists to match clients' particular needs, by keeping techniques flexible in order to suit individual styles, and by varying the time between interviews. They emphasize that psychotherapy is a "corrective emotional experience" achieved through forced insight and liberal use of supportive techniques. This latter approach highlights another counseling issue concerning the effectiveness of very direct therapist activity and liberal use of support.

Eric Berne developed a position called *transactional analysis* (1961). He postulates that each of us carries with him three basic ego states—parent, adult, and child—which we use to test reality. The main subject matters for the helping process are the defensive and gratification interactions of these states within and between individuals. For example, one person may react with his archaic "child ego" to the "parent ego" of another person in such a way that the communication is marked by manipulation or distortion. Berne calls these defensive interactions "games." He tries to help clients see more clearly the use of their various ego states and how they can strengthen their more adaptive adult ego. They do this through a progressive structural analysis of their own ego states, a transactional analysis of their communications with others, and analysis of the games they play with others. A key activity in transactional work is reconstruction and analysis of "life scripts," which are basically life-style histories. The stroke is a rewarding condition, such as love and attention. Transactional analysis devotes much time to the client's history of gaining and losing strokes in his or her life script. Transactional analysis incorporates methods from several theoretical positions, such as contracting and Gestalt awareness. For many counselors TA has become a viable and flexible theoretical framework.

SUMMARY OF RECENT PSYCHOANALYTIC POSITIONS.   In summary, the current directions and implications of neo-psychoanalytic theory are as follows: (1) greater recognition of the cultural determinants of behavior; (2) more concern with clients' present circumstances, especially people close to them, and less preoccupation with infantile development and traumata; (3) more emphasis upon the quality of the therapeutic relationship and how the client perceives it: (4) a deemphasis of sexual needs and aberrations, and increasing stress on other needs and feelings such as love, hostility, and ambivalence; and (5) a greater emphasis on rational ego functions in solving life problems.

Self-Theory and Phenomeno-logical Approaches

Self-theories are relatively new in counseling and psychotherapy. Although the concept of a "self" was postulated many years ago by Jung, McDougall, and others, a counseling approach based upon this basic concept was not specifically offered until Rogers's controversial volume, *Counseling and Psychotherapy*, appeared in 1942. Roger's position became known as "nondirective" because it was counter to the traditional counselor-centered methods of solving client problems. Rogers emphasized the client's creative responsibility for reperceiving his problem and enhancing his "self."

Rogers himself is a good example of a creative person at work. He has grown constantly in his counseling theory and practice over the last forty years. He was one of the first therapists to use audio recordings of his interviews, so the world could see what he actually did. From this breakthrough in interview technology Blocksma and Porter (1947) found that what counselors said they did and what they actually did in their recorded interviews were very different. This study set the patterns for decades of counselor education via audio and video recording.

The reader familiar with the problems of classifying counseling and psychotherapy theories may note the painful difficulties in systematizing them. In the present classification, the writers recognize that some theorists would not like their classification. Others can be classified in several places. Self-theorists, for example, cover a wide range of persons who regard themselves as psychoanalysts. Horney is a conspicuous example with her frequent use of the concept of self. Rogers identifies with the humanistic psychology group.

Rogers (1951) is generally recognized for having collected the most systematic set of assumptions and constructs on self-theory, as well as for applying the theory to counseling and psychotherapy in a humanistic framework. His "client-centered therapy" highlights an issue in counseling; namely, how much responsibility can be placed on clients for their own problem solving or psychotherapy? Rogers and his humanistic colleagues believe strongly in individual responsibility and power to act on their worlds. Many of the following summaries are taken from Rogers's thinking.

THE NATURE OF THE SELF. The "self" is a construct rooted in Gestalt and phenomenological psychology. It is typically defined as "the individual's dynamic organization of concepts, values, goals, and ideals which determine the ways in which he should behave" (Shostrom and Brammer, 1952, p. 8). It is the individual's consistent picture of self and is best represented by what he or she calls "I" or "me." Various terms such as "concept of self," "self-images," "self-concept," and "self-structure" are used to describe this personality construct. The main sources of these personal evaluations are direct experience and the values and concepts of parents which are incorporated as if directly experienced.

As with all constructs of this type, there is great danger in thinking of the "self" as a type of homunculus, or "man within a man," having personal qualities. The next temptation is to use the concept as a universal explanation for motivation and action problems. Rogers (1951) used "self" in the sense of awareness of being or functioning, not as a synonym for organism or a "place where."

The concept of self is a learned attribute, a progressive concept starting from birth and differentiating steadily through childhood and adolescence like an unfolding spiral. For example, one of the earliest manifestations of the self is the negativistic attitude of the two-year-old child when he begins to realize that he has an individuality of his own with pressing and distinctive needs and powers. This growing awareness of himself as a unique person is his concept of self. This self takes on various subjective attributes in the form of "I am" (his nature), "I can" (his capacities), "I should or should not" (his values), and "I want to be" (his aspirations) (Shostrom and Brammer 1952).

When people perceive themselves as behaving in a manner consistent with their picture of themselves, they generally experience feelings of adequacy, security, and worth. If they act in a manner different from the way they define themselves, they experience what is known as "threat" and feel insecure, inadequate, or worthless. These individuals, if they perceive no other alternative, may then defend themselves against this threat or inconsistency via one of the commonly described "defense mechanisms."

An example of this phenomenon is the young man who comes for counseling in an anxious state. His first attempts at handling the feelings of anxiety have been to deny or distort them. The client describes his mixed feelings about going to college and continues: "My parents keep telling me I can make it; my aptitude test scores indicate I can do it; I would like to do it; but I am somehow convinced I can't. I feel caught between, so I freeze when I take exams. I would like to junk the whole idea." The client continues to describe his discomfort and other symptoms.

The client's *self-definitions*, capacity concepts, and aspirations run partially along these lines: "I am a young adult; I respect my parents' opinions; I do not have the ability to do college work; I want a college degree; I want to be liked and admired." Yet, the client experiences the fact that he is in college now; his parents have expressed themselves and he values their judgment; the tests indicate that he has the ability to do the work. He is very much *aware* of the anxiety which results and is aware that this anxiety expresses itself in "exam panic." He does not yet perceive, however, that he is experiencing *threat* because his self-concepts are so incongruent with the data. The *symptom* is anxiety which is experienced when threat occurs. He is tempted to deny (defense mechanism) the conflict by running away from the situation. This evasive action may reduce his awareness of the threat, but not the threat itself. Unless counseling or other life experience breaks this defensive chain reaction and strengthens his self-concept, the defensive behavior (exam troubles, running away) will very likely increase susceptibility to further threat and guilt, thereby creating more distortion and more mechanisms. The preceding sequence is a summary of the self-theorist's threat and defense theory.

Another common example of the threat-anxiety-defense sequence is that of the young woman who feels a conflict between career and marriage. If she falls in love she would satisfy the need for marriage, but it would threaten her career. However, if she does well in her grades in school and spends much time on training instead of social activities, it would support her career needs but would seriously threaten her marriage goal. The preceding analysis of threat-defense sequences could be applied to this situation where there are two seemingly opposing self-concepts. In this case, the counselor tries to help the client recognize and accept both desires.

When the person above is not acting in accord with her self-concept, we might say she is maladjusted in the sense that her awareness of threat and anxiety, and her consequent defensiveness, are high. Her concept of self and her experience as perceived by herself are dissimilar, as indicated in Part (a) of Figure 8. The student in the former illustration who feels deeply that he cannot do college work, yet denies the significance of parental judgments and test data, fits this paradigm also.

Conversely, when the person's concept of self is in relative harmony with his perceived experience and he feels that he is acting in accordance with his values, ideals, and past experiences, we might say he has good adjustment. Our student illustration recast in hypothetical terms to match Part (b) of Figure 8 would say: "I'm convinced I can make it. My parents expect it; my grades and test scores all point to the fact that my plans are realistic."

Congruence is a significant term used by self-theorists, particularly Rogers (1951). It means the close matching of awareness and experience. If a client is aware of communicating a feeling which he is genuinely experiencing, his behavior is said to be congruent or integrated. If a client is *aware* of trying to *communicate* a feeling of love to another person, for example, yet he *experiences* hostility toward that person, the recipient of his feelings may experience an awareness of phony communication. The recipient is often aware, furthermore, of the unconsciously motivated defensiveness underlying the client's inaccurate communication. This illustration points up the clear incongruence between experience and awareness, because what the client is aware of and what he is genuinely experiencing are two different phenomena. This condition is also an illustration of the nature of defense from a self-theorist's viewpoint.

A further example of incongruence is the bored guest who insists he is having a wonderful time. Here the guest is aware of the incongruence between his real feeling of boredom and a desire to be polite. Rogers would say this is a type of incongruent behavior which is deceptive rather than defensive because he is aware that his communication is incongruent with his genuine experience of boredom.

The principal counseling implication of this theory of congruence,

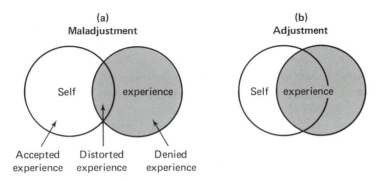

(a)
Maladjustment

(b)
Adjustment

Self   experience

Self   experience

Accepted
experience

Distorted
experience

Denied
experience

FIGURE 8. *Maladjustment and Adjustment from the Self-Theorist's Viewpoint.* Adapted from Rogers (1951, p. 526).

it would seem, is that the counselor's problem is how to help clients to face courageously the incongruence between awareness and experience so that communication of their real experiences is in full awareness and not defensively distorted.

FURTHER CHARACTERISTICS AND ASSUMPTIONS.   Although the "self" is the key structural construct, the principal assumption or central hypothesis of the self-theory group is that the individual has a self-actualizing growth tendency or need. The organism strives not only to maintain itself, but also to enhance itself in the direction of wholeness, integration, complete- ness, and autonomy. Hence, the client is believed to have the capacity and the motivation to solve his own problems. The main implication of this view is that the counselor's role is to create an interview "climate" and to use techniques which allow these natural growth forces to emerge in the direction of mentally healthy and creative behaviors. Thus, the self and growth theories are rooted in existential philosophy and humanistic psychology. Both are based on views of present existence and quality of living. Questions such as Who am I? What does my life mean? and What is real? are in the forefront. Existentialism emphasizes responsibility for individual choice and self-acutalizing goals.

Although the "self-actualizing tendency" is postulated as being bio- logically determined, the direction of the growth tendencies is assumed to be culturally determined by parents, peers, teachers, and other persons significant to the child. Since the individual tends to deny perceptions which conflict with his self-concept, these growth forces often become dis- torted in the developmental process. This condition often gives the picture of a person devoid of positive growth motives. There seems to be a strong belief on the part of the self-theorists that the positive growth forces will ultimately triumph. For example, independence will supersede dependence; integration will overcome disintegration; social behavior will replace antiso- cial behavior.

A third assumption, based on the point of view called *phenomenology*, is that people's "reality" is that which they perceive. External events are significant for individuals only insofar as they experience them as meaning- ful. The phenomenologists say that the way to understand individuals is to infer the "phenomenological field" from their behavior. In other words, to really know a person, the observer, or counselor, must know how the individual views his environment and himself. Thus, the term *internal frame of reference* has come into common use in counseling with the implication that counselors must try to perceive clients' perceptual worlds as closely as they can. This intimate understanding is a necessary prelude to "accep- tance" of the client's feelings. This viewpoint explains why the client-cen- tered counseling group focuses on deep understanding and acceptance of client attitudes. Thus, the phenomenological approach places a premium upon the empathic skill of the psychotherapist. Rogers has been the model of this skill of getting into the unique perceptual world of the client. A key assumption of client-centered counseling is that clients who have been heard in this understanding way are better able to become self-actualized.

Rogers (1951, 1961) has developed a tentative system of fourteen postulates which go beyond the basic assumptions summarized above. Much current effort is being expended to clarify his propositions and to submit them to rigid experimental tests. Grummon (1965) has summarized the assumptions and postulates of the Rogerian position in a form extremely useful for counselors. The research centers on how the conscious and unconscious states of the organism are organized and altered. It is a difficult problem, however, to relate the changes which are observed in client-centered counseling to the self-theory postulates, particularly the basic one of self-actualization. Examples of research efforts toward this goal are collected in Rogers's and Dymond's report (1954) and Truax and Carkhuff (1964).

A related group of personality theorists is the "need"-centered group. Maslow (1970), for instance, combines the self-theorist's basic postulates, such as the self-actualization principle, with basic human needs. He views the human being as an integrated holistic organism with a series of basic needs organized into a hierarchy of importance dictated largely by the culture in which he or she is raised. The psychotherapeutic process becomes a systematic need gratification through a very special type of interpersonal relationship. Maslow feels that his need gratification theory explains why so many people are helped by persons who are well-meaning but who are untrained in counseling technique and theory.

GENERAL IMPLICATIONS OF SELF-THEORIES. One of the basic contributions of this view for counseling and psychotherapy is that the experiencing individual becomes the center of focus in the counseling process. Since the client holds the power of growth and meaningful perception internally, the responsibility for change and the "locus of evaluation" of his or her experience must be within the client. The client's internal frame of reference is generally close enough to "objective reality" so that the counselor can follow meaningfully what the client is saying. The counselor, nevertheless, constantly must ask, "What is the client trying to say; and what does this mean to the client?" The counselor's understanding of the perceptual world of the client is then communicated to the client in fresh language. This condition facilitates further elaboration and clarification of feelings, which leads to insight, and in turn results in positive planning and action.

Another implication of the growth principle is that the counselor's attitudes in the interview must be so genuine, caring, and transparent that the threat to the client's self is reduced to a minimum. Reduction of threat allows clients to accept hitherto unaccepted parts of themselves and to express feelings never before admitted. Since they accept more of their previously denied and distorted experiences into their self-organization, they are in a better position to accept others and to achieve the characteristics of fully functioning persons as described by Rogers (1954, 1961).

A third implication is that the emotional quality of the relationship is the most significant therapeutic element. Wealth of information, diagnostic accuracy, and historical understanding, which are primary in some theories of psychotherapy, are secondary to the trusting "climate" created by the counselor's sincerity, warmth, acceptance, and sensitive empathic understanding. There is less concern about the *direction* in which clients will move and more concern about providing a *relationship* where they can freely and safely move in exploring their own feelings. When "delinquents," for example, are given this type of relationship, the expectancy is that they will move in a socializing direction because they see this as the most rewarding way to go. Thus, there is little emphasis upon changing basic motivations or habits. The self-theorist claims that these behaviors automatically change in a socially desired direction when the client's perception is more finely differentiated and when the client discovers for one's self more satisfying ways of meeting his or her own and society's needs.

A limitation of self-theory approaches is their lack of applicability to types of counseling stressing information, test results, persuasion, and environmental change. The self-concept is too narrow to encompass the full range of counseling problems. It is a confusing variable to utilize in counseling research because specific dimensions of the self are difficult to define and assess. For example, how are changes in the self-concept determined as a result of an educational-vocational counseling experience?

SUMMARY OF SELF-THEORY APPROACHES.   The principal mark of the self-theory group is its postulation of a self-concept. A second distinguishing characteristic is the belief in the innate positive growth potential or self-actualizing power of the organism. The main focus in therapy is on the relationship of counselor to client. In this relationship, the counselor's attitudes of honesty, trustworthiness, and genuine concern are crucial. A main difference from other dynamic approaches appears to be the effort to build and maintain a nonthreatening, anxiety-reducing relationship in which growth can take place from the very beginning. Another difference from other approaches is the increased amount of responsibility placed upon the client compared to that ascribed to the counselor.

BEHAVIORAL APPROACHES

Although the dynamically oriented theorists seek to understand conscious and unconscious conditions through inference, the behavioral group concentrates on objective study of client behavior and the learning process in particular as the source of hypotheses about counseling. Since the emphasis of this group is on behavior, their primary concern is to discover how the behavior was acquired and how it can be changed. A second emphasis is on cognitive processes and how these can be altered as a precondition for behavior change. The label *cognitive theories* applies to this group. A contemporary trend among theorists is to use the term *cognitive-behavioral* to describe integration of these two traditions. Meichenbaum (1977), in particular, has developed practical clinical procedures with children and adults based on research into how self-directed inner speech and imagery guide behavior change.

Behavioral counselors are concerned about outcomes of counseling also, although they insist that the goals be stated in observable terms. Krumboltz (1966), for example, states specific illustrative goals under three general types. They are "altering maladaptive behavior," "learning the decision-making process," and "preventing problems." Goals are stated differently for each client and generally are compatible with counselor values, but the goals are stated in specific terms which different observers could agree were achieved. In addition to the emphasis on outcomes rather than on process the behavioral approach stresses competencies in counselors that produce specific outcomes in clients.

Behavioral counseling is based upon behavior analysis. This process includes concepts such as observation of behavior, environmental determinism, functional analysis of behavior in terms of cause and effect, and the reinforcing conditions in the environment. When these observations and analyses are performed then the behavior technologist can assist the client to specify goals for change and design a specific set of conditions to bring about that change. A simplified process of behavioral counseling consists largely of determining with the client the behavior he or she wants to change, noting the conditions when it occurs through careful observation and counting, setting specific goals for change, and then evaluating progress in reaching the goals. Change methods consist mainly of increasing or decreasing a specific behavior. This may include, relaxation training, for example, to decrease the tension in the body; or it may include assertion skills training which increases the social effectiveness of one's behavior. Role playing to practice new behaviors, such as in an employment interview, are common methods of simulating the real life situation. Considerable emphasis is placed on homework to practice the new skills in everyday settings. Behavioral counseling uses many learning principles and methods, such as reinforcement and modeling, to be described in the next section. The focus is on doing something about solutions and change rather than discussing problems.

The Gestalt or field theorists are a rather independent group. They are included with the broad behaviorist group since they, too, stress learning and systematic behavior observation. The differences, however, between Gestalt approaches and behaviorism are more striking than their similarities. In many ways, Gestalt views, with their emphasis upon perception and their relation to phenomenology, are significant sources for the self-theory group's views.

Reality Therapy

Glasser's approach (1965) to counseling was developed in prison settings where a practical approach to behavior control was essential. *Reality therapy* draws on many methods and concepts and is applied to numerous settings. The main thrust is encouraging clients to act responsibly so that their needs are met. The focus is on behaviors that achieve individual intentions or desires directly and effectively, without jeopardizing others' needs. The counselor, for example, asks the client, "What are you doing—and does that get you what you need and want?" "How do you need to change to fill your need for respect, love, or esteem?" Clients get in trouble because they select behaviors which guarantee failure to satisfy these basic needs. Denial of reality is a common mechanism of such clients and is expressed in behaviors such as crime, alcoholism, paranoia, irrational fears, and even suicide (as an ultimate denial). The counseling strategy is to determine what clients need, how they are frustrating those needs, what strengths and resources they possess, and what they must do to themselves or the real world environment to live realistically with their own and the world's limitations. The focus is on constructive behaviors that increase self-esteem and respect for others. While there is an emphasis on quality helping relationships, the main focus is on changing client cognitions and behaviors such that they face reality. The methods and strategies of reality therapy are clear; but the age-old question of what is real, good, and responsible behavior is still puzzling.

Learning Theory

Historically, this group evolved from the Pavlovian conditioned-response approach to learning and the Watsonian behaviorism of the 1920s. Their objective orientation resulted in a heavy emphasis upon studying behavior in its most simple forms through the medium of animal experiments. Until recently these early experiments had little impact on counseling theory or practice. Mowrer (1950), Dollard and Miller (1950), Shoben (1949), and Shaw (1939), for example, made early efforts to integrate learning theory concepts with counseling principles. Behavioral concepts and research have had two types of impact: One is the development of a wide range of strategies, called behavioral counseling, to assist clients in counseling. The other is known as behavior modification—applying behavior technology to change individuals in group settings, such as classrooms.

Learning theory has been a promising source of productive experiments. Recent cognitive processes have modified the long-standing dominance of learning theory. The keystone in cognitive learning theory is self-directed behavior change. Some of the practitioners who have experimented with concepts such as operant conditioning and reconditioning in counseling are Krasner and Ullmann (1965), Krumboltz (1966), Bandura (1969), Eysenck (1952), Grossberg (1964), Wolpe (1958), Michael and Meyerson (1962), and Mahoney and Thoreson (1974). Most of these investigators follow the experimental leads of B. F. Skinner (1953), the principal exponent of operant conditioning principles in learning theory.

CHARACTERISTICS AND ASSUMPTIONS.   The learning theorist assumes, first of all, that most of human behavior is learned. It is assumed also that behavior can be modified by application of learning principles, some of which are discussed below.

Strictly behavioristic explanations of client behavior are based largely upon the theoretical works of Thorndike, Hull, Guthrie, Skinner, and Tolman. Mowrer and Miller, Shaw, Rotter, Shoben, Wolpe, Bandura, Krasner, and Krumboltz are some persons who have attempted to apply these principles to counseling. All these investigators start with the assumption that the person has *drives*. These drives are primarily physiological, but through social learning a vast hierarchy of secondary *motives* is acquired. These drives and motives propel the individual toward goals. From past learning, the individual acquires *expectancies* (excluded by some reinforcement theorists) that, if he seeks a goal in a certain way, he will achieve it. A *stimulus* or *cue* sets off the *response* which propels the client toward his goals. If the response is *rewarded*, it tends to be repeated. This sequence is described as an S-R model (stimulus-response). The individual *discriminates* among various stimuli according to past *conditioning*. Stimuli are assumed to be interchangeable if stimulus generalization occurs. The person learns to make a particular response to a once nonsignificant stimulus which happened to be around when he was making a response to a quite different stimulus. In an oversimplified way then, almost any stimulus can become associated with almost any response. The counselor's task becomes one of helping the client to identify undesirable stimulus-response patterns and then interfere with them or set up conditions for more desirable stimulus-response patterns. These patterns often take the form of very specific goals, such as approaching strangers to ask for information, which heretofore had been a deeply anxiety-provoking experience.

A key concept of the behavior approach is that of *reinforcement*. This is a rewarding condition which occurs when a stimulus-response sequence has been completed. The S-R pattern then tends to be repeated under similar circumstances and *generalizes* to other types of responses which are similar to the learned pattern. Also, response patterns which are repeated and not reinforced periodically tend to be *extinguished*, that is, disappear. The process of substituting one stimulus for another to get the same response, or of getting a different response for the same stimulus is called *reconditioning*, or in psychotherapeutic terms, *reeducation*. The concept of anxiety for the learning theorists is a type of nonspecific fear in which one is unaware of the source as well as the object of his fears.

Two principles of learning which have applicability to therapeutic processes are *operant conditioning* and *desensitization*. Operant conditioning is a procedure of rewarding behaviors as they occur so that they will be stronger and less likely to be extinguished. Examples are therapist praise, smiles, and nods for client statements which are interpreted by the client as approval. Desensitization is a process of exposing clients to increasing amounts of anxiety-provoking stimuli until they cease to elicit anxious responses. As this technique is described by Wolpe (1958), it includes special training in relaxation methods so that a relaxation response is substituted for an anxiety response to the same stimulus. Salter (1961) has developed a program of conditioned reflex therapy growing out of human and animal conditioning research. Emphasis is upon removing inhibiting behaviors, not symptoms, through environmental change.

An example of a learning-theory approach to counseling is Phillips's (1956) *interference theory*. Phillips stresses the contemporary assertive and choice-making behaviors of a person and leaves out concepts involving "depth" and "defense" in the personality. To change behavior in psychotherapy, then, the counselor sets up conditions which interfere with present behaviors and which teach the client new ways of responding to his environment. Phillips hits directly on one of the major issues of psychotherapy; namely, is it necessary to postulate a depth dimension of personality and invoke assumptions about an unconscious and defense mechanisms such as repression?

Another issue faced squarely by learning-theory advocates is that of experimental validation. The learning theorist strives valiantly to state his concepts, postulates, and hypotheses in forms which have behavioral correlates and which can be observed and studied in laboratory situations. Learning theorists criticize other theory-making efforts severely because the concepts, postulates, and hypotheses are "slippery," vague, and difficult to correlate with behavioral referents. However, learning theory does not offer utilitarian substitutes for some of the inferred structural and functional concepts of personality propounded in the dynamic and self-theories.

A key issue separating the behavioral group from dynamically oriented people is the nature of neurosis and the origin of symptoms. Neuroses were viewed historically as behaviors preventing intense anxiety from becoming conscious. Phobias and compulsions, for example, were regarded as casually learned behaviors which kept the personality intact and reduced anxiety from conflicts originating largely in childhood. Behaviorally oriented counselors look upon these so-called neurotic behaviors as learned responses in the process of drive reduction. Phobias, for example, are learned avoidance behaviors to be reduced through reconditioning methods.

Dollard and Miller (1950) were among the earliest investigators to link social learning theory with psychotherapy. Their views are still considered valid for a behavioristic rationale for counseling. Basic principles are *drive*, which is motivation for action, and *cue*, which is the stimulus for provoking a *response*. Strength of response varies with the intensity of the drive and the cue. A final concept is *reinforcement*, described above as a rewarding condition which tends to fix the behavior. Conversely, when behavior is repeated without reinforcement it is *extinguished*, or eliminated. This is an oversimplified sketch of the Dollard-Miller view, an approach to behavior change involving a blend of learning principles and psychoanalytic assumptions.

IMPLICATIONS AND LIMITATIONS FOR COUNSELING AND PSYCHOTHERAPY. Experimental psychologists generally do not attempt to draw parallels between laboratory conditions and the interview. Clinicians, however, make attempts to define counseling variables in learning-theory terms. They reason along the following lines: An almost universal condition of clients, from those who have superficial counseling problems to those who need deep psychotherapy, is some form of *anxiety;* the counseling relationship as experienced by most clients is *anxiety-reducing;* many defense mechanisms are anxiety-reducing also and have been reinforced so many times that they become fixed; although a defense mechanism, such as sarcasm, may reduce tensions, it is paradoxically self-defeating or socially maladaptive; hence, the defensive measure itself creates more anxiety.

Learning theory may some day shed more light on why counselor characteristics enable clients to feel secure and to learn more personally rewarding behavior in place of their maladaptive defenses. Pleasure experienced from smoother interpersonal relationships, for example, appears to have a reinforcing effect on the new behavior.

We need to know why some clients fail to learn more satisfying behaviors under the same conditions. Why do some clients persist in their maladaptive defenses even when they are very much aware of their source and of the pain they cause themselves and others? Many clients can label the dynamisms and symptoms with great aplomb, yet they do not seem able to act upon this knowledge.

How impulses can be inhibited in clients with immature characteristics and so-called character disorders is another problem which may someday be helped by learning methods. How can responses considered undesirable by the client himself be extinguished so that they do not recur? How can this inhibition of undesirable responses be accomplished without resorting to conscious suppression or unconscious repression?

Learning theory has stimulated the idea that the client should be encouraged to experiment with new behaviors for the purpose of enlarging his repertoire of adaptive behavior in social situations. He is often given tryout "homework" to do, for example.

How can the client be helped, furthermore, to *generalize* or *transfer* from *response sets* (Harlow 1958) discovered as rewarding in the counseling relationship to situations outside of counseling? Ivey and Simek-Downing (1980) describe their ideal of "intentional living" as the ability to be flexible in communicating with self and others in the same culture. They do this by developing a maximum of verbal and nonverbal descriptive sentences about the client's culture while in counseling. This flexibility in language enables clients to increase their response capacity to cultural demands and their ability to develop new thoughts and behaviors.

Rotter (1954) emphasizes that one psychotherapeutic task is to increase the *freedom of movement* of clients so that they are aware of, and can engage in, more activities which lead to satisfaction. After loosening the client's rigid perceptions of his or her situation, *expectancies* are built up which anticipate reward instead of punishment. Then, when the clients try out a new expectation of themselves, such as speaking before a group, their feelings of success about themselves are reinforced through people telling them they did a good job. The counselor's attitude of acceptance alone seems to be helpful in supplying positive reinforcements and positive expectancies. Clients may come expecting criticism for their exploits, but they find the counselor understanding and relaxed about the matter. This feeling of being understood and liked is a type of positive reinforcement which may lead to more generalized feelings of being liked by others outside the psychotherapeutic interview.

Although there is some agreement among clinicians interested in learning theory as to what learning labels can be applied to client behavior, they differ greatly regarding how active the counselor should be in promoting new learning. Some think the counselor is obliged to have clients spell out their problems so that they can perceive and redefine it accurately; then the counselor helps the client through suggestion and interpretation to build expectancies for more satisfying outcomes. The counselor tries to get the desired behavior, and then reinforces it.

Other counselors with a learning orientation feel that the first chore is to prevent the client's anxiety from generalizing to other stimuli and to allow expectation principles to operate. Next, the counselor attempts to help the client recognize distorted expectancies without using argument or pressure. Meanwhile, the counselor's accepting attitude conveys the idea that the client's difficulties are due to his confusion and lack of understanding rather than to "weak will power, orneriness, laziness, or perverseness." New behaviors are then elicited as tryout suggestions from the client rather than through direct suggestion from the counselor.

In some cases, the counselor may decide to intervene more actively, to teach the client *skills* which may be used to achieve the expected rewards. For example, the failing student may need improved study methods before he or she can experience the rewards of achieving the new expectancy of being the "successful student," which the student will very likely generalize to being the "successful person." Mahoney (1979) has developed a series of principles and practices of self-management whereby people can establish change programs for themselves without the intervention of a counselor or therapist.

The principle of expectancy has another implication in the phenomenon of transference. Transference, which will be described in Chapter 8, can be explained in learning terms as a series of learned client expectancies. Examples of such expectancies are that the counselor will be like other persons the client has known who are feared, disliked, or loved.

SUMMARY OF LEARNING APPROACHES. In summary, the learning approach to counseling and psychotherapy has great promise as a methodology of guided behavior change, especially since it is stimulating so much basic research on the counseling process. The participants in the Kentucky Symposium on learning theory, personality theory, and clinical research (Adams et al. 1954) concluded that learning theory, which is based on controlled and highly artificial experimental situations, has limited applicability to practical problems. They agreed also that personality and clinical theories which are based on clinical case observation do not have suitable forms for experimental testability. The Kentucky Symposium participants suggest that one way to mesh the two is to strive for more generality of learning theory and to be more concerned with finding means whereby results of psychotherapy could be measured with laboratory methods. Developments described in the preceding behavioral analysis section are a partial realization of this hope.

Critics of the learning approach to counseling feel that emphasis on objectivity and denial of unconscious manifestations leads to sterile, mechanistic, atomistic approaches, and that personality is too complex to study with the present method, which are designed to study lower organisms. The next criticism logically following is that theories based upon simple models have little applicability to complex human processes. Learning theorists aim to understand behavior in small, highly controlled samples and argue strongly against premature attempts to explain higher processes until methods for study of these processes are developed. The self-theory group is generally skeptical of the learning-theory approach because it tends to stress the process of learning rather than to focus on the client who is doing the learning.

Some critics are concerned that conditioning methods will be too effective and might be used to manipulate clients, as is the case with critics of behavior modification strategies. There is fear that freedom and individual responsibility will be reduced by the counselor who perceives his or her role as a human engineer controlling behavior in a psychologically determined utopian state.

Cognitive Approaches

There is a group of theorists who emphasize that mistaken beliefs or perceptions people have about themselves are the source of their psychological problems. Representatives of this view are Kelly (1955), Ellis (1962), Raimy (1975), Beck (1976), Singer (1974), and Meichenbaum (1977). Raimy points out misconceptions, such as "my parents never loved me," and how strategies such as identifying mechanisms for avoiding awareness and admitting mistakes can be utilized in counseling.

Rational approaches to behavior change assume that people are rational beings capable of changing their behaviors by altering their belief systems. Ellis's rational-emotive system of psychotherapy is an example. Ellis's rationale is that emotional distress is a result of self-defeating irrational thoughts with which the person continues to reindoctrinate himself. Change in behavior comes about when he changes his thinking. Examples of irrational premises which Ellis attacks are that one must be loved by everyone and that one must be perfectly competent in order to feel worthwhile.

Meichenbaum (1977) speaks of inner speech, or self-dialogues, as a means of altering behavior through cognition. He also developed a method of tension control he called "stress inoculation training," which uses a combination of behavioral and cognitive methods. Brammer and Abrego (1981) utilize a wide variety of cognitive and behavioral methods in their taxonomy of skills for coping with life transitions. Their intervention strategies include changes in perception of control, cognitive message awareness and restructuring, construction of external support systems, management of stress, and various styles of problem solving.

Neurolinguistic programming is one of the most recent developments in psychotherapy. It focuses on the language clients use to represent their worlds. Using a variety of methods, largely from cognitive psychology, psycholinguistics, and nonverbal language, therapists can identify patterns of belief and behavior. They look also for intent to change, potential for change, metaphoric language, and sensory cues to know how to have the most effective access to client experience. Counselors using this style of therapy attempt to enhance clients' awareness of their chief sensory modes of experiencing the world (mainly visual, auditory, or kinesthetic), gain access to their inner experiences through matching sensory channels, and then help clients to change their ways of experiencing their problems (reframing). Bandler and Grinder describe their system in a basic theory text (1975) and in a practical workshop format (1979). Implications for counseling of neurolinguistic programming (NLP) work are to be more aware of action language patterns (verbs and adverbs), sensory language patterns, and metaphoric language (images) to understand better how clients represent their worlds (representational systems). A key counseling goal and NLP objective is to assist clients in broadening their modes of experiencing the world and their sentences used to describe it. An additional counseling implication of NLP is that it provides an operational definition of rapport. The counselor, for example, watches for "accessing" cues such as "visual" words and then enters the client's world of experiencing through language that matches the client's visual symbols. As in other contemporary styles of counseling, to understand NLP one must gain experience either as a client or in experiential learning events led by expert models of the method.

Some cognitive theorists and practitioners attack the irrational beliefs of clients and the conclusions about themselves as a result of those beliefs. Ellis is the chief exponent of this approach (1962). He calls it his ABC method, where *A* is the objective event, *B* the person's belief about that event, and *C* how the person feels about the event. For example, a student fails an examination; he believes that people who fail are reprehensible human beings; and he feels that he is a no-good person as a consequence. Therapy consists in attacking this belief and the consequent bad feelings. In Chapter 9 on interpretation, more detail is presented on dealing with irrational thoughts, using Ellis's method of analysis.

IMPLICATIONS FOR COUNSELING AND PSYCOTHERAPY. Cognitive restructuring methods are basic to a large number of theories. Since counseling and psychotherapy are such verbal enterprises and since so many clients' problems involve irrational thinking, all counselors need to understand cognitive change methods.

Field Theories and Counseling Field theorists are often classed with the behavioristic group because of their emphasis on learning as change of perception and their stress upon systematic behavior observation. They differ, however, in several ways, and particularly with respect to their phenomenological approach to perception. Among field theories, Gestalt psychology has the more formalized approach and is represented by such familiar names as Koffka, Kohler, Wertheimer, and Lewin.

The Gestalt approach was introduced to the United States from Europe about the same time behaviorism reached full flower. The Gestalt movement was radically different from behavioristic movements in that it tended to deemphasize minute analysis of behavior into mechanistic stimulus-response bonds and stressed, instead, the dynamic organization of whole units of behavior and the necessity for people to put their fragmented selves together again.

Perls, Goodman, and Hefferline (1951) have developed a therapeutic approach called Gestalt therapy which stresses the applications of Gestalt psychology to psychotherapy. They emphasize problems of awareness, the whole self in creative contact with the environment, and the reshaping of one's sensory capacities. Perls's system of therapy claims a reintegration of Gestalt principles, Freudian structures, Reichian viewpoints, and the principles of general semantics. Perls also emphasizes the importance of the present encounter to encourage awareness of current feelings. He encourages the emerging Gestalt of personal integration and the recovery of lost potential through exposing defenses, "games," and escapes to the future. Perls does not explain or interpret to the client, but provides opportunities for self-discovery. Thus, Perls leans heavily in the existential, humanistic direction also.

Two principal contributions to counseling theory have been made by the Gestalt psychology group, as distinct from Perls's Gestalt therapy approach. These are principles of perceptual organization and the phenomenon of insightful learning. The Gestalt group postulates that psychological organization of the person tends to move in the direction of wholes or the "good gestalt." This means that the person tends to organize his perceptions simply and completely in order to reduce tensions arising from a state of disorganization. For example, when we see an incomplete drawing of a familiar object we tend to complete the details to make it a meaningful figure. The Gestalt group stresses the influence of the "field," that is, surrounding forces in the environment, on the organism.

Lewin, although not thinking necessarily of applications to psychological counseling, formulated some concepts of particular value to counselors. Lewin calls his theory a "topological theory" of personality because he used a mathematical model to account for the psychological field of the person (1936). He pictured the personality in his psychological field with field theory terms such as *vector* (direction) and *valence* (attraction power). He conceives a dynamic system of interdependent subsystems of personality which offer a considerable contrast to Freud's more historical deterministic system.

Lewin describes the person as "differentiated life-space" organized into energy systems. In this framework, the child begins life as a relatively simple organism; as he or she grows, the processes of differentiation and integration become more rapid. Along with growth comes more rigidity of boundaries within the personality. The tensions, or needs, developing from internal conflicts and from frustrations in goalseeking act as motivating forces. These forces impel the personality toward actions to alleviate the tensions or reduce the needs.

One implication of Lewin's theory for counseling is the importance of helping individuals to make barriers within their personalities more permeable so that they do not suffer from the dissociating effects of rigidity. Another counselor task is to help the individual keep goals within reasonable grasp in order to reduce the frustration concomitant with goal barriers; that is, help him or her to develop a realistic "level of aspiration." A consequence of frustration, for example, is to force the personality to make fantasy solutions. In severe cases, the individual so displaces reality with fantasy that the latter is perceived as reality.

The principal goals of the counselor, summarizing implications from Lewin, are to increase the life spaces of clients so that they have more flexibility in living, to help them reduce the rigidity of barriers which prevent them from reaching their goals (such as achieving better reading skills so as to obtain success in job or school), and finally to reduce the rigidity within their own personalities to allow an experience of freedom and spontaneity.

VALUES OF GESTALT PRINCIPLES. The first significant contribution of field theory was the influence of *perception* in behavior. The main princples of perception theory are summarized as follows by Combs (1954): First, the physical state of the organism determines the nature of what is perceived. Therefore, how the person behaves is a function of the state of the person's perceptual field at the moment. Second, perception is a function of time since the exposure must be long enough to allow sensory organs to function adequately. Third, perception cannot occur unless there is an experience, either concrete or symbolic. Fourth, the client's values and goals influence perception. In general, people perceive what they want to perceive, or are trained to perceive. Fifth, the ego and the self-systems selectively determine what is perceived. Sixth, experiencing threat (as previously defined) affects the range and quality of perception. Threat seems to narrow the perceptual field as well as to force the individual to maintain the integrity of his personality organization by various defenses.

The perceptual learning group, then, begins with the basic postulate that behavior is a primary function of the person's perceptual field at the moment. Syngg and Combs (1949), for example, emphasize the importance of understanding persons in terms of their unique realities or "phenomenal fields." This phenomenological view is a considerable contrast to the psychoanalytic view that behavior is influenced by deeply repressed historical events in the personality. The psychoanalytic theorist is inclined to say that how people behave now is a function of the meaning automatically given to events in terms of their unique past histories of repressions and "libido," or life energy, uses. The behaviorist, in contrast, would stress the importance of past learning and current environmental conditions.

Kelly (1955) has devised a system which he calls "constructive alternatism." This view is a perception theory wherein the client construes his world in a variety of ways; hence, the client is not bound to a particular set of constructs about his world. Kelly's fundamental postulate is that "a person's processes are psychologically channelized by the ways in which he anticipates events" (1955, p. 46). There are many corollaries and definitions in his "psychology of personal constructs," but it reduces to a perceptual learning viewpoint incorporating the personal history of the client as a basis for understanding the perceptions of the moment. There are many implications for counseling in Kelly's formulations, including the strategy of assisting the individual to change role constructs, or pictures of himself, as a basis for planned changes in behavior. Kelly's view differs from that of Rogers and the self-theory group in the important respect that Kelly does not postulate a "growth principle" impelling the client toward a "mature self."

Self-theory leans heavily on principles of perception. For instance, a significant part of the rationale of the self-theory group is that the counselor attempts to get within the perceptual frame of reference of the client so that he or she can see the world in somewhat the same way the client sees it. Since the client's reality is that which the client perceives, it is quite important that the counselor get a good look at the client's reality.

Related to the idea above is the client's need to "free his or her perception," which means making it less rigid and less subject to distortion. The counselor does this by allowing himself or herself to be used as a screen upon which the client can project his or her perceptions. The counselor reflects these back in ways which help the client to see that there are other ways of looking at the client's problem. The counselor encourages the client to explore feelings and ideas which heretofore had been outside of his or her awareness. This verbalizing process helps the individual to alter and extend the client's perceptual world so that he or she has more flexibility of choice.

A significant contribution of the perception researchers to psychotherapeutic counseling has been the development of projective techniques. Although they were instigated primarily as diagnostic personality instruments, they are important aids to counseling, as will be indicated later in Chapter 10. Rorschach, Murray, Beck, and Klopfer not only pioneered the projective instruments but also added much to the perception theory of personality.

Another important contribution of the Gestalt group to counseling is that of *insight learning*. Here, a process of searching for solutions leads to a "restructuring of the field," or reshuffling of relationships, which, in turn, often results in a sudden solution. Past experiences are seen in a different manner and events stand in a different relationship to one another. Insight accounts for the "Oh yes, why didn't I realize this before," type of response heard so frequently in counseling.

Insight is achieved in counseling by helping the client review his or her past experiences, arrange them for clear observation, search actively for new solutions, and then wait for the perceptual reorganization to take place. In an actual counseling situation, the client usually has some form of hypothesis about causes and some tentative solutions he or she anticipated trying. The counselor's job is to help clients loosen their rigid ways of thinking so that perceptual reorganization resulting in insight can take place. This is done through a thorough discussion by the client of feelings and ideas about relevant aspects of the problem. It is through the process of verbalizing that the client actually relives or re-experiences his or her past or present perceptions. Something happens within the perceptual organization of the individual when superficial knowledge about one's self and others is translated into deep understanding and the increased awareness which we label "insight."

The importance of an "incubation" period must be stressed here. The counselor and client may discuss many relevant aspects of the client's problem without a satisfactory solution being presented. Then, after a period of time, the client comes back with a fresh "set" to attack the problem, or he or she may have a solution which the client wishes to discuss in the interview. Insight often cannot be rushed. It seems to be spontaneous and sudden when it comes, but the surest way to bring it about seems to be through the counselor's success in creating an interview climate where the client can explore many relevant past experiences and present feelings with a sense of freedom and deep personal intensity. Insight is more likely to come when the client is "involved" with his or her problem; that is, when the clients' feelings have full sway in the deep reexperiencing of those feelings he or she has tended to deny, distort, or project. There also must be an intense desire to find a solution to the discomfort.

LIMITATIONS OF GESTALT VIEWS FOR COUNSELING OR PSYCHOTHERAPY.   The principal limitations of Gestalt views for counseling are their incompleteness. Perception theories aid considerably in hypothesizing how attitudes are learned and changed. Insight theory gives further enlightenment to these matters. The therapist or counselor is still in the dark, however, when it comes to setting conditions whereby perceptual changes and insight are accomplished. How intellectual understanding of one's feelings and thought processes can be translated into the deep awareness called insight is still unclear. Even more baffling is how the counselor can assist the client to *act* on his or her insight.

TRANSPERSONAL APPROACHES

Transpersonal methods are rapidly becoming a part of the mainstream of counseling and psychotherapy. A few years ago they would have been regarded by the majority of theoreticians as charlatanry, or at least as suspect. Most of the theories presented so far have been concerned with interpersonal and, to a lesser extent, intrapersonal issues. In any case, all of them have been bound to Western philosophical traditions. During the past few years the field of transpersonal psychology has spawned a number of methods which supplement the talk therapy, problem orientation, and hyperrational methods of the past four decades. Transpersonal approaches to counseling emphasize the wholeness of the person, the interrelation of elements of experience, intuitive modes of inquiry, transcendent or altered states of consciousness, and the human potential for creativity, joy, and fulfillment. Earlier emphases on the use of nonprescription drugs to alter consciousness gave this movement a bad reputation among counselors and the adult public. While the experimental use of drugs to expand consciousness is still associated with transpersonal psychology, other nonchemical modes of enhancing awareness and effectiveness are stressed. These include meditation, energy enhancement, spiritual enlightenment, and body maintenance through exercise, diet, and stress management. The transpersonal approach is a broad inclusive style of counseling and therapy; but modes of inquiry to supplement traditional empirical methods are intuition, inner search or centering, and the study of ancient religions and mystics (Tart 1975). The focus is on accepting, but transcending, self with its normal suffering and problems of living. Other goals are to achieve closeness to nature, ascertain the meaning of life, achieve ultimate peacefulness, gain access to energy centers, and experience pure joy and compassion. Transpersonal counselors use meditation, hypnosis, voluntary control of body processes through biofeedback, imagery, guided fantasies, dreams, and symbols from everyday language as vehicles for their counseling. The basic strategy of transpersonal counseling is teaching clients how to use data from their total person to achieve their potentials.

With the rapid strides being made in research on paranormal events also, such as ESP, it will probably not be long before methods of parapsychology find their way into the professional counseling room.

LIMITATIONS OF TRANSPERSONAL APPROACHES. The main limitation of transpersonal psychology at this point is its thin data base. Since the data are subjective, it is difficult to do research in the conventional manner on issues of interest to transpersonal counselors. The paradox is that this limitation is also one of its strengths—validation through individual experience. In addition, transpersonal methods are conveyed through teachers, or gurus, who often have charismatic appeal and sometimes extraordinary healing powers. It is difficult to separate method from person.

THE TRAIT-FACTOR APPROACH

Trait theorists see personality as a system of interdependent traits or factors such as abilities (verbal, numerical, memory, spatial, and so on), interests and values, attitudes, and temperament. Social traits and adjustment types are included also. The trait approach has a long history of attempts to classify people into dominant character types and to describe them in terms of test scores along various trait dimensions. The goal is to improve clients' decision-making capabilities.

Trait and factor approaches have been used widely by nonpsychotherapeutic counselors who are usually concerned with educational and career choice problems. The counseling problem becomes prediction of school and job success using an all-around appraisal of aptitude factors. Employment counselors, case workers, and school guidance counselors who assist people to make decisions using test data are using trait and factor theory.

The trait and factor group was influenced greatly by the early measurement movement in psychology. Psychometrics was concerned with measuring the various dimensions of personality in order to make accurate diagnoses and predictions of probable success. Paterson, Bingham, Darley, and Williamson were pioneers in the early attempts to make counseling an objective measurement-centered process. Thorne and Symonds did the same for psychotherapeutic counseling. They have written profusely about integrating the procedures of testing, case study, observation, diagnosis, prediction, planning of action, and follow-up, making this a formal process which has become known as professional counseling.

Other theorists are contributing sidelights to counseling. Factorial methods of statistical analysis are being utilized to gather data on the organization of personality. Cattell (1950), for example, has amassed considerable data on "trait clusters." Several major developments on aptitude factors have emerged in research centers. A number of test batteries based on factorial studies are available to the counselor and have influenced his theoretical model of personality organization and function. These developments will be explained further in Chapter 10 on testing.

Allport's views on the independent unitary trait (1937) have strongly influenced counseling groups. A large group of personality tests have been based upon the general premise that personality can be broken down into quite consistent generalized response units called "traits." Tests of traits such as social introversion, honesty, aggressiveness, cheerfulness, and self-confidence, for example, attest to the widespread infiltration of this view into counseling language. Allport's recent views have a more existential flavor. He has attempted a synthesis of many viewpoints on personality, particularly for counselors. He ties together behavioristic views about humans as reactive beings with dynamic views of humans reacting emotionally in depth, and humans "being-in-process-of-becoming" (1955). Allport argues for an inclusive theory which accounts for complex human motivation, aspiration, a balance between tentativeness and commitment, an adequate image of humanity, and a new and broader rationalism. Trait and factor theorists strive for this kind of complete understanding of their clients.

IMPLICATIONS AND LIMITATIONS FOR COUNSELING AND PSYCHOTHERAPY. Trait-factor theorists are devoted to an empirical study of the counseling relationship with only modest attempts at conceptualizing these observations into broad theories. Their pragmatic concerns seem to have led them to focus on the minute-by-minute study of the interview, factors or traits which can be measured and incorporated into prediction formulas, and a decision-making process to accomplish specific counseling goals. This decision process is detailed in Chapter 4.

A significant application of trait theory is in career development. Assessment instruments are used to help clients discover their strengths and limitations and then make sound decisions regarding a career plan. Holland's Self-Directed Search (1979) is an example of a program assisting clients to assess their career capabilities.

Another important practical concern is how to establish criteria of success in counseling and psychotherapy. How to relate events in counseling, meaningfully, to measurable outcome criteria of success is the subject of much current research effort. For example, what is the relationship between the degree of lead assumed by the counselor and clients' subsequent ability to assume responsibility for their own lives and to seek jobs, raise their grades, get along more amicably with their family, or just feel better? In this empirical method, there is little interest in the client's past except as it seems relevant in the counselor's opinion through the systematic case study.

The emphasis on objectivity, diagnosis, and prediction by this group of researchers on counseling led to some reaction and alarm. They were labeled *directivists,* with the implication that this method of counseling was: "Find out what's wrong with 'em and tell 'em." Misapplication of the diagnostic and predictive techniques and avoidance of more dynamic views led to abuses and extremes which stimulated much of the vitriolic writing on the directive-nondirective "controversy" during the forties. One of the more naïve followers of the trait-factor school of thought believed that if one collected enough facts about the client's various traits his behavior would make sense. We know now that mere cataloging of facts has limited value.

CONFRONTIVE THERAPIES

A group of therapies has emerged that confront the client in unusual ways. They depart from traditional approaches, but they do not have a systematic set of assumptions or methods. Exaggeration of the client's behavior is one method. The counselor asks clients to carry out unwanted behavior to an extreme by a method called paradoxical intent. An example is the person who fears fainting in elevators. The counselor takes the person to the elevator door and says, "You haven't fainted," then takes him or her inside and says, "You haven't fainted," and so on through the floors. Clients then see the absurdity of their behaviors in the paradox.

A label of *strategic therapy* is sometimes applied to this group which emphasizes therapy in natural settings outside therapy offices. This group focuses also on the cultural context of the person, assuming that his or her behavior makes sense in some context. They also look at people as parts of a system. Families are an example of a system, so that helping a client in a family means counseling in the context of the whole family (Satir 1972). Strategic therapists tend to focus initially on symptom relief, or behaviors which are troublesome to the client. Later they move into broader developmental issues and plans for life-style change. Suggestion is used freely, as in Erickson's style of hypnotherapy as described by Haley (1973). Farrelly and Brandsma (1974) use an approach called *provocative therapy,* in which they use unusual methods to achieve a response. For example, with a catatonic client who would not talk, Farrelly pulled hairs from her leg starting at her ankle and moving to her knee; whereupon, she said, "Stop it," and began to talk.

This group of confrontive therapists also deal with power issues directly, since many of the provocative methods come from the counselor's presumed power. The goal, however, is to empower clients, as soon as possible, to confront their own behaviors (Haley 1977).

This group of counselors, as may be clear, take considerable risks with their unusual methods, but they often take clients with unusually difficult problems by other theorists' definitions. So, if the goal is to get people to behave differently, then heavily confrontive, direct methods may be required.

PROCESS AND SYSTEM MODELS

Some study of counseling has been done by the process analysis approach. The process researcher focuses on the counseling process from the standpoint of procedures that work best for accomplishing a particular goal with a particular type of client in a particular institutional setting. The process approach is more empirical than eclectic. Theorists in this area have studied the interview, searching for elements which retard or accelerate interview progress and for factors which improve communication between counselor and client. Robinson (1950), for example, developed a "communications approach" which delineated the verbal dimensions of the interview. Problems were studied by means of recordings along dimensions such as "responsibility," "leading," "talk ratios," "planning statements," and "discussion units." Robinson was concerned with the effect of counselor attitude and technique on the client, without special regard to a particular systematic personality or learning theory.

The *systems model of counseling* is a comprehensive detailed model of the counseling process, based upon systems theory and operations research. A systems approach provides counselors with a framework for including their accumulated knowledge about relationships and helping as well as their cumulative empirical knowledge from research on the helping process. Flow diagrams from referral through evaluation of outcome provide a clear, logical series of steps for the process. Systems language, symbols, and flow charts are used to make this approach explicit. Stewart and his associates (1978) have analyzed the basic components of counseling and applied these principles to their approach, called systematic counseling.

Computer-Assisted and Programmed Counseling

A behavior-oriented development is the use of computers as a counseling adjunct or substitute. A system to conduct an automated interview is an experimental reality and is described and documented by Cogswell and Estavan (1965), Loughary, Friesen, and Hurst (1966), U.S. Office of Education reports (1969), and Super (1970). The client faces a teletypewriter linked to a computer. The computer begins, for example, by printing a question on the client's machine: "Do you plan to continue your formal education beyond high school?" If the client types "no," the next question is likely to be: "Which of these is most like what you plan on doing after high school? 1. Join the military service; 2. Go through vocational job training; 3. Enter an apprenticeship; 4. Get a job; 5. Decide later." Additional information and questions are sent back and forth depending on the answers of the client and the previously stored information about the client in the computer.

This approach has much promise for relieving the counselor of routine kinds of readiness work with clients. The system is programmed so that unusual responses needing individualized attention will be referred to a professional counselor through direct suggestion from the computer. While initial hopes for computer-assisted counseling were not realized, the computer has become a powerful adjunct to counseling for providing current information, especially in career choice.

Computers have been programmed such that student data can be screened by the computer and brought to the attention of the counselor like the warning light on a car instrument panel. Programs were developed to simulate counselors going through record folders. For example, printouts contain responses such as: "Student's grades have gone down quite a bit. Ask about this in interview. Possibly there are personal problems." Other possibilities include: "Student is a potential dropout"; "Low counseling priority. No problems apparent."

It is possible to link computer systems containing student data to other systems programmed with prediction data on college entrance, admission, and retention probabilities, scheduling, and other decision-making aids. Monitoring systems ensure that clients needing special attention are singled out. Unusual output indicating machine malfunction or inadequate programming also is brought to the attention of the counselor through monitors.

Validation for computer-assisted counseling comes from studies by Cogswell and Estavan (1965), Loughary, Friesen, and Hurst (1966), a comparison of programmed face-to-face counseling by Gilbert and Ewing (1965), and Wagman (1980). Loughary and associates studied the similarities between automated school counseling systems and human counselors in terms of pre- and postinterview assessment, and similarities in output, such as course selection. Client feelings about the computer were found to be favorable, although they preferred the human counselor. Some clients felt the computer was more helpful with certain kinds of prediction data, but they felt the human counselors had a greater amount of information to offer. The automated counseling system performed in a manner similar to human counselors in choice making and prediction such that the investigators see automated counseling as a valuable counselor adjunct of the future rather than a replacement.

The Plato DSC computer system is a recent example of personal dilemma problem-solving styles of counseling for college counseling centers (Wagman 1980). The model is a simple interactive system with a match between computer logic and client communication logic. This better match, along with improved computer technology in the seventies, produced a more workable system than the earlier efforts of the sixties.

The Gilbert and Ewing study in a college counseling service compared programmed counseling with highly trained and experienced counselors. Programmed counseling was compared to simulated programmed counseling (with counselor personal factor present) and normal counseling. Results indicated that, in terms of learning about one's self, each of the three methods produced some significantly greater performances. Generally, students preferred normal counseling, but they learned as much from programmed counseling. Studies of automated counseling have demonstrated the value of programmed assistance in certain kinds of planning and decision-making interviews. While the personal factor is still a relevant consideration in this type of counseling, apparently it is not as necessary as previously thought.

Decision and Choice Theory

While computers are aids in making predictions and plans, they also contain possibilities for developing models of the decision-making process. Programming is difficult unless objectives and a predictive system with alternatives and relevancy weights for each choice are determined. Gelatt and Brew (1980), for example, hold high hopes for counseling applications from decision and games theory developed in economics and mathematics. Counseling, especially of the planning type, needs more precise concepts and steps whereby significant life decisions are made.

A number of theories about how vocational choices are made by school-age youth have been developed. These are special variations of choice theory and will be reviewed in Chapter 14 in the context of educational and career counseling. Greenwald developed the view that all counseling focuses on decisions, even though feelings are important foci also. He has evolved an elaborate set of principles and strategies based on what he calls *decision therapy* (1973). The gist of Greenwald's theory is that people decide at critical points in their lives how they will respond to life's demands. Therapy consists of a rigorous reexamination of this sequence of decisions and their consequences.

SUMMARY

This chapter maintains the view that counselors and psychotherapists should have a consistent and explicit theory of personality to guide their practice as scientist-practitioners in therapeutic psychology. Although there is no one theory of personality which is suitable to frame the practice of counseling and psychotherapy, each position has unique implications for practice. The various dynamic, behavioral, and existential models of personality can be drawn upon to help understand this unique client in this particular setting. Each counselor must assume responsibility for developing his or her own approach to counseling.

3

Actualizing Counseling and Psychotherapy: A Multidimensional View

The title of this chapter states our views on a creative synthesis approach to counseling theory and human growth. The whole point to growth is to become one's true person and to realize all the potentials within one's self, that is, to continue actualizing into a responsible, fulfilled human being. In the preceding chapter we surveyed a variety of theories intended to achieve the goals of counseling and psychotherapy and described our creative synthesis approach. We emphasized that any one theory is not yet sufficiently comprehensive or systematic enough to guide the counselor through the multitudinous problems in everyday practice. Therefore, multidimensional view is described to cope with the complexities of the counseling endeavor. As counselors grow, their theories progress. Intuitive dynamic and existential theories become integrated with objective action approaches. The historical depth model of personality, which stresses inner drives and impulses to action, becomes reconciled with theories that emphasize the individual's present perceptual matrix, rationality, and conditioned behaviors.

We have struggled with the problem of devising a parsimonious, yet multidimensional, approach to counseling which involved selection of concepts that would hold up with growth, crisis, and prevention models, or which were at least workable for the majority of our clients. The selection of a personality model which had consistency for the universe in which we worked, and the selection of techniques which fitted our personalities, gave us a vocabulary and a frame of reference within which to verbalize, communicate, and test our observations about counseling relationships.

This chapter is our effort to make the events of counseling and psychotherapy more understandable to us, and we hope more understandable to the reader. We have discovered that it is much easier to develop a point of view for a restricted clientele in a special setting than a theory for counseling in general. Yet we know from our teaching and conferring with colleagues that most counselors work in settings with wide varieties of human problems requiring a multidimensional dynamic theory and a flexible approach to methods.

Other theories have made their unique and rich contributions to our thinking, for which we are grateful. We have added reflections, however, from our combined experiences in counseling and psychotherapy over a broad spectrum of clients and settings. Figure 9 represents perceptions

FIGURE 9. *Relationship of Actualizing Counseling and Therapy to Four Overlapping Historical Approaches*

of the current state of our thinking in reference to other wide and overlapping categories of theory. Major conceptual contributions to actualizing counseling flow from Gestalt psychology, an aspect of the phenomenological view. Perls's ideas about perception, awareness, and encounter in the present moment are examples. The humanistic contributions of Maslow on self-actualization, May on human encounter, Rogers on sensitivity to feelings, and Jourard on transparency and self-disclosures are central also. Cognitive-behavioral views such as those of Krumboltz, Lazarus, Bandura, Meichenbaum, and Mahoney emphasize behavior reinforcement, cognitive restructuring, and specific client goals. These views are important for actualizing counseling because they focus on problem solving and actualizing goals desired by clients. The cognitive approaches of Ellis (1962), Beck (1976), and others have been influential in their emphasis upon conscious and preconscious determinants of behavior, upon the use of present cognitive processes rather than past traumatic events, and upon the significant way in which humans intervene between stimulus and response by means of cognitive processes. Analytic views have made their impact in the form of levels of functioning, in focus on the ego, and with the phenomenon of defense. Transpersonal psychology has contributed many holistic principles of mind-body relationships and numerous techniques to explore our fantasy and dream worlds.

The principal tenets of actualizing counseling are progressive awareness and growth toward the actualized person. This growth process stresses responsible social action within a self-fulfilling framework. The term *actualization* was used originally by Goldstein (1940) to describe the becoming process of the organism. We use Maslow's and Goldstein's concept as a departure point, emphasizing the process term *actualizing*.

MULTIDIMENSIONAL SCOPE OF THE ACTUALIZING MODEL

A *developmental* or *historical* approach is a facet of actualizing counseling. As indicated in Chapter 2, there is considerable disagreement on the necessity for including an historical depth approach in one's conceptual framework; but we feel that even though our focus is on the present and the future, inclusion of a time dimension is very important to help the client understand the present and predict the future.

Each developmental stage has its unique problems and learnings which form the seeds of future problems. The counselor may work with the client at a particular historical level of development in the actualizing process in addition to immediate concerns. Thus, diagnostic statements are more meaningful as they are viewed in the context of a continuous growth process.

A *contemporary perceptual* approach is equally important, since we must know the client's unique outlook on his or her life at this moment in time. We need to know not only their current world view, but also perceptions of their immediate life space—not others' interpretations of it. Actualizing counseling, therefore, has a here and now phenomenological quality as a fulcrum on which the actualizing process turns.

An *action* or *behavioral* focus is central to actualizing counseling also, since it is behavior we wish to change, and not an illness we wish to cure. With this key assumption it behooves the actualizing counselor to become knowledgeable about behavior change concepts such as conditioning, reinforcement, generalizing, and others outlined in Chapter 2 to mobilize the client into constructive action. Actualizing counselors work with data in the solution of human problems and must have a rationale for including significant behavioral data from tests, for example, in helping the person predict and plan directions for actualization.

Because of the broad context in which most counselors and psychotherapists perform their helping functions, we feel strongly that a multidimensional approach must be utilized in maximizing their helpfulness. Frequently counselors must approach clients on a wide front, utilizing many interacting modalities of feeling, cognition, sensation, imagery, and action. For maximum effectiveness, however, it appears that counselors must focus on one or two modalities at one time, drawing on numerous techniques to reach client goals. For example, a counselor may focus on expression of feeling during the early stages, use fantasy to facilitate expression, move to a desensitization method to assist with management of specific fears, model new behaviors through role playing, interpret growth goals according to the polarity hypothesis, and set up a schedule of reinforcement to perpetuate new adaptive behaviors over the next few months. We are fully aware of the difficulties in attempting integration of the broad spectrum of theoretical views of personality and behavior change, but we are convinced that this task needs continuous effort by every counselor.

We see five dimensions comprising the actualizing point of view. A *philosophical dimension* is an essential consideration because of the emphasis on goals of actualization. We have a model of the kind of person who evolves in this growth process. This model incorporates a series of value judgments about the human condition and the nature of reality.

The *structural dimension,* a schematic conceptualization of personality organization, is a kind of cognitive map for viewing the actualizing process in a given moment of time. Closely related is the *dynamic* dimension, which emphasizes basic processes of growth and motivation. A *developmental* dimension includes much of what we know about human development.

Finally, a *research dimension* is essential to an enterprise as new and dynamic as actualizing counseling and psychotherapy. The actualizing counselor is a true scientist as described in Chapter 2. Counselors are curious, critical, truthful, logical, objective, and precise in this role, as opposed to their more subjective emotional functioning as a participant in the client's actualizing process. The actualizing counselor must strive to reconcile these frequently contradictory roles through employing them in a kind of synergic alternating of awareness, or as a check and balance system. We feel strongly that an overemphasis in either direction is not appropriate at this stage of development in actualizing counseling. Maslow has approached this problem in depth through his extended essay *The Psychology of Science: A Reconnaissance* (1966), recommended to the reader for more ideas on reconciling these conflicts.

The Philosophical Dimension

Counseling and psychotherapy, being such deeply human growth processes, constantly face questions of what values and goals to promote, how free the individual is or should be, and how much influence the actualizing counselor should have on client values. These questions will be discussed more extensively in Chapter 6 on the actualizing counselor as a valuing person. The purposes of this section, however, are to emphasize the importance of the counselor's philosophy and to present some philosophical assumptions underlying actualizing counseling. The vastness of this subject requires restating that this discussion is illustrative and does not do justice to the importance and complexity of this topic.

ASSUMPTIONS OF ACTUALIZING COUNSELING. Actualizing counseling is based in part upon the following assumptions:

1. Each person is a *unique human being* seeking actualization, even though he or she shares much "human nature" in common with others. A better term is Buber's "particularity" principle, a unique "thou" seeking to be realized.

2. While the actualizing principle has a futuristic quality in the "becoming" sense, it takes place in the *moment-to-moment growth* process. Hence, the "here and now" becomes the temporal focus of the process.

3. Human behavior is not determined by events (external or internal) as much as by one's own cognitive representations of events.

4. While much of human behavior is determined by personal history and forces beyond one's control, the actualizing process assumes that one's future is largely undetermined and one has wide ranges of *freedom to choose*.

5. The assumption of freedom places corresponding *responsibility* on the person for his or her own actualizing. One cannot depend upon others or blame others for one's growth or lack of it. Even though growth takes place in a social context, each person alone is responsible for his or her own life.

6. While some primitive behaviors are reflexive, hence largely genetically determined, and some are the result of chemical or neurological changes, a fundamental assumption of actualizing counseling is that *social behavior is learned* and changes in behavior follow an active learning process.

7. Most human learning is not automatic but, rather, is mediated through cognitive processes such as symbolic coding and selective attention.

8. Actualization is achieved primarily in *social interaction* with a counselor, teacher, minister, group, friend, or family; but it also can be achieved through self-help methods, such as meditation and imagery. Social interaction becomes the main vehicle for conditions of actualization, such as honesty with feelings, awareness of self, freedom of expression, and trust in one's self and others.

9. A reciprocal interaction takes place between thoughts, emotions, and actions such that a change in one tends to bring about a change in the others. Each person decides intentionally which modality begins the change process—thought, feeling, or action. To go from intention to action the person must move beyond awareness and intention to commitment.

10. Each personality contains the paradoxical state of *polar opposites* which are expressed and forced to awareness and action in the actualizing process. Examples are dependence and independence, affection and aggression, support and criticalness.

Goals of Actualizing Counseling and Psychotherapy

A philosophy of counseling must contain some indications of outcomes expected from the growth process. The following statements of personality growth are just that—ideals of the ongoing actualizing process and not fixed quantitative end points. While some of these goals are preludes to more remote growth stages and could be organized in a hierarchy such as Allport's and Maslow's schemas, we prefer at this point merely to list and describe some of our objectives of actualizing counseling and therapy.

There are three kinds of goals. The first is a category of *process goals,* which are means toward broader actualization. Examples are free spontaneous verbalization, and continued working through of problems. *Client goals* are the manifest purposes of the client's initial search for help. Examples are reduction of anxiety, desire for information, removal of annoying symptoms, making a crucial decision, or easing a situational pressure. Clients do not come initially asking to be "actualized." *Actualizing goals,* however, are broader, more generalized growth outcomes than solutions to immediate problems. It should be emphasized that these actualizing goals are tied closely to social values and the kinds of behaviors required to live effectively in Western culture. In another sense, these goals are characteristics of a theoretical model personality which would seem to "fit" Western cultural settings. This statement does not imply that psychological counseling leads to passive adjustment or conformity to a heavily bureaucratized world. The principal emphasis is upon developing the individuality of clients, at the same time helping them to see their social responsibilities for contributing to, and possibly changing, the culture about them. This discussion and the values to follow flow mainly from the humanistic tradition, since this approach to counseling emphasizes the potentiality of people for psychological growth. This view pushes the person beyond adjusting and coping with life.

1. *Independence.* The end point of any counseling effort is to help the client to become self-sufficient and to minimize his dependence on his physical and social environment. The client should be able to act decisively on the basis of increased awareness.

2. *Spontaneity.* Various phrases are used as synonyms for this goal, such as freedom to be, flexibility in meeting change, openness to one's own and others' experience, and reduction of rigidity. Spontaneity may be construed as the polar opposite of defensiveness. Rogers (1954) describes this characteristic as "increasing openness to experience." The world of experience for the client is no longer threatening. Clients picture themselves in a way more congruent with the way they are seen by others; therefore, they need not defend themselves as strenuously as they did before counseling.

There are objective indices of such a characteristic as spontaneity on psychological instruments. Rorschach protocols, for example, show how spontaneity follows as the constrictive control indices decline. Flexibility takes its place. Shostrom's *Personal Orientation Inventory* (1963) also has a spontaneity scale which measures this quality.

As a result of the decrease in defensiveness, the client is better able to perceive reality as defined by others. There is less rigidity of perception and less need to distort or narrow perceptions in the direction of delusions. As Rogers says:

> *He sees that not all trees are green, not all men are stern fathers, not all women are rejecting, not all failure experiences prove that he is no good, and the like. He is able to take in the evidence in a new situation,* as it is, *rather than distorting it to fit a pattern which he already holds.* (1954, p. 16)

A close relative of spontaneity is a concept called *tolerance for ambiguity.* One can live comfortably with value and factual conflicts or unclear situations. One can hold beliefs in a tentative fashion while sifting conflicting evidence. One is not compulsively bound to seek definiteness in all things.

Another related term used by Rogers is *getting behind the mask.* Successful counseling results in dropping the facade, the mask, or the role. One becomes more genuinely one's true self. In Jungian terms the *persona* decreases. As one of Roger's clients put it, "I haven't been really honestly myself, or actually known what my real self is, and I have been just playing a sort of false role" (1954, p. 11). It should be emphasized that one retains some of one's defenses and roles.

Counselors are not trying to "standardize" personalities in psychological counseling. Actualizing counselors strive to help people appreciate their own uniqueness, providing the unique qualities are not maintained at too high a price. There is also value in the client's appreciation of the other person's "particularity" and realization that people are basically alike in many ways. They have similar hopes, feelings, and thoughts, though their various roles and persona characteristics often make them appear to be vastly different.

Creativity is one consequence of spontaneity. Analytic psychotherapists, especially Jungian ones, place great stress upon developing a creative personality. According to analytic therapists, the client is able to use more of his or her unconscious feelings as servant rather than as master. Much of the energy heretofore used to defend feelings is now released to the other systems for the client to use more creatively. Maslow (1970) postulates that all humans are given this creative potentiality at birth, but that they lose it through the process of acculturation. The creative impulses must not be thought of necessarily as being applied to the arts, as in writing or music, but in more humble circumstances of everyday life. One can be a creative clerk, craftsman, teacher, or homemaker.

3. *Living Here and Now.* By this phrase is meant an increasing tendency to live each moment fully. The client tries to live so as to extract the richness of every moment. One does not try to anticipate life with too many ready-made answers. Rather, each moment is new; what one will do with that moment is something creative, hence, unpredictable. One's value structure, which is part of one's basic individuality, will assist one to act appropriately. As Rogers says in his reflective paper on the *fully functioning personality,* the individual is "dependable but not predictable" (Unpublished, p. 11).

The client, in terminating psychological counseling or psychotherapy, feels as if the job is not done, but just beginning. It is as if clients are on the right train, not exactly knowing where they are going, yet feeling that they are moving in the right direction. One is in closer contact with one's own feelings and goals, and is more aware of social values and goals. One does not, however, approach a new situation with a rigidly preformed structure. One's personality is flexible and the defensive walls permeable. One can make possible modifications of inner structures from each new experience. One is satisfied in the feeling that one never quite "arrives."

Rogers (1961) points out in his discussion of the fully functioning person that such a person enjoys an activity for the pleasure of doing it, not necessarily because it is a means to an end. Our American culture puts great stress on the value of *means* toward ends, and not enough stress, in our opinion, on the *ends* themselves. Some people, for example, feel it is necessary to rationalize golfing because it is good for their health— they get sunshine and air—and do not admit that the act of golfing itself is pleasurable.

Rogers's summary of his philosophical paper entitled *A Therapist's View of the Good Life* emphasizes the significance of a philosophy based on awareness and acceptance of one's own nature:

> *I believe it will have become evident why, for me, adjectives such as happy, contented, blissful, enjoyable, do not seem quite appropriate to any general description of this process I have called the good life, even though the person in this process would experience each one of these feelings at appropriate times. But the adjectives which seem more generally fitting are adjectives such as enriching, exciting, rewarding, challenging, meaningful. This process of the good life is not, I am convinced, a life for the faint hearted. (It involves stretching and growing, becoming more and more of one's potentialities. It involves the courage*

to be. It means launching oneself fully into the stream of life. Yet the deeply exciting thing about human beings is that when the individual is inwardly free, he chooses as the good life this process of becoming). (1954, p. 13)

4. *Trust.* Clients terminating successful psychotherapy have certain attitudes toward themselves which may be characterized as "self-confidence" or "self-worth." One trusts one's self and one's judgment. In deciding what course of action to follow in any question, one does not necessarily rely on rules, common-sense aphorisms, or mandates laid down by institutions or "social customs." Rather, one trusts one's judgment and does what feels right or appropriate—all things considered.

The last phrase, "all things considered," should be emphasized. The confident, self-directive individual does not just act impulsively or whimsically. As Adler points out, one considers consequences. One thinks, for example, of one's social responsibility. One trusts one's own inner promptings rather than depending exclusively upon external motivation to behave. One believes in one's self, as well as in other persons and institutions.

The stringent controls of the character level are relaxed so as to make their modification more possible. The authors incorporate the concept of *conscience* or the Freudian *superego* as part of the character level. The earlier learnings from parents regarding social values are more amenable to critical examination and alteration after a course of successful psychotherapy.

The authors are indebted to Rogers (1957, p. 8) for an illustration of how the process of achieving self-trust and confidence might work in a client. We can compare the personality to a gigantic computing machine. Since the client is now more open to experience, more data from his or her present situation as well as extensive data from past learnings are available. Since he or she is interacting more completely with the environment at any point, he or she has more access to data from within and without. The client can more properly evaluate and select relevant data for the solution of present problems. We feel that one reason people err in judgment is that they include data which do not belong to the present context and exclude data which do. Thus, people who exclude data from their present situation and react only in terms of memories and stereotypes from previous learnings, as if they were this reality, are in trouble. Prejudice functions this way. Or, conversely, people who react to present situations without the benefit of past experiences may be in trouble as well. The present data may be stored in distorted form. All reliable data are needed to produce the most appropriate answers to life problems.

Operating in the spontaneous, self-trusting manner cited above does not mean a client will avoid errors. But it is hypothesized that such a client will correct errors due to omitted or distorted data without guilt or self-punishing defenses. Learning to trust one's feelings and judgments, as well as one's intelligence and experience, is a difficult state to achieve. Many people tend to want direction from without, to be dependent upon someone else to tell them what to feel and what to do.

Learning to express one's feelings—to live them—is stressed by many writers of psychological literature. Fromm (1941), for example, emphasizes that the client "becomes alive" to his feelings. Knowing one's real feelings, expressing them in individually and socially satisfying ways is an extension of the psychotherapeutic process of uncensured emotional experiencing when the client *is* his anger, his fear, or his love. This experience of learning to like and trust one's self is one meaning of self-realization—of becoming a real person.

5. *Awareness.* A primary objective of actualizing is increased awareness, a sense of aliveness and responsiveness. One can perceive and appreciate one's environment freshly and more deeply. One has more of what Maslow (1970) calls "peak experiences," those intense emotional experiences accompanying life activities. This awareness includes experiencing the full range of behavioral possibilities in each of the polarities of existence. An especially troublesome polarity in human experience is the masculinity-femininity dimension. In Western, particularly American, culture males are expected to behave in conditioned stereotyped ways, and females likewise. Bem's research (1975) validates the numerous ways this dichotomy creeps into our culture; and she gives her rationale for androgynous behaviors where males can exhibit traditional female traits such as tenderness and females can be assertive in the traditional male fashion.

After becoming more aware of their innermost feelings over a long period of time, clients experience a greater range and a finer differentiation of feelings. They find that they do not live merely in terms of their intellects, but that they can experience feelings also. They can courageously and joyfully experience communication with more varied feelings. Again we quote Rogers's observations on this point:

> It seems to me that clients who have moved significantly in therapy live more intimately with their feelings of pain, but also more vividly with their feelings of ecstasy; that anger is more clearly felt, and so also is love, that fear is an experience they know more deeply, but so is courage. And the reason they can thus live fully in a wider range is that they have this underlying confidence in themselves as trustworthy instruments for encountering life. (1957, pp. 13–14)

Occasionally the phenomenon is called *freedom from emotional constriction.* This means the capacity to experience a greater range of feelings without consequent threat.

Brown (1940) expresses the experiencing of increased range of feeling in another way. Paraphrasing Freud, he suggests that one goal of psychotherapy is to help the client to love more easily and to hate more wisely. Occasionally clients come who can express only positive feelings, having been forbidden to express hostile feelings at home. It has been our observation that the necessity to suppress expression of negative feelings tends to have a constricting effect on expression of positive feelings also.

Finally, the reduction of painful anxiety is a criterion of successful psychotherapy. The client is relieved of incapacitating guilt and anxiety so that the uncertainty and insecurity he felt formerly are replaced with more certainty and optimism.

6. *Authenticity.* Being one's genuine person in relations with others is a way of expressing authenticity. Becoming more authentic through actualizing counseling is one way to overcome the alienation, loneliness, and meaninglessness felt by many people.

7. *Responsible Action.* Actualizing persons make judgments which enhance their own welfare and that of others. Their spontaneity, freedom, intentionality, and expressiveness are controlled and limited to the extent that they live in a real social world where consideration of others, commitment to family and work, and contribution to social good become a large part of their lives. They have the courage to resist social demands and trends which run counter to their own lives, however, and do not blame others for their adverse conditions. They take responsibility for their own choices and utilize their own style of problem solving.

The mature client can postpone and modify decisions about others at this moment in this situation. The latter idea is often called a "time-binding" facility with which the client is better able to postpone pleasures and goals. For example, the graduate student undergoes much immediate sacrifice and strain to reach the satisfactions of a distant professional goal.

While much actualizing behavior is concerned with inner development of pleasure and fulfillment, active outgoing interpersonal contact is equally significant. This focus includes an activist stance which concentrates on enhancing others' welfare and serving as an advocate for the weak, helpless, alienated, and deprived. This role also means functioning as a force for community change by attempting to transform community norms, attitudes, and behaviors to those more in line with the actualizing goals cited above.

8. *Effectiveness.* While overlapping and summarizing many of the actualized characteristics above, the goal of increased human effectiveness is central to actualizing counseling. Effectiveness in living is related to life stages, since effectiveness is defined in terms of the expectancies and skills the person possesses at his or her particular stage in life and particular cultural setting. The actualizing person meets life's demands effectively and flexibly at each of his or her developmental stages. Ivey and Simek-Downing (1980) use the term *intentionality* to describe an overall goal for counseling. A person possessing this quality can approach problems flexibly from a variety of viewpoints and can act with a sense of capability to develop new thoughts and behaviors appropriate to the present time and place.

The list above is not exhaustive of actualizing goals. Empirical studies of ideal growth have been made by investigators such as Maslow (1970), with his "self-actualized young persons," Rogers (1961) on personal growth, and Shostrom (1963) with dimensions of self-actualizing. Much of the counseling, mental hygiene, and existential literature is replete with statements of ideal maturation for our culture. Mental health is a term to describe this ideal mature state. Jahoda (1958) developed six key criteria after reviewing the extensive literature on mental health. These are:

1. Attitude toward self.
2. Degree of realizing self-actualization potential through action.
3. Integration of personality function.
4. Autonomy or independence of social influence.
5. Perception of reality.
6. Taking life as it comes and environmental mastery.

Key problems for counselors are to find observable indicators of the above criteria and then to specify the conditions for achieving them.

THE STRUCTURAL AND DYNAMIC SYSTEM OF THE ACTUALIZING MODEL

The following outline of structural and functional dimensions of personality is presented as an example of a way of conceptualizing the actualizing process. Several basic concepts characterizing this model will be described, followed by a detailed listing of functions and actualizing goals for each of the levels.

Five levels—facade, actualizing, manipulative, character, and core—are shown in Figure 10. They are hypothesized as interlocking energy systems with their unique functions to perform for the person. They represent rough levels of awareness from high awareness on the exterior to low awareness at the core level. The term *system* is used to denote the dynamic interactive characteristic of these functional levels, rather than to imply a static and rigid hierarchy of functions, or a structured topographical personality "map."

A DYNAMIC SYSTEM.   This is a key concept because it denotes the unstable changing character of the personality system. There is constant movement along the polarities in an interweaving fashion among the various levels. This idea is represented in Figure 10 as arrows moving across levels. The rhythmic flow through the levels of the model means that one can move freely from one level to another to begin awareness processes at one level and move to another, according to client need or situational demand. This idea does not imply a depth conception, as in psychoanalytic models, but rather the client's freedom to work at the most relevant level of the moment.

Another dynamic aspect, furthermore, is the current skepticism regarding the validity of the idea of stable traits of personality. It appears from Mischel's extensive review (1973) of the personality literature and his own research that personality is such a determined function of the person and his or her situation of the moment that we cannot make valid generalizations about the stability of traits.

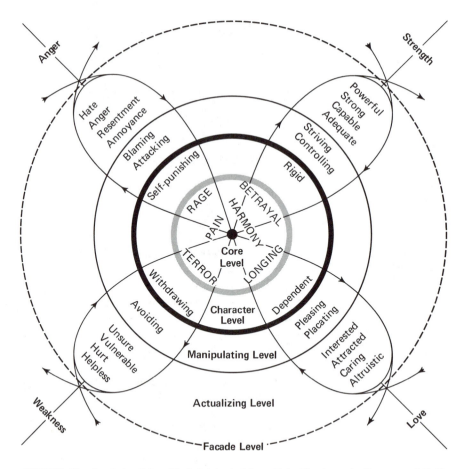

FIGURE 10. An Actualizing Model. Adapted from E. L. Shostrom, L. Knapp, and R. Knapp, *Actualizing Therapy* (1976, p. 137).

The term *dynamic* implies the action element so central to the actualizing model. We assume that awareness is moving continuously from vague experiencing into active behavior change in the direction of the client's specific goals and the general actualizing goals cited earlier.

ENERGY. It is assumed that energy is a characteristic of all personality levels and provides the motivational force impelling the person to action. It is predicated upon a biologically based need system. It is postulated that energy flows freely among the levels in the system. All levels are "grounded" in the body where feelings are expressed in the musculature.

POLARITIES. The actualizing model attempts to come to grips with one of the baffling issues in counseling, namely, the paradoxes inherent in the idea of feeling polarities. The idea of polarities in existence is an old one—for example, the idea that if dependence is a pronounced characteristic, a dormant independence opposite is present also. Leary (1957) brought the concept of polarities and continua of polar characteristics to the center of personality theory. This concept of polarities is central to actualizing counseling and therapy because we think that helping the client to become more aware of these polar traits and to accept their seemingly contradictory functions in our lives is a key actualizing goal. One of the additional goals, furthermore, is to develop both poles in the service of the person. In Maslow's research on self-actualizing people (1970), he found that they could express anger or tender love with ease. They were competent and strong, yet were aware of their weaknesses. In Figure 10 only four polar points, with illustrative feelings, are included for the sake of simplicity and because we regard these four points of anger-love and strength-weakness as key polarities. Others, such as dominance-submission, masculinity-femininity, dependence-independence, are significant also. The descriptive terms along the polar continua express the polar characteristics for that level of personality, for example, actualizing on the weakness pole has unsure and helpless feeling qualities.

Levels in the Actualizing Model

FACADE LEVEL. This level is defined as a permeable boundary between the actualizing level and contact with the interpersonal world. This permeability, indicated by a dotted line in Figure 10, varies with the person's needs for defense or freedom of contact. Openness to others, for example, can be thought of in terms of permeability of the facade.

The principal functions of the facade level are to *defend* the person from psychological threats from without; to "hide" feelings at the other personal functioning levels from others and to present a "public image" or impression. The facade functions are controlled largely by the manipulating or managing level. Here, the defensive functions, such as projection, deception, denial, and manipulation, are initiated. These defensive functions are learned in the process of development and become quite automatic, even though partially under the control of the manipulating level. They are part of our "programming" for survival.

An objective of the actualizing process is to make the person more aware of facade level functions, to make defensive maneuvering functions more serviceable to the person, and to place them more under the control of the actualizing level. For example, "game" behavior, as Berne (1961) defined it, has a deceptive or manipulative effect on others and has many "payoffs" for the person, such as social advantage and satisfaction of aggressive needs at the expense of others. Actualizing processes attempt to put these functions in juxtaposition with actualizing behaviors so the person can make some basic adaptive and rational choices and achieve some balance in expression of his or her polarities. Another goal is to achieve some measure of congruence between the public image put forth at the facade level and the private images one has of one's self at other levels. An example of such a discrepancy would be the person's behavior at a cocktail party. Here, the manipulative type of person responds in terms of what others expect rather than in terms of his or her private feelings. In other words, open, flexible, and congruent facade functions are the basic goals.

ACTUALIZING LEVEL.   This is the first level of awareness in the system. First, it serves an *objectifying function* such that people can look at themselves as both subjects and objects. That is, they can get outside of themselves to observe themselves as objects. Thus, it has many functions of an ego system in the analytic models. It is the equivalent of the "I" or "me" of everyday language. In the objectifying function, the actualizing level also is the locus of rationality and ordering of experience.

Through its rational functions, the actualizing level performs a type of filter effect for selecting stimuli to which the person will attend. This actualizing function includes symbolizing and externalizing much of the feeling which comes from the other levels within the system. As a symbolizing agent, the actualizing level helps the person to rationalize conflict by attempts to reduce apparent inconsistencies. Hence, the actualizing level contains the major integrating force.

Thus, one of the important related functions of the actualizing level is construing the world in a manner so as to make perceptions "fit." Following the above-mentioned symbolizing and filtering functions, this system organizes and attaches meanings to current sensations in light of past experiences. The actualizing system also compares perceptions with past experiences and data from the other levels.

When the actualizing level is functioning in the ways described above, which are effective and satisfying for the person, it is said that one has a "strong" actualizing system. The person is perceiving events as accurately as possible with his or her unique experience background. The person is aware of a feeling of competence to master both internal and external pressures and to reconcile polarities. The person is also aware of a feeling of value and individuality which is a goal in the actualizing process.

A second important function of the actualizing level is *action*. Many of the problem-solving, decision-making, and energy-mobilizing functions of the person have their locus here, as well as in the manipulating level, to be described next. The actualizing level is the locus of activity in the person, where actualizing behaviors are focused and find expression in interpersonal contacts.

A third function is serving as a vehicle for *expression of feeling*, usually in contact with others. In Figure 10, it may be noted that these feelings follow the axis of the polarities and are characteristic in both kind and intensity of the actualizing level. The aim in the actualizing process is to facilitate the active expression of basic polar feelings freely and appropriately. A function of the actualizing level is to translate the feelings in nonfunctional or dysfunctional forms from other levels such that the actualizing goals of the person are achieved. This is accomplished in the rhythmic style described earlier and illustrated with arrows in Figure 10.

MANIPULATING LEVEL. The chief function of this level in the system is to manage or control for purposes of protecting the person, manipulating others, gaining support from the environment, or coping with environmental demands. A key synonym for manipulating would be *managerial,* since one consequence of this level of functioning in interpersonal events is that the other person feels controlled. The manipulator functions without much feeling. This nonsensitivity to others is understandable, since the main function of the managing level is to protect the person. An overemphasis on this function leads to a "thick-skinned" protective reaction which is perceived by others as insensitive and rigid. A counselor may say, for example, "Are you aware that your need to defend yourself sometimes hurts people and shuts off their caring about you?" (From here the counselor works on specific actions clients can take to loosen their behaviors and increase their contact skills.)

CHARACTER LEVEL. This level functions as an identity base for the person. The basic personal styles, or character patterns, are stylized ways of responding to the world. For example, in terms of the basic polarities of the actualizing model, a character style would be the typical personal patterns of handling hostility, dependency, and rejection or acceptance of others. Much of the reaction is experienced by the musculature in the form of tenseness or by organ dysfunction, such as colitis. Holding back on feelings, for example, is associated with muscular rigidity.

    Another function of the character level is to provide a definition of self, that vague, undifferentiated part of the person which one defines as the "real me" or the "self." It is a learned pattern of responses to characteristic life situations which are expressed in the form of stereotyped responses along the polarity dimensions. As in the manipulating level, the character level performs essentially negative protective functions. The challenge of actualizing is how can one's basic character structure be made over sufficiently to act in the service of actualizing the whole person, instead of maintaining essentially stereotyped responses? The level of awareness of the person in regard to the character level is usually low. One of the goals of the actualizing process is to loosen the boundaries between the core and actualizing levels so that the basic character of the person can be modified sufficiently to serve the actualizing goals of that person. This process means taking risks so that the manipulating level can release sufficient controls to allow change to take place. This loosening process can be monitored to a limited degree by keeping in touch with body developments. For example, as the control and caution needs lessen, the body can loosen. Muscular rigidity is the body's way of communicating that the person does not consider that release of feelings or revelation of core polarities is safe.

CORE LEVEL. This center of the person is the locus of basic feelings and what is called popularly "human nature." Paradoxically, the core has the common elements of feeling polarities which characterize all human beings; at the same time, it defines the uniqueness of a person. It is the center of one's existence and has the function of providing a harmonious and satisfying home in a world of loneliness and isolation from others; or it can be a living "hell on earth" of accumulated painful feeling experiences of which one is only vaguely aware.

We have been impressed over the years with people's basic need for privacy—a place in their existence which is uniquely their own. We view the main function of the core, then, as providing this center of one's existence where the vectors of many polar feelings cross. It is here that much of the painful hurt of the past is experienced. It is often expressed in deep longing for contact as, "Why wasn't I loved?" or in a form of rage as, "Why wasn't I given the freedom to be?" Sometimes, an awareness of being rejected is experienced as betrayal. Core pain is thus a basic reaction to the denial of the person's fundamental right to exist as a person. The actualizing process consists, in part, then, of aiding the person to be aware of those feelings of hurt and denial, to own them, and to take responsibility for actualizing himself or herself to the point of effective and satisfying living.

The core level is the locus of experiencing positive and strong qualities also. These qualities are expressed frequently as awareness of well-being, harmony, peace, confidence, worth, beauty, oneness with nature or with the universe. One goal of the actualizing process is to bring these feelings to awareness and to reinforce them with actualizing level behaviors which validate the positive core feelings.

We view the core level, therefore, as being neither positive nor negative from an external judging point of view. It is much like Fromm's description of the unconscious, which he describes as follows:

> *In Freud's thinking the unconscious is essentially that in us which is bad, the repressed, that which is incompatible with the demands of our culture and of our higher self. In Jung's system the unconscious becomes a source of revelation, a symbol for that which in religious language is God Himself. In his view the fact that we are subject to the dictates of our unconscious is in itself a religious phenomenon. I believe that both of these concepts of the unconscious are one-sided distortions of the truth. Our unconscious—that is, that part of our self which is excluded from the organized ego—*contains both the lowest and the highest, the worst and the best [emphasis ours]. *We must approach the unconscious not as if it were a god whom we must worship or a dragon we must slay but in humility, with a profound sense of humor, in which we see that other part of ourselves as it is, neither with horror nor with awe. We discover in ourselves desires, fears, ideas, insights which have been excluded from our conscious organization and which we have seen in others but not in ourselves.* (1950, p. 97)

The core level is a powerful motivating agent in the person, since it is from here that much of the energy for action stems. If our hypotheses are correct—that is, that basic drives for security, sexuality, and aggression originate here through learned life experiences—then it is understandable what a dominating force the core could be in the personality. This is the case particularly in times of threat or crisis. The biological and anthropological evidence on the inferred nature of the core level is fragmentary and conflicting. Generally, people seem to come into this world with basically outreaching, cooperating, security-seeking need systems. In the normal processes of family life many frustrations and learnings are experienced which affect the person's basic outlook on life and himself or herself. It is assumed, therefore, that the feeling propensities and characteristics of the core level are learned rather than inherited.

Since core feelings are learned, and work in such individualistic ways to influence the behavior of persons, it is difficult to generalize about "human nature." While some people seem motivated by "blind" pleasure and seek to minimize pain and effort, others appear to be motivated by challenge and search. One goal of the actualizing process is that persons seek meaningful activity and meaningful relationships to fulfill complex longings for worth and dignity. This goal and the value premise underlying it have profound political implications as we visualize a society which makes possible full actualization of its members.

A basic principle of the actualizing process is to open communication between the core and the actualizing levels of the person. One of the main methods is release of affect through talk, body sensory work, fantasy, or other projective method. The safety of a counseling relationship offers the person an opportunity to face the frightening feelings of rage, deep longing for contact, terror, or rejection and betrayal by trusted persons. This relationship offers opportunities for release of these feelings to awareness and the companion approach of taking responsibility for constructive action to change one's behavior. This awareness serves to prevent use of these past experiences and feelings as excuses for not realizing one's potential for growth. Often the labored expression of these painful core feelings with a caring helper results in feelings experienced as harmony, peace, and well-being. In terms of our postulate of system energy, this energy that was so bound to the core feelings is now released for constructive use at the actualizing behavior level. A basic principle of many therapy models, the actualizing model included, is that release from emotional conflict equals available emotional energy for actualizing pursuits. This release of energy coupled with action methods for behavior change offers clients a wide spectrum of actualizing possibilites.

DEVELOPMENTAL DIMENSION

Counseling is frequently construed as a process of facilitating optimum lifelong development. In addition, each stage in life has its unique physical and psychological tasks to accomplish. Some of these tasks must be finished before moving to the next stage, such as achieving a sense of personal identity by late adolescence. Unless a clear answer to the question "Who am I?" is achieved by young adulthood, later years of life are preoccupied with answering it. If certain tasks are not accomplished by the expected age for that culture, a life crisis could erupt. Counseling is concerned with these developmental crisis points also. So, the value of a developmental perspective for a counselor is that it provides a kind of lifeline map to identify tasks and crisis points for each roughly defined stage.

The idea of life stages with definable boundaries is very controversial. Levinson and associates (1978), for example, identify a number of fairly stable stages in adult development separated by usually unstable transitional periods of one to three years. Brim (1977), on the other hand, says his data do not support the concepts of stages and predictable crises during life transitions. In the following section we present a few developmental counseling issues; but we refer the reader to specialized texts on lifelong development.

Recent developmental research and text writing have focused on cognitive developmental work (Collins 1977). These studies of cognitive competencies from infancy to old age help counselors decide what interventions are likely to succeed or fail at a given age. Examples are the findings on moral judgments and social role-taking ability. Designing psychological education programs on the basis of cognitive-developmental theory is another example.

GENERAL PERIODS OF GROWTH.   Lifelong development can be divided into two general periods: from birth to about thirty-five years, and from age thirty-five to death. The first mastery stage is one in which people have broad capacities for learning and building their lives. Unfolding intelligence and physical and emotional maturation are in their service to pursue countless goals which are both created and limited by their physical and cultural environments. In this period people develop habits to cope with parental demands; then they meet pressures to develop rational skills, acquire an education, enter and progress on a career.

At the end of this first period the individual's intellectual, physical, and emotional potentials have taken direction; habits have been formed; choices have been made; mastery skills have been developed; and a life style has been chosen. Following this first broad period people begin to think of ways to consolidate their gains. They have in some fashion mastered their economic and social environment. Efficiency and physical strength begin to diminish, and the maintenance period begins. The goals of youth begin to be replaced by the goals of maturity and old age. They find themselves beginning to scrutinize their values and to look for a way of life that will support and reward them and those they love until the end of life.

The idea of precise stages of adult development is not supported by sufficient data. What is impressive to us, though, is the increasing diversity with age. While it makes some sense to talk about the typical seven-year-old, it makes no sense whatever to describe the typical fifty- or seventy-year-old. Even retirement planning, for example, is no longer following the conventional counseling approaches because of the great variability in ages of retirement and perceptions of what that event means.

Counselors must study developmental psychology to understand the changing demography and the impact of social change on different age groups in a given culture. For example, counselors need to know what is happening to the older American adult group in numbers and use of psychological services. From census projections, for example, adults over age 65 by the year 2020 will comprise over 16 percent of the population, whereas only 11 percent are currently over 65 (Jarvik 1978). Where only 2 percent of mental health services clients now are from the elderly, it is estimated that demand for counseling will skyrocket when the current middle-age generation arrives in the older-age brackets. Myths about older adults are crumbling also. Their potential for growth is great and their mental declines are not as severe as once was believed (Butler 1975). Their special problems of facing multiple losses and the imminent prospects of death or disability, for example, are unlike those of younger age groups. Suicides among older adult white men are more frequent per unit of population than any other age group. Above all, counselors need to face their own biases about aging, their own fears of becoming "useless," and, finally, their own deaths (Schlossberg, Troll, and Leibowitz 1978).

BASIC PRINCIPLES OF GROWTH. Psychological growth has several general underlying principles that affect the counselor's perceptions. Growth is *progressive* and *cumulative;* that is, it moves by steps and through rough stages. Growth is *integrative* and *disintegrative;* that is, growth is a building- and fitting-together process as well as a tearing-down process. For example, childhood patterns must be disrupted before adult patterns become operative. These patterns are fairly stable and when undergoing transformation force the person into an unstable transition period. These transitions may vary from a month to two years and are characterized by discontinuity with patterns of the past. Such transitions usually call forth coping abilities the person didn't know he or she had and often are a means to growth. If a transition is "off time," such as a young person losing a spouse through death, the transition usually has crisis proportions and heads the person into an intensive mourning process. Even chosen transitions, such as job change or early retirement, involve a loss of some kind, and may thrust a person into a mourning process also. Counselors need to be wary of changes in people's lives and how these changes affect their coping capacities.

Psychological growth depends upon the twin principles of *maturation* and *learning.* Maturation implies a potential for development which unfolds under the proper stimulating conditions when the organism is ready to respond. Restrictive environments and restrictive adaptations of the individual, such as intense psychological threat, inhibit psychological growth. Finally, psychological growth is dependent upon contact with people. It is believed that one reason why the helping relationship provides a powerful growth medium is that special optimum human relationship qualities prevail.

The principle that growth takes place through intimate human contact is highly significant for the helping professions. The relationship techniques discussed in Chapter 7 have the purpose of establishing an environment between the therapist and the troubled client to provide a maximum climate for growth. The capacity to love is perhaps the most important growth ingredient. Fromm, who has written extensively on the topic of love, asserts that, "Analytic therapy is essentially an attempt to help the patient gain or regain his capacity for love" (1950, p. 87). He defines love as, ". . . the active concern for the life and growth of that which we love" (1956, p. 26). In a similar vein, Sullivan says, "Love begins when a person feels another person's needs to be as important as one's own" (1953, p. 246).

A principal quality of mature love is deep concern about the other person's welfare. We postulate that the experiencing of this kind of love from parents or their surrogates is necessary for normal growth. Experiencing and expressing love have special meaning for psychological growth and health of the individual at every stage from infancy through old age.

Some therapists say that people become "ill" when the conditions for growth are not fulfilled. But the problems with which the counselor and client struggle are not so much "mental illness" as they are inhibition of normal growth processes. In an individual client, these growth problems may take one or both of two general forms. On the one hand, the person may be experiencing diffculties which are endemic to his or her particular age level. On the other hand, problems inhibiting growth may be those which, considering age and capacity, he or she should have mastered earlier.

We further postulate that individuals are the product of all those experiences which they have had until the time they receive counseling or therapy. Moreover, the experiences to which they have been subjected in their early formative years determine, in large part, the type of adjustment that they will make at any later level of development. All individuals have "problems" in growing up. When these are solved successfully and successively, people are well equipped to progress in their psychological development. When the problems have been too threatening or too difficult to resolve, they falter in growth or develop a shield of defensive mechanisms which inhibits or distorts their creative potentials.

Research
Dimensions

Any approach to counseling must have an emphasis upon validation of concepts and methods. Otherwise, at best it is an anecdotal accumulation of therapeutic wisdom, and at its worst reverts to the occult and mystical. There are pressing ethical and scientific obligations to validate, with the best experimental means available, the procedures advocated. Unfortunately, experimental methods are not completely adaptable to counseling settings. We depend upon a rough empirical kind of validation called a tryout or pilot study; but we strive for more precise study of concepts and methods through a variety of disciplines. This research orientation to actualizing counseling and psychotherapy was described further in Chapter 2 and is emphasized throughout this book. It is mentioned here only to emphasize the open-ended tentative quality of all systems. One of our current obligations is to state our assumptions, strategies, and expected outcomes in such a way that they can be tested, not only in the rough arena of comparative case experiences, but also in the step-by-step detailed study of process and technique for achieving operationally definable goals of actualization.

We endorse Nevitt Sanford's idea (1966) that human problems must be studied from the point of view of culture or social context as well as individual psychology, and that we need a general personality-social theory to guide us. Study of isolated part-function behaviors does not necessarily add to a deeper understanding of complex social behavior, such as clients interacting with counselors or their families. In counseling research we are stymied by methods designed primarily to study segmental rather than holistic behaviors.

SUMMARY

A multidimensional point of view termed actualizing counseling and psychotherapy is described as a process of helping people to develop their life potentials. It includes philosophical, developmental, structural, dynamic, and research dimensions. Actualizing counseling and psychotherapy is based upon a model of the actualizing person as a developmental goal, rather than a cured state of illness or the mere solution of immediate life problems.

4

The Process
of Counseling
and Psychotherapy

In this chapter *process* is defined as the steps and changes that take place over time in counseling and therapy. The emphasis is on short-term processes. We describe process also in terms of the actualizing counseling and psychotherapy model elaborated in Chapter 3. The basic point of the process of actualizing is that the person changes from a condition characterized by a rigid style of responding to the world, dysfunctional creative and cognitive capacities, and a basically manipulative pattern to a more actualized response pattern.

Counseling is basically a problem-solving process involving many decisions and actions. Both in and out of counseling we are making choices constantly about what to do next. Heppner (1978) reviewed the counseling literature related to problem solving and found few studies exist that detail the process steps and how to lead clients into this process. He makes a convincing case for the position that counselors can teach problem-solving procedures to clients with data that already exist and that we need not wait for all the necessary studies to be completed. This is the view we take as we present this chapter. The list below is a general model for this decision-making process. These roughly sequential steps condense to two broad phases of *exploration,* in steps 1 through 5, and *action,* in steps 6 and 7.

Step 1: Stating concerns and establishing a need for help
Step 2: Establishing the relationship
Step 3: Determining goals and exploring alternatives
Step 4: Working on problems and goals
Step 5: Facilitating awareness
Step 6: Planning a course of action
Step 7: Evaluating outcomes and terminating

STEPS IN THE PROCESS

Step 1: Stating Concerns and Establishing a Need for Help

The process goal at this first step is to enable clients to state their concerns, problems, distress, or reasons for coming. Many clients have a clear purpose; but some do not. Their presenting statement may or may not imply a recognition of need for help, since clients at this early stage often do not have a strong sense of "ownership" of their problem. Clients may blame others or think they are victims of fate. Seldom have they made a firm commitment to work on their problems in an intentional, responsible manner. So, a second process goal is to determine the clients' recognition of need for help and readiness to commit themselves to the process. Much of the first interview is usually devoted to these issues of need and commitment. In terms of our actualizing model, the main process goal in this step is to work through the facade level resistance.

The process strategy during this first step is to attend to client statements and observe nonverbal behaviors for messages. Clients often come in with vague complaints and goals and very guarded reasons for coming. Their facade level is often functioning effectively to protect them. A second strategy, then, is to help clients clarify the nature of their concerns or problems. Further clarification usually is needed regarding client expectations and perceptions of the nature of counseling help and commitment to work under the counselor's counseling or therapy model.

It is important to realize that clients initially are hesitant to make a firm commitment to counseling, since this commits them to change. The prospect of change is frightening for most clients. Change means giving up something dear—a comfortable habit, a long-standing relationship, a prized thing, a cherished value, or even a painful feeling. This long-standing experience of letting go usually is painful and often sets off a mourning process. Counselors need to be sensitive to signs of distress and to be aware of this strong resistance to change in clients. Evidence suggests that there may be an optimal set for problem solving (D'Zurilla and Goldfried 1971). This set includes an awareness that problematic situations constitute a normal part of living, behaving as if effective coping with one's problems were possible, and believing that one has control over much of one's environment. A second group of problem-solving behaviors consists of identifying bothersome situations and labeling them as such (Heppner 1978). A third class of good client problem-solving behaviors is not to act impulsively or avoid the problem situation. These attitudes set the stage for steps to be described next.

Step 2: Establishing the Relationship

The main process goal at this step is to build a relationship which has characteristics of trust based upon openness and honesty of expression. It is important for the counselor to establish credibility as a trustworthy person at this point. A growing body of research (Barak and La Crosse 1975; Schmidt and Strong 1971; Strong and Schmidt 1970) supports the idea that how the counselor is perceived in terms of expertness, attractiveness, and trustworthiness determines the effectiveness of counseling.

The process strategy depends largely on how counselors use themselves as persons and the degree of skill they possess in applying relationship techniques, such as listening and reflecting. Additional readiness strategies to be described in the next chapter may be needed to get the relationship off to a productive start.

Step 3: Determining Goals and Exploring Alternatives

The principal process goal at this step is to discuss with clients what they would like to get out of the counseling process, especially if their presenting concerns and reasons were vague. This discussion averts the possibility that unrealistic goals and expectations emerge by default, such as viewing counselors as having extraordinary power to change client behavior or make people happy. Specific goals are usually discussed along with the kinds of behaviors which would be regarded as successful outcomes. Another process goal is to obtain a clear understanding of who is the client. Often in referrals, especially of children, it may be the teacher or the parent who is the "problem" and who possibly should be, therefore, the client. A further process goal at this stage is the determination of the *structure*, of how the process is going to proceed, of the nature of the goals, and the "contract" regarding ground rules and responsibilities. Further coverage of this topic is given in later chapters.

The strategy at this point involves discussing procedures for reaching the expected outcomes and negotiating any working agreements.

Step 4: Working on Problems and Goals

The process goals and strategies at this point are determined largely by the nature of the problem, the style and theory of the counselor, and the client's desires and style of communicating. Often this step involves further expression of feeling if the person is distressed or confused. In any case, it often involves further clarification of the problem since the presenting problem often changes with discussion.

CLARIFYING THE NATURE OF THE PROBLEM AND CHOOSING STRATEGIES. While defining the nature of the client's problem and refining his goals, an important process goal is to determine the best general strategy to use. A second goal is to be aware of what kind of resources one has as a counselor to facilitate achievement of these goals. In terms of our actualizing model, at this step the counselor is discussing issues with the client at the actualizing level described in Chapter 3. If the client's problem can be dealt with at this actualizing level by cognitive strategies, there is little use in extending client expectations or making complex commitments for working with the problems at other levels. For example, some clients' needs for information, planning, deciding, or problem solving require primarily a model such as the following which they can work out at the actualizing level with cognitive resources. An example is planning a career. While there are feeling and valuing elements involving other levels of the personality, it is primarily a cognitive process localized in the actualizing level.

The Problem-Solving Process

1. Develop a clear statement of the client's problem in terms of a goal to be achieved.

2. Describe the problem-solving or decision-making process.

3. Compile relevant data from interview, case material, and assessment instruments.

4. Discuss data and formulate action alternatives.

5. Apply relevant tests and diagnostic procedures to action alternatives.

6. Develop a plan and implementing action steps.

7. Try the plan in simulated or real-life setting.

8. Evaluate outcomes and amend the plan as indicated by data.

These steps are generalizable to a wide range of problems where the use of data and decision-making skills is needed to accomplish the actualizing goals of the person. Even though the counseling process may not focus on these precise steps, the client, faced with the necessity eventually to act, follows formal decision-making steps in a rough way throughout the course of counseling. An important outcome of all counseling is the client's understanding of the process and willingness to apply the process to future problems.

EXTENDED EXPLORATION OF FEELINGS. While the nature of the client's problem and goals may be such that formal attention to problem solving is not indicated at this step, a strategy decision must be made about what to explore further. Typically, with personal problems, feelings are explored in detail to achieve clarity and personal responsibility for them. Rogers (1958), for example, views the psychotherapeutic counseling process as a series of ongoing attitudinal changes. His opinion on the manner in which study of the process of psychotherapy should proceed is: First, observe the behavior of the client with as few preconceived notions as possible, or as Rogers states it, ". . . to steep oneself in the *events* . . ." (1958, p. 142). Then, from these observations come low-order abstractions and hypotheses which can be tested empirically. Rogers tries to grasp characteristics of the changes in the therapeutic process without thinking of them as fixed or static stages. The seven dynamic stages which he perceives in the process range from an early client condition of threat, resistance to change, and little communication, though a gradual loosening of feelings, assumption of greater personal responsibility for feelings, greater clarity and accuracy of perceiving feelings. Finally, clients experience their feelings as part of themselves. They no longer view themselves or their feelings as "objects" or as "problems."

CRITERIA FOR EXTENT OF FEELING EXPLORATION. Agency policy or counselor prudence may limit the extent to which the client should be encouraged to explore feelings. To help a counselor determine the depth to which he or she should allow the client to explore, the following criteria are suggested:

1. The nature and severity of the client's symptoms. For example, prolonged delusional thinking is almost always a sign of psychosis. Hysterical outbursts in which uncontrolled anxiety or hostility is poured forth is another example of a situation which is outside the purview of psychological counseling, and which in most cases is restricted to intensive psychotherapy aided by drug therapy.

2. Length and persistence of symptoms. If a behavior, such as stealing, for example, is persistent and difficult to explain with data at hand, there is a high probability that one is dealing with a pathological process.

3. The nature of the predisposing and precipitating experiences. Some clients, for example, have had a series of severe traumas falling within a short period of time. Deaths in the family, divorces, desertions, plus many small crisis-producing experiences, are examples. These experiences often mobilize more feeling than the client can handle in the interview.

4. Past stability and defensive functioning. A client who desires to express strong feelings and who has a history of stability and adequate defenses generally can be allowed to express emotions more deeply than the client who has a spotty psychological history.

5. Resistance to psychotherapy. Resistance to further exploration and probing by the counselor is a fairly reliable indicator of the sensitivity of the client's feelings and the rigidity of his defenses.

6. Extent and adequacy of the counselor's or therapist's training. Generally speaking, there is a direct relationship between amount of training and experience in psychotherapy or counseling and the depth at which the process may be pitched.

7. The problems of the counselor or therapist. Often the counselor is unable to handle feelings because the client's feelings touch upon sore

spots of his or her own. This condition should discourage the counselor from delving into similar client feelings.

8. The amount of time available. Time for the counseling or therapy series is significant in that the deeper the involvement in feelings, the more time to work the feelings through must be budgeted. This may mean a hundred or more hours.

9. Institutional policy on doing psychotherapy. Policymakers often dictate to the therapists in general terms how far they can go in probing for feelings and allowing the clients to express themselves. This is especially true in public school settings where personal counselors have consideration of parental and administrator attitudes as well as numerous technical problems to face.

VALUES AND LIMITATIONS OF EXPRESSING FEELINGS. This "ventilation of feelings," as it is sometimes called, has several benefits and limitations. The first value of emotional expression is the feeling of relief it gives from strong physiological tension. A second benefit is the awareness of relief from emotional pressure. A feeling of satisfaction and courage often follows because clients finally could admit having feelings which heretofore had been so alien. In addition, they feel a sense of security and freedom from the continuing and often onerous task of defending their feelings. This awareness of security often gives clients courage to solve problems. Thus, new creative energy is released. Previous emotional energy was so tied up with defending themselves that they had little energy available to use constructively. For example, if a client has discussed a fight he had with his father he often will be more ready to discuss other things, such as his own aggressive feelings. A final value of verbalizing feelings is that it prevents "acting out," that is, instead of directing aggression toward others, the client is encouraged to use symbolic means through language.

Intense expression of feeling, called catharsis, has several distinct limitations. If allowed to "ventilate" excessively, clients may feel so good afterward that they will feel it is unnecessary to go on to the causes of their difficulties and take the steps necessary to change attitudes and acts. They leave counseling for the time being with a condition described as a "flight into health." They will stay away then until their anxiety builds up to an intolerable point again. Some anxiety is necessary, however, and the optimal amount necessary for good working motivation is discussed in Chapter 7 under relationship techniques.

Allowing clients to have continuous palliative relief without working into the awareness and action phases of counseling may serve to reinforce repetitive neurotic patterns. Depression is an example. Allowing clients to talk at length about their miseries merely serves to reinforce their self-images of being miserable people. It is also as if they had an emotional tranquilizer each week without moving further toward self-understanding. There is little evidence available which might indicate that periodic, emotionally cathartic sessions have much psychotherapeutic value other than the temporary supportive effect of draining off excess tension. Some life experiences, such as confessionals in religious settings, relieve guilt but tend not to produce the type of insight and action necessary for personality changes. On the other hand, self-confrontation experiences such as those experienced by drug users in programs like Synanon often lead to profound personality change.

EXPRESSING FEELINGS IN THE ACTUALIZING MODEL. Step 4, working on problems and goals, in the actualizing model involves exploration of feeling at all levels. There is a rhythmic expression of feelings along polar dimensions from the actualizing level to the core and back in the other direction. For example, clients could explore feelings related to their value as persons or their intense fears, loneliness, or rage very early in the process. Clients are encouraged to feel anger when they perceive themselves as wronged, or to experience love feelings when responded to warmly.

The process goals of the actualizing model in Step 4 are to encourage clients to explore feelings significant to them in the moment and feelings along the polar dimensions. For example, the counselor may ask clients to exaggerate their hostility so as to become more aware of that basic feeling. The counselor may ask them to express the opposite feelings on the assumption that an excessive use of a manipulative device such as angry domination is a cover for the opposite potential. The extent to which clients respond to such an invitation to express feelings depends on their readiness as well as the conditions of trust established in the relationship. The goal is awareness of wide ranges and types of feelings so that clients can see them in relation to the pattern of their lives. Another key goal at this stage is free modulation of affect. The opposite condition of inability to modulate feeling freely is characteristic of seriously disturbed persons, especially those diagnosed as schizophrenic.

Process strategy at this step is to use whatever relationship method works to encourage free expression of feelings along the polar dimensions from actualizing to core levels.

Step 5: Facilitating Awareness

Various terms have been used to describe this step. We prefer facilitating *awareness* (of actualizing possibilities). Others have used *working through,* achieving *insight* or *understanding.* Awareness means self-knowledge from what one sees, hears, and feels. The process involves reexperiencing events and seeing one's life events in a different set with more clarity, integration, and breadth than before. The term *insight* can be defined the same way; but it has a close association with historical *insight therapies.*

The concept of *insight* has a varied history. Literally it means to *see into* or understand. In Gestalt psychology the term is used to describe the sudden perceptual reorganization leading to discovery or solution of a problem. An example is Kohler's experiment (1925) in which a chimpanzee suddenly discovered how to put various sticks together and pile boxes to reach a much-coveted banana. Insight in counseling and therapy has some of this sudden "aha" or "so that's the way it is" quality to it, in which significant detail stands out from the background. The classical psychoanalytic view of insight includes exploring, analyzing, and clarifying motives and mechanisms for reducing symptoms. Making unconscious motivation more conscious evokes insightful understanding and cures neurotic behaviors. The assumption is that when insight is achieved, the conflict or problem essentially solves itself or disappears.

Ellis (1963) contrasts usage of the terms *intellectual* and *emotional* insight. While an intellectual understanding of irrational and self-defeating behaviors is often a prelude to a deeper emotional experiencing of self-awareness, there is agreement among therapists that intellectual understanding alone contributes little to behavior change. Ellis emphasizes that emotional insight is a complex process of seeing, believing, thinking, wishing, and practicing. It is different qualitatively in that it involves more forceful committed behavior which leads to constructive action. A long chain of events precedes this state, however, and consists of clients admitting they are disturbed and are behaving irrationally, that their behaviors have antecedent causes, that they are reindoctrinating themselves to sustain their disturbance, that they now admit they can change their ideas and patterns of behaving, that they must accept and believe that their previous ideas were false, that they must actively challenge their assumptions by acting in a manner to change them, that their emotions are under their control, and that they realize that there is no way to remain undisturbed other than through their own efforts.

London (1964) is extremely critical of historical *insight therapies*. His work is largely an impassioned attack on psychoanalytic views of insight and a defense of *action therapies*. The major criticisms of insight approaches are that: therapists are inferring motives when they should be observing behavior to plan behavior changes; symptoms are assumed to disappear when self-knowledge (insight) happens; compared to behavioral (action) therapies, insight approaches take too long and hence and economically less feasible; and finally, the outcomes in insight approaches are more generally stated, whereas in the behavioral approaches they tend to be more specific and limited. To us, the point of London's cogent criticisms is that the counselor cannot depend primarily upon insight approaches, but must look to the best of the action strategies emphasized in Step 6.

The principal process goal of Step 5 is to work from feeling to awareness. An implied goal is to keep clients in counseling long enough to achieve whatever awareness is needed to reach their goals. Three critical points, therefore, must be faced in Step 5. The first relates to the tendency of many clients to leave counseling when they experience discomfort and pain while exploring feelings in Step 4. Occasionally clients experience a feeling of getting worse before things get better, because of the painful self-confrontation. Sometimes the opposite happens when clients feel such relief from the verbalization of feelings that they want to terminate.

A second critical point is reached when the client has expressed considerable feeling and becomes aware of being defenseless. It is as if the client becomes too aware too fast. While this point is critical, since a psychotic process already under way may be accelerated, the vast majority of clients have defenses and actualizing strengths which protect them adequately from various types of psychotic deterioration. The strategy here is to deal with feelings at tolerable levels of intensity. Edwin Shneidman, in conversation with one of the authors, suggested that this experiencing of intensive feelings was like a basement full of cats waiting to spring out. Uncovering or experiencing too many of the hidden desires, impulses, inhibitions, or thoughts of the past would be like opening the cellar door and letting all the cats out. It would be quite traumatic or even physically catastrophic. The therapist must control the relationship to enable the client to open the cellar door just enough to allow one cat at a time out to be examined and tamed. The succeeding sessions would be occupied with "taming more cats."

A third critical point is reached when the client, having gone through considerable work on feelings, reaches a point of well-being or elation. This experience frequently results in the client's decision to terminate with the conclusion that all's well now because he feels so good. Although there is some logic to the claim that the process properly could be ended when this feeling comes, the client often stops short of commitment to action. It is a difficult professional judgment to know when clients should be encouraged to continue so as to maximize productive outcomes, or let them terminate whenever they feel ready to do so, or seem unwilling to do something about their problems. The payoff for the hard investment leading toward awareness is what the client does with the awareness.

PROCESS GOALS AND STRATEGIES IN THE ACTUALIZING MODEL.   While the general process described above applies to the actualizing model also, we wish to describe further process events in the special language of the model.

An early process goal is to clue clients to their use of manipulative behaviors, since these forms by definition deviate from actualizing behaviors. The differences are often difficult to determine, as, for example, whether people are loving or if they are simply pleasing or placating. In addition to one's own rigorous self-analysis, one needs the feedback from a knowledgeable group to distinguish real love from pleasing behavior.

MANIPULATIVE RESPONSE PATTERNS.   Four illustrative manipulative responses are cited below. The first, *pleasing* and *placating*, is learned early when the child finds that this is an effective means to manipulate parents. This effect is accomplished often through reducing one's own significance by being a "nice guy," or by being "protective" or others, like a solicitous sacrificing mother. We assume that when people engage in these behaviors they are doing the best they know how at the moment. When being "nice," for example, it could be that a person is denying his anger—the polar opposite. Evidence of this condition is found in body responses of rigidity in neck and jaws, for example.

A second typical manipulative response is a *blaming* and *attacking* form. Instead of being angry, people blame or criticize one another. Instead of putting themselves down, as in placating, they destroy others by attacking. These people also deny tender or loving feelings. It is almost as if loving is to be hurt, so it is safer to attack others first. In extreme form this behavior becomes a struggle for survival. Again, the body reflects this conflict of polarities in the form of tension in vital organs and muscles.

A third pattern is *striving* and *achieving*, expressed through calculating and dictating behaviors. Instead of expressing genuine strength, the persons are constantly proving themselves, their capacities and superiority. They spend much time managing others for their presumed good. The calculating person is more indirect, getting one to buy his or her ideas. A father who persuades his children to go to college, for example, may care only about achieving his own goals. Here again, it is assumed that this type of person is denying the opposite dimension of weakness, a point of possible vulnerability.

A fourth manipulative response pattern is showing weakness by *withdrawing* and *avoiding* others (and problem situations). The person says, for example, "I can't. . . . You do it." They depend on others to think and act for them. By pleading innocent or weak, they avoid many unpleasant and threatening demands and responsibilities. It is a common and effective control device. Here strength is being denied, and the conflict is often reflected in body dysfunctions.

CHARACTER STYLES.   These styles, as described in the preceding chapter, are extensions of manipulative or controlling styles but are more fixed into the life style of the person and are more remote in the awareness scale. An important process goal, however, is to help clients become aware of these styles so they can become more actualizing or functional in their goal achievement. Some examples of these styles are the *dependent* people who use denial as their chief mechanism. For example, they seek love from others and rationalize their giving in to others' needs as an act of giving and receiving love. They get some nourishing satisfaction from this action; but it lacks the deeper satisfaction of expressing love from the core of their being. Another style is a *masochistic* type of *self-attack*. The *psychopathic* style blocks not only the expression of anger, but also the polarity of tenderness and love.

The striving, achieving tendencies evolve into a *rigid* character style. To appear strong and confident, for example, the person produces—becomes a "workaholic." The character style of the *schizoid* type is one of coldness and aloofness, but denial of this detachment and demands for understanding and approbation from others is characteristic also.

The basic process goal for all of these character and manipulative styles is awareness of how these styles are distortions of basic feelings. The key strategy is interpretation of how these distortions take place in development and how they serve to block the actualizing process in the present. Expressing these basic needs through body work is another fundamental approach to awareness of the denied feelings. Clients are encouraged to give up dysfunctional aspects of a character style and become more flexible and open to change. For more detail on theory and strategy of managing clients with manipulative and character problems, consult Shostrom's *Man, the Manipulator* (1968).

CORE GOALS AND STRATEGIES.   Since the core is the center of one's existence, a key process goal is to enable clients to get acquainted with their core characteristics as completely as possible. They learn to trust themselves rather than external authority. They learn to feel at home with their polar feelings of anger, loneliness, despair, and weakness. A further goal is the release of energies for creative activities from the core. This energy flows in effortless form into many life activities. It means listening to the wisdom of one's center and experiencing its harmonious possibilities.

Strategies for reaching these process goals are many and varied. The principal strategy is release of affect through talk and body work. When people experience core feelings of rage, longing, terror, or rejection in the safe confines of a supportive relationship, they are likely to experience feelings of harmony, trust, release, and confidence in themselves. People also experience surges of energy which now can be devoted to actualizing tasks.

Various fantasy approaches help clients get in touch with their centers. Numerous meditational styles aid this quest. Journal keeping as described by Assagioli in *Psychosynthesis* (1965) and by Progoff in his journal workshop manual (1975) provides a means of self-dialogue through writing. Dream analysis is another method to develop awareness of core feelings and symbols. Some of the qualities of the core are tapped in instruments such as the Actualizing Assessment Battery to be described in the next chapter.

THE ACTUALIZING PROCESS.   The whole point to the preceding discussion is to facilitate the actualizing process and to make this process function at the actualizing level of the person. This means, for example, that the more public functions of the actualizing level are congruent with the more private functions of the core. Actualizing means experiencing the outcomes outlined in the introduction to Chapter 3, which described the actualizing goals of existence.

*Step 6:
Planning a
Course of
Action*

While some counseling outcomes relate to understanding and comfort alone, most clients are faced with some form of action—deciding, planning, or doing. We do not subscribe to the assumption of most insight therapies that insight or awareness alone is sufficient for action. While there is a natural flow from awareness to action, it is not automatic. A wide range of cognitive-behavioral technologies is needed to move from the exploratory and awareness phase to the action phase. Therefore, the main process goal of Step 6 is to help clients put their newly discovered ideas and awareness into action in real life. In terms of the actualizing model this means well-functioning processes at the actualizing level to enable clients to move freely along their polar feeling dimensions, utilize their cognitive capacities without interference, live harmoniously with themselves, and function effectively in their interpersonal worlds.

Well-ordered life experiences offer the best therapeutic medium, once the client has sufficient relief from crippling feelings, has achieved some awareness of potential new directions, and has made a commitment to action. Maslow points out this idea very succinctly:

> . . . *major experiences can be therapeutic in the fullest sense of the word. A good marriage, success in a suitable job, developing good friendships, having children, facing emergencies, and overcoming difficulties—I have occasionally seen all of these produce deep character changes, get rid of symptoms, etc., without the help of a technical therapist. As a matter of fact, a case could be made for the thesis that good life circumstances are among the ultimate therapeutic agents and that technical psychotherapy often has the task only of enabling the individual to take advantage of them.* (1954, p. 311)

It appears from Maslow's thinking above that everything which has been described in the process thus far has been an attempt to prepare the client for therapeutic life experiences. Thus, the counselor or therapist makes herself or himself more and more dispensable through the clients' ability to utilize successfully their new skills in self-actualization. People can be taught new and higher level life skills much in the same way that dog paddlers can be taught the more efficient Australian crawl.

Step 7: Evaluating Outcomes and Terminating

The principal criterion for successful counseling and the key indicator for termination is the degree to which the client has achieved the goals of counseling. This decision to terminate is a joint effort on the part of the counselor and client, although it is the client who is the principal determiner of when the goals have been met. The process goal of termination is not taken seriously enough, in our opinion, since so much of counseling and psychotherapy is structured as open-ended with vaguely defined outcome criteria.

A significant part of the counselor's or therapist's thinking concerns his or her evaluation of progress toward goals. Some of the questions which go through his or her thinking are: Did the relationship help the client? In what respects did it help? If it did not help, why not? If the goals were not achieved entirely, what progress was made toward them? Some of the problems in answering these questions revolve around determination of the effect of counseling versus experiences outside of counseling which contribute to change, control of the variables in the counseling process itself, and what is known commonly as the *criterion problem*—reliable standards of change and means to measure them. Current approaches emphasize changes effected by specific variables such as reward, caring, and transference, rather than global approaches such as relationship therapy or rational counseling. Studies of process effectiveness have been done with the *experimental analog* technique and have been reviewed by Zytowski

(1966). In the laboratory, simulated counselor and client behavior are utilized to study therapeutic variables. For example, stress is induced in a client; a method such as reinforcement of coping behavior is applied; and the results and their transfer to extra-interview behavior are noted. This laboratory analog procedure holds promise for the future, but current studies are not yet sufficiently refined to affect counseling procedure appreciably.

One of the principal difficulties in evaluating counseling and psychotherapy is finding adequate and specific external criteria for judging progress, although, currently, internal criteria defined as client-determined goals prevail. Some of the criteria which have been used in the past are: *opinion* based upon observations of counselor or client that the goals were achieved; *performance* on a standardized test of personality, a projective technique, sociometric study, or a specially constructed test of information or attitude before and after counseling or therapy. Performance in the form of improved grades, occupational stability, job satisfaction, decreasing numbers of dropouts, or lost work time has been used, but with little success.

A second problem in outcome evaluation is the lack of sensitive instruments and techniques for measuring change as a result of counseling. These methods are still rudimentary.

We also need more knowledge about which counseling procedures will accelerate or retard progress toward the behaviorally defined goals. A troublesome question in counseling has been to explain the lack of positive results from evaluative studies. Often these results have been interpreted as indicating counseling does no good and that longer term therapy is less effective than short term. Eysenck (1952) promulgated this view with his widely discussed review on the effects of psychotherapy. Strupp's summary (1963) of the numerous critiques of Eysenck's findings on methodological and interpretative grounds leads one to discount his attack on the efficacy of psychotherapy. Eysenck's main criticisms of nineteen studies centered on comparison of treated clients with nontreated. He assumed that the control clients were as disturbed initially as the treated and that recovery criteria were the same for both groups. He concluded that about two-thirds of neurotic patients improved markedly within two years of onset of the difficulty whether they were given psychotherapy or not. He also implied that there was an inverse relationship between intensity of treatment and rate of recovery. He claimed 44 percent of psychoanalytically treated clients improved; 64 percent of eclectically treated clients improved; and those given only general attention by general practitioners, or given custodial care, improved by 72 percent.

Strupp and others have criticized Eysenck severely for procedural fallacies. These center on the unsuitability and noncomparability of untreated control groups, discharge criteria from state hospitals as being certainly different from psychoanalytic clinics, equating neurotic behavior to physical illness, and the difficulty of evaluating so-called spontaneous remissions. Eysenck also classified the dropouts as unimproved.

Sundberg and Tyler (1962) also criticize Eysenck's study on grounds of lack of sample comparability, uniformity in defining *improvement,* and information on type of therapy administered. This controversy revolving around Eysenck's critique highlights the problems of evaluating the helping process. Evaluation of counseling and therapy must consider comparable *samples* of clients and settings when comparing counseling experiences, definite and *comparable criteria of improvement,* concretely *specified outcomes,* and carefully described *procedures* used in the helping process itself. Research of the future will decide which clients, treated with which methods, by which type of counselor, will produce which specific outcomes. These comments are presented here to give only a taste of this complicated issue and to point out that the effectiveness of counseling and psychotherapy has become the hottest professional issue of the 1980s. Government at all levels is concerned with effectiveness since reimbursement for publicly funded treatment is a critical issue.

In a closer look at this entire issue of success and failure, Carkhuff and Truax (1966) indicated that some clients are helped and some are hurt by the process. When comparing treatment and control groups, one then finds no differences because the gains and losses cancel each other out. Treatment groups tend to show greater variability than controls in positive and negative personality change. It is a sobering thought that counseling may not only retard growth, but be a party to further failure. Research on these growth facilitative and retarding conditions is imperative if counseling and psychotherapy are to be dependable helping processes.

The literature on evaluation of counseling and psychotherapy is vast and confusing. The *Annual Reviews of Psychology* include lists of published evaluative studies for students interested in pursuing the details of this topic. One of the early and extensive studies of personality changes in counseling was done by Rogers and Dymond (1954). While all the significant outcome studies cannot be summarized here, a few more illustrative studies will be cited. Campbell (1965) performed a massive follow-up study of student counseling twenty-five years earlier where the counseled clients were more satisfied and had higher grades than a non-counseled control group. Using criteria of college achievement and satisfaction, Campbell found that the counseled group years later was less satisfied, more anxious, and had more complaints than a control group. This follow-up kind of study is fraught with many perils. How are comparable control groups chosen, and are counseling groups not full of concerns and problems which send them to counseling? Campbell's study illustrates the typical follow-up, control group type of design, and also illustrates the difficulties in assessing effects of counseling. In an early report of counseling and psychotherapy outcomes at the University of Minnesota Student Counseling Bureau, Volsky, Magoon, Norman, and Hoyt (1965) applied the best available evaluative techniques. While it is injust to summarize this massive study in a few words, its contribution lies in careful specification of counseling outcomes—changes in anxiety, defensiveness, and problem solving—and use of sensitive methods to assess these outcomes.

Counseling and therapy evaluation studies fall into four major categories: (1) follow-up studies of client attitudes toward their experiences by means of questionnaires or interviews; (2) the opinion of the counselor or therapist about changes which took place in the process and his or her estimate of the progress made toward the goals; (3) internal process studies based upon close scrutiny of the verbal exchanges, interview by interview. This method is best accomplished when the entire transcript is available from a tape. An example of client change would be the decrease in defensiveness exhibited in his remarks, or the signs of increasing client self-directedness manifested by comments such as, "I feel that I can really handle these feelings now," or "I think I can make a decision about what I should do when I graduate." Other studies have used estimates of tension reduction based upon client statements of relief from disabling anxiety through a measure called the *discomfort-relief quotient* of Dollard and Mowrer (1947); and (4) external methods based upon objective measures of behavior changes. Examples are using personality tests such as the Minnesota Multiphasic before and after a course of counseling, or studying changes in Rorschach protocols obtained before and after counseling. Shostrom's Personal Orientation Inventory (1963) and Growth Process Inventory (1980) are proving to be useful evaluation instruments for assessing outcomes.

The first two methods of counselor and client opinion of outcomes are based upon observations of the experience shortly afterward and are subject to the usual unreliabilities and biases of reporting. Though the third method, the internal, offers some significant ways of thinking about the changes taking place in counseling processes, it has great limitations for evaluating counseling success. The outcome criteria have a way of becoming the goals for the counseling and they become contaminated with many other changes. There is no effective way of knowing how permanent the changes are and what independent criteria might exist against which to match the internal criteria. The fourth method of using external devices has the limitation of not indicating what changes to attribute to the counseling and what to other life experiences. There are always the problems of reliability of the instrument and regression toward the mean to consider in studies that use standardized instruments.

Although the field of evaluation criteria and methods at present is very inadequate for the needs of practicing counselors, they still must strive to develop critical attitudes about their work. They must study developments in the area of evaluating counseling and psychotherapy with the aim of developing their own research designs for ascertaining the effectiveness of their work.

PLANNING A COURSE OF PSYCHOLOGICAL COUNSELING

From the preceding discussion the reader will note that the counselor or psychotherapist must make several judgments early in the process. The type and extent of help offered will depend upon the following factors.

Client Needs and Variables	The client has a problem to solve, such as choice of a mate, selection of an occupation, reaching a decision about divorce, or feeling more comfortable with anxiety. These expressions of client need may be construed by the counselor as problems to be solved in counseling and/or symptomatic expressions of deeper personality disturbances. An important first question is, "Who is my client?" The clients may be multiple, as in the case of a family. The general rule is that the client is the person who "owns" the problem, or is most motivated to proceed through the processes just described.

Treatability is another client variable affecting therapeutic planning. Does the client really want help? Is he or she motivated and ready? Is the client capable of profiting from the style of counseling or therapy I am able to offer? Is the client's character structure and defensive functioning such that he or she is not likely to change much? The therapist must realize that not every client can be helped. If most of the questions are answered negatively, the only realistic recourse is to judge the client unready to undertake counseling at the present time with this counselor. The counselor may be able to be of some limited service to such a client, however, in helping the client think through the immediate choice he or she is forced to make.

Which persons should get the most time is often determined by the personal preferences and social values of the counselor. We feel that the main criteria of who should get counseling or therapy should be whether the prospective client can profit from the services offered and whether this counselor is likely to help the client more than some other counselor. In other words, counselors should ask themselves whether they think clients would be better off with or without the help they can offer. It should be recognized that other agencies operate on such criteria as the greatest good for the greatest number, younger rather than older people, mildly rather than severely disturbed, or those who can make the greatest social contribution.

Clients' knowledge of psychology and the principles of counseling may or may not be an asset. Our opinion is that psychological sophistication can accelerate progress if the knowledge has not been too inextricably tied up in the client's intellectualizing defenses.

Diagnostic formulations regarding the nature and severity of the emotional problems are also factors. These topics are covered in a later section and in the next chapter.

Counselor and Agency Variables	The counselor's or therapist's assessment of the client's needs, problems, and condition for help affect the planning. The counselor's competence determines the level or intensity of counseling. The type of agency in which the counselor or therapist functions also determines level. For example, a counselor working in a high school situation has limits set by the policies controlling psychotherapeutic functions in that agency. The level

of counseling may be set at more surface and supportive levels no matter how competent the counselor may be. A counselor functioning in a clinic setting, where there are associates and specialists from other fields with whom he or she can discuss cases and share responsibility, can plan the counseling along broader and more intensive lines.

After considering the client, agency, and counselor-therapist variables, the counselor-therapist and client together must decide whether to proceed at all, the objectives or goals, length of time, and general style to be employed. The counselor-therapist takes the lead in this determination since he or she has primary professional responsibility for the process outcomes.

DURATION OF PSYCHOLOGICAL COUNSELING AND THERAPY

The duration of counseling and therapy is determined by the nature of the goals. The extent to which the client wants to get deeply involved and to stay involved is also a significant determinant of length. Many immediate goals, such as reduction of anxiety, formulation of career plans, and decisions regarding further education may involve just a few hours; whereas the achievement of a more general level of actualization may take many hours.

There is some research on the relationship between length of therapy and outcome (Morton 1949; Barten 1971; Small 1971; Sifneos 1972; Malan 1976). Most investigators concluded that time-limited counseling was effective for specific goals and for crisis management. Morton's study, for example, utilized a high degree of interpretation and emphasized learning principles, following Rotter's Social Learning Theory. Morton concluded that:

We can assume with an extremely high degree of confidence that brief psychotherapy conducted in a rational manner, following a systematic theoretical orientation, and utilizing vehicles appropriate to the theory, will result in striking and lasting changes of adjustment in subjects who were seriously maladjusted. (1949, p. 17)

While counselors may feel that they control the duration of a counseling relationship, there is evidence that the interaction and the degree of personality similarity between counselor and client determine length. In general, behaviorally oriented counselors contend that early specification of goals shortens the process. Mendelsohn (1966) found that similarity of counselor and client personality types was related to length of counseling, in that dissimilar types terminated shortly while similar types had varying length of contact. This kind of study suggests that we need better methods for matching clients and counselors.

Research by Muench (1965) on time-limited psychotherapy, is an example of careful studies on the effect of length on outcome. Muench found with various objective measures and therapists' judgments of change that differences in growth among short term (less than eight interviews), time-limited therapy (terminated at prearranged date from eight to nineteen interviews), and long term (twenty or more) were not significant. Findings were similar when the six most successful therapists were compared to the six least successful. This study suggests that controlled time limits for counseling can be imposed without loss of effectiveness.

To do brief time-limited therapy requires some information early in the process. While the following questions are typical for any intake interview, they are especially important to determine whether or not time-limited therapy is likely to be effective.

What does the client want from counseling?
  (To determine if time-limited therapy is realistic)
Will time-related therapy meet these expectations?
  (To determine if a reasonable match exists between expectation and possibility)
Can a short-term goal be formulated from client expectations?
  (To decide if a specific outcome can be achieved by a definite date)
What is the experience of this client with human relationships?
  (To decide if a working relationship can be established immediately)
What is the ego strength and actualizing capability of this person?
  (To determine if the person has strength to work toward change)
What is the person's recent history in regard to drug usage, hospitalization, alcohol consumption, or attempted suicide?
  (To find if hidden unresolved problems exist, indicating longer-term therapy)
What is the best strategy to achieve the client's short-term goals?
  (To decide if environmental change, emotional support, skill acquisition, or confrontation on intent to change is appropriate)

When it is determined that time-limited therapy is workable and in the best interests of the prospective client, then issues like how many sessions, what specific goals, and what kind of contract are faced.

Generally speaking, clients should be kept in counseling only as long as they seem to be making satisfactory progress toward the general actualizing goals of the process and toward the solution of their immediate problems. The ethics of counseling make this viewpoint imperative, especially when there are fees involved.

DIFFERENCES IN PSYCHOTHERAPY
WITH THE MILDLY AND SEVERELY DISTURBED

This book was designed for students in counseling and psychotherapy who deal primarily with clients classified as maladjusted normals, mildly disturbed, or neurotic. Some psychologists in clinics and private practice, however, work also with clients having psychotic characteristics. Since the

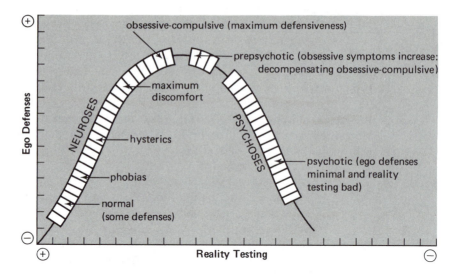

Figure 11. *Normal-Neurotic-Psychotic Ego-Defense Continuum.* Adapted from B. Klopfer, *Developments in the Rorschach Technique,* vol. 2. (Yonkers, N.Y.: *World Book,* 1956), p. 146.

counselor or therapist never knows what kind of client will walk in the door, it is highly important that he or she be well fortified with information of two types: (1) an understanding of behavior disorders so that he or she can recognize severely disturbed or psychotic persons; and (2) a clear recognition of his or her own competence and limitations in dealing with serious disorders both on an emergency and on a referral basis.

Figure 11 suggests a continuum for normal, neurotic, and psychotic conditions. It indicates that neurotics exhaust their defenses to the breaking point before their reality-testing functions deteriorate. The average neurotic, before psychotherapy, has a heavy wall of defenses. The psychotic, on the other hand, generally has little defensive strength and low self-actualizing capacity.

Psychotic people often have rich private worlds of reality, but their perceptions of the meaning of their external reality is distorted, thus giving a delusional quality to their thinking. Neurotics, in contrast, experience their outer worlds only photographically (filtered by defenses), as Fromm (1941) points out. Neurotic clients are very sensitive to outer stimuli but are defended staunchly from perceiving their inner worlds. In Fromm's conception of the healthy personality, both poles are present; inner and outer perceptions are both accurate, thus enabling clients to see the world more objectively and to experience their own thoughts and feelings subjectively without distortion or overreaction.

SUMMARY

Counseling is basically a problem-solving process calling for continuous decisions. In this chapter a summary of the process of actualizing counseling and psychotherapy was presented. The various stages in the process were linked to the levels of awareness in the actualizing model. Special attention was given to the action approaches at the actualizing level. Critical points in the process were identified and key problems at each stage were described. Counseling and psychotherapy outcomes must be evaluated to determine whether clients were helped or hindered in their search for actualization.

II

TECHNIQUES

5

Readiness and Diagnosis in Counseling and Psychotherapy

This chapter covers three topics of concern to counselors and therapists as they begin the counseling process—building readiness for counseling, obtaining data from case histories and tests, and psychodiagnostic evaluation. These topics concern counselors mainly in the early interviews as they think through questions of involving clients in meaningful, productive relationships, of determining clients' strengths and limitations, and of deciding what data are required for helping clients solve problems.

READINESS

Readiness for learning is a well-known educational concept. Children, for instance, are not "ready" to read until they have achieved a certain level of motivation, maturation, and basic skill development. Readiness for counseling and psychotherapy is similar in that certain conditions must be satisfied before counseling can take place. For instance, a study by Lipkin (1954) led to the conclusion that clients who view the counseling experience favorably and anticipate success undergo more change than those who are more skeptical.

A client may recognize that something is wrong in his or her life, but typically the client has to have this observation pointed out to him or her by someone else or wait for a crisis to emerge. A suggestion that the client needs help often provokes resistance—a type of protective defense against change discussed in Chapter 8. It is significant for this discussion because the typical client comes to counseling with some strong reservations.

Counseling cannot begin until people recognize a need for change and until they are ready to commit themselves to the change process. Our culture interferes with both of these steps. First of all, when people seek help for emotional difficulties, others often perceive them as weak or defective rather than viewing them as humans with limitations or special problems. Consequently, admitting to a need for help brings feelings of shame and embarrassment which too frequently lead people to block such needs from their awareness. Assuming this first obstacle of need for change is faced, common misconceptions about the change process interfere with the second step of actively seeking competent help and using it effectively. For instance, a professional helper may be viewed as having the power to effect changes in people they don't really want or as able to solve others' problems single-handedly rather than as a collaborator in a project requiring mutually cooperative efforts. A concern of this chapter, therefore, will be over methods for assisting clients in facing difficulties, seeking help, and utilizing the helping relationship effectively.

Even though clients may need assistance in pursuing help, overzealousness in these efforts should be resisted. Some groups, such as extremist religious cults and a number of the mass-psychotherapies, resort to a variety of deceptions to prepare recruits or clients for changes the group leaders have decided are in the clients' best interest. We believe this ends-justifies-the-means approach is both unnecessary and destructive. We support, instead, a facilitative process based on fully voluntary and informed choice, whereby a potential client is made aware of the strengths as well as the limitations of the particular counseling approach.

Factors Determining Readiness

Several factors determine "readiness" of the client for a counseling experience. They may be a function of the client, the therapist, or the context within which counseling takes place. Factors within the client may involve perceptions of the counselor and/or counseling process, intellectual or conceptualizing abilities, and openness to information about one's self.

Clients may view the change process as being similar to that of fixing an automobile. They expect the therapist to fix them with minimal involvement on their part. Elements of readiness such as this are covered under the term *structuring* to be discussed in Chapter 7. Alternatively, a client may take a dim view of a particular therapist on the basis of his or her reputation, or lack thereof (Rippee, Harvey, and Parker 1965), or on a cultural and socioeconomic gap which leaves the client skeptical of the therapist's ability to fully understand the client. Crider's study on conceptualizing ability (1946) found that the more intellectually able and psychologically sophisticated individuals have the best chances of therapeutic success. Individuals' openness to information about themselves usually is described in terms of the rigidity or flexibility of defense systems and levels of insight. A number of investigations have found a relationship between readiness and this flexibility and openness factor. For instance, Mendelsohn (1966) concluded that persons inclined to seek help were more open to exploring themselves, more willing to consider change, and more intuitive and perceptive (as defined by the Myers-Briggs scale published by Psychological Press) than those not so inclined. Similarly, Raskin (1961) found that increased motivation for treatment went with an increased awareness of one's psychological difficulties.

Most of the research on client readiness for counseling has studied isolated dimensions of expectancy. In a factorial study to identify the most relevant dimensions, Tinsley, Workman, and Kass (1980) found four component factors—personal commitment, facilitative conditions, counselor expertise, and nurturance. This was the first systematic study of the client commitment factor, although the importance of client commitment to change has been part of counseling lore for decades. High client commitment scores are a good prognostic sign, insofar as clients are expected to devote much time and energy to the process. The importance of preparing clients for their counseling experience with realistic information is underscored in a study by Wollersheim and associates (1980).

Raskin's study highlighted another important variable determining a client's readiness for treatment, that is, the therapist's readiness to treat that particular client. Clients who were liked by their therapists rated high on motivation. Results of Raskin's study along with findings of a national survey of psychotherapists conducted by Goldman and Mendelsohn (1969) showed that such clients tended to be imaginative, sensitive, curious, of high educational and occupational levels, and anxious. It seems that most therapists like to work with clients who are verbal, exhibit little pathology, and who are much like themselves. Critics of counseling have called this preference the "YAVIS Syndrome" (young, assertive, verbal, intelligent, socialized).

The context within which counseling takes place can also affect readiness significantly. For instance, if the physical setting is uncomfortable and lacking in privacy, clients may become ill at ease and distrustful. Similarly, some hospitals, schools, and colleges have an administrative policy or an unfortunate history of rumors which mitigate against an atmosphere of trust and acceptance. An example is having the counseling function closely tied to disciplinary activities rather than having disciplinary officers serve simply as a possible referral source. Lack of accessibility is another aspect of the counseling context which can seriously interfere with readiness. A disturbed client, for example, may arrive motivated to work. He is told he will need to make an appointment for a later date because the counselor is booked up. Often he loses interest to the point where he does not return. It would seem desirable to have an "intake" system to see clients, even if briefly, when they come the first time. This procedure would let them feel something is being done and would ascertain the degree of urgency for psychotherapy, counseling, or referral to specialists. Some counseling services maintain fixed open hours to avoid intake delays for urgent problems.

A significant contextual factor is the cultural, economic, and ethnic match of the counselor and client. While there is no compelling evidence to our knowledge that counselor and client must come from the same race or ethnic background to be effective, many clients have feelings about the issue. Sue (1977), for example, found that half of the minority clients he studied did not show for their second appointments, and a large number of these, when followed up, did not finish counseling later. Two implications emerge from cross-cultural counseling research. One is the necessity for counselors to have training in cross-cultural facts so that they can understand and deal effectively with clients different from themselves. The second is to acquire a broad kind of cultural awareness that Ivey and Simek-Downing (1980) stress is necessary for the majority of counselors, so that these counselors can escape their white, middle-class orientation and respond empathically to the needs of culturally diverse clients.

Methods for Readying Clients

One way of reaching people with problems is through *talks*. Heads of agencies and counseling service directors report that every time they give a talk to a public group on mental health, family problems, study methods, or child behavior, for example, there are numerous requests for services.

A second method of motivating clients is through creating an *institutional climate conducive to seeking help.* In schools, for example, this is particularly important, since very few student clients seek counseling voluntarily.

A third method for stimulating weakly motivated clients and for building better readiness in those already seeking such services is that of *instructing referral sources.* Counselors constantly must work on sharpening the awareness of referral agents through conferences with physicians, teachers, advisers, ministers, lawyers, personnel directors, and others likely to make the first contact.

Referral techniques and resources are complicated and unique to a particular community. The counselor education staff at Michigan State University has published a list of referral guides designed to help school and college counselors particularly, but the list has applicability to all workers and agencies which are faced with referral to another service.

1. Check to see if the school has used all its own available resources in helping the student before looking outside the school for help.

2. Try discussing an incipient problem with an agency or specialist before referral is urgent.

3. Try to discover what persons have had contact with the parent or student in regard to the problem, and what results were obtained from these contacts before making a referral.

4. Designate one person to be responsible in working with the patient and student in developing a referral.

5. Learn whether a community agency is already working with the family, for a consultation with that agency is the proper first step in considering a referral in such cases.

6. It is unwise and impractical to refer a student to community agencies without the knowledge, consent, and cooperation of his parents.

7. Keep in mind when telling students or parents about available services in the school or in the community that the teacher should explain both the functions and the limitations of these services. Do not give the impression that any specialist or agency has all the answers and can work wonders.

8. Do not coach a student or parent regarding how they might "wangle" hard-to-get services.

9. Let the student or his parent make his own arrangements for service whenever possible. Do not "spoon feed" the student by being more "helpful" than necessary.

10. Remember that in some cases, however, help may be needed by very immature, dependent, or ill students or parents in arranging an appointment or even in arranging transportation to the agency.

11. Secure a signed consent from the student's parents before releasing information to a social agency.

12. Help the agency or specialist by indicating which person should be the point of contact representing the school. (Michigan State University 1956)

A fourth device for promoting readiness is to give the prospective clients *information about themselves.* This is quite easy in a school or college setting compared to private or clinic practice. Generally, test batteries have been given, and personal records are completed routinely and cumulatively. The students are notifed that they can come in to discuss the test results. In a clinical setting inventories such as the classic Mooney Problem Checklist (1950), Shostrom's Personal Orientation Inventory (1963), or Berdie's precounseling checklist (1952) can be used. An example of an effort to integrate two standard psychometric instruments (Strong Campbell Interest Inventory and California Personality Inventory) into a package is "Guidepak" (Pick 1978). This is a computerized program to provide self-help data to clients to supplement counseling interviews.

A fifth significant source of finding motivated clients is through the *educational process* itself, such as courses in study methods, English skills, reading techniques, college orientation, psychology, and marriage preparation. Workshops in assertiveness training, human relations, or sex role awareness often generate interest in individual counseling.

Special *precounseling orientation* meetings are a sixth means of giving clients information about counseling and related functions such as testing, helping them formulate realistic expectations about counseling and the counselor's role, acquainting them with the philosophy of the particular counseling service, and reducing anxieties about the anticipated counseling experience. The results of early studies conducted by Richardson and Borow (1952), Stone (1948), Truax and Carkhuff (1964), and Glazer (1956) have supported the effectiveness of precounseling experiences.

Readiness during the Interview

Most of the preceding methods of establishing readiness are concerned with locating and motivating clients. Once the client is in the office, a counselor has a special problem in readiness. Attitude, setting, and technique are important factors. Counselors must be able to size up the situation to know if they should apply support techniques to ease clients' anxieties, or whether they should increase client discomfort to get them more emotionally involved and willing to work on their problems.

Counselors can be misled easily by the "facade" phenomenon. The client's resistance may result in opening the relationship on issues such as "no vocational goal," "poor name remembering," "stage fright," or "poor study habits," as the basic problem. We feel that the counselor should start at this level with the client and not jump to the conclusion immediately that this is a "facade" problem. Generally speaking, however, if the counselor's attitudes are appropriate, clients will come forth with a redefinition of their problems shortly. Attitudes which facilitate readiness to discuss problems are elaborated in Chapter 6.

Criteria which the counselor can apply to ascertain the client's readiness to move forward are positive attitudes toward the therapeutic process and a lowered defensiveness which gives an impression of spontaneity and eagerness to talk about problems. Impressions that clients are ready to deal with the emotional implications of their problems, articulateness which enables them to express ideas and feelings directly, and a general acceptance of the therapist's or counselor's role, structure, and style of counseling are further indications of client readiness. The counselor should be alert also to the client who may not be able to articulate problems or feelings directly, but by attitude indicates a desire to go ahead. Similarly the counselor should be wary of the client who is too glib about going ahead, and who uses interview talk as a device to avoid taking responsible action.

THE CASE HISTORY

A case history is a systematic collection of facts about the client's current and past life. This history may take many forms depending upon the style and preference of the counselor or therapist and the type of problem situation. A psychoanalytically oriented therapist, for example, would stress detailed facts of early emotional development through adolescence to present status. Counselors trained in the social work tradition would place considerable emphasis upon the environmental circumstances of the client and would also collect a detailed life history. Career counselors would collect only those items which have a direct bearing upon the client's work of selecting life objectives. A self-theorist would tend to ignore a formal, systematic life history, letting clients select items which were important to them. A counselor in the Rogerian tradition would not ask specific questions to fill in gaps in the story as given by the client because this might tend to throw the responsibility too much on the counselor's shoulders. Some counselors, in addition, feel that it is the client's present perception of his or her situation that is important, not the accurate systematic reconstruction of the past.

Limitations of Case History Methods

One of the key limitations of the case study method is the overemphasis upon counselor responsibility that is engendered by voluminous data collecting. The client feels that the therapist is collecting information from which the therapist will later formulate an answer to his or her "case." Since making a case history generally demands much questioning, it has the unfortunate effect of increasing client resistance to help and makes it more difficult for them to help themselves later. There appears to be a declining interest in data collecting among counselors. Meehl (1960) reported that his study of 168 psychotherapists' opinions revealed that just 17 percent regarded prior personality data collection as accelerating therapy.

Although the method may be limited through the possible danger of using data inaccurately, the danger that a counselor may allow his or her bias or a priori assumptions to enter, in regard to a particular case, is especially potent when collecting case data. The counselor may find, furthermore, that he or she collects much irrelevant and unreliable data during a systematic review of the client's life. Skilled counselors know the subtle distortions which often characterize a client's reporting of past events. Preoccupation with case data has the additional disadvantage of being very time consuming.

In addition to detracting from the job of building the relationship solidly, too much preoccupation with taking a case history may give counselors a false sense of security that they have a meaningful diagnostic and prognostic answer to their clients' problems. Mere data seem to have a morbid and powerful fascination for some counselors to the point that a neat collection of life facts gives the illusion that they understand the client.

Forms of Case Histories

CAREER COUNSELING SURVEYS. Case histories can be obtained in various ways. Career counseling generally requires a highly structured planning survey form designed to be completed by the client. Such a form covers: (1) basic *identifying information* such as name, age, and sex; (2) *educational information* such as school history, scholastic and activity record, subjects liked and disliked, and present educational status and plans; (3) *vocational history* such as part- and full-time jobs held, military experience, present and past occupational choices; and (4) *personal data* including health history, disabilities, parental and marital status, family background with data on socio-economic level, family aspirations, hobbies, personal problems, and the career ideas of the client. To these basic data supplied by the client and often supplemented by the first interview are added the data from *school transcripts, work samples, test profiles* of interest, aptitude, personality, and achievement. Holland's (1979) *Self-Directed Search* is an example of a coordinated career assessment and occupational exploration program. Based on Holland's theory of career development, the Self-Directed Search makes clients active participants in their own career exploration process, since they score and interpret their own results. Counselors can concentrate on those who cannot be helped by this program and supplement the efforts of those who choose to start the career exploration process themselves.

PSYCHOTHERAPEUTIC COUNSELING HISTORIES. With severe emotional problems, the case history may focus more attention upon a systematic social record such as the family history, and the record of interpersonal relationships with parents, siblings, teachers, and peers. The data are often collected by means of the interview—usually by an "intake worker." This specialist does not do the psychotherapy but collects information, determines eligibility and suitability for help, and checks with the local social-service exchange for information on previous agency contacts. The method is used mostly by multidisciplinary clinics and agencies dealing especially with children.

In private practice and in school and college counseling agencies, the data generally are collected by the person doing the counseling. The authors have found that it serves the best interests of the client to collect information on a systematic self-report form and to supplement this with data offered by the client in the course of a statement and elaboration of the problem. This procedure tends to avoid the pitfalls of the formal case history mentioned earlier, yet it gives the counselor basic data from which he or she must formulate hypotheses and decisions about the course of future relationships with his client.

The main justification for collecting facts by means of a systematic case history is to shed light on present problems. To avoid being sidetracked by clients who become preoccupied with, or misconstrue, details from the past, it is best to view such information tentatively and as one of many possible vantage points from which to build an understanding of present behavior. It should also be stressed here that concern for collecting systematic data should not interfere with establishing an effective helping relationship. Occasionally a detailed study is needed when the existing data are sketchy or unreliable. Case data are especially useful to assess the context for a client's present problem. Since problems rarely exist in isolation from others, it is useful to know, for example, what the client's current family circumstances are and what health history items may be relevant.

CUMULATIVE RECORDS. Most schools and colleges have record systems wherein basic data about the development of the student are maintained. The first step which the counselor must take when a student becomes a client is to check on the recency and reliability of the data already collected.

The fragmentary data of the usual school cumulative record make hasty, superficial judgment a grave temptation. A flagrant example is jumping to conclusions about a client's mental ability from group test scores and course grades. Another problem relative to cumulative records involves the handling of confidential data. The general rule found most suitable for school and college situations is to keep confidential personal notes in a separate highly secure file, with only official notations in the cumulative record. To fulfill school requirements, many states now have laws that give parents, and often students, the right to inspect the student's cumulative record. Many school counselors, for example, can testify that a student can be a "marked" person because of entries made about earlier misconduct. Now it is hazardous legally to do so.

The cumulative record can be a useful counseling tool to facilitate the readiness process. A counselor can formulate hypotheses about problems and can note discrepancies in data, such as the differences between John's test data and teachers' reports on his work. This preliminary exposure to brief case data saves valuable interview time. The counselor can spot possible "trouble" areas in the record, noting that the parents have been divorced recently, that he lists two addresses, and that he is alternately with each parent.

Some counselors prefer to start "with a clean slate." They feel they cannot trust the recorded data or even their own perceptions of data. They are afraid that their biases will affect their relationship with the client adversely. As in most other counseling issues, the value of records hinges on the individual preferences of the counselor and his or her care and skill in using them.

CASE WRITE-UPS. Counselors and psychotherapists vary in their opinions about keeping notes on clients. Those who take elaborate notes feel they have more material for therapeutic planning, interpretations, and predictions; the main arguments for not keeping extensive notes are that the confidential material might fall into unauthorized hands and the fact that the relationship has been between the counselor and client only. We take the position that some notes are necessary. Certain identifying information and a brief outline of the topics and plans discussed are essential to note trends in the counseling process. With a heavy counseling load, it is easy to get clients mixed up and to forget essential facts. The counselor may wish, or may be required, to put notations in the cumulative or agency records, but confidential material should be kept in the counselor's personal file only and destroyed after the client's termination.

OTHER TECHNIQUES. Clients can be asked to write autobiographies as a way of initiating thoughts about their current problems in light of their developmental histories. Formal journals or diaries serve this same purpose. Some journals can be structured around topics such as life transitions and choice points (Progoff 1975).

A variant of this method has been called the *time graph*. The client is instructed, for example, to outline topics such as father, mother, and home location on the vertical dimension, with the decades or years marked on the horizontal axis. Key life points, past and future, such as marriage, first job, anticipated retirement, and death, are identified. Such an approach can sharpen one's developmental perspective by highlighting significant patterns and discontinuities.

Another approach involves asking clients to write about a specific topic such as, "What I want to get out of life," or "My family." This can generate valuable material about self-perceptions, values, and readiness for counseling.

Poetry and art can be used when direct verbal approaches fail. Highly significant personal statements can arise out of discussions of a client's verse, sketches, or paintings.

PSYCHODIAGNOSIS

Concepts and Issues

Diagnosis in the medical sense means a process of examining symptoms, inferring causes, integrating observations and fitting them into general categories, and, finally, pinning specific labels on disease entities. Psychiatric or psychological diagnosis is a similar process of ferreting out causation and of naming symptom clusters—schizophrenia, for example, or reading deficiency, or anxiety state; but there is no clearcut psychological analogue to a medical concept like diphtheria or thrombosis, which have definite etiology. In these diseases it is mandatory that diagnoses precede treatment.

In the psychological era, however, the diagnostic process takes on several meanings and is not as clear as in medicine. Psychological diagnosis generally means a statement of the problems or present status of the client, probable cause of the difficulty, possible counseling techniques to solve the problems, and a prediction of counseling outcomes or future client behavior. A diagnostic formulation may also include a survey of the strengths of the client.

Types of Diagnoses

Psychodiagnosis has meant historically a descriptive *classification* or taxonomy of problems similar to the psychiatric classifications for neuroses, psychoses, and character disorders. This process is often called *differential diagnosis* wherein the clinician attempts to differentiate one disease entity from another. Various differential classification schemes have been devised for different types of pathological behavior. The American Psychiatric Association's *Diagnostic and Statistical Manual of Mental Disorders* (called DSM III) on types of psychoses, neuroses, and character disorders is the standard nosological reference for pathology (1980).

Field studies with the DSM III yielded reliabilities for diagnostic descriptions higher than those obtained with the DSM II. This apparently resulted from the increased comprehensiveness and specificity of the DSM III's diagnostic criteria. It should be noted, however, that the reliabilities for specific classes of personality disorders were comparatively low. Since personality disorders are characterized by maladaptive and enduring responses and since they are less acute than other classes of disorder, it is harder to distinguish normal from abnormal in unambiguous terms. Nevertheless, the DSM III is proving to be a more useful counseling tool to classify atypical behaviors.

In looking at nonpathological classifications used in counseling, Williamson (1939) proposed a sociological type with five categories: personality, educational, vocational, financial, and health problems. Bordin (1946) looked deeper, at the source rather than at the kind of difficulty, and developed five categories: no problem, lack of information, dependence, self-conflict, and choice anxiety. Pepinsky (1948) has a similar set of categories for student problems, including lack of assurance, lack of information, lack of skill, dependence, self-conflict (interpersonal, intrapersonal, cultural), and choice anxiety. Robinson (1950) has a simple three-category system based on discussion topics: adjustment problems (emotional and nonemotional), skill learning, and lack of maturity. These schemes vary with the times, type of agency, and clientele served. Each agency must develop a classification scheme useful for its own purposes.

The Missouri Diagnostic Classification Plan is one of the most manageable schemes developed for research reporting purposes (Callis 1965). It is built upon earlier systematic efforts of many diagnostic thinkers and contains two dimensions: problem-goal and cause. Robinson (1963) developed a two-dimensional diagnostic model emphasizing client present and past motivation and response patterns. Robinson suggests a four-step process utilizing his scheme: determine causes to plan differential counseling, determine counselor purpose clearly so efforts are relevant to the task at hand, study case intensively to know client style of response, and select bases for learning best suited to the present purposes.

Since most of the above diagnostic thinking grew out of counseling adults, Byrne (1958) proposes a revision of the earlier Bordin-Pepinsky categories, suited to high school clientele and possessing more current psychological relevance. Byrne suggests the following categories for further research: lack of information, lack of insight, lack of assurance, lack of problem-solving skill, immaturity in situation, and dominance by authority person or situation. Byrne's contribution is largely the use of psychologically meaningful categories rather than sociologically descriptive groups.

Diagnostic categorization of counseling clients serves mainly a reporting and research purpose, although the lack of basic agreement on the dimensions of personality and personal problems makes reporting difficult. There has been little effort recently to classify clients or problems according to causes. Pepinsky (1948) found that judges of case write-ups agreed with their reliability on classifying clients' problems by his scheme, but they have not proved sufficiently useful in planning differential counseling.

Diagnostic categories may be useful in certain environmental manipulations and for offering specific treatment such as remedial help for slow reading problems, but in their oversimplifications they do not help the counselor very much in understanding a client.

Shorthand labels such as "neurotic" do little to help the counselor, or the client either, since they tend to make the client into a stereotype which may not fit the dynamics of the client in question. If this type of labeling seems necessary, a descriptive phrase rather than a single term is preferable. This type of understanding is merely one basis for applying the most appropriate counseling or therapeutic techniques.

One of the issues in diagnosis, involving diagnostic categories, is reliability of classification. The evidence is conflicting. One study by Ash (1949) indicated that the reliability of diagnosing pathological categories was distressingly low, although this study has been severely criticized because of the inadequate categories involved. A later study by Schmidt and Fonda (1956) on the reliability of psychiatric categorization revealed a high degree of reliability and met the usual standards of research design. The principal limitation of such studies is semantic in that more sound categories of pathology need to be developed before this issue of diagnostic reliability can be resolved.

Purposes of Diagnosis

The main purpose of diagnostic thinking in counseling and psychotherapy is to plan differential treatment of clients. In the counseling framework the principal exponent of this view is Callis (1960, 1965), who makes diagnosis central to his planning with clients and research in counseling. The rationale for this kind of thinking is that the counselor must help clients decide whether, for example, they need information, suffer from lack of experience, or are experiencing distorted perception. Each of these conditions requires a different counselor approach—information giving, interpretation, or client self-discovery. No one counseling approach is equally efficacious for all behavior changes. Weiner (1959) adds evidence to this view with cases illustrating the significance of careful diagnosis in personal problems.

Our view is that diagnosis is a general descriptive statement identifying the client's style of life functioning. The purpose of diagnostic descriptions of behavior style is to motivate clients to change their behavior. Clients' confrontation with themselves as self-effacing or manipulative persons, for example, helps motivate them to change. Perls, Goodman, and Hefferline (1951) confirm this view from their clinical experience, and Shostrom (1967) builds a diagnostic description system around the concept of manipulation of others. Awareness of one's manipulative style is a first step in a client's actualizing process.

Behavioral therapy contributes much to diagnostic thinking with its emphasis upon clear specification of goals. It does little good to identify manipulative style, for example, without having a clear idea of what change is desired and what means are needed to effect the change. A mother, for example, who plays "judge" to her child can be given specific phrases to use instead. She can say, "I want you to," "I'd prefer," "I wish," rather than "You should," or "You must," or "You had better." Mother in these examples is clear and specific about her own feelings and expectations.

Observation skills are the main resource for obtaining the counselor's data. Systematic samples over several interviews where counselors attempt to control their own projections and interpretations are the main source of diagnostic data. Psychometric devices are another source of diagnostic data, but in our opinion the use of psychometrics for diagnostic purposes is diminishing.

A further purpose of diagnosis in counseling is that of *interpreting* case data, sometimes called *structural* diagnosis. Williamson (1939) uses the term to mean the *pattern of consistency* which helps to explain or describe the client's behavior. Diagnosis is the step following analysis of the data wherein the counselor selects, from the mass of case data, the relevant facts which form the basis for a prognosis and a plan for later counseling or psychotherapy. By a process of inference, the counselor is enabled to discover new meanings in the data which can be used in the therapeutic planning or which can be interpreted directly to the client. This rationalistic view of diagnosis assumes a certain lawfulness and consistency of behavior, and was developed primarily for student personnel counseling, which is heavily educational-vocational in character.

Klopfer (1956) emphasized the importance of collecting descriptive material on defenses used, and strengths and ameliorative factors in personality, as well as pathological signs when making a diagnostic study. This practice is in line with the general trend to make psychodiagnosis a descriptive rather than a classification process.

Thorne (1950), looking at the diagnostic problem even more clinically, asserts that an accurate diagnosis must be made before "rational treatment" can be planned and carried out. He gives, therefore, an elaborate rationale and procedure for accomplishing the "act of clinical judgment" in psychotherapy. Thorne, furthermore, depends heavily on tests for diagnostic aid in counseling and psychotherapy.

Thorne (1955) built his definition of personality diagnosis around the concept of personality integration, which is a dynamic process of organizing and unifying the behavioral field, as well as a phenomenological trait reflecting the organizational status of the person. The diagnostic process is partly one of understanding the various levels of organization existing at any given moment. In the diagnostic study, the person is examined to see if psychobiological substructures are intact and are supporting higher functions, if deep drives are being satisfied adequately and integrated with environmental demands, and if the person is able to use his personal resources to cope with life. In ascertaining the degree of integration, the diagnostician looks at the various levels of organization which the person uses to deal with his life situation. These levels vary from simple biological processes, such as digestion, all the way to complex learning and the person's style of life.

Cautions in the
Diagnostic
Point of View

There are dangers in the interpretive view of diagnosis described above. The incompleteness or inaccuracy of data, or oversimplification of complex human problems, often causes the counselor to overextend herself or himself on the diagnosing steps. The evidence cited later in this chapter indicates also that even the best clinical or statistical predictions are not reliable enough to formulate critical decisions.

The second major caution of this interpretive view is that it leads the counselor to become preoccupied with the client's history, to neglect present attitudes, or to ignore current behavior. The diagnostic process must be rooted in the individual's current psychological milieu to be effective in understanding him or her.

A third caution is that the clinician is tempted to utilize tests too quickly to aid in the diagnostic process. This act is likely to lead to a client expectancy of "answers" from the tests rather than from looking inside for the causes of his or her difficulties.

Losing sight of the client's individuality is a fourth difficulty in the diagnostic process. For example, the therapeutic psychologist may possess much comparative data on such things as intelligence measures and MMPI scores, but may lose sight of the subtle distinctions which make the client a unique person responding in his or her own individual style to common social stimuli.

Since diagnosis has been associated historically with pathology, there is a further danger that the clinician will be preoccupied with morbidity rather than hygiology of behavior. There are still too few terms to describe healthy creative personality states which would be comparable to the elaborate terminology of psychopathology. Therapeutic psychologists are devoted to a search for positive characteristics, asking such questions as, "What strengths does this client already possess?" "How much insight does he have now?" "What can we build upon?"

A final objection often cited for the heavily diagnostic approach to psychotherapy is that it leads to a judgmental attitude, a feeling that the therapist is going to "case" clients and then tell them what they ought to do. Responsibility is thus shifted too strongly to the psychotherapist, who is put in the tempting position of pontificating to the client.

Therapists following the Rankian tradition, however, tend to eliminate the early formal diagnostic steps. Rogers (1951) seems particularly adamant on the question of diagnosis. He claims that diagnosis, as understood in the preceding light, is an actual detriment to the psychotherapeutic type of counseling. Rogers does not ignore the significance of behavior causation, but he claims that the meaning of behavior lies within the particular way clients perceive their reality. Clients, according to Rogers, are really the only ones who can know fully the dynamics of their own perceptions and behavior. In order to change client behavior, therefore, a perceptual change must be experienced. Just getting more intellectual data about the problem isn't likely to help change that client's behavior very much.

Rogers feels also that a diagnostic point of view tends to pull the counselor away from a client frame of reference and to become too preoccupied with intellectualizations about the client. Certain counselors would be prone to this overdiagnosing because of their particular judgmental attitudes. Rogers claims, further, that therapy is diagnosis in the sense that it is the client who is experiencing the process and really does the diagnosing in terms of formulating his or her own experience in meaningful terms.

Another more subtle social danger is seen by Rogers (1951) in that too much emphasis upon diagnosis sets up the consequent temptation to make evaluative prescriptions. If clients rely on the "expertness" of the counselor, there is the potential danger of social control and influence where the counselor specifies the goals and makes the value judgments on whether a behavior is appropriate or inappropriate, mature or immature.

Rogers is criticized for his extreme view of diagnosis because he seems to set up a "straw man," in that the understanding of the client in a diagnostic sense is imposing understanding on the client. There seems to be an assumption that if one takes a diagnostic viewpoint, one is automatically judgmental. Bordin (1955) points out, also, that the clients' perceptual awareness is only part of their experience. They could achieve deeper understanding by making a more active contribution to the process.

Apart from Rogers's criticisms of the diagnostic position, there is another cogent reason or caution. Diagnoses are made partly for purposes of prognosis or prediction of clients' future behavior. Predictions based upon clinical judgment and clinical data are not what they should be, even for modest confidence. Clinical predictions, according to a review by Meehl (1954), are less valid than straight actuarial methods in which tests, for example, are used to predict behavior. One of the controversies in the psychological literature is the relative value of clinical and statistical methods for predicting client behavior. While some psychologists express confidence that, under the right experimental conditions, the clinical methods will show up better, the evidence to date is that statistical prediction is superior and that clinical prediction methods have many limitations for counseling.

Clinical prediction is based upon the assumption that clients are consistent within themselves. The diagnostician is concerned with ascertaining patterns of consistencies, with which projections can be made about behavior in the future. Meehl (1954) concluded in his review of the problem of clinical and actuarial prediction that the problem can be resolved partly by specifying the conditions under which each method works best. He hopes clinicians will not be forced to think of clinical versus statistical methods much longer.

Resolution of the Diagnostic Issue

We maintain a third view on the question of diagnosis. We find it difficult to escape the fact that the therapeutic psychologist must make some decisions, do some therapeutic planning, be alert for pathology to avoid serious mistakes, and be in the position to make some prognoses or predictions. It seems that the therapeutic psychologist is forced to play a delicate role between the Rogerian position of withholding judgment and attempting to stay within the client's frame of reference as much as possible, and at the same time trying to understand the client diagnostically.

It is proposed that we simultaneously understand diagnostically and understand therapeutically. This is done through a process of hypothesis or hunch making. Although counselors may decide to avoid some of the formal diagnostic steps, they develop, nevertheless, a series of hypotheses about such questions as: "How serious is this behavior?" "What would be the most appropriate approach at this time?" "How far should I attempt to go?" "What seem to be the basic dynamics operating (defenses, dominant needs, symptoms, environmental pressures)?" "What will the likely outcomes be?" The basic diagnostic questions, however, are: "What is going on?" "How effectively is the client responding to demands in his or her life?"

Hypotheses flowing from answers to the preceding questions are revised constantly until this client's style of life, basic relationships with people, dominant values, principal defenses, main strengths, and limitations fall into a pattern. Viewed in this way, the counseling process itself is, according to Pepinsky, a process of ". . . hypothesis formulation and testing, a process of approximation and correction. . . ." (1954, p. 198). Pepinsky goes further to indicate that what counselors do with their hypothesis making is to formulate a hypothetical client with behavioral descriptions in terms of the counselors' basic constructs and assumptions. In other words, counselors are thinking that if the clients with whom they interact at the moment behave like their model, then they can predict how their clients are likely to behave in the future. For example, we know from research and experience that depressed clients are potential suicide risks. We have a model of the suicidal person, and as the client tells us more about how he or she feels and what he or she has been thinking, we see the client conforming more and more to our model. This starts the prediction process going.

Action questions then come fast. Should I, as the counselor: (1) Refer the client immediately to a specialist, a hospital, or contact his or her relatives; or (2) Would referral upset the client even more and should I use some emergency support techniques? (3) Should I decelerate the rate of exploration of feelings, or cut discussion of them completely so the client does not become more depressed? (4) Should I stop counseling with the client as soon as I can conveniently shift responsibility to another therapist? (5) What other indications of pathology are present and what indications of personality strength does he or she manifest? (6) Is this a primary personality disorder or a secondary reaction to strong environmental stress? The answers to these questions will be indicated by the predictions made from our model. What the counselor is doing, in effect, is trying to verify a hunch that he or she has a likely suicide that requires a swift plan of action.

How the clinician thinks through this hypothesizing process is still quite mysterious and intuitive. Meehl (1954) speculates that the process is somewhat as follows: (1) collect data; (2) have a set of assumptions and some general laws about behavior; (3) generate a tentative specific hypothesis about behavior from comparing the case data and the assumptions; (4) collect further facts and compare them to reduce the number of possible hypotheses; (5) study the facts and hypotheses until a meaningful pattern emerges; (6) select tentative hypotheses; and then (7) make a specific prediction.

McArthur (1954) also reported some research and speculation on the clinical process. He found that successful predictions were made from the model or "clinical construct" each clinician formulated, rather than from a single test, theory, or case datum. The clinicians seemed to be using an inductive method by which they fitted the case data to a model person. From this model they made their prediction as to how the client would likely behave. McArthur indicated that they seemed to be using such a phrase as, "He seems to be the sort of person who . . ." (1954, p. 204).

Koester (1954) studied the diagnostic process by asking counselors to "think out loud" to a recorder while examining their case materials. He found that instead of a sudden insightful patterning of the data there was a more gradual buildup of the data into a more meaningful understanding of the case. Koester indicated that the steps that the clinicians seemed to follow were similar to a problem-solving procedure described earlier in this chapter: (1) collection and comparison of the data; (2) interpretation of the data; (3) formulation of hypotheses; and (4) evaluation of the hypotheses.

Like McArthur, Koester found that the total formulations were more meaningful when approached openly without the rigidity of a single theory or set. Those counselors who failed to revise their hypotheses because of negative or contradictory data appeared to be the most rigid and single-theory-centered.

An illustration of the use of the clinical diagnosis-prediction process may be had from career counseling. Here, the need to formulate hypotheses about the client's abilities, interests, traits, and experiences in relation to the best model of a successful insurance salesman, home economics teacher, or architect, for example, is particularly important. Clinical prediction methods must be used in career counseling to supplement the actuarial methods which stress test scores and validity coefficients. Career counseling, therefore, illustrates the interplay of clinical and actuarial methods of prediction.

Another illustration of the diagnostic process and of the utility of a separate diagnostic step can be found in the area of skill deficiencies. A client complaining of reading difficulties must go through a rational diagnostic procedure to determine the most likely combinations of causes such as visual, perceptual, emotional, experiential, or language deficiencies.

The clinical process in the illustrations from psychotherapeutic, career, and skill deficiency areas is going on continuously in the counseling process. Perhaps this is what writers like Rogers mean when they assert that diagnosis blends into the therapeutic process. A further observation on our part is that the further the client's complaint is removed from problems involving cognitive data, such as career plans and learning difficulties, the less distinct the formal diagnostic steps seem to become.

The function of career diagnosis is to achieve thorough understanding by both counselor and client of interests, aptitudes, personality characteristics, aspirations, family history, and work background so that the client can match these characteristics with job requirements. Although the preceding process is quite rational and logical, there is a danger in ignoring the attitudes underlying the more cognitive features, such as aptitudes. Just collecting information and collating it with career goals which seem to follow logically is oversimplifying a very complex process. In other words, diagnosis in the sense in which Williamson (1939) uses it, as understanding of the meaningful pattern of data, is essential to educational-career counseling. The counselor cannot shift responsibility as an expert in making this kind of prediction to the client or anyone else.

As implied earlier in this discussion, career counselors must make decisions about how emotionally involved they should allow the relationship to become. One of the most difficult decisions is if, and when, they should cap off a client's persistent effort to force the relationship into a psychotherapeutic model. Often the counselor can help reduce anxieties over unsettled plans for the future or difficult relationships with people without employing involved psychotherapy. But the diagnostic process comes to the counselor's aid in detecting atypical and dysfunctional behavior. This is the reason all counselors, regardless of their assignment or level, must be familiar with the signs of psychopathology or deviant behavior.

The Psycho-diagnostic Use of Tests

THE NATURE AND BASIC ASSUMPTIONS OF PSYCHODIAGNOSTIC TESTS.   Tests are one of the therapeutic psychologist's main tools. The discussion to follow will be mainly concerned with their diagnostic use. There are other uses of tests—interpretive, information giving, evaluative, and predictive—which will be described in later chapters.

The main purpose of all testing is to obtain samples of behavior in a standardized situation devoid of subjective judgment. Test results should represent objective factual material, whereas the subjective element enters into the interpretation of the factual results. Here, the therapeutic psychologist marshals his or her test data, case experience, and observations, into a series of diagnostic hypotheses about this particular client. In other words, the value of psychometrics in diagnostic assessment is as an *aid to observation*. It may seem paradoxical that we discuss the use of psychometrics in such detail here when we express so much caution and skepticism. Like most aids to observation, we view them as useful, but not as substitutes for careful observations by the counselor. Sundberg and Tyler (1962) have reviewed the evidence from many studies. It appears that personality psychometrics in general, and projective methods in particular, are not very useful in diagnosis.

Personality characteristics, furthermore, must be sampled frequently to assess changes. Personal characteristics should be studied also, in their social context, since personality is a product of social interaction. There is good evidence that even some of the difficulties in intellectual functioning, involving thinking, memory, concentration, and perception, have their roots in impaired interpersonal relationships.

A further assumption underlying psychodiagnostic testing is that the unique patterns of thinking and feeling uncovered by the tests are indications of the client's basic character structure. This structure is presumed to be quite stable and consistent.

USES OF PSYCHODIAGNOSTIC TESTS: (1) SCREENING.   Although it is beyond the purpose and scope of this book to go into psychodiagnostic testing in detail, it is important for counselors to understand the diagnostic uses of tests. One of the principal functions of tests for the therapeutic psychologist is as a rough "screen" for pathology. By giving a brief test battery at an appropriate spot early in the process, the counselor can get a clearer picture of the likely issues to be faced later. Severe pathology often does not show up until later interviews. By giving a projective technique or the Minnesota Multiphasic Personality Inventory, the counselor often can obtain a more clear understanding of current or more obscure pathology.

Similarly, on intellectual variables, the counselor often desires a quick estimate of the client's intellectual capacity and functioning in advance of more definitive data. A short vocabulary test such as the Stanford Binet or Wechsler Adult Scale vocabulary subtests can give these data. In addition, short tests like the Proverbs Test (Gorham 1954) give a quick, even though possibly unreliable, estimate of intellectual functioning. Oral reading tests such as the Gray Paragraphs (1923) offer the counselor another quick estimate of intellectual skills. The studies on culture bias of ability tests, and prohibition of many selection test procedures by the federal government on grounds of bias, warn the counselor to be extremely cautious in their use.

USES OF PSYCHODIAGNOSTIC TESTS: (2) PREDICTING SUCCESS OF COUNSELING.   Diagnostic screening tests can provide information regarding readiness for counseling, for example. There is support for the statement that the rapidity of achieving successful counseling outcomes hinges on ego-strength factors such as response adaptability, capacity to test demands of reality, and undistorted perception, as evidenced by research on the Personal Orientation Inventory. Therefore, the counselor can decide early in the process whether continued counseling with this client would be feasible or desirable.

USES OF PSYCHODIAGNOSTIC TESTS: (3) DETAILED INFORMATION.   There is no effective substitute for a diagnostic test in such skill areas as reading and arithmetic. Remedial help and concomitant counseling are often planned around information obtained in diagnostic achievement batteries.

Similarly, in personality trait areas, such tests as the California Personality Inventory or the Personal Orientation Inventory could give the counselor topics to explore directly without the circuitous route of client verbal exploration. For example, finding through tests that handling feelings of hostility is a problem helps to pinpoint sensitive areas early. This early detection may create less resistance to discussion of the problem later, since the client tends to perceive the test results as "objective evidence."

Counselors working on career planning problems find diagnostic information helpful, but the main focus in career planning is on prognosis. Detailed material on the important prognostic use of tests will be described later.

USES OF PSYCHODIAGNOSTIC TESTS: (4) DIAGNOSTIC FORMULATIONS. Pinpointing pathological types has been and continues to be a major forte of the clinical psychologist. Projective techniques such as the Rorschach and Thematic Apperception Tests have been used along with tests such as the Wechsler Adult Intelligence Scale to give a rounded picture of the perceptual, conceptual, and affective functioning of the client. While diagnostic accuracy in terms of classification still needs much development, the DSM III described earlier is a great improvement in reliability and usefulness over earlier editions. Despite these improvements we still face the problem of pinning psychiatric labels of illness and disorder on persons who are on the borderline between normal and disordered functioning. Many people do not clearly fit the classifications, which were based originally on clinical intuition (Frances 1980). From our perspective the chief limitation of the classification method of diagnosing is placing deviate labels on behavior that is essentially normal.

ACTUALIZING ASSESSMENT BATTERY (AAB). This battery consists of three inventories aimed at assessing aspects of the actualizing process. In contrast to the DSM III approach to problems and disorders the AAB stresses the positive qualities of people. These inventories are presented here in brief form to illustrate their use with our Actualizing Counseling and Psychotherapy model. This battery is used in promoting client readiness, in diagnosing the presence or absence of key actualizing attitudes and behaviors, and in assessing progress in counseling. These tests aid the assessment of intrapersonal as well as interpersonal dimensions of psychological functioning, just as a thermometer or stethoscope aids the medical practitioner in assessing dimensions of physical functioning. For detailed information about the nature of the battery, its research base, and its use, consult *Actualizing Therapy* (Shostrom, Knapp, and Knapp 1976). This reference includes a brief clinical report of a couple's relationship illustrating the application of this battery.

PERSONAL ORIENTATION INVENTORY (POI). This 150-item inventory is a measure of intrapersonal being. It is based on the theoretical formulations and the research of several humanistic psychologists such as Maslow, May, Perls, and Fromm. Items are grouped into two major scales and ten subscales. One of the major scales assesses inner- versus outer-directedness, while the other is a time-ratio scale assessing the degree to which one is oriented to present, past, and future. The subscales are designed to reveal degrees of self-actualizing, existentiality, feeling reactivity, spontaneity, self-regard, self-acceptance, constructive view of people, synergy, acceptance of aggression, and capacity for intimate contact.

When used in a counseling or clinical setting, the POI provides a fairly objective measure of the client's actualizing level, as well as offering positive guidelines for growth. Scales can be used in combination to assess polarities (such as aggression and contact).

CARING RELATIONSHIP INVENTORY (CRI).   This is a measure of inter-personal effectiveness applicable to a variety of group and individual counseling settings, especially those involving couples. The focus of the inventory is on the various elements of loving or caring, and is based on views of love by persons such as Fromm, Lewis, Maslow, Nygren, and Perls.

The CRI consists of eighty-three items concerning feelings of one member of a male and female pair toward each other. True-false responses are made, first as applied to the other member of the couple, and second as applied to an "ideal" mate. Two forms exist—one for females to rate males, and one for males to rate females. Development of the CRI was based on responses of criterion groups of successfully married or actualizing couples and of divorced, troubled, or nonactualizing couples.

The scales assess a developmental concept of love from early erotic forms to mature, altruistic, or "agape" forms of love. One of the subscales covers self-love (S)—the ability to accept one's own weaknesses, as well as to appreciate one's unique worth. This concept includes acceptance of one's full range of feelings toward the partner. Deficiency love (D) is a type of exploitative, manipulative love where the other person is regarded for what that person can do for one.

PAIR ATTRACTION INVENTORY (PAI).   This inventory is based on a dual theory which emphasizes attraction based on complementary needs and differences. Both complementarity and symmetry are assessed. The basic rationale is based on personality research at the Berkeley Institute of Personality Assessment which emphasized the presence of basic polarities, particularly anger-love and strength-weakness.

Research and usage so far indicate that divorced persons, and those seeking relationships outside marriage, have characteristic patterns and preferences. PAI usage suggests seven basic kinds of unconscious mate choices which operate in pairing relationships: nurturing, supporting, challenging, educating, confronting, accommodating, and actualizing. The actualizing relationship is considered in the context of this book as the preferred one. Some assumptions are that actualizing couples can be strong and weak, angry and caring. The couples can respond also with a freedom and creative rhythm not present in the other types of relationships.

PERSONAL ORIENTATION DIMENSIONS (POD).   This is primarily a research instrument at this point. It is designed as an extension and refinement of the POI. Dimensions assessed are: Orientation (time orientation and core-centeredness); Polarities (strength, weakness, anger, love); Integration (synergy, potentiation); and Awareness (being, trust in people, creative living, sense of mission, awareness of manipulation). Preliminary data indicate potential productive use with a variety of populations in colleges, churches, treatment centers, schools, and hospitals.

These tests together form a whole greater than their parts. Given as a battery, the AAB produces a six-page case study of the interpersonal relationship. It supplies information that would not be available otherwise by using the instruments independently of one another.

Early diagnosis and understanding of a therapeutic direction is especially essential for the counselor when dealing with couples in therapy. The AAB provides the counselor with an in-depth narrative study of the conscious and unconscious personality dynamics of both partners and how they each function as individuals in society. The kind of early understanding that this battery provides can expedite not only the understanding of the couple about themselves, but also their commitment to the therapeutic goals.

Health-model assessment data demonstrated by the AAB are relatively easier to share with clients due to the non-threatening nature of the language and terminology. As a result, defenses are not as irritated or stimulated in the client as with medical-model assessment data. This allows for more open and in-depth exploration and actual use of the profile data with clients.

SUMMARY

Three preparatory concerns face therapeutic psychologists. First of all, they must face the problems of motivating the reluctant or ignorant client. The case study is a second concern, expressed in the question: "What are the relevant data needed to help this client?" Various sources of data are available, such as case histories, cumulative records, time graphs, autobiographies, and essays. A third concern of the therapeutic psychologist is the form and extent of diagnostic formulations. Diagnosis is a process of describing client life style in such a way that it helps the client change his or her behavior in a more actualizing direction. As a means of describing causation and predicting future behavior, the diagnostic thinking process has great limitations. Clinical and statistical predictions are still too limited in validity to be used with confidence. The counselor can, however, look at the diagnostic process as a procedure for formulating increasingly more tenable hypotheses regarding the nature of the client's difficulties. Examples of such questions are, "How much pathology is present?" "How far should I attempt to take this client along the road to mature living?" "In light of the best evidence available, what seem to be the best answers to the client's search for a career or life objective?" Tests and case histories are valuable aids for the diagnostician in making preliminary estimates on the above questions, as well as in executing fine differential psychodiagnoses. The Actualizing Test Battery was described as an illustration of efforts to assess the characteristics of the actualizing person objectively.

6

The Relationship in Counseling and Crisis Intervention

The heart of the therapeutic process is the relationship established between counselor and client. In the preceding chapter, the importance of client attitudes in approaching counseling was emphasized. In this chapter, we examine the attitudes of the counselor as a variable in the relationship and how the relationship is used to help the client. In many ways the counselor is a model of how to establish and maintain a relationship. We shall describe relationship techniques in Chapter 7, after the discussion of counselor traits, since we regard techniques as *implementations* of the therapist's basic attitudes. Using helping techniques without appropriate supporting attitudes is usually counterproductive.

The relationship is important in counseling and psychotherapy because it constitutes the principal medium for eliciting and handling significant feelings and ideas which are aimed at changing client behavior. Thus, the quality of the relationship determines not only the nature of the personal exchanges, but also whether counseling will continue at all.

We are becoming increasingly convinced that the relationship in psychotherapy and counseling is a helpful agent in its own right. Many people do not have effective interpersonal relationships. The psychotherapist's task, therefore, may be seen as establishing whatever relationship the client is able to make, solidifying it, gradually freeing it of unrealities, and teaching the client how to maintain it. This is a positive picture of the therapist's instructional role, as opposed to a more negative, remedial or problem-solving role. This developmental role is also what makes the therapist's own relative freedom from neurotic distortion of central importance.

Before proceeding further, the concept *relationship* should be defined. We prefer the Pepinskys' definition of a relationship ". . . as a *hypothetical construct to designate the inferred affective character of the observable interaction between two individuals*" (1954, p. 171). It should be noted that in the definition, however, "relationship" refers to the *affective* or emotional elements of the interaction, which can only be inferred from observation of client behavior. We feel that a description of the relationship should include additional dimensions, many of which are paradoxical. In actualizing theory terms, a relationship provides the principal bridge for the actualizing personality levels of two people to make contact. Thus, defenses, interpersonal problem-solving skills, and polar feelings find expression in the relationship. While each basic counseling theory has a position on the significance and function of the relationship, recent research on relationship variables indicates that effectiveness of relating in terms of empathy, warmth, and genuineness did not show significant differences among three divergent theorists' interviews (Fischer and Paveza 1975).

CHARACTERISTICS AND DIMENSIONS
OF THE RELATIONSHIP

Uniqueness/
Commonality

Though certain general statements can be made about the therapeutic relationship, it is important to remember first that each client-counselor relationship is unique. The factors creating this uniqueness are as diverse as human differences. The unique factors include *counselor* attitudes, behaviors, and physical characteristics, in addition to *client* attitudes, backgrounds, and behaviors discussed in the preceding chapter. This uniqueness makes generalizing about counseling difficult. Each new counseling relationship is a fresh challenge to the counselor. Counselors cannot learn myriads of rules to cover all possible situations, yet we hold the view that they can function effectively in helping people if they know clearly their own personalities and goals, exhibit certain basic attitudes toward people, and demonstrate competencies in basic helping functions.

Another aspect of uniqueness in a therapeutic relationship is its distinction from other human relationships. While friends, relatives, and teachers have profound influence on behavior, one unique element of a counseling relationship is its structure, that is, its carefully planned and described process framework. Another unique element distinguishing counseling relationships from others is the counselor's ability to be objective as well as emotionally involved.

Because of its intimate nature, structure, and attitudes, the counseling relationship also has similarities to other human situations, for example, family, friendships, teacher-pupil, doctor-patient, and pastor-parishioner. In another sense, then, a counseling relationship is an extension of ordinary effective living processes.

Objectivity/
Subjectivity

A second way to look at the relationship is in terms of its objectivity-subjectivity balance (Oppenheimer 1954). This balance refers to the degree of emotional intensity of the relationship and the relative weighting of the intellectual and emotional elements. *Objectivity* refers to the more cognitive, scientific, generic aspects of the relationship, wherein the client is regarded as an object of study or as a part of broad suffering humanity. In extreme objectivity, therefore, a counselor would remain psychologically distant and would regard client views and values without personal judgment.

The meaning of objective counselor behavior for clients is that they feel the counselor respects their views, does not force his or her ideas on them, and looks at their problems rationally and analytically. It is observed often, however, that clients tend to reject such an objective attitude. They want the counselor to get emotionally involved and to be personally concerned about them. This subjective feeling of involvement is one basis for feeling "understood," and seems to offer the reassurance that the counselor knows how the client feels, and that he or she cares. Therefore, it is our observation that clients tend to be ambivalent about counselor objectivity-subjectivity in the relationship.

Objectivity can offer security for the counselor, also, since the essence of diagnosis is striving for an objective view of the client's situation. Therapists like to feel that they are aware of their own feelings at all times and that they avoid forcing values and solutions on the client.

The *subjective* elements of the relationship include emotional involvement in the form of human "warmth" and psychological "closeness," as well as intense interest in the client's problems. This behavior is often described as caring. The meaning that subjectivity has for the client is one of feeling understood. Conversely, some clients perceive counselor involvement as threatening, since they are "submitting" to the control of or "revealing" themselves to another person. They experience anxiety, therefore, over feeling vulnerable and feared loss of emotional control. This anxiety is especially strong when clients see the counselor allied with their externalized or rejected feelings. A client seeing the counselor, for example, as a loving mother becomes fearful of his own uncontrolled dependency needs.

The nature of the emotional interaction appears to be a key variable determining the quality of the relationship, or encounter. Counselors must be *aware of the various levels of their impact* on clients, and the clients on them. First, the counselor reacts at a friendship level, as one liking certain qualities in the other and experiencing pleasure at the meeting. Secondly, he or she reacts at a genuine personal encounter level, honestly and directly communicating. Then the counselor reacts at a more intense level of loving concern for the other person's welfare. The counselor must be aware also of possible erotic components of interaction, which if unrecognized may interfere with the counselor's effectiveness at other levels. Rollo May (1969) suggests that a real encounter involves all four levels.

The meaning of the subjective view for counselors is that in some cases they might respond to clients' problems as if they were their own. Yet, counselors must use their own generalized experiences and feelings as guides to experiencing the client's feelings. For example, how can counselors really know how it feels to be loving and hostile to a parent simultaneously unless they have experienced this feeling themselves and have been aware of the implications? This does not mean that counselors must have experienced all feeling situations. They must have recognized in themselves, however, those universal human experiences such as anxiety, depression, disillusionment, and self-dismay. They must have worked them through enough to be able to tolerate recognizing and empathizing with them in clients. One of the key issues in counseling is the extent to which counselors should reveal themselves as distinct persons and how much emotional involvement they should allow themselves. This issue will be covered in several contexts in the next few chapters.

The most reasonable goal seems to be that the counselor get emotionally involved to the extent necessary to keep the client emotionally involved; but the counselor's keen interest in helping should be tempered with some reserve and distance so that the counselor can accept attitudes and feelings expressed by the client or confront them objectively with as little counselor projection as possible. If counselors get too emotionally involved with clients, it is difficult to be objective about such attitudinal areas as religion, for example, or moral behaviors different from their own which may even disgust them personally. Counselors are objective, or "detached," in the sense that they regard these attitudes and behaviors as important manifestations of the client's personality. The difficulties in maintaining this position will be described later in the discussion of transference and countertransference phenomena.

Thus, it may be inferred that in counseling practice, objectivity and subjectivity are in a harmonic, yet paradoxical, relationship. This means that the counselor operates variously between the two positions and incorporates elements of both. For example, the counselor is deeply and warmly interested in the client, but not in the same sense as lovers would be interested in each other, or parents in children. Objectivity is needed in diagnosing, yet subjectivity is necessary to build the climate to use that diagnostic information to help the client. The term *participant-observer* is used in psychological circles to describe this dual relationship problem. The counselor participates fully in the intricate human interaction; yet, simultaneously, he maintains a detached observer role.

Cognitiveness/
Affectiveness
Cognitive relationship elements refer to intellectualizing, such as exchanging information, advising on courses of action, or interpreting data, whereas the affective elements refer to feeling expressions and exchanges. In manag-

ing the relationship, the counselor must know when to encourage rational examination and interpretation of the client's problem and when to encourage more exploration of feelings and their ideational connections. Communication is going on at both levels all the time, so it behooves the counselor to be aware of the relative weight of these factors at any given moment. Techniques for handling the connotive aspects of the relationship are described in the following chapter, whereas those techniques for dealing with the more cognitive elements are described in the chapters on interpretation and information giving.

Grater (1964) studied preferences of ninety-five clients for cognitive or affective counselor characteristics. There was a significantly greater focus on personal-social problems in the first interview for clients preferring affective counselors over more cognitively oriented counselors.

Ambiguity/
Clarity

The notion of relationship ambiguity, as developed by Bordin (1955), is a characteristic of a stimulus situation to which people respond differently and to which no clear-cut response is indicated. The counseling relationship is vague and ambiguous to the client. Counselors generally define themselves and the situation early by a process known as *structuring,* an effort to introduce some clarity to the relationship.

Ambiguity serves the function of allowing clients to project feelings into the ambiguous counseling situation. This is done easily, since humans tend to handle ambiguous stimuli in terms of their unique projected responses. This process of projecting feelings aids clients to become aware and concerned about their feelings, thus enabling counselors to know and deal with them through clarifying counseling techniques.

Too much ambiguity for some clients precipitates anxiety in their attempts to make something secure and structured out of the relationship. For example, being too permissive with clients early in the counseling process and encouraging too free exploration of feelings may make them panicky or, in extreme cases, provoke a psychotic episode.

There is some confusion in the relationship if the counselor is too definite a personality to the client or becomes too intimately known as a person by the client. For example, the helper behaves more like a friend than a counselor. Moderate personal ambiguity is necessary so that the client can project any desired role on the counselor. The issue is *social distance* rather than *emotional distance,* as discussed under the objectivity-subjectivity section. If counselors are too friendly with clients in the sense that they let themselves be known too early as well-delineated personalities, counselors will find that they feel compelled to "act themselves" too strongly in an interview situation. Thus, an interview might be pushed in the direction of social conversation or intimate friendship. This is a difficult matter to handle in the school situation, for instance, in which counselors frequently meet student clients on social and instructional as well as therapeutic levels.

In a clinical setting the problem of socializing with clients could create relationship problems. Most clinicians, therefore, still consider it unwise to socialize with clients. The expectancies of social relationships tend to be quite different from therapeutic relationships and tend to interfere with an effective counseling relationship. This issue is controversial, however, since a growing body of therapeutic literature and practice is stressing the importance of the counselor being a natural friendly human being with clients.

Responsibility/
Accountability

Accepting a client in a counseling relationship implies a willingness on the part of the counselor to assume some responsibility for the outcomes of counseling and some willingness to share in the client's troubles. Counseling is very serious business and must be matched by a seriousness of purpose and ethical commitment. Clients have responsibility as well, which they must assume in great part since it is their problem and behaviors which are at stake.

Counselors differ in their interpretation of the proportion of responsibility which each participant must assume. We feel that the counselor does not take responsibility for running the client's life or selecting the counseling goals. The acceptance of the relationship, nevertheless, places counselors in a responsible leadership position where they must protect the client and assume certain liabilities for the outcomes because of the influence of their own personalities on the relationship. The latter situation holds especially in psychotherapeutic relationships where clients make such crucial decisions as whether or not to get a divorce, leave home, commit suicide, change jobs, or drop out of school.

It is difficult to reduce the client's responsibility to a formula. The amount of proportional responsibility depends upon such factors as the age of the client, type of problem, type of agency setting, legally designated responsibilities, and professional expectations. There is no question but that the client is responsible for setting the goals of counseling since he or she owns the problem. Usually, if the goals are ethical and feasible, a counselor agrees to facilitate the process of achieving these goals. How accountable the counselor can be for the outcomes is a debatable professional issue. The trend, however, is to hold the counselor increasingly more accountable for outcomes in line with client and agency goals. In other words, counselors increasingly must be able to produce measurable results to demonstrate responsible professional behavior.

Some counselors control the responsibility factors by discouraging clients from making crucial decisions over such matters as divorce while in the counseling relationship. Such counselors claim that the relationship offers them a vehicle for exploring the ramifications of divorce which puts the client in a better position to make a sound decision and to live with it. The writers believe that responsibility cannot be handled so neatly in most cases. Counselors have more influence than they realize, because of their power and status as healers. They partake of some of the shaman's influence in more simple cultures. Some counselors have an added charisma which gives them even more influence. As a result clients tend to feel powerless, and this feeling is likely to be destructive to client self-esteem and growth (Stensrud and Stensrud 1981). Handling this power and influence humanely is a key counselor responsibility. The techniques of structuring and contracting described in the next chapter can help both counselor and client to face frankly the problems of allocating exclusive and mutual responsibilities.

Counselors working in an agency setting have a further responsibility to be loyal to the institution for which they work. The preceding discussion emphasized the client's and counselor's responsibilities to each other. Mutual responsibilities of agencies and counselors are controlled somewhat by ethical considerations, but they involve the hard realities of agency responsibility to provide adequate facilities and legal protection, for example. Counselors have responsibilities to their agencies to carry out agency policy. Although this aspect of accountability is not a dimension of the relationship, it has a direct bearing upon it and is occasionally in conflict with client interests.

The counselor's responsibility to the broader society is covered in the next section on ethics.

Ethical Dimensions

A distinctive mark of the professional counselor is ethical handling of client relationships so that both the client and society are protected. The counselor's value system is an important determinant of ethical behavior. Codes that summarize ethical principles are based on dominant social values. To cover questions commonly arising in counseling, the Committee on Ethical Standards of the American Psychological Association has published a code of ethical standards (1979); this code is continuously revised to reflect changes in cultural values. The American Personnel and Guidance Association (1981) also published a revised statement of ethical standards that were originally designed for school and college counseling settings. The APA code includes the following principles, stated here in greatly abbreviated form in order to indicate the general idea of the nine principles. It is important for all counselors to have personal copies of the entire code and apply the principles, subprinciples, and standards to specific cases.

1. *Responsibility.* Psychologists take responsibility for providing the highest possible standards of service.

2. *Competence.* Psychologists maintain their high standards of competence in the interest of the public and the profession as a whole.

3. *Moral and Legal Standards.* Psychologists' moral, ethical, and legal standards of behavior are a personal matter; yet they are aware of the impact that their public behavior could have on quality of service.

4. *Public Statements.* Public statements and advertising of psychologists serve the purpose of providing information to help consumers make informed choices. Therefore, they must be accurate and objective statements of qualifications.

5. *Confidentiality.* Safeguarding personal information obtained in the course of teaching, practice, or research is a primary obligation of the psychologist.

6. *Welfare of the Consumer.* Psychologists respect and protect the people with whom they work. Conflicts of interest and loyalties as well as evaluative or training procedures must be made clear to the consumer in order for participants to have freedom of choice regarding participation.

7. *Professional Relationships.* Psychologists give due regard to needs, competencies, and obligations of colleagues, other professionals, and organizations with whom or with which they associate.

8. *Utilization of Assessment Techniques.* Psychologists observe relevant APA standards when developing, publishing, and using assessment methods.

9. *Pursuit of Research Activities.* The psychologist carries out investigations with safeguards for the welfare and respect for the dignity of participants.

There are occasions when the codes do not apply specifically. They were intended to be guidelines only and reflections of a consensus of professionals. There are times when counselors must rely on their own experience and intuitive judgments flowing from their own personal ethics. When in doubt, it is common practice for the counselor to consult with colleagues about the specific issues and what is planned as a resolution. Many situations arise, however, when consultation is not readily available. For example, a counselor judges the client's problem to be beyond his or her competence, and a referral is considered. The APGA code says in Section B:

> *The member shall decline to initiate or shall terminate a counseling relationship when he cannot be of professional assistance to the counselee or client either because of lack of competence or personal limitation. In such instances the member shall refer his counselee or client to an appropriate specialist. In the event the counselee or client declines the suggested referral, the member is not obligated to continue the relationship.*

The preceding questions cover only a small sample of the many which face the counselor in everyday practice. Since they involve elements of judgment as well as fact, it would be well if the counselor consulted with colleagues concerning questions of ethics in difficult cases. Counselors should look also into their own ethics and areas of bias to find possible sources of doubt and value conflict about the ethical implications of their behaviors. Finally, one of the most important safeguards against unethical behavior is knowledge and experience. When in doubt about an ethical problem, it is usual practice to discuss the issues with a group of professional colleagues, using their consensus as a guide.

There are other significant questions to be answered, such as, what causes unethical practice? Is damage or discomfort to the client as a result of ignorance or inadequate training unethical? Schwebel (1955) asserts that unsound judgment and ignorance, though dangerous and having important selection and training implications, are not, strictly speaking, unethical. He hypothesizes further that generally it is self-interest which causes unethical practice. By *self-interest* Schwebel means seeking personal profit, self-enhancement, security, and status at the expense of others. Conflicts often arise, therefore, over the infusion of the counselor's values into the process. Recent emphasis on the methods of self-disclosure of counselors in the relationship poses a related ethical problem. While the client's trust may be enhanced by the counselor revealing his or her true feelings and values, it could have a compelling impact on client values bordering on the unethical. Wrenn (1958) stressed the personal values of the counselor as a basis for counseling ethics. He states, in addition, that ethical behavior on the part of a counselor involves more than subscribing to a code of ethics; a feeling of responsibility to relate behavior to ethics is necessary as well.

CHARACTERISTICS OF THE THERAPEUTIC PSYCHOLOGIST

A principal consideration in building a relationship is the counselor's personality. A counseling follow-up study by Forgy and Black (1954) tends to confirm this assumption that the counselor's personality and counseling style are important, although they found that it was the interaction of counselor personality and method which accounted for differences in counseling effectiveness. The changes could not be attributed to counselor personality only, nor to methodology exclusively. Seeman (1949), in a study of career counseling, concluded that methods are not as important in accounting for differing client reactions as are characteristics of "warmth, interest, and understanding." Fiedler (1950) compared three differently oriented groups of experienced therapists with three groups of inexperienced therapists. Fiedler found that for experienced therapists, personalities and experience, rather than different methods, accounted for differences in therapeutic outcomes. Though serious questions have been raised about Fiedler's methodology and interpretations, there is sufficient evidence of the importance of counselor personality to warrant extended discussion.

While Gardner's exhaustive review of relationship variables (1964) revealed much research on ideal therapist characteristics and their positive relationship with client progress, research is still not sufficiently definitive to select counselors on these characteristics.

Many of the traits and attitudes to be discussed may seem idealistic; nevertheless, they provide yardsticks against which counselors can measure themselves. What are the characteristics of the effective counselor or therapist? While it had been popular for years to compile lists of characteristics of counselors thought to be significant, we are well along in research on traits of effective and ineffective counselors and therapists. An early APA

Committee on Training in Clinical Psychology, for example, compiled a list of traits which were difficult to specify behaviorally. Other lists have been compiled subsequently by Cox (1945), Cutler (1954), and Graver (1948). Cottle and associates (1953, 1954) and Combs (1969) described how counselors differ from other defined helpers, such as teachers. The methods were largely standardized tests of traits correlated with specific counselor behaviors. This line of investigation was not very productive of useful data about effective counselors. The following discussion of counselor characteristics is derived largely from experimental studies on effective counselor characteristics, as well as from our own experience.

*Person-
Technician
Balance*

Counselors and psychotherapists have two strong and balanced components: personal relationship skills and technical qualifications. Clinicians such as Strupp (1963) support this view. The actualizing counseling approach is replete with suggested techniques for developing effective technicians for behavior change. In addition, counselors must always be in a conscious process of personal growth so their personal actualizing efforts will serve them as well as their methodologies. There are abundant data now to validate the view that counseling effectiveness is maximal when a counselor can relate to clients in warm, understanding, and self-revealing ways. In this manner he or she serves as a personality model for the client.

Several references will be made to the data of Rogers (1953), Truax and Carkhuff (1964), and Combs (1969) on facilitative relationships characteristic of counselors. They found that counselor characteristics of warmth, understanding, positive regard or caring, concreteness of counselor expression, and transparency or realness create conditions for greater client self-exploration. These characteristics in turn result in greater behavior change in a client than if these "facilitative conditions" were not present in optimal amounts. Our problem in counselor selection and training is to find means for assessing these characteristics reliably. Carkhuff's scales on facilitative dimensions have been used extensively in assessment and research (1969).

Before describing counselor characteristics further, we wish to reemphasize what we feel to be some focal points of this book:

1. Counselors and therapists are engaged in helping others in a professional capacity. But, more important, they are human beings with personal weaknesses and actualizing problems of their own. The therapist has the capacity to grow; as teachers learn from students, likewise therapists learn daily from clients. Counselors must take continuing responsibility for their own personal growth through counseling for themselves, group experience, and other self-renewal experiences, such as those described by Gardner (1965) and Brammer and Abrego (1981).

2. Professional counselors are experts in helping others, but they have no mystical solutions. Their technical training can be helpful, but only the continuous attempt to increase their own self-understanding and awareness makes them believe in what they attempt to do with clients.

Counseling and therapy are only partly technique; the rest is subtle human effectiveness through personal relationships.

3. Each client with whom one deals is a unique expression of human nature; hence, the textbook generalization never applies completely. Also, counselors must respect themselves as unique persons.

4. Thus, counseling and therapy can be viewed as a laboratory for the actualizing of both participants. Each client can help a counselor or therapist shed new light on his or her own personal integration.

5. A central emphasis for enlightened counselors or therapists must be the development of a core of valid technique which fits their theory, along with flexibility for learning new ideas each day and for discarding old approaches which no longer apply.

Intellectual Competence

To comprehend the enormous complexity of the human personality and to handle the involved abstractions of counseling theory the counselor must be considerably above average in general intelligence. Related to intellectual competence is the requirement of vast knowledge of the culture acquired through general education and varied living. Intellectual and cultural breadth is significant also, since one basis for understanding varied clients is to have familiarity with the cultural environments those clients have experienced.

Counselors believed for a long time that didactically presented knowledge about counseling improves effectiveness. Growing evidence from studies such as Joslin's (1965) indicates that, in training situations with school counselors, rated counseling competence has a low relationship to measurable knowledge about the process.

Spontaneity

What was said about spontaneity as a characteristic of the actualizing personality in Chapter 3 applies especially to the counselor. It has been mentioned several times that counseling is not a rigid mechanical application of formulas for producing behavior changes. The counselor's responses to client statements and feelings must be immediate reactions of the counselor's total being at that moment. Counselors must be free to move naturally, quickly, and easily in their thinking and feeling in order to adapt to the subtle nuances of client behavior.

While no concrete suggestions can be offered concerning how this characteristic is acquired, it seems to be a by-product of thorough preparation in counseling theory, attitudes, and methodology plus a nonrigid mature personality relatively free from threat.

Acceptance and Caring

It is questionable how much attitudes can be changed by advice, persuasion, or threats. Client attitudes appear to change most effectively in the presence of other growth-producing attitudes. The client experiences acceptance, for example, as a feeling of being unconditionally understood, loved, and respected. This attitude of positive acceptance is the counseling equivalent of a basic form of altruistic love (Sorokin 1950). The evidence and logic presented by writers such as Fromm (1956), Montague (1950), May (1953), and Sorokin (1950) attest to the therapeutic power of altruistic love. For the past few years counselors looked to philosophy, theology, and anthropology for their concepts of therapeutic love. Psychologists have studied the components of love through ingenious experiments with primates. Harlow's (1958) studies of mothering are examples. In the context of long range developmental studies, Harlow found that primates fed and raised under varying conditions of maternal deprivation developed maladaptive behaviors which in human terms would be described as neurotic and sociopathic. Examples are infantile sexual behaviors, excessive and inappropriate aggression, and reduced affectional interaction. It was apparent that the deficient quality and quantity of early affectional relationships with the mother or mother surrogates had a profoundly negative effect on their later behavior. Spitz's (1949) earlier studies with children in foundling homes further support common sense observations about the powerful qualities of love relationships. Infants not fondled by home personnel had an unusually high mortality rate compared to those who obtained some human attention. Until more evidence is accumulated, however, one should be cautious about overgeneralizing in regard to the curative effect of love.

The counselor is in a position to provoke love relationships in the interview which can have constructive or destructive effects on the client's security system and capacity to give and accept love. As long as clients have unfulfilled affectional needs, the counselor's management of love in counseling will be a crucial therapeutic variable. Observations seem to indicate that people who have received sufficient love, particularly in early development, learn to be happy with themselves and to love adults around them, which, in turn, enables them to direct considerable altruistic concern to all human beings later on.

Caring is often communicated through touch. While counseling research findings support the effectiveness of nonverbal communication generally, touch has its special issues and risks. Sometimes clients feel anxious when touched; others feel the warmth and caring intended; some attach sexual overtones; and some feel patronized if in a lower status. Certainly, counselors need to exercise their best judgment about this issue since research offers little help. A few guidelines, such as making the gesture appropriate to the situation, not imposing more intimacy than the client desires, and not communicating a negative or power message, might help. Alagna and associates (1979) studied the effects of touching with mixed sex pairs. They concluded that counselors can use touch effectively in counseling, but that this complex behavior had a number of limiting boundaries that made both counselor and client potentially vulnerable.

Some counselors and psychotherapists may have reservations about using the ambiguous term *love* in a counseling context. *Caring* is a term meaning much the same as love, and includes the component of unconditional regard for the client's welfare. This care can be expressed in an aggressive critical fashion as well as in situations where correction or discipline are involved.

Shostrom's Caring Relationship Inventory (1966) is an experimental attempt to measure the essential elements of caring, or love, in couple relationships. It helps clients to discover the spurious, as well as the growth-producing, elements of love in their own persons.

Unconditional positive regard is another euphemistic term used by counselors to describe this deep concern for the client's welfare and personhood. Truax (1963), for example, found unconditional positive regard as an effective treatment variable in his study of treatment in psychosis.

Nygren (1953) contrasts the eros and agape types of love—eros referring to the ancient Greek term for a self-centered, erotic love which satisfies the organism's desires. Agape refers to a type of love in which a person seeks to assist other people to grow, contributes unequivocally to the welfare of the love object, and allows the loving person to be used for self-enhancement of the loved. Acceptance, as defined in therapeutic terms, has many of the attributes of agape.

Another characteristic of acceptance is *spontaneous motivation*. The presence of concern for the other person is a natural outgrowth of the basic attitudinal structure of the counselor's personality. Acceptance is *altruistic* in the sense that the other person's welfare is sought, not exploited.

Acceptance attitudes are *nonjudgmental* in that the counselor holds a "neutral interest" in values held by the client. This appears paradoxical when we assume that the counselor wants to promote the welfare of the client as the counselor views that welfare. The counselor tries to say in effect, however, "I neither approve nor disapprove of your behavior and attitudes, but I deeply respect your right to feel as you please and your right to act or feel differently from me." The counselor makes clients feel that no matter how they feel toward the counselor it doesn't matter, and that the counselor won't judge them for seeking help.

BASIC ASSUMPTIONS UNDERLYING ACCEPTANCE.   Holding an attitude of acceptance presupposes several basic assumptions. First, acceptance is based on the idea that the individual has *infinite worth and dignity*. In other words, human values are extremely high in the value hierarchy of the counselor. A **second** basic assumption is that it is the person's *right to make his or her own decisions* and lead his or her own life. This assumption is based upon a third even more basic assumption that the client has the capacity or *potential to choose wisely* and *to live a full, self-actualizing, socially useful life*. A fourth related assumption is that each person is *responsible for his or her own life*. The counselor's value system must be such that he or she will enhance this sense of self-respect and self-responsibility in clients and in herself or himself. As we indicated earlier in this chapter, while discussing responsibility, counselors must realize that they cannot solve problems for clients.

The basic assumption of many counselors, particularly of those leaning toward the client-centered group, is that there exist within the individual creative growth forces which, when released by the counselor's acceptance, will allow the individual to grow toward the model of the self-actualizing personality. Rogers (1951) cites evidence from several fields which appear to support this assumption of growth needs. Allport's concept of "propriate striving" as a positive, goal-directed, motivating force deep within the personality supports this basic assumption also (1955).

The assumptions and attributes of acceptance are rooted deeply in American democratic philosophy, which in turn is based strongly in the Hebraic-Christian cultural traditions. The Leibnitzian philosophical position of viewing the human as an active, growth-motivated organism has contributed much also. The blend of eighteenth-century emphases on universal human rights and values with nineteenth-century views on human uniqueness and individuality has created a rich background for twentieth-century counseling philosophy. Thus, the present cultural and educational climate in the western world appears to favor these assumptions and attitudes. This climate is making it easier for counselors to learn and apply basic attitudes leading to client self-actualization.

A summary definition of acceptance has been stated by Rogers (1951) as being a positive attitude toward people which views them as persons of worth and dignity with the right to make their own decisions. We have postulated that the major element of this positive attitude is a form of love. Being loved in this accepting sense makes clients more capable of loving themselves and others. Perhaps the following is the dynamic of acceptance: When clients have experienced attitudes of acceptance, they are able to take this attitude and experience it in the same way toward themselves. Once they have accepted certain characteristics about themselves, they are able to accept those ideas, experiences, and drives which are a part of their basic selves, but which, up to now, they have been denying or distorting. Evidence from studies by Truax and Carkhuff (1964) support this idea of greater self-confrontation in the presence of warmth and understanding.

SELF-ACCEPTANCE.   There is some evidence for the circular idea that acceptance of others is based on acceptance of one's self, and that self-acceptance is based largely on being accepted by others. Several early studies (Phillips 1951; Sherman 1945; Zelen 1954) point to the significance of self-acceptance and other positive self-regarding attitudes as basic for acceptance of others. The significance of these findings for counselors is that they must accept themselves before they can accept clients sufficiently well to help them. The significance for clients is that acquisition of self-acceptance and understanding puts them in a position to accept and to receive social rewards from others. Fromm (1956) points out that one great difficulty with this principle is that our culture frowns on self-love yet extols loving others. This difficulty seems to stem from our cultural inability to differentiate *selfishness* from *self-respect*.

VALUES OF ACCEPTANCE.   A point of great significance for the acceptance attitude is that clients get involved in the counseling process when clients sense that the counselor really cares about what they think and feel, that the counselor can and wants to help them, and that they will not be judged. Counseling then begins in earnest and becomes meaningful.

A second value of the acceptance attitude is its effect on the *psychological climate* of the interview. By psychological climate is meant the emotional tone resulting from the personal interaction of the client and counselor. The climate may be described, for example, as warm, cold, serious, or frivolous. Conspicuous examples of emotional climates are those surrounding funerals or football games. Porter (1950) defines psychological climate more narrowly as those elements of a situation which have implications regarding valuing one's self as a person. In other words, the counselor's attitudes affect the interview climate which, in turn, influences clients' attitudes toward themselves—attitudes of confidence, worth, and competence, for example.

The counselor, in addition, tries to keep a fairly consistent or stable attitudinal climate so that clients can express themselves freely without expecting disapproval, criticism, argument, or other traditional responses they expect on the basis of their past experiences. This accepting climate, and the fact that the counselor does not react toward them as others have reacted, makes a favorable situation, we believe, for learning new responses and extinguishing old nonadaptive behaviors.

A third value of acceptance is its salutary effect on *defensive* attitudes. Why does acceptance have such power to counteract defensiveness? A partial answer may be found in the description of personality presented in Chapter 3, which viewed the individual as being protected by a facade of protective mechanisms—mechanisms employed to reduce psychological vulnerability. Rationalization, denial, justification, projection, and development of symptoms were a few examples.

What happens when clients feel threatened? Their previously learned defenses are mobilized. They are like the old man in the fable who, when the wind began to blow, wrapped his coat around himself even tighter. You will remember that in the story it was the sun, with its warm rays, which created the atmosphere or climate which made the man want to take off his coat. Acceptance, similarly, is that attitudinal set of the counselor which seems to create in the client a feeling of being so comfortable in the counselor's presence that the client need no longer keep his or her guard or defenses up.

ACCEPTANCE—WHAT IT IS NOT.   The following are some mistaken notions about acceptance. *Approval* or agreement is not acceptance. Accepting a person means neither approving nor disapproving of what he or she says or feels. It means simply taking him or her as a person with the right to feel and think differently from the way we think and feel, no matter how unfair, absurd, negativistic, wholesome, social, or pleasant the person's expressions may be. That clients, early in the counseling process, may misinterpret the counselor's acceptance attitudes as agreement with what they say and feel is a real counseling hazard.

A second misconception may occur over an attitude of *neutrality*. Acceptance is a *positive, active* attitude toward the client. It says in effect, "I *like* you even if I may not necessarily agree personally with all you think or feel." Another way of stating this idea might be, "I see, appreciate, and value these ideas and feelings along with you. You, the essential you, matter more to me than what you say or do."

A third distorted notion of acceptance is to equate it with *sympathy*. Sympathy goes much farther than acceptance, in that the counselor actually begins to feel in the way the client does—with a strong empathic response. The counselor actually feels sorry too as he or she becomes more emotionally involved. Acceptance, however, is more detached. The counselor says in effect, "I understand how badly you feel, although I do not personally feel that way." Sympathy, while intended as a supportive device, has the added disadvantage of tending to *minimize* the feeling of the client. A sympathy attitude says in effect, "You poor person, I feel so sorry for you since you cannot help yourself; let me give you encouragement and help." Clients feel incapable of handling feelings by themselves and feel that they must look to outside support. The net effect is the creation of a psychological climate in which dependent and evasive behavior is learned. When the need in the counselor to offer sympathy is strong, it is suspected that this is an expression of his or her own dependency needs.

A fourth misinterpretation of acceptance is equating it with *tolerance*. Although tolerance may be a desirable social trait, in a counseling relationship it connotes "putting up with." It implies a negative acceptance rather than a positive one, as well as a more superficial kind of respect for personality. The tolerance attitude implies that there is a characteristic, such as race difference, of which the counselor is aware, and about which the client senses he or she is trying to be tolerant.

Understanding and Empathy

Counseling and therapeutic writings are replete with suggestions to *understand* clients as a special way of being with them, yet the term is seldom defined in behavioral terms. Effective counselors seem to be able to understand their clients more than ineffective counselors can, according to several studies (Fiedler 1950; Heine 1950). Porter (1949) made a useful distinction between understanding diagnostically and understanding therapeutically. *Understanding diagnostically* refers to the intellectualized descriptions of the client's behavior. Examples are the information obtained through testing or observation for making diagnostic judgments for use in career planning. As one would expect, this aspect of understanding enables the counselor to make predictions about clients' overt behavior and their self-descriptions. The test, then, of the degree of counselor's diagnostic understanding would be the extent of their ability to describe, interpret, and predict client behavior.

Understanding therapeutically refers to feeling reactions on the part of a counselor which enable the client to feel understood, accepted, and empathized with. An attitude of therapeutic understanding emphasizes seeing clients as they see their experiences. As Gendlin (1962) so aptly described it, understanding empathically is sensing the meaning which the client is experiencing so as to help the client focus on that meaning. Raskin (1974) studied eighty-three counselors from eight different therapeutic orientations to arrive at a description of the ideal therapist. They agreed highly on the ideal qualities, and most put empathy in the first rank. Yet, when examining the recordings of six expert therapists, Raskin found many short of their ideal. Empathy, even though not a very operational concept, has been studied extensively and has proven to be a key ingredient for obtaining constructive outcomes in classrooms as well as in counseling (Aspy 1975).

Therapeutic understanding appears quite unrelated to the counselor's knowledge about the client (Fiedler and Senior 1952). Effective therapists, although not able to predict their client's self-descriptions much better than the poor therapists (Fiedler 1950; Luft 1950), were rated significantly better in their ability to establish and maintain a warm, accepting relationship. In this connection, one of Fiedler's significant findings was that there was substantial agreement among skilled therapists of three different schools of therapy as to what constituted an ideal therapeutic relationship. The skilled therapists of different schools agreed more with each other on definitions of the ideal relationship than with the unskilled members of their own school (Fiedler 1950). If Fiedler's results can be interpreted at face value, it seems that understanding therapeutically is closely related to therapeutic competence.

The evidence is not all positive, however. Lesser's study (1961), although limited in scope to a few counselors and clients, found that the generally accepted idea of empathic understanding being related to client progress did not pertain. Even though all clients in his study made progress as measured by Q-sorts on ideal-self perceptions, this progress was unrelated to measures on an empathic understanding scale.

In a series of studies on the conditions which promoted constructive personality change in college and hospital clients, Truax and Carkhuff (1963, 1964) found that a sensitive and accurate attempt at therapeutic understanding of the client was very facilitative. This is an empathic response to the client's being, which clients perceive as meaning they have been understood. Truax and Carkhuff found that nonpossessive warmth and counselor genuineness were variables which, in addition to understanding, promoted client growth. The rationale for the effectiveness of these ingredients is stated by the investigators as follows:

> The greater the degree of the therapist's accurate empathic understanding of the client, the greater the degree to which the therapist shows unconditional or nonpossessive warmth or integration of the therapist within the relationship, and the more intense and intimate the therapist in the relationship, the greater will be the degree of the client's interpersonal exploration and the greater will be the consequent extent of positive behavior change. (1964, p. 861)

In other words, if counselor conditions as described above are present in the relationship, clients feel more free to be themselves and face their problems. Empathy has been stressed as a key variable in counseling success. Little direct evidence from client satisfaction outcomes is available to support this enthusiasm; and Gladstein (1977) cautions us that, in light of this thin data base, counselor-educators should be cautious in their emphasis on empathy.

Effective counselors apparently need both diagnostic and therapeutic types of understanding. Yet they may find that attempting to use both types of understanding is difficult indeed. There is a strong tendency to be preoccupied with the cognitive aspects of client difficulties and to overlook the connotive implications of their confusion and indecision. For example, while attempting to see the client's reasons for seeking financial aid, for finding social work more suitable than teaching, or deciding which marital prospect appears most promising, the counselor might tend to ignore the threat to the client's independence involved in the financial aid, or the need to dominate children in the career choice, or the extreme dependency interfering with a marital or occupational choice. In some cases, perhaps, more emphasis needs to be placed on the reality level of the client occupational choice rather than on the intricate feelings regarding their parents' wishes for success through them. This point is especially pertinent for many school counselors and advisers whose positions are structured around career planning. We assume that the really effective therapeutic psychologist has the capacity to keep the understanding emphases in balance and to know when to stress one aspect of understanding over the other.

THE INTERNAL FRAME OF REFERENCE.   Another useful concept in understanding the client and in assisting the counselor or psychotherapist to understand the meaning of empathy is that of the internal frame of reference (Porter 1950; Rogers 1942). This concept is defined as the attempt by the counselor to perceive the client's phenomenological world as seen by the client. It means the attempt to think *with*, rather than *for* or *about* the client. By frame of reference is meant simply point of view or the observational vantage point. Rogers cites an example of the counselor's thoughts as he assumes this role:

> To be of assistance to you I will put aside myself—the self of ordinary interaction—and enter into your world of perception as completely as I am able. I will become, in a sense, another self for you—an alter ego of your own attitudes and feelings—a safe opportunity for you to discern yourself more clearly, to experience yourself more truly and deeply, to choose more significantly. (1951, p. 35)

An example of a counselor's thinking from the *external* frame of reference would be, "What is causing this difficulty, and why is he so preoccupied with marital problems?" The counselor thinks, "This fellow is in bad shape;

I've got to find out what is wrong and try to help him save his marriage." An example of the *internal* frame of reference thinking would be, "You see this as a very disturbing experience, and you want to do something about it." The counselor thinks, "I must try to understand how he looks at this problem and to help him clarify his own thinking about it so that he can make a decision in line with the best interests of all concerned."

As an aid in conceptualizing the problem of getting within the client's frame of reference, see Figure 12 (Shostrom and Brammer 1952). In stage (1) the client and counselor are in an ordinary social interaction situation where *S* listens and *C* talks. The perceptions are formed largely on the basis of the unique past experience of each participant. Each moves down his or her respective experience lane as in stage (3). Often the counselor, who characteristically assumes the external frame of reference, tries to get the client to come into his or her lane—to see things his or her way. Under certain circumstances this may be a legitimate objective, but it does not necessarily help in understanding the client.

When counselors assume the internal frame of reference, however, they try to make their perceptual framework match that of the client as in stage (2) of Figure 12. Stage (4) illustrates what happens when counselors try to get into the client's lane. At least temporarily, they attempt to think and feel the way the client does.

Learning to assume the internal frame of reference and to stay within it seems to be particularly difficult. As one contemplates the reasons for this difficulty, the following examples can be considered.

Language differences constitute a major obstacle. As the adult tries to understand the adolescent or the child, or as the easterner tries to fathom

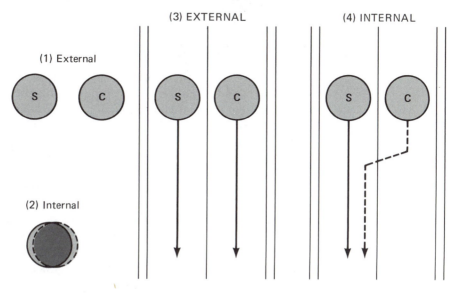

FIGURE 12.   *The Internal and External Frames of Reference*

the particular lingo of the westerner, it seems that the symbols used have different meanings to different people. This is a problem of semantics which has received much attention in the psycholinguistics literature of recent years.

Biological differences are obviously another barrier. The difficulties experienced as a man tries to assume the feminine frame of reference, and vice versa, can be easily understood.

A current issue in counseling is whether white or black counselors working with clients of a different race can really empathize with their clients since they share so little common experience. It takes unusual empathic ability to transcend these differences.

Socioeconomic differences often cause client and counselor to be in different semantic worlds. Counselors, for example, having from five to eight years of college training, have difficulty assuming the frame of reference of those with little formal education. A thorough understanding of social class differences and their significance, therefore, should be part of every counselor's training. There is abundant evidence of the need for this type of understanding in studies by Havighurst (1953), Warner (1949), Postman, Bruner, and McGinnies (1948), Schwebel (1965), Ivey (1979), and Sue (1977).

Related to cultural differences are *experience differentials.* Counselors, having life experiences different from their clients, can only see the client's world imperfectly in the light of their own frames of reference. Finally, *age differences* influence understanding, in that one who has lived longer often finds it difficult to "see" the significance of the conflicts and frustrations of a much younger person. Teachers, for instance, often forget "how it feels" to be a student.

It was felt that a brief analysis of some of the obstacles to assuming the internal frame of reference would help to punctuate the necessity for striving very hard for broad life experiences, as well as for asking ourselves the questions: "How does he look at this problem?" "How is she thinking and feeling about this matter?" "What is he trying to say?" This attempt at understanding the client by means of assuming the internal frame of reference pays heavy dividends in a better relationship and more appropriate counselor responses to the client's feeling and thinking.

Empathic response is another way of viewing understanding. Empathy is related to the German *einfühlung,* which means *feeling into.* An illustration is the response of the crowd as the highjumper clears the bar. All vocalize *umm-mm* and lean forward as the jumper goes up. Bowlers often experience similar feelings when they "empathize" the ball. Similarly, counselors tend to "feel into" the attitudes of the client as they are being expressed. Although this capacity to empathize aids the counselor in maintaining the internal frame of reference, there is a tendency to get overinvolved emotionally, the dangers of which have been described previously.

The question of how a counselor manifests empathic qualities is answered by the quality of verbal responses which capture the essential feeling messages of the client. Reflecting these messages with caring concern leaves the client with a feeling of being warmly understood.

Warmth and Human Encounter

Closely related to therapeutic understanding, caring, and acceptance attitudes is *warmth,* a term used to describe an aspect of the relationship. Warmth appears to encompass the sensitive, friendly, considerate, and responsive elements of the counselor personality. *Relating easily to people* is a phrase often used to describe an aspect of warmth. Manifested warmth seems basic for an effective relationship. Truax and Carkhuff (1964) found with their warmth research scale that nonpossessive warmth was an effective therapeutic ingredient, and that the higher the level of this variable the more evidence of constructive personality change was noted.

The friendly conversation, preceding and interspersed in the process, however, adds little to the progress of counseling. It has been called "sawdust" by Rogers (1942), meaning that it helps to maintain a friendly climate but doesn't result in much therapeutic progress.

Consideration for clients is rooted in respect for them as persons and is another way of manifesting warmth. This counselor attitude conveys a feeling to clients that they are worthy of respect (a feeling which many clients do not have for themselves). Consideration is shown also in the ordinary courtesies of social communication, such as offering a chair and showing concern for the client's comfort. Consideration is shown through the intense interest exhibited in clients so that they feel they are important and worthwhile persons to the counselor, not just research subjects or practice "guinea pigs."

Bugental (1964), in describing the mature therapist, uses the term *encounter* to describe the therapist's willingness to "be there with" the client and yet take responsibility only for his or her own (the therapist's) authentic personhood. The counselor serves as a model for authenticity.

Another external manifestation of warmth in a relationship is the honest smile. This behavior is the test of the genuineness of the counselor's attitudes. Clients can sense when counselors are "just trying to be nice" and when they experience genuine pleasure in knowing their clients as distinct people.

Freedom

This corollary attitude of acceptance characterizes a freedom and lack of authoritarian and judgmental attitudes in the counselor's personality. *Permissiveness* was a term used in the past to describe therapeutic freedom, but accrued negative connotations reduced its descriptive accuracy. The counselor says in effect, "You may discuss anything you wish here without fear of judgment"; hence, he or she is neither offended nor shocked. Counselors allow clients freedom to be themselves and to grow.

A completely laissez faire attitude, however, would operate to the disadvantage of the client, since the relationship would be too ambiguous.

If allowed too much free expression, the client may fear loss of emotional control and suffer anxiety. As indicated in the discussion of catharsis, too free an expression of feelings may serve to erode client defensive structures to the point where they are at the mercy of their feelings and may move toward a psychosis.

A counselor who is too permissive could be extremely cruel to the client who is vulnerable to anxiety. Such a client might flounder without direction. The counselor would abuse his or her own freedom if he or she were facetious. An extreme sample would be the client who came into the office and announced, "I just killed my mother," to which the counselor replied, "Did you use an axe or a knife?" The client assumes that counselors take their professional responsibilities seriously, and responses of this type tend to destroy respect for them.

The counselor's authority role often belies attempts to acquire a permissive attitude. The counselor's personal prestige, specialized knowledge, and professional "halo" make an atmosphere of free expression difficult to achieve. Counselors are tempted at most to use their authoritarian status to urge clients toward definite goals or, at least, to select the content of the interviews. The desirable amount of authority or direction to be given is the least amount consonant with the goals of the particular counseling case and the least amount which is comfortable for both. Techniques for implementing these attitudes will be clarified later under the subject of structuring. When used appropriately, therapeutic freedom allows clients more spontaneous expression of their feelings, thus allowing them to understand and accept the feelings.

Congruence and Transparency

There is growing evidence that, in order to elicit open, honest self-confrontation by the client, the counselor must manifest these qualities. There is little evidence, however, concerning what kind of self-congruent behavior is therapeutic. Does this mean telling the client one's own problems? In a group therapy situation, Branan (1967) found that use of the counselor's self-experience did not increase perceived counselor genuineness significantly; yet Schutz (1971) places leader self-revelation in a central place in group work.

Various terms are used to describe the condition of genuineness-realness, congruence, transparency, and authenticity. There is more than just self-awareness and nondenial of feeling in counselors. They must present themselves as real persons in the interview encounter. A common behavior running counter to this idea in counselors is the facade of professionalism—a kind of protective personal distance. In the Truax and Carkhuff studies (1964), there was a significant tendency for counselors rated high on the genuineness and self-congruence scales to have clients who were rated most improved or having the most constructive personality change.

The counselor must, above all, be honest and sincere in his attitudes. Counseling cannot be a masquerade. Honesty, as used here, is not perceived in moralistic terms but as a characteristic of *straight-forwardness.* Beginning counselors, for example, learn quickly that if they try to be accepting without truly feeling this way inside, clients do not take long to find it out. It is this quality of honesty which again distinguishes communication in the interview from ordinary social conversation. In much of social communication both parties keep up a "front," hence conversation is often a game of mild deceit. It seems that when clients experience a relationship in which this deceit is not present and when they feel that the counselor is serious and "on the level" with them, they realize that they can drop their own facades and can accomplish little by being deceitful themselves.

In order to be completely honest, it is necessary that counselors recognize frankly their own errors—that they make errors of judgment and technique. Therapists can more easily recognize and correct errors when they can admit their possibility. Their perceptions and humble acceptance of error, however, must be balanced by a mature tolerance for the inevitable mistakes, especially the more trivial ones. Clients seem to have a remarkable tolerance for counselor error providing other aspects of the relationship are adequate. This attitude of alertness to error serves as a useful antidote to counselor complacency, or what is known as the "pedestal syndrome," or the "Jehovah complex." Bugental (1964), in describing characteristics of the mature therapist, mentions humility as a consequence of counselors' awareness of their limited knowledge and the awe they experience in the presence of potential growth. Bugental mentions further the need to accept normal guilt for being a therapist. This condition results when sensitive therapists realize that they are not doing all that can be done for persons who trust their lives to them. These are further illustrations of the need for counselors to face up to the real business of being human in the very sensitive relationship of counseling.

The studies of Truax and Carkhuff on therapeutic variables have been cited often in this chapter. Not only are they models of research procedure, but they also give valuable leads for process conceptions and counselor selection. They found that effective counselors are people who can sensitively and accurately understand clients, allow themselves to express warmth, be genuine, and still retain their integrity in the relationship. These conditions encourage clients to manifest the same characteristics, resulting in deepening self-exploration and self-awareness, which then make possible more constructive personality change. They also found that low therapeutic conditions resulted in ratings of client behavior indicating deterioration (Carkhuff and Truax 1966). Thus, counseling can have negative effects; this may help to explain why so many studies of counseling outcomes come out negative, and why so much credence is placed in Eysenck's findings (1952) which question the efficacy of therapy. Positive growth indices are canceled out by the deteriorative effects of some counseling relationships.

We feel that, at this point in the discussion of counselor characteristics, it must be mentioned that the counselor is not some sort of inert, bland agent to be manipulated at will by the client. In attempts to accept the client wholeheartedly and to enter into a close relationship, the counselor or therapist *risks* as much as the client. Counselors, too, must open their facades to make the relationship effective. The risk element involves the possibility of failure or rejection by the client and, if this happens, the counselor may lose part of herself or himself. The counselor accepts this risk as the price of being human.

To help counteract tendencies to be incongruent, studies of matching client and counselor on compatibility variables have been performed. Fry and Charron (1980), for example, found that in their study of cognitive style and compatibility clients improved in their self-exploration skills and ease of relating to their counselors. These general findings have been confirmed in similar studies (Packer and Bain 1978; Meara, Shannon, and Pepinsky 1979).

Flexibility

Carnes's study (1949) of counselor flexibility points up the necessity for this vital trait in the counselor's character. Therapists must be flexible in the use of their counseling techniques and attitudes as they move along all the dimensions defined at the outset of this chapter. Sometimes they must be objective, and at other times subjective. Often they utilize techniques which are primarily affective; at other places they are primarily cognitive. For example, they may explain a point about client responsibility to create clarity; at other points they may deliberately promote ambiguity, as will be explained in Chapter 7. Sometimes counselors focus on aspects of client problems which are common to men and women in general. Then again, they may dwell upon the unique problems of particular clients. The essence of the creative synthesis view is flexibility in utilizing all approaches and methods as they seem appropriate and effective in achieving the anticipated client outcomes.

SUPPORT AND CRISIS

Nature of Support

The therapeutic relationship, in addition to being the vehicle for the development of awareness and action, serves a broad supportive role. As we said earlier, an awareness of anxiety reduction and a feeling of security on the part of the client are the results of a suitable emotional response from the counselor. The essence of support, then, is this feeling of general well-being, and satisfaction of "affect hunger," as Levy (1963) describes it, which the client experiences in the presence of certain counselor attitudes.

Support may be viewed in four ways. Its implicit form is the supporting nature of the relationship itself. The acceptance, warmth, and other characteristics of the counselor are construed by the client as security provoking. The client experiences support when the relationship bridge is broadened so that feelings can flow freely between the core and actualizing systems, as well as between counselor and client personalities. Rogers, for example, speaking of the counseling relationship says, "It is experienced as basically supporting, but it is in no way supportive. The client does not feel that someone is behind him, that someone approves of him. He does experience the fact that here is someone who respects him *as he is,* and is willing for him to take any direction which he chooses" (1951, p. 209). We agree with Rogers in principle, but there appear to be crises when actual support techniques need to be applied. This effort to support a client also may seem to contradict earlier statements about the use of anxiety and distress for motivating change. The principles of flexibility and timing, however, make it possible for the therapist to be accepting at times, more supportive at other times, and even threatening at appropriate points.

A second type of support experienced by the client takes the form of reassurance and a change to a low stress environment. There is a large group of counselors who feel this type of support is necessary with clients experiencing loss or hurt, especially in the early phases of counseling. Thus, whether support is offered explicitly through a medium such as reassurance or only through the implicit support of the relationship itself is up to the sensitive judgment of the counselor.

Support may be experienced by clients in a third manner when they feel the counselor assuming more responsibility for leading the interview, carrying the major verbalizing load, and making decisions. While this shift in responsibility may have a supporting effect, it should be viewed as a temporary expedient for reducing anxiety only. *The danger of prolonged support of this type is primarily that of reinforced dependency and reduced capacity to assume responsibility.*

A fourth function of support is in the form of crisis intervention, which is described in the next section.

Management of Crises

Crises are produced by two sources of stress—external events such as disasters, death in the family, sudden unemployment, or severe illness, and internal events. Internal sources, while aggravated by external events, are such conditions as suicidal feelings, acute alcoholism, despair, or bad drug trips. Crises are characterized by severe stress, disruption of life routines, acute frustration, and feelings of anxiety and helplessness. Crises associated with situations such as death are usually of short duration, especially if the normal grief process has ensued. Developmental or existential types of crises, such as going off to school, entering the army, or facing a conflictful choice, usually are more prolonged. In Western societies crises usually are viewed as severe problems to solve; whereas in some Eastern societies—for example, the Chinese—the language symbol for crisis is danger plus opportunity. From an actualizing viewpoint, therefore, counselors need to ask how crisis methods might move the client from comfort and equilibrium to higher levels of growth. At least when the crisis has passed clients should ask themselves what they learned from that experience.

An appropriate supportive relationship provides hope—the best antidote for despair and grief. Currently, helping agencies are experimenting with a multiple impact strategy with families, where several specialists offer immediate and comprehensive help to a family undergoing a crisis. Here, a team of specialists meets the family right at the hospital, in case of severe accident, for example, and provides intensive help to get the family functioning as normally as possible. Crisis centers, run largely by volunteers trained in basic crisis helping skills, are part of almost every large community. Much of the supportive contact work is done by telephone. Skills for managing crises are presented in detail in *The Helping Relationship: Process and Skills* (Brammer 1979).

Lavelle (1979) compared two styles of dealing with crises—*behavioral* and *affective*. The affective style emphasized clarification of cause and effect, linking present and past behaviors, and summarizing common themes. The behavioral style emphasized probing, focused commands, formal analysis of the client's difficulties, and suggesting potentials. The behavioral style elicited significantly more alternative-related and future-tense statements but significantly fewer coping statements compared to the affective style. One implication for counseling style is to stress flexibility and multiple roles for crisis intervention.

Crisis intervention methodology and strategy has become a specialized helping field. In addition to the usual helping skills, drug therapy may be a useful medical adjunct in severe emotional pain. The goal usually is restoration to precrisis equilibrium. Aguilera and Messick (1974) summarized the key steps in crisis intervention as: (1) Assessment of the person and problem (for example, danger to self or others?); (2) Planning the intervention (for example, to restore equilibrium); (3) Intervention to explore feelings, gain intellectual understanding, explore coping mechanisms, and reopen the social world; (4) Resolution of the crisis (for example, reinforce coping mechanisms).

The Rusk model (1971) is a second process model used widely in crisis work. The first effort to validate the steps was done by Beers and Foreman (1976). They found that the process was useful and that it included most of the accepted contemporary counseling ideas related to crisis intervention. Rusk's steps are: (1) Counselor presents self as concerned helper; (2) Client is encouraged to express and discuss affect; (3) Counselor empathizes with expressed affect; (4) Counselor gains information about the crisis situation; (5) Counselor helps client formulate a statement about the problem; (6) Counselor and client agree on strategies to resolve crisis-induced stress; (7) Counselor and client review and implement mutually established strategy for management of the stress and ways of coping with future stress.

The most common type of crisis is associated with loss, or impending loss, of a loved one, a prized job, health, or physical strength. For example, Kübler-Ross (1975) has described the five stages persons facing death go through: denial and isolation, anger, bargaining, depression, and acceptance. Part of the counseling task is to help clients work through these stages.

Values of Support

A supportive relationship has four primary therapeutic values. One of its principal values is that it helps to reduce excess anxiety and consequently develops security and comfort. The emotional presence of the therapist enables the client to feel worthy, loved, and respected. This aspect of support waxes and wanes according to the needs of the particular client at various points in the process. Those clients feeling inadequate, grief-stricken, unworthy, and uncomfortable, lonely, or fearful about losing control of their feelings are given the specific relationship help they need. For example, the inadequate person is led to feel that here in the therapist is a pillar of strength on which he can lean temporarily while he develops confidence and strength.

While the focus here is on support through counseling relationships, we must realize that most of the support, for young adults at least, comes through friendships. An extensive study by Parham and Tinsley (1980) revealed that young adults value friends who are accepting, trustworthy, and confrontive. Less important were empathy, expertness, and directness. While the participants did not avoid professional counselors for help with emotional problems, they tended, first, to seek friends who were open, genuine, concrete, accepting, and nurturing. These findings fit with studies on why young adults select friends for help rather than professional therapists (Tinsley and Harris 1976).

A client can feel also that for the time being he or she does not have to be big and strong, mature, and capable. In other words, clients feel they can walk before they are expected to run. This may seem, at first, to be promoting dependency, but its value lies in allowing clients to express their security and dependency needs, accept them, and interpret them later. It seems wise to go along with clients' dependency a short while so that they do not feel that the counselor is just another paternalistic adult anxious to push them into maturity. Some older clients, for example, are dependent economically and physically as a normal course of their aging. These older clients need to accept their growing dependency while striving to maintain their self-esteem.

Grief-stricken or suicide-prone people can feel that here is someone who understands how they feel and with whom they can share troubles. A supportive relationship helps clients who are fearful of their impulses, to feel that it is all right to have the feelings, to express them, and to realize that they won't get into trouble. In addition, counselors may help clients to control their feelings by techniques designed to decrease the emotional intensity of the discussion.

A second value of support is the assurance it gives to clients that they can be helped—for example, that they can make realistic plans, that they can improve their studies, or that they possibly will save their marriage. Clients in a state of anxiety often have a hopeless feeling about their problems, or feel theirs is a unique case. The counselor's calm, accepting, reassuring manner can be a powerful supporting medium for these clients, such that they experience hope and confidence in the future.

A third value of support is the awareness it gives clients of their freedom to change their views or behaviors. By fully accepting them, counselors say, in effect, that though they may not agree with the clients, they can be receptive to their views at the moment. Thus, clients are not given the reassurance that they are right about their present views. If clients feel overly reassured about having, for example, a picture of themselves as very shy persons, they may tend to feel guilty about changing this picture. In other words, they do not feel "caught" in their present attitudes and are able to try out new responses. Support enters again when they try out the new response which may get them into even greater difficulties temporarily.

A fourth value of a supportive relationship is that it prevents the client from accepting abortive solutions to problems. It encourages the suicidal person, for example, to explore alternatives to suicide. Clients can feel that they do not have to take impulsive actions which may get them into even worse trouble. For example, a person may see that becoming more settled in his or her feelings before going ahead with divorce proceedings might save later regrets. Similarly, hospitalization may support the client until he or she is better able to work rationally on his or her problems.

Limitations of Support

Since counselors are supportive when they help clients meet their emotional needs, it is obvious that this condition offers mixed blessings. One liability of oversupport is the resentment or guilt clients may feel when they are aware of their dependence on the counselor. Some clients, in addition, are deeply threatened by too much "warmth" or emotional closeness, possibly because they have not yet learned how to handle a close human relationship. A second limitation is the strong dependency that may develop through prolonged support. This significant counseling condition is discussed in Chapter 8 under the topic of transference.

A third limitation or misinterpretation of support is that of sympathy. We have discussed the implication of sympathy earlier in this chapter. It should be emphasized again that liberal use of support may have a ring of insincerity or exaggeration.

Resentment against the apparent shallowness and stereotypy of liberal reassurance is a fourth limitation. The attitude that "everything will come out in the wash, so don't worry" has been offered many times by important people in the client's life. He or she knows that things don't always turn out all right, so the client is threatened by what appears to him or her to be insincere, stock techniques.

SUMMARY

Psychotherapeutic and counseling relationships have several basic dimensions, such as uniqueness-commonality, objectivity-subjectivity, cognitive-affective, ambiguity-clarity, and responsibility-accountability. The counselor has the difficult task of recognizing and dealing appropriately with these seemingly paradoxical elements of the relationship.

Since therapeutic effectiveness hinges so much on the quality of the relationship between counselor and client, basic attitudes of the counselor are highly significant. The attitudes of acceptance and understanding have considerable consequences upon the psychological climate of the interview. This climate which these attitudes create holds important implications for the client's evaluation of his or her own personality. A key to an effective attitudinal climate is the counselor's assuming the internal frame of reference, which is an attempt to understand the client by taking the client's view of his situation. The counselor must have additional characteristics of warmth, intelligence, flexibility, humility, and a willingness to share the responsibility.

One of the principal functions of the relationship is to provide support for the client, especially in crises. Support is the promotion of comfort and security through the construction of optimal conditions of living. Support is considered generally to be an aim of psychological counseling and is often a condition necessary before more cognitive solutions can be found.

7

Relationship Strategies and Methods

The purpose of this chapter is to present methods for relating easily and effectively to clients, promoting client comfort and feelings of being understood, and encouraging client exploration of feelings. In the preceding chapter on counselor attitudes, an assumption was made that techniques are limited unless there is full understanding of therapeutic goals, fundamental counselor attitudes, and theoretical assumptions from which the techniques emerge. In other words, there is a danger of becoming too "technique-conscious." One characteristic of a charlatan is blind adherence to pat techniques applied indiscriminately to all clients.

Techniques, on the other hand, are somewhat personal in that counselors develop varying styles and techniques best suited to their own personalities and their estimates of client needs. Techniques are, after all, primarily media for defining and redefining relationships with people. Useful techniques, in addition, have stood the test of time in practice; in many cases, they have been validated experimentally. An example with a strong empirical base of such training is the microcounseling approach of Ivey and Gluckstern (1974, 1976). This method breaks relationship skills into fine, teachable components such as attending, questioning, and summarizing.

We emphasize a variety of techniques and flexibility in their application. This emphasis on flexibility fits our actualizing models. These relationship methods are useful in dealing with problems at the facade level in handling resistance. They also have a modulating effect on feeling awareness and expression at other levels, particularly with feeling polarities. Relationship strategies are especially useful in encouraging expression of feelings along the basic polarities of loving and directing anger, for example. Thus, modulating in this context means the process of expressing a full spectrum of feelings along any polarity in a manner which achieves the growth goals of the client.

Keeping the above considerations in mind, we offer the following discussion on methods as possible ways the basic attitudes and concepts of the counselor and psychotherapist might be manifested. We would like to point out also that most of the following methods can be described behaviorally and can be taught as skills. We would like to point out also that there has been abundant research on counseling skills the past twenty years. Almost any verbal response method will have its supporting data; but the research methodological and classification issues are so great that consistent results and firm conclusions are rare. We know, however, that methods have differential effects. To determine these differential effects, for example, one study by Ehrlich, D'Augelli, and Danish (1979) found that feeling-type counselor responses encouraged two and a half times as many client affect responses as advice types and twice as many as open questions. So counselors need to give close attention to the kinds of responses they make to achieve the results they want.

OPENING TECHNIQUES

The first task upon meeting a client is to establish a feeling of trust. Earlier books on counseling and psychotherapy speak of building rapport, a condition of mutual understanding and comfort. Counselors establish this condition by living their accepting, warm attitudes and manifesting deep interest in clients, rather than by applying a kind of technique. Some of the accumulated experience of counselors in beginning the relationship is summarized in the following topics.

The Greeting   If counseling takes place in an office, the counselor's initial interest in a client is manifested by meeting the client in the reception room with a firm hand clasp (if socially appropriate to age level and subculture), greeting the client by name, and escorting him or her courteously into the office. If not in an office, the usual informal greeting customs appropriate to the subculture of the client would prevail. Ordinary human courtesy, therefore, goes far in opening a relationship satisfactorily.

The Topics

Counselors vary in their opinions on how to open an interview. Starting with an urbane or trite conversational topic might result in a more strained relationship than if clients were allowed to state their business frankly and immediately. This problem illustrates an area of artful judgment required of a counselor and reflects his or her personal style.

Counseling generally deals with problems that are personal and loaded with anxiety. It is often difficult to face these problems squarely and immediately, particularly in the presence of a strange person of uncertain trustworthiness. The counselor must resolve the client's fear and restraint, which is natural in a new setting, by making the client moderately comfortable. Sometimes it helps a client to mention a "conversation piece" in the office such as a picture on the desk. Clients often feel comfortable with this conventional way of starting a human relationship. It should be emphasized, however, that such openers are merely "ice breakers" to enable the client to start perceiving the therapeutic attitudes of the counselor. There is just as much danger that the relationship will get off on a conversational bent as on a "cold," resistive start.

As an additional note of caution, an effective relationship can be established just as easily on a nonverbal basis by a warm and friendly "waiting-for-you, my-time-is-yours" appearance on the counselor's part, and secondly, by competently meeting whatever lead the client gives for a starter. If a client is motivated to seek help, counselor initiated "small talk" may tend to show a kind of disrespect for this need. Furthermore, too much "small talk" might imply that the counselor needs to protect the client from the reality of the situation. Generally, a lead something like "would you like to tell me what brings you here?" is most realistic and honest. In summary, the first remarks are largely matters of counselor preference or style.

The Physical Arrangements

One of the determinants of a good working relationship is believed to be the physical condition of the room. There is no research on this problem, so we depend upon opinions of counselors. While some counselors work across a desk, we feel this sets up communication barriers. Yet sitting face to face at close range is too threatening for some clients. Counselors need to experiment with the most effective arrangement.

Other physical arrangements would seem to be taken for granted, but it is our experience that often they are overlooked by counselors. It is axiomatic, for example, that clients never be placed in a position where they must face the light. This means that, if it is necessary to face the client toward the window, the blinds or drapes must be closed.

Another consideration is the nature of the client's chair. The possibilities for a good counseling relationship seem to be improved through installation of comfortable chairs for both counselor and client. This represents quite a change from traditional arrangements whereby the counselor is afforded a comfortable swivel chair and the client is given any available straight chair.

The Attitudes   A degree of mysticism seems to surround the client-therapist relationship. Counselors sometimes give the client the impression that therapy is a form of magic and that the therapist is endowed with special powers which make him or her able to help people. In our experience the relationship bridge is built best on a feeling of the natural human relationship. It is assumed here that counseling is a unique, human interaction which differs only slightly from other human relationships. The counselor may explain that there is nothing mysterious about counseling or psychotherapy, for they are largely processes of planning, relearning, and confronting one's self.

As with all other techniques, building a relationship is rather fruitless unless the counselor possesses the characteristics detailed earlier in Chapter 6. Ethical behavior must prevail. Above all, the confidential nature of the interview must be maintained. Counselors working in colleges and universities often are tempted to use illustrations from their own counseling experiences in classes in counseling, mental hygiene, and psychology. Such procedure is doubtful, yet counselors are apt to follow this practice unless they are aware of the damaging effects this may have on relationships with future clients.

REFLECTIVE RELATIONSHIP TECHNIQUES

Reflection of   In the actualizing approach to personality described in Chapter 3, it was
Feeling   emphasized that much of personality is beyond awareness. Reflection technique helps the individual to go beyond the actualizing system to become more aware of obscure feelings of the core and to deal with them more effectively. What seems to happen is that clients talk of their feelings as "it" or "them"—something apart from themselves. This tendency of the client to deny ownership of his or her feelings at first serves a useful defensive function. The reflection technique, however, focuses on the subjective element of what the client says. Reflection emphasizes the pronoun "you" in the phrases, "you feel . . ." and "you think. . . ." Reflection serves a useful purpose in that it leads the client to think of the feelings and ideas being expressed as part of one's own personality and not outside one's self. Thus, reflection is a useful intermediate technique to be used after the initial relationship has been built and before the information-giving and interpretation stages in the process are begun.

Reflecting feelings is a skill and, as such, can be learned by understanding and practice. Phillips and Agnew (1953) found from their data that reflection is definitely a learned helping skill, and that it is not commonly used in general interpersonal relationships by nonclinically trained, or even able and mature people. With the prevalence of communications skills training, however, and the emphasis on listening for feelings, reflection of feelings is becoming more of an everyday occurrence (Allmon 1981).

It is apparent from the chapters so far that to get clients to express their feelings is an important process goal. While all the basic helping skills of attending, reflecting, and nonverbal encouragement facilitate expression of feelings, Hill and Gormally (1977) found, in a careful study, that probing methods produced more discussion of feelings than either reflection or restatement. Modeling examples by the counselor is another effective method to get client self-disclosure of feeling (Zarle and Boyd 1977). Thus, many counseling skills are needed to elicit feelings.

The Nature of Reflection

Reflection of feeling is defined as the attempt by the counselor to paraphrase in *fresh* words the essential *attitudes* (not so much the content) expressed by the client. The counselor attempts to mirror the client's attitudes for his or her better self-understanding and to show the client that he or she is being understood by the counselor. The word *fresh* is emphasized because, perhaps, the most glaring reflection error of the novice counselor is to express the reflection in words already used by the client. In a humorous anecdote, in which the counselor repeated almost verbatim the client's statement, the client's reply was, "What's wrong with the way I said it?" It is preferable to use sufficiently different words with an air of intense interest and effort to understand, such as "You seem to want to make a decision, yet you find it so hard to do so."

The word *attitudes* is emphasized in the definition of reflection in order to make the counselor aware that he or she must be able to grasp the underlying feeling about what is being said, not just the content. Therapy is often likened to a river, with the ripples on the surface corresponding to the content. But more important are the undercurrents—the feelings underlying the content. It takes considerable skill to develop the sensitivity necessary to identify these feelings immediately and to mirror them back as soon as the client has completed his or her statements.

A word of caution about client feelings is worth expressing. A common misconception arising from an emphasis on feeling is that the expression and identification of feelings have in themselves some great intrinsic merit. The conclusion often drawn is that feelings are more important than intellectualizations. Expression of feelings is encouraged by the reflection technique. Its effectiveness, however, seems to reside in the idea that the expression of feeling is a means to self-confrontation, and not an end in counseling.

Feelings are thought by the client to be subjective and not to be trusted. They tell the client of danger when there is no danger, of presence of symptoms when he or she is tired and discouraged. The expression of feeling, therefore, is to make possible the discovery of the idea which underlies or is attached to the feelings. The client should be taught to *trust* the expression of feelings. A person in a panic state, for example, is helped if allowed to express his or her feelings. The air is cleared of smog and, as a result of the clarification, the client can examine and deal with the underlying basis of his or her insecurity.

Individuals, through the aid of their actualizing capacities, are the evaluators of their experience. Feelings do not possess evaluational quality; they are not "right" or "wrong." Ideas, however, possess truth or falsity. But evaluation of thought is only possible after feelings have been clarified.

This is why reflection of *content* is unwise in the early stages of therapy but appears to have real value in later stages. Thus, clarifying feelings leads to clarification of the *ideas* and *experience* underlying these feelings.

Reflection of Nonverbal Experience

A form of reflection in actualizing counseling which goes beyond reflection of verbalized feeling is reflection of experience—a method of "reading" behavior. This is a technique where a counselor observes the posture, gesture, tone of voice, and eyes of the client. The counselor reflects back not just the client's intended *feelings,* but also the message from his or her *observed nonverbal behavior.* Our actualizing therapy view states that much of our expressive potential is projected in our posture, movement, and voice. Actualizing counseling assists the individual to discover and use directly the energy that was expended in these projections.

Reflection of experience technique confronts the contradiction of *what* clients say they feel and what the counselor *sees or observes their total organisms saying.* Some examples follow:

c: You say that you are angry but your eyes appear to say to me that you are hurting inside.

c: You say that you hate me but I seem to hear caring in your voice.

c: You say that you love her but every time you talk about her your fists clench.

Actualizing counselors must have the courage to reflect their own percepts of the client as well as to state the client's intended or stated feelings. This requires confidence in one's ability to observe what is going on right here and now.

Sharing of Experiences

Actualizing therapy holds that the relationship between client and counselor is a key dimension of the therapeutic process. This relationship may be thought of as a *continuum of personal responsiveness* with *reflection of feeling* at the one end, with *reflection of experience* in the center, and with *sharing of experience* at the opposite end. By *sharing of experience* is meant the honest effort of the counselor to share her or his own experience with the client in the moment. Thus, *sharing of experience* is *modeling* for the client and encourages clients to share their experience. The therapist is modeling how to be a person and is not simply a technician mirroring the client's verbalizations. This stance requires risking and a willingness to share with the client the therapist's personal feelings at the moment. The following are examples:

TH: It makes me angry when you let her get to you like that.

TH: I get uncomfortable when you *always* hurt and never let yourself feel any other feelings.

TH: Your intellectualizing is boring me and I am getting sleepy.

Identifying Feelings

In teaching the technique of reflection to new counselors, we found it helpful to list and categorize the nature of human feelings so as to assist the novice in the immediate recognition of the feeling expressed. Reid and Snyder (1947) found considerable variation among counselors in their ability to name feelings expressed by clients. There was high agreement among counselors rated as good, however. This implies that ability to reflect is partly a matter of general counseling skill and experience.

In general, it may be said that feelings fall into three broad categories: postive, negative, and ambivalent. Positive feelings are those which are ego-constructive and self-actualizing, while negative feelings are generally ego-destroying. Ambivalence refers to the presence of two or more contrasting or conflicting feelings expressed or implied at the same time toward the same object. In clinical counseling, it is found that such feelings underlie a great many interpersonal relationships; therefore, it is particularly important for the counselor to spot these apparent contradictions and to reflect them to the client. It is important for the client to see and to accept seemingly contradictory attitudes toward the same person, for this can be a source of great tension. One of the goals of psychotherapeutic counseling is to realize that one can both love and hate the same person at the same time.

The following list gives some examples of labels which fall into the two arbitrary categories of positive and negative feelings.

Positive		Negative	
Happiness	Self-worth	Guilt	Disgust
Security	Love	Resentment	Antagonism
Gratitude	Optimism	Fear	Rebellion
Self-confidence	Contentment	Depression	Rejection
	Warmth		Hostility

A beginning counselor who can observe and identify common feelings will find it easier to reflect these feelings more quickly and confidently. The ability to sense fine shades of client feeling is dependent largely on the empathic capacities of the counselor.

Difficulties in Reflecting

STEREOTYPY. A common error is made in reflection when the counselor uses a stereotyped introductory phrase, such as, "You feel. . . ." This procedure, if it is not varied, will tend to arouse client feelings of resentment and attempts to analyze the process hypercritically. The following variations are suggested:

Use of the word that expresses the feeling; for example: "You were mad (sorry, confused, etc.) when that happened."
"You think. . . ."
"You believe. . . ."

"It seems to you. . . ."
"As I get it, you felt that. . . ."
"In other words. . . ."
". . . is that it?"
"I gather that. . . ."
Inflection—intonation of various words to express the reflection; for example:

CL: It really hurt me to hit her.

C: It *really* hurt. (Note: This is an exception to the general rule of not reflecting content.)

TIMING.   Another error which counselors seem prone to make is that of waiting for clients to stop their comments before reflecting. When much content and little feeling are expressed by the client, this is not serious. As counseling develops, however, a great many feelings may come rapidly. This condition often necessitates interrupting the client so as to focus on and emphasize significant feelings. It is also easy to make the opposite error of interrupting clients too soon and completing their sentences for them.

SELECTION OF FEELING.   When Rogers introduced this reflection technique it became associated with the Rogerian label, *nondirective*. A cursory examination of the technique suggested that since the counselor was only repeating feelings which already had been expressed by the client, the counselor, therefore, was not *directive*. A closer scrutiny of this technique reveals, however, that any reflection requires that the counselor *choose* from the verbalization of the client those elements which he or she feels have greatest quality of feeling and are in greatest need of clarification. This means that the counselor, in a sense, is highly direct and confrontative in using this technique.

Porter (1950) made a significant contribution to the use of reflection technique when he suggested that the counselor must learn to avoid the "four common errors of reflection." A paraphrased and illustrated summary is presented below.

CONTENT.   "Reflecting content" is an error in counseling which consists of reflecting back client statements in essentially the same words that the client used. When counselors do this, they do not convey understanding, but merely repeat blindly what has already been said. Their reflections, moreover, are generally met with denial rather than acceptance.

CL: I've always just considered medicine because my father always dictated to all of us boys what we should be.

C: You've always sort of considered medicine because your father dictated to you and your brothers what you should be.

A counselor who uses these techniques is fortunate if the first interview lasts over five minutes. The counselor who has a "knowledge-of-acquaintance" in reflecting techniques might reflect in the following manner:

C: You just went along with him since you never thought of disagreeing with him?

This is an attempt by the counselor to get below the surface and to touch on the undercurrent of feeling expressed by the student. The counselor disregards the words of the student in favor of the feelings being expressed.

DEPTH.   The counselor who fails to respond to the same degree of depth in feeling as expressed by the client is also not reflecting accurately. Some counselors are consistently too shallow in their reflections. Others are consistently too deep, and the reflection becomes an interpretation. An illustration follows:

CL: I want to be an engineer, but I just can't drive myself for four long years without her. . . . I just can't do it. . . .

C: You'd like to be an engineer, but you'd also like to get married.

The reflection obviously is too shallow. A more accurate reflection might have been:

C: It's just too long a grind without her.

Or, the counselor might have reflected:

C: You just wouldn't be able to live without her for four years.

This reflection perhaps is "too deep" and might be met with denial or by a change of subject on the part of the client.

MEANING.   It is also important that the counselor not *add to* or *take away from* the meaning of the client's statement. An illustration of such procedure is as follows:

CL: I just can't see myself as an accountant sitting at a desk all day.

C: You don't think you'd like the idea of having to balance budgets, and making profit-and-loss statements, day in and day out.

It is obvious that the client did not say all that the counselor did. The counselor has read much more meaning into the statement. The counselor might have taken away meaning by a reflection of the nature of the following:

c: You just don't like indoor work.

To be accurate in reflecting the proper meaning on the surface appears easy, but too often the counselor responds from his or her own frame of reference rather than from the client's frame of reference.

LANGUAGE.   Experience by many trained counselors indicates that the counselor should always use the language most appropriate to the situation. Here is an example of a poor use of language:

cl: I just seem to be shy with girls. I just can't be friendly.

c: This inferiority complex seems to be extremely active in these hetero-sexual relations.

The errors the counselor made in the reflection are mainly overinterpretation and pedantry as well as absence of feeling.
     It should be emphasized that although reflections should be accurate, an inaccurate remark may still promote interview progress if clients perceive that the counselor is trying to understand them. For example, the counselor may say, "So you resent your father for doing this?" The client responds, "Oh no, I actually admire him for it." While inaccurate from the client's viewpoint, the remark may still be effective since the client feels compelled to clarify his or her feelings and correct the counselor. The net effect is often further self-exploration.

*Types of
Reflection*

IMMEDIATE REFLECTION.   This type consists of reiterating a feeling immediately after it has been stated by the client.

SUMMARY REFLECTION.   This involves "tying together" several feelings. This summary method is diagrammed in Figure 13. The summary reflection

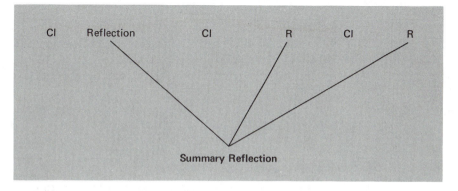

FIGURE 13.   The Summary Reflection

is a method of bringing together in one statement several feelings expressed previously. An illustration is, "From your descriptions of your family relationships, school experiences, and now your new job, you seem to have strong feelings of personal failure in all of them."

TERMINAL REFLECTION.   This is a technique of summarizing the important aspects of the entire counseling hour. Terminal reflection may also include certain content material which summarizes the proceedings of the hour.

Reasons for Effectiveness of Reflection

It seems appropriate in the discussion of this technique to examine some of the possible reasons for its effectiveness in achieving the goals of counseling.

Reflection helps the individual to feel *deeply understood*. Most disturbed clients are defensive and feel misunderstood. When confronted with this technique their fear of feeling misunderstood diminishes. The clarity with which the counselor reflects their deepest unverbalized feelings can cause disturbed clients to feel deeply understood. Thus, reflection serves a supportive function and is used most effectively in the early and middle phases of counseling.

The reflection technique helps to break the so-called neurotic cycle, often manifested in marital counseling and expressed by such phrases as, "She won't understand me and therefore I won't understand her." The counselor, relying on the reflection technique, helps break this tenaciously held line of reasoning.

Reflection impresses clients with the inference that *feelings are causes of behavior*. Perhaps the most significant contribution that reflection of feeling makes to the counseling process is that it affords a vehicle for conveying understanding of causes. Feelings are elusive and often difficult to control. Frequently we feel that we do not understand ourselves because of the emergence of strange or unwanted *feelings*. When another human being tries so genuinely to understand us, and appears so capable of clarifying for us the elements of our own experience which are cloudy and fearful, this human being comes to be valued by us. Reflection serves, therefore, as a clarifying and simplifying function.

Reflection keeps the *locus of evaluation* in the client. Another reason that reflection is so effective is that it challenges individuals to take responsibility for themselves. It subtly suggests that a value system is not something inherent in any experience or object, but that value is placed on it by the individual. Bombardment of the individual with such phrases as "you feel" and "you think" and "you believe" teaches people that they are the evaluators of their own experience and that values are alterable. Clients see that values are judgments made by individuals based upon their experiences. Values are also alterable if and when new experience gives new evidence. The term *locus of evaluation* is helpful here. In the early phases of therapy clients tends to put the locus of evaluation of their behavior *outside* of themselves in parents, friends, or social groups. Toward the end of counseling, the individual finds that one can place and must place this evaluation of behavior in one's self. Clients learn that they own their feelings.

Proper reflection gives clients the feeling that they have the *power of choice*. A current tendency in our culture has been to shy away from assuming personal responsibility and to trust the "expert." The specialist is expected to tell us how to rear our children, to advise us on marriage or divorce, to choose our career, to advise in matters of love making, budgeting, ad infinitum. In matters of personal concern, the result is a continuous cycle of helplessness. The more the expert is consulted, the greater the feeling of helplessness, the greater the need for further advising. In counseling, the aim should be to create self-direction in the client. The reflection technique along with the lack of advice on these matters encourages the individual to achieve this end of self-help.

Reflection *clarifies client thinking* so that they can see the situation more objectively. Reflection technique by its very nature involves an attempt by the counselor to draw out essential elements of the client's conversation for reconsideration. The natural result of such a procedure is to mirror to clients the high points of their thinking, and to enable them to clarify their present situation and to see it in a more objective and focused fashion. Clarification, a technique which summarizes the substance of the client's verbalization, is designed to accelerate client awareness through simplification of their wandering and scattered responses without feeling they are being "pushed."

Reflection helps clients to *examine their deep motives*. When counselors concentrate on the individual's feelings rather than the ideational content of his remarks, they are reaching the individual at a deep motivational level. This observation is illustrated by the common question with which all of us have been faced: "Why did you do that?" The answer may have been, "Because I felt like it." People often do things just because they "feel like it." Feelings are manifestations of the needs and drives which compel us to act. Careful scrutiny of our feelings leads us to examine the motivating forces underlying these feelings. This process is illustrated by the comment, "Well, I felt like it because. . . ." The word *because* often leads us right to the core motive or experience.

ACCEPTANCE TECHNIQUES

Nature and Value of Acceptance Techniques

This is a simple technique of responding mainly with short phrases, such as "mm-hm," "Yes, go on," which imply attitudes of attention and acceptance. It is employed usefully in the early stages of counseling when much content or narrative material is produced, often without much associated feeling. Acceptance techniques are employed also in the later stages when clients are delving deeply into themselves and bringing out painful material. It is simply a verbalization of the attitudes of acceptance of the counselor which say in effect: "Go on, it's safe, you needn't be ashamed of expressing how you really feel." The values of expressions like, "I see" or "Uh huh," are that they reinforce discussion and provide a bridge between ideas, which gives a smooth flow to the process.

Elements of
Acceptance
Technique

Simple acceptance technique has at least four major observable elements. The first is simple *attending behavior,* largely maintaining eye contact. Eyes are very expressive for most people and are a key vehicle for counselors to express acceptance and caring. Second is the *facial expression* and nodding of the counselor. The counselor must convey genuine interest in her or his face. The counselor who puts on a feigned expression of interest will be discovered by the sensitive client.

Third, *tone of voice* and inflection tell the client whether the counselor is accepting, even if he or she uses conceptually meaningless vocalizations such as "mm" instead of words. Of course, counselors who speak so quietly that clients must strain to hear them hamper the process by conveying an impression of disinterest. But the counselor who speaks with an overbearing voice conveys an impression of dulled sensitivity to the expressions of the client or is exhibiting his or her own needs for controlling the interview.

Distance and posture are a fourth consideration in acceptance. If the counselor leans over and sits comfortably close to the client, the client will infer a friendly attitude. This conveying of "towardness" as opposed to "away-from-ness" by posture is important, since the former attitude conveys the qualities of openness and sincerity of the counselor. Since many clients are hypersensitive to cues like these, they may interpret the slightest negative gesture of the counselor as rejection or disinterest. Yawning, crossing and recrossing of legs, grasping the arms of the chair tightly are examples of such negative cues which are easily discerned by the client.

Ellis (1955), in surveying the literature on couch and face-to-face therapy positions of clients, concluded that face-to-face therapy was preferable, partly because acceptance techniques could operate more effectively. In terms of a microcounseling approach, the above acceptance methods have came to be known as attending behaviors (Ivey and Authier 1978).

STRUCTURING TECHNIQUES

Nature and
Value of
Structuring

Structuring technique is the counselor's definition of the nature, conditions, limits, and goals of the process. In other words, structuring provides clients with a framework or orientation for therapy. They then feel that the relationship has a rational plan. Structure provides them with a counseling road map and with a dossier of their responsibilities for using the road map, thus reducing the ambiguity of the relationship. Clients should know *where* they are, *who* the interviewer is, and *why* they are there. Thus, the structure of counseling has three elements; the first is implicit in that the very setting and known role of the counselor automatically set limits that are generally understood by the client. The second element, formal structuring, consists of the counselor's purposeful statements to explain and limit the counseling process. The third, or contractual element, is described later in this chapter.

The use of May's analogy (1939) to illustrate the nature of implicit structuring may be helpful: Each person is traveling through life as though he or she were in a boat going down a river. Without the structure of the riverbank the water would flow in all directions. The banks of the river provide the limiting factors which guide the boat and give it added power to go downstream. Individuals, likewise, are free to make their own choices, but always there seems to be a frame of reference which limits and gives direction to those choices.

Another illustration of the directional value of structuring is provided by a former client: "It was kind of like going down the highway on a foggy night. I drove my own car but the counselor provided the illuminated white line in the middle of the road for me."

The therapeutic value of setting limits can be distilled to the following general principles: (1) limits should be *minimal,* consonant with the security of the client and therapist; (2) limits should be applied *nonpunitively;* (3) limits should be *well defined* in regard to such things as action, time, and number of appointments; and (4) limits should be structured *at the proper time.* Too early or too rigid structuring may destroy a relationship. Sue and Sue (1977) make the case for structuring when counseling with minority clients since their unfamiliarity with the client role in counseling may hinder their success.

Dangers of Inadequate Structuring

It appears that the therapeutic process is a miniature social condition in which individuals can utilize their freedom, but in which they must simultaneously accept the limits imposed by that freedom. The counselor who fails to provide structure would be unfair to many of the clients who have no notion of what counseling is all about. In this age of consumer rights and regulations it is a legal as well as an ethical obligation to present accurately what the client is buying. Curran stresses this point:

> A confused person is likely to approach the first interview feeling a minimum of responsibility for himself and a maximum of fear, insecurity and defensiveness. Continued miscues on the part of the counselor in structuring the relationship seem to cause the client to depend on the counselor and to feel rejected and hostile if the counselor refuses to solve his problems, and finally in defensiveness and fear to flee the interviews and not keep subsequent appointments. (1944, p. 189)

Structuring, therefore, has value in preventing such early misconceptions about counseling as magical cures, fast help, single causes, advice giving, smooth sailing, inevitability of cure, and counselor responsibility. By focusing on the positive learnings and roles of client and counselor, and the reasonable expectations of the process, many misconceptions can be offset. This aspect of structuring, by the way, must be a continuous process.

It is Rogers's opinion that the structure of therapy can be provided for the individual at the nonverbal level; that is, the client will "get the idea" as he or she participates in the process. This may be true with highly sophisticated clients but does not seem to be adequate for average clients. Ingham and Love, on the other hand, suggest that undesirable insecurity develops when structuring is not provided:

> *The patient may at first feel that his task is unorganized and formless and that there are no rules. Then he experiences a strange feeling of helplessness and dissatisfaction. It is as though the therapist did not care what he talked about or how he spoke of it.* (1954, p. 81)

Lack of structuring arouses anxiety in clients and perhaps accounts for some counseling failures. It is important, therefore, that the structure be made a *means* to enhance the security of the relationship and not an *end* in itself. Otherwise, permissiveness and acceptance values are lost. Structuring in the beginning phases of counseling must be approached with caution, since there is a danger of conveying a feeling that the counselor has a definite preconceived way of doing things which the client had better follow as an ultimatum. Another danger is that the counselor might convey an impression of how clients ought to feel rather than encouraging them to feel the way they really feel.

Sherman (1945) found that failure to structure, so as to leave the client too much on his or her own resources early in the process, results in strong resistance. A feeling for the right amount of structure for each individual client is a paramount counseling skill. If structuring is done badly, it can be a relationship barrier. Similarly, if it is ignored in institutional settings, the results may be equally undesirable, since the client may build unreal expectations about the outcomes. Structuring has a positive value if it reduces the anxiety of clients who are not cognizant of the dual roles of their counselors or are not aware of situational limits which exist. An example is the counselor who has instructional or administrative relationships with a student. The counselor must point out that these relationships are different from his or her relationship as a counselor, and that authoritarianism will not spill into the relationship.

The counselor's compulsion to structure frequently, to set the client straight, may be a symptom of his or her lack of assurance. Another caution in structuring is the tendency to imply that the relationship will continue with this particular client. It may turn out that the counselor will decide not to work with this client or that the client may not be suitable for this counselor. Hence, the client or the counselor may feel too committed to the relationship if it has been overstructured. Overstructuring can be avoided by matching degree of structure to the conceptual level (need for structure) of the client. Clients vary considerably on need for structure, and the importance of matching intervention method with the person is supported increasingly with data (Stein and Stone 1978).

Types of Structure and Contracts

Earlier, we described structuring as a technique which defines the limits and potentialities of the process. Paradoxical as it may seem, the provision of clear-cut limits provides the client with permission and power to change. Structuring methods extend to contracting, which is an agreement on how and when counseling goals are to be achieved.

CONTRACTS. Several theories of counseling use the term *contract* to describe structuring agreements. Some contracts, especially with young clients, take on a formal character. They list privileges extended, responsibilities incurred, bonuses or sanctions, how and by whom the contract is to be monitored. Contracts have characteristics of *specificity,* that is, clients know exactly what is expected of them, and *feasibility,* meaning it is within the capabilities of clients to carry out. Contracting works most effectively when the client is acquiring or getting rid of a specific behavior, such as smoking or excess eating. The key value of a contractual form of structure is that a counselor knows when he or she has been successful—that is, when clients reach the goals they agreed to work on, and in the way both agreed. Contracts tend to focus on expected *outcomes.*

TIME LIMITS. Perhaps the time limit is paramount in school and other public agency counseling, in which only a limited amount of time can be given for each interview. The counselor, therefore, must explain at the onset of the interview just how much time is available. We suggest that when time limits are presented, clients very often hasten the therapeutic processes in an effort to accomplish as much as possible in the time available. This suggestion applies to short five- or ten-minute interviews as well as those lasting longer. An example is, "We have forty-five minutes; let's see what we can accomplish."

A second aspect of time limits concerns the time required for the process as a whole. It appears that one of the contributing factors to the success of psychoanalytic therapy, for example, is that the analyst emphasize very carefully to the patient that the process might take two to three years and will be costly. It is admitted that many clients cannot accept this, but at the same time, for the clients who can, the process seems to be facilitated. The counselor, in similar fashion, indicates that to reach the agreed goals, several sessions will be required. The counselor is careful to point out, however, that no commitments can be made as to specific outcome. For example, a counselor might say, "Ordinarily we get together a couple of times to go over the test data and other material collected, then we spend a session or two helping you plan a specific course of action. In all, it should take four or five hours to get where we want."

In more emotional problems counselors may feel that they do not want to become committed to a long-term therapeutic relationship. Structuring may help them prevent misunderstandings with clients, as the following example shows:

c: We have been talking about "first-aid" methods for a while. Perhaps we had better talk a bit about where we go from here. As you realize, we cannot become committed to a major personality overhaul (pause).

cl: I see, more of a tune-up job then.

In structuring time limits the counselor must guard against being overanxious for the client by making promises or raising false hope, or even by stating that counseling "is a good investment." Promising success violates one of the ethics of psychotherapy. An optimistic counselor attitude, however, creates client confidence in the process as well as assists an insecure and anxious client to begin working confidently.

Although it is difficult for counselors to make definite long-range time commitments to clients, they should discuss fees frankly and early in the first interview. Phone calls and missed appointments, generally, are billed, since this fact is part of the contract. The counselor who does not charge for long phone calls and uncanceled missed appointments plays into the manipulative client's hands. Also, it is not sound therapeutically because it does not take cognizance of the *reality* of the relationship. A clear contract should help on these issues.

ACTION LIMITS.   There are also what might be termed action limits. The counselor does not limit verbal expression, no matter how absurd, unfair, or foolish it sounds; but there are certain feelings which cannot be permitted direct expression in *action*. Younger clients, for example, cannot break windows, or destroy furniture and equipment. They can say they don't like the therapist, but they cannot physically attack the therapist. As Rogers (1942) points out, hurting the therapist may arouse the child's deep guilt and anxiety in relation to the only person who can help him or her. Fear of retaliation and threat of withdrawal of this unique kind of supporting relationship may destroy the possibility of therapy.

ROLE LIMITS.   In educational, industrial, religious, or medical settings we find that the counselor often has dual roles: teacher-counselor, supervisor-counselor, administrator-counselor, minister-counselor, and physician-counselor. This means that these people also have a role of authority in the life of the client, as well as the role of nonjudgmental listener. These roles must be so structured. The teacher, after a hearing, points out to John that he must take certain prescribed courses whether he wants to or not. Thus, one role of the advisor is to maintain the school structure. A foreman, counseling one of his men, cannot permit him to come and go on the job whenever he wishes. A teacher cannot permit a student client to avoid handing in class work. These are limits defined by the *role of authority* which these people also have.

In situations which make it necessary for the counselor to take dual roles, the use of the "coat analogy" is often helpful. The following is an example of how it may be used:

c: Well, Jack, before we start I want to clarify my role with you. You might say I wear two coats around here—my teacher's coat and my counselor's coat. When I wear my teacher's coat, I have to be evaluating and judging to a certain degree in order to state your progress as a student. When I see you personally, however, in a relationship such as this, I am wearing my counselor's coat. This means that you can feel free to talk about anything you like and I won't hold it against you or make judgments about you. Okay?

PROCEDURAL OR PROCESS LIMITS.   If counseling is to be successful, clients must accept the nature of the process. In the first place, clients must accept their *responsibility* for carrying on the major share of the interview. There are certain things they must know to utilize the process most effectively. Ingham and Love (1954, pp. 79–81) suggest six basic process values which must be conveyed to clients in the early structuring remarks and through basic attitudes.

1. ". . . that it is appropriate and good to investigate ourselves." *This means facing his disturbing problems as much and as fast as he is comfortably able. This value suggests that there are causes of his difficulties which can be known and understood.*

2. ". . . that it is better to investigate than to blame." *This approach conveys the idea that there is a difference between a "bad" person and the "bad" act. The counselor stresses that he is trying to understand, not blame him. Thus, he will be better able to accept what he discovers within himself.*

3. ". . . to regard emotion as a real and important thing. . . ." *This value stresses the idea that emotions and their free expression are important realities and not signs of weakness.*

4. ". . . that there must be relatively complete freedom of expression." *The idea emphasized here is that the emotional importance of a topic, not its social acceptability, is the criterion of topic choice. This means that swearing, sex topics, and unconventional ideas are acceptable.*

5. ". . . the use of investigation of the past in developing an understanding of the present. . . ." *This focus on the past is a controversial value among counselors and therapists.*

6. *A series of process values centering about the client's present view of his world are often mentioned in structuring. These are his capacity for human relationships, his own individual importance, and his own life values and morals as a basis for further changes through counseling. A keen interest in the client's basic style of life is indicated.*

STRUCTURING PROCESS VALUES. It should be emphasized that all of the aforementioned process values need not be made explicit. Clients have differing needs for explanations about how counseling proceeds. Generally, the counselor lets clients bring up their own topics, and as it becomes apparent that they have misconceptions, or feel bewildered, helpless, or dissatisfied with this new experience, the counselor aids them through structuring. The counselor should start counseling on grounds familiar to clients and get them involved in the main job of counseling as quickly and comfortably as possible.

A second important use of structuring as a means of describing the process comes in the *handling of direct requests for advice*. In general, we recommend reflecting the feeling underlying this request first. This often allows the client to continue and to see his dependency as a problem. It is often necessary, however, actually to define this limit, as given by the following example:

CL: Can't we do something about this? The tension is really getting me. Can you tell me what to do? It might help both of us.

C: I can understand how desperate you feel; but we have found that there are certain answers that only the individual can give himself. By working together I think that we can arrive at some answers for you.

Unfortunately, it is easy to give the client a feeling of getting the "brushoff" with a response like this. The anxious, dependent client tends to miss the structuring and reassuring intent of the counselor's response and may interpret it as, "So, you are another one who doesn't want to help me."

A third use of process structuring is to present to the client the philosophy underlying the method of counseling. Porter (1950, p. 60) gives an example of this method:

Counselor: "I don't believe I know much about why you are here. The Dean mentioned you some time ago, but I know very little about it."

Frank: "Well, the Dean and Professor R. wanted me to see you. They said you were a good psychologist, and that if you studied me you might be able to diagnose my adjustment. They think I'm not getting along very well and if you diagnosed what was the matter, you would be able to help me."

Counselor: "They think you need some help, and you are trying to do what they wish?"

Frank: "Well, they say I'm not doing as well as I should, and if you studied me, you could say why."

Counselor: "Well, now I'll tell you, Frank, I really haven't had much luck helping students with problems that the Dean thinks they have. I don't know whether I can be of help to you along that line or not. When a student is concerned about some problem that he *thinks he has, then frequently we can work out something together, but otherwise, I don't believe I get very far. I wonder, quite aside from what the Dean thinks about you, whether you feel there is anything about your situation that is causing you concern?"*

Frank: "Well, I don't know—I suppose I don't live up to my ability."

Counselor: "That is something you feel a little concerned about?"

Frank: "Yes, I don't know, I guess I procrastinate; I just don't get things done on time. I don't see why. I've thought about that a lot and tried to analyze it but I don't seem to have helped it."

Counselor: "So you feel you really do procrastinate, and that you've been unable to do anything about it."

Timing of Structuring

Cardinal principles of structuring are that it is a continuous and individualized process. With some clients who demand more structure or seem to be confused, formal structuring of the process must come early. With others, the formal structuring can come later when attempts to shift responsibility to the counselor are made. With other clients who seem to take to the process easily, a very minimum of formal structuring is necessary in the beginning. In fact, if too many structuring remarks preface counseling, the client may experience them as constricting and annoying. Sophisticated clients expect that the structure will grow out of the relationship rather than be dictated to them in a formal, instructional manner. Day and Sparacio (1980) summarized the basic themes of structures from their survey of the literature. One theme dealt with practical issues such as length and time of counseling, appointments, and other procedural matters. The second theme covered consumer issues such as outcomes, records, costs, risks, rights, and methods. Process issues involved definitions of counseling, how to begin a session, statement of client goals, and role descriptions for counselor and client.

From this presentation the reader may rightly infer that structuring is a controversial issue in counseling practice. Some writers emphasize its value, while others stress its limitations. We have attempted to present various sides of the issue so that counselors can develop a style most effective for themselves.

LISTENING TECHNIQUES

Listening is an active attending process with little or no verbalization. It may seem strange, at first, to give prominence to listening as a technique of counseling. Yet, all the systems of helping skills give listening a prominent place. It is our conviction that therapeutic listening is a technique that must be learned. Perhaps this is so because the ethics of social conversation in our culture discourage silence. Hence, we have learned to become uncomfortable with silences and to regard long pauses as synonymous with a social vacuum. Beginning counselors often feel that when pauses are long they are not doing enough for the client. The appropriate mix of counselor response and listening is one of the most difficult counselor behaviors to learn.

The Meaning and Handling of Client Silence

In evaluating the significance of a pause, the time of its occurrence and whether it was initiated by client or counselor are significant. A long pause initiated by the client early in the initial interview conveys a different meaning to the counselor from one occurring later in the process. Pauses made by the client early in the interview may reflect embarrassment or resistance. As the counseling progresses, silence gradually comes to be a vibrant communicative medium for support, emotional expression, and thought.

In addition, it should be emphasized that counseling interviews are characterized by pauses of varying lengths from a few seconds to several minutes. It is difficult to assess the meaning of all pauses and no attempt is made here to catalog these possibilities. The following are offered merely as suggestions for interpreting and handling interview silences initiated by either counselor or client.

Any discussion of silence requires that recognition be given to two types: negative or rejecting, and positive or accepting. Socially, we often use the "silent treatment" as a form of rejection, defiance, or condemnation. In social situations, when we argue with people we are saying in effect that we respect them enough to want to change them. The negative silent treatment, however, says coldly in effect that the other person is not even worth talking to. Unfortunately, before a proper counseling relationship is established, it is possible for a client to interpret early silence in the interview as being this negative or rejecting type. This is true particularly when clients are still afraid of what the counselor is thinking about them. Appropriate acceptance techniques frequently have a reassuring effect, so that clients feel they do not have to impress the counselor.

A second meaning of silence is that the client or counselor has reached the end of an idea and is merely wondering what to say next. An extended pause may mean, also, that both have lost their way temporarily and that the interview has become confusing to both. The client may realize also that he or she has come to the end of the conversational period and must get down to work. Characteristically, there is an extended silence before getting down to serious work. The counselor can help the client over this hump by saying something like, "It is sort of hard to get down to serious business." The counselor's silence points up dramatically the transparency of small talk in later interviews. If the pause is of this "thought-collecting" type, it is considered wise not to interrupt. Tindall and Robinson (1947) found in study-improvement interviews that this type of contemplative silence accounted for half the pauses.

A third meaning of silence is that of hostility-motivated resistance or anxiety-motivated embarrassment. This is true particularly when the client has been called for or sent in. At first, the client may be waiting cautiously for the counselor to make all the first moves and may answer or comment in short words or phrases followed by a long expectant pause. This kind of silence is an effective client manipulative device.

The pause with a fourth meaning may be the signal that the client is experiencing some particularly painful feeling which he or she is not ready to verbalize, whereas consciously he or she may want to express the feeling desperately. The counselor may say something like, "It is all right if you want to wait until words come along," or "It seems hard to say what you want at times, doesn't it?" Without pushing the client, the counselor might say, "Perhaps if you gave me some hint where your thoughts are moving, maybe I can help you put them into words." We have facilitated expression in this type of client by handing the client a pencil and paper without comment so that he or she can write what the client wants to say as a starter.

In the resistive type of silence the participants may appear to be engaging in a contest to see who can outwait the other, like children trying to stare one another down. This may be owing to a preconceived notion of counseling in which the client expects the counselor to ask questions, or has a cautious "wait and see" attitude. This silent response may indicate to the counselor that there is a need for structuring or for a brief exploration of some personal items to get the client talking. The counselor may provoke the hostility-motivated client to talk by making a disarming reflection, "You don't feel like talking just now, do you?" Another way is to ask her or him to interpret the silence, "What do you think has brought this about?" However, the client may consider that the counselor who takes the attitude of, "Well, I'll wait until you decide to talk," or who pauses too long, is rejecting the client.

If shyness seems to be the difficulty, it might be overcome if the counselor starts with some items from the client's life history, for example, "Here we've spent quite a bit of time together and you haven't mentioned your mother (pause)."

A fifth meaning of silence might be labeled as "anticipatory," wherein the client pauses expecting something from the counselor—some reassurance, information, or interpretation. Tindall and Robinson (1947) found that counselors were quite sensitive in assessing and responding appropriately to this type of pause.

A sixth meaning of client pausing is that they may be thinking over what they have just said. In this case interruption of the pause may be inappropriate, since it might destroy the client's train of thought and may throw the interview off the client's main theme.

Finally, a pause may mean that the client is merely recovering from the fatigue of a previous emotional expression. Here again, quiet acceptance of the silence is probably the best approach.

The problem for the counselor in the preceding illustrations might be simply stated as follows: Shall I interrupt the pause or shall I wait and let the client go on? In general, our view is to let the client assume responsibility for going on when he or she was responsible for pausing originally. This avoids interfering with a forward-moving activity. Yet, the counselor must be alert to those situations in which it seems best to support clients over rough places rather than to force them to face their problems, feelings, and responsibilities before they are ready. Problems of handling the negative silence are treated in the following chapter under *resistance*, which will be defined and illustrated. In any case, the counselor is asking himself or herself continually during the silences, "What is going on?"

Values of Counselor Listening

It is one of our basic assumptions that listening of the positive and accepting type is a most promising counseling technique. The counselor's silence forces the client to talk. Similarly, being in the presence of another silent person often moves the client's attention to the task at hand—the client's problems. Silence on the part of the counselor then can have the value of focusing responsibility on the client.

A second value, emphasized from research with the Rorschach technique, indicates that introversive persons may be deeply creative individuals, with rich inner lives. They should not necessarily be seen as people inferior to the more socially valued extroverted individual. In counseling, clients discover that they can be silent and still be liked. Perhaps it is this acceptance of silence in the client which gives the less articulate person a feeling of worth and thereby helps people to accept themselves for what they are. By feeling accepted as a shy and quiet person, a client is able then to experience this same attitude toward himself. The following case comments by Rogers suggest the therapeutic value of silence.

I have just completed the strangest counseling case I've ever had. I think you might be interested in it.

Joan was one of my very first clients when I started counseling one half-day each week at the local high school. She told the girls' adviser, "I feel so shy I couldn't even tell her what my problem is. Will you tell her for me?" So the adviser told me before I saw Joan that she worried about having no friends. The adviser added that she had noticed that Joan seemed always to be so alone.

The first time I saw Joan she talked a little about her problem and quite a bit about her parents of whom she seemed to be quite fond. There were, however, long pauses. The next four interviews could be recorded verbatim on this small piece of paper. By the middle of November Joan remarked that "things are going pretty good." No elaboration on that. Meanwhile the adviser commented that the teachers had noticed that Joan was now smiling a friendly greeting when they met her in the halls. This was unheard of before. However, the adviser had seen little of Joan and could say nothing of her contacts with other students. In December there was one interview during which Joan talked freely; the others were characterized by silence while she sat, apparently in deep thought, occasionally looking up with a grin. More silence through the next two and one-half months. Then I received word that she had been elected "woman of the month" by the girls of the high school! The basis for that election is always sportsmanship and popularity with other girls. At the same time I got a message from Joan, "I don't think I need to see you any more." No, apparently she doesn't, but why? What happened in those hours of silence? My faith in the capacity of the client was sorely tested. I'm glad it did not waver. (1951, pp. 158–59)

Apparently the therapeutic value of spending time with someone who understood her and who had faith in her ability to solve her problem was helpful even though little was said.

A third value of counselor listening is that, after a significant expression of feeling, the client is allowed to think and to come up with profound awareness. Had the counselor forced continued exploration or verbalized too much, the awareness might not have followed. The client often uses silence to delve deeply into feelings, to struggle with alternative courses of action, or to weigh a decision. Clients want to feel that the counselor approves of their doing this, and that they are not letting the counselor down by this behavior. In fact, one extreme style of therapy, called the silent interview method, consists almost entirely of this nonverbal type of communication wherein the therapist conveys to the client the therapist's understanding that the client is struggling with deep, difficult feelings. Hence, one value of silence is that it forces depth of client penetration into feelings.

A fourth value of counselor listening is that it reduces the pace of the interview. Often the counselor senses that the client is rushing, or that the counselor feels compelled to push too hard. A counselor can reduce the intensity and pace to a more tolerable level for both participants by making the pauses longer. The counselor suggests in effect, "We are not in a hurry; take it easy." Thus, counselor silence in later interviews tends to have a beneficially calming effect on the client.

In a study of counselor pauses, Tindall and Robinson (1947) classified the pauses of the counselor giving educational skills counseling into three types: deliberate (for emphasis), organizational (for transitions), and natural termination (to close counseling). Organizational pauses, in the vast majority of cases, helped most to clarify the subject discussed and prepared the way for information to be given by the counselor. Clients generally responded only after a deliberate or natural terminal pause. It is apparent, however, from Tindall's and Robinson's study that pauses have many different meanings to clients, and that counselors must use them naturally.

Difficulties in Using Listening Techniques
In the training of counseling psychologists, we have found that it has been necessary to teach toleration of client silence without embarrassment. To the untried therapist a minute of silence seems like an hour. He or she has, consequently, an overwhelming desire to interrupt the client's thought. Porter (1950) suggests that one of the errors of reflection is that of completing sentences for the client. Many clients find it difficult to state what

they mean precisely without fumbling for words. Therefore, a very common error that inexperienced counselors make is to put words into the client's mouth, or in some way to take the conversational initiative away from the client.

Using listening technique does not mean being passive or uncommunicative, however. There has been a growing conviction among counselors, arising from studies and clinical experience, that activity level of the counselor is a significant variable in client response, and indeed affects whether the client stays in counseling. It is difficult to do conclusive studies on such a variable as counselor activity-passivity, but Heller, Davis, and Myers (1966) surveyed the literature and conducted a laboratory-type study on effects of interview style. They suggest that clients verbalize much more actively, rate counselors as more friendly, and continue in counseling when counselors are more active than passive and silent. While these terms need more definition to be useful as guides to counselors, such evidence contradicts long-standing views that interviews should start with low structure and a more passive stance to allow the client to do more projecting and talking.

One of the most difficult aspects of using the listening technique is keeping silent when the client wants to talk. A greater proportion of client talk, however, is not necessarily an indicator of a more effective working relationship. Carnes and Robinson (1948) analyzed 353 discussion units from four types of counseling interviews. They concluded that ". . . a high talk ratio is not necessary to a good working relationship but it is good insurance (1948, p. 639).

The relationships between insight and talk ratio in the above study were inconclusive; although, with study skill interviews, insight tended to be associated with low frequency of client talk. In other words, when counselors explained things in study skill interviews, clients apparently gained more insight than they did if they, themselves, talked. For therapeutic problems, Carnes and Robinson found that it was not the amount of client talk per se which was related to awareness, but rather the relative amount of client talk within the framework of a particular counseling style. In other words, keeping silent and just getting the client to talk more will not necessarily lead to greater awareness. A counselor can talk too much or too little at the wrong times.

The most definitive relationship in the Carnes and Robinson study cited above was found between client talk and amount of client responsibility assumed for the discussion unit. (The discussion unit is the verbal exchange between client and counselor on a discrete subject.) When clients felt primarily responsible for interview progress they talked more. It is interesting to note also that Carnes and Robinson found that the stronger the counselor's lead, the less the client talk. The general conclusions of Carnes's and Robinson's study are that the causal relationships between desired interview outcomes and amount of client talk are not clear, and that it is not possible, therefore, to use the amount of client talk as a measure of counseling effectiveness.

LEADING TECHNIQUES

General Principles and Values of Leads The term *lead* is used with two meanings. One usage refers to the extent to which the counselor is ahead or behind the client's thinking, and the extent to which the counselor directs the client's thinking or "pushes" the client into accepting the counselor's remark (Carnes 1949). Bugental (1952) uses the term *impact* to describe the counselor's influence on the client and the interviewing process. Counselor questions, for example, would have a high impact compared to the accepting vocalization "mm." Silence would have a lower impact or lead.

Robinson (1950) uses *lead* in a different, but related, sense. He construes *leading* in counseling to mean "a teamlike working together in which the counselor's remarks seem to the client to state the next point he is ready to accept" (1950, p. 66). In addition, Robinson compares leading to the act of passing a football down the field so that the receiver's path passes the flight path of the ball at the same time. All techniques can be rated according to degree of lead involved, but in the present discussion the topic will be limited to general leading as a technique by itself.

The value of leading is that the counselor is enabled to retain or delegate varying amounts of responsibility for counselor-client talk and to generate more client responses.

Using Leads Three general usages of leading are recommended. One principle is to lead *only as much as the client can tolerate* at the present level of ability and understanding. Enough old material must be mentioned to form a bridge of understanding to the next new idea. Robinson (1950) uses a ladder analogy to indicate that the counselor is not more than one rung ahead of the client, hence, close to his or her needs and interests. A lead too far ahead of the client generally arouses resistance to counseling. Similarly, too little lead may annoy clients who feel that the counselor should carry more of the responsibility for the interview talk.

The second general principle of leading is to *vary the lead*. The amount of lead changes from topic to topic or within a discussion unit so as to match the pace and lead of the client.

A third principle is *to start the counseling process with little lead.* For example, begin the counseling process with relationship techniques which have low lead, until the relationship is well established. Then increase the lead as needed with information and interpretation, which are useful in developing awareness.

The *indirect lead* may be used to help clients elaborate upon a topic of their choice. Examples are, "Would you explain that a little more?" "How do you mean that?" This type of lead is used also in the form of general questions to start an exploration, such as "What would you like to talk about today?" "Is there anything more you would like to discuss?"

The *direct lead* indicates the area of discussion desired from the client and is akin to the probing techniques discussed in Chapter 5. Examples of the direct lead are: "Tell me more about your father"; "Suppose we explore more fully the idea of teaching"; "What do you think that means?" Asking the client a question, whether rhetorical or for information, is a means of shifting responsibility to the client. Conversely, if the client asks many questions of the counselor it may indicate more than a desire for information or interpretation; it may mean the client is expressing a need to shift responsibility to the counselor.

Interpretive techniques which are described in Chapter 8 employ various degrees of lead. Leading utilizes Robinson's (1950) principle of moving ahead of the client just enough to stimulate growth. The concept of lead is introduced in this chapter, however, to emphasize that some degree of lead is always present in the relationship techniques which the counselor uses. Even silence is a leading technique, since lack of verbal response on the counselor's part causes the client to make a judgment about the significance of the material just presented. Thus counselors, through their manipulation of the pauses, often are responsible for the direction of the interview.

REASSURANCE AND SUGGESTION METHODS

Nature and Value of Reassurance

One relationship technique which has wide utility for conveying support is reassurance. In Chapter 6 the concept of support was introduced as a necessary ingredient of the counseling relationship. Reassurance is essentially a type of reward which has a reinforcing effect on behavior and builds expectancies for future rewards. The counselor suggests directly, or in effect, that, "You are a capable person; you can be consistent; you can be reasonable; you can be organized; you can feel better; you can solve this problem."

Reassurance also is a process of fitting counseling to the client's present belief system. Reassurance encourages exploration of new ideas or tryout of different behaviors. In this capacity reassurance is a temporary expedient to keep the client in the relationship. Kelly (1955) compares reassurance to the proverbial string and baling wire which is used to hold structures together until more solid or productive work can be done. Reassurance also prevents fragmentation of the client's ideas, even though eventually the client may want to change his or her maladaptive responses.

A second value of reassurance is the means it provides to reduce anxiety and insecurity directly. Although anxiety in the proper amount is a positive motivating force to keep the person in counseling, excess amounts interfere with the therapeutic process. Reassurance tends to keep the anxiety generated by the counseling process itself under control by assuring clients that they don't have to explore feelings too fast. This use of reassurance is particularly valuable in controlling anxiety outside the relationship, for example, over weekends and vacations. An example is offering simple suggestions to a mother who is having problems with her child, such that weekend crises are lessened.

A third value of reassurance is the reinforcing effect it has on new patterns of behavior. It is often difficult to launch a new course of action, even after significant insights have been achieved. The client often feels discouragement, leading to loss of confidence. An example is the student who is attempting to improve her failing grades. Reassurance in the form of praise for her attempts, assurances that she will pull through the temporary setbacks, and the encouragement of confident attitudes generally help her to retain or regain her new behaviors.

Reassurance is thus a form of expressing implied counselor value, a form of promising improvement which we feel is wholly consistent with an eclectic frame of reference that places value on the counselor's honest expression of his or her own feelings as well as those of the client. This expression of counselor feelings must be consonant with client welfare, however. We feel that the counselor's failure to express reassurance when he or she honestly feels it is a form of therapeutic dishonesty. A counseling relationship which does not allow any expression of feeling puts the counselor in a form of emotional straitjacket which may be harmful to the relationship.

Using Reassurance

The *approval* or *acquiescence remark* is one means of reassurance. Its purpose is to give the client some feeling of security about the ideas or feelings he or she is expressing. Expressing approval of the client's remarks tends to have a reinforcing effect also. An example is:

CL: It seems that people resent being criticized or told they are wrong.

C: That's right; a very interesting observation and a good rule about personality.

This technique goes beyond acceptance; it is actual agreement with the client. Though generally reassuring, it may be hazardous, because clients may feel they cannot change position without admitting error. Thus, the approval technique tends to have the unfortunate effect of rigidifying the client's thinking. The client may be communicating feeling on a different meaning level also, so a reassuring counselor response may be disruptive.

The counselor who suggests that there are other ways of thinking and acting builds expectations of success in clients. For example, the counselor assures clients that they can change themselves and that counseling can be an effective means to help them change.

Prediction of outcomes is a phrase used by Kelly (1955) to describe the consequences of counseling or psychotherapy over the following few days. Avoiding sweeping predictions, the counselor makes a limited forecast about how the client is likely to feel between conferences. An example is: "We've been talking about your problems in a more intensive fashion. You will probably find that you will be more uncomfortable and moody the next few days. Don't be alarmed, because this is part of the process. You will be able to handle it all right."

Postdiction of outcomes is a related reassuring technique, also described by Kelly. An example is, "It is my guess that during the last few days things have been tougher for you to handle. We opened up many sensitive areas last time which have upset you during the week. Is this correct?" Another example is, "Perhaps you were disturbed by our session last time; but this is a normal part of the process." The reassuring value of such comments comes from the client's impression that his or her behavior makes sense to the counselor and is predictable.

The *interview conditions* tend to be reassuring. As we pointed out in our earlier discussion of support, it is the acceptance, structured limits, attention, affectional warmth, and outward signs of friendship in the counselor which have a powerful reassuring effect. This is true particularly with children, whose behaviors can often be drastically changed through the reassuring effect of emotional support. Thus, meeting specific emotional needs of the client is one of the key uses of reassurance.

Factual reassurance can be given to the client who feels his or her problem is unique. When the client knows that many other people suffer from the same feelings, the fearful bewilderment may subside. Related to this point is the reassurance that the problem has a solution and that the cause of the difficulty is known. Thus, people can tolerate anxiety and annoying symptoms when they know that they are, very likely, temporary reactions to their basic problems. Clients also feel reassured that they can reach specific objectives, such as achieving an educational goal, formulating a vocational plan, getting better grades, or saving their marriages.

Often, the counselor's reassurance of his or her clients that they do not have to feel ashamed, guilty, or alarmed about their problem helps. The client can feel that the problem does not have to be viewed moralistically, but as a personal problem to be solved in an objective way.

Reassurance that the best of help available to science will be given to a client is an often successful means that the counselor can employ to reduce the client's anxiety about the efficacy of treatment. Sharing diagnostic and prognostic formulations with the client when they are favorable is a very convincing type of reassurance.

Reinstating defenses is another psychotherapeutic "first-aid" method. Clients may be using a defense, such as vigorous sarcasm, to handle their hostilities. In the course of counseling, such a client sees the inappropriateness of the extrapunitive tendencies. But the client has not worked them through sufficiently, so he or she develops incapacitating migraine headaches which appear to be manifestations of intrapunitive hostility. Clients are better off if they are "given back" their former defensive mechanisms through being encouraged to express their hostilities more outwardly—the social consequences of which are less severe than the personal consequences of repressed hostility.

A *support system* is an important outcome from a supporting relationship. While this is partly a goal to replace the supportive counseling relationship, it is also an important coping skill to have for future problems. Counselors can help their clients to identify and use their support network. Who are the significant people in a client's life? What differential functions do they perform—nurturance, information, motivation, pleasure, constructive feedback? How is the client using the network? What alterations and additions does the client need? A network is especially useful in crisis situations, so we do our clients a great service through helping them to identify, assess, use, and develop a personal support network.

Using
Suggestion

Suggestion is a powerful supportive tool when used in the context of a helping relationship. We need to recognize that we are giving suggestions in subtle ways all the time. While the counselor gives direct suggestions under conditions of high client receptivity, the goal is to teach clients more creative imagery so that they can perform self-suggestion, or autosuggestion, on their own initiative. Several conditions make the use of suggestion possible to improve client functioning. The prestige and attributed power of the counselor is an influential beginning. A relationship of trust and confidence is a second positive variable for suggestion. Having the client at ease, relaxed, calm, and receptive is an essential condition. The counselor's soft, calm voice aids this state of receptivity. Under these conditions telling clients that they are calm and relaxed, yet alert and energetic, makes them even more receptive to natural and sincere suggestions that they are, for example, competent to pass an impending examination, confident in social situations, able to remember names, or able to curb their appetite for sweets. They imagine themselves able to do these things in the future also, and with the same confident, competent, self-regarding attitude. The emphasis is on having positive qualities, not on the removal of negative images. Then it is suggested that clients can do this imaging on their own initiative. They can develop this state of relaxed alertness or "flow" by themselves.

The reader might ask whether the methods just described are applications of hypnosis. There are similarities between suggestion and hypnosis since the latter is primarily a hypersuggestive state induced by more direct and formal methods than those described above. Being ready for positive suggestions is a kind of trance state; but it is much lighter and more limited than traditional hypnosis. Because of their manner, language, and status, counselors have the power of suggestion, and they need to become more aware of it and to develop more explicit methods to use that power constructively for client development.

This suggestion method has great potential for helping clients to function at higher levels of effectiveness and pleasure (Barber, Spanos, and Chaves 1976).

Limitations
and Cautions

Limitations of reassurance methods are mentioned in the following paragraphs in order to acquaint the student with the fact that reassurance is a two-edged sword in many ways. It can be most helpful when utilized properly as a reinforcer in the situations described, and most detrimental when used indiscriminately.

Levitt

Reassurance is a technique which is particularly vulnerable to misfiring. Reassurance is so easy to use that there is a temptation to be overliberal. Direct verbal reassurance is a vehicle so common in everyday human relationships that it may be stated fairly that reassurance is much overused in counseling. A frequent misuse of reassurance, for example, is in false concealment of the true nature of a serious situation. This is an ethical problem as well as a procedural concern.

Reassurance is used crudely in the approach that "everything will come out in the wash." The "just relax, everything will come out all right" attitude and the old aphorisms, such as "every cloud has a silver lining," serve only to create resentment in clients.

Reassurance might be interpreted by a very disturbed person as artificial and insincere sympathy. Reassurance, at best, is a temporary expedient and the counselor must be reconciled to the possible slowing of progress if he or she uses it. There is the obvious limitation that the whole relationship can be put in jeopardy because subsequent events do not bear out the optimistic predictions of the counselor.

Reassurance has the additional liability of promoting a dependency relationship between client and counselor. The periodic need for reassurance is a type of substitute satisfaction for real accomplishment. The responses reinforced by reassurance tend to become fixed learnings, and the client feels a strong need to get reassurance from this particular person. Some clients use reassurance as an excuse not to change their behavior.

If clients interpret reassurance as agreement, they may limit themselves in the sense that they will feel guilty about changing their behavior or experimenting with new methods of viewing their problems. In other words, they may feel trapped in their present efforts and may think that they can't find any solutions to their problems.

It has been stated earlier that reassurance is most valuable in supporting the anxious, distressed client. It can be grossly misused if given to the client who is already overly aggressive or self-confident. This type of client needs discouragement of her or his often insensitive, rigid, egocentric behavior, rather than support for it.

Use of suggestion has some liabilities for the client. In a suggestible state the client can be influenced easily; so he or she would be vulnerable to an unethical practitioner. Even ethical counselors need to be fully aware of their power when the client is in a suggestible state. Counselors must see that this power is not abused; there must be no unwarranted influence on client values or behaviors.

TERMINATING SKILLS

The effective termination of counseling is as important for successful outcomes as the establishment of the relationship. How neatly the counselor "settles the dust" or "ties up the package" determines the ease with which clients can assume complete responsibility for themselves and the extent to which their progress toward their goals can be determined.

Since the problems and procedures for closing interviews and changing discussion units during the counseling process are related to techniques for terminating, these are considered together in the following discussion.

Terminating a Discussion Unit

A discussion unit can be closed by the summary reflection described earlier, wherein the counselor ties together the loose ends of several related ideas. The net effect of this summary is to give a feeling of closure and progress to the client, whereupon the client generally proceeds to another topic.

A second device for ending the discussion unit is a *capping technique.* This consists of shutting off the flow of talk or feeling in such a way that the client does not stop talking or feel rejected. Frequently the counselor senses that the more the person delves into feelings the more uncomfortable he or she becomes, or the more dissociated he or she seems to get. When the counselor feels that clients' defenses are not sufficiently functional to protect themselves, he or she helps clients regain their defensive armor through capping techniques. The counselor does this with the hope that it is a temporary expedient, and that the client will be more ready to attack the conflict at a later time.

Capping techniques consist of *changing the subject* to something less intense. The subject can be changed back to a topic previously discussed, the original symptoms, or a new and less loaded topic. Reducing the *length of counselor lead* and the general *pace* of the interview often reduces the client's discomfort, resistance, or undesired feelings toward the counselor. The counselor can help to decelerate the pace by *pausing* longer and more frequently. In order to cap exploration which has become too intense, he or she can *reduce the frequency of interviews.* It is well known in counseling and psychotherapeutic practice that the intensity of the relationship varies directly with the frequency of interviews per week. The counselor, for example, may suggest meeting every two weeks instead of once a week. Sometimes reassurance that there is plenty of time to work through the problems helps to take feelings of pressure off the client. Increasing the amount of *counselor talk* has a "shutting off" effect on client communication, thus preventing deeper exploration of problems.

There may be times, also, when the quality of the relationship is such that the counselor can use *direct interpretation* to terminate a topic. An example is, "You are getting quite disturbed about this. Suppose we drop it for a while and go on about your plans after graduation." Clients may need further explanation for changing the subject and reassurance that they can come back to this topic at a later time.

Terminating an Interview

The counseling literature contains very little information about the nature of skills for terminating an interview. Yet, most counselors would agree that it is important that the interview be drawn to a definite close and not left with the client feeling that nothing had been accomplished. Beginning counselors report that ending an interview is one of the most difficult tasks they face. The following are some "tricks of the trade." The reader should note that detailing of such methods can be carried to the point of misleading absurdity. Ordinary honesty and natural courtesies common to our culture are the best guides.

Reference to time limits is one natural way to remind the client that the hour is up. No matter what the length of the interview, it is important that the counselor inform clients at the beginning of the interview that they have a fixed length of time. In a clinical setting, a forty-five- or fifty-minute period is usually standard. In other settings, such as public schools, a much shorter time may be more appropriate. Interview time is a matter of agency policy, case load, and the purpose of the interview.

Generally, it is felt that a minimum of forty-five minutes is needed to deal with clients' most pressing problems. This allows clients a few minutes for "warmup," wherein they move slowly into the main content of the interview and pick up the loose threads from the preceding session, and gives them a few minutes at the end of the hour to "pull themselves together." This is especially necessary after a therapeutic counseling session which delved deeply into feelings.

In school counseling, however, time and case load pressures often force the problem to be stated and analyzed in interviews of ten or fifteen minutes. In any case, as long as the time limit is set, the successful conclusion of the interview can be more assured. At the end of the interview, for example, the time limit can again be brought up by such a statement as, "Our time is nearly up; when would you like to come back again?" or "Well, that does it for today" or "It seems we've reached the end of the hour." This provides an easy transition to the calendar, the door, or the receptionist.

Summarizing is a second means of terminating the interview. This can be done by the counselor, the client, or as a collaborative act. When the counselor sees that the interview is drawing short, he or she can summarize the essential factors of the interview. Again, the terminal reflection technique can be used if the counselor is disposed to summarizing the essential feelings which have been expressed by the client during the interview. A topical summary to reflect the major content of the interview would be in order also.

From the counseling literature it appears that client summaries are used widely. The counselor asks the client for a summarization of key feelings and ideas as follows: "Tell me how you think the situation looks now," or "Now suppose you tell me what you think you have accomplished in this interview."

The counselor usually precedes the collaborative summary with such a phrase as, "Suppose now we take a look at what we have done today. As I see it, we have said. . . . Perhaps you could state how you have seen it."

Reference to the future is a third and graceful way for the counselor to terminate an interview; at the same time, an indication of his or her desire to maintain the relationship is made by the use of a statement which would refer to subsequent meetings with the client. Such a statement would be as follows: "I see our time is about up today. When would you like to come in again?" or "Would you like to make it at the same time next week?" or "I have Thursday at three and Friday at two open. Which would you prefer?" It is important to end in a warm positive tone, following the setting of the exact date and time, with a parting phrase such as, "Fine, I'll be expecting you then at two next Friday," rather than a doubtful "Then you'll come next week at two?"

Fourthly, *standing up* is frequently a persuasive technique for ending the interview. With particularly difficult clients, such as obsessive-compulsive people who do not wish to terminate the contact, it may be necessary for the counselor to stand up as a more blunt means of indicating that the interview is finished. This can be done gracefully at a "low point" before the client has a chance to delve into another topic of conversation. In more formal situations, especially with adults and at the end of first interviews, the offering of the hand as a parting gesture is helpful, too.

Subtle gestures are a fifth category of cues to close the interview. While most counseling contacts close naturally at the fixed time, some clients continue to chat on. Most counselors develop certain gestures to indicate that the interview is to be terminated and that it is time for the client to depart. Examples of counselor cues which even the most obtuse client can perceive are to glance at his or her watch or desk clock, and lean forward. It should be mentioned that the counselor should be alert to and evaluate the wisdom of common devices such as fidgeting, distractibility, irritability, and shuffling desk papers to cue clients that the hour is up.

Ushering clients to the door and opening it for them could aid a graceful and prompt departure. Ordinary courtesy demands that the counselor rise with clients and walk to the door with them. This makes it much easier for the client to leave than it would be if the counselor left the whole burden for terminating the interview upon the client.

Summary notes are a sixth useful aid to terminating interviews. In certain types of counseling where decisions are being made, some counselors find it useful to jot down notes while the interview is in process. They may have another sheet with carbon between so that at the end of the interview the client is handed the carbon of the counselor's notes. This is especially important in career planning, where data are profuse and significant. Many counselors feel that the client will remember the interview if they make a concrete summary of the salient features of the interview. Other counselors encourage clients to make their own notes, thus encouraging independent action.

The *"homework" or "prescription" method* can be utilized as a terminating device. Herzberg (1945) suggests the use of the "social task"—doing something like joining a folk-dance group before the next interview. Sullivan (1954) also suggests giving the client something to do between interviews. Examples would be: "Before you leave I'd like to suggest a little 'homework' . . ." or "I wonder if you could give some thought to these questions which have arisen in our conversation today (mention items)." Counselors from most theoretical positions rationalize homework of some kind to encourage generalization of interview learnings to real life.

Related to the activity approach is the *arrangement for tests* or *occupational reading* if the problem is primarily educational or vocational. This is another natural way to end the interview. It should be stressed that endings are arrived at cooperatively and by counselor suggestion; they are not coerced.

It is important that the interview end on a note of positive planning in that clients know exactly what they are going to do. If the counselor is ambiguous about plans or expectations concerning the client, he or she may arouse insecurity and confusion.

One of the rules in terminating an interview is to start *tapering off* in intensity a few minutes before the scheduled end. A counselor should never let a client leave without allowing the client to pull himself or herself together again and to reduce the feelings stirred up by the interview. Yet this very condition makes it difficult for the client to leave. Clients tend to relax when they feel the pressure is off and often become very spontaneous. They will try to detain the counselor with new and interesting material. Counselors can hold to their structure, or they can use the "five-minutes-more" technique. This technique is ushered in as follows: "I have a few minutes between the interviews. I'll share them with you. You may have five minutes more if you wish. Then we will have to close for today."

The counselor may decide that the material coming out is so significant that it warrants using the "extra hour" device if by chance he or she has the next hour free. One might say, "I have this next hour free; I gather this is a significant area for you. Suppose we take more time, then, while the matter is still hot." This hour may be extremely productive since the usual defenses may not be prepared for it. The client is likely, therefore, to be exceedingly spontaneous. It is our experience that material often comes out in this hour which very likely would not arise in interviews for which the client is more "set."

One danger of the "extra hour" technique should be mentioned. Once an extra hour has been given to a manipulative client, he or she may try to get extra hours again and again. The approach would be "You helped me then—why don't you again?" It may also result in the client remaining superficial in the first hours as his or her defenses get reset. In any case, this technique is useful if used with discretion.

Regardless of the device used to end the interview and to get clients out the door, the interview should end on a positive and friendly note. The counselor should not adopt a cold, neutral attitude, in an effort, perhaps, to avoid deciding for clients whether they will continue and when they will return.

Techniques for terminating interviews, in summary, should be planned in advance, and should be friendly, definite, and collaborative. These characteristics are necessary in order to help the client feel wanted, focus on accomplishment, know what to do next, and realize that he or she collaborated in solving the problems.

THE PROBLEMS.   Practically speaking, no case is ever closed in the sense that the problem is "solved." Effective counseling opens possibilities of client growth which are never finished. Yet there comes a time in the process where either client or counselor feels that the client should be placed completely on his or her own resources. How does the counselor tell when closure has been reached? Clients often give cues that their expectations of counseling have been satisfied or that they have hopes of reaching their goals on their own efforts, such as, "Well, I guess this answers my questions," or "I feel much better about it now."

Generally, the counseling process tends to terminate spontaneously when the client's goals have been reached. A series of elaborate studies of the counseling process indicate that client responses tend to become more positive and self-directive toward the end of counseling (Seeman et al. 1949).

There are other cues which the counselor can use to effect closure. A crucial factor is fulfillment of the counseling contract. Reference should be made to the goals set in the first interviews and the contractual agreements which were negotiated. Were the expected outcomes achieved and to what degree? Counselors can watch for indices that the general goals of counseling have been accomplished. Client goals might be understanding of self and problems, an intellectual awareness of solution and direction to the problem, diminution of such symptoms as anxiety, and, most importantly, behavior improvement. The counselor must be wary, however, of the "hello-goodbye" and "flight into health" phenomena. Clients often experience feelings of euphoria and completion after an interview or two. They may feel that their problem is solved when their symptoms subside after a cathartic interview. They feel better and frequently wish to terminate counseling. Yet, the counselor realizes that no lasting behavior changes have been achieved and that such clients will be back as soon as another decision or crisis upsets them.

A distinction must be made between termination of the process by the client and by the counselor. Clients terminate counseling for many reasons. There may be completion according to the structure or contract. They might stop because of a disruption caused by resistance, ignorance about counseling, trauma, impasse, time, finances, or a feeling that the counselor is no longer needed.

The question naturally arises as to why clients leave counseling rather than become addicted to it. In addition to the cost in time, and sometimes in money also, clients may experience pain and humiliation at having to face further personality change or to achieve a higher stage of self-actualization. Or, in successful cases, the functions that were once located in the counselor are now the clients' property. Clients no longer have a "need" for counseling since what they have learned in the process has now become part of themselves and their way of life.

Counselors terminate counseling, in contrast, when they feel that the goals of counseling have been achieved, or when lack of progress on the formal or implied contract does not warrant, in their opinion, continuation of the relationship. Many counselors, once the problem is delimited, structure the time limits of the process in such a way that when this limit is reached closure proceedings are begun. For example, the counselor starts the closure by saying something like, "Well, here we are nearing the end of the term when we said we would try to finish off our counseling. Suppose we examine where we have been, where we are now, and our next steps." This method of terminating at fixed limits has great drawbacks and some danger in that the person may not be ready to terminate, or may be ready long before the structured limit. However, we think that client anxiety, which often accompanies lengthy counseling, is alleviated when they can anticipate the approximate time of closure.

Often the counselor's skill and patience are tried by the dependent client who resists assuming personal responsibility for his or her life. The counselor can only have faith in the client's capacity for and interest in personal growth. It is assumed here that lingering feelings of dependence upon, affection for, or resentment against the counselor (to be defined under "transference" in the next chapter) have been resolved. These feelings may show in relatively short informational or supportive types of counseling too, if a client, lonely or dependent, simply cannot face the deprivation of the counseling relationship, even though the most pressing problems have been resolved. A useful procedure with this type of client is to space interviews in increasingly longer intervals prior to final closure.

STEPS AND METHODS OF CLOSURE.   The first step to close the interviews is *verbal preparation*. The client is reminded of the time limits agreed upon in the initial interview. For example, "Well, this is our fourth and last interview. . . ." Statements of client growth as a lead to termination of contacts may be expressed as follows: "You seem to have achieved some important awareness about yourself, and some realistic plans; do you think you can go it alone from here?" Other examples are: "It seems we have come to a point where you can work this out by yourself," or "You seem to think that you can carry on from here without further help from me. . . ."

The counselor should then work out a *final summary statement* with the client. This may be a general review of accomplishments, arrangements for referral or follow-up, or preparation of a plan or written summary. Examples of written summaries made during counseling on careers can be found in the workbooks of Bolles (1977) and Borow and Lindsay (1959).

Another step the counselor may take is to leave the door open for possible *follow-ups*. This is especially necessary in short-term, highly structured interviews. Abruptness is avoided when the counselor can say something like, "Drop in to see me when you are around campus," or "When you try it alone for a while you may wish to drop in to review how things are going." It is debatable how much this type of "open-door" policy should be encouraged, since it has possibilities of renewing the dependency of the client and of laying the counselor wide open for attempts to reconstitute the relationship. However, with a younger client in a school situation, the counselor may wish to establish "standby" contacts to observe their development or to give further information. An interest inventory may be used; for example, "It is a good idea to take inventory of your developing interests occasionally. . . ." This type of statement generally has a reassuring effect on clients and permits continuous observation in standby relationships.

A variation on the third step is possible *referral*. If the counselor has gone as far as he or she feels capable of going, or if another type of therapist or agency is going to take responsibility for the relationship, referral technique is used. Here it is important that the counselor structure the nature of the referral in order to pave the way for easy transition to the new relationship without revealing the nature of that new relationship in advance. As indicated in Chapter 5, reasons for referrals should be discussed carefully with clients so they do not get the "run-around" feeling. Clients must convince themselves that the referral is necessary or helpful. If the counselor were to say, "I think you ought to see a psychiatrist about this," the client would be likely to be resistive or frightened. To avoid these possible negative responses the counselor might say, "Our consulting psychiatrist might be able to help us on this problem. Would you care to make an appointment?" These same principles apply whether referral is to the school librarian, a social agency, the speech therapist, employment agency, or physician.

Another consideration the counselor should keep in mind in making referrals to outside persons is the desirability of mentioning two or three names, say of physicians, from which the client may choose. It is assumed, of course, that the counselor is familiar with the intake and eligibility policies and conditions of the agencies to which he or she refers clients, as well as the policies of one's own institution regarding referral channels and procedures. Schools, for example, have definite channels established for handling relationships with social agencies, courts, and professional persons in private practice.

The fourth step is the *formal leave-taking*. What was said about concluding the final phase of the individual interview applies here, with emphasis upon parting with a cordial and confident tone. It should be recognized by the counselor that the steps just cited do not always unfold smoothly. The client may make several abortive attempts to operate alone with a newly discovered insight, only to be forced to return to the same or another counselor.

Before leaving this topic of termination, the authors would like to examine Thorne's concepts of overtreatment and undertreatment (1950). Thorne places the responsibility for determining the safety and appropriateness of termination squarely with the counselor. Some of the attitudes counselors have which tend, according to Thorne, to result in undertreatment are: "therapeutic nihilism," in which the counselor has a pessimistic attitude that his or her counseling will not work with this client, as a result of which he or she gives up; "diagnostic failures," wherein the counselor fails to find or deal adequately with pathological processes and so terminates counseling prematurely; "passive methods," with which a counselor fails to deal actively enough with client problems; "lack of confidence" in attempting to counsel difficult cases; "lenience" in not following up clients persistently; and "overwork" of the counselor from taking too many cases, which results in rushing through appointments, or even reaching "burnout."

Though these dangers may be valid for certain cases, Thorne cautions that the counselor may err on the side of "overtreating" also. By this he means that a counselor might carry the client beyond the point of ethical treatment, or beyond the point of his or her competence. Some overtreatment may result from a conscientious attempt to be thorough, thus perhaps reinforcing the dependent client's need for constant support. However, a loose type of relationship over an extended period may have a prophylactic effect which would prevent further deterioration of the client's problem-solving ability. As in so many other areas of counseling methodology, counselors must assess the situation, weigh the advantages and disadvantages of their courses of action, and then use their best judgment.

SUMMARY

The techniques for implementing the basic principles of relationship in the preceding chapter have been classified into eight categories—opening, reflecting, accepting, structuring, listening, leading, reassuring, and terminating. Each method has its unique values, as well as limitations for creating the optimal kind of relationship necessary for the development of insight and self-actualization. In the next chapter, some of the conditions which present difficulties in building and maintaining an optimum relationship and applying relationship techniques will be explored.

8

Barriers to Actualizing Relationships

Counseling and psychotherapy are interpersonal processes that have identifiable barriers. The purpose of this chapter is to identify those barriers to building and maintaining a relationship, whether formal counseling or friendship. *Transference, countertransference,* and *resistance* are three conditions that may help or hinder the relating process, depending on how they are expressed and handled. Some sensitive therapists feel that use of these terms intellectualizes a very personal relationship too much. Describing warm feelings toward a client, for example, as countertransference depreciates the deeply human quality of the relationship. Students wishing to understand conceptually the subtle interplay of feelings in counseling relationships, however, need some thinking tools. This objective approach need not interfere with appreciation of the more nonrational and subtle interpersonal events. This point is emphasized to reassure counselors that they are dealing with normal feelings and that they need not feel guilty for having genuine and varied feelings toward clients or for experiencing normal gratifications from the helping process. Similarly, they should not be disturbed when clients possess strong and varied feelings toward them.

The three terms above are central to psychoanalytic technique, which is where they originated. Since these concepts are so significant for psychotherapy and counseling, they will be described and illustrated in detail.

TRANSFERENCE

Nature of Transference Feelings

After examining the original writings of Freud and the elaborations of Fenichel, Fromm-Reichmann, Alexander, French, and others, it appears there are several meanings of the term *transference*. In a broad sense, the term refers to any feelings expressed or felt by the client toward the therapist, whether a rational reaction to the personality of the therapist or a projection of earlier attitudes and stereotypes.

We favor the view of the existential therapists (May, Angel, and Ellenberger 1958). Neurotic clients do not really "transfer" their feelings about family members to the therapist. Instead, as May says, ". . . the neurotic is one who in certain areas never developed beyond the limited and restricted forms of experience characteristic of the infant. Hence in later years he perceives wife or therapist through the same restricted, distorted 'spectacles' as he perceived father or mother" (1958, p. 79). Hence, the problem of transference for neurotic clients is primarily one of delayed development and their perception of the present situation through the colored glasses of past experience. May (1967) further cautions that too much dependence on a traditional view of transference as the re-creation of personal relationships from the past leads to a diminished significance of the present encounter with the therapist. It can rob clients of personal responsibility for their feelings in this moment, and it can serve the therapist as a protective screen to avoid the threat of direct encounters with clients. This positive approach to transference emphasizing encounter is a significant characteristic of actualizing counseling.

Historically, transference meant the process whereby client attitudes formerly expressed or felt toward another person important to the client were unconsciously "transferred" or projected to the counselor. For example, feelings of love, hate, ambivalence, or dependence at one time directed toward a parent are now irrationally repeated with the psychotherapist as the object.

An intensive development of the transference process is called the *transference neurosis* by psychoanalysts. Colby (1951) describes three usages of the term *transference neurosis:* a person with a severe neurotic condition exhibiting transference feelings, a simple transference condition, and a severe form in which a heavy proportion of the client's infantile problems are focused on the therapist. Transference is a necessary component of the analytic process wherein the person transfers his or her intrapsychic conflicts into the interpersonal relationship between therapist and client in such a way that it replicates other neurotic relationships past and present. The analyst then uses the transference as a vehicle of therapy.

Transactionally, transference and countertransference can be viewed as interaction problems of ego states. For example, the client's natural child ego state may be rebelling against the amount of responsibility demanded by the therapist, who is speaking from his or her adult ego state. Interaction problems also can be viewed as "games" between counselor and client. A client, for example, may play "the stupid game," manifested as resistance to perceiving strong reality pressures clearly. A behavioral therapist might construe this same example as learned avoidance behavior.

In the therapeutic use of the transference neurosis, the psychoanalytic therapist does not view transference as a *problem,* but rather as a fortunate circumstance making the neurosis available in miniature. In existential terms, the transference feelings expressed by clients give the therapist valuable information on how they perceive and manipulate their worlds. Strupp (1963) is convinced that the transference relationship is not only a rich source of interpersonal data but has a validity of its own and should be studied more intensively.

Sometimes the term *transference* is used as a synonym for relationship, as in the phrase, "The transference was established early. . . ." We feel that this usage is too loose. In this sense, the psychotherapeutic relationship described in earlier chapters could be considered as a type of transference because feelings of mutual attraction are present. An equally vague usage is to regard transference as any expression of feeling toward another person.

Rogers (1951) states that transference feelings develop when the client perceives that the other person understands her or him better than the client understands herself or himself. The way of viewing transference, whether as hostility or dependency, depends largely on the degree of threat involved.

We view transference as a concept midway between the classical Freudian view, with emphasis on the past, and the position that all feelings currently expressed toward the counselor are transference. In other words, transference is viewed as a type of projection of the client's past or present unresolved and unrecognized attitudes toward authority figures and love objects—toward the therapist. This projection is done in such a way that the client responds to the therapist in a manner similar to the way he or she responds to other love objects. Clients build certain expectations of therapists and their roles through this transference process. The client may expect the therapist, for example, to be supporting; or he or she may expect the therapist to be a punishing or controlling agent. In other words, transference is a term describing how the client construes the therapist and how the client behaves toward the therapist.

Intensive transference, commonly found in extended psychotherapy, is regarded as a type of relationship which goes beyond that considered desirable or optimal for counseling. A concept of degrees of transference relationship is illustrated in Figure 14; the client enters the counselor's presence with the usual mixed feelings people have as they meet strangers. Since counselors and therapists generally are cordial and emotionally warm, the relationship bridge begins to widen and client feeling flows more freely

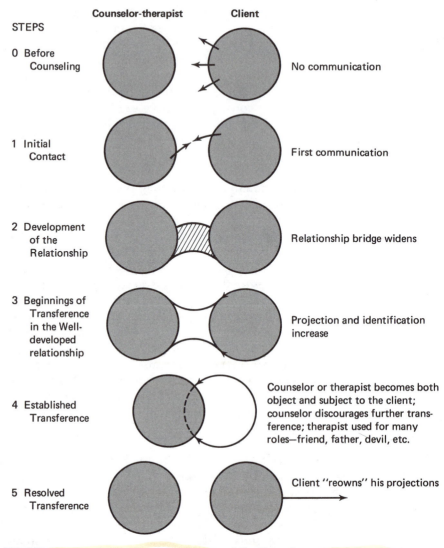

FIGURE 14. Development and Resolution of the Transference Relationship.

toward the counselor. At this point, the transference relationship begins. Clients with strong affection or dependency needs may project these so intensively at times that the client's perception of the counselor is grossly distorted. An extreme example of this idea is the unusual client who literally hugs or throws himself or herself upon the psychotherapist. Often, clients with weak actualizing capacities must "use" the therapist's strength. In this sense, transference may be a necessary prelude to building the client's own actualizing strength. Gelso (1979) points out how all clients enter counseling with a wish (usually below awareness) to be dependent and to have needs for affection satisfied.

Parenthetically, we believe that Step 4 of Figure 14 illustrates a fundamental distinction between counseling and psychotherapy. The counselor develops a close personal relationship with clients, but does not encourage or allow strong transference feelings as does the psychotherapist.

The resolved or broken transference relationship is conceptualized in Figure 14 as a complete emotional detachment, with the vectors of the client's feeling moving away from the counselor as a person and in the direction of investing feeling in other mature human relationships. Clients, in other words, take their projections back.

Transferences may be designated as positive or negative. A positive transference would be made by clients when they project their feelings of affection or dependency to the counselor, perhaps perceiving him or her as a loving, helpful father or mother. A negative transference would be made by clients when they project their feelings of hostility and aggression. These transference feelings change form, sometimes quite suddenly. For example, a client may experience warm feelings toward the counselor while describing his or her problem, yet feel fearful and resentful for having told "all" or for having exposed his or her perceived "weaknesses." Often the client's positive transference will change to negative feelings when the counselor doesn't give all the reassurance or advice expected. Sometimes clients respond to the counselor in a manner similar to that used during childhood "confessions" to their real parents.

ORIGINS OF TRANSFERENCE FEELINGS.   As we explained in the preceding material, transference feelings have their roots in the client's life experiences. The counselor's personal reactions to the client or his or her institutional role (minister, dean, or physician, for example) arouse selective feelings in the client. Counselors should be aware of feelings which they might elicit from clients. These feelings might be very normal social reactions to what the counselor is, says, or does. As illustrated in Chapter 7 on the nature of the relationship, the more ambiguous the counselor personality, the more opportunity the client has of projecting inner needs and attitudes rather than of responding socially and rationally to the situation. The nature of the physical setting of the counselor's office also seems to have a pronounced effect on the client's emotional responses to the counselor, although little is known about this phenomenon.

Transference as "Being Deficiencies": A Gestalt View

Most of us have had the experience of a first contact that was experienced as real and meaningful. Yet, at other times, there was little, if any, meaningful contact with the other. Freud believed that in any prolonged contact, such as a therapeutic or employee-employer relationship, there is a transfer of many emotional responses once felt in the client's relationships with past significant others, like parents. Our reflections about transference have led us to believe that the relationship cannot be accounted for simply by the client's relationship history. For example, we cannot view hostility once held toward parents as accounting for hostility expressed in the here and now. So, it is not what the client *has been,* but what the client *has not been* that is involved. It is a failure of development—a failure to move from environmental support to self-support—and this failure is a heritage from the past. Perls, in Gestalt terms, calls this "the unfinished situation" (1973). A person's hostility can be seen as a manipulation of the present situation so as to avoid contact. In other words, it is the client's fantasies of expected support, fantasies which stem from his or her *lack of being,* and not what was and has been forgotten, which is the essence of the transference. Thus, client histories are really their backgrounds of existence or being—a record of how they have become what they are.

People do not come empty-handed from their past. They bring various means of manipulating their environments. But they tend to lack self-support—an essential quality for survival: their manipulations minimize their self-support; and these manipulations are endless. For example, people break promises, play stupid, forget, lie, and continually ask questions. These manipulative behaviors annoy, embarrass, and exploit others. Thus, client styles of manipulating others are a form of transference.

Client fears of rejection and disapproval are a form of resistance. So they manipulate therapists or employers by putting on a mask of the "good child." They "bribe" with submission or pseudoacceptance of requests. So, from the Gestalt viewpoint, clients are not persons who *had* problems, they are persons with continuing here-and-now problems.

Clients need the means by which they can solve present and future problems by themselves. This self-support requires that clients become truly aware when and how they are manifesting their problems and how they can solve them in the present. This action requires that they experience their problems in the here and now rather than in the past. To achieve this focus in the present, clients must repeat the basic sentence: "Now I am aware that. . . ." The use of the word *I* develops the client's sense of responsibility for his or her feelings and thoughts. The word *aware* provides clients with a sense of their own capacities and abilities of which they had not been aware. *Awareness, contact,* and *present* are key words to describe "Being in the now." Thus, transferences can be viewed as "being deficiencies," where clients manipulate present relationships. They can learn to change these deficiencies through awareness and living authentically in the now. Bugental (1965) confirms our idea that authenticity is a central quality of being. A key counseling task is to help clients become aware that their resistance to change is their defense against being authentic. Bugental sees transference as a process of falling away from authentic communication with the counselor.

Implications for Counseling and Psychotherapy

Since the counselor depends primarily upon a relationship of mutual trust and acceptance for success, a strong transference, especially of the negative or hostile type, tends to interfere with his or her counseling effectiveness.

The psychotherapist, on the other hand, does not necessarily view transference as an interference. He or she uses transference-type feelings to help clients recognize what they are trying to do with the relationship to the therapist—for example, how they may be trying to manipulate the therapist. The client's demands help the therapist to understand what sort of person the client is trying to be or wants to be. The transference relationship, therefore, provides valuable clues for later interpretations to the client on how his or her interpersonal relationship mechanisms are functioning.

Counselors recognize also that, though they do not depend upon a transference relationship for effective therapy, it is important to recognize that transference feelings are present in varying amounts. For example, there are the clients who fear counselors, depend on them, love them, or expect varying roles of them. These responses may be regarded with the classical view that they may be projected self-regarding attitudes related to earlier experiences with parents; nevertheless, they must be recognized and handled effectively in the Gestalt manner described above to maintain client involvement.

Clients are often aware of these feelings and express them openly. Wood (1951) analyzed five completely recorded client-centered counseling cases. He found only 61 out of the total of 1,900 client responses dealing directly with a discussion of the relationship. Qualitatively, however, there were a number of responses which indicated a deep emotional involvement with the counselor. The following excerpts are illustrations:

> *(Second interview)* "... it seemed to me that as we were talking along, that you, not only as a counselor, but you as an individual, were getting sort of excited about this thing too, just as I was. And that, well, at times, you were no longer a counselor to me, but you were just another person that I was talking over this problem with."* (1951, p. 74)

> *(Fourth interview)* "As a matter of fact, a peculiar thing—I hate to admit it—(laughs) is that, except in the last two interviews, I don't believe I've been much concerned with your reflections. You probably realize I've been moving pretty fast, and somewhat running up the middle of your spine at times without, uh, knowing it, desiring to go ahead. A sort of manic euphoria (laughs). But I guess I've done enough to you today."* (1951, p. 74)

Client-centered or phenomenological counselors, in particular, do not regard a transference situation as a significant therapeutic problem. The result is that persons using the client-centered style of counseling rarely confront intensive transferences, and they reflect them as they would any other feeling. Rogers's writings suggest this procedure:

> *In client-centered therapy, however, this involved and persistent dependent transference relationship does not tend to develop. Thousands of clients have been dealt with by counselors with whom the writer has had personal contact. In only a small minority of cases handled in a client-centered fashion has the client developed a relationship which could in any way be matched to Freud's terms. In most instances the description of the relationship would be quite different.* (1951, p. 201)

Another cause of low-intensity transference phenomena in counseling might be the counselor's approach to a transference feeling. He or she does not usually try to analyze deeply the manifold ways in which the client manipulates his or her life relationships. Instead, the counselor utilizes reflection and acceptance techniques which aid clients to see that the transference feelings reside within their own inadequate perception, and not within the counselor.

Counselors tend to regard expressions of negativism, hostility, and guilt as manifestations of resistance in an incomplete growing-up process. Some counselors handle transference feelings with interpretation of the unconscious impulsive nature of those feelings, whereas other counselors, dealing with the same feelings at a more superficial level, tend to use a variety of responses, including reflection of feelings. Some counselors, furthermore, look upon the helping task as a continuation of the maturation process which has been incompletely guided by the client's natural parents. The counselor generally tries to help clients understand and accept their feelings and see what they have been trying to accomplish with their attitudes. After gaining a more rational understanding, they can take their projections on the counselor back to themselves, so that, for example, they can be less dependent. The client also is helped to understand in which ways his or her former behavior was ineffective in reaching the goals of effective living.

Often, the client persistently tests the counselor's sincerity through repeated criticisms, unrealistic expectations, aggressiveness, resistance, and irritability. Gradually, however, clients feel "safe" in dropping their defensiveness and changing their perceptions of themselves and the counselor. Clients, for example, find themselves able to reconstruct satisfactory relationships with others as well as with the counselor, since they learn they may not always expect counteraggressive acts when they are hostile to others.

Negative transferences often follow positive transferences. When clients suddenly realize they have been idealizing or have been depending upon the counselor, they begin to perceive the counselor as he or she really is rather than in the client's "God-like" image. This is the counselor's welcomed cue of client growth. The counselor must help clients work through these feelings of disillusionment, however, by "giving back" their projections. The situation is analogous to "falling out of love." The lover, in fairness to his former beloved, returns her projections of idealized images (romantic love) so that her actualizing mechanisms are restored to their former state.

Not all negative feelings expressed in the interview can be construed as transference feelings. Instead of being projected to the counselor, they may be directed inward. Intrapunitive hostility or guilt, for example, can contribute to depression. Though the counselor must be alert to clinical forms of depression which should have more extensive treatment, he or she can interpret anxious and mildly depressed feelings as a sign that the client is struggling with important feelings. For example, the counselor says in effect, "If we stick together, we can make use of these feelings because they show us that we are very close to something important."

THERAPEUTIC FUNCTIONS OF TRANSFERENCE FEELINGS FOR COUNSELORS. While strong transferences toward the counselor often complicate his or her task, it should be recognized that this process serves significant functions for the client. The awareness of freedom to express previously repressed irrational feelings is a unique experience which often reduces anxiety.

Transference serves to build the relationship by allowing the client to express distorted feelings without the usual counterdefensive responses. For example, clients with a "chip on their shoulders" expect their irritability to arouse counterhostility from others. When the counselor does not react as expected (by getting irritated), the client can safely reduce his or her defensiveness. Hence, clients have less need to feel guilty because of hostile impulses, and less need to project hostility on others. This refusal of the counselor to respond to client projections is one of the main vehicles for accomplishing therapeutic goals. For example, if the client's former human relationships have been characterized by rejection or devaluation, the counselor is very accepting and warm. If the client has felt exploited and abused, the counselor is careful in making demands upon that client. The general principle here is that counselors should not fit themselves into the client's projections so as to satisfy the client's neurotic needs. If the counselor fulfills the client's expectations, there is the possibility the projections will be perpetuated by virtue of having been reinforced.

A second function of transference, implied above, is to promote client confidence in the counselor through wise handling of transference feelings. Such feelings also have the net effect of amplifying clients' emotional involvement with their problems, thereby enabling them to stay in counseling.

A third function of transference is to enable clients to become aware of the origin and significance of those feelings in their present life through interpretation of those feelings. The transferred feelings, along with their maladaptive behaviors, tend to disappear with insight so that they can establish more satisfying and mature relationships with people.

WORKING THROUGH TRANSFERENCE FEELINGS AND PREVENTING DEEP TRANSFERENCE RELATIONSHIPS. The counselor's main task is to encourage free expression of feelings while simultaneously keeping the transference attitudes from developing into a deep transference relationship. Several general suggestions for handling and resolving transference feelings follow.

1. A primary technique for resolving transference feeling is by means of *simple acceptance,* as one would handle any type of client feeling. This procedure enables the client to "live out" his or her feelings, "take back" his or her projected feelings, or continue to express them more freely in the interview. The client recognizes, then, that transference feelings reside in herself or himself and not in the counselor.

2. The counselor may ask *clarifying questions* regarding the forms of anxiety which the client seems to be manifesting. An example would be, "You seem to be unloading on me today. Why do you suppose this is happening?" This statement is a prelude to the interpretation likely to follow, but it explores the client's attitude first and gives him or her the opportunity to do his or her own interpreting.

3. The transference feeling in the client's statement may be *reflected.* For example, the counselor might state, "You feel that we shouldn't discuss this because it may make *me* uncomfortable."

4. The counselor may *interpret* the transference feelings directly. For example, "Sometimes when people feel they have been telling too much, they get insecure about their relationship with that person. Do you suppose this is happening here?" You will note that, even with the use of interpretation, the counselor seeks the feeling response of the client, since it is his or her distortion of human relationships and feelings which very likely are at the root of the difficulties. The main goal of transference interpretation, then, is to clarify the relationship between the client's earlier interpersonal experiences and his or her present behavior. A second goal is to reassure the client that these feelings and their resolution are a normal part of the process.

The interpretations generally emphasize present problems and crises and do not dwell on earlier experiences. Interpretations also come relatively late in the process so as to allow the counselor to accumulate data from which to make valid interpretations. Sometimes interpretations come as "shock treatment" where the counselor says in effect, "Congratulations; you are now able to take these projections and see them as existing in yourself." (The counselor then may go on to explain the nature and function of transference feelings.)

As the client becomes comfortable with the counselor, a common question on transference would be, "Toward whom else have you had these feelings you are feeling toward me?" Such a question suggests to the client that feelings toward the therapist may be directed genuinely toward him or her, but that they should be considered in terms of the idea that feelings at the moment are often attempts to relate past expectations to the present.

5. The following suggestion by May that the counselor should focus on *what* is going on now in client feelings rather than *why* provides a most fruitful technique for handling the difficult problem of transference:

> *In existential therapy "transference" gets placed in the new context of an event occurring in a real relationship between two people. . . . The only thing that will grasp the patient, and in the long run make it possible for her to change, is to experience fully and deeply that she is doing precisely this to a real person, myself, in this real moment. . . . Part of this* sense of timing *. . . consists of letting the patient experience* what *he or she is doing until the experience really grasps him. Then and only then will the explanation of* why *help.*

This is a point the phenomenologists make consistently, namely, that to know fully what we are doing, to feel it, to experience it all through our being, is much more important than to know why. For, they hold, if we fully know the what, the why will come along by itself. (May, Angel, and Ellenberger 1958, pp. 83–84)

The general principle here is that not all feelings automatically need be construed as transferred from the past, but may be the result of a genuine present encounter between counselor and client, or between client and client in a group.

6. In general, calling attention to the transference causes the client to react in the opposite manner. Therefore, counselors usually adhere to the principle of calling attention to negative transference feelings, but not calling attention to the positive transference unless it has reached a level where it is interfering with therapeutic movement.

7. A common method for handling transference is to regard it as a form of *projection*. The counselor can test this idea by asking the client to reverse the projection, and to encourage repetition until the statement is felt by the client as that which he or she is really feeling. The following is an example:

CL: I have the feeling that you don't like me.

C: Can you reverse that statement?

CL: You mean, I don't like you!

C: Yes, can you say that again louder?

CL: I don't like you!

C: Say it again louder.

CL: I don't like you!

C: True or not true?

CL: I guess that's true!

8. The counselor may also interpret transference feelings as expressions of "being deficiency," as described earlier in this chapter. An example using a role reversal method follows:

CL: You don't help me.

C: What do you want me to do?

CL: To say something helpful.

C: You be me and say something helpful.

CL: OK, Gloria, you ought to stand on your own two feet and think for yourself.

c: Now be yourself and answer.

CL: You are right!

9. The counselor may *refer* the client for more extensive psychotherapy if the relationship develops to an intensity which is beyond his or her competence and responsibility.

Types of Transference Feelings

The following discussion covers more problems on transference and illustrates the use of the principles discussed above.

Ambivalent *authority* feelings are commonly transferred to the counselor. In middle class society, which provides the bulk of the psychological counselor's clientele, authority feelings are exceedingly mixed. The client, in addition to having possibly both dependent and hostile feelings about authority figures, becomes anxious when he or she divulges personal information to the counselor. The emotional material may come up too fast for him or her to handle, resulting in anxiety and a possible breakdown of control mechanisms. His or her feelings may change suddenly to hostility directed toward the counselor for allowing him or her to tell so much.

The following excerpt illustrates an authority-type of feeling transfer (the client is a nineteen-year-old single woman who has spent two previous interviews describing her feelings of inadequacy and hostility toward her father):

CL: I just can't talk any more.

c: You feel run down like a clock spring?

CL: No, I'm just finding it harder and harder to talk to *you.*

c: You feel that I as a person am making it harder for you?

CL: Well, yes, I mean (long pause and signs of distress).

c: You mean that somehow I remind you of someone—like your father perhaps?

CL: Yes, I never thought of it that way; but I guess most men do; but you just sitting there looking at me (pause) bothers me.

c: When you think of me as a man, you get the same mixed up feelings as you do when you think of your father. Is that it?

CL: When I really think about it, I know I haven't any real reason to (pause) well, to think of you as my father. It seems silly, but it makes me feel better to know why I feel this way.

(Followed by further discussion of relationships with father.) The counselor in the excerpt tried to maintain an attitude of understanding and acceptance. He had listened to her outpouring of feelings for two sessions. Mild interpretation from the counselor led her to see that her growing difficulties in expressing herself were not due to the counselor's austere paternalistic attitude, but were more the projections of her own feelings about men in general, and her father, in particular. She realized that she could be secure and that she had no palpable reason for feeling that the counselor was censuring her or that he represented father to her. This reperceiving experience, as well as the intellectual awareness of projection, tended to reduce her defensiveness. Thus, she could perceive the counselor as he really tried to be—a personality who understands and accepts rather than evaluates. Rogers emphasizes the value of the above perceptual change in clients:

> The whole relationship is composed of the self of the client, the counselor being depersonalized for purpose of therapy into being "the client's other self." It is this warm willingness on the part of the counselor to lay his own self temporarily aside, in order to enter into the experience of the client, which makes the experience a completely unique one, unlike anything in the client's previous experience. (1951, p. 208)

On the other hand, counselors need to recognize the developments in consciousness that have taken place the past few years in relationships of male counselors with female clients. There are many issues and resentments around traditional female roles and the fact that the preponderance of clients are women. Male counselors, in particular, need to appreciate the subtle feelings involved with changing roles and perceptions of women about being clients and patients with male service providers. In terms of the sixties and seventies the feminist point of view was that, for some male counselors, there was a tendency to view women's problems as personal rather than as manifestations of and inability to meet cultural demands and female role definitions.

The following example illustrates a type of transference feeling involving *dependency* (this is a first interview with a nineteen-year-old woman):

CL: I'm not doing so well in school.

C: Mm-hm.

CL: I thought you could help me by telling me what I'm doing wrong.

C: You are confident that I can help you improve your school work possibly by analyzing your procedures?

CL: Well, yes; I've heard you have tests and things.
(After further structuring the role of the counselor and client and further elaboration of the problem, the client is still thinking along dependent lines.)

CL: I certainly hope these tests give me the answers. I know they aren't very accurate; but with your experience with them, you should be able to tell me what I should do.

C: While you recognize the limitations of tests, you still feel I will be able to suggest a definite course of action. However, I will interpret the results to you and discuss them with you in such a way that you will be better able to decide.

CL: Well, I guess that is what you are here for, aren't you?

In the preceding example, it became clear that the client was depending on the counselor to solve her problem. In spite of the counselor's patient acceptance and later interpretation of her dependency, the client continued to look for further support without much evidence of awareness. The counselor's effort to shift responsibility gently back to her was met with a negative transference remark. The counselor, realizing that his own personality or technique might be arousing this aggressive transference, finally decided that continuation of this relationship would merely reinforce the client's dependency and would very likely arouse some countertransference feelings. Therefore, he decided to structure a referral to another counselor.

While hostile or affectional transference feelings seem to be more adequately resolved by counselors, it is this persistent form of dependency which appears to give them the most difficulty. The dependent client insists that the counselor take over the decisions and self-mangement. This dependent attitude generally shows up early in counseling, so that the counselor can decide whether his or her skills can cope with the alternating apathy and aggression often accompanying the dependency. Clients frequently do not obtain the solutions and support they seek; hence, they become defensive. The resulting aggression severely tests the counselor's judgment whether to inhibit his or her own negative feelings and maintain an attitude of acceptance and understanding, or to react more openly with feelings.

Another danger in dependency transference is that the client's desires to solve his or her problem may be outweighed by wishes to prolong the counseling. It is often necessary to put a "brake" on the regressive-dependent type of transference feeling early in the process, before it becomes a persistent response.

Rogers (1951) offers the hypothesis that a dependent transference arises when clients feel they are being evaluated and that the evaluation has more accuracy than their own self-estimates. The net effect is to decrease self-confidence and to increase dependency. Use of techniques, such as interpreting a test score, or reassuring expressions such as, "It is normal to feel that way," or interpretive remarks such as, "Maybe you do not resent her as much as you thought you did," convey the idea that the counselor has a high degree of omniscience; hence, the client feels relieved to place responsibility for decisions on the counselor. In other situations, the counselor is not afraid of assuming responsibility toward the client for a prolonged period before working through the unconscious emotional aspects of the transference.

In amplifying the hypothesis in the preceding paragraph, Rogers suggests that as the client explores feelings more deeply, he or she becomes more threatened. Then there generally is a tendency to displace or project these threatening feelings to the counselor. This feeling of threat and its accompanying anxiety often result in more dependence, which usually takes a long time to resolve.

Schuldt's data (1966) suggest that clients discussed dependency themes if counselors approached this topic forthrightly, and, conversely, clients tended to avoid the topic if the counselor did so. In studying the dependency theme over the total process, he found significantly more client dependency responses during the early stages than the later stages, although the counselor approaches to these dependency responses remained consistent throughout the process. Schuldt's data suggest that amount of dependency expressed is related to many complex therapeutic variables, but that the counselor's approach-avoidance manner is a likely contributor to the degree of client-expressed dependency.

A third common type of transference attitude is that of *affection*. This feeling is elicited largely as a function of the understanding and accepting attitude of the counselor. A client with strong needs for love and attention will often respond to the counselor's "warmth" with feelings ranging from friendly interest to intense erotic love.

Since this interview may be the first relationship in which the client has experienced genuine acceptance and in which he shares his deepest feelings, it is easy to understand how intense positive feelings, even of intimacy, may develop. This development of feeling, unless recognized, becomes increasingly more difficult to handle by both client and counselor. It was this type of situation which, in the early days of formal psychotherapy, produced so many rumors of irregularities in the conduct of therapists. This is another reason for counselors to limit the buildup of strong transferences. However, these positive feelings elicited by a counselor's accepting attitude can be utilized to create understanding of need deprivations.

Three classes of feelings—hostility, dependency, and affection—were utilized here for expository purposes. It is important to remember, however, that feelings exist in a vast array of types and combinations, although the basic techniques for dealing with all are similar.

In the concluding phases of counseling or therapy, it is necessary that any strong residual transference feelings be discussed frankly with the client and broadly interpreted. Clients must be made aware, for example, that they must become less dependent on the counseling relationship as well as on the counselor, since the present relationship is about to terminate. The affection felt toward the counselor, in addition, must be generalized to include all human beings. Any resentments lingering toward the counselor must be completely understood by the client in light of the total psychotherapeutic discussion of parents, siblings, and so on. Thus, the client is not left struggling with unresolved feelings dredged up during the counseling.

In counseling, the diminution of transference feelings is due to increased client awareness of previously unaccepted, distorted, or partially known experiences. In psychotherapy, there is usually a more pronounced personality change, and the decreases in transference problems run parallel to personality changes.

Transference Problems in Groups

Transference problems are compounded in group therapy. Every group member perceives the counselor incorrectly because of transference distortions around such issues as authority, dependency, and autonomy.

According to Yalom (1975) there are two major approaches to transference resolution in group therapy: consensual validation and therapist transparency. The counselor, for example, may encourage a group member to validate his or her impressions of the counselor with those of the other group members.

A second technique is to acknowledge one's fallibility openly. The counselor shares feelings and acknowledges or refutes motives or feelings attributed to him or her. The counselor could say, "I think you touched a place where I am not entirely free myself. Maybe you could help me see what's wrong here." Another example might be, "Here we all are trying to face reality . . . I am one of you on the same quest." The counselor might also tell the group members when their comments match his or her internal experience. An example is, "I've never heard you challenge me that way before. It's scary, but also very refreshing." So group leaders need to be models of transparency themselves, yet cope with the group's transference feelings directly.

Summary of Transference

In this section, transference was described as a largely irrational part of the counseling process wherein the client projects to the counselor self-regarding attitudes and unresolved feelings from earlier human relationships. Intensity of transference seems to be a function of the type of client involved, setting, length of counseling, extent of emotional involvement, counselor personality, and counselor technique. Although the expression and working through of transference feelings has therapeutic values, it is the intense feeling or involved relationships that create counseling problems. For intensive counseling, however, the development and working through of transferences are considered to be a significant part of long-term relationships.

The resolution or working through of transference feelings is accomplished if the counselor maintains an attitude of acceptance and understanding, if he or she applies reflection, questioning, and interpretive techniques appropriately, and if he or she is willing to share some of his or her own feeling reactions to the client's transference. In any case, transference is a normal condition of every relationship.

COUNTERTRANSFERENCE

Nature of Counter-transference Feelings

The reader may have deduced from the previous discussion that countertransference refers to the emotional reactions and projections of the counselor toward the client. In an extensive review of the writings on countertransference, Cohen (1947) concluded that, although the term transference has fairly standard meaning, countertransference has not. Winnicott's (1949) "objective countertransference," wherein the counselor's resentment of the client, for example, is based upon some objective antisocial or psychotic behavior which would be objectionable to any human being, is on one end of the continuum. Fromm-Reichmann (1950) separates Winnicott's type from the more subtle forms, such as counselor reactions to client transference feelings. Alexander and French (1946) include all attitudes of the counselor toward the client. Other writers include only affectionate or libidinous feelings under countertransference.

We view countertransference broadly to include conscious and unconscious attitudes of the counselor toward real or imagined client attitudes or overt behavior. It is the expression of the counselor's humanness. It may be simply a feeling of the moment which is a genuine response between two human beings; it also may be a form of counselor projection. Examples follow:

1. Genuine expression:

C: You are very pretty.

CL: Thank you very much.

C: You're welcome.

2. Projection:

C: You are very pretty.

CL: Thank you very much.

C: I suppose you react that way to all men who say that?

One of the counselor qualifications mentioned in Chapter 6 was that they have insight into their own immaturities, prejudices, objects of disgust, anxieties, and punitive tendencies. No counselor is free of these feelings. Unless counselors have an awareness of their attitudes, however, their responses to client statements will all too frequently be tainted with their own feelings. These negative attitudes tend to have a destructive effect on the relationship by arousing negative transference feelings in the client. Positive countertransferences, made by counselors, can be even more deleterious, since they are less apt to recognize them and the client is more upset when they are withdrawn.

There are positive and helpful countertransference attitudes in the form of facilitating counselor traits described in Chapter 6. Attitudes of acceptance are essential in building a therapeutic relationship. The counselor, furthermore, must decide how much of a "real person" he or she must be to the client.

Since handling client feelings is reported to be one of their principal difficulties, countertransference complicates the problems of beginning counselors. These counselors are relieved to know that it is commonplace to have some mixed feelings about the client. In addition, the client is an overvalued person in the beginning counselor's life because of his or her own strong desires to succeed in counseling.

There are few studies with implications for the subject of countertransference, but Chance (1958) studied the attitudes of counselors toward their clients and found that, as therapy progresses, the clients become more alike in the counselor's eyes. The results of this study suggest that as counselors anticipate client progress, clients become more like the counselor's projected "generalized client," rather than more sharply differentiated people.

Countertransference can lead to negative effects on clients. Hadley and Strupp (1976) summarized their views on the negative effects of counseling around several themes. All of these factors are counselor misjudgments or due to ignorance or rigidity of style. *Misassessment of the background* of the person (culture, meaning of psychopathology, motivation, ego strength, age factors) comes from pushing the client too fast or probing too deeply. Applying the *wrong technique* with a particular client out of ignorance or unrealistic confidence and allowing *transferences* or *countertransferences* to get out of hand add to the possibility of a negative effect. *Communication difficulties* and inability to recognize and confront client cognitive distortions, such as overgeneralization, add to the probability of failure as a counselor. *Lack of a focal point* or theme, where the counselor allows discussion of anything or focuses too narrowly, is a factor in failure. *Mismatch* of counselor and client as described in Chapter 6, or where the counselor is inflexible or blind to alternative theories of causation or methodologies of treatment, is a contributing factor. *Ethical misconduct,* where the counselor violates a confidence, holds the client too long in counseling, or lets the counseling process just drift, is an additional factor predicting failure of counseling.

Sources of Counter-transference Feelings

Counselor anxiety is the prime source of countertransference behaviors. The counseling relationship mobilizes anxiety from former relationships in a manner similar to transference. The anxiety patterns in the counselor may be classified into three types: unresolved personal problems of the counselor, situational pressures, and communication of the client's feeling to the counselor by empathic means.

The first category, the counselor's unresolved personal problems, needs little explanation. The main solution here is counseling for the counselor. Even after personal counseling, counselors must continue to increase their self-awareness to minimize countertransference.

Situational pressures are tied to the counselor's problems but also may aggravate latent feelings. An illustration follows: A counselor had just come from a fatiguing meeting. He had to wait a few minutes for a late client who, noting the austere facial expressions of the counselor, apologized profusely. The client felt that the counselor was provoked with him, when in reality it very likely was the emotional exhaustion and frustration experienced by the counselor in a previous hour which caused him to respond so severely to the client.

Situational pressures exist for counselors in the form of their feeling responsibility to see that the client improves, or feeling that their professional reputation is at stake if they fail with this client. As a result, counselors "try too hard," by pushing the client, and thereby may defeat their own purposes. Counselors must be on guard so that their anxious feelings of frustration when a client does not improve are not transmitted to the client.

Related to situational pressures are heavy case loads and long counseling hours which result in excessive fatigue. Prolonged efforts of this kind, or just the boredom of months of counseling without breaks, lead to a condition called by many counselors the "burnout effect." This is a condition of chronic fatigue, apathy, mild depression, and loss of motivation. In severe and persistent form, it has led counselors to leave the field of counseling (Maslach 1976; Edelwich and Brodsky 1980). This vulnerability to burnout requires that counselors seek renewal experiences regularly. These refreshment experiences go beyond the usual vacation, since they require a reexamination of basic values and thorough assessment of life-style competence.

Support networks have been a key factor stressed in recent behavioral science research findings (Maslach 1978). A study by Casas, Furlong, and Castillo (1980) is an example of such research and it underscores the importance of a support network for helping counselors, especially minority counselors, cope with stress. The study found that those counselors who said their support group was adequate (70.4 percent) reported significantly less stress than those without an adequate support network.

A third source of countertransference is communication of client feelings to the counselor. When counselors tend to be overly sympathetic, is it because they have unwittingly responded to a strong bid for sympathy and attention? When counselors feel themselves becoming anxious or resentful, is it owing to the contagion of the client's anxious feelings? That this happens frequently is possibly due to the counselor's special training in alertness to client feelings. The counselor then responds empathically to minimal cues, such as changes in posture, voice, and manner. The counselor may not be aware that the stiff jerky walk from the reception room to the office, the grating voice, or the loud aggressive talk of the client generate tensions in him or her.

Counselor responses to client hostility were studied by Gamsky and Farwell (1966) in an experimental situation. They found that counselors reacted in a negative manner when the hostility was directed at them. Counselors so threatened reacted with significantly more reassurance, suggestions, and information than at other times. Experienced counselors handled the hostility better than the less experienced.

It should not be overlooked, perhaps, that in addition to the empathic explanation, the preceding behaviors are also related to the counselor's past personal problems. One of the ways the counselor manifests anxiety is to emit impulsively a verbalization of his or her own—a question, comment, or change of subject which may not technically be relevant to the counseling process at the moment. The net effect is often disruptive from the standpoint of stopping or diverting the flow of client feelings, throwing him or her off the loaded topic, or creating more transference feelings. An example is the counselor who has difficulty working with teen-age youth because his or her own unresolved teen-age problems are reenacted.

In addition, the counselor may reveal anxiety by uneasiness. Reusch and Prestwood (1949) studied the transmission of feelings in an experiment which involved psychiatrists listening to recordings of therapeutic interviews. The investigators found that the emotional tone of the listeners varied significantly with the rate of speech, use of personal pronouns, and frequency of expression of feeling. A relaxed client resulted in a relaxed listener. Those interviews heavily laden with anxiety resulted in listener reports varying from being ill at ease to being angry.

Any discussion of the source of countertransference attitudes would not be complete without mentioning the counselor's value structure again. As indicated in earlier chapters, the very nature of the relationship puts the counselor in a position of influencing the client. This happens even though he or she claims to be objective and nonjudgmental. It is difficult for counselors to avoid conveying the feeling that they regard emotional maturity, for example, as an important goal for counseling. It is quite easy for the client to guess by emotional implication, if not verbally, the values which the counselor holds after a discussion of moral problems.

The counselor conveys two types of values to the client—those on how to live, and those on how to behave in counseling. There is no question professionally that a counselor can convey counseling process values which facilitate counseling. Examples are: "It is important to express how you really feel here." "It is all right to tell me how much you resent your aunt."

There is considerable question as to how far counselors should go in promoting their own moral concepts or styles of life in the interview. On the one hand, it may be desirable to help a racially prejudiced client to perceive others in a less rigid manner consonant with his or her capacity for insight; on the other hand, it might lead to unfortunate consequences to specify a particular type of religious faith.

There are two reasons for restricting value projection. One is that the counselor might succeed. We cannot safely trust even a sophisticated counselor to be a "cultural high priest" where he poses as the best judge about right and wrong or appropriate or inappropriate beliefs. If it is felt that the client needs more information and clarification in the area of religious values, for example, it is preferable in our opinion to refer him or her to a reliable minister from whom there is clear understanding that he or she will receive instruction in values consonant with his or her needs and subcultural identity.

Another reason for restricting this activity is that the counselor's deliberate efforts to influence the client's values might fail. The unsuccessful attempt might interfere with a good therapeutic relationship by promoting an unwanted negative transference attitude. Yet, a counselor is an expert in the process of living and applying principles of behavioral science. The counselor constantly must be aware of the client's personal standards and beliefs also. He or she must try to see these values as the client sees them and help the client utilize them for the client's own benefit. The counselor must keep up with the fast-changing value scene in society at large and in extreme subcultures so that he or she can help the client to gain perspective and make wise choices.

Ingham and Love suggest a technique for handling the instances where the client is aware of the counselor's values. The counselor explains the situation by saying, for example, "You've picked up something of my feeling about marriage. I don't mind your knowing what I think about it, but it doesn't mean that you should follow my ideas" (1954, p. 78). Here the counselor admits he or she has given his or her values and allows the client to accept or reject them, yet does not refute his or her own feelings.

The Professional Identity Defense

Gottsegan and Gottsegan (1979) described a form of countertransference they call the "professional identity defense"—an unconscious need to defend one's professional image at the expense of the client. They believe it stems from taboos set up by currently fashionable therapy "schools" regarding what must not be allowed to happen in therapy. Some examples are: (1) blindness to client data that require a response different from an orthodox "school" response; (2) blaming the client when things don't go right; and (3) conducting the therapy in a rigid stylistic manner so it comes out the counselor's way.

A protection against the professional identity defense is to try new therapeutic techniques. Until counselors actually experience the new techniques, they must not summarily reject them. This approach is consonant with the theoretical position we described in Chapter 2, namely, that counselors must not rigidify their responses or acquire a theoretical identity too quickly. This means becoming a creative synthesizer and continuing to integrate new concepts and methods.

Signs of Countertransference Feelings

The following checklist of illustrative signs is offered to enable counselors to test themselves. Hopefully, it will help to distinguish positive therapeutic feelings from anxious or defensive countertransference involvement with clients.

1. Getting sleepy, or not listening or paying attention, not hearing client's messages clearly.

2. Denying the presence of anxiety and thinking, "I feel all right about this topic and should feel upset; but I don't." (If there were no anxiety present, why would the counselor even think about it?)

3. Finding it difficult to shift positions or experiencing one's self "tighten up."

4. Becoming sympathetic rather than empathic or becoming over-emotional in face of client's troubles.

5. Selecting certain material to reflect or interpret and wondering afterward why this material rather than some other material was selected.

6. Consistently reflecting or interpreting too soon or incorrectly (and the result cannot be accounted for on client resistance grounds only).

7. Underestimating or missing the client's depth of feeling consistently.

8. Feeling an unreasoning dislike or attraction for the client. Getting angry at the "unappreciative" client.

9. Being unable to identify with the client. For example, when the client feels upset, the counselor feels no emotional response.

10. Overidentifying with the client, as in becoming aggressively sympathetic when the client cites maltreatment by an authority figure.

11. Discovering a tendency to argue with the client, beoming defensive, or otherwise vulnerable to client criticism.

12. Feeling that this is a "best" or "worst" client.

13. Being preoccupied with the client in fantasy between sessions, even to the extent of thinking of responses to be made.

14. Being habitually late in starting interviews or running over the hour with certain clients.

15. Attempting to elicit some strong affect from the client by making dramatic statements.

16. Being overconcerned about confidential nature of work with clients.

17. Feeling the compulsion to do something active; hence, making too strong an impact with "shotgun" interpretations and suggestions.

18. Dreaming about the client.

19. Being too "busy" to see the client or complaining of "administrative duties."

20. Working excessively hard with clients to point of fatigue, then complaining of overwork.

An insidious form of countertransference expression is compulsive advice giving. This "if I were you" approach is so exceedingly common in everyday human relations that it tends to spill into counseling relationships also. The counselor may feel the need to convince the client that the course of action discussed is best for him; yet the advice, persuasion, or reassurance is motivated more by the counselor's personal needs. A possible motive for advice giving is extrapunitive hostility. It is a way of controlling others, depreciating them, and elevating one's self to a dominating role. There are conditions, however, where *information* and *opinions* can be offered. These conditions are discussed in Chapter 10 on information techniques.

A common form of countertransference feeling is the idea that the client must somehow like the counselor and that the counselor must please the client. Though the relationship is built upon mutual trust and cordiality, there are times when the counselor must risk this client admiration. For example, sometimes counselors must help clients see that they must give up important things, and that removal of pleasing behaviors is sometimes painful.

Fiedler (1951) found in his studies of the factors in the counseling relationships that the poor, or nonexpert, counselors had the tendency to "not hear," "ignore," or communicate poorly with clients. The expert counselors had these tendencies significantly less often. This study suggests that such countertransference signs, as Fiedler found, are not a great problem for experienced therapists.

For counselors who feel that they are not vulnerable to countertransference tendencies, a revealing and sobering exploratory study by Fiedler is cited. He found that there was a high relationship between therapeutic competence and lack of negative countertransference attitudes. Fiedler's method consisted of comparing the similarity of the counselor's and the client's self-descriptions. The counselor's "ideal" description, then, was used to determine the nature and intensity of countertransference feelings. An implication of this study is that, as counselors grow in counseling experience and personal understanding, their harmful countertransference attitudes diminish.

Resolution of Counter- transference Feelings

Although little research has been done in the area of resolving a countertransference, there is a body of clinical experience which may be useful to the counselor in handling feelings toward the client. Increasingly, encounter group experiences are helping not only beginning, but experienced counselors to become more aware of their feelings toward clients.

LOCATING SOURCES OF FEELINGS.   After awareness of the feelings the first step consists of the counselor asking, "I wonder why this is so?" This question is precipitated by the feeling that the counselor is not communicating with clients. The following list of questions should give counselors additional reasons to ponder their countertransference attitudes.

A Counselor's Guide to Self-Criticism[1]

Why did I make this particular response to this student's remark? What was behind it?

What was I reacting to when making this remark?

[1] Adapted from Johnson (1946).

What was I endeavoring to convey to the client?

Why did I ask that question?

Was it really asked for purposes related to helping the client?

Was I merely curious?

Was I really being judgmental by asking that question?

Why did I feel impelled at this point to give advice?

Was it because I felt that the client expected me to have all the answers?

And did I respond by being all-wise?

Why did I become so emotionally involved with the client who felt so unloved and insecure?

Could it be that basically I too still feel unloved and unlovable?

Why did I want (or did I not want) to bring the parent, husband, or wife of this client into counseling?

Can it be that I have overidentified with the client and have already rejected the spouse? (or the parent?)

Why in this first interview did I talk so much instead of letting the client tell his or her story?

Was it because I felt I had to impress the client with my own knowledge so he or she would return?

Why does it upset me when appointments are broken?

Is it because I am really insecure and uncertain concerning my skill?

Why am I so reluctant to "let go" when the counseling with a client has reached a good termination point, or when I know the client should be referred for a different kind of help?

Am I using the client for my needs or am I letting the client use me?

Counselors must accept the fact that they have varied feelings about clients and that they will be changed somewhat by the counseling experience. Counselors must also be aware that they have anxieties coming from insecurity in the counseling role and the client's expression of anxiety.

Counselors must control their tendencies to give reassurance to the client because of their own needs for reassurance. For example:

CL: Sometimes I feel like screaming out loud in a quiet place like the library. In fact, I feel so tensed up at times I feel like wringing somebody's neck till he dies.

C: It is all right to feel that way. After all, thinking of killing isn't the same as murder.

This counselor response is likely to arouse more anxiety in the client, whereas the following response would recognize the main feeling, tend to tone down the reassurance, and yet not show the counselor's anxiety (even if the counselor realistically pictures himself as a possible object of the client's homicidal feelings):

c: Sometimes these feelings do seem hard to control and we feel an urge to let them go at times. Perhaps you would like to mention some experiences with other people or situations which make you feel this way.

Counselors control their anxiety through the knowledge that nonpsychotic clients rarely assault counselors and that hostile, threatening language is often a clever device used by disturbed clients to frighten counselors.

SUPERVISORY ASSISTANCE.   First of all, every counselor who feels uneasy about his or her responses to a client should admit to the possibility that these comments are a form of his or her own projections. All that may be necessary is to admit to this possibility frankly with a supervisor or colleague and attempt to change. There are times in the professional life of all counselors when they must admit that certain types of personalities make them defensive or are beyond their level of competence. They can handle this problem by assessing the client as "too hot to handle" and referring the client to another therapist. An additional recourse is the supervisor or a colleague with whom a counselor can discuss, with considerable candor, the feelings involved, without breaching the confidences of the relationship. For example, a counselor may recognize that he has trouble with hostile, aggressive women; hence, he might suggest that such a client change counselors. Again, discussing this problem in a counseling relationship or in a case conference with a supervisor helps counselors resolve their own feelings (Langs 1978).

DISCUSSION WITH THE CLIENT.   Though there is no objective evidence to indicate that it is expedient to discuss countertransference feelings with the client, we have found a mild reassuring and interpretive reference occasionally helpful in allaying anxiety. For example (this is a second interview with a thirty-three-year-old married woman, after a discussion about an involved marital problem):

CL: Well, there it is—straight from the shoulder.

c: You feel you have told the story quite frankly. Perhaps you have noticed that there are times when things you say may seem to disturb me a bit. I trust though that you will not hold back any feelings for fear of disturbing me.

CL: I appreciate your telling me this. It might make it easier to talk to you.

Another example wherein a counselor rationalizes his or her unwarranted intrusion follows: The counselor has just interrupted the client and says, "I'm sorry; I didn't intend to stop you. Sometimes we are so eager to help we interrupt your train of thought."

COUNSELOR GROWTH.   Counselors can use their own awareness of themselves as reflected through the therapeutic process to enhance their own growth and resolve their difficulties. Cohen (1952) cites an example of a psychotherapist who doubted his own intellectual adequacy and habitually overrated and competed with his more intellectual clients. This situation made it difficult for the counselor to help the clients who use intellectualized defenses against their own anxieties. Similarly, the "burnout effect" cited earlier can be allayed or avoided by careful attention to a personal growth program of renewal, rest, and recreation.

REFERRAL TO GROUP COUNSELING OR THERAPY.   Another technique for handling a countertransference is to require that the client discuss his or her problem in group therapy. For example, if it is obvious that a woman client has strong affectionate feelings toward a male counselor, he can ask that she talk about this matter in a group therapy situation. This procedure depersonalizes the problem and removes much of the possibility of any undesirable countertransference reaction.

EXEMPLARY ENCOUNTER.   If, instead of seeing the client-counselor relationship as one which is active on the part of the client and passive on the part of the counselor, the dialogue is seen as an *encounter*, then the counselor will not be afraid of expressing and introjecting his or her own feelings of anger and frustration. A counselor's awareness of countertransference dangers, and willingness to admit that "this may be my problem," provide the client with an open model of humanness and expression which will help the client more than an overcautious counselor who is constricted because of countertransference fears. We see a danger in becoming too cautious for fear that countertransference may cause trouble. This caution could result in excessive "friendly, warm, and respectful" behavior. Epstein (1977) warns that avoiding one's hostile or angry feelings is not always beneficial. Clients who feel worthless often tend to feel even more worthless when their counselor is always warm. By recognizing and being honest about his or her own anger the counselor can set appropriate boundaries for himself or herself and the client.

ANALYSIS OF TAPES AND VIDEOTAPES.   An additional source of countertransference awareness is through use of audio- and videotape recordings. A frank discussion with fellow staff members of the countertransference aspects of their work samples will reduce the danger of introjection of the counselor's projections into therapeutic work.

Summary of Countertransference

The purpose of this section is to impress upon the reader the significance of the counselor's irrational attitudinal responses. Another purpose is to suggest ways of resolving these feelings. We support the hypothesis that the counselor's attitudes are one of the most important determinants of interview climate. A counselor can resolve feelings toward the client by recognizing that he or she has countertransference feelings, by examining himself or herself concerning why the feelings exist, possibly admitting that he or she should not work with this client, and by using the recognition of countertransference feelings as information to enhance his or her own personal growth outside the interviews through counseling or encounter group work.

The next section contains a consideration of the phenomenon of resistance, which draws upon elements of the transference and counter-transference discussion; yet, the resistance phenomenon has unique characteristics of its own.

RESISTANCE

Nature of Resistance

One of the principal realities of building and maintaining an effective counseling relationship is the presence of resistance. Resistance may be viewed as a special defensive form of transference and a key function of the facade level. The term *resistance,* as we use it, refers to a characteristic of the client's defense system which opposes the purposes of counseling or therapy.

The term *resistance* was introduced by Freud to indicate unconscious opposition toward bringing unconscious material into consciousness, as well as the mobilization of repressive and protective functions of the ego. Transactional theorists would construe resistance as an elaborate "game" with definite "payoffs."

The existentialist view of resistance is stated by May as follows:

> . . . *this is an outworking of the tendency of the patient to . . . renounce the particular unique and original potentiality which is his. This "social conformity" is a general form of resistance to life; and even the patient's acceptance of the doctrines and interpretations of the therapist may itself be an expression of resistance.* (1958, p. 79)

Perls states cogently from the Gestalt viewpoint that all resistance represents the client's refusal to be self-supportive. Therefore, he or she has to be confronted with the "gain" he or she gets from such resistance. An example as Perls would respond follows:

c: What does it do for you just to sit there?

cl: Then I don't have to work.

c: You really don't want to help yourself?

cl: Well, yes and no.

c: Be the yes and no!

cl: Well, the no self says, "I enjoy frustrating you." The yes self says, "but I've got to do it myself."

Resistance, like transference, has different implications for counseling as opposed to psychotherapy. In general, counselors see resistance as something which opposes progress in problem solving and therefore is something which the counselor tries to reduce as much as possible. Other counselors, in contrast, see resistance as an important phenomenon for intensive analysis. If they can understand the client's unique form of resistance, then they will be more likely able to help clients understand and change their personalities. The aim of counseling, therefore, is not just to ascertain the client's defense system or to "find out his or her secret." Rather, it is the significant question, "How does the client hide his or her secret?" A significant part of counseling, therefore, involves the intensive awareness and study of resistance and transference feelings.

Resistance exists in varying amounts in all interviews and may be viewed as being at the opposite end of a continuum from free emotional expression. Daulton's (1947) and Sherman's (1945) data appear to support this thesis of a continuum relationship. Haigh (1949) found a significant inverse relationship between defensiveness in early interviews and later expressions of positive attitude.

Resistance may vary from rejection of counseling and overt antagonism, on the one hand, to subtle forms, such as hesitation and inattention, on the other. Clients may say: "I know what I want to say, but I can't say it"; 'I'll have to leave early today since I want to study for a test"; "I don't think that applies in my case"; "I'm sorry I'm late, but I almost forgot about our interview"; I thought you were supposed to be the expert." An obvious form of resistance is *embarrassment*—the tendency to make contact and retreat at the same time. *Blocking* or blank spots may be interpreted as restraining oneself and taking responsibility for it. *Not seeing or hearing* are tendencies which definitely can be labeled as resistance.

Although resistance is present in some degree in all interviews, it is seldom recognized by the client. Hence, resistance exists largely as an unconscious phenomenon and is manifested by rationalizing one's behavior and by assuming an ambivalent attitude toward counseling. Clients want help, yet they resist the very help they seek. This ambivalent client attitude is one of the most baffling situations confronting the inexperienced counselor. Even experienced counselors occasionally cite resistance as an excuse for not establishing an effective relationship.

Freud emphasized that the ambivalent and paradoxical attitude is a normal state of affairs in therapy. Many counselors typically regard resistance as a normal mechanism which functions independently of therapy, to prevent disturbing feelings from coming to awareness.

The degree to which it is necessary to focus upon resistance to grow and reach the goals of therapy illustrates further the different levels of counseling, as indicated in the following examples:

1. Reflective level I:

CL: I can't seem to be successful as a salesman—I just can't get along with other people.

c: You've pretty well ruled out selling then? Have you considered some of the other occupations on which you score high on the Strong-Campbell Test?

Reflective level II:

c: You find it necessary to keep people distant from you.

2.   Action suggestion level:

CL: I can't seem to get along with my supervisor.

c: Since this seems such an obstacle, let's look at some techniques for getting along with such people.

Interpretive level:

c: You seem to have much resistance to working with persons in authority.

Usefulness of Denial Defenses

Richard Lazarus (1979) has suggested that we need to reassess the idea that facing facts, or "reality testing," is one of the main ways of avoiding resistance. In fact, Lazarus suggests that denial (refusing to face the facts) and illusion (false beliefs about reality) are useful in coping with stress and may be healthy strategies for certain situations. He goes further in saying that a temporary disavowal of reality helps a person get through the devastating period of facing death. The person can later face the facts and mobilize coping efforts, but, at first, denial appears to be useful.

Lazarus distinguishes between threat and challenge to illustrate his point. Threat is a state in which a person feels blocked and coping skills are inadequate. Challenge, however, actually facilitates functioning and growth, in the long run.

Another implication of threat theory is that we can teach coping skills by helping students to change maladaptive strategies to adaptive ones. An example of maladaptive self-talk would be, "This exam is too tough for me." A more effective self-statement would be, "I may be a bit anxious during the exam, but it may actually help me do better."

Denial can be a useful coping defense when one is trying to recover from the severe emotional effects of loss. Riggs (1977) sees resistance mechanisms performing useful homeostatic (stabilizing) functions for clients.

Sources of Resistance

There appears to be general agreement among counselors that resistance arises when the client perceives the counselor, topic, or situation as threatening. Since anxiety is present in response to threat, clients are compelled to defend themselves further against the anxiety through behaviors which are resistive in nature. It is a curious paradox that people often pay for counseling and then spend so much energy working against the very change they are paying for. It is the counselor's task to align himself or herself with the side of the client that wants to change. Clark (1977) agrees that it is important to work with client resistance rather than against it, especially since it is such a prominent feature of long-term counseling.

Resistance can be classified conveniently as "internal" or "external" in origin. Internal resistance comes from within the personality structure of the client and is a generalized response to threat; external resistance is provoked as a result of the counseling setting, the impact of counselor technique, or countertransference attitudes.

INTERNAL RESISTANCE.   One common source of internal resistance is the tendency of anxious clients to retreat from usually painful attempts to explore or alter behaviors. It represents a fear of growing, or not wishing to be self-supportive.

There seems to be anxiety associated with change in life status or attitude. Clients fear the expression of anxious or hostile feelings because they have learned to anticipate judgmental labels such as *immature, lazy,* or *neurotic.* These feelings seem to be most manifest when clients express feelings too fast, in which case they feel that they are exposing themselves to the anxiety of ego-relevant stimuli faster than they can judge the safety of these stimuli. Crider (1946), in his study of the hostile personality, found repressed hostility, especially in persons fearing expression of aggressive feelings, to be a prominent source of resistance.

The term *facade* is used to describe another form of *internal* resistance. Facade refers to the initial statement made by a student client—for example, to explain his poor showing in college. Examples are: "I guess I hang around with the gang too much"; "I must be in the wrong major"; or "The army is going to get me soon"; "My study habits are no good." Although these statements serve a useful function as reference points for further discussion, they are very often rationalizations and expressions of resistance. Clients seem so captivated by the simple logic of their statements that they often find little motivation to overcome their resistance and explore the situation further.

Another phenomenon creating resistance is reification anxiety; that is, the client's fear that to put feelings into words will make the condition real. An example of this basis for resistance is reluctance to express anxieties about having cancer, of death, or of losing love.

EXTERNAL RESISTANCE.   Some counselors are convinced that external resistance grows out of poor technique. Rogers, in his earlier work on counseling, offers the hypothesis that resistance is not necessarily ". . . an inevitable part of psychotherapy, nor a desirable part . . . ," and that what resistance is present appears to come from attempts to accelerate or to cut the process of therapy short (1942, p. 151).

An illustration of *external* resistance is the case where the counselor has made modest suggestions about improving study efficiency. The client may be anxious about carrying them out because of a supposed feeling of closeness or obligation to the counselor. Clients may resent being "drawn in" to this type of relationship at this stage of development, or they may have experienced family relationships where children were obligated to return helpful favors in kind. The counselor's suggestions here create a negative transference which interferes with counseling effectiveness.

Another illustration of counselor technique which arouses resistance is a situation where the counselor gets too far ahead of the client, and reveals it by reflecting an implied feeling or offering a premature interpretation.

CL: "My parents are always criticizing me and threaten to stop giving me money for school."

C: "You resent your parents for these things they say and threaten to do."

CL: "No, not exactly, I don't dislike my parents for it, I think they are right in lots of ways; I'm wasting my time here at college, really . . . I shouldn't be talking about them like this."

Here, reflection and interpretation, although not very likely accurate, pinpointed feelings which could not be recognized and accepted at this stage.

Another cause of external resistance is related to lack of proper readiness. Clients may misunderstand the counselor's role or they may not have faith in the value of verbalization. Clients may not realize that counseling takes time; therefore, they may resent spending the time which they could devote to other less-threatening activities. Clients may be embarrassed to admit that they have problems which they are unable to solve by themselves.

The counseling relationship itself presents a paradoxical situation to the client. The accepting atmosphere encourages free expression of feeling, yet the client often is neither ready to express nor prepared to accept his or her own feelings. The relationship tends to force the premature examination of his or her own feelings, thus creating a source of considerable resistance. A common device clients use for manifesting this type of resistance is to talk about someone else's problems. An example is the case of a mother who worried about her fourteen-year-old daughter's behavior. The mother felt guilty, in addition to having intense feelings of failure. When the counselor encouraged the mother to talk about her own feelings, she felt compelled to continue discussing her daughter's difficulties.

English (1948) cites further examples of situational anxiety as an obstacle to an optimal therapeutic relationship. He found that using lead techniques low in intensity early in the interview left clients dominated by their anxieties. English indicated that he found it necessary very often to reduce some of the anxiety temporarily by taking a greater lead and giving more support.

MIXED SOURCES OF RESISTANCE.   In addition to client's perceptions of threat in the interview or anxiety concerning their own impulses, other conditions cause resistance. Conditions such as fatigue, disease, mental deficiency, foreign language barriers, and psychoses cause resistance. The schizophrenic, from one point of view, exemplifies his resistance through withdrawal into hallucinations, muteness, or general negativism and projection. The neurotic may manifest resistance defensively through rigidity, concern over details, irritation, argumentation, or playing "stupid."

Knowing the sources of resistance, particularly the internal type, should be reassuring to the counselor who tends to feel personally responsible for the resistance he or she encounters. On the other hand, since counselor manner is the trigger for so much resistance, counselors must study continually their techniques and professional setting in order to reduce external resistance cues.

Positive Functions of Resistance

In addition to the protective or defensive functions of resistance for the client, there are valuable clues which resistance provides for the counselor. A principal value of resistance for the counselor is that it gives an indication of general interview progress and the basis for diagnostic and prognostic formulations. Noting resistance symptoms is the first step toward taking appropriate measures to ignore, reduce, or utilize them.

A second function of resistance is the glimpse into the client's defensive structure which it affords. The presence of resistance tells the counselor that the client does not wish to explore these particular feelings further at this moment. Areas involving morals and deeply held beliefs are usually defended rigidly. Hence, resistance symptoms inform the counselor when he is treading temporarily in taboo territory. When these areas of threat become known, therefore, they offer the counselor much valuable interpretive information. Resistance is the counselor's cue that perhaps his usefulness has ended as a therapeutic agent and that counseling should be formally terminated. Rogers (1946) comments that clients often change their feelings of warmth and acceptance toward the counselor to resentment when they no longer feel the need of the relationship. This manifestation, therefore, may be a healthy indication for terminating the relationship.

Resistance acts as a protective mechanism for clients through keeping acute anxiety under control, and through avoiding disintegration of their defensive structures prior to establishment of new constructive behaviors. In this sense, resistance often serves a useful decelerating function for the early stages in the counseling process.

Manifestations and Classifications of Resistance

Although it is futile to attempt to list the myriad forms of resistance, it may be helpful to indicate some of the subtle as well as glaring examples of resistance. We feel that a distinguishing mark of the experienced counselor is the ability to recognize resistance and deal with it appropriately.

Resistance may manifest itself in a number of negativistic ways. For example, the client criticizes the counselor, expresses dissatisfaction with the results of counseling, fails to hear or to understand the counselor, comes late or fails to keep appointments, remains silent, forgets the fee, engages in intellectual discussion using complex psychological terms, expresses negative attitudes toward psychology, desires to end counseling prematurely, is unproductive in associations or with unfamiliar material, introduces irrelevant topics, makes unreasonable demands on the counselor, is pessimistic about counseling, or expresses skepticism about interpretations.

The client's resistance may take less aggressive forms as, for example, agreeing unequivocally with everything the counselor says, refusing to get emotionally involved, being overly cooperative, prolonging a dependency transference, maintaining persistent facetiousness, forcing the process into a semantic wilderness of abstractions and philosophical notions, pressing the limits of the relationship by asking for overtime, perhaps, and expressing strong interest in the counselor's personal life. Shostrom's concept of manipulation (1968) is useful in helping clients define ways they manipulate others, including counselors, in order to resist changing themselves. Berne's (1961) concept of client "games" is a further illustration of client avoidance of emotional realities.

Two scales for organizing signs of resistance, and one study on scaling signs in order of intensity, have been reported in the counseling literature. From a hypothetical base line of ideal free expression, Bugental (1952) postulates five levels of symptom intensity varying from *lagging* through *inertia, tentative resistance, (true) resistance,* to *rejection.* The headings used by Bugental are illustrative of the behavior he is describing.

At the *lagging* level, the client shunts responsibility to the counselor, is sluggish in response, distractible, and concerned with intellectualization rather than emotional content. Understanding is difficult for the client, who must ask for frequent clarification from the counselor.

The *inertia* level contains more pronounced disinterest manifested by short answers, disregard of counselor leads, and fatigue.

Tentative resistance includes indications that the client is unwilling to continue the interview. Some indications are: arguing, excessive qualifying, showing physical tension, and inhibiting expression of hostility, anxiety, and guilt feelings. Bugental regards this type as temporary, but of crucial importance in the interview, since it is while he is manifesting tentative resistance that the client vacillates between more active resistance and cooperation.

True resistance is described as an intensification of the tentative type with more open and direct attack or withdrawal behaviors, such as making vague or diffuse answers to counselor questions, remaining silent, assuming a hostile attitude to counselor leads, questioning the competence of the counselor, or using vituperative language.

The most extreme form of resistance in Bugental's framework is described as *rejection.* The forms are generally extreme, such as terminating the interview by direct request, making hostile remarks about the counselor or institution, or refusing to communicate sufficiently.

Sherman developed a similar five-point scale on which interview units may be rated for amount of resistance.

> *1.   Definitely resistive—rejects counselor point of view or manner of structuring interview in a somewhat belligerent manner, refuses to talk about a real problem, or attempts to close interview.*
>
> *2.   Somewhat resistive—rejects counselor point of view or suggestions but in a polite manner, does not talk freely, or may show a tendency to contradict counselor.*
>
> *3.   Apathetic—takes no initiative, but accepts counselor suggestions usually in a noncommital fashion.*
>
> *4.   Counselor and client work together fairly well—talk together rather freely, although there may be some friendly parrying to advance points.*
>
> *5.   Counselor and client work together on a real problem—talk very freely, feeling of mutual respect is marked.* (1945, pp. 57–61)

Daulton (1947), extending the work of Sherman, studied forty-eight interviews of twenty counselors. She found that the most frequent and intense forms of resistance were rejection of counselor suggestions and denial of counselor statements. Reticence in expressing feelings was rated as frequent but not intense. It seems that these findings would indict counselor technique as a potent source of resistance.

The counselor must evaluate the significance of resistance signs in light of the individual client's expressed feelings. Some clients exhibit many verbal symptoms of resistance because of a less-inhibited personality and a strong verbal fluency; in contrast, others are excessively cautious or suffer acute distress before they actually verbalize their resistance. In other words, the signs and symptoms cited above do not have the same meaning for all clients. The "life style" of the client and apparent voluntary control over resistance determine the significance to be attached. As Thorne has stated, "Many clients, particularly in the higher intelligence groups, conduct their human relations as they would a game of chess. Every move is more or less deliberately calculated" (1950, p. 238).

Research on resistance phenomena is meager. In addition to the studies cited above, Mowrer (1953) produced a series of studies on the relationship between two parameters of the therapeutic process—psychological and physiological tension. Hypotheses that increases and decreases in resistance are associated with measurable tension changes have been studied. The principal techniques used to prove these hypotheses have been subjective ratings by subjects on "tension" and "happiness," palmar sweating, and discomfort-relief quotients derived from analysis of interview recordings. The tentative results indicate these approaches to be valuable means of studying observable changes in tension as a result of therapy.

Techniques for Handling Resistance

In one sense, all of the readiness and relationship techniques mentioned in preceding chapters are designed to build a relationship and, consequently, to reduce or to prevent resistance. How this is accomplished is an intensely practical problem for the counselor, because the resistance variable determines to a considerable extent whether a client will leave counseling or continue. We assume at this point that the main aim for the moment is to keep clients in counseling and to prevent their loss of confidence in the counselor.

Davis and Robinson (1949) studied the resistance-handling techniques of experienced counselors and found great variation in frequency of use and type. Those techniques used most often by counselors, according to the study, were questions, personal reference, approval, reassurance, nonpersonal illustration, and humor. Davis and Robinson had little to offer on the evaluation of the differential effectiveness of these techniques and indicated that frequency was not necessarily a measure of effectiveness. These authors found frequent use of personal reference techniques, such as, "I think . . ." and "I would do this. . . ." However, the frequency finding should not be construed as endorsement of this dubious device.

In the same study, Davis and Robinson found that counselors were strongly tempted, when encountering resistance, to use techniques of sympathy, reassurance, approval, humor, research citations, personal experience, anecdotes, and rhetorical questions. The investigators concluded that these techniques alone were not sufficiently effective to close discussion units effectively. The only exception was approval techniques (a support device) which was associated with high rapport in discussion units on vocational problems. A discussion unit is a discrete interview topic in Robinson's (1950) research designs.

The counselor's first step in dealing with resistance is to become aware of possible external causes in himself or herself and the influence of the amount of lead in his or her techniques. The counselor then can take judicious steps according to the following suggestions.

1. The *noting-but-disregarding technique* consists largely of ignoring the symptoms, but it includes alertness to increased resistance. Mere presence of mild resistance does not mean the counselor should do something about it. The content of the discussion unit which arouses resistance is examined for possible adjustments in lead. The counselor realizes that this type of resistance is a normal artifact of counseling. Instead of blaming himself or herself or the client, the counselor concentrates on understanding the unique defensive style or security operations of the client. Resistance indicates to the counselor that the psychic balance in the client is in favor of repression and anxiety control rather than expression.

2. *Minor adaptations technique* is applied by the counselor when he or she feels that something must be done actively to reduce the client's resistance if it has reached the second level in Bugental's and Sherman's systems (pronounced inertia, with an outward appearance of cooperation). Obviously, there are no rigid rules about the most efficacious thing to do. The main goal is to reduce the client's defensiveness and to maintain exploration of his or her problem. Generally, at this level, no attempt is made to change the topic.

One of the minor adaptations which counselors use is *lessening the emotional impact* of the discussion by moving to a more intellectually loaded aspect of the topic which has aroused the resistance. This tends to reduce the pressure felt by the client. Examples are referring to test results, using a nonpersonal illustration, or asking a question which can be answered in a matter-of-fact casual way. Rhetorical questions can be especially useful when anticipating resistance during the interpretation of personality-appraisal results.

A second minor adaptation technique is a *change of pace* effected by lessening the length of counselor lead, pausing, or shifting posture to a more relaxed state.

A third minor adaptation technique counselors can rely upon is the *judicious use of humor,* which often eases the tension felt by the client. This must be a natural and spontaneous act, however, since a strained or awkward use of humor, or use with an implication which makes the client appear ridiculous, will "backfire" on the counselor in the form of increased resistance.

Supportive and accepting techniques, as described in the preceding chapter, are often the keys to reduction of resistance, particularly when the client can accept the counselor.

3. The *temporary diversion technique* involves redirection of interview content to less-threatening areas when it appears that clients cannot protect themselves adequately by their own defenses. The strategy is to return to the painful subject at a later time. This technique is used with resistance which is hindering, but not yet obstructing interview progress.

The principal element of diversion technique is changing the subject gently. Secondly, counselors limit their own ego involvement in the process by assuming a more detached and disinterested attitude. This device has the effect of taking pressure off the client by reducing the speed and intensity of the interview. Korner (1950) speaks of a "disengagement" technique wherein counselors examine their own ego involvement in the interview and personal threat in the presence of resistance. In applying this technique, the counselor changes the tone of the feeling of the interview rather than the topic; hence, it is difficult to cite illustrations. The counselor assumes a more reserved and cautious bearing, limits interpretation, or reduces the speed and intensity of the interview.

A third diversion technique is the citation of related research findings, illustrations, a suggested test, or bibliotherapeutic reading matter. These devices often provide the needed change of pace without straying too far from the subject.

4. *Direct manipulation techniques* are used when the client appears to be aware of his or her feelings of resistance. Their use assumes a fairly effective working relationship and a well-structured interview. Because these conditions take time to build, direct manipulation techniques are more useful in later interviews. The counselor says, for example, "You have been spending a great deal of time talking about things you wanted to talk about; now let's talk about those things you don't want to talk about."

Interpretation of the resistance, a principal direct technique, involves an explanation of what the client is doing to resist. This technique helps clients develop a tolerance and acceptance of their own resistance, as well as an intellectual understanding of its uses and the difficulties caused when resistance gets out of hand. The counselor expresses his or her own acceptance of the resistance along with the interpretation. This acceptance helps to decrease the likelihood that the client will take offense at the interpretation. Examples are:

CL: I just can't talk about it.

C: You feel that sex is a topic to be avoided. Perhaps you can see that this tendency is serving some useful purpose which we cannot yet understand.

CL: Yes, that makes me feel a little better about it.

An example of interpretation of a transference-type problem follows:

C: (replying after the client has made a series of skeptical comments about the counselor after a preliminary exploration of family relationships) Do you see that your feelings toward this relationship of ours are possibly related to your feelings about your father? You felt you couldn't trust him and now you unconsciously see your father in me.

CL: I never looked at it quite that way before. I'll have to think about that.

Reflection of the feelings of resistance often is effective as a direct technique when the client appears to have an intense feeling, such as guilt, about resisting. It is an effective technique in the earlier interviews where interpretation might be premature.

Referral techniques are needed occasionally when intensive resistance is encountered. Counselors should assess their own therapeutic competence carefully before penetrating the defenses of a highly resistant client. Sometimes, if a counselor shifts the client to another counselor he or she can remove the source of external resistance which has been inhibiting therapeutic progress.

Threats in veiled form, though a last resort, are useful occasionally in a high-risk attempt to motivate a resistive client to change his or her behavior. This situation would be apparent where the counselor's role included, in addition, that of dean, personnel manager, or other authoritarian position. For example, a student client having academic difficulties has been resisting discussion of the problem. The counselor may say, "If you don't want to work this out, I suggest we stop getting together."

5. *Direct confrontation* or direct questioning in depth around the resistance theme may be required. For example: "What is your objection to . . . ," or "You are now playing the protection game. What is it you are protecting?" A more extreme position a therapist may take is, "So you don't want to play the therapy game? It makes you happy to frustrate me, and so you win the battle with me and lose the war with yourself?"

6. *Resistance in groups* often occurs under the claim of equality. Clients often assert early in the group process that they feel exactly the same about all of the other group members. The counselor leader must help members differentiate their feelings about one another more sharply. Yalom suggests that the following questions help this differentiation:

> *"Who are the members of the peace and tact movement in this group?"*
>
> *"Toward whom in the group do you feel most warm?"*
>
> *"Whom do you most envy in the group?"*
>
> *"If you were angry, at whom would it be?"*
>
> *"If you were on a date with Albert, what kind of an experience would it be?"* (1975, pp. 134–135)

Secondary gratification from playing roles in a group often leads to resistance. When a client has an image to project or a group role, such as being most influential, most wise, or most sexy, the consequence is often obstruction of the group's work. Clients are often unwilling to relinquish their gratifications from these roles. Encouraging members to share feelings after being excluded from the group or from the therapist because of such roles is often useful to reduce such resistance.

7. *Body experiencing* can sometimes help; that is, to flow with the resistance and experience it in one's body. Gendlin (1978) proposed that experiencing the resistance directly in one's body is an important coping strategy. The following interview excerpt illustrates how this approach might proceed.

C: Oh, so you are afraid to experience your anger?

CL: I'm not really angry.

C: Can you let yourself experience how afraid you could be to experience your anger?

CL: I don't think so.

C: Let's suppose you are angry. How would you feel about it?

CL: I wouldn't like it.

C: Would it be scary for you if you were angry?

CL: Yes.

c: Let's suppose you let those scary feelings be felt inside your stomach.

cl: They are a "tightness."

c: Increase the tightness.

cl: They go away!

c: It often happens that when you let your body experience a feeling, the physical expression reduces it.

Summary of Resistance

Since one of the counselor's key professional problems is helping clients to overcome resistance, this section was devoted to a discussion of the nature of resistance in individual counseling, illustrating and classifying its manifestations, and suggesting appropriate methods of handling the resistance. Resistance was regarded as a normal part of the counseling process.

SUMMARY

Although transference, countertransference, and resistance are ever-present phenomena in the counseling process, the counselor must deal judiciously with these conditions to keep the process moving toward satisfactory termination. Transference feelings, the projections of stereotypes from the past to a counselor, have an ambiguous status in counseling. Transference feelings can be useful psychological data. They also can hinder counseling progress. Countertransference, the transference feelings of the counselor, is a tendency which must be recognized and resolved by a counselor before counseling can progress satisfactorily. Resistance is the natural blocking of interview progress and must be resolved by a number of counseling techniques—from ignoring the resistance to direct interpretation. Resistance signs serve as useful cues concerning sensitive personality areas, general interview progress, and the nature of the client's defensive structure.

9

Interpretation and Body Awareness Strategies

The purpose of this chapter is to present strategies for developing understanding through interpreting and body awareness methods. Interpretive illustrations for the different levels in the actualizing counseling and therapy model are presented.

NATURE OF INTERPRETATION

It is difficult to formulate a neat set of principles about interpretation of personality data because the style and content are determined by the assumptions one makes about behavior change and personality function. Therefore, several illustrative styles are presented early in this chapter with some generally applicable principles and cautions cited later. Levy (1963) emphasizes that the interpretive process involves placing observational data in the framework of a theory. Then the theory is used to make further propositions about the observed behavior that are consistent with the theory.

The kinds of data which may be interpreted to a client usually are classified by psychologists into two broad categories. Some data are derived from test results presented and explained to clients in terms of statistical expectancies or, as in the case of projective techniques, as hypotheses for further consideration. Interpretation of such objective data will be discussed in Chapter 10.

The data in the second category are derived from intrapersonal data revealed during the counseling process. Interpretations of these data have the purposes of making the client more aware of relationships among personal experiences and of transforming dysfunctional feelings and behaviors into actualizing behaviors.

DEFINITIONS OF INTERPRETATION

Interpretation has been defined as an attempt by the counselor to impart meaning to the client. Interpretation means presenting the client with a *hypothesis* about *relationships* or *meanings* among his or her behaviors. Interpretation from this viewpoint gives the client more freedom in the resolution of his or her problems. Interpretation varies with one's theoretical viewpoint because, in part, it is a process of *imposing meaning* on events. It is not a quest for some mythical true meaning of an event. Interpretation merely brings a fresh look at the behavior in the forms of different language, new frame of reference, or revised theoretical outlook. The ultimate criterion of interpretive effectiveness is whether it facilitates behavior change in the direction desired by the client.

Interpretation, like so many psychotherapeutic terms, is construed differently by therapists. A classical psychoanalyst, for example, would label many of the techniques described in the previous chapter as interpretation. Remarks intended to confront clients with the nature of their resistance would be considered interpretation by some therapists as well.

Interpretation techniques are used by psychotherapists of most theoretical viewpoints. Client-centered therapists generally do not favor the techniques defined above and appear to restrict their methods primarily to clarification and reflection of feelings. The client-centered view holds that interpretation fosters resistance and puts too much therapeutic responsibility on the counselor. We believe, however, that most reflections of feelings are really mild or conservative interpretations. Whenever counselors reflect feeling, they must always *select* from the material which the client has presented. These feelings are emotionally toned ideas which the counselor judges to be the most significant of all that have been expressed. Therefore, reflection of feeling is interpretive in the sense that the counselor's judgment of significance is involved. The counselor, through additional efforts to clarify feeling, generally adds more meaning than the client did originally. On this issue, client-centered counselors would claim that they are not interpreting because they try to remain completely within the client's meaning framework. The evidence and opinions are contradictory.

There is a continuum of differences between reflection of feeling and interpretation, with much blending of the two. It seems, furthermore, that the alternatives are not either interpretation or reflection, but rather *what kind* and *degree* of interpretive-reflective response the counselor chooses to use.

Client-centered and Gestalt therapists, particularly, emphasize the liabilities of overintellectualization. There is a growing body of evidence, however, which supports the interpretive techniques of the cognitive restructuring psychotherapies. Most impressive to date is a study conducted by Rush, Beck, Kovacs, and Hollon (1977) which showed Beck's cognitive psychotherapy to be more effective than pharmacotherapy in the treatment of depressed outpatients. Also noteworthy is an investigation by Lipsky, Kassinove, and Miller (1980) which indicated that Ellis's rational-emotive therapy produced more significant changes in an adult outpatient population than supportive therapy.

A CONTINUUM OF INTERPRETIVE METHODS

REFLECTION.   In the chapter on relationship techniques, great emphasis was placed upon reflection of feeling. The key idea underlying reflection of feeling is that the counselor goes no further than the client has already *explicitly* gone with verbal productions, although the counselor is selective in what he or she reflects.

CLARIFICATION.   A technique which goes slightly beyond reflection is called "clarification," which means clarifying to the client what is *implicit* in what the client has just said. Clarification, therefore, reflects relationships or meanings for the client which are *suggested* or *implied* in the feelings or ideas brought out by the client's actual responses. Clarification deals with material which, in the judgment of the counselor, is just beyond the awareness of the client. Clarification requires knowledge of psychodynamics and mechanisms of which the client is usually not aware. The counselor adds strong cognitive elements to his or her reflection of feelings. It gives the client a feeling of forward movement in that it verbalizes material which the client may have felt only vaguely. It is analogous to the pacing of a young racehorse by a more mature one. The counselor goes far enough beyond the client's conscious verbalizations to stimulate further thinking, but not so far that he or she loses the client.

CONFRONTATION.   A third point on the interpretive continuum is a technique called "confrontation." Here the counselor brings to the attention of the client ideas and feelings which are *implicit* but of which the client is unaware or which he or she refuses to acknowledge. In using this technique, the counselor confronts clients with their own words, but relates past to present, pointing out similarities, differences, and discrepancies of which they are unaware at that moment.

DEPTH INTERPRETATION. Finally, in depth interpretation, the counselor introduces new concepts, relationships, and associations which are rooted in the clients' experiences, but which are considerably beyond their awareness. Some examples of the above levels of interpretation follow:

CL: Last night I was really bothered by a wet dream I had which involved a little seven-year-old girl who looked partly like my baby sister and partly like my little daughter.

1. Reflection:

"It was really disturbing to have such a dream."

2. Clarification:

"It bothered you to have an experience which suggested erotic impulses toward your daughter or sister."

3. Confrontation:

"You apparently have similar erotic impulses toward your daughter as you reported you had toward your little sister."

4. Interpretation:

"You are becoming more free to admit your past and present impulses toward those whom you love, even though it is disturbing to express feelings that are so strictly forbidden in our society."

Clarification Methods

ASSOCIATIVE TYPE. The counselor presents a hypothesis which draws together or makes associations between the client's explicit or implicit thoughts or feelings. Four major forms of association can be distinguished:

1. *Similarity.* The counselor may draw together two ideas with similar content as follows: "What you are saying now about your wife appears to be very closely related to the feelings which you expressed about your mother a few weeks ago. Would you say that is a fair statement?"

2. *Contrast.* The counselor may associate two dissimilar ideas. An example of this form would be: "I gather, from what you said, your feelings about your father are almost the opposite of those you have about your mother."

3. *Contiguity.* The counselor may associate ideas which are close in space and time. For example, "You seem to get these feelings of tension whenever you come into the biology laboratory?"

4. *Distance.* The counselor may associate ideas or feelings which are far apart in space and time. For instance: "You seem to have many of the feelings toward this person that you had toward your mother several years ago under similar circumstances."

The counselor may relate feelings or ideas to each other which have been evident in prior sessions and which seem to have some relevance to the client's present expressions. The counselor may thus be said to reduce the distance in time and space between the client's feelings and thoughts in order to make them more comprehensible, to stimulate finer differentiations, or to promote integration of feelings and ideas.

SUGGESTIVE TYPE. In this type, the counselor suggests to the client certain ideas and feelings which are related to material already presented. Suggestive clarification verbalizes this connection. An example is, "You seem to understand that your feelings of hostility might be at the root of your social difficulties."

Suggestive clarification differs from general interpretation in that nothing new is brought out in the interview except that which is only dimly in awareness or, by remote implication, suggested by the client's comments. In contrast, by the general interpretation method, hypotheses or meanings are imparted to the client which may or may not have been suggested by the client.

Curran (1944) uses the term *forking response* to describe a situation where it is important, in the counselor's opinion, to bridge superficial problems in order to reach deeper concerns. The counselor accepts the client's feeling that perhaps the problem goes beyond the one just stated, and the counselor broadens his or her reflective response to include references to the deeper problem. For example, a client is describing at length his scholastic difficulties and has included a few references to girl problems implying a lack of information on sex. The counselor responds, "School work has been difficult for you and it seems to have been complicated by problems with girls. I gather that sex is part of the difficulty. You seem to feel that all of these things are tied together." This response opens the way for the client to talk about his more emotional concerns and is an open invitation to move away from the topic of scholastic difficulties to the underlying problems.

Suggestive clarifications can be classified into five general categories:

1. *Pacing Clarification.* Here counselors word statements in a manner which will pace the client. In other words, counselors move just a little ahead of the client's thinking, but in the direction which they believe the client is going. An example follows:

CL: It's difficult to talk about these things.

C: They are painful to you. (Implying that growth is often painful.)

CL: You might put it that way—and yet I need to face them.

C: It's painful, and you feel it necessary to discuss it; yet would you say it is a relief too? After you talk about them you feel better? (Introduces a clinical principle.)

CL: Yeah. Once I get it out it doesn't seem so strong anymore.

C: It's like an internal cleansing process.

2. *Selective Clarification.* Using this form, the counselor selectively emphasizes feelings or ideas expressed by the client which the counselor judges to be of therapeutic significance even though these feelings or ideas have not yet been given this weight by the client. An example follows:

CL: I just feel so all alone. I have no one. I guess I'm just weak. You don't like me either, do you?

C: You don't think much of yourself? (Relates to self-concepts.)

CL: No, I don't. Oh, I guess I'm not that bad—there are some things about me which I like.

C: Some good, some bad, and some between. (Reflects ambivalent self-regard.)

It may be noted here that material relative to the client's self-concept is suggested to him directly.

Should counselors select the most important feeling to comment on, or should they reflect all those that have been stated? Though it may be desirable to give summary reflections in later interviews, it is our opinion that responses should be short in the first interviews because of the client's need to get release.

3. *Labeling Clarification.* Here the counselor utilizes some of the common psychological labels which may assist clients in understanding their situation more concisely.

CL: I just can't seem to get to the things which really bother me. I keep talking about all kinds of irrelevant things.

C: Let's learn a new word today. Would you say that you are kind of "resisting" the process?

CL: Yes, that's it.

One danger of this method is that the discussion may become too abstract and may sound like the table of contents from a textbook.

4. *Clarification of Unhealthy or Untenable Attitudes.* Many adjustment problems of normal people relate to unhealthy or untenable attitudes which are acquired in experience. Sometimes this takes the form of "canned thinking," where people act or believe certain assumptions about human behavior which they have learned from people without psychological sophistication. Bugental suggests other ways in which clients have crystallized their attitudes in unhealthy neurotic thinking. Many of these perceptions have come from general cultural attitudes and not from the personal experience of the client. He gives the following as examples:

> *Something is wrong with a person who feels both love and hate toward the opposite sex; you should be devoted to your spouse, and if anyone else interests you, it shows you are fickle or over-sexed. It is childish to want something you can't have. If you've once given up a habit, you should never feel any desire to practice it again. If one doesn't try to be the best in whatever he does, he's*

giving up, a quitter. The easy way is, ipso facto, the wrong way. If you have to learn *how to get along better with people, it isn't natural. Normal people (or, other people) know why they do anything and want to do whatever they do. If I were only in the right field, I would want to work hard and wouldn't have to force myself.* (Unpublished, p. 5)

The counselor should be sensitive to ideas, beliefs, or attitudes such as those given in the examples and suggest their fallaciousness through clarification. The following is an example:

CL: I hate my father. And there's no reason for it. It makes me feel awful because it's a sin to hate your father—especially if there's no reason for it.

C: You feel that a person just shouldn't hate his parents, especially if there is no reason for it?

CL: Yes, don't you think so?

C: Many people do have such feelings; we call them ambivalent feelings—feeling both ways about the same person. I gather, however, that this is objectionable to you.

5. *Humorous Clarification.* This type employs the use of humor by the counselor to help clients regard their situations more light-heartedly. Crying and laughing seem to be fraternal twins. Psychotherapy is not a laughing matter, but there are times when the introduction of humor may facilitate the growth process. Humor seems to help the client gain perspective and makes anxiety bearable.

CL: I hate this place, and everybody in it, including you. You make me so damn mad just sitting there.

C: Boy, you're really giving me both barrels today, eh?

CL: Yes, damn it; real shotgun barrels, too.

C: I guess this is the season for counselors.

Humor in this instance implies acceptance of the client's feelings and may serve to reduce guilt feelings. The counselor can also use it to reduce or put in perspective a client's strong feelings. It can also be a kind of "capping off" effect.

It should be mentioned that the use of humor in therapy, although effective at times, should be done with caution. It certainly should not be used to satisfy the counselor's basic needs, nor should it be used with anxious, guilt-ridden clients. Generally, humor should not be used until the relationship is well established.

GENERAL GUIDELINES FOR INTERPRETATION

Although there are no universally valid rules for interpretation, there are some guidelines which, if individualized and applied judiciously by the counselor, can help the client toward awareness.

WHAT TO INTERPRET. The content of interpretation is determined by the particular stage in the counseling process. In the early interviews it may be necessary for the counselor to interpret attitudes toward counseling and the meaning of resisting efforts. Counselors keep interpretations very general and tentative at first, the main purposes being to explain the process to the client and to open up new areas for consideration.

Later, interpretations take the form of explanations of how defenses function to keep us from becoming aware. Here, in the middle of the process, the counselor makes interpretations more specific in terms of his or her basic theory. Toward the end of counseling, counselors make the interpretations more general and vague to encourage clients to do their own interpreting. Counselors also have the goal of closing issues, rather than stirring up new problems. So, interpretations become fewer and more general toward the end of the process.

WHEN TO INTERPRET. Perhaps the most important consideration in the use of interpretation is that of timing. In general, interpretations are made very cautiously and, in the counselor's judgment, not until the client is ready to accept them and is at the point where the client can almost formulate the interpretations by himself or herself.

It is wise for the counselor to interpret, or to elicit interpretations from the client, after that client has gained some awareness of the subject area of the proposed interpretation. In other words, interpretations should rarely be offered "blindly." There are occasions when clients may be accelerated by a thoughtful "shot in the dark."

In nondirective therapies, reflection of feeling dominates the early phases of counseling, followed by the tentative formulations of clarifications. In the later stages, when awareness must be expanded and insights tested, general interpretation in terms of a specific theory, as illustrated later in this chapter, is used. Figure 15 illustrates the time relationships of this technique to the counseling process.

More direct approaches assume that a new conceptualization of the presenting problem and a clearly understandable rationale for treatment are established in the initial phase of counseling. This direct view holds that many clients come in feeling out of control. So, the sooner a conceptual framework can be offered which imparts hope and defines the counseling rationale, the sooner the client will become motivated and involved in counseling. This approach is well illustrated by Meichenbaum, Turk, and Burstein (1975). It should be noted that these alternative conceptualizations could be foisted upon the client or developed through a collaborative proc-

Techniques	Reflection of Feeling	Clarification and Confrontation	Interpretation in Theory Terms
Time:	First Interviews	Middle Interviews	Later Interviews

FIGURE 15. *Timing of Interpretations*

ess in which the client became an active participant. We favor the latter approach since it promotes more sustained client motivation for counseling.

There are times when interpretation may be inappropriate because the counselor senses that the emotional dam of the client may break. On the other hand, clients can be prepared for interpretations that would otherwise be highly threatening by establishing a context of unconditional acceptance as described in Chapter 7. For example, the counselor could discuss a "hypothetical" situation close to something the client is experiencing, explaining to the client that the situation is given to make a point. The counselor can then demonstrate that even if the client had done this hypothetical act, he or she could accept this and still feel worthwhile as a person. Frequently, this method frees clients from the fear of lowered self-esteem so they can express themselves more freely.

Often counselors make interpretations early in an interview so that there will be sufficient time to work through the client's reactions. This is true especially when potentially threatening interpretations have to be made.

There are occasions when interpretations are given more appropriately toward the end of the interview. In these situations it is necessary to prepare the client carefully and to present current documentation to support the interpretation. There are occasions also when counselors could suggest interpretations at the end of the interview to stimulate the client's thinking between sessions.

General Methods of Interpretation

TENTATIVE APPROACH. Counselors frequently are critical of their more active colleagues because they feel that their interpretations are given dogmatically and without finesse. This is a gross misconception, because even the highly direct cognitive counselor generally suggests interpretations rather than stating them harshly. He does not say, "This is the way it is"; but rather, "This appears to be this," or "This seems to be this way with you."

FREE ASSOCIATION. Especially in the early stages of interpretations, it is important for the counselor to stay *with* the client and not to get too far ahead. The counselor should not give the impression he or she is a detective trying stealthily to observe, diagnose, and influence the client. A main goal is to help clients become aware and to do their own interpreting. This is done through a process of loosening client thinking so that new relationships become more apparent. Loosening is facilitated by encouraging more free association. For example, the counselor reminds the client to "Say whatever comes into your mind"; "Let yourself go"; "Don't try to be consistent and logical"; "Just give me parts of ideas"; "Say it, even if it seems vague or unimportant to you."

Free association is a fundamental technique of psychoanalysis. As Sullivan suggests, however, "trying to tell patients what is meant by free association, and trying to get them to do it, can be quite a problem" (1954, p. 83). He recommends that the best way to handle this problem is for the counselor to demonstrate it to clients by having them associate to a particular question which may arise in the interview, for which they have no answer. For the counselor to ask them at that time to talk at random about the question often gives a convincing demonstration of the effectiveness of this technique. An example might be:

C: You seem to be stuck on this question of the importance of your mother's influence on you. Suppose you try stating the word "Mother" and then follow it with as many words as come to your mind in rapid-fire order. Get it?

CL: I think so . . . Mother—nice—soft—does things—silly—mad—stupid—damn her.

C: You really resent her doing so many things for you, and yet you like it, too?

This fragmentation and association of ideas often lead to relationships which the client might never have discovered. When the free association leads to significant areas, the counselor may then accelerate the reintegration process again by using short-lead interpretations, such as questions. An example would be, "This discussion reminds you, then, of how your past ways of looking at your parents and your present feelings are similar?" One of the goals of the counselor here is to move among the different levels of client thinking, pointing out parallels and contrasts.

A cardinal goal of all counselors is assisting clients toward *self-interpretation*. The client must get the insight, not the counselor. Karpman (1960) developed a self-interpretation method which he has labeled *objective psychotherapy*. Here the client gives the counselor the preliminary case data from which the counselor formulates questions. The client takes the questions home to write out answers and weave in materials from his reading. When the client returns, he and the counselor discuss the written materials and do further interpretation. From this discussion, an additional set of questions is formulated. At certain places in the process the counselor gives the client interpretive memoranda which the client comments upon in writing.

Because so much written material is involved, the Karpman technique appears to require more than average intelligence, cooperation, and persistence from the client. It is offered here as an additional device to encourage client participation in the interpretation process. The ultimate usefulness of this device, however, must depend upon the adequacy of interpretations made both by the client and counselor, and upon an evaluation of whether this intellectualized approach reinforces defensive intellectualization—a form of avoiding confrontation of feelings.

PHRASING INTERPRETATIONS.   Phrasing is a significant element of interpretation. It is suggested that counselors use "soft" words which imply tentativeness rather than certainty, such as "perhaps; will you; it's possible; do you suppose; I wonder if; would you buy this; does this seem to fit." These carefully chosen words tend to minimize resistance.

Thorne (1950, p. 301) suggests some acceptable phrasing for interpretations and suggestions:

"Would you buy this idea. . . ."
"Is this a fair statement. . . ."
"What would you think of. . . ."
"For what it's worth. . . ."
"You feel this is the only solution. . . ."
"Ben Franklin had a saying. . . ."

The best interpretations are phrased in the client's own terms and constructions. The counselor does not have to use the exact words of the client, but he should maintain the same general style and concept level.

Thorne (1950, p. 302) suggests some *unacceptable* phrases which are often cited in criticisms of interpretation:

"I think you should. . . ."
"The only thing for you to do is. . . ."
"If I were you I would. . . ."
"I'm going to tell you what to do. . . ."
"There's only one right way to do it. . . ."
"I want you to do this. . . ."
"There is a better way to do it. . . ."
"You must try to do this. . . ."
"If you don't do this you may be sorry. . . ."

COUNSELOR INSECURITY AND HOSTILITY.   Interpretations should not be made on the basis of projected personal experience of the counselor. Neither should the counselor reason that "this worked in another case; so it should apply here." If the counselor feels insecure about an interpretation, he or she would do well to avoid it.

Hostility from clients is encountered frequently and should not disturb counselors or tempt them into arguments with clients. Interpretive techniques occasionally provoke client hostility, and the fact that this feeling is aroused and that the interpretation is not accepted gives the counselor valuable data. Perhaps it would be better if the interpretation were dropped and raised again at a more opportune time.

REPETITION.   Repetition is an important interpretive principle. Since a useful and valid interpretation may be resisted, it may be necessary for the counselor to repeat the interpretation at appropriate times, in different forms, and with additional supporting evidence. Clients often achieve understanding after this kind of concerted effort (Raimy 1975).

Although repetition is an important learning principle, it is important that counselors reexamine their interpretive hypotheses and try to understand the supporting evidence, rather than pushing them repetitively on the client. One of the best tests is whether the therapist's hypothesized model of the client's dynamics can explain the *resistance* to the interpretation as well as the interpretation itself.

INTERPRETIVE QUESTIONS.   Interpretations are hunches or hypotheses based upon client observation more than they are declarative statements of fact. The question, therefore, is a common format for a confrontative type of interpretation. These questions vary from general leads such as, "Would you care to discuss this idea a little further?" through moderately structured questions such as, "How do you mean that?" "What does this mean?" "Wouldn't you like to talk about it?" "How did that make you feel?" to highly structured interpretive questions such as, "Do you think, then, that perhaps you distrust men because your father did not treat you well?"

In a special approach to questioning, Boileau (1958) suggests that often the client is endeavoring through some behavior to satisfy a certain basic need. His mode of expression or way of satisfying this need may be inappropriate. The problem, therefore, is not the need, but is more the manner of expression. He recommends that the counselor simply ask the client, "What's wrong with that?" This starts the client exploring his behavior to determine the root need. The client typically reacts with all of the social moralizing which prohibits such behavior. The implication of the question, however, is that he can go on with this type of "acting out" if he so desires. However, continued questioning of this type usually leads him to an evaluation wherein he determines whether or not this behavior is to his greatest interest and advantage. The main limitation of this technique is the danger of incurring client resistance. The following example illustrates Boileau's method:

CL: I just have to buy new clothes all the time.

C: What's wrong with that?

CL: Well, you just can't spend all your money that way.

C: Why not?

CL: You wouldn't have any money left.

c: So—

cl: You'd starve!

c: Oh?

cl: I know, there are other needs that we have to satisfy, besides being pretty.

Another approach to questions in psychotherapy is the idea that therapy is not so much a process of giving quick and easy answers as it is a process of assisting clients to ask themselves appropriate questions. An example of a basic question that needs to be faced squarely by any client is: "Shouldn't you be concerned about yourself, too?" As several writers, notably Rogers (1951) and Snygg and Combs (1949), have suggested, the preservation and enhancement of the self is a most important need. Fromm (1956) suggests the importance of recognizing the significance of self-love and respect. As indicated in Chapter 7, each client, from our experience, must cope with this basic problem of self-love. By the use of appropriate questions, the counselor can assist clients to ask themselves some of the basic questions which lead to answers needed for self-acceptance and a healthy personality.

Limitations of Interpretation Although much has been written about the value of interpretation for promoting awareness, there have been strong arguments and some data advanced against the overuse of the technique. The principal limitation cited is that interpretation is threatening; hence, resistance is aroused which blocks spontaneous new perceptions and understandings. Interpretation may have the effect of reducing client self-explorations. Bergman (1951), for example, in studying recorded interviews, found that when counselors interpreted at the client's request for evaluation, there was a significant drop in further self-exploratory responses.

Interpretation technique may tend to overintellectualize the client's problems prematurely, thus encouraging the use of interpretation as a type of defense mechanism. This happens because the client is searching for all means possible to keep feelings from awareness. The client isn't ready to invest responsibility for control of feelings in the counselor.

On the other side of the above argument, it should be emphasized that there is a tendency on the part of many counselors to think that interpretation is simply intellectual. This is not so, because many counselors are most effective in utilizing interpretation to get *emotional involvement.* The following response is an example:

c: You've told me about your family as though you were a disinterested observer; what do you feel when you are with them?

Another example:

c: You've several times lost the train of thought as you got around to the topic of your mother's death; I wonder if you're hesitant to show how deeply it still affects you?

ILLUSTRATIVE STYLES OF INTERPRETATION

Interpretation Methods in the Actualizing Model

The methods to be described in this section usually come later in the process when the relationship is well established and the counselor has enough data. The goal of all interpretive actions in this section is to encourage transformation of manipulative and character styles into actualizing behavior styles—the most functional in the hierarchy of behaviors. The following discussion is based on the actualizing counseling and therapy model described in Chapters 3 and 4.

INTERPRETING MANIPULATIVE STYLES. As people grow they need to feel loved; but life experiences threaten this feeling as people are manipulated by parents and significant others. Through these experiences, they learn to avoid the pain and to manipulate for survival. Manipulations are basically patterns of survival by which people adapt to their environment without the necessity of feeling. Figure 16 shows some manipulative patterns of the basic polarities with eight illustrative manipulative styles.

MANIPULATION ANALYSIS. Description of primary manipulation is the first step in manipulation analysis. As the client talks, the therapist begins to see a pattern emerging in which the individual is utilizing one or two of the basic manipulative patterns shown in Figure 16. For example, clients may continuously resort to the patterns of helplessness and stupidity, or they may utilize power plays and blackmailing techniques. Once the pattern becomes clear, the counselor *describes* to the client what seems to be his or her primary manipulative game or style. Manipulations are then analyzed from the standpoint of gains or payoffs. The active manipulations are seen to have possible *coercive* controlling values, and the passive manipulations to have possible *seductive* values. Gains are analyzed from a short-range, as well as from a long-range, viewpoint. Clients are asked to state what they see as the short-range gains received from the particular manipulation. For example, manipulations are most often used for control of others, exploiting others, avoiding situations, structuring time, and seducing others to work for one. From the long-range point of view, however, they can be shown to be self-defeating, because they alienate individuals from others and keep them immature and dependent, rather than mature and self-supporting.

Restoring inner balance is the second concern in manipulation analysis. The principle of inner balance is illustrated by the rhythmic loops seen in Chapter 3 which showed movement between the polarities of anger-love and strength-weakness. At any given time, a client might be at any one point on either of these polarities. If, for example, a client is mildly

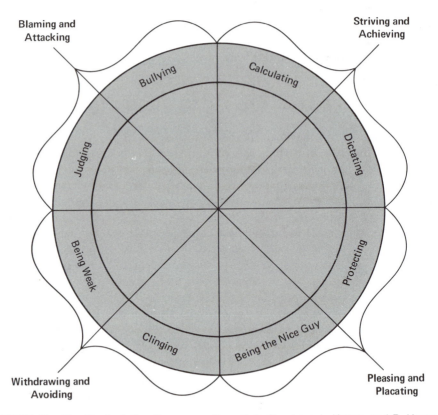

FIGURE 16. **The Manipulative Processes.** From E. L. Shostrom, L. Knapp, and R. Knapp, *Actualizing Therapy* (1976, p. 139).

angry, the therapist will facilitate his or her expression in one of two ways: by encouraging *exaggeration* of the expression of anger, or by encouraging *reversal*—the expression of the opposite polar dimension. In the latter case, the therapist is likely to encounter some resistance from the client, since this is not where the client is at this moment. Thus, it may be more appropriate for the therapist to encourage the intensification of the feeling of anger. The therapist's purpose in asking clients to exaggerate the manipulative tendency is to allow them to experience its apparent foolishness when expressed to such an extreme. The therapist may ask the client to express the opposite pole of the manipulative pattern he or she is demonstrating. For example, a person who is playing weak may be asked to try to play a dictator. The reason for this technique is the fundamental hypothesis that the exaggerated expression of any manipulative pattern is indicative of the underdevelopment of the opposite pattern. For example, playing weak by expressing hurt is usually indicative of covering up a strong need to express the vindictiveness that a dictator-type might feel. Expression of dependency is covering a deeper need to control others. Playing the role of a nice guy, a person may attempt to make others feel guilty for contesting him. He is often covering a need to express his hostility. The protecting person, in his need to feel responsibility for others, is often covering his need to be omnipotent. The therapist, in using this method, however, must constantly be aware of the principle of resistance and not *demand* the expression of any feeling but rather *encourage* feeling expression.

Integration, the final step in manipulation analysis, involves merging both active and passive dimensions into a unified working whole. In order to do this, the therapist continues to encourage clients to express all of their active and passive potentials, so that they might appreciate that actualizing involves the integration of all their polar styles into a unified whole. The actualizing person is like an ice skater who skates freely from one potential to another, creatively employing each in his or her movement through life.

In this connection, the client must realize that *self-defeating* manipulative behavior may be naturally transformed into more self-fulfilling actualizing behavior. Dictating can be transformed into leading, playing weak can be transformed into empathizing, and so on, as illustrated in Figure 17.

CHARACTER STYLE INTERPRETATION. Character styles refer to constellations of enduring response dispositions (that is, personality traits), which have significant maladaptive consequences for intra and/or interpersonal func-

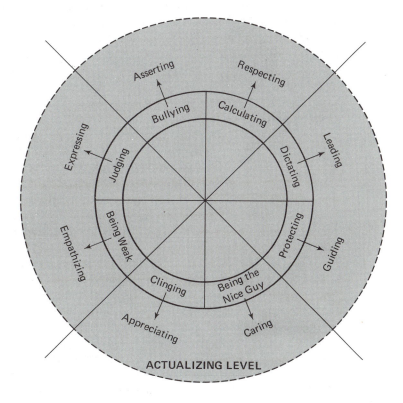

FIGURE 17. *Manipulating Styles to Actualizing Styles.* From E. L. Shostrom, L. Knapp, and R. Knapp, *Actualizing Therapy* (1976, p. 142).

tioning. They are distinguished from manipulative styles on the basis of the degree of rigidity of behavior and the extent to which core values have been lost from awareness. The correspondence between the basic manipulative and characterological style categories is as follows:

1. Pleasing and placating often are transformed into an *oral character* style. Such persons need *love,* but they feel abandoned by parents or significant others. They feel dependent and fear isolation.

2. Blaming and attacking may lead to a *psychopathic character* style in which attempts to discredit potential sources of criticism become so extreme one becomes convinced of the world's culpability and, consequently, engages in cruel and exploitive behavior without guilt.

3. As one begins to strive and achieve to the point of excluding pleasure from one's life, a *rigid character* develops. Success becomes the sole focus, and the fear of failure becomes a motive which drives the rigid character to a weary and joyless state.

4. Manipulative withdrawing along with rigidity and pervasive avoidance characterize the *masochistic character.* Such persons persistently denigrate themselves. They have little faith in their ability to cope with the world or to get along constructively with others.

5. The *schizoid character* does not exhibit a particular manipulative style, but, rather, results from dissociation from one's own emotional and perceptual processes. The schizoid character is like the masochistic type in that both avoid others. The schizoid, however, has no underlying desire for intimacy.

As the therapist and client discuss the client's present and past relationships, manipulative and character styles are uncovered. The client becomes aware of his or her primary manipulative patterns and learns to understand the muscular character styles that reinforce manipulative patterns. Character problems tend to be expressed in taut musculature. The client's body expresses the feelings of distrust and hostility in three ways, according to Kirsh (1973): (1) *Holding*—tight, spastic muscles bind feelings inside the body; (2) *Flaccidity*—flaccid, unusually flexible muscles also bind feelings; and (3) *Hyperactivity*—muscles become hyperactive so there is an inability to maintain feelings.

Each of the three basic personality levels has unique ways of dealing with feelings. At the level of manipulation, feelings are *avoided;* whereas they become *defensive* or *hostile* at the character level. Finally, at the core, these feelings merge into pain and hurt. When clients experience these feelings, they become aware of muscle tightness.

THE CHARACTER DIALOGUE. This strategy has a heavy confrontational quality designed to elicit and deal with strong feelings and bodily action. Most clients will respond to all four basic character styles, but they will respond in particular to the ones that seem most characteristic of those they experienced with their parents. Once counselors hear that certain parental admonitions obtain responses, they tend to focus on them.

The counselor, using the technique of *character dialogue*, "plays" the role of parents and significant others, expressing the negativity, abandonment, and rejection that they used to manipulate the client earlier in life. This process releases angry feeling, *character feelings* which in earlier years the client probably handled with tantrums. Part of the current procedure is to encourage body involvement in the form of kicking, pounding, or screaming "No!" repeatedly as refutation of parental patterns of behavior. Further illustrations of character interpretations may be obtained in *Actualizing Therapy* (Shostrom, Knapp, and Knapp 1976).

*Body
Awareness
Techniques*

INTRODUCTION TO BODY AND FEELINGS.   One of the ways for people to get in touch with their bodies is to help them become aware of expressions that express body messages. The following phrases illustrate this awareness of the body: "You *rub* me the wrong way." "I feel *touched* by that." "You get under my *skin*." "Get off my *back*." "I can't *stomach* this." "You give me a pain in the *neck*." "I can't *stand* that." "I don't have the *guts* to do it." "You *depress* me." Everyone has heard or used these expressions many times, and yet most people are not usually aware of the significance and accuracy of the body as a vehicle of expression.

A here-and-now approach to living suggests continuous attention to the body and what it is expressing at every moment. This assumes that one's body can be trusted as a reliable indicator of one's feelings. The recent body therapies—in particular, the Reichian and Bioenergetic—make this important assumption. Alexander Lowen says:

> *A person experiences the reality of the world only through his body. The external environment impresses him because it impinges upon his body and affects his senses. . . . If the body is relatively unalive, a person's impressions and responses are diminished. The more alive the body is, the more vividly does he perceive reality and the more actively does he respond. . . . The aliveness of the body denotes its capacity for feeling. In the absence of feeling the body goes "dead." . . . The emotionally dead person is turned inward: thoughts and fantasies replace feelings and actions. Despite this mental activity, his emotional deadness is manifested physically. We shall find that his body looks "dead" or unalive.* (1967, pp. 5–6)

Lowen further describes the therapeutic task and the relating of the body to feeling:

> *Looking at the body and listening to it is a continuous process. A patient's tone of voice tells me where he is, not his words. His words can lie. The body doesn't lie. The eyes may lack feeling, i.e., be dull or vacant, but that says something. His voice may be a monotone and that, too, is a sign. The lack of movement is as revealing as movement itself. But of even greater importance is the way a person holds himself, i.e., his psychological character structure.* (1972, p. 4)

Some Eastern approaches to problems of living, such as the Zen form of Buddhism or Yoga, stress attention to natural body processes. Proper breathing is central to Zen and Yoga meditational forms, since focusing on the body aids "turning off" cognitive processes and slowing down metabolic processes. Part of the effectiveness of meditational methods used increasingly in the Western hemisphere, such as Transcendental Meditation, is due to attention to the body. A recent line of investigation on meditational forms is Benson's work (1975) on the "relaxation response." This response is the common ingredient in all forms of meditation. It is elicited by continuously focusing one's attention on a single object or event (for example, a word or one's body experiences). This focused attention has been found to produce positive physiological effects, such as lowered oxygen consumption and blood pressure. The reduction in stress levels resulting from ten to twenty minutes of experience with the relaxation response has been shown to endure throughout the day and to be unduplicated by processes such as sleep.

Relaxation methods have been used frequently as adjuncts to counseling skills. While various forms for inducing a relaxed state exist, some on tapes and records, most current forms are adapted from Jacobson's early physiological research (1938). It is a progressive form of alternately tensing and relaxing muscles with relaxation messages to muscle groups. For example, one begins with the top of the head and moves progressively through muscle groups until one's whole body is relaxed. Once clients have learned this method thoroughly, they can relax in a few seconds with autosuggestive messages to "relax."

In action strategies relaxation skill is basic to anxiety reduction. The theory is that relaxation responses replace and reciprocally inhibit feelings of anxiety in the presence of cues which have previously elicited anxiety. There is a growing body of research, however, which is challenging this desensitization theory. For instance, Gillan and Rachman (1974) found that training in muscular relaxation could be omitted from the treatment of phobic clients without adversely affecting results.

After an extensive review of the literature on this issue Marks (1978) concluded that, "The overwhelming controlled evidence is that to achieve lasting reduction in fears or rituals, systematic training in muscular relaxation is redundant and time wasting" (1978, p. 501). Marks maintains that time is better spent on straightforward exposure to the fear or ritual-evoking stimulus in which the client remains in its presence until able to manage the resultant feelings. It is interesting to note also that controlled clinical studies, such as that by Hafner and Marks (1976), fail to support the assumption made by Stampfl (1967), namely, that it is beneficial to arouse anxiety maximally during exposure through a process called implosion.

A fuller awareness of one's body and emotions can be augmented by sensory awareness training and proper breathing. Holding one's breath is associated commonly with anxiety. Breathing opens up one's excitatory processes and helps one to feel anger, for example. Since breathing is associated with energy metabolism, proper breathing helps one to release feelings. Clients can also get in touch with muscular tensions and body rigidities through breathing exercises. When clients become aware of their bodies, they are more open to awareness of feelings; and when they are aware of feelings, they become more aware of their actualizing potential. This positive focus of energy is a substitute for tying energy to defensive and manipulative behaviors.

As with the lowly amoeba, human beings are constantly expanding and contracting, observed most easily in our pulse beat and respiration. People are either reaching toward the environment or withdrawing from it. Emotions, similarly, can be thought of as either expansive or contractile. Anger, for example, is expansive, as blood sugar and energy flow to one's muscles. Anxiety, or fear, tends to be a contracting emotion. Sadness is also a constrictive emotion, the withdrawal seeming to take place in one's arms and chest. When withdrawal becomes a permanent style, the emotions become bound up in muscle contractions, and the normal expansion and contraction process is stopped. This event happens to many people who have been hurt by the environment and by others.

Maintaining a rhythm of contact and withdrawal requires an understanding of one's self and one's body, of the fact that people *are* their bodies. It also requires hearing, touching, and seeing other people. Such contact is not possible without an awareness of physiological processes that make human contact possible.

BREATHING METHODS.   First, clients must learn to breathe correctly, since breathing is one means by which a person feels excitement and identification with his or her body. Since most people, when they are anxious or afraid, hold their breath to some degree, they should try to breathe as a baby breathes, from the diaphragm. In doing the exercises that follow, therefore, one should breathe from the diaphragm, by thinking of the diaphragm as a balloon that collapses when exhaling and expands when inhaling.

EXPRESSING THE ANGER DIMENSION.   One of the easiest ways to begin expression of anger is simply to have a "family argument." One person is asked to say "Yes" to another, and the other is asked to respond "No," while at the same time reflecting on past experiences of being required to do something the person did not want to do. The technique is to go back and forth, "Yes," "No," gradually increasing the volume and bodily participation. The exercise puts the participants in touch with their anger and their wants. Standing up to the other person, even making a fist, increases bodily involvement. It has been suggested that the jaw is the place where repressed hostility seems to center, so people are encouraged to stick out their jaws to one another in such a "fight." This also facilitates awareness of anger in the whole body.

A second way to get in touch with anger or hostile feelings is for two participants to turn back to back and begin pushing each other, gently "fighting" each other with their buttocks. During such an exercise one can easily discover feelings of anger. Although some people feel rather childish and foolish at first, these feelings, too, serve the purpose of the exercise, which is to help reactivate a more basic, childlike approach to one's feelings.

A third method for getting in touch with anger is for two people to interlock hands and push each other. If they can find a rhythm in their pushing and in allowing themselves to be pushed, they can discover the "joy" that comes from being able to communicate anger. It is joyful to feel one's capacity to relate rhythmically.

EXPRESSING THE LOVE DIMENSION.   The opposite end of the anger dimension is the caring dimension. In exercises for expressing this dimension, two participants, working together, can begin to feel their caring for one another by both saying "Yes," instead of saying "Yes" and "No." Saying "Yes" to each other warmly can help two people begin to discover their caring. Then, turning their backs to one another, they can rub each other's backs—this time, tenderly. Each begins to feel warmth—a loving, caring feeling—that can be expressed and received in a physical way.

Another effective caring exercise is the "facial touch." Most people, as children, were touched often by their parents. One way for people to discover their ability to care for one another is to touch each other facially as a parent might touch a child. For example, one person may say to another, "I'd like you to close your eyes now and I'm going to touch your face. I'd like you to feel that I'm your father (or mother)." Then he or she may go through a touching and talking sequence something like this: "This is your hair, and it's very soft. This is your forehead, and beneath your forehead is one eyebrow, which comes down here and goes up there, and the other one goes up like this and down like this. And these are your eyes (touching the eyes very softly). Your eyes are soft, delicate, wonderful. One eyelash comes out here and one eyelash comes out over here. And this is your nose, the bridge of your nose comes out to a very nice point and then goes out here toward your cheeks. Your cheeks are red and soft and beautiful. Below your cheeks are your lips. This is your upper lip, and it's soft and red and very lovely, and below your upper lip is your lower lip, and it's very nice and soft and beautiful. Below your lips is your chin, and your whole face comes down like this toward your chin and is very, very pretty."

Simply to say this to another person while touching him or her often brings tears to the person's eyes. This may seem a simple exercise, but if one is willing to take the risk of going through it, this physical expression of tenderness can be a very meaningful demonstration of the importance of caring.

EXPRESSING THE STRENGTH DIMENSION.   Stamping one's feet firmly on the ground, for example, gives a real sense of feeling one's strength, for the lower half of the body is where people get their support. In this series of exercises, people try to get in touch with their own strength. If one *stamps one's feet* firmly into the ground until one begins to feel the muscle strain in the calves and thighs, the feet will seem to become firmly planted in the ground, like the roots of a tree. This helps one feel a sense of strength and self-support.

A second exercise, helpful to developing strong resistance to manipulation in one's environment, is to lie on a bed with both knees up and to pound the bed with both fists and say, "I won't give up." Both movement and voice should express conviction. In this experience, clients often move to the opposite polar dimension and cry.

A third method for feeling strength is for the client to hold the weight of someone's head in his hands. The client's partner sits or lies down, and the client then lifts his or her head. In lifting or holding the partner's head, one begins to feel the strength of being trusted by another.

EXPRESSING THE WEAKNESS DIMENSION.   Just as holding another person's head enables one to feel strength, the ability to put one's head into another's hands helps one feel weakness or vulnerability. The person playing the weak role in this exercise lies on the floor and pretends to be a child again, perhaps only six months old and still not able to get out of the crib. The other person acts as his or her parent, and tries to make the "infant" feel its volnerability, its weakness, as he or she lies on the floor. When the "infant" is ready, it raises its hands, reaching for the "parent" and saying to him or her, "Will you help me?" It is important that this be a plea, not a demand. It should express great need: "I want you to help me, I need your help, will you please help me?" When this exercise is done seriously, it often brings tears to the eyes of the person playing the weak role. It also brings a feeling of strength and worth to the parent figure, who experiences having another person reach out to him or her. In the last part of this exercise, the "infant" reaches for the "parent" and allows himself or herself to be lifted up. As the "infant" is lifted off the floor, he or she can rest in the arms of the parent figure—rest his or her weight on the parent's body. In doing so, the "infant" experiences, more fully than in any other exercise, his or her own weakness, vulnerability, and need. Conversely, the parent figure feels great strength, capacity, and ability to cope.

A second technique for getting in touch with one's weakness is to stand with one's back to a couch, bent forward, with all weight on one's feet. The feet should be approximately fifteen inches apart, with toes turned in slightly. The fingers touch the floor out in front for balance. The knees are bent forward, and then slowly brought back so that a tremor in the legs begins. The vibration is accompanied by a tingling sensation in the feet and legs. Respiration now begins to deepen. When standing this way becomes painful, the client is instructed to fall backward onto the couch. The client is usually in tears by this time, and group members are instructed to touch and comfort him or her. The point of the exercise is to experience falling and surrendering to one's weakness and vulnerability. This exercise is illustrated in the film *Three Approaches to Group Therapy* (Shostrom 1974).

In a third exercise to get in touch with one's vulnerability or weakness, clients are asked to stand with their feet about thirty inches apart, toes inward, knees bent as much as possible, back arched, and hands on hips. The counselor then grasps the client's arms at the elbow and pushes him or her forward and down. As the client slowly lets himself or herself down to the floor, the client experiences deep feelings of vulnerability and surrender.

The ability to get in touch with and surrender to one's feelings of weakness and vulnerability is an aim of actualizing counseling. Everyone is afraid to give in to feelings; but, in particular, people are afraid of being weak. They feel they must be in control at all times. To surrender is to accept one's losses. The fear of falling is related to the fear of surrendering to another, especially parents and others who have manipulated one. As individuals overcome their fear of falling, they give in more readily to their bodies and their feelings.

GENDLIN'S FOCUSING.   Gendlin (1978) has developed a procedure whereby one can understand and integrate the relationships among thought, feeling, and bodily sensation. He calls this process "experiential focusing." His hypothesis is that words come from feelings and that feelings lead to freshly sensing one's bodily feelings. The following verbal exchange illustrates how a focus on feeling experience is achieved:

CL: I don't care about getting close to anyone. It makes me uncomfortable. *(Intellectualizing)*

TH: What is "it"?

CL: I'm afraid when I get too close to anybody. *(Feeling)*

TH: How do you mean?

CL: I get *really scared* of closeness! *(Deeper Feeling)*

TH: What makes that happen?

CL: I've been hurt too many times. *(Whole Problem)* My body becomes tight and freezes up in any intimate relationship. *(Bodily Response)*

Gendlin supports the goal of bringing together thinking, feeling, and bodily responses in therapy. He believes that sequences like the above illustrate that all therapeutic interactions are part of a *loosening process* that leads to freedom of expression and greater capacity to solve problems.

Cognitive Approaches

The focus of interpretation for the cognitive therapies is upon adaptive thought processes that lead to constructive behavior change. Cognitive therapies can be categorized in three groups, cognitive restructuring, problem solving, and coping skills.

Several assumptions about the most proper material for interpretation are held in common by this group (Ellis 1966). To begin with, past traumatic events are viewed as far less influential in the generation of emotional disorder than the particular way one responded to these events and the way one continues to respond to present events. Consequently, an emphasis is placed upon the cognitive mechanisms which presently sustain one's difficulties rather than on how one may have become disturbed originally. Cognitive therapists also assume that almost all important material is just below the level of awareness rather than deeply hidden and is relatively easy to find if the right questions are asked. In addition, dreams are not necessarily viewed as the royal road to the unconscious, as in psychoanalytic approaches, but are considered to be extensions of mechanisms which operate during waking hours. So, specific life events and cognitive responses to those events form the bases of interpretation.

The potential interpretive domain does not include all possible verbal expressions, fantasies, and behaviors, but is limited to a few key assumptions and belief systems. In addition, interpretations based upon the cognitive learning approach regularly go beyond the simply expository (for example, showing a client how he or she is overly dependent). The cognitive counselor attempts to explore the underlying cognitive mechanisms which sustain a behavior problem.

The process of interpretation is typically a collaborative, scientific effort between counselor and client whereby clients are taught how to differentiate facts from hypotheses and how to use observable data to verify or discredit personal hypotheses about their problem behavior. Clients are then shown how, through new kinds of thinking, they can replace invalid cognitions with more adaptive or rational thoughts.

ELLIS'S RATIONAL-EMOTIVE APPROACH.   Rational-emotive psychotherapy "is based on the assumption that human beings normally become emotionally disturbed through acquiring irrational and illogical thoughts, philosophies, or attitudes" (1949, p. 3). The therapist analyzes the client's feelings of hurt, anger, fear, and guilt, and shows ". . . him that these emotions arise not from past events or external situations but from his present irrational attitudes or illogical fears about these events or situations" (1949, p. 3). To Ellis, therefore, "Emotion itself is conceived of as *largely being a certain kind, a biased, prejudiced kind of thought*" (1949, p. 3).

Because it is believed that clients vigorously and forcefully continue to indoctrinate themselves with irrational self-statements and thereby sustain their disturbances, Ellis maintains that only an equally vigorous attack on these ideologies, initially on the part of the therapist and eventually by the client, will be sufficient to combat them. Interpretations are given several times when clients may be ignoring or misinterpreting them. This active approach to interpretation is often misconstrued as telling the client what he or she is doing and how to change. Typically, however, such confrontive interpretations are made through Socratic questions which lead the client through a process of self-discovery and questioning his or her own thinking (Ellis 1966).

Some of the major illogical ideas or philosophies which have been learned and believed by troubled individuals in Western culture are described by Ellis in the following excerpts. We quote them in full so the reader can get a more complete picture of the kinds of values and ideas which Ellis suggests as replacements for what is often regarded as irrational thinking. The following excerpts illustrate the problem of broadening the client's value possibilities and perceptions of his or her world so as to find the most effective means of construing his or her life circumstances.

1. The idea that it is a dire necessity for an adult to be loved or approved by everyone for everything he does—instead of his concentrating on his own self-respect, on winning approval for necessary purposes (such as job advancement), and on loving rather than being loved.

2. The idea that certain acts are wrong, or wicked, or villainous, and that people who perform such acts should be severely punished—instead of the idea that certain acts are inappropriate or antisocial, and that people who perform such acts are invariably stupid, ignorant, or emotionally disturbed.

3. The idea that it is terrible, horrible, and catastrophic when things are not the way one would like them to be—instead of the idea that it is too bad when things are not the way one would like them to be, and one should certainly try to change or control conditions so that they become more satisfactory, but that if changing or controlling uncomfortable situations is impossible, one had better become resigned to their existence and stop telling oneself how awful they are.

4. The idea that much human unhappiness is externally caused and is forced on one by outside people and events—instead of the idea that virtually all human unhappiness is caused or sustained by the view one takes of things rather than the things themselves.

5. The idea that if something is or may be dangerous or fearsome one should be terribly concerned about it—instead of the idea that if something is or may be dangerous or fearsome one should frankly face it and try to render it nondangerous and, when that is impossible, think of other things and stop telling oneself what a terrible situation one is or may be in.

6. The idea that it is easier to avoid than to face life difficulties and self-responsibilities—instead of the idea that the so-called easy way is invariably the much harder way in the long run and that the only way to solve difficult problems is to face them squarely.

7. The idea that one needs something other or stronger or greater than oneself on which to rely—instead of the idea that it is usually far better to stand on one's own feet and gain faith in oneself and one's ability to meet difficult circumstances of living.

8. The idea that one should be thoroughly competent, adequate, intelligent, and achieving in all possible respects—instead of the idea that one should do *rather than always try to do* well *and that one should accept oneself as a quite imperfect creature, who has general human limitations and specific fallibilities.*

9.   The idea that because something once strongly affected one's life, it should indefinitely affect it—instead of the idea that one should learn from one's past experiences but not be overly attached to or prejudiced by them.

10.   The idea that it is vitally important to our existence what other people do, and that we should make great efforts to change them in the direction we would like them to be—instead of the idea that other people's deficiencies are largely their *problems and that putting pressure on them to change is usually least likely to help them do so.*

11.   The idea that human happiness can be achieved by inertia and inaction—instead of the idea that humans tend to be happiest when they are actively and vitally absorbed in creative pursuits, or when they are devoting themselves to people or projects outside themselves.

12.   The idea that one has virtually no control over one's emotions and that one cannot help feeling certain things—instead of the idea that one has enormous control over one's emotions if one chooses to work at controlling them and to practice saying the right kinds of sentences to oneself (1958, pp. 40–41).

Ellis adds that there is more to therapy than changing some beliefs, but he does not seem to believe that it is necessary, as in psychoanalysis, to focus on historical events to show the client how he or she *became* disturbed or to depend on relationship variables for behavior change. Rather, he feels that after any necessary support or ventilation of feelings, emphasis should be placed, from the start, on *attacking* the client's irrational beliefs and on showing how he is *sustaining* his neurosis by still believing them. He then teaches clients how to *reverbalize* and *rethink* these ideas in a more logical, self-helping way. Finally, he encourages clients to engage in *activities* which will prove the validity of their newly formed and valid assumptions about life.

COGNITIVE PSYCHOTHERAPY.   Rather than focus on the content of cognitions Beck (1976) emphasizes the form or style of a client's thinking. Some examples are: dichotomous (events are construed in simplified black-and-white terms); overgeneralization (a person may conclude that he or she is a failure because of a particular mistake); personalization (one may indiscriminately blame oneself for almost all that goes wrong); and selective abstraction (a person may regularly attend to the negative features of life and overlook or discount the positive).

It is worth noting that both Beck and Ellis interpret both the style and content of a client's cognitions and that the above distinction is a matter of emphasis. Beck's manner of interpretation is less direct than Ellis's style. Beck emphasizes the tactful use of questions which lead to client discoveries. He also encourages a warm and supportive relationship and recommends careful timing for interpretations. While Beck emphasizes personal discovery, Ellis shares his hunches about what a client might be telling himself or herself in instances where the self-discovery process is going slowly.

Beck looks for the "schema" of the client—a general principle of life that governs feelings about events. An example is looking at life as a struggle with others seeking to destroy one. This schema then acts like a colored dye through which clients run their life experiences. This idea of schema is similar, in our opinion, to Ellis's client belief system that underlies behavior problems.

SELF-INSTRUCTIONAL TRAINING. Rather than viewing cognitions as the cause of emotional distress, Meichenbaum (1974, 1977), in his self-instructional training procedures, sees cognitions as part of a series of responses initiated by some stimulus. As such, they are believed to be one link in a chain, which can be most effectively broken at this ideological point. The counselor's interpretive job is to assess the role of a client's cognitions in maintaining the maladaptive behavioral chain. Clients also need help to develop more functional cognitions which then lead to functional responses as substitutes for less compatible responses in the chain.

This orientation response chain leads Meichenbaum to focus more on cause-and-effect relationships between various responses (that is, cognitions and behavioral acts or emotions) than upon the rationality of a given cognition, as does Ellis. Consequently, cognitions are interpreted on the basis of their adaptive and relational qualities, regardless of whether or not they seem rational in and of themselves. Whereas Ellis distinguishes normal from abnormal behavior on the basis of the irrationality of the content of one's thinking, Meichenbaum makes this distinction on the basis of how well one copes with these irrational beliefs.

Meichenbaum's manner of interpretation has been determined, in part, by the work of Luria (1961) and Vygotsky (1962) on the development of internalized control. Luria maintains that a child develops self-control by following first the verbal instructions of others, then by regulating personal acts through audible self-talk, and finally by learning this self-talk to the point that it becomes automatic. Meichenbaum's method of interpretation parallels this process. An adaptive set of cognitions are selected in collaboration with the client and then modeled by the therapist who talks out loud while performing a particular task. Clients perform the task under the therapist's direction, then under their own overt verbal control, and, finally, under the guidance of their own private speech.

PROBLEM-SOLVING AND COPING-SKILLS THERAPIES. These two approaches look at behavior disorders in terms of the *absence* of adaptive cognitive skills rather than, as in the case of cognitive restructuring, in terms of the presence of maladaptive cognitions. They differ, however, in that problem-solving therapies focus on deficits in cognitive processes or skills when a person is free from stress, whereas coping-skills therapies analyze deficits which occur within the actual problem situation. An example of problem-solving deficit is described by D'Zurilla and Goldfried (1971), who interpret disorders in terms of an inability to specify a problem, generate alternative solutions, and use means-ends thinking to evaluate and choose a particular alternative. Meichenbaum's (1975) stress-inoculation training emphasizes learning coping skills, especially skill in identifying nonadaptive self-descriptive statements which emerge in stressful situations. Counselors, therefore, need a variety of views on the place of cognition in behavior change. Some instances require an attack on the client's dysfunctional belief system; some demand an interpretation of the client's thinking in terms of Beck's criteria. At other times, counselors need to look for deficits in problem solving and coping skills. In the next section another cognitive approach is described—interpretation of the client's personal constructs.

KELLY'S PERSONAL CONSTRUCT INTERPRETATION. Kelly (1955) considers the material of interpretation to be the personal construct, which he defines as an anticipatory concept or predictive idea which the individual utilizes in dealing with the events or experiences of his life. Kelly, therefore, sees interpretation as a process in which events of life are compared and contrasted with one's constructs. A client makes a generalization about himself which he utilizes as a construct to predict his life events and behavior. For example, he might have feelings of inadequacy which would result in his predicting failure at a task. Unless this construct is related to the events of life, it is meaningless. The interested reader will find Kelly's system of constructs elaborated in his two-volume work (1955). It is too detailed to present a complete picture of his methods here.

A Gestalt View of Interpretation

Gestalt therapy, especially as interpreted by Perls (1969), is concerned with producing awareness through focusing on the here and now. Perls asks "what" questions, such as, "What are you doing now?" This method draws attention to immediate behaviors and avoids the distant intellectualizing that sometimes goes on when "why" or "cause" questions are posed. He draws attention to discrepancies in behavior such as, "You say you are afraid, but you are smiling. A frightened person does not smile." Clients are thus forced to do their own interpretation when their behavior, or disjointed fragments of behavior, are brought into focus in the present. This confrontative strategy also helps clients to recognize and "take back" their projected feelings to objects and persons.

Gestalt theory suggests also that learning through interpretation means discovery learning. The person has a new experience. He or she is made aware of his or her press for environmental support through various manipulations—playing stupid, using flattery, or being helpless. The person is led to lean on his or her own resources and to assume responsibility for his or her own behavior.

The key interpretive problem in Gestalt counseling is to work through what Perls calls the *existential impasse.* This is the critical point where the client's environmental support has diminished and the client feels he has not reached the point where he can cope with life by himself. The counselor's interpretive problem is to help the client get over the impasse and to take responsible risks. In the "safe emergency" of the relationship the client discovers that exaggerations and catastrophic expectations exist in his or her imagination. Finally, the client sees the total Gestalt of his or her life in the actualizing efforts.

MENNINGER'S NEOANALYTIC METHODS. Interpretation is an important method in psychoanalytic therapy. Karl Menninger (1958) presents a scheme for identifying various types of interpretation in terms of the time sequence and theoretical constructs of analysis.

1. Preparation for interpretation:

Having identified some connections, or certain common elements, in a considerable number of events in the patient's life, . . . the next step is to further the preparation for real interpretation. (1958, p. 136)

2. Real (content) interpretation:

Sooner or later, the therapist is in a position to say something like this: "This thing, then—(this trick, this experience, this defense, this defeat)—happens to you repeatedly; it seems to happen especially to you. You seem to have something to do with its happening. Perhaps it doesn't just happen, possibly you actually do it. You have done it before. Perhaps you have some hidden purpose behind it, a purpose which was once valid but which is no longer valid. This can be seen as what Fate does to you; but let us look at what you do with your Fate!" (pp. 136–37)

As Menninger recognizes too, such interpretations tend to be hard blows to clients. They will attempt to justify, to "not get it," to theorize, to digress, to dawdle at some of these interpretations.

3. Interpretation of resistance:

Instead of rubbing his nose in it, so to speak, one proceeds to the interpretation of the resistance. One says in substance "You do not want to see this for certain reasons." First, one points out that such resistance exists, then one points out how it manifests itself; then one points out its obvious purpose (and, of course, if one doesn't know what its obvious purpose is, then the patient's cooperation has to be enlisted in that search). In general, of course, the purpose is to avoid seeing the unpleasant truth. (1958, p. 137)

4. Transference interpretation:

It (the real interpretation) may be further obscured by various transference patterns and purposes; the patient may be bribing, defying, or seducing the analyst. (1958, p. 137)

It may be seen, above, that transference, as we have already mentioned, is a form of resistance to real interpretation which is yet too painful to accept.

5. "Working through" or repeat interpretations:

> . . . *Resistance will often cover with the same obliviousness the repetition of the same old pattern, so that all that was won by painstaking labor seems to be forgotten. . . . We have to begin (over and over) again from the beginning.* (1958, p. 138)

> *This necessity for "working through," for the analyst to repeat interpretations until they are taken hold of is a reflection of the extension of the neurosis into many different aspects of or events of the patient's life. His defensive structure isolates these events from one another, so that he is not aware of the common tendency running through them. In the language of some learning theorists, the "transfer" or "spread of effect" of the insight from one situation to other situations is limited or blocked. In Freud's words "One must allow the patient to get to know his resistance. . . ." Hence the necessity of repeating the interpretations as the patient repeats his neurotic behavior in different contexts.* (1958, p. 138)

GROSSMAN'S HYPERBOLIC APPROACH.   A type of value reorientation approach to interpretation is described by Grossman (1964) as hyperbolic therapy. This is an effort to adopt an exaggerated form of the client's defenses, impulses, and conscience. These vary from a rational supportive stance to a "devil's advocate" approach using humor, sarcasm, and ridicule when appropriate. The rationale is to shock or press clients so that they see themselves in more clear relief. The counselor does this by being more like the client than the client is herself or himself.

SPECIAL INTERPRETIVE ADJUNCTS

Written Communications

Written communications have become an accepted adjunctive method for individual counseling. Pearson and his contributors (1965) have reviewed the advantages, disadvantages, and future uses of various documents such as diaries, letters, creative writing, and notebooks on fantasies and dreams. While many counselors are skeptical about the value of such materials and their use in avoiding interpersonal contact, many others are experimenting with written communications as an adjunct to counseling and have become enthusiasts for the method. Progoff's journal method (1975), for example has been refined into an elaborate schema for recording and interpreting personal data.

Fantasy and Metaphors   Another stylized way of introducing an interpretation is to put it in the form of a fantasy (daydream), even using picture language like a metaphor. An example is, "I have a fantasy about what you have just said. I picture you walking down a path in the woods, coming to a fork in the path, and being undecided which one to choose. You unconcernedly flip a coin and run joyfully down the path chosen by the coin. How does this fit?" Hopefully, the fantasy is close to the client's awareness and triggers new ways of perceiving himself or herself through further discussion. The limitation is that in using this skill the counselor shifts all the way into the client's frame of reference, thus forcing the client to deal with him or her (or the fantasy). Sometimes it is useful just to give one's reaction in the form of a metaphor, such as, "Most of the time I perceive you as a great big soft teddy bear who stays in any placed position." Gordon (1978) has developed the use of metaphor as a central thrust of his counseling. These metaphors take the form of parables, fairy tales, myths, or short verbal images to give clients a mirror onto which they can project their life circumstances and choice conflicts. The metaphor then suggests a possible solution.

SUMMARY

This chapter includes a variety of interpretive approaches and illustrations along with selected body awareness methods. Interpretation is the principal technique the counselor uses during the awareness phase of the counseling process. The major goal of interpretive techniques is to promote client understanding and self-interpretation that lead to mature self-actualizing action.

10

Information, Tests, and Action Strategies

This chapter is concerned with two basic strategies: (1) the use of data as a tool for planning and decision making; and (2) the use of behavior-changing methods that mobilize clients into action.

ADVICE AND INFORMATION-GIVING STRATEGIES

To the man or woman in the street, counseling and psychotherapy are almost synonymous with giving advice. Offering "common-sense advice" in a friendly manner is probably the oldest form of counseling, the aim being to offer substitute attitudes and behaviors for those the client holds. It is an appeal to the client's intellectual powers through logical reasoning and evaluation of his or her experience.

Advice giving is generally accompanied by a heavy dose of persuasion because the counselor, in giving the advice, often has a personal interest in seeing that the client follows it. This point is valid, particularly, when a teacher-counselor's value to colleagues or superiors, for example, is judged by the behavior changes he or she effects in student clients. Although professional counselors give valid information when it seems appropriate, they seldom use advice of the "Here is what I think you ought to do" variety, mainly because it is a projection of the counselor's own values and styles. The importance of using proper informational techniques, however, was emphasized in Yalom's study of groups (1971), where information giving was one of the ten most significant methods of promoting constructive change.

Use of Advice and Suggestion

Persuasive advice giving is a standard technique used by unsophisticated persons. Nevertheless, there are occasions when advice in the form of suggested alternate courses of action for the client to follow might be indicated. The word *suggested* should be emphasized so as to leave the evaluation and decision about the course of action with the client. Examples are those situations when a parent is exploring possible ways in which she has been mishandling her young child, or when a client feels caught on the horns of a dilemma about which occupation to select, and for which the counselor suggests additional possibilities.

Sullivan (1954) distinguishes between *prescriptions for action* (suggestions), which he advocates, and outright *advice,* which he condemns. He claims that good advice is usually an elaboration of the obvious and an insult to most clients; advice based on incomplete or faulty data is often dangerous.

The use of suggestion and opinion is most appropriate when it is known in advance that the contact will be short and where a relatively inconsequential life decision must be made quickly. The counselor recognizes that this is a superficial, intellectualized approach which generally does not affect basic attitudes. If used sparingly and cautiously on normal people with situational problems, little risk is involved. Normal people generally are capable of evaluating suggestions and rejecting them when not acceptable.

Thorne (1950) suggests the use of persuasive advice in crisis situations where cooperative action of several people must be secured to prepare clients for major readjustments and to prevent emotional trauma. Examples are situations where reorganization of families is undertaken in cases of hospitalization, divorce, imprisonment, loss of job, or financial crisis. Complex classroom changes in school situations, for another example, usually require the concerted efforts of several people, obtained through the medium of persuasive recommendations.

Experiments in short-term counseling have been made from time to time. These studies often involve persuasive informational techniques. An example is given by Herzberg (1945), who uses persuasion and intellectual appeal to change behavior by manipulating the inhibitory powers of the personality. Much research is needed on the rationale and techniques of persuasion, suggestion, and advice giving before these methods can be advocated unequivocally as effective short-term counseling techniques.

In family counseling much use is made of suggestions, such as on child behavior management, to try out during the week. These interventions are not offered as advice, although they might be so interpreted by clients. The important question is, does the intervention result in positive behavior changes in the client?

Limitations of Advice and Opinion

One of the greatest limitations of advice giving for counselors is the temptation to use it indiscriminately and profusely. If they give advice excessively it may court strong resistance from clients, even to the point of causing them to terminate the relationship. Strong dependency relationships may be built up when the counselor meets demanding overtures for solutions to a dependent client's problems.

A chief danger, however, is that a counselor may be tempted to give advice which is not in the client's best interests, because it is a projection of the counselor's needs, problems, and values. This is known as the "If I were you . . ." approach. The client may take the counselor's advice and suggestions, then, later, find that they were not valid. Bach (1954) observed that in group therapy, advice giving originated when the persons giving the advice perceived the problems brought up by others as consciously or unconsciously their own. In other words, interest in giving advice is aroused when we identify with the person having problems similar to our own.

Even if a counselor's values permitted direct advice giving, he or she cannot know enough about a person's situation to decide what that person should do concerning such questions as, "Should I get a divorce?" or "What occupation should I enter?" If the client follows the counselor's advice, the client's situation may change so that the original opinion is obsolete, perhaps even dangerous. There is also the risk that the counselor will be blamed if things do not work out right. In any case, jeopardy to the relationship hardly warrants the risk involved in choosing sides in the client's conflicts.

Counselors using the client-centered approach to counseling are critical of advice giving on the grounds that its use shifts the responsibility for solutions to the client's problems onto the counselor, and limits client opportunities to make their own changes in fundamental self-evaluative attitudes.

The issue on the use of suggestive advice boils down to the old problem of good judgment on the counselor's part. The weight of counselor opinion, however, seems to be against the use of straight, opinionated advice. It certainly has gross limitations for extensive psychotherapeutic types of counseling. A distinction must be made, furthermore, between giving valid information and offering opinionated advice of the personal projection variety. Methods for presenting information to a client are offered in the following sections.

Case Management Skills

The management of cases often involves suggestions which might be classed as advice. Occasionally the counselor must advise referral, hospitalization, or some other significant move which, in his or her professional judgment, would be in the best interests of the client. Counselors constantly must evaluate themselves in terms of what they can do with clients. They must also assess client life circumstances in light of their ability to profit from counselor services. Finally, the institutional setting must be appraised in terms of what kinds of services can be safely and legitimately offered. Often, the conclusions drawn from appraisal of these factors must be communicated to the client in the form of suggestions of steps to be taken next. The principal issue here is what is the extent of accountability assumed or assigned?

TESTING AND OBSERVING STRATEGIES

It is assumed that students and practitioners reading this volume are familiar with basic principles of measurement and are acquainted, also, with commonly used tests. This section will cover some of the questions involved in the functions and choice of tests, as well as in the use of tests in counseling. Tests are viewed in this chapter as tools to be used in the therapeutic process and not as central emphases. We feel that tests have been used too profusely in counseling in the past, largely because they have been a convenient "screen" to hide a lack of counseling knowledge, and an "escape" from facing the real problems of facilitating client growth. Clients have reinforced this practice in their frequently stated reason for counseling, that is, "to take some tests."

One of the key contributions to clinical practice is the predictive use of tests to help clients make decisions and plans. There is also a continuing trend in the therapeutic use of tests, in addition to their traditional diagnostic use of helping the counselor formulate hypotheses about his client.

Functions of Tests

Tests help the counselor in surveying and diagnosing personality characteristics and problems with the aim of giving the client useful information about his or her own personality. A counselor who locates problem areas by means of personality inventories, problem checklists, and temperament tests often accelerates the client's exploration of problems and economizes exploratory interview time.

Clients come to psychotherapeutic and vocational counselors expecting to take tests to find out more about themselves; hence, they expect direct and useful answers from the tests. For the psychologist in a clinic setting, in contrast, the survey function of testing may be important for helping the counselor obtain hypotheses or to verify some of his or her hunches about the functioning of the client's personality. Here, the client takes tests without necessarily expecting to have the results given to him or her. In fact, some of the interpretations under clinical conditions frequently would prove very mystifying and threatening to the client.

Testing, especially personality appraisal, for personnel selection and upgrading purposes is under fire. Accusations of bias toward minorities and the poor, as well as invasion of privacy, have curtailed the use of tests for all purposes. The American Psychological Association has published a set of standards for use of psychological tests to reduce misuses and abuses of psychometrics (1966).

The diagnostic function of tests with children is well recognized. Counselors rely extensively upon tests for assaying reading and learning difficulties, for example, where several hours of interviewing would be needed to get the same information.

Bordin (1955) proposes that an important area which the counselor may analyze with tests is client sense of reality, by having clients try out their self-expectations through their own behavior samples on tests. Just as one tests one's abilities in athletics through tryout experiences, clients can test perceptions of their abilities and traits through the medium of testing. A by-product for clients of this reality-testing experience is the development of a desire to explore motivations and capacities further.

Discovery of interest and value clusters and assessment of life style is another use of tests and inventories in counseling. Clients generally know their manifest interests well, but they have little idea of how they compare with individuals in known groups, such as men in general or college women. It is this relative standing on definitive norm tables which gives tests their value for appraising the client's interests, aptitudes, achievements, and other personality variables. Thus, an important question which tests help to answer for the client is, "How do I compare with others with whom I will be competing?"

A third significant function of tests is the prediction of behavior. Aptitude tests are examples of instruments which take behavior samples from which the counselor can make inferences about the client's ability to pursue a particular educational or vocational plan. Predictions are made in terms of probabilities of success in a given program. The probabilities are directly related to the specific validities of the tests used.

Selection of Tests

In many clinical situations, standard batteries of tests are administered, such as Wechsler or Stanford Binet, Rorschach or MMPI, and the Actualizing Assessment Battery. Yet, for many clients, tests must be selected to bear more appropriately upon age and unique problems. In career planning, selection of tests is especially important because of special needs for accurate prediction.

Most often counselors select the tests which they think would be most useful from a standard checklist, much in the same fashion that a physician writes a prescription. This method puts the responsibility upon the counselor. Being, of course, the expert in the matter of appraisal, the counselor should have the prerogative of determining the tests to be used.

The counselor should suggest tests when clients reach the point of feeling a need for more data about themselves for the decision at hand. Clients may wish to know, for example, whether they have enough scholastic aptitude to succeed in college. They also may desire an interest inventory to help ascertain the major most likely to give them satisfaction. This principle of timing in test selection is especially important in counseling. If the counselor proposes personality tests at the outset, the client may come to overvalue them as a means for suggesting solutions to personal problems, rather than coming to depend upon the relationship to reach self-actualizing goals. If the counselor suggests them too far along in the process, it is very likely that the client may tend to feel that the counselor is baffled by his or her case or that it is more serious than was thought at first. The counselor must sense the most appropriate point early in the process when tests can be given and when it can be explained to the client that this procedure is routine.

When the client expresses a desire for more data, the counselor may then bring up the topic of tests and suggest specific types which would give the kind of answers sought. At this point, the counselor would do well to explain that sometimes tests can give helpful data on the problem and sometimes not. It should be stressed, however, that the client should have a genuine desire to take the tests as an outgrowth of his or her feeling the need for more data.

Principles of Using Tests in Counseling

Until recently, test interpretations have been performed in interviews. A number of studies have been carried out with school-age clients comparing group and individual methods of test interpretation. On understanding and memory of test scores, the results have consistently shown no differences between group and interview settings. A replication study by Walker (1965) revealed that with high school clients there were no significant differences in ability to recall scores in group and individual settings, but personal acceptance of test scores was significantly higher with individual procedure. In the same study, different methods of presentation were used, and effects on students of varying mental ability observed. A further conclusion was that no approach is equally satisfactory for all clients and that a variety of test interpretation methods must be utilized.

Presentation of test results by means of programmed materials has supporting studies to substantiate its effectiveness. Forster (1966), using a prepared program manual with college freshmen clients, found that such methods were effective in promoting accurate self-estimations from tests without emotional reactions often associated with low scores. Forster's results demonstrated significantly greater gains in self-estimation with programmed materials than with counseling interviews. The Gilbert and Ewing study of programmed counseling (1965) cited in Chapter 2 utilized information in program form and had findings similar to Forster's study. Holland's research growing out of development of his Vocational Preference Inventory (1965) resulted in a self-help program called "Self-Directed Search" (1979). This is a systematic method of helping the client move through a career choice problem. These studies suggest that test interpretations might be done more economically and more effectively by means of carefully prepared programmed materials for self-help than in conventional test interpretation interviews.

The following principles of interpretation were developed from best-known practices and research at the present time.

1. The first rule of test use is to *know the test thoroughly.* This means more than knowing just the manual. The test should have been taken by the counselors themselves and should have been investigated in the journals and in such collections of critiques as Buros's *Mental Measurement Yearbooks* (1978). The weaknesses and limitations, as well as the strengths, of the test should be known to the counselor.

2. *Exploration* of the client's reasons for wanting tests and past experience with tests is undertaken. The client's expectations are important data to be considered, since he or she may be expecting much more than tests can reasonably be expected to perform. Some clients have been to several counselors and have taken tests with each, yet they are still searching for the magic answer which they hope tests will reveal. Further testing adds little to these situations, and more of a psychotherapeutic approach is needed to help them understand their compulsive searching.

Clients have often been traumatized by tests made earlier in school. They may regard them with deep suspicion, skepticism, or outright hostility. As a first step, the counselor should determine the client's feelings about the threatening aspects of testing to avoid distortion of the results of the interpretation and possibly failure of the counseling itself. Adults, especially, seem to feel threatened by any kind of testing, whereas adolescents have had so many tests in school that most of them seem to take tests without emotional difficulty.

Hills and Williams (1965) studied the effects of interpreted test scores on client self-knowledge and self-acceptance in educational-vocational counseling. Clients who did not get results which corresponded with their ideas about themselves did not experience increases in self-acceptance and self-understanding. This kind of study emphasizes the need for counselors to be keenly aware of the emotional impact of test scores.

3. *Structuring* of the test interpretation session is especially important to prepare the client for meaningful, undistorted information. The counselor must ascertain the client's knowledge of the limitations of testing as well as the values for giving various self-information. An example is a discussion of the fact that tests do not give answers to problems. This is done in a casual manner to allow the client to ask questions and react to the counselor's introduction to the test interpretations. Test interpretation should grow out of the general discussion of the client's problem, with the counselor stressing how tests add to the pool of data about the client's personality.

4. The *meaning* of the scores should be established early in the discussion. That is, the client should know clearly what type of measure is being discussed—interest, aptitude, achievement, or personality. Most counselors probably could cite instances when they have been annoyed or embarrassed

later by having a client interpret his or her interest inventory scores to a parent or friend as abilities.

5. The *frame of reference* of the test results should be specified clearly. That is, the client must know at all times which norm group is being used so that he or she has some yardstick for judging how high a high score really is. In helping clients to estimate their chances of success in a liberal arts college program, for example, it makes a tremendous difference whether they are being compared with high school seniors or college freshmen at the institution of their choice.

6. *Test results,* not scores, should be given to clients. If tests are given with their expectation that they will be informed of the results, they are entitled to know the outcomes. Numerical scores are merely technical symbols for use by the counselor. Clients generally have just enough information about the meaning of numbers, such as I.Q.'s and percentile scores, that they tend to fix on the single score as "their score." Numbers are thus subject to the distortions which reflect the client's stereotyped meanings. Perception is focused, then, on the score symbol instead of on the meaning behind the symbol.

The counselor would do well to use trait terms and descriptive phrases such as, "Your high capacity to use language and to do verbal reasoning . . . ," instead of, "Your high scores on the scholastic aptitude test. . . ."

A corollary to this rule is to avoid using exact scores in interpretation. The lack of sufficiently high reliability in most tests indicates that the score symbol reported by the psychometrist represents a range or band of possible scores about the reported score. Brief mention of this phenomenon to clients often dispels their tendency to repeat requests to be told their reported scores.

Although counselors and psychotherapists are familiar with standard errors of measurement, it would be well for every counselor to pause periodically to examine data on reliability and the fact that it must be very high for the test to be useful. It should be noted, for example, that a typical correlation of .50 between scholastic aptitude tests and grades reduces the error of prediction over chance by only 13 percent. A correlation must be around .70 before error reduction reaches 30 percent and half the variance can be accounted for. The correlation must be almost .90 before the percentage of error reduction is 50 percent.

A third important point, relative to interpretation, concerns the language used to convey the relative significance of test results. In light of a lack of research on the matter, there seems to be a consensus that the counselor should use broad categories in presenting the client's relative rank. For example, if the client's rank is in the middle range of the distribution, the terms *average, high average, low average,* or *middle range* are meaningful. If around the 70th to 85th percentile range, the phrase *high* or *upper quarter* or *upper 15 percent* is descriptive, although the term *high* has unfortunate value connotations for many clients. The terms *low* and *below average* certainly have negative associations for many clients. Phrases implying rankings for low scores, such as *lowest 10 percent of machinist apprentices,* are meaningful without stirring negative self-regard feelings.

7. Test results should always be *verified.* Another way of stating this principle is that test results should be presented with an air of tentativeness. This cautiousness is especially important until further data are collected to verify the test results. Again, knowledge of all the various sources of unreliability in test administration and reporting leads counselors to the position that they should never accept test scores at face value.

There are many ways to check the reliability of a test score. Comparison of the score with past academic achievement gives a rough check on scholastic aptitude scores, although grades themselves are notoriously unreliable. Giving an additional test, especially an individually administered form, is desirable when the results are suspect. Interest inventory scores can be checked from case data on hobbies, reading, and activity interests.

As a corollary to the principle of verification, the counselor should never use a score in *isolation.* Test results should be woven in with other case data to check on the validity as well as the reliability of the test score. Decisions which people make as a result of counseling interviews are most often too consequential for the counselor to risk making predictions on skimpy and unconfirmed data.

8. *Counselor neutrality* in imparting test results is important since it is so easy to slip into evaluative phraseology. Examples of evaluative phraseology are: "You did extremely well on this test." "The results look pretty good; I think you will be pleased." "I think this test means that. . . ."

The test results should speak for themselves without the counselor's personal value projections. Clients, in addition, should formulate the evaluations for themselves. It would be preferable for the counselor to avoid overpersonalizing scores by indicating something like, "Adults with results like these seem to find college work quite easy," or "People with results like these would very likely find engineering training very difficult."

9. *Meaningful and clear* interpretations should be the counselor's constant aim. Clients should make their own evaluations, as indicated in the previous principle. However, they should not have raw data thrust at them for interpretation. Neither should the counselor explain the meaning of test results in technical language. Ambiguous reporting of test results invites distortion of the interpretations, since clients can more easily project their own meaning into the results.

If counselors are overcautious in making interpretations, however, they encourage the client to become overanxious and, consequently, to distort them. Though counselors should not go beyond their data, they should be willing to state their predictions with forthrightness when reasonably certain that the client would be able to accomplish a planned course of action, such as attending college.

Diagrams and profiles aid the counselor in giving meaningful interpretations. Counselors vary in their opinions on the appropriateness of showing a profile to a client, because the client tends to look for identifying labels and specifics. Unless used properly, the profile may be very misleading, as in the case where several tests are reported on one graph, yet each has differing standardization groups. Tests having comparable scores because of a common standardization population, such as some of the recently developed aptitude batteries or standard interest test profiles, can be presented on a single graph so that comparisons among tests in the battery would have meaning relative to each other.

10. Accurate *prediction* is the principal aim of testing. Test results should be stated in terms of statistical predictions. This rule hits at the heart of the testing problem—that of validity. So few test batteries have been developed sufficiently, or standardized according to the local population, that the counselor has the principal difficulty of giving probability figures to clients. It would be fine if the counselor could say, "Three out of four students with results like these succeed in law," "A person with results like these has a 60-percent chance of succeeding in engineering." In spite of the general absence of these more exact probability figures, the counselor can still rely on probability language in which to couch his or her interpretations. A counselor may say, for example, "With results like these the chances are very high that one could succeed in a liberal arts program."

11. *Client participation and evaluation* is another aim in the test interpretation phase. Interaction between client and counselor is valuable because it gives the counselor constant information regarding how the client is receiving the interpretation. In a study by Dressel and Matteson (1950) it was found that more self-understanding and satisfaction were associated with high client participation. Asking the client an occasional question, or asking if he has questions, often prevents the counselor from going off into long didactic soliloquies concerning test data. Pausing occasionally to allow the client to react serves to increase his or her assimilation of the results. Perceptual research by Kelly (1947), interpretation studies by the Bixlers (1946), and studies of memory by Bartlett (1932) point out clearly the tendencies of clients to hear selectively and distort and forget what they hear. So much of the research growing out of the Gestalt psychology approach, such as Wulf's classic studies (1922), bears out the tendencies to reproduce figures more in line with the "good gestalt." Clients, then, unconsciously distort their perceptions in ways which make their sensory data more understandable and meaningful. There is the presumption here that this perceptual distortion phenomenon also takes place in test scores which are laden with threat potential. The counselor must be alert to these tendencies so he or she can help the client perceive the results as accurately as possible, and see the distorting effects of the counselor's own motivational structure.

12. The interpretation of *low scores* to normal clients is one of the most difficult problems the counselor must face. We have found from experience that it is best to start the interpretation period with the client's high scores. This tends to build the confidence which is so helpful to acceptance of low scores later.

A second helpful device the counselor may use is to test clients' readiness to accept low scores by asking them to predict what they think their relative ranking might be on the trait in question. Clients often have a good hunch of how they rank. The counselor then makes a statement confirming the hunch with the test results. However, if the client does not have a clear idea of how he or she ranks, and if he or she is emotionally ready for the results, the counselor should present the results factually and wait for the reaction. The counselor should be ready for whatever feelings may be elicited—surprise, disappointment, pleasure—and be prepared to reflect these and help the client work them through.

The counselor should be especially cautious and tentative in giving low scores, since they may be fallible. The client who achieves scores which do not seem to be confirmed by other case data should be questioned to discover the cause. That is, the counselor should determine if the client suffered from excessive fatigue, test anxiety, misunderstood directions, or improper test readiness. The counselor should entertain the possibility that unreliability due to the test itself might be a factor.

13. *The appropriate conceptual level* for phrasing test interpretations is very significant if the client is to understand test results. If the counselor uses phrases such as *scholastic aptitude* or *linguistic aptitude* with many clients, for example, he or she conjures up a stereotype of foreign language ability. It would be much more appropriate to use the client's symbols and to speak in terms of *ability to use words.* Asking questions to test the client's understanding of the interpretation is one technique to help the counselor stay on the most appropriate conceptual level.

Tests,
Inventories,
and Projective
Techniques

PAPER-AND-PENCIL PERSONALITY INVENTORIES. These inventories are divided into three general categories—those which propose to measure presence and strength of such traits as dominance or submission, presence and strength of emotional problems, and, finally, the extent to which the client has feelings and problems similar to a standard diagnostic category such as hysteria.

Paper-and-pencil tests of the trait-measurement type have little utility in counseling because they do not give the counselor clear information with which to assess discrete traits or trait clusters. In our opinion, the tests have a second limitation because the counselor could not relate the tenuous traits to anything meaningful, even if he could find them. Few useful validity coefficients have been worked out using trait-type inventories.

The Actualizing Assessment Battery (AAB) (Shostrom 1963) is an example of a paper-and-pencil approach to measuring self-actualization. The California Psychological Inventory (Gough 1952) is another example of a descriptive type of inventory used in general counseling. The AAB tests, which now have been used in many validity studies, emphasize mentally healthy and actualizing qualities rather than pathological characteristics. Clients can be given this battery at the beginning of counseling to measure their self-actualization; then it can be given again at the end of counseling and compared with the original as an indication of growth toward self-actualization. Combined together, these tests form a whole greater than their parts; given as a battery, they produce a six-page case study of interpersonal relationships and supply information that would not be available by use of the instruments independent of one another.

Early diagnosis and understanding of a therapeutic direction is especially essential for a counselor when dealing with couples in therapy. The AAB provides the counselor with an in-depth narrative study of the conscious and unconscious personality dynamics of both partners and how they each function as individuals in society. The kind of early understanding that this battery provides can expedite not only the couple's understanding of themselves, but also clarify the therapeutic goals.

Assessment is relatively easier to share with clients due to the nonthreatening nature of the language and terminology of the AAB; therefore, defenses are not as irritated or stimulated in the client as by medical-model assessment data. This allows for more open exploration and use of the profile data with the clients.

The AAB is also useful in group psychotherapy or growth groups. Test results can be shared among group members, and goals or plans for group exploration can be agreed upon after discussing assessment profiles. The AAB has been used specifically for this purpose and has been especially useful with marriage or couple groups.

Besides serving as a diagnostic and therapy tool, the AAB is useful in training counselors and clinicians in objective personality assessment. Its test profiles are relatively simple, clear, and well defined in comparison to many other personality instruments. In addition to being a useful system to familiarize the beginning student with the process of assessment and its therapeutic uses, the AAB is a tool that the student will be able to utilize at a later time in professional practice.

Adjustment inventories, which purport to inventory personal problems, are useful in providing an opening wedge for discussion of the client's problem. Adolescent clients, especially, have resistance mechanisms which can be modified by personality test results because they are so curious about their own personalities. However, the questionnaire type of adjustment inventory often is unreliable, and its use tends to divert the client from real problems to a defensive preoccupation with test results.

The third type of personality inventory, which measures the degree to which a client has symptoms judged similar to psychiatric categories, is mainly useful in rough-screening. The Minnesota Multiphasic Personality Inventory (Hathaway and McKinley 1942) is an example. It has a "can opener" function also, to help clients get to the descriptive level of their adjustment problems more quickly. The MMPI helps counselors make diagnostic formulations, although they must exercise great caution in using the diagnostic categories of the instrument literally.

PROJECTIVE TECHNIQUES.   Another category of personality appraisal devices is the projective technique group which allows the client to project his or her own unique perceptions upon ambiguous stimuli in the form of ink blots, pictures, and three-dimensional objects.

Projective techniques are useful to help counselors make diagnostic formulations, as well as to give them leads for counseling.

A picture-story type of instrument, such as the Thematic Apperception Test, is used in counseling or therapy principally for client self-interpretation. Several studies by Bettleheim (1947), Deabler (1947), Jacques (1945), and Morton (1955) indicate the usefulness of having clients interpret their own stories. Morton found the TAT an especially useful device to expedite brief psychotherapy, since the themes and their interpretations tended to center the client's attention upon immediately pressing problems and their solution. One of the strategies of short-term psychotherapeutic counseling is to get clients to talk about present perceptions of their problems, the nature of their defenses and goals, rather than dwell upon past events.

Deabler (1947) uses the TAT as a device to reflect back important client attitudes so that further expression of feeling is facilitated. Clients then suggest their own interpretations, thereby generating insights more quickly than they would if the counselor were to use direct methods of interpretation.

Rorschach protocols can also be used to get immediate data for therapeutic purposes. Although the Rorschach cannot be used by clients in self-interpretation, as can the TAT, the findings from the content and the psychogram can be used to stimulate much therapeutically valuable material from the client in the early phases of counseling, or to get him or her off a resistance "plateau" later. For example, the counselor may interpret the life-style elements of the Rorschach psychogram as follows: "As this instrument is interpreted, you give the picture of a person who has difficulties establishing satisfactory interpersonal relationships, or as we say, relating to others. Does this fit with your estimates of yourself?" Often, if the counselor makes this type of interpretation early in the interview, he or she can pinpoint the defensive areas faster than if he or she allowed the client to approach them through the often tortuous channels of free conversation and resistance.

Pepinsky (1947) describes more informal projective methods for counseling through use of common objects, such as room furnishings. For example, Pepinsky, referring to a landscape picture on the wall, would casually ask clients how they felt about it. One typical response was given, as follows, when a bright client was describing her disturbances over her failing midterm reports:

C: You would like to relax. Would it help you to look at my picture here? (Points to picture on wall.)

CL: (After a brief pause.) I'm looking at it, but I don't like it.

c: Can you tell me more about that?

cl: (Clenching her fists.) The branches of that tree—they seem to be clutching for something they never reach—just like me. (Bursts into tears.)

Pepinsky summarized the values of the picture device as allowing the client to feel at ease in dealing with a stimulus which seemed external, thus enabling the counselor to get more verifying data with which to firm up his or her diagnostic formulation. A further value was that of keeping the responsibility for analyzing the problems directly on the client.

There seem to be many implications and many promising leads in the use of projective devices in counseling. A few examples are given here of some of the possible uses. Serious clinical students have access to many books on projective techniques which will enable them to go far beyond the brief introduction made here. The whole area of the use of projective tests in psychotherapy, however, needs more study before definite statements can be made of the utility of the methods.

EXPRESSIVE MOVEMENT.   Observation of the posture, speech, artistic productions, and gestures of clients has always been a rich source of data for counselors to make inferences about their internal world. Fidgeting and sweating are especially valuable nonverbal indicators of the general state of tension in the client. An essential skill of counselors is ability to read nonverbal body messages accurately.

INTEREST AND VALUE INVENTORIES.   Inventories in this category have utility primarily in educational and career counseling situations. They help clients to compare their casually stated or manifest interests with their solicited opinions on an inventory. According to their measured interests, clients are compared with other groups having known interest patterns, such as men in general, or engineers. By helping the client to see that the various approaches to interests corroborate each other and that his or her interest patterns are consistent, the inventories serve a supportive function in counseling. Conversely, inventories help to point out indeterminate or immature interest patterns. If a counselor should find that an adult client has no dominant interests, it may have much clinical significance, suggesting that the dynamics of his or her personality should be investigated. A lack of interests may mean, for example, that the client is incapable of identifying with a group, that he or she has general emotional immaturity, or that he or she is inexperienced. Patterson (1957) indicates that the emotionally disturbed client tends to be interested in creative talent and social-service types of occupations, which may be interpreted as escape into the arts or into service activities.

A second value of interest and value inventories in counseling is that they shed light on client self-concepts.

As a third use, interest inventories may be used by the counselor to predict the amount of satisfaction a client will derive from a given occupational area. Strong's research (1955) on the value of interest inventories in predicting later vocational choices and work satisfaction is illustrative of this function. Inventories of interest are limited largely to mature adolescents and older clients who have more stable interest patterns than younger clients. Sometimes, however, a general inventory made early in adolescence can give the client a general idea of the relative strengths of his or her interests, according to such broad areas as mechanical and clerical.

The problem of the use of specific tests in counseling is a vast topic and beyond the scope of this volume. It is assumed that the general reader is familiar with tests commonly used. If not, we recommend Anastasi (1976) and Cronbach (1970) as good sources.

APTITUDE AND ACHIEVEMENT TESTS.   There is extensive literature on aptitude and achievement testing. The purpose of this section is only to point out some of the principal informational uses of this type of test in the counseling relationship.

One function of aptitude and achievement tests is to give the client support. Frequently clients feel "stupid" or "inadequate" without factual bases for such feelings. If used along with psychotherapeutic techniques, a test of aptitude for scholastic work, for example, can help to give clients a more realistic indication of approximately where they would stand relative to the group in which they would compete. This group may be the general population, college freshmen, engineering freshmen, art students, or other groups for which the test is normed. It is often reassuring to clients to have more accurate knowledge of where they stand so that more realistic planning can be undertaken.

A second function of aptitude and achievement tests in counseling is to give the counselor a basis upon which to make predictions of the possible success of a client in a given general or specific effort. Examples are predicting success for a client in engineering training, a college liberal arts program, or a teacher selection program. Validities of tests and prediction tables are not as useful as counselors would like, though such tests are better than choices based upon whimsy.

Aptitude testing often serves a third, but oblique, function in counseling. If the client is threatened easily by judgmental situations, doubts his or her ability, or has discrepancies between ability and ambition, the testing program catapults these anxieties forcefully into the relationship, where the counselor can deal with them psychotherapeutically.

The main purpose of all testing in counseling is to provide clients with reliable and valid information about themselves so they will be able to make wise choices.

ACTION STRATEGIES

Since a key client goal is to act in some way to solve a personal problem, counselors need methods to help clients move from insight, awareness, or understanding to action (deciding, choosing, planning, and doing).

Counselors must help clients choose the best strategy for their problems—a basic decision-making process or behavior-changing process. We do not assume, as some theorists do, that awareness or insight is sufficient for the client to act appropriately. We will describe some illustrative methods in two basic strategies—one a general problem-solving model, and the other a cluster of skills for changing specific behaviors. These action approaches, furthermore, are some specific things a counselor can do to bring about mastery and behavior change goals at the actualizing level of our theory. The theoretical and experimental base is social learning theory, especially as advanced by Bandura (1969), and cognitive behavior change, as described by Meichenbaum (1977).

It is assumed also that the action strategies discussed below are carried out in the framework of an effective relationship. Mickelson and Stevic (1971) found, for example, that client information-seeking behavior was more effective when the action methods were conducted by counselors manifesting high-level facilitative conditions of warmth, empathy, and genuineness than by counselors skilled in action methods but low on facilitative conditions.

Problem-Solving Process and Skills

PROCESS.   The steps below follow general problem-solving sequences and are applied to many problems, but most of the illustrations are in the area of educational and career planning as exemplified by Krumboltz and Sheppard (1969). These steps are similar to our general counseling problem-solving process outlined in Chapter 4. These general steps are:

1.   Establish a *relationship* and get the client *involved.* The client must be interested in the process and have hope that he or she has the power to make decisions that will influence his or her life profoundly.

2.   State and clarify the *problem* and determine *goals.*

3.   Explore *alternatives* to the apparent solutions.

4.   Gather relevant *information.* This may take the form of active seeking and reading, statements of fact by the counselor, simulation games, films, or tests.

5.   Explore *implications* of information and *consequences* of the alternatives.

6.   Clarify *values* that underlie personal choices. Clients must know what they desire and the order in which they value those desires. The counselor leads the client into exploration of interests, competencies, family circumstances, social expectations, and realities.

7.   *Reexamine the goals,* alternative choices, risks, and consequences. A final check on understanding the information and implications is made before the final decision.

8.   *Decide* on one of the alternatives and formulate a *plan* or course of action implementing that decision.

9.   *Generalize* the process to new life situations.

10. *Try out* the plan for implementing the decision with periodic *reevaluation* in light of new information and changing circumstances.

Most people have limited life experiences in making formal decisions and are generally unfamiliar with this rational process. Therefore, many clients must be taught this process through problem-solving interviews, direct trial-and-error experiences, and simulations, such as "Career Games," "Marriage Games," and "War Games." Young clients often ask outright, "What shall I do?" "What course should I take?" "Should I try drugs?" "What career should I choose?" "What college should I apply to?" Instead of giving advice or opinions it is preferable to say, "I can't tell you because I don't know what is best for you; but I can help you decide for yourself what to do. Would you like to learn how?" There is abundant evidence that school-age youth make poor-quality decisions about many areas of their lives (Gelatt and Brew 1980).

Decisions in the area of interpersonal problems, such as sexual behavior involving previously learned response patterns, are more complicated. Solutions to these problems involve relearning methods, as well as rational problem-solving described above. Adult clients who face difficult choices, such as what to do with rebellious children, dependent relatives, errant spouses, or changes of work locale, must be taught this same problem-solving process as a substitute for acting on impulses, stereotypes, or advice.

SKILLS.   Most problem-solving skills are combinations of those described in other contexts: problem identification, goal setting, informing, interpreting, diagnosing, and evaluating feedback. There is a skill applicable to Step 3, generating and weighing alternatives, called *force-field* analysis. This skill utilizes physics concepts of fields of force and polarized valences. It is a method of comparing personal and social forces which are propelling clients toward goals and distracting them from goals at the same time. Force-field skills are applicable to many kinds of decision-making situations. The client's goal is stated briefly at the top of Figure 18, and the direction of solution is indicated by an arrow. The forces pushing him or her toward an alternative goal (in this simple illustration, to reduce weight by three pounds a week for six weeks) are indicated by a plus sign, and those working against him or her by a minus sign. After listing the + and − forces, clients can see more clearly where they are in relation to the feasibility of their goals. They can then rank the forces on their strength by rating each from 1 to 3. Now the client can decide on a strategy of strengthening the + forces or weakening the − forces. If it is a conflict-of-choice problem, each alternative goal can be analyzed and then compared.

Goal statements are derived from problem statements and have characteristics of specificity and clarity of expected outcome. A client says, for example, "My problem is that I'm lonely; it really hurts." The skill of stating goals comes in when deciding the best time to urge the client to stop talking about loneliness and start talking about a goal for new

GOAL: Reducing weight by three pounds a week for six weeks

+	Rank	—	Rank
Spouse likes me thinner	1	Like rich food	3
Better for my health	2	Dislike diets and diet foods	1
Live longer	3	Lack knowledge of low-calorie foods	2
Clothes will fit better	1	Will smoke instead of eat	2
Less fatigue	3	Three pounds seems too much in a week	1

**Balance
Point for
Forces**

FIGURE 18.   Illustration of Force Field Analysis. From L. M. Brammer, *The Helping Relationship: Process and Skills* (1979, p. 136).

behavior that can reduce the loneliness. Restated, the goal might be to relieve some of the loneliness by making two new acquaintances during the coming week and exploring common interests with them. While making new friends often doesn't relieve the loneliness totally, at least it is a tangible start. So, counselor and client can work on specific actualizing behaviors which will reach these goals.

Behavior-Changing Skills   MODELING. Modeling is a method of learning by vicarious experience or imitation, such as watching the performance of others. The research evidence (Bandura 1969) suggests that a wide variety of behavior can be changed through modeling. Common sense experience attests to the power of examples also. Clients tend to do what the counselor does. If counselors use colorful street language to express themselves, so will the clients; if counselors disclose personal data about themselves, the clients will be more inclined to do so also. One of the problems in helping interviews is that clients do not know what to do, and verbal explanations often do not help. If the counselor models expression of feeling, this gives the client a clearer picture of what behavior is expected. Another problem is that the counselor's behavior must be at a higher level of functioning than the client's performance so that he or she has a behavioral model to work up to (Carkhuff 1969).

Role playing is another example of vicarious behavior where clients can see, through roles performed by others, what is expected. If they are fearful of approaching an employer about a job, for example, the counselor can perform the role of an applicant (the client), while the client acts as the employer. The two then continue until the client sees other ways of acting in an employment interview. Then the clients try on the new behavior themselves through reversing roles and having them critiqued repeatedly until they learn the new behavior to their satisfaction.

A third example of modeling effectivenss is the removal of fears by observing fearless behavior in a model, acquiring information about the feared object, and finally, having a direct experience with the threatening object with no ill effects. This type of situation would be effective with fears of snakes or of making speeches, for example.

Modeling seems to be most effective when the model has characteristics of credibility, competence, knowledge, and influence. If the models possess qualities similar to counselors, they are effective. Advertising methods take advantage of these facts. An implication of these findings for counselors is to discover which qualities are most attractive to clients and then use them as guidelines for selecting models.

Modeling can be done by live, filmed, or taped methods. Although live methods have some advantages, such as maintenance of interest, filmed versions allow for more careful emphasis on the behaviors that one wants to model. An example of a helping situation with delinquent boys, which utilized live college-age models, is the work of Sarason (1968). Adolescent boys observed special modeling of the following situations: (1) career planning; (2) motivation and interests; (3) attitudes toward work and education; and (4) utility of socially appropriate behavior. When the boys observed socially acceptable models, they improved their own planning skills and ability to think in socially positive terms. The models were attractive to the boys, and role-playing methods sustained their interest.

Filmed models have also been used with effectiveness. Hosford and Sorenson (1969) used audio tape and filmed models successfully with fourth to sixth graders who wanted to speak up more in class. Motivating teenage students to do the investigational work necessary to career planning is a problem also. Stewart (1969), using group models on audio tape, found that students improved their interest in career information and more actively explored sources of information after listening to the tapes.

General principles of using modeling are:

1. Determine which features of a model would be most *attractive* to the client.
2. Decide upon the *objectives* of the modeling.
3. Choose *believable models* similar to the clients in age, sex, and race.
4. Decide if *live or simulated modeling* would be more appropriate and practical.
5. Design a *modeling format, script,* or role-playing sequence.
6. Conduct the *modeling exercise.*
7. Discuss the *client's reactions* in terms of feelings, learnings, and suggestions.
8. Recognize that *informally we are modeling behaviors constantly* for clients.

REWARDING. At several points in this book we have described the reinforcing, or rewarding, effect of various helping procedures. This section will develop this idea as a consciously applied skill. The basic idea is that rewarded behavior tends to be repeated. Another striking characteristic of rewards is that a wide variety of events can have reinforcing functions. We can use reinforcement: (1) to overcome behavior deficiencies (as in encouraging a client to plan ahead); (2) to change undesirable behavior (as in chronic stealing); and (3) to maintain present responses (as in encouraging statements of feeling).

Although the idea of using rewards to shape behavior is a simple one, there are some pitfalls. Most of the principles of reinforcement have come from animal learning studies in which animals were deprived of food and water, which then became the reinforcers. Since human responses are so much more complex, rewards have varied meanings. In helping situations we depend mainly on words, which have different effects depending on the cultural background of the client. Praise words, such as *good job,* for example, are used commonly, but soon lose their effect because of overuse, and because they have differing levels of potency for different people. Verbal rewards are most effective when the counselor and client are working toward common goals. They are resented as blatant manipulation when used to influence clients in ways that are not in their apparent best interests.

Some *general principles* in using reinforcement as a skill are that the reward, or incentive system, must be capable of maintaining a high level of action over a *long period.* In other words, we want the learning to be lasting. Secondly, we want the reward to be dependent on the appearance of the behavior we want. We want the *desired behavior rewarded,* which is difficult in ordinary life situations because the reward is often badly timed or is given haphazardly. As a result, the undesired behavior is rewarded. Finally, the reward must be *strong* enough and given *often* enough for the desired behavior to be repeated. We also want the behavior to *generalize* to similar situations when the rewards are not present, as in being able to solve problems in other contexts. This reinforcement process is aided by using natural settings, varying the reward, and rewarding conditions systematically.

The *general strategy* for using rewards is to plan them selectively in a pattern so that the desired behavior is emitted in the form and sequence desired. This is a *reinforcement schedule* or *contingency.* We apply these stimuli (such as praise) in the appropriate strength and frequency until the appearance of the desired behavior is as strong and as frequent as required. With children, tangible reinforcers such as toys and candy are used. Adults respond to money, usually. The strategy begins with finding the *appropriate type* and *strength* of reinforcing agent.

Using tangible reinforcers is very controversial since some claim it to be similar to bribing. This argument is not relevant here because bribery is "pay" before the act, whereas reinforcers are given after the act is performed. Tangible reinforcers have a place if they are *not* used: (1) to *control* others; (2) to reward an act required in *daily living;* (3) to stop undesirable behavior (such as giving ice cream to stop crying; (4) to *replace* intrinsic rewards (such as self-satisfaction); (5) to *affect* others *adversely* (such as favoritism with rewards). When tangible reinforcers are used, it is understood that they are an expedient to get the desired behavior more fixed and that they should be reduced as soon as possible. It is hoped that more *intrinsic* personal rewards will take their place and that people of all ages will outgrow their dependence on "gold stars." We must recognize, however, that people seemingly never outgrow their need for praise and affection, so these usually remain through life as powerful reinforcers in the helping process.

Generally, it is desirable not to use "if-statements" to get desired results, because they imply doubt about the person's willingness or ability to do the task. For example, one could say, "If you learn this vocabulary list, you can eat lunch." A preferred method is to say, "When you have completed this task, you can go outside."

A final word on strategy of reward is to *praise the action, not the person.* An example is, "I liked the way you helped Bob this morning, Jim," rather than, "You are a good boy, Jim, the way you help others."

This process may sound very mechanical and manipulative, but we are describing a behavior change technique used in an ethical context where these methods are used with the client's knowledge and consent. If we are interested in the effects of these methods on the group, we can use these same principles at a social system level. Individual performance can be made contingent on the group performance and vice versa. We may design double reinforcement contingencies for the person and the group. For example, we can influence the degree of support, cohesiveness, productivity, and level of responsible behavior in individuals and groups by planning a suitable system of rewards.

There are many opportunities to use rewards in helping interviews or groups. If we want the client, for example, to focus on feeling expression, our attention to these expressions, as well as overt praise, will tend to increase this behavior. If initiative in seeking information to solve his or her problems is important, there are many ways to show approval in a reinforcing manner. This discussion of reward should make us more aware of all aspects of our counselor behavior which have a reinforcing effect on the client's behavior.

Reinforcement has a decided effect on client interview behavior, as demonstrated by Ryan and Krumboltz (1964). Using verbal reinforcers, such as *good* and *fine,* and approval nods in decision-making interviews, they were able to effect significant increases in client deliberation and decision responses. Similarly, a study of rural youth in group settings done by Meyer, Strowig, and Hosford (1970) revealed that information seeking behavior can be increased considerably in eleventh graders by reinforcement methods. They found also that counselors could be taught to use these skills very quickly.

A summary of rewarding skills in the helping process follows:

1. *Reward performance,* not the person.
2. Determine the reward most *appropriate* to the client, considering unique interests, age, and setting.
3. Utilize *social* rather than tangible reinforcers.

4. Apply the reinforcer as *soon* after appearance of the desired behavior as possible.

5. As an *ethical* matter, obtain the understanding and permission of the client when using rewarding methods.

EXTINCTION.   Extinguishing skills are closely related to reinforcing methods since behavior gradually subsides and eventually disappears when it is not reinforced. Thus, the skill element for the counselor is applying extinction in systematic ways. Behavior can be changed by discontinuing the rewards. If the client wants to change an undesirable behavior, for example, the counselor assists him to identify the conditions that are reinforcing it and then removing or weakening them.

Characteristics of extinction are that: (1) *rates* of extinction are *variable* and depend upon the regularity of reinforcement, the effort required to perform, perceived changes in the reinforcement pattern, and the availability of alternate reponses; (2) *avoidance behaviors* can be extinguished by prevention of punishing consequences; (3) behavior is *displaced* rather than lost since it can be reinstated quickly through reestablishing the reward schedule; (4) using extinction does *not guarantee* that more desirable behavior patterns will emerge.

Usually, after extinction of the undesirable behavior, efforts to elicit and reward desired behavior need to be undertaken. Behavior changes can be brought about most effectively by a *combination strategy* of extinguishing undesirable behavior along with modeling and reinforcing desirable behavior.

Methods of extinction include: (1) simple *removal of reinforcing conditions* (as in not attending to an overly talkative client); and (2) gradually *changing the external stimulus* for an undesirable behavior, for example, by exposing the person in small increments to a fearsome situation, where the fear is minimally elicited and the fear response is blocked. Gradually, the fear will be neutralized. One method for doing this is through "behavior rehearsal," a kind of role playing. The counselor and client play scenes from actual problem situations. The method works well with clients who want to be more assertive. In this case, the counselor poses problems for the client involving asking favors, making complaints, or refusing a request, in a gradual way, until the most difficult situations are encountered. Time is taken for critiquing the experience and for occasional modeling where the counselor takes the role of the client. The client is urged to try the new techniques under conditions where anxiety arousal is least probable. The advantage of this behavior-rehearsal method is that it involves the client in actively solving a close-to-life problem.

The main implication of extinction phenomena is to know how to change undesirable client behavior by removing the rewarding conditions. Does intense attending behavior, for example, always reward the desired client behavior? Are there some behaviors such as tendencies to overintellectualize, or to talk to the floor, that we would like to extinguish by altering the reinforcing stimuli? In summary, then, counselors can use extinction by showing the client how he can remove rewarding conditions for un-wanted behavior. Counselors can help, also, by neutralizing undesirable emotional behaviors, such as fear of crowds, by gradually exposing the client to fearsome situations and by helping him or her to avoid punishing consequences.

AVERSIVE CONTROL. This skill related to reinforcement and extinction involves a process of removing undesired behaviors through use of "punishing" or "aversive" stimuli. The principal theory of how aversive control works is that the punishing effect results in a conditioned fear which has an inhibiting or suppressing effect. Aversive control is used to help reduce undesirable and persistent responses which are self-reinforcing. Examples are self-punishing activities in children, and unwanted smoking, overeating, and drinking in adults. To be used successfully, however, aversive methods should be paired with a positive reinforcement program for desired behaviors. Usually, other forms of help are needed, since aversive control methods deprive the client of much pleasure. He must be unusually cooperative and desire behavior change intensely.

Elements of aversive control are: (1) Introduce an aversive stimulus at the *time the person is engaging in the unwanted behavior*. Standard efforts for problem drinkers, for example, have been to combine an emetic with the drink so as to cause nausea and vomiting. Dire warnings of impending cancer are given to smokers when they light up. Temporary banishment from the group is effected for stealing property. (2) Develop a *positive reinforcing schedule for new behaviors* when the noxious behavior has ceased. (3) Be alert to *undesirable side effects* such as excessive fear arousal or unwanted negative attitudes toward the counselor who suggested or administered the aversive stimulus.

Sometimes aversive consequences can be imagined with desirable effects. Clients are asked to create situations in their fantasies which are like the ones they face. For example, the client is having great trouble fighting a demanding mother. He wants to avoid his strong responses, so with the aid of the counselor he can imagine his demanding mother and work out alternative responses to her.

DESENSITIZATION. Desensitization is a method of reducing the emotional responsiveness to threatening or unpleasant stimuli by introducing an activity which is incompatible with the threat response. Sometimes this process is known as *counterconditioning*. For example, fear of speaking up in class is associated with an incompatible pleasant and relaxed feeling. The unpleasant response (fear) cannot be experienced when the pleasant response (relaxation) is present. Most desensitization activities are concerned with introducing relaxation in the imaginary presence of anxiety, although they have been used with feelings of anger and guilt also. Occasionally, desensitization is used in combination with modeling and reinforcement.

Desensitization methods were developed initially by Wolpe (1958) and were refined by him and numerous other behavioral scientists. There are several steps in desensitization procedure: (1) discussion of conditions under which the problem occurs; (2) explanation of the method and its rationale, as a learning process, to the client; (3) relaxation training; (4) construction of an anxiety hierarchy; and (5) working through the hierarchy.

Steps 1 and 2 are straightforward explanation. Step 3, relaxation training, follows any of the various methods, such as Jacobson (1938), for inducing relaxation. Step 4, hierarchy construction, is conducted at the same time as the relaxation training takes place. Essentially, the hierarchy is a list of twelve to fourteen anxiety-producing situations around the same theme, such as taking tests. These situations are ranked by the client from lowest anxiety at the top to highest anxiety at the bottom. It is desirable to go over the list with the client to determine the strength of each and the equality of intervals between items. They should be evenly spaced as to their potency in arousing anxiety. In the "fear of testing" example, they would be arranged from "waking up on the morning of the test" all the way to "opening the cover page of the test booklet."

The items in the hierarchy should be similar to, or represent, the client's real life experiences. They should be sufficiently detailed to help the client imagine a clear image of the incident. Items should include a broad sample of situations where the feared incident, for example, might take place. The client should be able to see herself or himself as actively involved rather than passively observing.

After the hierarchy is constructed and checked, the working-through process (Step 5) is begun. In the relaxed state, clients are asked to imagine a few neutral scenes, such as a path in the forest. Then, they are asked to project themselves into the real problem and are given the top item in the hierarchy (lowest in anxiety). They are asked to indicate with a signal, such as raising an index finger, if he feels any anxiety. If so, relaxation exercises are undertaken again briefly. Then the counselor returns to the hierarchy, reading the same item, and proceeding in the same manner through the hierarchy. If successful, the client should still feel generally relaxed even after imagining the most potent anxiety-provoking situation on his or her list.

The following list is a summary of desensitizing skills:

1. Discuss *problem* with the client.
2. Decide if desensitization is *applicable*. (Desensitization might be indicated when a special isolated fear situation needs to be faced.)
3. Teach *relaxation* routines.
4. Construct *hierarchy* with the client.
5. *Test hierarchy* for rank order of *potency* and *evenness* of intervals between items by asking client, "Which is more anxiety-provoking, A or B?"
6. Conduct *desensitization* by reading from the list, the least potent first, in about thirty-minute sessions.
7. Check for relaxation and *repeat items* from the hierarchy until re-

laxed—stop and go back to relaxation methods if the client cannot go on without anxiety.

8. Complete *entire hierarchy* (usually twelve to twenty items).

SEMANTIC ANALYSIS STRATEGIES

Semantic analysis in counseling is more an approach to problems of communication than a series of techniques. The basic postulate of the semantics approach is that emotional disturbances arise largely from misuse of words, lack of clear understandings, and distorted meanings caused by malfunctioning of the client's symbolic processes. Through the use of clarification, restatement, and interpretive techniques, the client is helped to correct faulty language habits. Ellis's rational psychotherapy (1958) uses this technique heavily, and neurolinguistic programming methods work on semantic issues also (Bandler and Grinder 1979).

By using the semantic approach, counselors can correct faulty client thinking concerning unrealistic ideals. The counselor, thereby, can prevent the frustration and disappointment that result from the client's efforts to achieve "success." Johnson (1946) called the tendency to set unrealistic goals, the "IFD disease"—idealization, frustration, and demoralizaton. Enabling a client to define goals more accurately helps to avoid this semantic pitfall.

Clients who have difficulty in assigning accurate symbols to feelings and ideas present another type of problem in communication. One of the principal values of counseling is that it provides a verbal structure for emotions. The client becomes able to verbalize ambivalent feelings, for example, and to see that it is possible to construe one's self as having two opposing feelings toward the same person at the same time.

Counselors may use semantic analysis to correct loose thinking—another problem in communication. Loose thinking is generally accompanied by "ververbalization" and characterized by a frantic search for meaning. The individual who ververbalizes is really avoiding thinking. The counselor can encourage tighter thinking by asking the client frequently what is meant by his or her statements, or by attempting to restate and clarify the ideas just stated by the client, or by encouraging longer pauses.

Sometimes rigid thinking, along with underverbalization, is symptomatic of semantic difficulties. The use of stereotypes, prejudice, dogmatism, single causes, absolutism, and "either-or" are examples of thinking difficulties of this type. The counselor can help clients to see, for example, that human traits are not dichotomous, but exist in all shades and combinations. Ellis's (1962) rational approach to helping clients ferret out the faulty assumptions they make about themselves helps clients correct inaccurate conclusions about themselves. An example is, "I make mistakes; therefore, I am an incompetent person."

Semantic analysis, then, is an approach to the problem of expressing feelings by describing them accurately so that the client can handle them in a problem-solving manner, and so that he or she can see the relationship between feelings and thoughts. Semantic analysis also helps the counselor clarify meaning, tighten thinking, analyze assumptions, and make the client aware of tendencies to abstract and to confuse symbols with reality. Thus, the client can move closer to self-actualization when he or she stops asking vague questions and stops accepting ambiguous answers.

BIBLIOTHERAPY STRATEGIES

The use of literature to help people with problems is a very old practice. Reading is used for two purposes in counseling—information and psychotherapy (formerly called bibliotherapy).

The Informational Use of Reading

The informational use of library materials covers such situations as educational and occupational study in career counseling, sex and marital education in family and marriage counseling, and religious instruction in pastoral counseling. Reading materials are used in these situations mainly to economize time in the counseling hour. The client is given the responsibility, for example, to look up material on training institutions for law or to read occupational pamphlets related to law as a career.

The counselor's suggestions for relevant reading are generally accepted without question by clients, although he or she must include some motivational factors to stimulate the client's independent exploration of the materials. The suggestions for reading are introduced at a time when the client seems to exhibit a need for information. Principles for using specific types of informational material will be covered in Part III on their applications to various human problems. It should be noted that many of the principles using bibliotherapeutic materials apply to general informational reading matter.

The key use of outside readings is to promote the idea of self-help, that is, that clients have capacities for developing their own problem-solving methods and generating solutions on their own initiative. This is not to say that reading about a problem leads to effective action regarding it; but it is a start.

The Bibliotherapeutic Function of Reading

In his review of the literature on bibliotherapy, Brower (1952) indicated that there is little data bearing on the usefulness of bibliotherapeutic techniques. Many counselors, however, attest to its usefulness with certain types of clients. The intelligent client seems to make most use of reading as a source of self-help.

There are two types of bibliotherapeutic literature. One type—fiction, biography, and inspirational literature—offers much in the way of varied expressions of human experience. Shrodes (1943), for example, compiled excerpts from well-known literary works. The materials are classified into sections devoted to such topics as family life, economic pressures, and emotional conflicts. This approach to reading about human problems through literature helps clients broaden their understanding of human motivation and culture conflicts. It is claimed also that literature offers the client the opportunity to share experience, which can be therapeutic. Many clients find that reading the Bible and other religious literature provides them with much emotional support.

The other type of bibliotherapeutic literature, popular psychology books on personal growth, is designed to give useful information for solving human problems and covers practical principles and facts on adjustment problems.

One of the values claimed for bibliotherapy in counseling is time saving. Reading materials appropriate to the problem serve as a device to start clients thinking about related features of their feelings. Often clients are so eager for information that the counselor may resist giving it to prevent the relationship from starting on a too highly intellectualized basis. Suggesting some special reading, however, satisfies the client's need for specific information, yet enables the counselor to avoid the tendency to get involved in a question-answer sequence. Such efforts are frequently resistance devices of the client.

A second value of therapeutic reading is that it provides the client with more familiarity with the terminology of testing, mental hygiene, defenses, and emotions in general. The semantics values for the client of finding more exact language to express ideas and feelings seem to be encouraged by proper reading.

A third value of therapeutic reading is that it stimulates thinking. Clients run across ideas which may increase their awareness. A mother, for example, finds that while she has been telling her child that she loves him, she has not been accepting many of his characteristics. The child, in turn, interprets the mother's behavior not as loving but as rejecting. Reading about such ideas encourages clients to do their own interpreting.

Bibliotherapy, as a final value, enables the counselor to give support. When clients are anxious about their problems it may help to read about such problems. They find that others have the same feelings and same problems. They discover that their marital difficulties, for example, are not as unique as they thought.

Limitations of
Bibliotherapy

We have pointed out some of the functions of bibliotherapy which are cited by psychotherapists as being helpful for some clients. Bibliotherapy has limitations as well. One of the foremost is the fact that people tend to rationalize their problems when they read about them. Hence, any readiness for counseling which they may have had could be reduced, and their neurotic defenses could tend to become aggravated rather than diminished. Reading could become a type of resistance to, or even substitute for, going ahead with counseling.

A second limitation of bibliotherapy is that it encourages clients to think that the reading is helping them to solve their problems. Unless the reading is carefully described as being an *aid* to counseling, clients may substitute the vicarious participation and pseudoinsight they gain from the reading for the painful experience of genuine growth to be gained from the counseling relationship itself. It is estimated that few behaviors are changed through reading. It is feared also that too many of the so-called insights achieved through reading turn out to be as ineffective and elusive as the New Year's resolution.

There are, in addition, the clients whose anxieties are reinforced by reading about emotional problems. They see themselves in every case, and, if suggestible, acquire more symptoms for their defense repertoire. This personalizing tendency is particularly acute in paranoid individuals and in clients with weak defense systems.

Principles in Using Bibliotherapy

Knowledge of the books the counselor recommends is a first principle. Counselors who refer clients to books with which they are not familiar run the risk of misleading them and might fail to meet their needs or their level of sophistication. Missing the client's level of understanding could have deleterious effects on rapport. This principle puts a severe burden on a counselor to keep abreast of literature and to keep the titles in his immediate memory. This familiarity enables him to suggest books not only appropriate from a content standpoint but also for age, experience, and language level.

The counselor should *evidence confidence* in the suggested reading to interest clients in it and to make sure that they consider the ideas presented. Readings are *suggested* rather than prescribed.

Timing is a third significant principle the counselor must consider to ensure that clients properly understand and accept the idea of reading. The counselor does not want to convey the idea that the client's problem is so simple it can be solved by reading a book rather than working it out through the counseling process. Neither does the counselor want to convey by poorly timed suggestions that he or she can no longer help the client and that reading might be a way out of the therapeutic impasse. A significant timing principle is to make the suggestions during a period of low resistance. The counselor who suggests readings at a time when the client is struggling with a feeling or when he is rolling toward insight will annoy him or her and be considered as lacking understanding.

Discussion of the results of the client's reading is important to ascertain the effect of the reading. The client can ask questions and point out ideas which were especially valuable. Often, related passages can be read aloud for clarity. It is very important that distortions and misunderstandings be corrected at this point and that a realistic evaluation of the ideas is made. Some significant questions are: How authoritative was the writer? How recent is the material? Some books written in the forties and fifties do not reflect current psychological thought. Are opinion and fact clearly differentiated? So many popular writers are not scrupulous about the factual bases of their opinions.

Lists of suggested readings and mimeographed tables of contents can be used to stimulate reading. Books and pamphlets, often with passages underlined, can be left in the waiting room for clients to browse through and to borrow. Often the browsing itself directs a client's thought process and produces significant material for the counseling hour. The following is an example:

CL: I was reading an article in one of the journals in the waiting room. It discussed reasons why people are apt to create marital problems for themselves. I don't believe that writer had all the answers. I could think of some reasons that the author didn't mention.

Smaller doses of reading seem to be more helpful than larger amounts. A pithy article or pamphlet is often more helpful than a book. It is easier for the counselor to pinpoint suggestion in a short work, since so much material extraneous to the client's immediate concern may distract him or her and dilute the emphasis desired.

SUMMARY

Information and action strategies are important to counseling. The use of advice and suggestion is appropriate under some counseling conditions. The principal danger in advice giving is that it often becomes a projection of the counselor's needs and values. Procedures designed to solve problems and change behavior directly through self-helping methods are suggested. Tests of personality, interest, aptitude, and achievement are widely used informational tools designed to give the client information about himself with which he can make wiser decisions. Tests are highly technical devices necessitating special training in their careful selection and use. Semantics principles help clients to sharpen their ability to think about their problems and to communicate more clearly. Informational reading and bibliotherapy are techniques designed to give the client valid ideas for use in planning his or her future and solving present problems. Methods for helping a client move from awareness to action are covered.

11

Group Principles and Methods

THE HUMAN POTENTIAL FRAMEWORK

The increasing popularity and widespread use of the group experience as a force for personality change is affirmed by Carl Rogers:

> . . . the intensive group experience is one of the most rapidly growing phenomena in the United States . . . because people . . . have discovered that this group experience alleviates their loneliness and permits them to grow, to risk change. The encounter group brings persons into real relationships with persons. . . . It has been estimated that at least 5 million persons have now had an encounter group experience in the United States. (1968, p. 29)

Maslow has said,

> If ordinary [individual] therapy may be conceived of as a miniature ideal society of two, then group therapy may be seen as a miniature ideal society of ten . . . in addition we now have empirical data that indicate group therapy . . . can do some things that individual psychotherapy cannot. (1970, p. 263)

Individual therapy is analogous to a lecture in college, whereas group therapy is the laboratory. Each is necessary for total learning. In the laboratory of the group clients are afforded opportunities to try out a new "stance" in life and to experience and express the values to which they are committing themselves. If the number of people going to group therapy is added to the number of those who have sought encounter group experiences, Rogers's estimate of 5 million (made originally in 1968) should now perhaps be increased to at least 10 million. Those seeking encounter group experiences as well as those seeking group therapy are well-functioning people who want to improve. The fact of their numbers seems to belie the stigma that pervaded earlier decades of group attendance.

Kagan (1970) has asserted that clients in groups have vague irrational fears that seem to be nearly universal. Specifically, these are:

1. The counselor might hurt or reject them. [Fear of exposing weakness.]

2. The counselor might make an affectionate, intimate, or dependent demand on them. [Fear of intimacy.]

3. The client's own hostile impulses might be expressed toward the counselor. [Fear of anger.]

4. The client's own affectionate, intimate, or dependent needs might be acted out toward the counselor. [Fear of loving.]

To these we add a fifth: The client's own strengths or competencies might need to be asserted. [Fear of strength.]

As suggested by our bracketed interpretations after the above comments, it is apparent that Kagan is referring to the fundamental polarities of actualizing counseling and therapy. Kagan asks, "Would it be possible to confront people with these general concerns? Would such confrontation serve as a stimulant or facilitative device to encourage clients to become aware of their own specific concerns?" (1970, p. 47). We believe that our interpersonal system does exactly this. (See Figure 19.) Kagan's list of group fears parallels the polarities of anger, love, strength, and weakness of actualizing counseling and therapy described in Chapter 3.

It is apparent, then, that group methods are growing in popularity, not so much as clinical methods to help the seriously disturbed, but as media for assisting the already functional person to achieve higher levels of functioning and awareness. This awareness in turn can lead to increased effectiveness, greater humanness, and further actualizing of his or her potentials. Present trends indicate group approaches may largely supplant individual counseling and psychotherapy because of their effectiveness in leading to behavior change. The increased attendance at group events has removed much of the social stigma of any kind of help, since groups appeal to people already functioning effectively.

Task groups, in contrast with growth groups, focus on problem solving and specific agenda functions, such as committees. In this chapter we describe growth groups only. Organizational development, which focuses on the organization as the client system, deals with group issues of problem solving, goal setting, communicating, and leadership development. These group functions in the organizational context are also beyond the scope of this book.

Distinctions between counseling and psychotherapy cited in Chapter 1 hold for group counseling and group psychotherapy. The focus of group counseling is on group dynamics and interpersonal skills rather than on basic personality changes. Group counseling is preventive and developmental as well as remedial. It has specific goals and is usually oriented around problems. In addition, the members may be experiencing situational crises. Usually group counseling is carried out in institutional settings such as schools, colleges, and clinics (Corey 1981). Groups go through process stages as in individual counseling. Gazda (1978) describes four stages in group development—exploration, transition, action, and termination. The T-group is a special educational group form where the members focus on improving their communication skills and interaction styles in the laboratory atmosphere of the group. The Bradford, Gibb, and Benne collection of papers (1964) presents a rich fare of theory and practice with T-groups. Group psychotherapy, conversely, has been a standard term for a problem-centered, crisis-oriented method of clinic and private practice settings. The most significant differences between the two terms are intensity of emotional involvement and agency setting. Counseling groups in schools work on a common theme, interest, or problem area, such as academic achievement or getting along with parents. Group counseling deals more with present attitudes and behaviors and less with past difficulties and intrapersonal problems. Exploration of feeling usually is more controlled during group counseling than in group psychotherapy, which not only permits, but encourages, members to express intensive core feelings, such as intense hatred.

A number of additional terms are used commonly in group literature. Group dynamics refers to the general principles of group interaction and communication. Groups are described variously as "sensitivity" training (largely obsolete), "T-groups" (mentioned above), "encounter" groups (from existential viewpoints), and "conjoint" family groups. Applications of group principles stressing openness with feelings, leading to self-awareness and improved human relations, have been made to industrial, educational, governmental, clinical, church, and family settings. These general approaches emphasize personal growth for people already functioning well, rather than solving intense personal problems. They also differ from counseling and therapy groups in their emphasis on the "here and now" of present group interaction and communication skills, rather than on problems and feelings of the past. The spread of the T-group model for improving human relationships has great portent for the future. If many people can become skilled group leaders in family, community, and work settings, and if the trend toward greater public acceptance of human relations training continues, there is the likelihood of a "chain reaction" toward improved human relations. This, hopefully, will lead to confidence in people helping one another and using experts mainly as teachers of leaders and as monitors of group development experiences. This development could be a potent force in counteracting the alienation, fractionation, and dehumanization felt particularly by persons living in cities and working in large organizations.

DEVELOPMENTS IN GROUP WORK

Actualization
Groups

Developments in group work such as the actualization group, assertiveness training, consciousness raising, and life planning and life renewal groups are focused extensions of basic group work. Actualization groups differ from general encounter groups in that they focus on precise outcome behaviors. These intensive group experiences are conducted for periods as long as twelve weeks or as short as a two-day weekend. There is a dual emphasis—didactic (lectures, films, demonstrations), and experiential (exercises and encounter groups. Zimet (1979) introduced a group concept he calls "Short-term DTCs" (Developmental Task and Crisis Groups) which focus on developmental transitions, such as from childhood to adolescence. These groups focus on life-stage issues and transitional crises (Erikson 1959; Sheehy 1976).

A fundamental theory of general actualization groups and workshops proposed by Shostrom (1976) is: "The group is the individual turned inside out." By understanding the various manipulative patterns shown by members of a group, they learn to see potentials that exist within themselves. Shostrom and Satir describe four manipulative response forms—avoiding, blaming, conniving, and placating. The basic theory of group change is to create an actualizing person with characteristics of contacting, affirming, confronting, and engaging.

The Actualizing
Model Applied
to Group Work

This approach draws heavily from the group encounter and group therapy literature of the past twenty years. We have synthesized these varied approaches into a model for the actualizing group. For example: the feeling emphasis of the client-centered approach is prominent; the interpersonal skills element of the National Training Laboratory T-group model is a strong feature; the confrontational strategy of Perls's Gestalt approach is evident; the body methods of Lowen are included; the open encounter emphases of Schutz and the behavioral skills laboratories are part of the actualizing model. A unique feature of the actualizing model, however, is its emphasis on evaluation and measurement strategies to assess outcomes through instruments, such as the Actualizing Assessment Battery and specific coping skills inventories.

GOALS OF ACTUALIZING GROUPS. The goals of actualizing group work cover broad outcomes to match the actualizing values cited in Chapter 3, as well as the specific outcomes expected by individual participants.

One can be strongly self-expressive and yet be responsive to one's perceived weaknesses, for example. We see the group process as providing a unique learning setting for growth on these broad polarities as well as for developing specified life skills.

WORKING WITH POLARITIES IN THE GROUP. This section is based upon the discussion of the actualizing model of Chapter 3 and is linked to the theory in the following manner. The basic polarities functioning within each person are represented as the intersecting whorls in each circle (representing each group member) in Figure 19. Within the person there is a rhythm between his or her own primary polarities and the polarities of other members of the group, represented by the lines linking the individual circles in Figure 19. This process broadens each person's perspective of the group and the various roles developing for each.

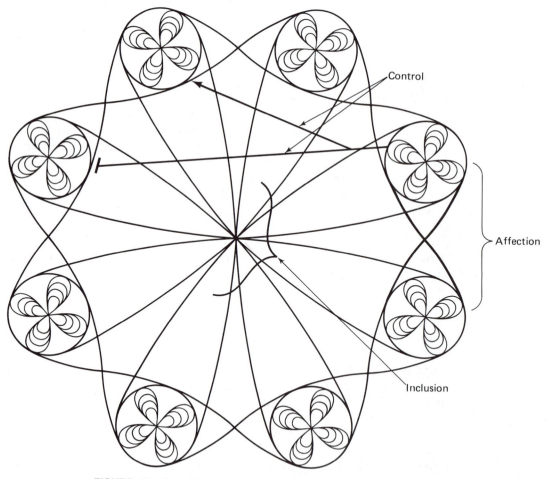

FIGURE 19. Polarities in the Actualizing Group. Adapted from E. L. Shostrom, L. Knapp, and R. Knapp, *Actualizing Therapy* (1976, p. 192).

GROUP ENERGY. The group has its special energy system, much more complex than the dyadic relationship in individual work. This energy field in a group is experienced by the perceptive members; but it is a difficult phenomenon to capture and study in any reliable manner. Yet, experienced leaders have known about the group energy phenomenon for some time. In a small group of eight to ten persons, each person seems to radiate an energy field up to several feet. This common experience is illustrated when a prominent or particularly powerful person enters a room. John Kennedy is reputed to have had this effect on people. His energy was perceived immediately. In terms of implications for group work strategy, Schutz (1975) emphasizes the importance of assessing and following the energy of the group. Signs of such energy are the postural and voice cues exhibiting stress or enthusiasm, for example. Contrast this phenomenon with the low level of energy associated with intellectual discussion of problems or outside issues.

POWER. Another issue to be perceived and dealt with effectively in the actualizing group is how power and influence are used and balanced. They may be used in manipulative or actualizing ways and can have enormous influence on a group in either direction (Shostrom 1976). For example, one implication of balancing power roles in a group is the practice of selecting group members, sometimes called "hawks," who have strong aggressive influence already, and less assertive and influential members, sometimes called "doves." The potential awareness of these polarities in individual members with this kind of selection offers, for example, greater opportunities for individual growth along this polarity.

EXPRESSION OF INTERPERSONAL NEEDS IN THE GROUP. Three basic interpersonal needs have been identified by Schutz (1975)—inclusion, control, and affection. We use them to help understand the interactions of the group and the individual needs of the members. These dimensions are identified in Figure 19. By inclusion is meant feelings of being prominent, significant, or worthwhile as a group member. It manifests itself, as indicated in Figure 19, as a reaching out and focusing of energy toward the center of the group. It means searching for togetherness, belongingness, attention, and response. This may take manipulative forms, if thwarted, as if the person were saying to herself or himself, "I'll make them pay attention to me in any way I can."

The second need to be concerned about in actualizing groups is control—the need to manipulate others, have authority over them, or dominate them. It may be expressed as a polarity in the form of need to be dominated or manipulated. These polarities are represented in Figure 19 as the attack (←) or push (⊢) symbols. Confronting behaviors such as blaming, attacking, controlling, and conniving are examples.

The third need is affection, for close relationships between group members. It usually takes place in pairs (dyads), rather than in some global group-living sense. It is expressed in the symbolic form of the embrace

($\times$) in Figure 19. Again, polarities are involved as expressions of affection directly or avoidance of closeness.

BEING IN THE NOW.   Being in the now can be seen as a primary goal of actualization group counseling and group therapy. It means focusing on feelings in present time. The most important clues therapists have are their own feelings. Experienced therapists learn to listen to their own feelings. Yalom (1975) says they are as useful to him as a microscope is to a microbiologist. To be one's feelings in the now requires an orientation to living which we call *being* in contrast to *doing*. *Being* is basically an internal process of sensing and experiencing feelings way to the core. *Doing* is basically an external process of achieving or changing things. Changing from an external to an internal focus requires modeling by the therapist of being and feeling. An example of how painful this process of change really can be for some clients is Yalom's case of "The Man Who Could Not Feel."

> *Mr. Steele sought therapy for a single, sharply delineated problem: "I want to be able to feel sexually stimulated by a woman." Intrigued by this conundrum, the group searched for the answer. They investigated his early life, sexual habits, fantasies, and finally, baffled, turned away. As life in the group continued, Mr. Steele, a regular attender, seemed peculiarly impassive. He spoke in a monotone and seemed entirely insensitive to others' pain. On one occasion, for example, a member in great distress announced in sobs that she was illegitimately pregnant and was planning to have a criminal abortion. During her account she also mentioned incidentally that she had had a bad marijuana trip. Mr. Steele, seemingly unmoved by her tears, persisted in questioning her intellectually about marijuana effects and was puzzled when the group turned on him because of his insensitivity. So many similar incidents occurred that the group came to expect no emotion from him. When he was directly queried about his feelings, he responded as if he had been addressed in a foreign language. After some months the group formulated a new answer to his oft-repeated question, "Why can't I have sexual feelings toward a woman?" They asked him to consider instead why he couldn't have any kinds of feeling toward man or woman.*
>
> *Changes in his behavior occurred very gradually and were mediated via an investigation of his autonomic expression of affect. The group wondered about his frequent facial flushing; he described his gastric tightness during emotionally laden episodes in the group. On one occasion a very volatile girl in the group called him a "god-damned faggot" and said that she couldn't relate to a "psychologically deaf and dead" individual and threatened to leave the group. Mr. Steele again remained impassive, stating that he wasn't going to "get down to her level." However, the next week he told the group that after the meeting he had gone home and cried like a baby. When he looked back at the course of his therapy, this seemed to be a turning point, and gradually he was able to feel and express sorrow, fear, and anger with others. His role within the group changed from that of a tolerated mascot to that of an accepted compeer. (1975, p. 341)*

GENERAL STAGES OF GROUP GROWTH. *Inclusion:* These same need dimensions cited above describe Schutz's (1975) conceptions of group growth. Inclusion is the first stage, where new members express concern about how much in or out of the process they see themselves. It is a time of decision on how much commitment to the group one is going to make. It is a time of keen concern about how members see themselves in relationship to the total group, that is, where they fit in. This anxiety is expressed, for example, in overtalking, withdrawal, exhibitionistic behaviors, or telling descriptive stories about previous group experiences.

CONTROL. When the group has become somewhat established, concerns are expressed about who is in charge, who administers the sanctions and rewards, how much power does a member have. Manipulations through both strength and weakness strategies become apparent. Attacks on the leader (often in the form of questioning his or her competence) become evident, as examples, at this stage.

AFFECTION. When issues of control are resolved, affection concerns become prominent. Positive feelings, as well as hostility, are expressed to one another. Jealousies and pairings become evident. There is heightened emotional expression generally.

The tire-changing metaphor is useful here. Just as the mechanic tightens each wheel nut enough to keep the wheel in place, so each person in the group is attended to "once over lightly" early in the process in terms of his or her feelings. Then the bolts are tightened further until the wheel is firmly in place. Similarly, each member's needs for inclusion, control, and affection are worked through until they are satisfied.

SEPARATION. In most groups this is a critical stage of development. For continuous groups, where members leave one at a time. This is not a key issue; but the weekend encounter group, or the ten-week group, must face termination feelings. As groups terminate, they tend to resolve their affection, control, and inclusion needs in reverse fashion. First, personal feelings of loss and gain (positive and negative) are dealt with. Next, discussion often focuses on the leader and how the group members have rebelled at or complied with his or her methods. Finally, the group discusses the feelings of termination and possibilities of continuing the group. Sometimes the "fantasy reunion" phenomenon occurs here when the group makes elaborate plans to come together at a future time, names and addresses are exchanged, but the future meeting rarely occurs.

Family Groups   Group methods with families have become very popular with agencies and private practitioners. Some school systems described by Zwetschke and Grenfell (1965) have developed family counseling programs as a means of helping children make a better adaptation to the learning environment through improved home environments. Whole families come to the sessions, sometimes for one to three days over a weekend. McGregor (1962) reports such a successful family counseling venture with a combination of group and individual interviews over a three-day period. Usually a crisis precipitates the process, and the family can change quickly under conditions of high motivation.

Satir's system of conjoint family therapy (1966) is a particularly significant development in group methods. According to Satir, most individual therapy deals with an "identified patient." But to treat him or her alone is impossible without understanding his or her role and status, as well as the values and norms of the interpersonal group from which he or she comes.

A family is an individualized system of feeders and the fed, directors and the directed, supporters and the supported. A client is someone having a problem of growth in the family. The problem in part is deciding what he or she needs to do to survive in this system. A symptom is a behavior which is considered sick, bad, stupid, or crazy by members of the family system. It always takes at least two people to make a behavior: the feeder and the one fed.

Satir stresses that group communication is always at two levels: the literal and the metacommunicative. This second level is the message about the message, since it covers feelings and intentions toward the receiver. Family therapy deals largely with these message levels and patterns.

Satir classifies communication patterns in five groups or targets:

1. Where the literal message is one of *agreement*
   Where the affective message is *pleasing and placating*
2. Where the literal message is *disagreement*
   Where the affective message is *blaming and attacking*
3. Where the literal message is *changing the subject*
   Where the affective message is *being irrelevant or withdrawing*
4. Where the literal message is *being reasonable*
   Where the affective message is *conniving*
5. Where the literal message is *reporting oneself*
   Where the affective message is *making a place for others*

Family therapy is an attempt to get families into pattern or target 5 above. This process of actualizing communication is illustrated in the film "Target 5" (1967) by Satir. Typically, according to Satir, when Father plays the "pleaser" (pattern 1), Mother plays the "blamer" (pattern 2), and child plays "irrelevant" and withdraws (pattern 3), we may have a schizophrenic family! Often the child's communication "games" evolve from the interaction that he or she sees and hears in the family. In effect, children are conditioned to behave with certain communicative patterns as they grow up. Thus, family therapy is a form of deconditioning malfunctioning communication patterns.

Satir utilizes behavior therapy techniques in the following ways:

1. Many of the communication patterns of family members reflect fear. Even psychiatric labels are reflections of fear communication patterns. Paranoids, for example, are constantly fearful that the senders are criticizing them. Clients with schizoid tendencies garble their messages out of fear of being understood! Thus, one of the basic techniques of good therapy, and especially family therapy, is that technique of *deconditioning fears.*

2. Therapeutic methods are also very supportive, especially of the younger family members. Therapeutic support is a companion method for deconditioning.

3. Communication patterns which are clear and direct instead of phony and manipulative are *rewarded.*

4. Finally, the leader behaves in the family group session as a *model,* doing and saying that which will encourage similar behavior in the family.

Satir suggests a definition of transference as it relates to the interpersonal system of the family, namely, relating to another in terms of certain *expectations* from one's past. For example, if there were no anger allowed to be expressed in his or her family, the client would transfer this same expectation to the therapist. Patients in mental hospitals have been known to improve greatly while there because that was the expectation of the therapeutic community. Then, when they return to the family system, the expectation is that they will flop, which they often do!

This discussion of transference reemphasizes the importance of family therapy. If the client's behavior toward the therapist is characteristic of his or her communications with mother and father, why not help the client deal with the family more *directly* by seeing the client and family together? This removes the burden of change from the identified client only. He or she can be seen as someone who is already trying to change the family's system of behaving. If clients are seen alone and are urged to increase their efforts by themselves, they often receive more intense criticism from the family.

Communication training is considered by Satir as a central feature of family therapy. She differentiates between the functional and the dysfunctional communicator. The functional communicator:

1. Firmly states his or her case.
2. Clarifies and qualifies.
3. Asks for feedback.
4. Considers feedback.

Dysfunctional communicators are vague and send incomplete messages. They use pronouns vaguely, such as "it," "we," and so on. They often do not send messages at all and then behave as if they have.

According to Satir, *all messages are requests.* Whenever a person is communicating he or she is not only making a statement, he or she is also trying to influence the receiver, or to ask something. The receiver, in turn, must respond, because people cannot avoid communicating. Family therapy, therefore, is a workshop on message-sending and message-receiving skills in a family setting.

Marathon Groups

A form of intensive group work popular during the sixties is known as *marathon therapy.* This development has been described by a number of writers, especially Bach (1966). It is an intensive, living-in kind of therapeutic experience with a group of about twelve, a therapist, and a cotherapist or two. It may go on for twenty-four hours or more, with little time taken for vital functions. The total honesty and free expression of feelings over an intensive and extensive period of time results in greater transparency of feelings for some than would more spaced sessions. Marathon groups are not necessarily "one-shot" sessions, since follow-up sessions are conducted frequently. Sometimes a weekend is spent, with three intensive sessions interspersed with short sleep periods. Most evaluative data are in the form of personal testimonials about how one's life style has changed. Few data are available about the permanence of changes when participants return to Monday morning routines without reinforcement for new-found gains. One criticism is that current practitioners do not screen candidates for marathon groups with sufficient care; a person with weak defenses or latent emotional crises would be especially vulnerable.

Research on Groups

Abundant research comparing group and individual methods with controls has appeared in the last few years. Results are conflicting because of the difficulty controlling treatment conditions and specifying the methods of the counselors. Some groups are more effective and some leadership styles are more effective, depending on the peculiar characteristics of the counselor (Yalom, Lieberman, and Miles 1971). Combinations of methods appear to be most efficacious in behavior change. A study by Katahn, Strenger, and Cherry (1966) is an example. They used group counseling with a form of systematic desensitization with test-anxious college students. Results indicated a significant rise in grade average and a reduction of measurable anxiety.

Questions for additional research are: What personality changes are effected by group process? How do these changes affect behavior and how permanent are they? What undesired "side effects" of group process take place? Are group experiences deleterious to the welfare of some persons? What are the best combinations of individual and group experience to maximize growth? What are the best time intervals and lengths of sessions for maximum growth? Are marathon sessions more effective than spaced sessions? What kinds of persons can profit most by group experiences? How can trust conditions be accelerated in groups? Are certain group experiences, such as T-groups, more effective in changing attitudes and traits than other types of educational experiences? What is the effect of leadership style on group outcomes?

A productive application of group methods is to use the group leader as a change agent in a social system. More research is needed on organizational development and planned change through group process. Productivity of small leaderless groups compared to more structured groups is also a continuing subject of research. See Bradford, Gibb, and Benne (1964) and Havelock's change agent's guide (1973).

Self-help groups that utilize healing forces in the group have grown greatly since their early forebears such as Alcoholics Anonymous and Recovery, Inc. Berzon and associates (1968, 1969) experimented with leaderless growth groups called Planned Experiences for Effective Living (PEER). Their studies and subsequent evaluations indicated such groups have some strengths, but the results are too equivocal to recommend this pattern for all groups.

GROUP EFFECTIVENESS.   The question whether group techniques do, in fact, yield enduring positive personality change (Gibb 1971), or actually result in psychological damage in some cases (Yalom, Lieberman, and Miles 1971) has only recently been subjected to objectively quantified assessment. After analyzing 106 studies, as well as examining 123 additional studies and 24 recent doctoral dissertations, Gibb stated, "The evidence is strong that intensive group training experiences have therapeutic effects. . . . Changes do occur in sensitivity, ability to manage feelings, directionality of motivation, attitudes toward the self, attitudes toward others, and interdependence" (1970). The term *interdependence* refers to interpersonal competence, teamwork in problem solving, and effectiveness as a group member. Because interdependence is also one of the chief goals of actualizing counseling and therapy, we believe Gibb's research summary is significant.

Yalom, Lieberman, and Miles conducted a study of encounter group styles in which 210 Stanford undergraduates were divided randomly into seventeen different groups. Two of the groups were led only by tape-recorded instructions, and the others were led by professionals whose philosophical approaches included Gestalt, transactional analysis, Synanon games, "Esalen eclectic," and others. In contrast to Gibb, the Stanford researchers found the rate of casualties to be an "alarming and unacceptable" 10 percent. Casualties were defined in terms of psychiatric problems such as severe depression. Chances of "clear, positive benefit" proved to be about one in three. Only 16 percent of the participants had "peak experiences" during the course of the groups. Gimmicks and structured exercises did not prove especially valuable. In conclusion, Yalom, Lieberman, and Miles emphasize that it is important to keep deep respect for the self-preservatory functions of defenses, and that to encourage attack in an effort to dislodge a person from familiar defenses is cruel and often counterproductive. The Yalom study also has implications for leadership style. Those leaders with either a strong, confrontative style or a pronounced laissez faire, low-key style were least effective and had the largest number of group "casualties."

The results of the Yalom study confirm certain tenets of actualizing counseling and therapy. Expressing anger is good, but sustained levels of anger are unproductive and need to be balanced by love and support. Furthermore, the study concludes that both feeling *and* thinking need to be expressed in the group.

RATING SCALE FOR CURATIVE DIMENSIONS.   How does group therapy help clients? Yalom's research (1975) partly answers the question. His data suggest that there are ten curative factors to judge the effectiveness of the group. His data suggest further that these dimensions operate in all therapy groups but that the goals and leadership determine the differential importance.

Based on Yalom's work, Magden and Shostrom (1974) constructed a rating sheet, which included eight dimensions of group effectiveness. This rating sheet can be used by trained observers watching groups or films of groups in process. The following dimensions are used in this rating form:

1.   *Catharsis.* Group members often ventilate feelings and/or experiences.

2.   *Group as a second family.* Group members identify the therapist and/or other members in family roles.

3.   *Awareness.* Group members become more aware of their thoughts, feelings, and/or bodily responses.

4.   *Group cohesiveness.* Group members appear involved in the group.

5.   *Receiving information.* Group members appear open to instructions, advice, and suggestions from the therapist.

6.   *Imitative behavior.* Group members model their behavior after the therapist.

7.   *Faith in the process.* Group members' behavior suggests that the group process will work for them.

8.   *Giving and receiving help.* Group members appear to help one another through support and reassurance.

The two additional dimensions listed by Yalom (1975), but not utilized on the rating sheet, are:

9.   *Universality.* Group members appear to get insight into the "universal commonness" of their ideas, feelings, and behavior.

10.   *Altruism.* Group members appear to feel a sense of caring or love for one another.

The Magden-Shostrom rating form was used in research conducted at a meeting of the American Psychological Association (1974), where the film series *Three Approaches to Group Psychotherapy* was rated by 200 psychologists. The group sessions were conducted by Everett L. Shostrom (actualizing therapy), Albert Ellis (rational-emotive therapy), and Harold Greenwald (direct decision therapy). The purpose of the study, reported by Magden and Shostrom (1974), was to relate the eight dimensions measured by the rating form to the three approaches to group therapy presented in the films. Analysis of the data indicated that Shostrom averaged highest of the three leaders on all dimensions of effectiveness. Ratings were significantly different on all dimensions except number five (receiving information), and the rankings were consistent for all rating groups, regardless of their own theoretical orientation (Magden and Shostrom 1974). Results showed also that this rating form can be used to evaluate the effectiveness of a group session within a two-minute period.

OUTCOME STUDIES WITH THE PERSONAL ORIENTATION INVENTORY (POI). The Personal Orientation Inventory has been used widely in studies on group effectiveness. In a review of instruments in human relations training, Pfeiffer and Heslin have noted:

> The POI, perhaps more than any other instrument described in this book, measures the things talked about by people in human relations training. For this reason it is an excellent training device. It awakens people to important dimensions of life and ways of viewing the world and themselves that they may well not have considered previously. (1973, p. 100)

Many of the early studies considered here contained a number of methodological shortcomings, but because of the importance of objective data in this area, a review and integration of findings to date seems appropriate.

The POI has been successful particularly in measuring the effectiveness of group work in a variety of settings. For example, of fifteen studies reviewed by Knapp (quoted in Shostrom, Knapp, and Knapp 1976), seven dealt with adult samples, seven with college student samples, and one with high school student samples. Eight of these fifteen studies incorporated a control group. Sample sizes, an important factor in statistical interpretation, ranged from 14 to 135, with results in four of these studies being based on responses from fewer than 30 subjects. Perhaps of greatest importance in the review of these studies, however, are the effects of such variables as length of time over which the changes are evaluated and comparisons of the effects of different encounter techniques. Before undertaking studies evaluating effects of such variables upon outcome of the encounter group experience, adequate measurement techniques are required. As mentioned, the availability of the POI has accelerated research in this area.

A number of studies have demonstrated changes in self-actualizing following encounter group experience. A summary of the results of these major studies is presented in Shostrom, Knapp, and Knapp (1976).

To examine the effects of a program of Transcendental Meditation on self-actualizing, Seeman, Nidich, and Banta (1972) administered the POI to an experimental group of twenty college students, and to a control group of twenty, prior to the initiation of the program and two months following completion of the program. The mean difference for the experimental group on the Outer/Inner support dimension was significantly higher than that for the control group. Significant mean changes in the positive direction were also obtained on five other scales.

A number of controlled studies using the POI as a criterion have demonstrated significant changes, immediately and after three months, as a result of human relations training (Byrd 1967; Alperson, Alperson, and Levine 1971; Banmen and Capelle 1971, 1972; Bebout and Gordon 1972; Reddy and Beers 1977). These representative studies cover high school student, high school teacher, church professional, and general adult populations. In the area of military drug treatment programs, Knapp and Fitzgerald (1973) report significant before and after changes on five scales of the POI.

The studies reported above are based on the criterion of self-report of changes taking place as a result of group experience. While the POI has been demonstrated to be a sensitive instrument with which to systematize and assess these self-reports, there is always the big question of what these perceptual changes mean in behavior. Does the participant in an actualizing group really move into actualizing behaviors?

The question of "faking" to look better on a posttest looms large also. This issue has been studied with the POI. While knowing the concepts and rationale of the POI makes it possible to improve one's score, it is fairly resistant to efforts to make a good impression (Braun and LaFaro 1969; Wareheim, Routh, and Foulds 1974).

PRINCIPLES OF GROUP DYNAMICS

The principles which underlie groups at work may be classified into three categories: leader behaviors, discussant behaviors, and content analysis. Students of group dynamics can utilize the following outline for analyzing group behavior in terms of the three categories.

Typical Leader Behaviors   Groups may function with varying degrees of leadership ranging from leaderless to a strong professional group leader. Berzon and Solomon (1966) present a series of studies in leaderless group methods for encounter and therapy groups. They found that under some circumstances, self-directed groups using prepared program materials were feasible and effective in changing behavior.

The importance of leadership style for producing destructive as well as constructive outcomes was emphasized in the Yalom study cited above. This study found that leaders who were extremely active or passive had the least constructive outcomes. Implicit in the actualizing model is a leader behavior characterized by more active participation and responsibility than the more nondirective style of leadership. Yet, the leader does not dominate the group. He or she tries to "read the group" in a sensitive manner and does what appears most appropriate to achieve the actualizing goals of the group. The leader leads actively in terms of giving information, making process observations, or using confrontative or supportive interventions as indicated. He or she tries to model actualizing behavior as much as possible without setting himself or herself up as a paragon of such growth. The following list is suggestive of the various possible group maintenance functions performed by a facilitator of an actualizing group. These are general process behaviors. More specific strategies and methods are presented later in the chapter.

Problem Setting. In a problem- or issue-oriented group, the leader states the issue or question to which the group is to address itself. This may occur at the outset or at various points in the discussion. The statement is made without indication of what solution should be reached or which side the leader favors.

Process Moderating. The leader calls on some members or asks others to withhold comment; he or she may ask for order or attention. This category has nothing to do with content of the discussion but only with the process.

Sentiment Testing. The leader seeks to learn the balance of opinion in the group. He or she may call for a show of hands or may simply state his or her impression of the trend of opinion and ask for confirmation.

Idea Developing. The leader seeks to aid in the clarification and development of ideas before the group by restating, summarizing, or contrasting them. He or she does not inject new material, but seeks to make issues more clear or to insure more general understanding.

Monitoring. The leader reminds the group of limits and constraints under which it is operating (for example, time limits, authority bounds, ground rules).

Energizing. The leader seeks to motivate the group to its self-assigned task. He or she may cite reasons for its work or simply enjoin the group to greater activity or chide it for inactivity.

Group Serving. The leader may perform service functions for the group (for example, keeping notes, recording on a blackboard, distributing paper, adjusting lighting). There may be no verbal aspects to this function.

Content Participating. The leader takes part in the discussion, as another member, without exercising leadership functions in any way.

Leaders also utilize certain *process facilitation techniques* with a view toward carrying forward the discussion of their group. The following list is a partial compilation of such techniques:

Initiating. The leader proposes new ideas, procedures, or orientation. Major content is not derived from previous work of the group but mainly from "within" the current speakers.

Amending. The leader develops ideas already before the group. He or she may add new "twists" but basically modifies more than initiates.

Supporting. The leader lends emphasis, reason, or other aid to ideas already before the group. He or she does not seek to change them, but only to accelerate their acceptance.

Opposing. The leader may question, challenge, or detract from ideas before the group. He or she may seek to change them and to influence the group to reject them.

Summarizing. The leader brings out common or contrasting ideas before the group, reduces issues to essentials, and focuses or clarifies points.

Controlling. The leader may seek to control who will talk, when, or how much; he or she may intercede for less vocal members.

Informing. The leader provides information to the group (sometimes in response to a question), often simply to supply data, but he or she may have a secondary intent to influence the group. However, the main aspect of this function is to transmit facts or what are offered as facts.

Leadership Strategies

ACTIVATION OF THE HERE-AND-NOW.   Yalom suggests group leaders think "here-and-now." When they focus on present realities long enough, they influence the group strongly toward the here-and-now time frame. Whenever an issue is raised in the group, for example, the leader thinks, "How can I relate this issue to the group's primary task? How can I make it come to life in the here-and-now?" (Yalom 1975, p. 134).

The leader moves the group topical focus from outside to inside, from abstract to specific. If a client describes a confrontation with a spouse or roommate, the therapist-leader may inquire, "If you were to be angry like that with anyone in the group, with whom would you be?" If a client comments that he or she lies, or stereotypes people, or manipulates groups, the therapist may inquire, "What is the main lie you've told in the group thus far?" or, "Can you describe the way you've stereotyped some of us?" or, "How have you manipulated the group thus far?" (Yalom 1975, p. 134).

FOCUS ON PROCESS ORIENTATION.   In making process comments the leader initiates the process of change by escorting his or her group through the following sequence:

1. *Here is what your behavior is like.* Through feedback and, later, through self-observation, the patient learns to see himself as others see him.

2. *Here is how your behavior makes others feel.* Members learn about the impact of their behavior on the feelings of other members.

3. *Here is how your behavior influences the opinions others have of you.* Members learn that, as a result of their behavior, others value them, dislike them, find them unpleasant, respect them, or avoid them.

4. *Here is how your behavior influences your opinion of yourself.* Building on the information gathered in the first three steps, patients formulate self-evaluations; they make judgments about their self-worth and their lovability (Yalom 1975, pp. 155–156).

ACCEPTANCE OF BASIC PREMISES.   The therapist-leader's goal is to guide clients to a point where they accept any or all of the basic premises listed below. This list is adapted from Yalom's list of premises (1975).

1. *Only I can change the world I have created for myself.* *Responsibility* pervades every part of the therapeutic process. Yalom refers to being "responsible for . . ." by being "the basis of . . ." or the "cause of . . . ," the "author of . . ." something (1975, pp. 157–158).

2. *There is no danger in change.* Yalom recommends that the therapist makes an as-if assumption about the client: "You act now as if you feel there would be considerable danger if you were to change." The therapist then assists the client to clarify the nature of the imagined danger. Then, the therapist proceeds to discredit the likelihood of this danger happening.

A second approach to feared danger is to encourage the client to commit a feared act in the group. Since the feared calamity does not, of course, ensue, the dread is gradually extinguished. A client, for example, may avoid aggressive behavior because, at a very deep level, he or she fears that his or her murder impulses might be unleashed. The therapist helps such clients to express their aggressive feelings in small doses in the group. Examples would be feelings of annoyance at being interrupted, irritation at members who are habitually late, and anger at the therapist for charging fees. This is basically a de vivo kind of systematic desensitization, described in Chapter 10.

3. *To attain what I really want, I must change.* Clients often persist in behaving counter to their best interests. For those clients therapists suggest looking at the *payoffs* for maintaining one's present behavior. Once clients realize what they "really" want, they conclude that they must change to attain these wants.

4. *I can change, I am potent.* Explanations provide a conceptual system to clients by which they can order events in their lives into a coherent pattern. To name something or to place it into a logical, causal sequence is to control it.

All theories of counseling are based on imaginary "as if" structures. They all say, "You are behaving (or feeling) *as if* such and such a thing were true." Concepts such as superego, archetypes, masculine protest, the parent-child-adult ego states do not really exist; they are psychological constructs created for our expository convenience. Thus, the novelty of the therapist's explanation from the actualizing frame of reference not only gives clients a fresh way of viewing themselves in their worlds, but the fresh concepts also give them a renewed sense of control over their lives.

Member Behaviors

Although members often utilize some of the foregoing techniques also, it is possible to identify certain unique characteristics of member behavior.

FREQUENCY AND VOLUME.   Occasionally groups are concerned about participation norms. Here a process observer can perform a useful function. Participant frequency of each group member can be found simply by tallying each of the group member's responses. When a member speaks for a longer than average period, the tally can be underlined. When the volume is particularly loud, the tally can be blackened so as to indicate the strength of the response.

TYPES OF APPEAL.   In any discussion, the speaker's appeals and group influence can be determined. Sometimes this influence will be grossly explicit and sometimes more subtle. Some examples follow:

Appeal to reason and logic . . . . "it seems only reasonable"
Appeal to interest . . . . "should be interesting"
Appeal to sanity . . . . "don't be foolish"
Appeal to decorum and good taste . . . . "not in mixed company"
Appeal to enjoyment . . . . "might be fun to . . ."
Appeal to a need, such as dependence . "would help us to . . ."

INDIRECT INFLUENCES.   Many influences on group members are implicit and indirect, since they are not a part of the topic or discussion content. Some examples are: personal characteristics (sex differences, age differences, physical-size differences); status characteristics (vocation, position, community or civic activity, educational background, experience); and nonverbal "signaling" techniques (contrasting voice volume, pounding the table, sex appeal, fidgeting and restlessness, silence followed by strong activity, staring). In making these observations, it is useful to watch for individuals whose behaviors are at variance with those of the group as a whole—for example, those who make a soft-spoken response when everybody else has been shouting. Thus, though one may watch a particular individual, it is well to be aware of the whole group as a frame of reference.

INFLUENCE PATTERNS.   Certain persons in the group seem to have the power to be "addressed to" more than others. Some group members seem to draw and often monopolize the attention and expressions of the group.

Some process observations focus on *content* of the group's work. The following are examples:

TOPICAL DEVELOPMENT.   In listening to a discussion, particular attention can be given to the "life history" of the topics. Though it is not possible or necessarily desirable to be highly precise about this historical analysis, nevertheless, the following scheme can help: How does the topic arise—from one individual, from the interactions of several members, from some other topic? How does the group work with the topic—by arguing contrasting aspects of it, by illustrations and examples, by emotional appeals, by responding to the influence of particular members? What changes occur in the topic as the group works on it—a part gradually displaces the topic as a whole, it is expanded and generalized, it is gradually lost sight of, it is thoroughly examined and concluded? What is the eventual fate of the topic—it is dropped, it becomes a part of the group's product, it is blended with other topics?

TOPICAL CONCURRENCE. By concurrence is meant the degree to which a second speaker seems to understand, accept, and extend the subject matter of the first speaker. The second speaker does not necessarily agree with the first, but he stays with the same general ideas. Often he or she builds on the previous idea. Following is a scale demonstrating four types of concurrence:

1. *Concurring:* No new content areas are opened; there is direct agreement or disagreement or repetition.

SPEAKER A: I think we should try to get more time to do the job.

SPEAKER B: I agree; or, I don't think we need any more time; or, Yeah, we don't have enough time.

2. *Expanding:* The same basic content area is covered, but it is expanded, developed, amplified, or illustrated. The next logical step is taken, or a direct challenge to the preceding remarks is made without bringing in a new focus of attention.

SPEAKER A: I think we should try to get more time to do the job.

SPEAKER B: If they want more than a hasty piece of work, we certainly need more time; or, There's no use seeking more time until we've seen what we can do as it is; or, Look, if we've got to plan the next meeting, arrange for the speaker, and do all those other things, then we've got to have more time.

3. *Altering:* The topic covered by the first speaker is only generally the same as that covered by the new speaker; a major change of emphasis or application is made; the ideas previously expressed are given quite a different turn.

SPEAKER A: I think we should try to get more time to do the job.

SPEAKER B: Yeah, we certainly need it to settle this question about whether to have a lecture or a film. If we're going to use a film, we have to decide which one. I think it should be . . . ; or, No, it isn't more time we need; it's more good ideas; time won't help us until we start really producing. . . .

4. *Changing:* The previously expressed ideas are ignored or given only a perfunctory recognition in what is essentially a new topical development.

SPEAKER A: I think we should try to get more time to do the job.

SPEAKER B: Yes, that's a good idea. Now about those films we were talking about. It seems to me that . . . ; or, What's the name of that film we saw last week?

While the preceding discussion pertained to general group functions, the following material applies especially to counseling and therapy groups. Usually when the client comes for therapy, he or she is seen individually by the therapist first, so that the therapist knows the client well before placing him or her in a group. A group is selected which seems to meet the needs of the client, as well as the client's meeting the needs of the group. The client may then continue to meet the therapist individually once a week and also work in the group once a week. He may reduce the number of individual visits, depending on the setting and problem.

In group counseling, clients usually are selected because of common characteristics, such as underachievement or behavior problems. They usually do not obtain collateral individual counseling but depend on the group for their vehicle of change.

Selection of Group Members

BACKGROUND. One of the first questions that usually arises is, "Who should be in a group?" For a long time, counselors and therapists suggested that members be selected according to diagnostic problem categories. Joel and Shapiro (1950) contend that problems and dynamics should be relatively similar, but that diagnostic categories should be forgotten. Winder (1945) holds that, whenever possible, the members should be chosen so as to have fairly homogeneous backgrounds. This opinion is shared by Coffey (1948). Cohen (1947), however, feels that a calculated attempt should be made to include varied personality types in the composition of each group: for example, one or two outspoken or aggressive individuals, several mature and stable personalities, and several depressed, anxious members. From experiments with grouping of individuals for therapy, Glatzer (1956) found that judicious groupings of varied personalties was important for optimum therapeutic movement. Powdermaker and Frank (1953) concluded from their research that, except for alcoholism, none of the attributes usually considered in grouping—age, intelligence, education, marital status, clinical diagnosis—are significant in themselves, either in determining which clients are suitable for group therapy or in selecting those to be treated in the same group. Similarities or differences in any one of these factors may be important in a particular group under special circumstances, but their effects can be understood only in terms of their importance to the issue with which the clients are concerned at the time. Bach (1954) states that the selection of an individual client is really meaningful only in relation to the factors of group dynamics in the particular group for which membership is being considered. A focus on family remarriage problems, for example, determines group composition by age and sex. Type of problem is also a factor. The success of the Synanon movement with persons addicted to hallucinogenic drugs is an example. Alcoholics Anonymous is another.

Bach has introduced a theory of grouping which he calls the "Nuclear

Expansion Theory." Here, the group is started with two or three members, and the expansion is made according to the identification and similarity needs of these particular individuals. We agree with Bach's view on selection of members.

MAINTAINING GROUP BALANCE.   Fundamental to the decision of placement is the concept of "role" vacancies in a group. A key strategy in forming actualizing groups is to select, or to add, persons with balanced polar opposites. This means, for example, including persons with various traits, such as love and anger, dominance and submission, to give variety to the group and to enable persons to have models and growth stimuli for traits opposite to their own. In other words, it is not desirable to have all angry types, or all bullies, or all nice guys. This selection not only promotes more effective interaction (such as energizing the group), but it also facilitates growth along each polarity. It is felt by most group therapists that groups should have a balance of roles represented. These various personality types give the group material to provoke discussion of common human problems and transference relationships. Some of the many possible role needs for a mixed group are illustrated in the following examples:

1. Father figure or "critical parent."
2. Mother figure or "mother hen."
3. Sex object or "sweetheart."
4. The prodder or facilitator of discussion.
5. The "warm, understanding" member.
6. The adolescent or "delinquent" member.
7. The referee or "compromiser."
8. The religious, "self-righteous," or moralizing member.
9. The "devil," Don Juan, or "wolf."
10. The "snob."
11. The "good wife."
12. The "bad wife."
13. The "good husband."
14. The "bad husband."
15. The "executive" or "very important person."
16. The "woman-hater."
17. The "man-hater."
18. The "masculine" woman.
19. The "feminine" man.
20. The "learned scholar" or "professor."
21. The "working man."
22. The "castrating female."

Placement in a particular group, therefore, would be determined partly by role vacancies which exist in a group.

A further consideration in role placement is that of the individual needs of the client. Placement is often made when the new member is expected to identify with, or will feel close to, other members. Predicted hostility to other members can be a criterion for placement also.

SEX AND AGE COMPOSITION. The most common group is composed of mixed sexes, unless there is a definite reason for like-sex grouping. If one assumes, however, that the therapy or counseling group must be viewed as a part of the transference phenomena, then, as Slavson indicates (1947), a mixed group may favor the tendency to act out problems in a therapeutic fashion. Slavson states that during certain stages in the treatment process, clients develop libidinal desires directed toward the therapist as a parent surrogate. These can be displaced or retransferred upon fellow group members who resemble parental images.

When considering the age composition of a group, Joel and Shapiro (1950) suggest that mixed groups are most natural. Older persons offer more significant transference and identification opportunities for younger members, and vice versa. Bach (1954), who uses the principle of heterogeneity in the selection of his clients, contends that it is not desirable to mix very young adults having had little sexual and social experience with more experienced adults.

CRITERIA FOR EXCLUSION OF MEMBERS FROM GROUPS. When selecting certain members for groups, Hobbs (1951) has found that there are several types of persons who tend to disrupt or hinder group progress. They are: (1) psychologically sophisticated persons who use knowledge of psychodynamics cruelly on others; (2) extremely aggressive or hostile people who destroy the atmosphere of acceptance and freedom essential to the success of the group; and (3) people who are continuously in close contact with each other outside of the group.

Bach uses four personality criteria for exclusion of members from groups: (1) insufficient reality contact; (2) extremes of culturally tabooed or illegal behavior; (3) the dominant character who would be a chronic monopolist of discussion; and (4) those with psychopathic defenses and impulsiveness (1954, pp. 18–22).

SIZE OF GROUPS. In organizing an actualizing group, the question usually arises as to how many persons should be included. Size is important because it can be a barrier to effectiveness of communication. A suggested minimum number for an effective social unit is three to five. Ten to twelve would be the maximum. It is generally agreed by group therapists, however, that eight is an optimum number. Loeser, for example, has several properties which he thinks are characteristic of the therapy group with four to eight members:

1.   It is large enough to dilute basic drives to safe and easily handled levels.

2.   It is large enough to provide a variety of intragroup transference potentialities to suit the needs of each person at any given time.

3. It is large enough to avoid the strong positive and negative polarity of reaction of the dyad (two-member group) and triad (three-member group) and hence is more enduring. It cannot be destroyed by one or even two people.

4. It is large enough to permit heterogeneity and diversification of psycho-dynamic types and thus implement the group interaction process.

5. It is large enough to permit acting out in a diluted and workable manner.

6. On the other hand, it is small enough to be handled by a therapist with a minimum of leadership and control. The therapist can maintain his or her uncritical, permissive, and passive role, all of which are necessary for effective therapy.

7. It is small enough to operate without strong or numerous rules or regulations. Beyond a few simple rules such as hours, meeting places, etc., very few regulations need to be introduced.

8. It is small enough to permit each member a reasonable amount of attention and time, but large enough to remove the tensions of face-to-face talking. The passive individual can remain inconspicuous until his or her confidence is built up before he or she need take on an active role. (1957, pp. 11–12)

Hobbs (1951) and Joel and Shapiro (1950) contend that more interaction is obtained if the group is not large, since discussions led from within the group can operate more effectively. Such discussions are desirable, because leadership from within the group seems to be preferable to thera-pist leadership for controlling monopolists and for drawing out shy mem-bers. The "postsession technique," described later, is essentially such a discussion which operates most effectively when the number of members is small.

SEATING AND PHYSICAL SETTING. The group is arranged in such a way that all participate in an easy and informal manner. For effective participa-tion, the group members must be able to see and hear each other easily. The circle arrangement seems to facilitate participation better than rectan-gular table arrangements. The use of a table should be avoided, for it can serve as a psychological barrier to free interaction. If there are cothera-pists in the group, they should sit several seats away from the therapist in order to avoid having the focus of leadership in one area. Another factor of importance is that each client should have the opportunity to choose his or her own chair.

The physical settings in the room must be conducive to group proc-esses. It is desirable that the room be furnished to some degree like a comfortable living room.

SESSION LENGTH AND TIME INTERVAL. The length of the sessions and the time interval between them have been found to be as important in group therapy and counseling as in individual work. The number of sessions and the length of each vary according to the particular therapist. Some counselors and psychotherapists contend that as many as three meetings a week are preferable, because continuity and intensity of personal interaction are facilitated by the greater frequency of meetings. If three meetings are held, they generally continue for one hour (Joel and Shapiro 1950). Other groups will agree to have only one or two meetings a week, with one-and-a-half or two hours of actual work (Hobbs 1951; Bach 1954). Generally, group counseling sessions are held once a week for an hour to an hour-and-a-half to keep the emotional involvement factor under control. Marathon approaches emphasize fewer but longer and more intensive sessions.

Hinckley and Hermann (1951) found that the majority of group members from the Student Mental Hygiene Clinic at Minnesota preferred meeting one hour a week. Sessions longer than one hour were tried but were found to be unsatisfactory. Usually the first hour was very active and productive, but the succeeding hour was much less productive. In general, it may be said that therapists differ in their opinions about length of session, but group therapy meetings usually last from one to two hours in length and are conducted about once a week.

Role of the Cotherapist in Group Therapy

It is not uncommon for groups to employ the services of two therapists. The second therapist acts as an interpreter-observer in many instances, or he may remain quite passive. The question often arises whether or not two therapists in the same group setting are conducive to group progress. In our experience, it is most helpful to have cotherapists. The facilitative role is then performed by one therapist, the interpreter-summarizer role by the other. The cotherapist role also permits a training situation to exist, wherein trainees can function in this real leadership role.

From psychoanalytic theory one might hold that the cotherapist is better played by a female, so that both "mother" and "father" roles are played by the therapists. In terms of Fromm's theory, however, one therapist can play the mother role of being accepting and permissive, while the interpreter-summarizer role is more akin to Fromm's idea of father love, that is, love with expectations and demands (1956). Joel and Shapiro (1950) contend from their experience that the presence of two therapists, especially if they are of the opposite sex, more readily revives the family situation.

Closed and Continuous Groups

There are two kinds of groups—closed and continuous. In the closed group, the same members are maintained throughout the life span of the group. This is often the case in educational settings where groups run the length of the academic semester. In the continuous group, replacements are made when a member leaves.

There is some degree of speculation among certain therapists whether closed groups offer more advantages than continuous groups. Some think that the closed group has more advantages because data can be accumulated and the group composition kept constant. If members drop out, however, because of an unavoidable circumstance, it may make the group unduly small. An advantage of an open group is that a new member, who has just come to the group, sometimes fosters a reworking of rivalries and competition in the group. Also, a new member may help therapeutic movement through a consolidation of group feeling. New members may reduce their defensiveness by identifying with other members who have already overcome theirs. The presence of less-advanced group members appears to have some actualizing potential for the older members, since the older members gain therapeutically through the experience of sharing and helping new clients adjust to the group.

The Use of Videotapes

Videotape has proven to be a valuable resource for providing "focused feedback" to the group (Miller 1970; Robinson 1970). Berger (1968, 1970), for example, noted that client response to the first playback session differed from response to the later sessions. At first, clients attended primarily to their own self-image. Later, they respond more to their style of relating to each other and with the group's process.

STRATEGIES OF GROUP THERAPY AND MULTIPLE COUNSELING

The leader should be, first of all, competent in individual counseling and therapy techniques. In group therapy he uses all of the relationship, interpretive, and informational techniques discussed earlier in this volume. In addition, he must use other techniques which are unique to, or which must be adapted to, group work. Some of the strategies and techniques mentioned are illustrative only. This topic is so broad and is developing so rapidly that intensive study and coleader training experience are necessary to become competent as a group facilitator. These techniques are presented in the following sections.

Structuring and Contracting

Theories of group psychotherapy and multiple counseling emphasize how the group provides support, stimulation, and reality-testing opportunities. In the group setting, clients have an opportunity to express themselves freely. Support is provided for the member by the reassuring social climate of the group, in which members feel safe in saying what they want to say. The therapist, however, often initiates group discussion by some type of structuring in the first session. Hinckley (1951) gives examples of this method, as follows: One therapist explains, "We are here to learn about ourselves and to help each other manage our natural feelings in more comfortable ways. Now, my name is ———, as most of you already know. Perhaps the simplest way of beginning is for each of us to introduce ourselves and to say something about ourselves." Another therapist comments, "In group sessions we come together to talk over some of the feelings we have which may be causing us discomfort. By finding out how much we are like other people, we sometimes feel better. Also, we may learn how other people handle some of their worries." A third therapist states, ". . . and there will be times in our meetings when it will be very hard to talk about our feelings because they may be painful to us. No one need talk of his troubles, though, until he is ready." A fourth therapist says, "Most of us can feel a little better when we learn to share, that is, talk out some of our troubles. This is possible in here. When we are able to get along comfortably in a small section of society like this group, perhaps later we will feel comfortable in larger groups. Shall we introduce ourselves now and begin by telling a little about ourselves? We don't have to speak of painful matters immediately."

In the structuring process the therapist should make it clear why the clients have come together. The members should be aware of the fact that conflicting feelings and attitudes are the basic reason for the formation of the group. It is also appropriate to state some advantages of group therapy so that clients can anticipate realistic results. It should also be stressed that what goes on in the group is strictly confidential.

The reassurance of structure is needed because group therapy is generally a new experience for clients. Further reasons and techniques of structuring are covered in Chapter 7.

As an aid to helping clients form a realistic "set" toward the group experience, the authors use the following guidelines for communicating in actualizing therapy groups:

1. Always use "I," never "them," "they," "we," "you," "us," and so on.
"I feel."
"I think."
"I am."
2. Avoid "but," "although," "because."
"I feel hurt today"—*not* ". . . because I was hurt by my husband."
"I don't like you"—*not* ". . . but I don't like people like you."
3. Attempt to verbalize your feelings and thoughts in the *here-and-now* situation. Even past and future experiences should be expressed in the present: "I am going to group today and I feel tense"—*not* "I was driving here today and felt terrible." Feel terrible *now*!
4. When addressing a fellow group member, talk to him or her directly, eye-to-eye contact, and *don't* use the third person when relating to him or her. "I like you"—*not* "I like him," or "I like her."
5. Be constantly aware of what your body wisdom is saying to you (listen to your tensions, boredom, joys, and so on, and communicate these to the group). This is best done by listening to your voice.
6. When you are spoken to, *listen* intently and try to *hear* what is said and with what feeling it is being expressed.

7. The one question that should not be asked is "Why?" For example, if someone expresses caring for you, please don't ask why! Be responsive to the other person. How do you feel when this person cares for you?

Bach (1954, pp. 29–30) has prepared a *group therapy contract* in which six procedural principles are structured for the new group member. The new member signs this sheet when he or she accepts group membership. We have modified this preparation sheet for use in our practice and present it here as an example:

New Group Member Contract

1. *Size of group:*
The group's size is limited to a minimum number of six and a maximum number of ten clients.

2. *Admission of new members:*
When an old member leaves the group, his or her place in the group will be filled by a new member. The selection is made on two bases: (a) which group is best for the prospective member, and (b) which prospective member is best for the group.

3. *Extraoffice meetings:*
The regular office meetings of the group with the therapist, while of central therapeutic importance, are only part of the total program. Experiences during the postsession between members of the group provide important material for self-observation and analysis. No extraoffice meetings other than postsession meetings are allowed.

4. *Sharing of mutual experiences:*
Group members usually adhere to the principle that everything anybody says, thinks, or does which involves another member of the group is subject to open discussion in the group. In other words, the emotionally important experiences of any member are shared by all members. There are no secrets *inside* the group.

5. *Ethical confidence:*
In contrast to Principle Number 4, everything that goes on within the group—everything!—must remain an absolute secret as far as any outsider (nonmember) is concerned. Anyone participating in group therapy automatically assumes the same professional ethics of absolute discretion which bind professional therapists.

6. *The group's goal:*
The group goal is free communication on a nondefensive, personal, and emotional level. This goal can be reached only by the group effort. Experience shows that the official therapists cannot "push" the group; the group has to progress by its own efforts. Each member will get out of the group what he puts into it. As every member communicates to the group his feelings and perceptions and associations of the moment as openly as he can and as often as he can, the group will become a therapeutically effective

medium. The goal of free communication is freedom to be oneself most fully and comfortably.

I have read the above and agree to cooperate fully.

Signed: _____

The "Going-Around" Technique

The going-around technique is often used as a warm-up device by the therapist to pitch the communication at a more emotional and less intellectual level. Each member describes his or her feelings about how every other member in the group affects him or her emotionally. This is usually done from neighbor to neighbor, "going around" the group circle. This technique is particularly useful in situations involving "newcomers." Older group members give their first impression to the newcomer in a casual manner. Then the newcomer has an opportunity to do likewise with the group members.

The Communica-tion-Training Technique

Since a basic process goal of all groups is to promote communication among group members, the facilitator presents (at appropriate times) the following communication rules:

1. The principle of *direct communication* is stated to the group as follows: "We never withhold feelings that we have about another person in the group. When we communicate these feelings we look directly at the person to whom we are talking, and we use his name or the pronoun *you.*" A poor example would be (talking to group in general): "I think Bill is not facing this problem with his wife." A better example would be (talking directly to Bill): "Bill, I think you are not facing this problem with your wife."

2. Making statements is preferable to asking questions. The principle of *question analysis* is stated as follows: "Whenever we ask a question, we must state the hypothesis behind our question." A poor example is: "What was your wife's reaction?" A better example is: "I was curious about your wife's reaction because I wondered if she reacts like my wife does."

3. The principle of *advice analysis* proceeds as follows: "There is a strong tendency to project our needs, wants, perceptions, and meanings to others. Whenever we give advice we must speculate on what it was in our own life experience which has made us so alert to this particular advice." A poor example is: "Why don't you leave your wife?" A better example is: "I think you ought to leave your wife, since you have the same situation which caused me to leave my first wife."

The Psychodrama or Role-Playing Technique

The role-playing technique permits the client to apply playful acting-out of his problems as a serious attempt to understand his conflicts. The value of this method lies in the fact that participants reveal feelings and tensions without the burden of shame. It facilitates presenting a situation with fewer words and with greater clarity than can be achieved with the ordinary discussion methods. Driver (1954) claims that role playing is an effective alternative for talk and is an excellent warm-up device for discussion.

Role playing as a counseling technique often helps clients gain a better perspective of themselves and others. It can be used, for example, to practice social situations which are difficult for the client. Even when it is used in a group situation by qualified workers, emphasis should be placed on the fact that many complications can arise if it is not used properly. Bach (1954) warns of the possible traumatic effect of premature externalizing of threatening materials through role playing.

Some of the major types of psychodramatic procedures in a group therapy setting, as adapted from Del Torto and Cornyetz (1945), are described below.

1.   *Role reversal* is a procedure which allows two individuals to exchange roles. Role reversal is used in the following example: Mother and daughter figures might be discussing what would be a reasonable hour for the latter to come home from a date. The daughter could exchange roles with the mother to see her side. Conversely, the parent could be afforded the frame of reference of the daughter.

2.   *The double technique* allows a second individual to assume the identity of the subject. This is a technique whereby two identities may seem merged into one. Functions of the double are illustrated in a situation in which one individual has to make a decision. For example, when meditating over whether or not to buy a new car, one might be in doubt about its being a good buy. A double ego, in this situation, would function as the subject's conscience and desire, and would verbalize the conflict in a low tone of voice at the same time the subject was verbalizing his or her dilemma.

3.   *The soliloquy* is a technique to make known "hidden" thoughts of role-playing participants. Another purpose of the soliloquy is to clarify and fix newly gained insights. For example, in a conference, each individual is allowed to speak his piece. Then, as the scene is "frozen," each is asked to soliloquize or to speak out what feelings are going on in his mind which he is not expressing. For example, he is asked, "What thought occurred? How do you really feel about the other person?"

4.   *The mirror technique* is an attempt to allow subjects to see themselves. It is used when it is thought to be helpful to see themselves in action. For example, a subject may wish to observe himself or herself at a given task, such as a job interview. The person serving as the substitute ego is placed across from the subject and mimics his or her behavior.

5.   *Periodic stimuli technique* is a method used to test the client's range of expansiveness within the role. It is designed also to test his or her spontaneous adaptation to surprise elements. For example, a situation might be created where the subject is an artist working in a studio. At periodic intervals the director may send in a landlord demanding rent, a complaining sponsor, or a cantankerous model. The basic situation is not changed; only the stimuli are varied.

6. *The hidden theme technique* brings out the subject's ability to perceive a behavioral theme in a social situation and to create an appropriate role to deal with it. For example, a subject is sent out of the room. She is told beforehand that, when she returns, a social situation will be in progress and that she should relate herself meaningfully to the situation that is going on.

7. *The mute technique* is used to reveal nonverbal resources for communication and expression. A theme is given to the subject and other clients with instructions that they communicate by gestures and bodily movements. An example would be a card game involving four people who are allowed to communicate only by gestures.

Expression of Polarities

Primary emphases of actualizing counseling and therapy are awareness and expression of inner polarities so as to achieve ultimate integration and actualization. The actualizing counselor, therefore, does not simply role-play in the Moreno interpersonal sense. Instead, with the counselor's help clients role-play the polarities within themselves and the differences between themselves and others in fantasy. The following are examples (Shostrom 1976):

C: Be your lonesome self.

CL: I feel so blue and unhappy; I just need people.

C: Now be your strong opposite self.

CL: Oh, quit being such a weakling. You know that you don't need anybody else but me.

C: Now be the weak one again.

CL: What good are you?

C: Now be the strong one and answer.

CL: Without me you're a machine with only one wheel; but with me we drive the machine together.

C: Now be the weak one and answer.

CL: Gosh, I never thought of that. I guess we can be strong when we work together.

The above is an example of an individual *listening* to both weak and strong sides of himself. Through the conflict, antagonistic poles become complementary. When both sides of ourselves are accepted, integration comes more easily.

Kaplan (1978) suggests a variation on Gestalt leadership technique utilizing "right-brain, left-brain" concepts. He asks a client to go around the group telling each member first a message from his or her cognitive, or left-brain side, and then speaking to that person from his or her right, or more intuitive, side. This process would be reversed, leading to more flexibility and integration of the rational-intuitive polarity.

The Summary Interpretation Technique

Usually after forty or forty-five minutes of the therapeutic hour have elapsed, the group therapist or cotherapist finds it propitious to make a summary interpretation of what has happened in the hour. We feel that this summary task is best performed by a cotherapist, rather than by the therapist. The latter usually has a facilitative or management role, and would find it difficult psychologically to perform both the summary interpretation and the facilitative role.

The interpretation technique has been found helpful in giving the group a picture of what has happened during the hour. We have found the following types of summaries to be useful:

1. *"Theme" summaries:* Hobbs (1951) suggests that group therapy is much like a musical composition, in that there are certain "themes" which run through group conversation. The cotherapist identifies these themes in the summary. An example is: "Tonight we have been talking about competition. Sally and Jack see themselves as always running away from it. In the area of romance, Bill says he just gives up, or disposes of the possibility of winning. In interpersonal competition, we have decided that we have to define the problem clearly. This means defining the assets and liabilities of our competitors and then defining our own assets and liabilities. We can then decide on which techniques we ought to use. Doreen is competing now with another woman for her husband. One thing she can do better than this other woman is to be a good mother to her children and a good wife to her husband. She has decided this is one of her chief assets which she can develop. We have also discussed the idea of 'shooting against our own par'—that is, competition with oneself is one of the best ways for improvement. This method doesn't hurt anybody in the process. Jim does this in his golf game—and we can do it here too."

2. *Individual analysis summaries:* Sometimes the discussions of a group do not center on a particular theme, but the individual group members discuss their own unique problems. The cotherapist then summarizes more individually, as for example: "Our discussion tonight has focused on four people, and I'd like to say something about each of them. We might call these people by certain pseudonyms.

"Alex here is Accepting Alex. He wants to be so accepting of everybody, because he has learned that this is what good psychologists do. But this is only half the story. Before we can really accept others, we first must learn to accept ourselves—both the negative and positive parts of ourselves. When Alex is able to do this completely, he'll not have trouble accepting others' positive and negative sides too.

"Doreen we might call Doormat Doreen. She has spent seventeen years being a doormat for her husband, and now she wants to change.

She has been thinking that one way to do that is to take off from teaching this year so that her husband will not have the money she makes to depend on. But Les and Sam are in agreement that a better way would be to continue teaching, since just sitting around might make her more depressed and tired than before. Les found that out in his own experience. Furthermore, we know that most of us get more tired from underwork than overwork. If Doreen then continued to teach, she could keep her own money and really be selfish for once in her life.

"Will we might call Un-Warm Uncle Will. He just doesn't want to admit he is warm, and yet Doreen has shown us that he really is. He doesn't want to be this way, and for the first time tonight has asked us to pull him down from his stand-offish position. He has humbled himself to do this, and I think we can help him."

3. *Interpersonal dynamic summaries:* Instead of focusing on the individual problems of clients, the therapist can describe the interpersonal dynamics of feelings which have been taking place in the hour. An example is: "We have had many feelings shown here tonight. Some of them have been obvious, others not so obvious. Pete and Ted have both openly expressed their warm feelings toward Connie. Jack has expressed hostility by saying that he doesn't like her because she is so pretty, that everyone likes her, and that rejection is good for such a person. But after analyzing this feeling we find that Jack is saying this because he fears that if he were to express his real feelings of warmth to Connie, she might reject him, so he takes the offensive instead by rejecting her first. But he finds that this isn't very satisfying, because it leaves him feeling, as he says, lousy."

These methods of interpretation may be combined in summarizing the session; they are presented separately above for purposes of clarity in exposition.

The Postsession Technique

One of the techniques recommended by Bach (1954) is the postsession technique. This is a procedure of allowing the group to remain after the therapeutic hour for the purposes of integrating the accomplishments of the hour and for the purpose of preparing one another for further therapeutic work. Bach sees the following goals for postsession work: (1) therapeutic reinforcement of insight gained in the work session of the group; (2) preparation to deal with difficult and resistance-evoking material through the development of social alliances; (3) opportunity to release pent-up tensions that were instigated but remained unleashed in the clinical work session; and (4) provision of experiential data on neurotic set-up (acted out transference) behavior for later working through.

There are several basic rules which must be observed with the postsession technique. First, the group members must stay together as a group. There must be no postsession pairing off and departing from the group. Group members are told that, other than in the postsession, they must not socialize outside the group. Furthermore, all material discussed in the postsession should be brought out ultimately in the regular session. Clients are encouraged in their individual sessions with their counselors to discuss what happened in the postsession

Nonverbal and Body Awareness Techniques

Since words are often difficult means for expressing experiences, group leaders use various exercises designed to increase self-awareness and mobilize energy. Schutz of Esalen Institute, for example, has developed a program of group fantasy, bodily movement, physical release, and drama as media for expressing and increasing awareness of feelings. To accomplish these goals, encounter groups make use of a number of exercises in relaxation, stretching, touching, pushing, and striking. Sensory awareness, or "awakening," is developed through activities such as dancing and art work, with the goal of increased pleasure and joy. Interpersonal relationships are enhanced through exercises emphasizing touching, competitive activities, and physically breaking into the group circle. In the ensuing discussion, members become more aware of their impact on others and the meaning of their own feelings.

SUMMARY

Group techniques to develop interpersonal as well as intrapersonal dimensions have been presented. General considerations for development of groups, such as selection, composition, size, physical setting, time, facilitator roles, and closed versus continuous groups, have been outlined. Research, particularly on learning outcomes, has been a prominent group development.

It was suggested that the effective group facilitator must be familiar with all the individual techniques presented in this book. In addition, certain supplementary group strategies were presented. Some of these techniques are: structuring, "going-around," communication training, psychodrama, group summary and interpretation, and postsession meetings.

III

SPECIAL AREAS
OF
APPLICATION

12

Counseling and Psychotherapy with Couples and Families

COUNSELING COUPLES

Couples counseling is tied closely to therapeutic psychology; however, it has a unique history (Allen 1975). In the past, couples counseling was performed, for the most part, by clergymen and social workers in churches, public welfare agencies, and family-service organizations. Counseling of couples has become such a specialized activity that some states, such as California, require a special license to advertise as a marriage and family counselor. This category includes persons from varied professional backgrounds. In addition to their respective basic professional organizations, many marriage and family counselors belong to the American Association of Sex Educators and Counselors or the National Council on Family Relations.

Historically, social workers have worked mainly in agencies with low-income families who have not been able to seek professional help on a private basis. More recently, however, social agencies have begun to develop services designed for the middle-income group (Fizdale 1957).

Family-service agencies have become part of almost all large community-service rosters. This service gives total family counseling, as well as marriage counseling, to middle- and low-income groups. Numerous psychiatrists, psychologists, and social workers perform these services in private practice also.

The development of marriage assistance as a specialty dates back to such pioneer work as that of Stone, who established the first marriage consultation center in New York in 1929, and of Popenoe, who established the Institute of Family Relations in 1930. Much pioneer work has been done by Emily Mudd since 1932, when she established the Philadelphia Marriage Council. These people established marriage counseling as a specialty separate from family casework.

Specialists in working with sex problems and sexual enrichment in couples have become popular on the individual counseling and group scene. Sexuality topics in couples counseling and special workshops have become widespread owing largely to development of several strategies of sexual dysfunction treatment in addition to increasing public awareness of enrichment potential and admission of sexual problems. Some of these strategies are aimed at sexual enrichment primarily through educational media and sensory awareness. Other strategies, such as sensate focus, apply mainly to partners with some kind of sexual dysfunction, such as impotence. Masters and Johnson (1974) have done the basic research and development on treatment of sexual disorders. While their methods focus on sexual functioning, they view their work in the broader perspectives of caring relationships and pleasure outcomes. A key method is sexual enrichment through *sensate focus*—a method designed to reawaken pleasurable bodily sensations and feelings through touch activities and clear emotional communication.

*Issues In
Couples
Counseling*

PHILOSOPHICAL ISSUES.   We take the position that a counselor or therapist does not have the right to decide whether or not divorce is the best solution for those who seek marital counseling. Marriage counselors can assist in the actualizing progess of the persons concerned, whether or not divorce is a part of the solution.

The counselor should recognize that there are some couples whose emotional separation has been of such long duration, with so much bitterness, that reconciliation is not likely. Where great personality damage has been done to one or both individuals, reconciliation may be a dubious answer anyway. This does not mean that divorce is the only solution. A couple may be helped to live together in relative harmony and security even though the goal of a close marriage is impossible.

In some instances, a separation is the only means by which a marriage can be saved. Frequently this leads to final dissolution of the marriage. However, separation may help individuals face the realities of living instead of blaming each other for their problems. If a counselor can help the couple to stop quarreling over petty issues, it may be possible for one or both of them to do some basic growing. Later, they may be able to cope with complex marital interactions on a more constructive basis. Separation is seldom instigated by the counselor. Usually it is one reality factor to be considered in a particular counseling situation.

THEORETICAL ISSUES. A debate has been conducted in professional journals and books on how counselors should view marital conflict and plan their counseling. Three threads dominate this controversy: psychodynamic positions, behavioral marital therapy, and systems-oriented methods (Gurman 1980). The psychodynamic approach emphasizes the past and focuses on the individuals in the partnership. Behavioral technology emphasizes the present and focuses on skills needed to solve the problems in the marriage. The systems approach views the couple as a unit interacting with each other and others in a complex environmental matrix. Strategic therapy, growing out of the Palo Alto group on communication theory, focuses on present problems of the partners and how families can be restructured to be more functional and to communicate more effectively (Madanes and Haley 1977; Jacobson and Margolin 1979). In an attempt to reconcile the differences and to integrate the methods Gurman (1980) makes a strong plea for moving beyond the constraints of single models of marital change. He proposes the same view that we have throughout this book. Gurman goes further to predict that couples therapy of the 1980s will fall short if it does not consider a dual approach to helping individual members integrate their behavior and the family as a system to improve its functional capacities.

EFFECTS OF DISRUPTIONS ON CHILDREN. Sometimes a separation is a necessary transition to final divorce. It can facilitate reasonably amicable postdivorce relations and minimize unnecessary bitterness that likely will react unfavorably on the children caught in the middle. Thus, one of the most common considerations in divorce is the effect it will have on the children involved. Despert, in an analysis of the effects of divorce on children, says: "Divorce is not the costliest experience possible to a child. Unhappy marriage without divorce—what we shall call emotional divorce—can be far more destructive to him than divorce" (1953, p. 18). Recent data from a thorough study of sixty families with 131 children by Kelly (1981) refuted these findings. She found that how the decision to get a divorce was made was the critical factor affecting children. High anger and verbal assaults, for example, had a damaging effect on children. She concluded also that children could live better in a conflicted marriage than go through a traumatic divorce. Marital conflict was not related highly to inept child rearing.

Mahler and Rabinovitch, among others, list ways in which marital conflict may affect a child's development adversely. The following list is an adaptation of their discussion of marital conflict and children:

1. The child is made a buffer between parents; either or both turn to the child for satisfactions not obtained from the partner.

2. The child is made a pawn—something planned for, conceived, and used to cement a marriage already in jeopardy.

3. The child is made a confidant to either or both parents who are hostile to each other, thus burdening him or her emotionally beyond his or her capacity.

4. The child is hurt by impulsive actions, such as confronting him or her with major decisions or changes.

5. The child is subjected to recurrent or violent scenes, sometimes alternating with periods of false peace.

6. The child is exposed to protracted subtle discord, such as "the predivorce uncertainty."

7. The resolution of the oedipal phase is made difficult, since it is accomplished through identification with the parent of the same sex.

8. The child's period of dependency on mother is prolonged, since his or her dependency phase has been arrested at this level (1956, pp. 50–54).

When divorce takes place, the counselor frequently can help clients assist their children through this difficult period. Despert (1953, p. 42) thinks that the child of estranged parents needs to know that: (1) he or she is not to blame; (2) his or her parents still love him or her; (3) something is wrong—but not, as he or she fears, everything; (4) parents are not gods but human beings who have made mistakes.

Unfortunately, bickering families not only tend to diminish actualizing behaviors, but they also tend to perpetuate their unhealthy patterns in the marriages of the next generation. Marital counseling, in many instances, is the most direct and suitable approach to breaking this vicious circle. The conclusion is that there is no one best way to solve marital difficulties for the best interests of the children.

If divorce does take place, the effects on the children are further complicated by the now common occurrence of the remarriage of one or both parents. If marital or family counseling is needed, the counseling is affected by the complex interrelationships of the new marriage, as indicated in Figure 20. Children, jealous of the attention given by a parent to a new spouse, very often become difficult; step-parents, seeking love from their new spouses, often see the children as interfering with the new relationship; the obligation to include children in the total family decision-making process often creates many problems. Children of the two families become part of the marriage counseling, and the marital problems of one couple affect the family of the other couple.

The discussion above has suggested the complexity and consequences of the problem and has implied that it is frequently impossible that any solution will be absolutely constructive for everyone concerned. The following discussion can only outline some of the major problems in the complex area of marital counseling and suggest some techniques for handling them.

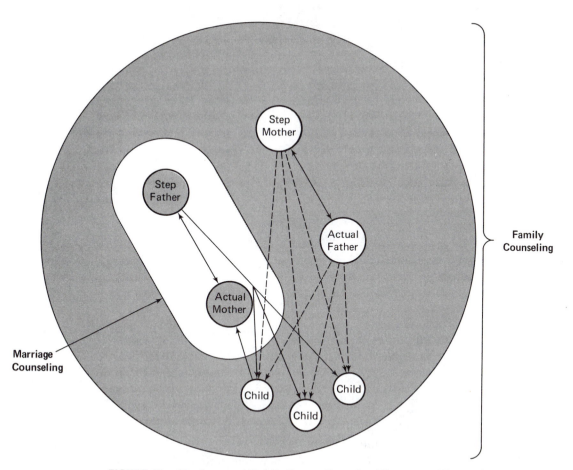

FIGURE 20. Marriage and Family Counseling after Divorce and Remarriage

Models of Couples Counseling

Couples counseling differs from other types of counseling in that one or both of the partners seeks help because he or she believes that their relationship is in difficulty. It is this emphasis on the problems of the relationship itself, at least in the early stages of the counseling process, which makes couples counseling a specialty.

Foster (1956, p. 213) has contrasted individual psychotherapy and marriage counseling in the two figures which follow. In Figure 21, illustrating psychotherapy, the therapist is directly connected with the client, who, in turn, is concerned directly with his or her symptoms, developmental history, character structure, and reality.

In Figure 22 Foster (1956, p. 214) shows a direct, individual connection between the separate entities of marital counselor, husband, wife, and the marriage. In addition to the symptoms, developmental history, and reality with which husband and wife are individually concerned, the marriage substitutes its own conflict patterns for the individual character

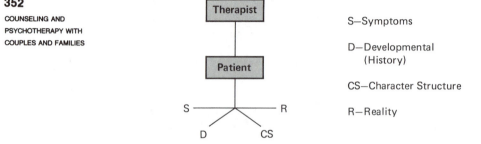

FIGURE 21. *The Individual Psychotherapy Model.* Adapted from Foster (1956).

structures. Thus, it is important to note that individual psychotherapy is very much a part of marriage counseling; but to this is added the emphasis on conflict patterns within the marriage, as well as the marriage symptoms and developmental histories. This means seeing both partners at the same time in most cases.

Foster distinguishes marriage counseling from psychotherapy in that the former must deal with a third element, the marriage relationship, as well as with the individual histories and conflicts of husband and wife. However, he does not make clear the dynamic relationships among these three elements. The naïve or inexperienced marriage counselor tends to focus on the *relationship* in marriage counseling only, concentrating on such problems or symptoms as bickering and unkindness. Consequently, he or she attempts to smooth out the relationship between husband and wife. The result, generally, is superficial. Marital psychotherapy usually means that the therapist begins with the individual spouses themselves and their unique problems. Thus, the marriage therapist works with the individual

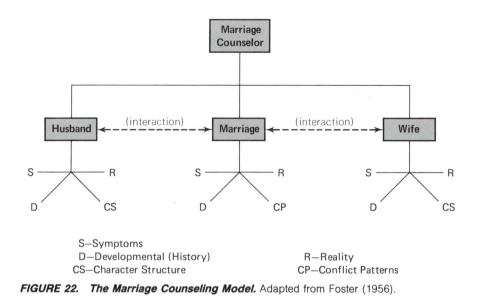

FIGURE 22. *The Marriage Counseling Model.* Adapted from Foster (1956).

first and then with the relationship. Marriage counseling does both but tends to focus on relationship problems and seeing the couple together.

Finney (1964) describes a "partnership psychotherapy," which consists of interviewing two clients at the same time. These may be a couple or persons of the same sex and age but total strangers to each other. Sharing and mutual stimulation draw on the advantages of group therapy while retaining the personal focus of individual interviews. Finney found this method had not only economy values but additional therapeutic outcomes as well.

Enrichment Models

A strong trend of the seventies that promises even greater acceleration in the 1980s is marital enrichment. Churches have sponsored many "marriage encounters," growth centers have offered workshops in marriage enrichment, and numerous popular books have been published on enrichment (Mace and Mace 1976; Otto 1976; Sawin 1979; Hoff and Miller 1980). The movement has controversial outcome research, but the consensus of specialists in marriage counseling is that it is a potent force in helping marriages that are dull or have gone dead but have potential for resurrection. Enrichment strategies work best when there is an intact relationship and the conflicts are not irreconcilable.

Marriage enrichment is more of a philosophy and a process than a program. The thrust is prevention and renewal rather than remediation. The basic content of enrichment programs, however, includes communications improvement, affective skills, self-esteem work, and taking care of "unfinished business." The principal limitations to this approach are the emotional, placebo effects, meaning the emotional high that is experienced after an enrichment weekend. Then the couple goes home to face the hard realities of behaviors that haven't changed much and old conflicts that are still unresolved. On the other hand, the positive effects are that the couple has a different perspective on their relationship and new skills to apply in everyday life such that a renewal effect is experienced eventually. A key is follow-up to see that the new awareness and skills are used in their daily life together. This is why some enrichment programs build in a couples support component, where couples get together regularly over the months following the original intervention.

According to Hoff and Miller (1980), the main long-range goals of enrichment work are to: (1) increase awareness of self and mutual empathy; (2) increase awareness of strengths and potentials; (3) increase mutual self-disclosure; (4) increase intimacy; and (5) develop skills in communication, problem solving, and conflict management.

Infidelity Problems

An analysis of marital conflicts leads to the conclusion that a basic problem is lack of healthy self-regard in one or both partners. Infidelity is often a symptom of not having achieved this major actualizing goal. The typical spouse, not feeling a sense of personal worth or love from husband or wife, may seek to prove lovableness by engaging in an extramarital affair. Counselors find, however, that simply eliminating the third person in a triangle does not help. What is required is a type of therapy that helps the individual to develop feelings of worth and adequacy. Once this is achieved, he or she will be able to see the neurotic need that is being met by an affair and to express hostility to his or her spouse for not having loved him or her more. The spouse responds typically by recognizing the dependence on the errant spouse. Finally, with these unexpressed and unrecognized dependencies having been worked through in an actualizing fashion, the relationship is likely to improve.

Horney describes the multiple factors involved in reactions to infidelity. The counselor often must deal with the spouse not involved in the infidelity also. Her discussion illustrates the meaning of such problems from the viewpoint of this other spouse.

> *There are a number of reasons that might explain why she feels and acts in this way, quite apart from a genuine hurt about the breach of confidence. (1) It may have hurt her pride that the husband could be attached to anyone but herself. (2) It may be intolerable to her that her husband could slip out from her control and domination. (3) The incident may have touched off a dread of desertion. (4) She may be discontented with the marriage for reasons of which she is not aware, and she may use this conspicuous occurrence as an excuse for expressing all her repressed grievances, thus engaging merely in an unconscious campaign of revenge. (5) She may have felt attracted toward another man and resent the fact that her husband indulged in a freedom that she had not allowed herself. (1942, pp. 283–84)*

The Reconciliation Decision

The course of reconciliation in marital counseling may be diagrammed as in Figure 23. What is suggested here is that, initially, marital counseling causes the marital relationship to get worse rather than better. Thus, the general idea developed in Chapter 4 that "you often get worse before you get better" holds true here also. In Figure 23 the course of marital therapy suggests that, at first, the spouses seem to separate psychologically. For this reason, it is unwise in the initial phases to focus on reconciliation, as indicated at Point 2. To do this would be to limit the necessary expression of hostile feelings toward one's spouse. Counseling brings out these hostile feelings, many of which have remained dormant for years. The expression of such negative feelings enables the client to come to the end of Point 1 —decision—more easily. Here he or she comes to regard himself or herself as a person of worth and dignity who does not need to stay with the marriage at any cost. This is the "brink of disaster" point, as far as the marriage is concerned.

Awareness of these facts, however, leads clients to make a choice.

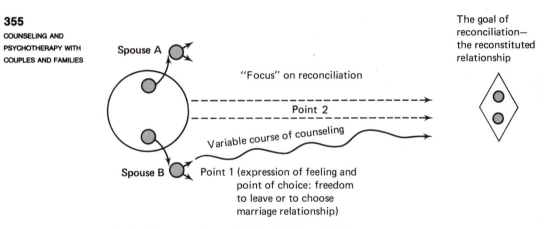

FIGURE 23. The Process of Marital Counseling.

They can be free of the marriage; but they are free also to *choose* marriage and not be neurotically bound to it. When they make the latter choice, they are able to relate effectively to their partners for the first time. Parenthetically, this means that it may be unwise for the client or counselor to focus consciously on "saving the marriage at all costs" if the process is to run its course and the risks are to be taken realistically.

In light of the above discussion, it is asserted that the area of marriage counseling is but a special application of actualizing counseling and therapy. Marriage counseling is more extensive in scope, however, since it deals with multiple relationships, as well as with the personalities of the persons involved.

Partnership
Problems

Until recently the main problems of young people as far as partnerships and sex were concerned were whether to get married or not, and whether to have sexual relationships before marriage or not. Now the choices are so many with the advent of the "pill" and the presence of widely variant values on sexual relationships. There are basic choices to be made among various forms of partnerships—the temporary marriage or "trial marriage," just "living together," homosexual relationships, premarital communes, "swinging" in various forms, in addition to conventional marriage. Even after the marriage choice is made, there are forms of group marriage, communal living groups, and various swinging options for the marrieds. This state of affairs makes counseling, of an informal type at least, all the more attractive for those persons faced with these decisions on what is best for them.

Skidmore and Garrett indicate that the "basic aim of premarital counseling is to assist the prospective partners to gain a better understanding of themselves, of each other, and of what marriage entails" (1955, p. 323). It is most difficult to categorize certain problem areas as being unique to *pre*marital counseling. However, there are a number of considerations that are basic to this subject, relating to counseling young people.

The Problem of Partner Choice A basic consideration in premarital counseling is the obvious question of partner choice. Psychologists have pointed out that many choices are based on some form of neurotic attraction. Mittelmann, for example, lists some common types of neurotic attraction, fitting in with our model of manipulation described in Chapter 3.

1. *One aggressive and sadistic versus one dependent and submissive.*
2. *One self-sufficient through emotional detachment versus one demanding love.*
3. *Mutual attempts at domination.*
4. *One neurotically ill versus one extremely considerate.*
5. *One with fluctuating helplessness and assertiveness versus one fluctuating in responsibility and disappointed desire for love.* (1956, pp. 82–83)

One of the major jobs in premarital counseling is to help young people determine the extent to which their choice of partner is actualizing for them or not. Fromm (1956) suggests the criterion that to love someone because you "need" that person is neurotic; to need that person because you love him or her is healthy. Fromm points out also that love in this sense is both an emotional feeling and a decision.

Maslow (1970) suggests also that marriage between self-actualizing people is a merging of feelings and intellectual choices. The choice is *felt* to be right. Their cognitive acts confirm their feelings, or vice versa. This reciprocal confirmation and convergence process takes place in varied ways with the individuals involved.

The Nature of Love and Commitment A second area of prime concern in premarital counseling is dealing with the meaning of love. Few people have ever taken time to develop any clear concept of love, much less to evaluate what that love means to them as individuals. When asked, most people are likely to say that they married for love; but often they cannot verbalize what they meant, or what they mean now when they say they love or do not love their mates.

Frequently a person's concept of love does not distinguish between "romantic love" and "mature love" between man and woman (Branden 1980). Romantic love has cultural roots in the past; but it survives in the present, nurtured by an endless barrage of fairy tales in movies, magazines, novels, and on television. The media cater to the susceptible daydreams of the immature and tend to make them addicts of romantic emotionalism. This happens because in their immaturity they appear unable to understand, let alone grow into, mature love relationships without assistance.

A counselor needs to be familiar with common psychological interpretations of love and the processes of loving. Although a thorough analysis cannot be made here, certain generally accepted ideas concerning love will be described as they affect the problem of premarital counseling. In our earlier discussions, caring was expressed as a way of manifesting love. Shostrom's *Caring Relationship Inventory* (1966), described in Chapter 5, identifies some of its dimensions. The CRI includes seven concepts of love. *Affection* reflects the capacity of the client to feel a sense of unconditional concern for another. It is charitable, compassionate, and appreciative. Its potential liability, however, lies in the overintense expression of these affectionate feelings such that a vague perception of ownership of the other person develops, or a feeling of obligation is incurred. Whether in parent-child or partner relationships, this manipulative tendency (in our actualizing model terms) needs to be recognized and changed. In an actualizing relationship, the sincere valuing of the other is a helpful antidote to regarding the other as a thing to be manipulated.

Friendship is another level of caring in the form of unconditional acceptance of the personhood of the other. It involves feelings of mutuality, equality, and appreciation. Again, the danger is that with manipulative twists this quality becomes exploitative.

The *eros* form of love and caring is characterized by romantic and erotic qualities. It is closely associated with sensory qualities from physical contact. It can be expressed in a manipulative form also as seduction or using the body of the other without much concern for the feelings of the other.

Empathy forms in the CRI reflect the capacity to feel for another, as described in earlier chapters on the nature of the counseling relationship. It is based on mutual appreciations, commitments, and common interests. Its manipulative form is pretense that one is empathizing, but then one does the opposite. An example is a spouse saying, "I know how badly you feel when I'm gone so much." Then he does nothing about it.

Self-love is appreciating one's individuality, feeling a strong sense of personal worth, and accepting one's weaknesses. Self-love moves into the manipulative category when one treats one's self as an object, prostitutes one's self, or allows others to exploit one.

Being love is a type of admiring, respecting feeling which does not extract conditions or reservations. *Deficiency love*, on the other hand, views the other for what he or she can do for one. Love is viewed as a means to gain other ends than solely being with the person.

Romantic love is a special form of the eros type described above. It needs to be faced honestly by prospective partners. It is defined as the projection of an individual's emotional needs onto a love object. Romantic love is the search for the ideal mate. This ideal mate personifies all the perfection and divine attributes that the individual feels he or she lacks or needs. Mature love, by contrast, comes only after a knowledge of and experience with the loved partner. It may follow a "period of disillusionment" associated with romantic love. "Falling out of romantic love" results from a shattering of the idealized, romantic love illusion. One "falls out of love" because one does not work through the period of disillusionment to a new conception of love based not on projected needs, but on a realistic appraisal and deep valuing of each other as unique persons.

"Counterfeit" or "profane" love are terms referring to manipulative forms not uncommon in marriage conflict. Counterfeit love can be recognized when the relationship is degrading, exploitative, possessive, violent, antisocial, irresponsible, sadistic, or masochistic. These are the symptoms that point to the need for more actualizing before a normal love relationship can be developed.

Fromm lists the following distorted ideas that many people have in regard to love: (1) They "see the problem of love primarily as that of *being loved* rather than that of loving." (2) They "think that to *love* is simple," whereas to find the correct love object is difficult. (3) They feel that love is beyond understanding, and they cannot learn how to love (1956, pp. 1–4).

Fromm states, furthermore, that mature love includes four basic elements: (1) ". . . the *active concern for the life and growth of that which we love.*" (2) *Responsibility* for the needs, physical and psychic, of the other. (3) *Respect* for the other, the ability to see a person as he is, to be aware of his unique individuality. (4) *Knowledge* of self, of the other, and of the nature of love (1956, p. 26).

Many other psychologists and philosophers emphasize that loving involves learning to give and receive love and that the needs of the other must be considered at least as important as one's own; otherwise love, mature love, does not exist. Maslow, for example, expresses it as follows: "One person feels another's needs as if they were his own and for that matter also feels his own needs to some extent as if they belonged to the other" (1970, p. 249).

Gibran emphasized that mature love requires "spaces in your togetherness." "Stand together yet not too near together: For the pillars of the temple stand apart, and the oak tree and the cypress grow not in each other's shadow" (1923, pp. 16–17). The idea that love is not possession, incorporation, or destruction was further described by Gibran when he said, "Love gives naught but itself and takes naught but from itself. Love possesses not nor would be possessed. For love is sufficient unto love" (p. 14). "Love between man and woman may be defined," Blanton writes, "as a relationship in which each helps the other to preserve and enlarge the life of the other" (1956, p. 83).

The nature and expression of *commitment* are key issues here. We see three types: a commitment of *concern* which is much like caring described above, a commitment of *obligation* based on promises and pledges, and a commitment to *growth* which is mutual assistance toward personal development. Masters and Johnson (1974) describe one kind of commitment based on agreed, or implied, responsibilities to care for each other or to give each other pleasure. There is a kind of give-and-get norm established. They use the term "commitment of concern" (p. 235) to describe a contrasting type of commitment where the partners feel a mutual obligation to each other, not out of compulsion, but from free choice. Masters and Johnson see this mutual concern about each other's welfare as the basis for pleasure, especially sexual pleasure, in a relationship. We emphasize an additional quality of commitment, namely, the mutual feeling of desire to enhance the actualizing growth of the other.

There is no blueprint for telling how a counselor can help clients understand and feel the meaning of these concepts. Each individual must discover what love means and how he or she can become lovable and loving in his or her own way. However, an awareness and a willingness on the part of the counselor to interpret these formulations on the meanings of love can greatly assist clients in their search for understanding and expressing love.

Sex

Fromm suggests that the neurotic individual often seeks to establish intimacy with another by sexual contact rather than through a gradual association. "Such experiences of sudden intimacy are usually short-lived and unsatisfying" (1956, p. 53). Sexual desire is often mistaken for love, and frequently sexual desire is motivated by other character needs. Fromm suggests four: (1) the anxiety of aloneness; (2) the wish to conquer or be conquered; (3) vanity; (4) the wish to hurt or even to destroy (1956, p. 54).

Faulty sex education or nonactualizing sex attitudes learned in childhood are frequent sources of trouble. Clients are often helped by facing the feelings that these early experiences developed within them. Frequently, if the counselor gives specific sex information, he or she can rectify problems based on misinformation or lack of knowledge. In the process of sex education, the counselor can be reassuring and helpful by giving specific information, although it is important that he or she make the client realize that it is not faulty information but distorted attitudes that are the seat of the real trouble. If not used carefully, the "sex manual" approach can be grossly misleading.

It is important that during premarital counseling the counselor impart an understanding of the relation of sex to love. In order to complete a human relationship, it may be said that biological desire must be joined with love as it has been described heretofore. Masters and Johnson (1974) describe a process of building relationships consisting of attraction, caring, commitment, pleasure, more caring and commitment, and more pleasure (and so on in an ever intensifying and renewing pattern). They are using pleasure largely, but not exclusively, in a sexual sense. A common social value we have inherited through our Hebraic-Christian tradition is that sex is one means of expressing love. This means that unless both elements are present, there is a "psychic prostitution."

Differences between Men and Women

Closely related to understanding the love relationship in marriage is understanding that the differences between men and women are more than physiological. Again, the client may need help in understanding how his or her attitudes toward his or her own sex role and that of the opposite sex developed. Early lack of proper sex-role identification or early resentments relating to sibling rivalries may be the source of much hostility in marriage. Clients may need considerable assistance in learning to understand, on an emotional level, just what their responsibilities and privileges are in regard to marriage.

Jung was a great exponent of psychic sex differences. He pointed out that women operate in terms of the "Eros Principle" and are basically feeling or intuitive in their approach to life. Men operate on the "Logos Principle" and tend to be more intellectual, systematic, and power-centered in their approach (1933). Fromm, too, suggests some basic character differences in men and women. The masculine character he describes by such terms as "penetration, guidance, activity, discipline, and adventurousness." The feminine character he describes in terms of "productive receptiveness, protection, realism, endurance, and motherliness" (1956, pp. 36–37).

Cultural stereotypes of masculinity and femininity have been in a considerable state of flux. Consequently, what it means to be a man or a woman has been changing so much that it is difficult to maintain a distinctive role identity other than childbearing. The Freudian stereotypes of the Victorian era and the Hebraic-Christian mandates on women's roles especially have diminished in influence. Maleness and femaleness were defined largely in cultural terms of fatherhood as protective and aggressive, and motherhood as nourishing and receptive. The "feminine" man or the "masculine" woman was considered a curious aberration. Such stereotypes now seem chauvinistic, arrogant, and rigid. Actualizing counseling and therapy is concerned with helping each person discover his or her most comfortable and effective male-female role behavior. This process often involves choices of when to blend with cultural expectations, when to flout them, and when assertively to change them. The range of choices is now far greater than it has ever been before. The price, however, is increasing choice anxiety.

The main therapeutic implication of the preceding opinions is that each individual needs to recognize that his or her partner has different needs, has had different experiences, and of necessity looks at life differently, and reacts to life's demands in a different manner. This area of psychological sex differences illustrates why a counselor probably will have little success in helping the client develop new attitudes if he or she relies solely on authority. Actually, the conflict between a man and a woman needs to be understood in terms of the two unique personalities. What is *this* woman like? What is the personality pattern of *this* man?

A further counseling implication is that an understanding of cultural and physiological forces at work can take some of the sting out of the conflict between the sexes; but essentially each human being must learn to accept and develop his or her own sex role in relation to his or her past experiences, present situation, and future goals. In practice, it is noted that once the client has been helped to understand, accept, and enjoy his or her own role, he or she can then be helped to accept the fact that the differences of his or her mate need not be a source of hostility. He or she can see that they are an important basis for enriching the marriage and his or her personal life. He or she sees that learning to value differences is a measure of personal and marital maturity. Consciousness-raising groups have great potential for helping men and women appreciate what it is like to be of the opposite sex. Typically, this goal is accomplished in a small group setting with either same or opposite sex membership going through exercises which force a confrontation with one's attitudes toward one's own and the opposite sex.

Empathy   Although the subject of empathy was discussed at length in Chapter 6, its relevance for marriage counseling will be elaborated here. Murphy makes the following distinction between empathy and sympathy: "Empathy is 'direct' apprehension of the state of mind of another person, without, as in sympathy, feeling as that other person does. In sympathy shared attitude is the chief matter" (1947, p. 985). It is important that the counselor, building on an understanding of the differences between men and women, as well as on the basic concept that each personality is unique, help the marital client to develop insight into the personality, feelings, and behavior of his or her partner, that is, to have *empathy* for the partner.

Too frequently an individual's background has not prepared him or her for any further stage in human relationships than a sympathetic role. When empathy is not experienced, such an individual often feels there is no basis for the relationship. Consequently, the marriage appears doomed, unless mutual empathy can be developed. Skidmore (1956, p. 69) lists empathy as one of the four major bases for building confidence and security in a marriage.

"I would never do that," "How can he feel that," "I can't understand why she would ever say such a thing," are all attitudes that may be approached from the viewpoint of developing empathy. Of course, the counselor's own ability to empathize with the client frequently can be used as a meaningful starting point for the client. The client knows, or can be helped to realize, that the counselor's acceptance is not the same as approval or sympathy. Having received an empathic response, the client then may be more ready to show empathy for others.

Experiencing empathic responses from a counselor sometimes suffices to stimulate a client's potential growth. In other cases, the counselor can demonstrate to clients their stubborn resistance to empathy and can use himself or herself as model to lead clients to deeper understanding of their defenses and development. Without empathy there can be little basic acceptance between human beings. Growing empathy between husband and wife can be a measure of improvement in their marriage relationship.

Communication   In some marriages, one or both individuals have such distorted means of communication or undeveloped skills in communication that even in casual conversation they misinterpret simple facts. Poor communication, then, becomes a focal point of many quarrels. The individual first may reduce exaggerated expressions of hostility standing in the way of understanding the more basic causes of his or her conflict by learning to recognize precisely what others mean or what they feel.

Accurate communication in a marriage not only can reduce hostility based upon misunderstanding, but it can also be a basis for developing a feeling of closeness or oneness within the marriage. It is a practical means for alleviating the loneliness that so many people feel. Following are examples of skills to be learned and used cautiously for improving communication:

1. Repeat what the first person says. Try to rephrase it in your own words and try to see the other person's frame of reference. (See Chapter 7 on reflection techniques.)
    a. Ask, "When you say so and so, do you mean this and that?"
    Example: "When you say I am too strict with the children, you mean I shouldn't have punished Bobby for taking the cookie?"
    b. Ask, "What do you mean by such and such?"
    Example: "In what ways do you mean I am uncooperative?"
2. Learn to recognize that people express themselves differently.
    a. Some people express affection or any other emotion by words—some by behavior.
    Example: Some people say "I love you"; others bring a bunch of violets; and others keep the house in tiptop repair without being asked.
    b. Just because something isn't expressed verbally doesn't mean it isn't felt.
    Example: The individual who is "never" hostile outwardly may express it by illness, sarcastic jokes, or sly innuendoes.
3. Reduce generalities to a minimum.
    Examples: "You *never* smile when I come home." "*All* men make life miserable for their wives."
4. State your own feelings clearly first before expecting your partner to express his feelings. Make clear "I . . ." statements.
    Negative Example: "Do you think we ought to move now?"
    Positive Example: "I think we ought to move . . . for the following reasons. . . ."
5. Distinguish the *situation* from the *person:*
    Example: "I would like to talk to you longer, but I have someone in the office and I can't *now.*"
6. Set aside time for communication regularly, even when there is no particular problem to resolve. Use communication as a preventive measure to head off incipient problems.

Hayakawa's theorem is pertinent here: "Misinformation breeds in an information vacuum."[1] An example follows: If communication between

---

[1] From personal communication with Dr. S. I. Hayakawa.

persons A and B is bad, A then makes guesses. The longer the time that elapses, the less A's "information vacuum" resembles reality. For example, John is expected home at seven o'clock. As the time elapses past this hour, his wife begins to make more and more false assumptions: "Has he been in an accident, or is he drunk, or has he been killed?"

Special Personality Adjustment Problems in Marriage

There are often deep personality problems that are seriously aggravated by marriage. These problems include alcoholism, gambling, extreme jealousy, compulsive nagging, chronic complaining, and violent temper. Moralistic admonitions to do the "right thing" will not help these individuals. In most instances, they need considerable individual help to move from a basically manipulative and exploitative approach to people toward a more actualizing state.

In addition, the partner of a client with these types of problems frequently can be a deciding factor in the outcome of therapy. The "innocent" partner needs help in understanding the reasons for the original marital choice, reactions to the partner's present symptoms, how the problem has been aggravated, and finally how he or she can realistically help his or her partner.

Special Areas of Conflict in the Marriage Relationship

It would be presumptuous and unwise to suggest specific answers to problems that commonly arise in the marriage relationship. Nevertheless, practicing counselors must be aware of these problems and, as suggested earlier, must know the right questions to ask. The following list concerns problems on which there must be some consensus in marriage. It must be remembered, however, that disagreement is only symptomatic of a poor relationship, and that before the relationship is dealt with, individual therapy on pertinent personal conflicts generally must be handled by the counselor.

1. *Finances.* Is an inability to agree on finances a cover-up for more basic disagreements? Which partner (or is it both) is immature in handling finances? Are financial difficulties a symptom of overall immaturity? What significance does money have for this individual and his or her partner?

2. *Social Life.* Do these individuals actually have different social aims? Are they temperamentally different in terms of sociability? Is each lacking in an understanding of the other's social needs? Why is one of them placing great emphasis on social life? Is there basic dissatisfaction with the demands of family living generally or of this marriage specifically?

3. *Parent-Child Relationships.* Is there basic disagreement in regard to discipline? Has either of these individuals a distorted idea of discipline? Is there overidentification with a child or the children by either parent? Is there jealousy of one parent's closeness to a child? Is the parent-child difficulty a displacement of hostility? Is there a resentment of the responsibilities of marriage expressing itself through parent-child difficulties?

4. *Religious and Life Values.* Are differences in religion being used as a cover-up for other differences? Why did this couple marry in the first place? Why is this couple now having difficulty with a difference they evidently felt could be resolved before marriage? What does religion mean to each of these individuals? How much real effort have they made to resolve this difference? How important were religion and other general life values to these clients while they were growing up?

5. *In-Laws.* Are the in-laws the problem or is it the client's attitude toward them? If there is not unity in handling this problem, how much unity is there on other problems? Is jealousy a major issue? Is one client complaining about his or her in-laws because his or her own parents are the problem? How mature is this individual in terms of maintaining his or her own independence?

6. *In-Family Triangle.* Why is this individual alarmed by his or her partner's having close ties with someone else in the family? Was this ever a close marriage? Is this client basically possessive? Is the partner expressing hostility by overdevotion to some other family member?

7. *Extramarital Relationship.* How has this client failed to build a marriage that meets the needs of the partner? Is he or she overly hostile or overly forgiving? Is this client really interested in reestablishing the marriage? Or is this client playing the martyr role? If this is the client who has "strayed," is he or she overly repentant or overly defiant? What was he or she trying to accomplish by extramarital entanglement? What kind of individual did he or she pick to make the triangle, and why did he or she pick this individual?

8. *Job Pressures.* Why are job pressures impinging upon the marriage? Is the individual really in a dead-end job or the wrong type of work? Does one or both have resentment or shame in regard to the job's prestige or income level? Are the hours of work really excessively long or is the job used as an escape from the home? What goals did this couple have originally in regard to economic status? Is the wife jealous of the husband's career?

9. *Inadequate Self-Actualization.* Is this individual really bogged down with too much responsibility and too many pressures? Does he or she really want to help himself or herself or does he or she want some magic solution? Is this client unprepared for the responsibilities of family living? Are there practical things that could be done to give this individual some opportunity for creative activity that he or she has not tried? Is this client really trying to pull away from the marriage?

10. *Different Cultural Background.* What part did defiance of family play in the original choice of each other? Is one enjoying basically what she or he considers a superior role? What does this couple have in common? Is one using cultural differences to cover up more basic dissatisfactions?

It should be emphasized, of course, that the counselor must not ask the client these questions directly. Rather, the counselor should use them to develop his or her own awareness of what is behind the client's problems. It might be well to reemphasize here the importance of the counselor's periodic analysis of his or her own reactions to the client's problems. Counselors must remember that their own standards will not necessarily serve as a solution for this particular client's problems.

Going one step further, it should be understood that these questions about cultural backgrounds may be a means whereby the counselor can lead the client from a superficial approach to consideration of deeper problems. The goal is to make the client understand how the problem developed, what underlying attitude is reflected, and what it symbolizes in the marriage. Knowing the client's cultural background will help the counselor to decide which of the client's remarks he will choose for reflection.

11. *Sexual Conflict.* Though mentioned in the introductory paragraphs as a problem in marital relationships, sexual conflict is considered again here to emphasize its importance as being an especially difficult problem. Clients eventually report sexual adjustment problems, although at first they obscure them by many resistive types of rationalizations. Marriage counselors generally work on the underlying psychological problems of the couples rather than directly on the sexual problems, since the sexual maladjustment is so often merely symptomatic. There are situations, however, where problems of inadequate knowledge and technique contribute to the difficulty, or where physiological problems are present. The latter problems should be investigated and dealt with first by specialists competent to diagnose and treat them.

There is considerable variation in the client's willingness to go beneath the surface of the problem confronting him or her. The client should be the main person to determine the length of marital therapy and the depth of insight to be achieved. Frequently, the manner in which the counselor helps the client to think about the problem, even on a superficial level, will make the client seek deeper counseling. It is not a matter of forcing clients against their desires, but of planting ideas that can come to fruition later when clients are more ready. For this reason, the counselor's understanding of the broad implications of presenting symptoms is an important facet of his or her proficiency.

Strategies and Issues in Marital Counseling

Therapeutic techniques having particular application to marital counseling are:

STRUCTURING.   In the beginning phases of marital therapy, this technique is frequently very important, particularly with unsophisticated clients who know very little about the process.

There are several basic attitudes that are important for the counselor to structure to the client early. Following are some of the basic counselor attitudes that must be communicated verbally to the couple. The therapist does not tell the couple how to run their lives. He or she does not function as an arbitrator, telling the couple who is right and who is wrong. He or she does not act like a top sergeant or parent substitute, telling them what to do. He or she is not a tattletale. He or she does not place blame, nor is his or her goal to give approval. He or she plays no favorites, but is equally interested in helping each client to realize more satisfaction from the marriage.

However, the therapist may structure the process by telling the couple that he or she has had training and experience in helping people to understand themselves and their partners. His or her purpose is to help them to understand how others have solved similar problems. The counselor hopes that by helping clients understand how their problems originated, they will develop insight and techniques for handling present and future difficulties.

Frequently, only one marriage partner is willing to be counseled. The other may come to the counselor but usually does not participate beyond the most superficial discussion. In such cases, the counselor can structure the relationship by suggesting that marriages often have been helped when one partner takes the initiative. The cooperative client can learn to build a better life for himself or herself within the marriage as well as to improve the marriage itself. It is not unusual for the noncooperative client to change as a result of the observable changes actuated by the cooperative client.

FEE PROBLEMS.   With the low-income family, finances are likely to be one facet of the family's problems. For this reason, the low-income group traditionally has received counseling in a social agency where financial aid was available. In the middle-income group, high fees can aggravate a marginal problem. In many instances, this condition shortens the counseling process to a few sessions, thus jeopardizing the effectiveness of the work.

The best generalization that can be made concerning fees seems to be that it is desirable for the client to pay a fee reasonable for his or her income level. A broad definition of a reasonable fee is one that does not substantially increase the client's problems. The fee does, however, put enough pressure upon him or her to work at problems conscientiously.

HANDLING INFORMATION AND BUILDING SKILLS.   In the third element of marital counseling, concerning the marriage itself, information is more important than in some other types of counseling. The counselor must exercise as much skill when giving information as when performing other forms of counseling, and it is often the crucial factor in improvement. Basic to successful information giving is the attitude with which the counselor presents data. When information is given suggestively as a basis for the exploration of ideas, and not pontifically or as reinforcement for preconceived ways of thinking, the client can be helped to grow.

Skill building in areas of communication or sexual technique is a key intervention strategy. This is not usually done in a counseling relationship itself, but more in a workshop setting with several couples. Communication exercises take the form of practicing the kinds of rules cited in the previous section, in addition to learning how to express resentments and appreciations more clearly. In the sexual area, the methods of "sensate focus" described in the introduction to this chapter are examples. Films are used commonly in this process to show models of sexual practices and to increase awareness. Many sex technique films are available, but few on the intricacies of relating in a caring manner exist. "Touching: Importance for Human Growth" is an examination by Ashley Montague (1971) of the importance of touch in human development.

REFERRALS IN MARITAL COUNSELING. The marital counselor frequently finds it necessary to make special referrals. Ideally, he or she should be well informed about, and have direct contact with, the available resources in the community.

Some clients may, in the counselor's opinion, need a complete referral. The individual may be so seriously dysfunctional that custodial medical care may be indicated. Finance or other broad family problems may suggest a casework approach; hence, a complete referral to a community agency would be preferable.

At times, the counselor may continue to work with the client under a partial referral arrangement. If there are physical symptoms, such as headaches or stomach ailments, it is essential that a physician decide if they require medical care, or at least whether counseling and medical care can be carried on simultaneously.

The establishment of a working relationship between a psychologist and an attorney makes for the facilitation of cross-referral between psychologist and attorney. In marital counseling, it is often necessary for the psychologist to refer clients to an attorney for pertinent information concerning marital laws, adoption, and annulment, for example.

Clients with a marriage problem are often in trouble legally as well as psychologically. One client, for example, revealed that she had completely repressed a former marriage. Skillful legal help assisted her in dissolving the first marriage without social incident or involved legal maneuvers. Another young man was assisted immeasurably during premarital counseling by an attorney when the legal problems surrounding a premarital pregnancy came up in the therapy.

MULTIPLE-COUNSELING. Whether one or two counselors should handle one marriage is a question that cannot be answered definitely at the present time. It depends on the couple, the counselor, and the setting in which the counseling is done. We have used both methods, although research is needed on this point to help decide on the better procedure.

The following material explores the arguments for and against relying on more than one therapist. A general rule seems to hold that if the problem involves intensive psychotherapy for each partner, two therapists would probably be indicated. If the problem were primarily one of marital counseling on relationship problems, one therapist or counselor would probably be sufficient and satisfactory.

The counselor who sees both partners in a marital dispute has the advantage of participating in a relationship with both and seeing the likely reality or distortion of the material each presents to him or her. Mittelmann (1956, p. 93) feels that the advantages of one counselor working with a married couple are as follows: (1) The counselor secures information that makes him or her more able to perceive accurately the problems of both partners. (2) The counselor can see the distortions or omissions in the material from one or both of the partners. (3) During times of stress for one of the partners, the counselor can modify the behavior of the other, which was complicating the problems of the partner.

Even in cases where one counselor is definitely indicated, the counselor has a difficult role to play. Mace (1956, p. 30) thinks that, "As a rule the relationship between the two individuals with whom he is counseling is initiated by conflict. In the presence of mutual hostility and recrimination, the marriage counselor must remain impartial and maintain the confidence of both husband and wife." In many instances, this is not an easy task.

Mittelmann (1956) points out that special transference problems may develop where one counselor sees both husband and wife. This transference is expressed by one partner in the form of concern over whether or not the therapist agrees with his or her evaluation of the other partner, fear that the therapist is siding with the other partner, and wish-fulfillment fantasies that the therapist will change the other partner by magic, thus saving the need for working out his or her own conflicts.

Mittelmann (1956) states, furthermore, that the counselor who handles both marital partners needs a reliable memory to know from which partner he got what information, the capacity to withstand the usually sustained rivalry and attack of both partners, the ability to be impartial but not neutral, and the courage to take a clear-cut stand in critical situations concerning who contributed what to a dispute. In other words, the therapist should behave like a benevolent, impartial, and firm parent to keep quarrels from getting out of hand.

Sometimes the counselor may find that what he or she says (or doesn't say) is so distorted or misinterpreted by one or both that the marital conflicts become exaggerated beyond repair. Under these circumstances, two counselors, particularly if they can work in close collaboration, can do more effective counseling than one.

Mittelmann (1956) suggests two reasons against using one counselor with both parties: If one of the partners seems paranoidal in the sense of blaming everyone for his or her problems, and therefore would probably blame the therapist for the termination of the marriage, it would seem more wise to have two therapists work with the partners. Secondly, if one spouse objects to working with the same therapist as the other, or if such a client were advised to go to the same therapist, he or she might refuse to be treated at all and might hide all resistance to help behind the cloak of objections to concurrent therapy.

One of the advantages of having separate counselors for each of the parties in a marital conflict is that the transference and memory problems suggested by Mittelmann above are avoided. Each partner perceives his or her problems in a unique way; and to get into the frame of reference of just one of the perceivers of a marital dispute often is much easier. Furthermore, since the counselor does not have to remember who said what, he or she does not have the problem of keeping confidences.

If each partner has his or her own therapist, the therapists should confer at regular intervals in order that they may cooperate in the therapy. It is important for each of them to remember that he or she received the information from the conference. Some disadvantages of the dual-counselor approach are that it is more time consuming and complicated, since it demands regularly planned conferences between therapists.

In the later stages of counseling, separate therapists and "joint sessions" or multiple-counseling can be introduced. As counseling continues, husbands' and wives' perceptions of their relationship become more congruent. Then counseling of both partners at the same time by two counselors may be helpful. The two counselors may rely upon a profitable technique, at this time, of appearing particularly understanding of their respective client's partner.

Another technique is that of asking one spouse to interpret what the other has just said to the other's satisfaction before being allowed to state his or her own views.

Group therapy, as an adjunct to individual psychotherapy, can be of immeasurable help in overcoming marital problems. We have developed two principles for utilizing supplementary group methods: husbands and wives are always placed in different groups; communication between them on what happens in their own groups is not allowed. Sometimes a program is arranged so that during the first four weeks, only spouses of the same sex are placed together. During the second four weeks, they participate in a mixed group, but not with their own spouses. Finally, husband and wife are assigned to the same group. After the first eight weeks, they are more ready to understand each other.

Some ways in which group therapy can be helpful to couples are: overcoming feelings of being isolated, different, or inadequate; catharsis and reassurance from talking without disapproval or condemnation; development of communicative skills and their transference to husband-wife discussions at home; awareness of the roots of sexual maladjustment in early experiences; insight into the many factors that militate against a complete sexual response; and breaking down of previously unrealistic sexual expectations.

COUNSELING FAMILIES

There is a long history of therapy with children in individual sessions, but only recently have methods been developed for prevention as well as for intensive treatment of family problems through natural family groups or groups of families. In Chapter 11 the principal group approaches applicable to family problems were discussed. The purposes of this section are to review the main strategies for working with families and then to focus on special counseling issues in working with children and adolescents.

A body of methodology around family group work has developed. Satir (1966, 1972) teaches what she calls "conjoint family therapy," which emphasizes treatment of the whole family as a unit and may include several family units in a unitary therapy group. What is known as strategic therapy or family systems therapy has become a standard method of dealing with dysfunctional and disintegrating family units (Minuchin 1974; Andolfi 1979). Diagnostic and treatment methods are combined to give the therapist maximum information to use in interpretation without destroying individual responsibility. There is an emphasis on appreciation of differences among family members, an effort to open communication, and a reconstruction of the flow of family life chronology.

There has been a controversy in the literature on family counseling during the seventies over individual treatment within the family versus treatment of the family as a system. The second issue has centered on defining the dimensions of family therapy more precisely, including how family therapy differs from individual work. Madanes and Haley (1977) explored the issue of individual versus system treatment and concluded that while there is fair agreement that the family context rather than the person with the problem is the focus for family counseling, there is no agreement on how to approach the general problem of counseling the family. Some counselors focus on the person while keeping him or her in the family system. Others lift the person out for counseling, tending to follow the traditional medical treatment model.

Additional issues that divide family counselors center around the theoretical issues discussed in Chapter 2, namely whether to focus on past traumatic events or on the present reinforcing conditions, to give interpretations toward insight or provoke action, to solve the present problem or aim for personal growth. Madanes and Haley (1977) support our actualizing counseling point of view in their warnings against the family counselor who uses the same set of methods with every person, no matter what the problem—and then justifies such interventions with a limited theoretical rationale.

There is abundant evidence that the current trend in family counseling is to view the person's problem in the context of the family system, to focus on the present, and to emphasize the solution of the present problems rather than long-range goals for personal growth.

There is a well-known style of family therapy known as Adlerian, after basic principles propounded by Alfred Adler earlier in this century. While there are many derivatives from his basic work, one of the modern developers was Dreikers (1948), who advocated simple methods parents could try with children to give them responsibility for their own behavior. His strategy was to see family members separately, then together, to work out ways of meeting the power and influence needs of all. A key part of the therapy is to anticipate and work out the special needs of children due to their ordinal birth position in the family.

Much family therapy procedure was developed around problems of fairly intact middle-income families. The problems of low-income families are quite different. Minuchin (1966) has developed a series of techniques called "conflict resolution family therapy," specifically designed for low socioeconomic families. It takes into account the psychological restriction and impoverishment of children from these families and their characteristic ways of handling conflict.

There are experiments in intensive marathon types of family treatment where families are assembled for weekends of continuous confrontation. Families can take advantage of the motivation of the family crisis and learn to stay in the situation long enough to work through the stress. An example is described by McGregor (1962) under the title *multiple impact therapy*. Here a family is brought together for intensive study and treatment by the guidance team for two days. As a result of working through problems at the height of the crisis, more dramatic changes can be effected. Group sessions are supplemented with intensive individual counseling interviews. Sometimes the therapist brings his own family to these intensive weekends to add to the naturalness of the human interaction.

Most family therapy methods have been developed in clinical or nonschool agency settings. There is a trend to involve families within the circle of school counseling functions. Fullmer (1978) describes an adjunct to individual counseling called *family group consultation*. It is an effort to improve communication within families and to develop more awareness of mutual impact on various family members. Three or four families are included in one group, and families more experienced with the method are used to help new families introduced to the group.

A growing problem for families is the care of elderly members. Although most grandparents live independently from their children, there is concern about the older person's welfare and care. When elderly family members become disabled or incompetent to manage their own affairs, great strain is placed on families, some of whom are unable to cope with the demands (Otten and Shelley 1977; Halpern 1978). A specialty called *gerocounseling* has emerged to help both families of older adults and the older adults themselves cope with the problems of aging. Counselors working with older adults need some adaptations of general counseling methods, just as those working with children need special skills and tools (APGA 1979, 1981).

COUNSELING CHILDREN

Evaluating results of counseling and psychotherapy with children is difficult. Levitt (1957) concluded, after reviewing the earlier treatment literature on psychotherapy with children, that untreated children improve about as much as treated children over time. These results, similar to Eysenck's analysis of adult therapy, suggest that we must be cautious in claiming results for psychotherapeutic methods with disturbed children. On the other hand, the data are too inconclusive to be pessimistic about helping methods with children; there may be a cancellation phenomenon operating also when results of various studies are averaged. As in adult cases, some are helped and some are actually hindered in their growth by formal therapy. Evaluation studies then indicate an averaging effect, which hides the true growth of individuals.

Special Counseling Problems with Children

The most apparent difference between child and adult is in the level of communication they use. The dependence of the child on adults forces the counselor to consider the needs of these close adults along with those of the child. Because children are pliable, and because their defenses are not as entrenched as are the adult's, there seems to be less stability in therapy. This condition makes it impossible to predict any permanency in the changes that take place. Because of these difficulties, the counselor must accept more responsibility for directing and protecting the client (Watson 1951).

COMMUNICATION. Poor communication is a difficult obstacle for a therapist to overcome when counseling a child. Such a child is restricted in ability to communicate for two reasons. The child's capacities to differentiate and integrate his or her outer world with his or her inner feelings are incompletely developed. Conceptual thinking and verbalizing abilities are at a relatively primitive level, with many gaps, inaccuracies, and elements of magical thinking present. The second reason is that the child has had so little practice communicating that his or her conversation is not a reliable or even intelligible bridge to the therapist.

Because of the child's limitations in adult styles of communication, the counselor must rely on a behavioral rather than a verbal medium for a solution to the difficult problem of achieving adequate communication between herself or himself and the child. For this reason, the use of play therapy as a communication medium and a therapeutic technique has been common practice. The therapist, in addition, must be skilled in reading the child's bodily nonverbal communication.

DEPENDENCY. Because of the child's dependency, some adult is always involved in a child's therapy. The importance of the role of the adult depends on the age of the child and the adult's sense of responsibility toward the child. A close adult, usually the mother, is frequently the *informant* through whom the therapist is able to obtain a preliminary history of the child and to obtain assistance in the therapeutic planning. The conference with the mother also gives the counselor an opportunity to evaluate the mother's role in the child's problems, her own emotional disturbances, and some idea of the family relationship. Also, it is an opportunity to establish a good working relationship with the mother, which is especially important if the child is to remain in the home. Without the assistance of the parents, the child is not likely either to progress or to be kept in therapy.

HELP FOR PARENTS.   Since the child's difficulties are tied up with those of the adults who created his or her problems, it is often wise for the counselor to insist that one or both parents cooperate to the extent of entering therapy themselves. There is increasing evidence from the therapeutic experience, especially that of psychoanalysis, that disordered behavior in the child has frequently been taught unconsciously as a result of observing the parents act out their repressed feelings and impulses. This approach assists the parent to create better personality growth conditions in the home.

Parental attitudes and behaviors are decisive in determining the developmental progress of their children. Thus, therapy for a parent can play a decisive role in changing the child's environment from one of unmanageable threat to one of security and love. Beverly (1941) implies that parents often see things in their children that are not there and try to force attitudes on the child that are impossible to accept. Occasionally it will be impossible to persuade the adult to participate in any form of therapy. When this happens, the counselor may gain some measure of reassurance from Axline (1947), who reports several instances of successful child therapy in which no adult was counseled.

Skills training for parenting is a commonly used strategy for dealing with parental problems. Some approaches, such as Gordon's Parent Effectiveness Training (1971), are highly concentrated communication skills packages and programs. The program focuses on methods of active listening, for example, and ways of managing conflict so that both parent and child end the confrontation as "winners."

THERAPIST RESPONSIBILITY.   Since the child is less able to absorb stress than the adult and has very little control over his or her environment, the therapist must often assume a greater responsibility for the welfare of the child by giving direct help. As children experience success where they had formerly only experienced failure, they will begin to realize that the world is not as hostile and defeating as they had thought. Sometimes a summer camp experience or a new school will provide this change. The therapist may act specifically as a child advocate by arranging a transfer to a new school or by reporting abuse of a child to the proper authorities.

AWARENESS OF NEED FOR HELP.   In contrast with adults, children are less aware of a need for help because their limited experience tells them, "This is the way things are." They seldom refer themselves for therapy; instead, they are usually brought in or sent in because they have displeased some adult. Consequently, they seldom come to the therapist with a conscious desire for self-exploration, as do most adults. Children will usually say that they "have no problems" but that their parents or teachers think they have. Axline reports the case of a disobedient twelve-year-old boy who enters the playroom and says, "Well, here I am. I just came because

. . . I can't understand what mother was talking about. She said that you would help me with my problems, but I don't have any problems" (1947, p. 30). In spite of this beginning, the boy had told the counselor of his troubles with his stepfather, the substitute teacher, and his peers at school before the end of the first session. He had also selected a medium (puppets) through which he could act out his problem. After this first session, the child usually looked forward to returning to the sessions.

It is often more difficult for the therapist to establish a common purpose with a child than an adult. The child is less able to understand the role of the therapist. His or her past experience conditions him or her to think of adults as authority figures who deal out rewards and punishments. The child's expectation of reward, for example, may make the child try to please the therapist by acting the way he or she thinks a good child should and by avoiding expressions of hostility. Fear of punishment may increase the anxiety so that his or her emotions become even more diffused.

ENVIRONMENTAL MANAGEMENT.   In addition to the helping environment created in the interview, specific steps must be taken frequently to order the broader environment in helpful ways. This may take the form of "milieu management," such as arranging for a private sleeping room at home, or it may be a type of behavior modification, such as keeping track of reinforcing conditions provided by parents. The main point is that interview strategies usually have limited success with children, whereas environmental management is a more powerful behavior-changing intervention.

VOLUNTARINESS.   The child cannot discontinue therapy when he or she wishes. Even though the therapist maintains that it should be up to the child to decide to continue or to quit therapy, in reality a parent or teacher may insist that the child continue until certain unacceptable behaviors are changed.

GROUP THERAPY WITH CHILDREN.   Axline (1947) and Moustakas (1953) found it helpful for the child to experience peer relationships within group therapy. Slavson (1950) found also that many children can be helped toward insight in a group situation. He reported that children substitute the therapist for their parents rather than develop a transference relationship in the adult sense. Their ties to their parents are still primary and intense, so that other adults are subsidiary. Many of the family techniques described earlier apply specifically to children.

Counseling Goals and Strategies with Children   In developing a relationship with children, counselors must be aware of the techniques mentioned in Chapters 6 and 7, but they must adapt these methods to the maturity level of the child. They must respond to the child's feelings just as they do to adult feelings. Because of the real communication barrier imposed by the child's immaturity, the therapist frequently has to develop other means of understanding and interpreting feelings and behaviors to the child.

In the counseling of adults, counselors are frequently assisted in their understanding of the client by inferences drawn from observing facial expressions, mannerisms, gestures, and other body movements. In children, such behavioral expressions are frequently the principal conveyance of the child's feelings. Therefore, the success of the therapist depends in large degree on his or her ability to observe, understand, and interpret the child in action. Since children use gestures as a means of expression to a much greater degree than adults, and in turn give personalized meanings to the gestures of others, the counselor must be mindful of his or her own facial and body movements and the interpretation the child might give to them. For example, if the counselor should suddenly raise his or her hand in an explanatory gesture, the counselor might frighten the child. Likewise, raising his or her voice or even prolonging silence might be interpreted as anger. From such reactions, the counselor may infer some of the principal learnings of the child, as well as how the counselor may best convey accepting, loving attitudes to the child.

Some counselors suggest using the same words very small children use to avoid talking over their heads. Axline mentions the value of reflecting the gestures of the small child. For example, if the child stamps his or her foot, the counselor stamps his or her foot, or if the child shakes his or her head, the counselor does likewise. Other therapists feel that what one says is not important as long as the reflection conveys an honest empathy of feelings.

However, there are a few general suggestions that apply to all children. The therapist's responses should be brief, relaxed, and natural. Care must be taken also to avoid talking down to the child, acting like an authority figure, or engaging in baby talk.

It is often helpful for the counselor to sit on a low chair or on the floor so that he or she is at eye level with the child. This seems to help create a "we" feeling that adds to the rapport of the counseling session.

The counselor must at all times be aware of the sensitivity of the child to the sincerity of adults. One often hears the comment "You can't fool a child or a dog," with the implication that they are able to sense the true intentions of adults through their pretended intentions. The aphorism "What you are speaks so loudly I can't hear what you say" is a strong reminder to the counselor.

In summary, the counselor can help to overcome communication barriers by paying attention to the expressive movements of the child. The counselor's verbal responses should reflect the attitudes and feelings of the child in simple, relaxed, natural phrases and gestures. By keeping responses simple and sincere, the counselor helps to build understanding and a relationship bridge that will permit the child to change his or her attitudes and behavior.

GOALS OF CHILD THERAPY. Primary goals of child therapy are to help children develop centering and actualizing strength so that they can cope more successfully with themselves and their environment. One hypothesis here is that these goals come about when the child is exposed to a good therapeutic relationship. A second hypothesis is that to facilitate behavior change the environment must be managed so as to produce actualizing outcomes. As children gain awareness, they learn to grow emotionally and to gain faith in themselves as responsible individuals. Moustakas (1953) suggests that there are three basic attitudes inherent in this good relationship: faith, acceptance, and self-respect.

The attitude of faith is intangible. It is reflected when a child considers himself or herself to be an important person—one having something important to offer others. If children come from homes in which the emotional climate is negative and critical, however, they are not as likely to have such faith in themselves. Jourard and Remy (1955) suggest that persons' self-appraisal is closely related to their perceptions of their parents' appraisal of them. To overcome the often negative effects of parental judgments, the therapist must believe sincerely in the child's ability for self-growth. This belief can be expressed to the child with such remarks as "What do you think?" or, "I'm sure you know more about that" or, "How you feel is the important thing."

If the counselor is able to build a relationship of faith and acceptance, self-respect is not difficult to achieve. When the child realizes that his or her feelings and interests are understood by the counselor, he or she believes that the counselor is sincerely interested in him or her. For example, the counselor's attitude might be as Moustakas has stated it: "These are your feelings and you have a right to them. I shall not try to take them away from you, to divert you from them, or to deny them to you, for they are a part of you, and I shall honor them as I do all aspects of yourself" (1953, p. 5). The respect of counselors thus goes a step beyond acceptance because, through their respect, the child has the freedom to express negative feelings. They also imply that the child does not become an inferior person because he or she holds "bad" feelings (Baruch 1953).

The therapeutic process in play therapy seems to pass through three definite stages, similar to the process discussed in Chapter 4. At first, the emotions of disturbed children are diffused, undifferentiated, and very negative. They are angry and afraid of everyone because they have lost contact with the source of their frustrations and fears. In the playroom, they either want to destroy everything indiscriminately or they wish to retreat in silence and be left alone.

As the relationship between the therapist and the child grows, the child is able to express anger more specifically. Pounding, smashing, and the desire to kill may still be present, but it is likely to be directed toward a particular person, such as a parent or sibling. In this second stage, the child releases and expresses negative feelings directly toward the people in his or her environment who have made him or her feel inadequate. It is assumed, of course, that the parent has been prepared for these events. As the child releases negative feelings and as they are accepted, the child begins to feel as a more worthy person. Hence, he or she is able to express more constructive feelings (Baruch 1953). He or she is free to explore the polarities of his or her existence.

The child shows a great deal of ambivalence in the third stage. For example, he or she still expresses specific anger, yet at the same time shows kindness. The child will love and fondle the doll one moment and spank it harshly the next moment. These ambivalent reactions are often intense in the beginning; but gradually, as the more positive feelings emerge, clients enter the final stage of the therapeutic process. Now, they see themselves and their environment more realistically. For example, a seven-year-old boy said of his five-year-old sister, "She's pretty cute sometimes, even if she *is* a spoiled brat."

During the growth process, then, the child's anger and fear move from a diffused feeling to a focused and specific feeling, which he or she is able to express verbally or in play. As children learn to express these negative feelings specifically, they begin to express positive attitudes occasionally. Finally they are able to separate more realistically their positive and negative attitudes toward their environment. This process of actualizing combined with the environmental management strategies described below provides the child counselor with a wide range of behavior-changing intervention methods.

Even though awareness is limited to the maturity level of the child, it is conceded that such awareness can be gained by the small child without verbalization (Axline 1949). The behavior of the child changes as a result of experiences in play therapy. The bully becomes a helper without explanation. Just as a chimpanzee can learn to solve the problem of reaching food by putting two sticks together, so the small child is able to bring together different ideas from his or her experience that help him or her solve problems. This therapeutic process does not occur automatically in a play situation. It is made possible by the counselor's responding with constant sensitivity to the child's feelings, accepting his or her attitudes, and conveying a consistent and sincere belief in the child's worth as an individual.

Play Therapy   The techniques of play therapy evolved because children are unable to express themselves adequately on a verbal level. Play seems to help children develop more elaborate and effective techniques for controlling their environment and appears to give them an opportunity to interact with an adult who takes a different attitude toward them (Watson 1951). The purpose of this section is to provide the reader with enough description to get a solid feeling of play therapy methods.

HISTORY OF PLAY THERAPY.   The use of play therapy as a technique dates back to the analytic movement, when Anna Freud used play to win children's friendship and when Melanie Klein (1949) developed a "Play Analysis," which in principle was true to the psychoanalytic tradition. Rogers, although not the first to state it, hypothesized that the individual had a strong capacity for self-direction and growth. Axline (1947) then applied Rogers's client-centered philosophy to children at play. Axline cites examples that imply that immature and dependent children have the capacity for self-direction and growth. The parents of some of her children would not enter therapy. Others of her children came from public institutions, and the adult supervisors were not directly concerned with them. Despite these limitations, the children apparently were able to overcome traumatizing experiences. This is possible because as a child undergoes a personality change, however slight, his or her environment is no longer the same. The child's stimulus value to others changes, and as a consequence he or she is perceived and reacted to in a different way.

ROOM AND MATERIALS.   Play therapy requires a playroom and materials. The room should be brightly colored, cheerful, and soundproof if possible. The walls and floors should be of a type easily cleaned and of a material that will withstand clay, paint, and mallet attacks. A washroom with hot and cold water should be accessible. For research and teaching purposes, the therapy room can be wired for tape recordings. Also, if the room is provided with a one-way mirror and is wired for sound, observations can be made without the child being aware of the observer. If observations and recordings are made, it is assumed that the ethical requirements have been met.

The list of materials used successfully in play therapy grows each year. Klein (1949) used only a few primitive toys laid out on a low table. Axline (1947) suggests a long list of "acceptable toys." Many other toys have been used with success. The success of Lebo (1955) in using toys that had not been recommended by any other therapist suggests that there are no apparent limitations with respect to play devices that may assist a child in working out his or her problems. It seems wise to select a wide variety so that the child may find a personally convenient medium for expressing his or her particular feelings.

SOME TECHNIQUES.   Many experiments have been reported in which dolls provided a highly adequate means for working through problems. Dolls generally appealing to young children are simple as well as suitable for exploring many different problem areas. Since the child's problems stem frequently from family relationships, a complete family of dolls—father, mother, brother, sister, and baby—is essential. Dolls can help the child to work through sex anxieties and to accept sex differences. Dolls and a bottle with a nipple are a must for the small child who is working through dependency needs.

Toys that are used often by children in expressing aggression are guns, trucks, soldiers, masks, and inflated plastic figures. Axline found it convenient to use a sandbox placed flat on the floor as a background for the doll house, furniture, and family. She found that sand was a good medium for expressing aggressive feelings. The child buries toys in it or uses it to represent rain, snow, bombs, or any number of other imaginative symbols. Puppets are very popular with older children between the ages of six and twelve. They provide a helpful means for role playing with readily identifiable figures, such as hero, villain, mischievous monkey, horrible alligator, or giants (White 1956).

Finger and easel painting are very popular with some therapists. Shaw (1934) and Alschuler and Hattwick (1947) have had success with these media and hypothesize that color offers many clues to the nature and degree of emotional life of the child. Messing materials, such as finger paints and clay or sand and water, are popular with children who are having difficulty working through early training conflicts.

CONTROLLED VERSUS FREE PLAY.   There is a difference of opinion as to whether play should be controlled or free. Levy (1963) controls the play by selecting definite toys that he feels the child can use to work out his particular conflicts. Levy seems to make no attempt to point out feelings to the child, to develop transference, or to promote changes in behavior; yet, he has been highly successful in therapy with children between the ages of two and ten.

From the child's history, Levy decides the probable cause of the child's present problem. For example, a boy of seven had nightmares of being bound and tortured. He would awaken with cries of pain. Levy learned that two weeks previously some of his classmates had tied him to a tree and pretended to torture him. A little later, a story had been read in school about two knights who nailed an innkeeper to the door of the inn. These two experiences were highly threatening because of their strong similarity to a traumatic experience the boy had a few years earlier when he had been wrapped in blankets for the puncture of his eardrums without anesthesia. Levy set up the playroom with dolls to represent a knight, a doctor, and boys. There were toys to represent the inn, rope, tree, and blankets. Using the toys, the boy worked through his experiences, and the symptoms were removed in four sessions (1963). This illustration does not imply that a rapid solution is usual. Most problems require many more sessions for satisfactory resolution.

Levy finds that children under six are helped apparently without their knowing why they were sent to the clinic and without perceiving any relationship between their play and their behavior at home. There is a possibility that Levy's success reflects the fact that fantasy and reality are not strictly differentiated at the younger age levels (1963). The success of Mann, using a similar process, supports this hypothesis (1957).

Axline (1947) and Moustakas (1953) insist on a free choice of materials. They set the playroom up in the same way for all children and with all equipment available for the child to use as he or she pleases. Spontaneous choice of materials is less artificial; the child selects his or her own media and proceeds at his or her own speed. The therapist may not even know the problem that the child is working through. Axline reports a little girl who would make a limping clay man, punch holes in him, tear him to pieces, and finally bury him. She continued to make and destroy the clay man at each session for several weeks. Not until after the girl was dismissed did the therapist learn that the mother was considering marriage to a crippled man.

Special play techniques for dealing with child frustration have been presented in films such as those produced by Vassar and Sarah Lawrence colleges. These techniques, developed by the late Eugene Lerner, suggest that an individual may react in many different ways to a frustrating situation according to his or her present needs. It is suggested that as a child learns to overcome these obstacles in play, he or she gains insight into the solving of other frustrations in his or her life. Several children in succession play with an adult who presents a series of play obstacles. The child is first presented with a situation in which the adult's and the child's car meet on a narrow track. The adult says, "We meet in the middle. How can my car pass?" The child's verbal or action response gives the counselor an idea as to the child's dependency, aggressiveness, or fear of authority. Ruch suggests three responses the child may make to this question (1948, pp. 474–75). The child may turn his or her car around and go back so the adult's car may proceed; he or she may poke at the adult's car or hit the adult's hand; or he or she may coyly answer the adult's question in the negative and then slowly ease the adult's car back out of the way of his or her own car.

The adult has his or her doll stop the child's car. What happens? Is the adult's doll run over or asked to ride? In play with the cars, the adult says, "Let's see who can get there first." The therapist observes if the child must always be first or if he or she must never win. Does the child permit the cars to crash, and if so, does he or she seem to enjoy the crash or does he or she appear frightened?

When playing house, the adult asks, "May my doll come into your house?" After a short time the role is reversed. When the child's doll wishes to enter the house, the therapist says no and notes the child's reactions. A wide variety of situations similar to Lerner's may be used to explore the child's feelings and reactions.

Both free and controlled play seem to have merits in assisting the child to work out his or her problems. The success of the various methods, as used by different therapists, suggests that counselors can be versatile and use discretion, either selecting the media themselves or allowing the child to do it. It should be pointed out that there does not appear to be an adequate rationale for explaining the success of play therapy. Just as in adult therapy, there are many hypotheses springing from the various theoretical positions.

LIMITS OF PLAY THERAPY.   It is important that the child be permitted great latitude of self-expression in the playroom, with fewer restrictions than he or she experiences outside. However, it appears equally important that children observe certain limits if therapy is to progress. These limits must be well defined and concrete but need not be mentioned to the children until they threaten to break them. In this way, they learn what they are permitted to do as they explore the relationship with their counselors. The children become aware of their manipulative efforts with adults and the effects of manipulative adults on them.

Well-defined limits within the therapeutic framework have as their purpose the preservation of reality, the psychological security of the child, and his or her health and safety.

The first element of reality to be considered is time. There must be a definite time to begin and to end the session, regardless of how interesting the play may be. This is a necessary consideration for the counselor who works on a schedule, and children learn that freedom is not unlimited and they are encouraged to focus their activities within a definite time limit. Another element to be considered is the rule that materials may only be used inside the playroom and cannot be taken home. However, the counselor may permit the child to take home the pictures he or she paints or simple toys that he or she constructs of paper or clay if this seems important to increase feelings of worth. In such situations, it is wise for the counselor to instruct the parents regarding how they should react. Parents can demonstrate interest by asking the child to tell them about his or her handiwork and taking time to listen to his or her story.

The child should not be permitted to destroy irreplaceable items or to throw a toy through the window. Giving children unlimited freedom with property does nothing to teach them the reality value of possessions or help them channel their feelings into less aggressive and destructive behaviors. Too much freedom very likely will increase their anxiety. Most therapists follow the general rule of forbidding the child to hit the therapist, since striking an important person in his or her life may create guilt feelings or reinforce openly destructive behaviors.

Health and safety considerations rule out any behavior that will harm children. For example, should they wish to break a glass bottle against the wall, drink the paint water, or throw sand in someone's face, the therapist would stop them.

Bixler (1949) suggests three mechanisms for enforcing limits: (1) The therapist may reflect the child's desire or attitude, for example, "You are very angry—you would like to hit me." (2) The therapist may verbally express the limitation, for example, "You can't hit me but you may hit Bobo." (3) The therapist may control the child by physical means, perhaps holding his or her hands or sitting him or her firmly in a chair and saying, "You may pound with this mallet." If the child continues to try to fight, the therapist must put him or her outside the playroom for the remainder of the session. Counselors must not be punitive in their attitudes but must carry out exactly everything they say they will. If they do not, they invite more aggressive behavior. However, in their firmness, they must make children understand that their actions are being rejected and not they themselves. Bixler suggests that limits in the playroom may be as important for progress as acceptance of the attitudes that provoke the behavior. This is similar to the idea on acceptance discussed in Chapters 6 and 7 on permissiveness and structuring in adult counseling.

The playroom with its equipment is but an aid to the attainment of a primary goal of child therapy—helping the child establish a working relationship with a permissive adult. When the counselor can act as a permissive parent, he or she creates an emotional climate that stimulates the child to verbalize and dramatize conflicts in play. This helps the child to extend himself or herself, to expect warmth from an adult, and thus to learn that all adults are not punitive.

*Behavior
Management*

This section contains an overview of the behavior-changing strategy known as behavior modification. It is a method widely used by parents, teachers, and community agencies to control and change children's behavior. Behavior modification is based upon the experimental work done by Pavlov on conditioning and later work by Skinner on operant behaviors. It assumes our environment controls our behavior through providing and withholding reinforcements, or rewards. Therefore, if one wants to help people change their behavior, or change it for them if this seems indicated, as in the case of hyperactive children, then one must control the contingencies, or reinforcements, in the environment. Paying attention to a child while he or she is doing an approved act, or giving a treat after he or she performs a reading lesson satisfactorily, are examples. These reinforcements tend to insure that the behavior will return, although the schedule for reinforcing must be planned to insure this repetition. The assumptions and methods are similar to those described for behavioral counseling in Chapter 2.

While behavior modification methods involve a complex technology and vocabulary too extensive to deal with here, our purpose is to point out that this strategy is widespread and effective for changing child behavior. The key limitations cited for the methods are that they work too well, in that they are easily subject to abuse in the form of controlling behavior. To obtain conformity, for example, a parent, teacher, or counselor may manage the environment to the point where spontaneity, initiative, and risk taking could be controlled to the detriment of the child's actualizing. While depending on environmental management, one deemphasizes free and responsible choice by the client. Many adults are fearful that these methods will diminish responsibility and other actualizing capabilities in people. Therapists, and collaborating parents, need to understand that behavior modification is a technology which can be used for enhancement of, or as a detriment to, the actualizing process.

COUNSELING PARENTS OF YOUNG CHILDREN

*General
Principles*

Since parents are largely responsible for the happiness of their children, one way of changing the child's environment is to change the behavior of the parents. For this reason, the child counselor often insists that parents enter therapy as well. Modern American parents suffer considerable confusion over childrearing, an intensity of confusion not shared with past generations. Earlier parents were guided by traditional childrearing practices not available to modern parents, who are bombarded with multiple and conflicting principles of parenting. The "child experts" don't seem to have consistent answers either, so parents are understandably confused and deficient in self-confidence and knowledge.

Parents have two broad and overlapping kinds of problems. First, the parent may have anxieties and problems not strictly related to the child, but which are passed on to the child through attitudes of tension, emotional inconsistency, strictness, thoughtlessness, and the like. In such cases, the procedures are the same as for adult counseling, but with efforts to help the parent understand the effects of his or her behavior on the child.

Secondly, the parent may be well intentioned but inadequate through ignorance of a developmental perspective to understand that everyone passes through certain physical, mental, and emotional phases in growing from infancy to adulthood. This knowledge is usually very reassuring to parents and helps them anticipate and meet problems of development with more confidence. Children's behavior must be evaluated in terms of the norm for particular age levels, although parents need to be cautioned about the atypical samples and overgeneralization. The developmental approach gives parents a framework in which limits can be set. Parental guilt, anxiety, and punitive attitudes can then be reduced or eliminated. Parents want accurate information on normative behavior.

Some of the persistent developmental problems encountered by a counselor working with parents of young children are aggressiveness, sexual tensions, elimination problems, and relating to other children. Specific ideas for parents in dealing with these problems are beyond the scope of this book, but abundant literature exists on childrearing and research on child development.

Manipulative and Actualizing Parent Models   Just as children learn many ways to control and manipulate their parents, so parents apply a wide range of manipulative techniques to their children. Creating guilt through emphasizing "shoulds" is one of these. The manner in which love is given or withheld is another example. One of the principal counseling approaches used with parents is to help them perceive these manipulative ways of managing their children's behavior and to move to more actualizing forms of communication.

The actualized parent emphasizes self-responsibility in his or her child and is aware of the child's need for autonomy even though painful to the parent. He or she is willing to "let the child go," even at great risk, to become an actualizing person in his or her own right. Counseling with parents emphasizes the problem of shifting responsibility for choices from parent to child and of helping the parent interpret the limits of freedom to the child.

COUNSELING ADOLESCENTS AND THEIR PARENTS

The adolescent is too mature for play therapy techniques, but since he or she is still a dependent with special developmental problems, some techniques additional to those used with adults are applicable. The developmental outlook assists adults in understanding the adolescent as well as other age groups. At the same time, a counselor should believe in adolescents' potential to solve their own problems and actualize themselves when they understand themselves and their particular problems. Counselors are asked by parents and teachers to be of help with certain typical adolescent concerns. Some of these typical developmental concerns are choosing a career, deciding on higher education, relating effectively to peers, finding a place in society or deciding to change it, managing sexual tensions, finding a satisfactory relationship with parents on a host of issues, and, finally—emancipation from home. High school counselors find that this developmental period is a specialty in itself.

A characteristic difficulty in working with adolescents, and one which makes it difficult to keep them in therapy, is their impatience. They want the answers right now. Since adolescence is a transition stage from childhood to adulthood, it is usual to find conflicts and confusion relative to long-term satisfactions versus immediate pleasures. The counselor can assist the adolescent to realize that his or her impatience is part of this conflict and help him or her make realistic choices. A further characteristic is dependence on peers for help rather than seeking adult assistance. The suspicion growing out of perceptions of adults as untrustworthy and not "with it" is an obstacle to counseling.

Counseling Parents

Goals in counseling parents of an adolescent are to help them channel his or her feelings into constructive activities and to understand his or her behavior. A parent is often reassured to learn that rebellious behavior is a necessary part of growth and emancipation from parents. This phase of development can be less painful for the parents and the adolescents if awareness of the growth process is gained before serious misunderstanding develops.

Baruch (1953) suggests that parents need to give their adolescents three things—*understanding, practical sex information,* and *help in becoming an independent person.* Adolescents should be encouraged to express their feelings without fear, and parents should attempt to accept their right to express hostile feelings. This view may be very threatening to a parent, which suggests that the parent can't understand the child's feelings unless the parent understands his or her own feelings. This parental lack of insight is one of the reasons why it is so necessary that parents enter therapy with the adolescent. As parents learn to talk out their true feelings with the child, they learn to understand themselves and their child better.

The parents can be assured that the youth needs their help in learning to express feelings and to control impulsive actions. Baruch (1953, p. 69) suggests five ways of channeling negative feelings into socially acceptable actions: (1) verbalizing the grievance; (2) writing out the bad feelings; (3) drawing pictures of the hated person; (4) painting, modeling, and dramatizing; and (5) playing games, such as tennis, golf, checkers, or chess, in order to work out family or peer battles.

To understand their adolescents, parents must realize that their children's present and past feelings cause them to act the way they do. Behind unacceptable actions are negative feelings that may have had their origins in early childhood. These feelings not only result from what actually happened but are also tied up with the child's fantasy of what happened. This fantasy also plays a part in the imagined attitude of the parent toward the youth (Baruch 1953). If a child felt a lack of love, of trust, or of a sense of belonging in his or her early life, he or she will tend to find it difficult in adolescence to feel at home with his or her peers. Therapy with the adolescent must uncover basic feelings from childhood that are causing ineffective actions in adolescence.

The parent needs assistance in learning to help the teen-ager avoid dangerous behavior and still allow him or her optimal personal freedom. This may be accomplished in two ways. First, the parent may anticipate certain interests and provide opportunities for the needed activity with a structured environment. Ball leagues, hot-rod clubs, camping, and fishing and hunting trips are examples. Secondly, the parent can be taught to accept the youth's negative feelings and verbalize them back to him or her. If the parent can accept the negative feelings, it is easier for the adolescent to accept them and thus eliminate his or her guilt feelings. Finally, parents must realize that there is the "generation gap" and that customs, entertainments, and mores are changing rapidly.

Parents often complain, "What about me? I have feelings too." They need assurance that it is sometimes necessary for them to express feelings also. They should express anger, and then, if they have regrets, say so in sincere humility. Usually, the parent is surprised at her or his adolescent's understanding and acceptance when he or she, as a parent, admits a problem too. This deidolization goes a long way toward building rapport between parents and children and toward building teen-agers' respect for parents' feelings.

Parents need assurance that limits on adolescent behavior are still necessary. Youth must accept the necessity of following certain customs and rules. Baruch suggests three reasons for limits which can be understood by the adolescent: "This is important for health and safety. This is important to protect property. This is important because of law and order and social acceptability" (1953, p. 11).

Dynamics of Parent-Adolescent Relationships

The problem, from the therapist's point of view, is to help the adolescent secure as much freedom as he or she is able to handle and to help parents accept the risks of this freedom. There are certain difficulties that make it hard to achieve this goal, even if the therapist has tried. The following devices, derived largely from Wickes (1927), are suggestive of the numerous maladaptive ways parents use to control adolescents.

1. Utilizing love as a dominating and holding force to satisfy personal needs in the parent that "may happen when the parent is disappointed in other human relations and, pouring out all the pent-up emotion on the child, also feeds himself upon the child's love" (1927, p. 90).

2. "Placing the youth under a burden of gratitude and sense of duty because of values received" (1927, p. 90).

3. Treating youth as emotional toys; thus, not allowing the child to reach for greater maturity.

4. Prolonging one's own youth beyond its rightful time. "Daughters are kept the little girls; the son begins to assume the place of the youthful lover" (1927, p. 96).

5. Being overstern and authoritarian on the parents' part and refusing to allow the child to break the submissive role.

6. Being too weak and too ready to yield, on the part of the father, and being unable to accept his responsibilities. "This may inspire only contempt in the son; thus the adolescent problem of freeing himself becomes too easy, and his contemptuous attitude is carried over toward all the struggles of life. A weak and acquiescent son, having a similar identification, may gravitate toward failure—even as his father has done. He is inclined to present his father-identification as an excuse for his own failure to meet life" (1927, p. 99).

7. If mother is the stronger parent, she represents not only love but authority, thus making it more difficult for the son to break away and establish independence. He may now fear the power of women, as he may acquiesce and lose his masculine attitude. Furthermore, he may break the bond completely and consistently undervalue women in an effort to deny their power.

8. Being suspicious and unreasonable, on the part of the mother toward the father, may create a similar unconscious attitude toward men on the part of the daughter.

9. Holding inappropriate attitudes, on the part of the father, may furnish the daughter similarly inappropriate expectations toward men in general. For example, if he is too fond of her, there is a danger that the daughter will find herself unable to break the close bond for marriage. She goes through life looking for her father's image in a prospective husband. If he is too dominatingly devoted, the daughter may repudiate his overinsistent demands and repudiate him. "She is frequently suspicious of men and their demands upon her. She senses sexual motives where none really exist, or if they do exist she refuses to see their normal aspect in adult life" (1927, p. 106).

Conversely, indifference and neglect on the part of the father may cause feelings of inferiority and may motivate the daughter to go about looking for a father surrogate who will give her the fatherly devotion she has missed. Other girls may feel only hatred and resentment toward such a father. Lacking the proper discipline, which is a part of development, she is torn by a conflict between rebellious aggressiveness and a desire for submissiveness.

It is the counselor's job to become thoroughly acquainted with dynamic patterns such as those illustrated above and to place them in the perspective of the child's and parent's lives. As a result, both can see more clearly what is operating among all family members. All the counseling skills described in earlier sections of this book are needed to do this job well.

SUMMARY

Couples counseling is a term applied to helping both partners in an intimate relationship. The case for interdisciplinary collaboration is illustrated. Premarital issues are explored in sexuality and relationships.

Some of the basic problems in counseling and psychotherapy with children, young adolescents, and parents revolve around achieving accurate communication, handling dependency feelings, working with the whole family, and helping clients to become aware of their need for help, while still keeping the relationship voluntary. Play has been found to be one of the best media for therapy with children. The principal goal of individual and group therapy with children is to help them achieve strong egos so they can cope with their environmental demands and their own inner pressures. Behavioral strategies are compared to play therapy. Counseling with parents involves many problems common to the development of young children, such as sexual and elimination problems, excessive aggressiveness, and unresolved dependency. Adolescents have their unique problems also, in the form of vocational choices, sexual adjustment, and relationships with parents and peers.

13

Counseling on Life Style, Careers, and Rehabilitation

Choosing a satisfying life style is one of the principal developmental tasks of life. In terms of our actualizing model, it involves all levels of awareness in the person, from values clarification at the core level, analysis of basic character styles, and development of rational choice methods at the actualizing level. This life-style choice incorporates what was once called vocational planning, but now this choice includes a much broader range of choices covering type of community life, desired family structure, avocational activities, as well as range and kinds of friendships and partnerships. Career planning packages and programs put careers in the context of life planning over the entire age spectrum. Bolles's self-help manuals (1977, 1978) stress a process of balancing and getting out of what he calls the three boxes of life—work, education, and retirement. Bolles uses the box metaphor to describe the compelling quality of each of these three life conditions and how people must struggle to free themselves. His manuals are examples of how a person makes the complex series of choices leading to a satisfying life/work plan. While these types of materials are useful checklists to make people aware of what they need to know and do to plan their lives, we know of no evidence that makes the do-it-yourself workshop approach superior to consultations with career counseling specialists. The complexities of the life decision-making and planning process and the technical resources needed are such that a counseling relationship appears a necessity to us.

Life planning is considered an integrated process involving many values and choices. This state of affairs offers a great challenge to actualizing counseling and therapy to provide a range of counseling methods and the most appropriate kind of relationships to help people make responsible choices and plans to sustain them for their lifetimes. Life-style counseling, combined with group experiences where values are explored, strengths and resources are inventoried, problems are examined, and plans are formulated, offers such a comprehensive approach.

Since a significant part of life planning involves productive work, a large part of this chapter will be devoted to careers and to the companion topic of educational planning. Since handicapped persons have special problems of actualizing in the career area, this topic will receive attention as well.

The social consequences of career choices are considerable. The principal values of professional career counseling services to society are the discovery, utilization, and conservation of human talent as a humanistic goal. Appropriate career choice is especially significant in view of the multiple career changes people now make in a lifetime to keep up with rapid changes on the job scene, as well as to match their careers to their evolving life style. Career counseling for the handicapped is wise social policy also.

Counseling and the collateral area of appraisal cannot become manipulative tools or instruments of national policy, however, since this would violate our values about freedom of choice. Therapeutic psychology seeks to help clients become aware of their assets, limitations, and opportunities in all possible areas so that they will make wise choices and will use their unique talents if they care to do so. We believe that when individuals know their talents and use them in ways of their own choosing, the effects ultimately will be best for the society in which they live. In addition, counseling serves broad social purposes through helping individuals overcome obstacles to effective learning and achievement by means of remedial and rehabilitative planning and action.

CAREER COUNSELING

Career choice has been regarded historically as *vocational guidance*—a process of helping the client to choose, prepare for, and succeed in a given occupation. This process was centered around counseling, which consisted largely of examining data about the client and looking over the occupational possibilities to find a specific career goal, whereupon an educational plan was formulated to reach that goal. Although this rationale is still basic, there have been recent changes in the perception of the significance and scope of career counseling. A significant change is from *occupational* guidance, oriented to a group of possible entry choices, to *career* guidance, emphasizing the process of progressing from one level to another. Another change is the concept of continuous career planning over life. The data about rapid professional obsolescence, for example, emphasize the need for continuing education. For many persons this means retraining in midlife for a vastly changed job classification or for a wholly new career. It is commonplace now for a person to anticipate three or four major career changes in his or her lifetime. Another significant development has been support for career education and counseling by the United States Congress, which has become part of a national labor and education policy. This career education commitment resulted in large-scale financial support for training, research, and development programs in career counseling.

Career counseling is a task of therapeutic psychology. Vocational psychology cannot be singled out as a special branch of counseling and psychotherapy, largely because career counseling must be accomplished in the context of the individual's total life style and in relationship to his or her subculture. Optimally effective career counseling, therefore, cannot be an isolated and mechanical process of matching people and jobs.

Career counseling goals can be construed in several ways. First, and most commonly, career counseling is a process of confirming the choice already made by the client. Many clients have done a fair job of assessing themselves and their opportunities and of making tentative choices, as a result of other life experiences with parents and teachers. Second, career counseling is a process of clarifying vocational objectives. People are collecting information about careers and their personalities all the time, but they have difficulty interpreting the meaning of the data and stating the choice problem precisely and in the context of life-style planning. Counselors can help this type of client perceive their problem in clearer terms. The third manner in which career counseling is helpful to clients is that it allows them to discover facts about themselves and the working world that they had not known before. The most revelatory aspects are those in which occupational choices are broadened to include many which the client had not considered originally.

Therapeutic psychology is uniquely suited to accomplish this broad goal of effective career planning as part of life planning. The techniques described in earlier chapters, plus some special tools uniquely suited to educational-vocational planning, are the principal requirements for effective career choice. It was pointed out in Chapter 4 on the counseling process that planning problems differed somewhat from other types of personal problems because there is more emphasis on rational problem-solving methods and more involvement of the actualizing level functions. It should be emphasized, however, that any career counseling worth its salt includes considerations of the client's polar attitudes, aspirations, and core feelings. Career choice, from the research results reported to date, is not a strictly rational process. Neither is it a process of choice making on the basis of a few interviews with a counselor. Research supports the idea that career decisions are the product of a long series of life experiences and learnings that come to a focus in the interviews with the counselor.

Theories of Career Choice

Psychoanalysts view the origins of a person's interests as a response to an ego need for recognition and status satisfactions. They explain career choices on the basis of unconscious needs, as illustrated by the person with aggressive tendencies wanting to be a policeman. There is little research evidence to support this point of view.

Roe (1956) has formulated a series of hypotheses to account for the early determinants of interest. These determinants are basic human needs and early family experiences of acceptance, avoidance, and emotional concentration. These early experiences influence the general orientation of the child toward things or people. Roe has classified occupations according to eight clusters, such as service, technology, and entertainment. She also classifies them in levels from professional to unskilled. Roe hypothesizes that the clusters can be identified in terms of major orientations toward people and objects and that the early life experiences of the child predispose him or her toward certain major occupational groups.

Ginzberg (1951) viewed career choice as a process covering three developmental periods—the fantasy (six–eleven), the tentative (twelve–seventeen), and the realistic choice (eighteen up). Ginzberg indicated that he thought the process was largely irreversible, a result of many compromises of values and opportunities, and a function of the person's perception of the job rather than a realistic view of work. Criticisms of Ginzberg's study center around the inadequate design, the lack of description of the compromise process, and the fact that he ignored the phenomenon of occupational mobility.

Carter (1944) claimed that the individual's vocational attitudes develop from efforts to adapt to direct family and social pressures and to his or her own perceptions of needs and capacities. Client interests develop from identification with an occupation and are confirmed through tryouts in that career field. Eventually, the individual incorporates the occupational demands into his or her self-concepts and the occupational interest becomes relatively stabilized. Others, such as Bordin (1955), feel that occupational interests are by-products of personality traits and self-concepts in particular. Interests shift when the self changes or when the individual's stereotype of the particular occupation changes.

Super's theory (1951) is that occupational choices are implementations of the self-concept. According to his theory: A person is qualified for many occupations; each occupation requires a characteristic pattern of abilities and traits (with wide tolerances); since individual self-concepts and social situations change, the process of choice is continuous due to growth, exploration, establishment, maintenance, and decline; the career pattern (level, sequence, and duration of occupations) hinges on parental socioeconomic level, ability, personality, and opportunity; vocational development is mainly that of developing and implementing a self-concept that is the product of interacting heredity, physical factors, opportunity for various roles, and the extent of approval from superiors and peers; compromises between individual and environmental variables, between self-concepts and reality demands, are made through role-playing opportunities in fantasy, counseling, school, or work; satisfaction depends on the extent of adequate outlets for personality needs, a work situation in which a congenial and appropriate role can be played. Super's Career-Pattern Study (1954) consists of longitudinal and horizontal research on how children and adolescents make their career choices. He used actuarial, life-history, and career-pattern-analysis methods to study the career choices of youth.

Holland (1966) has formulated a developmental theory of vocational development with a final focus on six personal types—realistic, intellectual, social, conventional, enterprising, and artistic—from empirical goal, role preference, activities, and self-concept summaries of each group. Realistic persons, for example, prefer physical and technical activities, hold conventional economic values, and hold social and esthetic values in low importance. They see themselves as masculine, practical, conventional, submissive, and uncreative kinds of persons. This developmental theory helps the person facing a career choice to consider the complex personality dimensions of occupations in a systematic and realistic manner.

Appraisal and Diagnosis

For didactic purposes, the career counseling process will be divided into three elements: appraisal and diagnosis, information methods, and counseling techniques. The methods and areas of appraisal are summarized in Figure 24. The various methods of appraisal in career counseling are listed in the outer circle, and the matching areas to be appraised are indicated in the inner circle.

Most of the methods listed in Figure 24 are designed for appraising the personality characteristics that are close to the surface and to aid in diagnosis of the more manifest career-choice problems. Hence, this discussion will focus on those personality levels that are related to the problems of career choice and career developments.

The diagnostic process in career counseling follows the principles of diagnostic thinking cited in Chapter 5 and is designed to clarify the client's choice problem. The following material illustrates some of the diagnostic formulations built on appraisal instruments. Detailed use of specific tests will not be discussed because there is so much information available elsewhere.

APTITUDE APPRAISAL. One of the counselor's first diagnostic tasks is to note the congruence or discrepancy between the client's aspirations and aptitudes. The first step a counselor should take to accomplish this goal is to ascertain the client's vocational aspirations and knowledge. General mental-ability tests, along with special aptitude measures, then, are administered to infer the client's relative capacity to perform job functions or his or her potential to succeed in specified tasks or curricula. This procedure

FIGURE 24. *Areas and Methods of Appraisal in Career Counseling*

may be applied to many individuals, such as the seventeen-year-old boy who wants to be a lawyer but for whom reliable and valid aptitude measures indicate he is in the lowest 10 percent of the college freshman population on scholastic aptitude.

Aptitude measures may be applied as well to the student who is performing beyond a comfortable level of achievement. This student is called, in educational terms, an "overachiever." Although it is desirable, perhaps, to emphasize high achievement, experienced teachers note that many clients of this type achieve above their rated aptitudes even though performance is not emphasized. Many of these clients experience much anxiety about status and failure; some even pay the heavy price of emotional distress later as a result of allowing their inordinate ambition to outstrip their capacities.

Aptitude tests may be applied to a third type of client—the so-called underachiever. This client has known aptitudes but ones he or she is not using to the fullest. The person may not be using his or her aptitude to the utmost because of a deep-seated motivational difficulty, educational-skill deficiency, or health problem. For this type of client, a more refined diagnostic process must be initiated.

Aptitude discovery is a further problem in appraisal. A client, for example, finds that as a result of the aptitude survey he or she has potentialities in the area of numerical reasoning and arithmetic problem solving that he or she did not know existed in vocationally significant strength.

Two additional types of clients confronted are those without tangible aptitudes and those with many high aptitudes. For the former, career counseling is difficult because training and placement of such clients is a problem. The problem is made even more difficult if the clients or their parents have unrealistic aspirations for certain occupational pursuits. For the latter type with multiple aptitudes, the counselor's difficulty often reduces to determining which of the high aptitudes fits other factors of the client's interests and opportunities.

INTERESTS, ATTITUDES, AND VALUES. Although aptitude appraisal is a matter of capacity and vocational performance, interest and value measurement are concerned with vocational satisfaction. Various measures purporting to appraise interest are correlated closely with measures of job satisfaction. Aptitude is not so related as far as we know now.

The client with a conflict between interests and measured aptitudes—that is, with a diagnostic problem in the interest and value area—is confronted often in counseling. Such a client, for example, may have much interest in science but little aptitude necessary for work in that area. A counselor may note, however, the existence of artistic talents. The counselor may reconcile the discrepancy by suggesting that the client consider, perhaps, becoming a scientific illustrator.

Another type of client presenting a diagnostic problem to the counselor, has measured interests not related to stated interests or ambitions. For example, a client chooses to be an engineer because he or she likes to manipulate and repair mechanical objects. However, the pattern given on a standard interest test is that of social service with no measured interests in common with persons in engineering.

The client who has no well-defined interest patterns is another type the counselor encounters. Such a client may lack interest maturity as a cause of his or her condition, especially if he or she is an adolescent. There may be no dominant pattern nor even an above-average interest area. The person's life experiences, out of which interests develop, may have been constricted. The solution may lie mainly in waiting a few years until a crystallized pattern develops. Strong (1943, 1955), for example, found considerable instability of interests in men younger than twenty-five. This lack of significant career interests may have some clinical meaning in that the client cannot get interested in anything or identify with a particular family of occupations because of some more involved value commitment issues.

Counselors occasionally meet clients who have unused or undiscovered interest patterns that are revealed by inventories. This condition creates counseling problems since the discovered interest pattern may be related to a field that the client cannot enter because of limited finances, family, religion, or some other socially constricting circumstance.

Part of the diagnostic picture in career counseling is the relationship between interests and values. Values are prime motivating characteristics that should be explored in any career counseling process. Their importance for career planning is contained in fundamental questions such as, "What is my philosophy of life?" "How do I feel I want to use my life?" "What is important to me?" These questions are closely bound up with occupational choice, but there is little research to indicate the ways in which material related to these fundamental questions can be used effectively in career counseling. The counselor must depend on his or her skill in helping clients clarify their attitudes about these important questions and in helping them find activities that fulfill the demands of their philosophies. Some instruments, such as the Strong-Campbell Interest Inventory (1977), are useful to the counselor to help clients identify their dominant interest-value clusters.

PHYSICAL AND EMOTIONAL ADJUSTMENT.   Counselors make attempts to appraise emotional factors related to career predictions, but not very much is known concerning the influence of these factors. There are few validity studies of personality traits or styles of life related to specific occupations. Apparently, there is considerable intraoccupational variability on such personality traits. Emotional problems, however, have a direct bearing on occupational success, in that attitudes toward authority, hypochondriacal tendencies, and other emotional adjustment problems, involving neurotic and psychotic characteristics, affect the client's ability to obtain and hold employment.

Physical factors play an important part in the counselor's diagnosis of occupational problems. These factors will be considered later under rehabilitation problems. As noted in Figure 24, there are many other considerations that must be made in career planning—finances, family situation, opportunities, and pressures from teachers, relatives, and friends.

Special Information Techniques

Although we covered the general topic of using information in counseling in Chapter 10, there are several types and sources of information especially useful in counseling on career problems.

TYPES OF OCCUPATIONAL INFORMATION.   Occupational information covers quantitative data, such as the number of people employed in certain occupations, and qualitative data, such as the structure and description of occupations. The several types of information that a career counselor must know are occupational structures, facts, and trends. These data serve two general purposes in counseling—exploration and verification (Rusalem 1954). The exploratory function is performed in the early phases of counseling before the client makes a career decision. Browsing through occupational readings, seeing occupational films, evaluating part-time jobs, and watching selected television programs offer direct or vicarious tryout experiences. Early education experiences through the school curriculum help also (Weinrach 1979). Rusalem's data (1954) point out how these exploratory experiences are emotionally toned and how they become part of the self-concept. Clients, during this exploratory phase, must get "the feel" of a career in addition to the usual stereotypes.

The verification function of occupational information comes late in the process when clients observe or read about occupational material to verify their tentative choices. They may actually try out the occupation to test the congruence of work reality with their expectations and self-concepts. For example, a prospective medical student obtains summer work as an orderly to check on the reality of his perceptions of medical environments.

The United States Department of Labor conducts continual occupational research designed to keep up with the changing job scene (Fine 1955). Classification is based on the assumption that workers are involved to varying degrees with things, data, and people. It is focused, therefore, on what the worker does on the job. Jobs are broken down into eight components, some of which are: interest, aptitude, temperament, educational development, and work performed. Twenty-six worker functions, such as computing, analyzing, serving, and copying, are weighted and organized into a hierarchy according to requirements for each job and not according to skill level. For example, a plumber is given a weighting of 6 on precision working, 3 on computing, and 1 on taking instructions (Fine 1955). This line of research has shown great promise in career counseling, particularly for those occupations requiring specific on-the-job training rather than broad general types of advanced education.

Occupational classification schemes are useful to the counselor as a means of orienting the client concerning his or her career objectives, on a level which the client can understand. They are valuable, in addition, because they suggest occupational goals that might otherwise have been overlooked in a systematic search for suitable occupations.

The counselor needs all the facts on various occupations his or her client is considering in order to describe to the client what demands each occupation will make. It is apparent from Ginzberg's (1951), Holland's (1966), and Super's (1951) research that it is not the external objective reality of the occupation that enters into career choice as much as the client's subjective perception or idealization of that occupation. Hence, there is much need for transmitting accurate and comprehensive job facts to clients. Most of this information is obtained in job analysis surveys performed primarily by the U.S. Bureau of Labor Statistics. The specific kinds of career information needed in career counseling are as follows: opportunities (current and long-range), compensation (salary or wages and supplemental benefits), hours (number and regularity), entry levels, and related jobs, qualifications, and restrictions (physical characteristics, marital status, memberships, licenses, certifications, examinations, and special personal qualities and training requirements).

Sources of Occupational Facts

Occupational facts found in thousands of occupational books and pamphlets are usually classified according to characteristics considered important for persons entering the occupation, or characteristics and duties of the jobs. There are three main sources of such information: federal agencies, commercial publishers, and trade associations. The Bureau of Labor Statistics and the Bureau of the Census generally do the basic research. These data are published in a variety of government pamphlets. Many of these occupational data are written up in attractive format and style by commercial publishing firms. Trade associations publish a plethora of occupational information, mainly of the recruitment type.

The counselor should note the *source* of the data in estimating the reliability and usefulness of the information for his or her client. He or she should note also the *date* of the publication and of the underlying basic research, since out-of-date occupational data can be very misleading. Data on salaries, which have changed very rapidly, become out-of-date quickly as well. However, most descriptive information remains valid over a long period of time.

Agencies in which career counseling is performed compile the occupational data in libraries called in most places "career centers." The data are classified by an alphabetical or numerical scheme such as that of the *Dictionary of Occupational Titles* (U.S. Employment Service 1965). Often a specialist librarian is employed to locate information for clients and to perform the monumental chore of keeping the information current. Several bibliographic sources contain compilations of current publications of value in career counseling. State departments of education and employment often have special services for counselors in the location and dissemination of occupational literature. A current development is computerized information which is retrieved directly by the client. Printouts from the system contain the most compatible career options, and supporting data, which match data about the client. Career development centers often join a network which provides the printout terminal services and maintains the system.

The study of occupational trends is another source of useful data to indicate future prospects of occupations. The numbers of farmers and laborers, for example, have declined considerably and clerks, technicians, and semiskilled workers have increased greatly. As in the case of occupational-structure information, these quantitative data are useful mainly for the general orientation of counselor and client. A client, for example, would not desist from choosing farming as an occupation merely because the

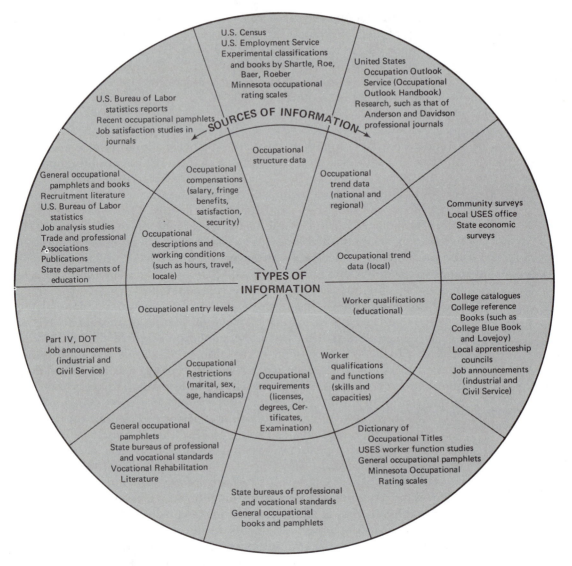

FIGURE 25. A Summary of Types and Sources of Occupational Data Needed in Career Counseling

national trend for employment of farmers was way down. Local occupational trends, however, might influence very much the choice of an occupation if the client were planning to stay in the local community. The principal problem here is that local data are most often nonexistent or outdated. School or community college counseling directors sometimes take leadership in conducting a community survey of local economic, population, and job trends with the aim of predicting employment opportunities for young workers entering the labor market.

The Occupational Outlook Service of the Department of Labor is one of the best sources of information on national occupational trends. A significant tool for the counselor is the *Occupational Outlook Handbook* (U.S. Government 1977) and its supplements, which contain trends and other pertinent data on occupations and are revised frequently.

National economic trends are useful data for counselors since they give clues to areas of potential employment. An example is the increased need for atomic energy for power purposes and rocket propulsion for transportation, which, in turn, requires the reorganization and building of entire communities around atomic and rocket industries. These industries call for new skills and training in the research, development, manufacture, and operation of novel machines and processes. The phenomenon of population mobility demands that counselors keep up with national, state, and regional occupational trends, as well as those in their local communities.

In the preceding paragraphs it was emphasized that counselors working with career-planning problems must have a vast array of occupational data at their fingertips. In Figure 25 we have summarized the types and major sources of occupational data for use in counseling. The sources of the occupational facts are listed in the outer ring, and information from those sources is located in the inner ring.

Counseling Methods for Career Planning

Career counseling is more than a rational process of matching an appraisal of the individual and appropriate occupational information into a career plan. This process involves careful integration with a life style which may be planned, or which evolves without much formal choice. Career counseling, according to Super (1951), is largely the implementation of the client's self-concept. This means that the client perceives himself or herself as behaving in a certain manner, with status, pleasures, social contacts, and other values satisfied through his or her occupation. This is why career counseling cannot be a simple process of fitting "a square peg to a square hole." Weinrach (1979), writing generally about career counseling, emphasizes that such counseling is a process of expanding the freedom and range of choices for the person.

SURVEY AND EVALUATION INTERVIEWS. Early in the career-counseling process, counselors collect data on the client from which they make predictions about probabilities of the client's success in training or work. Data are collected largely from the interview, a personal-data summary blank, case records, and test instruments. The data are weighted informally by the counselors from their experience and are then put in a type of multiple regression equation by means of which they make predictions. This process was described more in the diagnosis discussion of Chapter 5.

Newer methods of thinking about prediction problems, such as Information and Decision Theory (Gelatt and Brew 1980), include the application of logic and mathematics to the interaction of predictor variables and their relation to the final decision to be made. Much information and more useful theories are needed on how career predictions are made. It seems that the best that can be done at present is for the counselor to make the most accurate hypotheses possible on the basis of the most valid and reliable clinical data, and utilize the best of the present statistical prediction methods with tests and computer technology.

Early interviews in career counseling are marked by preoccupation with the reliability and validity of data from interviews, surveys, records, and tests. Counselors are asking themselves constantly what kinds of criteria (successful educational plans and vocational pursuits) are related to all the data being collected. Counselors should also ask themselves how they can bring the client more closely into this predicting, decision-making process.

THE SYNTHESIS INTERVIEW.   The counselor reviews material from the first interviews, examines the personal data summary, reviews test data and computer printouts, and compiles relevant occupational information. The client considers the interpreted test data, reviews his or her own values and feelings, and collates findings with the results of his or her independent occupational study. The client and counselor discuss these data in the synthesis or decision-making phase of the process. The synthesis interview ordinarily consists of the test interpretation, a discussion of occupational data, and then a discussion of these and earlier data. Counseling techniques mentioned in earlier chapters are used throughout the process.

ESTABLISHING THE OCCUPATIONAL OBJECTIVE.   Prior to the synthesis interview the client has done his or her own occupational study. This study may have been performed in a career center as part of a class, or it may have been accomplished specifically for this interview.

From the synthesis interview a career plan is formulated. Generally, this takes the form of specifying the general areas of greatest promise, such as science, service, or business. Then, depending on the client's age and need to be specific, goals of a more exact nature, such as machinist, typist, engineer, or elementary teacher are specified. This more specific selection usually is the culmination of a long process of vocational exploration and study, so that the choice naturally evolves out of the data. Often, however, the choice must be made in a short time to prepare for a training program or immediate employment. Such was the case with many veterans seeking career counseling. Typically, the counselor administered several tests, made his or her predictions, and then came up with several specific objectives in preferential order so as to formulate an immediate training plan. Similar "crash" decisions tend to be made in rehabilitation and employment, settings where time is a factor in moving heavy case loads. This shortening of the career-choice process is to be regarded as an expedient when viewed from a broad actualizing viewpoint. Career counseling should have built-in arrangements for follow-ups. Furthermore, there should be a thorough understanding with the client that a specific choice made in such a short time is strictly tentative.

Counselors must be aware of the rapid changes in occupations. Conventional occupations are disappearing and new ones arrive daily. Clients must be helped to think of career fields rather than specific occupations. Data are accumulating to indicate that the present high school student will change careers many times in his or her life. Even if his or her chosen occupation retains its general form and function, the obsolescence factor requires retraining every few years. This fact must be considered when making long-term educational and career plans with school-age youth.

The counselor suggests career ideas for further exploration. The client then makes his or her own decisions on the objective. Counselors may give specific occupational data from their knowledge and experience, but it behooves them to be right. It is preferable, therefore, that they use the source of the data verbatim to avoid distortion. There is evidence, such as that of Speer and Jasper (1949), which indicates that it is the counselor's presentation of occupational data that is most effective in selecting suitable goals. Independent reading on the part of the client, in itself, was not of much value in selecting suitable career goals. Counselors, therefore, must take a more active role in presenting occupational facts and guiding client readings. Counselors should point out that occupational information is more than just facts about jobs. It should be presented in terms of a way of life, of a relationship between worker and job, and relationships among workers. Fine (1955), for example, points out how persons planning careers "fit in" to the jobs performed. In family and school environments a person can be creative, be himself or herself, be expansive and spontaneous. Most jobs, however, are dull and require that the client conform to expectations, that he or she be a team member. Fine emphasizes how lack of understanding of this fundamental principle leads to frustration, hostility, and general job dissatisfaction. In other words, the counselor must consider career planning in terms of the values, life experiences, and expectations of the client. It is for these reasons that the career counselor must have a thorough understanding of therapeutic psychology and must place career planning in the broader context of choosing life styles.

The counselor has an additional responsibility to show clients how their occupational objectives do or do not *fit the data*. The counselor then must let clients come to their own conclusions. The counselor can show clients how their tentative objectives fit into organizational patterns and job families. The counselor may have organizational charts of typical industries related to the client's interest to show how a geologist, for example, fits into the organizational structure, or how a school psychologist fits into a public school administrative organization.

An important principle in presenting occupational information is *timing*. The client should be ready. Generally, the client is ready when he or she is aware of his or her characteristics from the appraisal phases, and is wondering what relationship they have to career choices. The counselor judges that the client is ready, for the most part, when he or she begins to ask for information.

THE EDUCATIONAL PLAN.   After the client has selected the general occupational area and made some specific occupational choices in preferential order, a plan is made for obtaining the necessary education to achieve the objective. This education may take the form of college, trade school, or on-the-job training. Methods and tools for accomplishing this plan are discussed in the next section under educational counseling.

Many counselors prefer to have the client leave with some kind of plan on paper. Hence, various career and life-plan brochures can be made that list the client's principal career choices, educational plans, and general profiles of test results. An example of such a life plan is described in Loughary and Ripley (1979). In a process as complicated as career and educational planning, distortions of the life plan take place over a period of time; hence, a summary of the results would tend to reduce distortion, at least in the factual elements of the program.

TRYOUTS AND FOLLOW-UPS.   It is necessary to convey to clients the idea that general area choices, specific objectives, and training plans are tentative until confirmed by tryout. This can be done without undermining the client's security. It is deemed unwise and unethical for the counselor to imply that, after taking some tests and talking things over for a few hours, the client has found the answers to his or her life plans.

Because of the process nature of career counseling, it is necessary to try the plan and reevaluate the objectives in light of the educational or occupational tryout. Follow-up interviews are arranged to check on the adequacy of the objectives and the preceding counseling.

Preretirement Planning

Increases in the numbers of upper middle-aged people and removal of mandatory retirement regulations make retirement planning a complex process. The abundance of studies on retirement satisfaction also indicates how individualized the process of planning for retirement must be. For example, some people thrive on an activity theory of retirement, where they must remain in meaningful activity, sometimes related to their former employment, to remain happy. Others prefer to be totally disengaged from any meaningful work and want to enjoy protracted leisure. Then, there are the mixtures in between. The preretirement planning literature is clear, however, that to enjoy one's later years, life must have meaning and purpose, health must be maintained, and finances must be adequate to one's chosen life style. The numerous choices that enter into a retirement life style and the maintenance of one's health and solvency require special skills of counselors. Some even specialize in preretirement counseling and conduct workshops in retirement planning. The demands for these services will increase given the demographic trends for older adults.

EDUCATIONAL COUNSELING

Educational counseling consists of two distinct types of counseling assistance: educational planning and remedial help. Educational counseling has acquired special social significance in light of talent searches and encouragement of the academically able student.

Educational Planning

SELECTING A TRAINING INSTITUTION.   This type of counseling is aimed essentially at helping clients select the most suitable educational goals and the best fit of educational institutions. Several factors must be considered in helping a client select an educational institution: scholastic aptitude sufficient for admission and retention, financial capacity, and suitability of the college program to the client's interests, general educational needs, and career goals. There are several characteristics about an educational institution that a client must consider also. Does it have suitable living facilities? What is the reputation of its faculty? What is the placement record for its graduates? Is it accredited by the regional accrediting agencies and by the professional associations for the particular curriculum being considered? Other factors, varying in significance from person to person, must be considered, such as the size of the institution, and extracurricular programs. Research on college environments is providing accurate comparative descriptions of colleges to help students choose wisely; but the rapid changes in higher education and patterns of attendance are making these studies obsolete quickly.

Some of the standard references the client may rely on to make a thorough study of educational institutions are: the *College Blue Book* (Macmillan Information Division 1979), Greenfield's *National Directory of Addresses and Telephone Numbers* (1981), *Lovejoy's College Guide* (1979), *Barron's Profiles of American Colleges* (1980), and Peterson's and Davis's *Education Directory: Colleges and Universities* (1979–80). These references are used to supplement information from the catalogs of the individual colleges. All students planning to take educational counseling must be familiar with them.

PREDICTING SUCCESS IN TRAINING AND EDUCATION.   One of the principal problems a counselor must face in educational planning is making predictions of probable success in a specific program in a given college. Many institutions have predictive indices, or at least a validity coefficient based on a correlation between a standard aptitude measure and grades in that college or curriculum. These validity coefficients generally fall in the low fifties for Pearson correlations. For the counselor making predictions about training success, the previous grades of the client in high school are still the best reference since grades generally have higher validity than a standard scholastic-aptitude test. For example, the counselor can fairly accurately predict success in the first year of engineering training in college relying on high school grades, mathematics achievement tests, and general scholastic-aptitude tests (Layton 1954). There has been a strong trend toward grade inflation among colleges and high schools, however. This tendency to constrict the range of grades given has changed the predictive accuracy of earlier grades and weakened prediction formulas.

So far, studies in the area of predictions indicate that it is much easier to predict success in training for an occupation than to predict success in that occupation. There are more definite criteria of success in training, such as grades and completion of the program. Obtaining criteria of success in many professional occupations is very difficult. Hoyt (1966) surveyed the cumulative evidence from studies predicting occupational success on the basis of grades. He found very low correlations generally between college grades and various criteria of occupational success, which suggests that factors other than scholastic ability enter into the criteria of success.

FINANCING TRAINING.   An important consideration in college planning is finance. Major sources of tuition, besides parental subsidies and savings, are scholarships, fellowships, and loans. Counselors working in areas of educational planning should have financial-aid bulletins of the major colleges. The current procedure used by colleges in awarding financial aids is the package plan. This is a mix of loans, tuition waivers, scholarships, and part-time work experiences suited to the needs of the student and the financial condition of the family. Financial status of families is determined by the College Scholarship Service, a national nonprofit organization that compiles detailed financial statements from parents and forwards this information to colleges at the parents' request.

REMEDIAL ASSISTANCE.   Although overcoming educational deficiencies is more an instructional than a counseling responsibility, the counselor practicing in an educational institution comes face to face with this problem frequently. We take the position that the counselor must be able to diagnose remediation problems in order to recommend steps to remedy deficiencies, or to make suitable referrals to remedial specialists. The availability of diagnostic testing instruments for assessing the achievement level and the precise areas of difficulty, as well as a dearth of experts in remedial assistance, make such diagnostic studies by counselors feasible and necessary. Appraisal instruments, along with supplementary diagnostic interviewing, often can be used to indicate to a client where the causes of his or her difficulties lie.

DIAGNOSTIC SKILLS.   Knowledge of diagnostic procedures in basic skills is of value to both the counselor working in educational institutions and to the private practitioner. Achievement problems are a key reason for referral in a school or college. In private practice, the psychologist spends much of his or her time with clients having difficulties in schools. The psychologist is in a key position to work with problems of educational achievement also, because of the complex psychological factors usually operating in cases of low achievement. There may be combinations of emotional problems, educational-skill deficiency, low motivation, physiological handicaps, or lack of practice in the basic skill. A thorough diagnostic and remedial program, therefore, calls on the skills of many specialists. The psychologist often is selected to coordinate the various specialists' diagnostic studies and to make recommendations to the tutors, teachers, or remedial specialists.

Although it is beyond the scope of this book to describe educational diagnostic methods in detail, some of the areas to be investigated are mentioned to give the counselor without orientation in these skills some background. There are two areas of investigation—general study methods and reading. Several inventories exist for diagnosing study difficulties. An example is the Brown-Holtzman *Survey of Study Habits and Attitudes* (1955). Though inventories identify problem areas, they do not differentiate between habits of good and poor students. An early study at Ohio State University revealed that even superior students used widely variable and unrecommended study procedures. The students apparently were superior in spite of their study methods (Danskin and Burnett 1952).

Diagnosis of educational problems should start with a good *physical examination* with particular attention to sensory and metabolic factors. Secondly, a close look at *motivational factors,* with special emphasis on personal problems, should be taken. There are generally many complicating factors in achievement deficiencies; however, attitudinal difficulties are often at the root of the problem. One should not overlook the possibility that emotional problems are the result as much as the cause of educational achievement problems. Achievement problems often reveal some deep-seated hostility toward parents or a confusion of values. These problems indicate counseling perhaps more than remedial educational techniques.

The counselor should examine *basic skills* and *knowledge,* which underlie achievement. Some of these are rate and flexibility of reading; level of comprehension and vocabulary; interest; quantity of reading; and interfering habits such as finger tracing, word reading, regression, and vocalization. These diagnostic data enable the educational counselor to formulate the client's problem more accurately than the usual "I can't concentrate" or "I can't read fast" type of offhand symptomatic statement of the client. This diagnostic survey enables the counselor either to make a referral to a remedial specialist or to offer some suggestions from his or her general knowledge in the field of remediation.

REMEDIATION.   Generally speaking, counselors do not perform remedial instruction since individual tutoring is so time consuming. Counselors can spend their time so much more profitably in other types of services. Most agencies offer remedial-type courses, which give the client an opportunity to learn basic skills over a fixed period of time in a group or clinic setting. Though there are many books and pamphlets available for self-help on educational problems, there is no evidence to indicate that a person improves his or her skills substantially by reading a pamphlet. The educational counselor may use the pamphlet-reading technique on a prescription basis, however, to give the client some background for later conferences on specific learning and study skills. The pamphlets and time-study schedules are useful as diagnostic devices to help a client find areas of weakness. Pamphlets are useful when a lack of learning techniques is not at the core of the achievement problem, but something more basic in attitude and approach to learning tasks.

REHABILITATION COUNSELING

Rehabilitation is a process of restoring clients with handicaps to the fullest possible usefulness to themselves and society. It is estimated the there are in the United States over three million disabled or severely handicapped persons in the productive years between fourteen and sixty-four (U.S. Department of Education 1963). Of these, two million come within the scope of services offered by vocational rehabilitation programs. Most of these two million could achieve happy and productive lives through suitable work. Vocational rehabilitation services offered through the states and assisted by the United States government have been working with this group since 1918. These programs have been able to help clients overcome their dependency and contribute to their society. The programs, furthermore, have enabled clients to achieve personal satisfactions, which come from engaging in productive work and avoiding the stigma of social and economic liability.

The Vocational Rehabilitation Act of 1965 and the Rehabilitation Act of 1973 broadened the concept of rehabilitation from original legislation in 1920 to include any person who has been hurt by life. This includes not only the physically and mentally handicapped, but also the culturally deprived and the socially handicapped, such as released prisoners. Counseling plays a vital part in this rehabilitation process. Counseling techniques for handicapped persons are little different from counseling for the able-bodied. Occupational distribution of the handicapped is roughly similar to that of persons who are not disabled. State bureaus of vocational rehabilitation employ special counselors, many with master's degrees in counseling, who are trained in the rehabilitation process. The U.S. Veterans Administration employs counseling psychologists to perform similar rehabilitative functions in veterans hospitals, with more stress, however, being placed on the counseling function.

The vocational-rehabilitation process covers many services to the handicapped client. In addition to the diagnostic and vocational counseling techniques described in this book, there are orderly sequences of services, such as physical restoration, training, psychiatric treatment, provision of training materials, maintenance while training, placement, license acquisition, and furnishing of equipment, such as vending stands, to establish a business under the supervision of the agency.

Generally, the process proceeds according to well-established steps, beginning with the *intake interview*, which includes orientation to the service and determination of eligibility, assignment to a counselor and the *initial interview*, the *case study, psychological evaluation, counseling*, formulating the *rehabilitation plan, training* and/or *placement,* and *follow-up* (U.S. Department of Education 1963). These steps are aimed at promoting maximum vocational usefulness as soon as possible.

Existential ideas have been infused into the rehabilitation process. Easton and Krippner (1964) point out the special existential problems of the handicapped in areas of apathy and meaning, motivation to assume responsibility for choice and action, and the meaning of pain. It takes the client beyond mere adjustment to a more creative approach to life with his or her disability.

Interest in professional counseling organizations has grown rapidly in rehabilitation circles during the past few years. In 1957, the American Rehabilitation Counselors Association was organized as a division in the American Personnel and Guidance Association. Division 17, Counseling Psychology, of the American Psychological Association also has many psychologists working primarily in vocational rehabilitation. The National Rehabilitation Association is another professional group available to rehabilitation counselors. To meet rising expectations for standards of service, a Council on Rehabilitation Counselor Certification establishes experience and educational requirements and also administers a competency examination for the certificate. This council is composed of representatives of the major professional rehabilitation counselor organizations.

The
Rehabilitation
Counselor

Vocational rehabilitation counselors must have the same helping skills and knowledge that persons in other helping professions must have. They are professional caseworkers since they usually handle the client's problems from the first interview to satisfactory placement, follow-up, and coping adjustment. Their counseling functions are very much like those described in this book, with special emphasis on psychometrics and career counseling. They must be conversant with medical and psychiatric terminology and must be familiar with community service agencies and educational institutions. In state agencies, they are expediters and coordinators of many services to clients.

The vocational rehabilitation counselor, therefore, must be a versatile person. Many lists have been drawn up to indicate what he or she should know to do the job well. Cantrell (1958) studied the matter of training rehabilitation counselors by asking a large number of counselors in the Veterans Administration, officials of state vocational rehabilitation centers, and counselors in private practice what they felt was important in training and how they would rank the material in usefulness. Though there were some disagreements in rankings among the three groups of practitioners, the average rankings, from first to last choice in significance, for their work as vocational rehabilitation counselors were as follows:

1. Counseling theory, principles, and practice.
2. Professional activities, including ethics, duties, interprofessional teamwork, professional growth, and public relations.

3. Supervised field work, including visits to agencies.

4. Psychological information, including developmental, abnormal, personality theory, and effect of disability on personality.

5. Testing principles and practice.

6. Occupational information.

7. Casework history, principles, and method.

8. Rehabilitation, including history, philosophy, legal, and administrative aspects.

9. Social and community resource information.

10. Medical and related information, including knowledge of physical restoration resources.

11. Research and statistics methods.

It was noteworthy in Cantrell's study that the practicing counselors considered counseling the very center of the process of rehabilitation and felt that the major emphasis in training should be on counseling. The other areas, such as medical information and case methods, were considered necessary supportive elements to the counseling relationship.

The problems of defining rehabilitation counselor tasks and evaluating counseling performance have been investigated by Muthard and Miller (1966). This kind of research is limited by the varying conceptions of counselor role and by differing views of evaluating successful rehabilitation counseling in qualitative terms as well as number of case files closed. On the one hand, pressures for agency accountability stress the number of people placed in jobs and the closure of the case; on the other hand, the quality of life and general coping capacity of the client requiring more extended counseling are contrary pressures.

SUMMARY

Life planning involves a broad approach to choices of life style, partners, living locale, and careers. Therapeutic psychologists often specialize, or become involved at some point, in problems of career choice, educational planning, diagnosis on remediation problems, and rehabilitation counseling of the handicapped. Though there are various theories on how career choices are made, there is much agreement among counselors that suitable career choices have profound consequences for individual actualizing and for society. Educational and vocational counseling draw heavily on appraisal and diagnosis functions, yet retain counseling techniques as the core of the process. The principal sources of data used in educational-vocational-rehabilitation counseling are tests, case histories, client self-evaluations, clinical observations, occupational information materials, training directories, and tryout work experience.

14

Counseling
and Human Values

The question of what I am going to do with my life is raised frequently
in actualizing counseling and psychotherapy. It comes in the form of choices
of life style or of value conflict. Terms such as *human revolution, human
potential,* and *human intentionality* put this basic question of purpose and
meaning in a broad social context. The main purpose of this chapter is
to examine the place of basic human values in counseling and how counselors and psychotherapists manage value-choice issues and methods.

Psychology as a science and a profession has become more concerned
about values, including the value assumptions underlying science itself.
The term *value* in this context is defined as a firm, conscious or unconscious
belief in the worth of an idea or feeling. For the purposes of this chapter,
the philosophical problem of the origin of values and the absoluteness
or relativity of values will be treated only incidentally.

VALUES IN THERAPEUTIC PSYCHOLOGY

Another purpose of this chapter is to examine some of the value relationships between therapeutic psychology and religious counseling. We shall
use Wrenn's description of the two approaches: ". . . religion and psychol-

ogy complement each other. Psychology contributes to an understanding of the *nature* of self and of one's relationships with others, religion to an understanding of the meaning and purpose in life, and the *significance* of these same relationships. Both may contribute to more effective living" (1958, p. 331).

In actualizing counseling and psychotherapy terms, the valuing process takes place primarily in the core of the person, with rational choice-making largely an actualizing function. This means that the person looks inward toward the core for value guidelines. He or she is "inner-directed" rather than "outer-directed." Outer-directed persons seek answers for value questions largely outside of themselves. They value expert opinion on these matters; they look to authority and tradition for answers to difficult life questions. They attempt to please others through manipulative behaviors and operate largely at a rational facade level. One goal, then, of the actualizing process is to encourage the actualizing person to look within for cues and guidelines and to learn to trust what he or she uncovers from his or her core being. This does not mean turning inward for answers exclusively, but to find the best balance between inner and outer criteria of evaluation. The actualizing model offers a wide spectrum of methods to deal with this search for awareness and inner support as well as for decision-making skills in acting out value choices.

In the psychological literature generally, there appears to be an awakening interest in philosophical problems underlying the psychological study of man. Mowrer, for example, states that psychology perhaps ought to examine its long-fostered assumption that the nonphysical elements of personality (conceived popularly as man's mind or spirit) serve the body (1957). Although personality grows out of needs to serve the body, Mowrer wonders whether the "mind" has its peculiar needs, characteristics, and survival demands also. He realizes that this is a disturbing question since the topic moves from the traditional pale of naturalistic observation to the area of the "spirit"—a traditionally religious subject. Yet, psychologists are becoming increasingly concerned about the subject of values clarification, psychological "survival," and the "human tragedy." Human problems, especially, have become such an acute social concern that practicing psychologists are willing to examine all available means of helping clients to survive psychologically. Apparently, they are willing to do this even if it means going beyond traditional laboratory and strictly behavioristic methods of studying and helping man.

It is a truism that counselors deal with fundamental problems of actualized living, namely loving, becoming an independent person, handling normal guilt, and gaining a mature perspective on the frustrating and tragic incidents of everyday life. We are aware of the difficulties in approaching the topic of values in the context of therapeutic psychology. This chapter is offered as a starting point for the student who may not have done much previous reading or thinking about the numerous value problems confronting client and counselor.

Psychological counselors have been reluctant to face the possibility that they might have functions and responsibilities that could be termed broadly as *religious*. This reluctance has been due to the empirical tradition, basic philosophical differences between social science and theology, alleged emotional extremes and hypocrisy in much of organized religious behavior, and the counselor's own spiritual ignorance or conflict. More psychological counselors are recognizing, however, that religious sentiments and feelings become powerful positive or negative motives in their client's lives.

Traditionally, psychology has been biologically oriented. The early models and scientific procedures of the late nineteenth century were based on physiology and physics. Darwinian philosophy had considerable influence on psychologists' view of man as a continuation of the animal world and subject to the same natural laws. Early American psychology added a functional note to the biological models imported from Germany. There was a very strong effort to divorce psychology from its earlier philosophical roots and to make the understanding of behavior a strictly scientific venture.

We do not advocate a return to rationalistic and other philosophical methods as a substitute for careful observation and rigorous experimentation. Psychology as a science must remain firmly planted in scientific methods and critical thinking. We are in accord, however, with the trend in psychological services to examine the methods and assumptions of psychology in regard to their adequacy for understanding basic human problems and helping people to deal with them more effectively. Part of the difficulty is that the hunger for knowledge about human nature and efforts to assist people with their problems is making premature and unrealistic demands on such an infant endeavor as scientific psychology. Nevertheless, the therapeutic psychologist is faced with the practical reality (or at least the pressure) for looking beyond scientific methods and psychological techniques to help clients with values beyond the behavior change process itself.

The assumption that it is necessary to go beyond empirically validated psychological techniques in helping clients with value problems puts the therapeutic psychologist squarely in the area of traditional religious concern. Here again, the history of psychology at some points has run counter to formal religion. Freud's writings, for example, are well known for their indictment of organized religious endeavors. Freud asserted that much of religious dogma and behavior are projections of unconscious wishes. In addition to the maligning of, or indifference toward, formal religious belief, there has been an attitude of suspicion toward professional psychologists who had any strong personal religious beliefs. They were automatically suspect because of the assumed interference these beliefs had with an attitude of objectivity so necessary for their profession.

Jung's attitude toward religion was that the client's present belief system should be used in such a way that it would hasten his or her recovery of healthy attitudes. This view was a radical departure from the Freudian position, which, as described above, tended to regard much of formal religion as a form of abnormality. Jung is reputed to have advocated finding God within experience as part of the individuation process (Glover 1950). The "God within" the racial unconscious of the Jungian system is then equated by many persons with a transcendental "God without." Jung admits that it is not the business of the psychologist to establish or even investigate objective truth regarding the existence of God. He states, furthermore, that neither is it the psychologist's business to construct a pseudoreligion out of primitive yearnings or myths. Jung tries to stay close to empirical facts in this realm and to concentrate on the oak rather than on the acorn (1933).

White (1953), a priest as well as a psychologist, approached the problem of God and the psychology of the unconscious in a spirit of compromise. He attempted to tie together the idea of an external reality, called God, with the inner nature and psychological realities of man. Kunkel (1955), a psychiatrist, also made efforts toward reconciliation of the two realms into a "religious psychology." The elements of this collaborative relationship are naturalistic observation and depth psychology. They are used to help understand behavior on the one hand, and to give purpose and direction to behavior on the other. Kunkel feels that a human helping relationship such as therapy and the goals of maturity need both approaches working together.

Efforts were made even earlier to tie more closely psychotherapeutic methods and assumptions to those of religion. Putnam, a New England physician of the early twentieth century, tried very hard to encourage his psychoanalytic colleagues to join him in efforts to broaden the base of psychoanalysis so as to include problems of the larger community and the cosmos. His proposals to tie a religiously oriented metaphysics to psychoanalysis met with strong resistance and some outright rejection in both Europe and America. This resistance persisted until such contemporary writers as Fromm (1950), Mowrer (1957), White (1953), and May (1953) reopened the question without suggesting that psychology compromise on its scientific bases.

A Point of View   We are discussing values in this book because clients often confront counselors with problems concerned with value conflicts, such as handling guilt over immoral behavior, meeting crises, overcoming deep-seated anxieties, feeling worthwhile, and relating to something significant. Counselors are often put in a difficult position when clients expect more of them than help in gaining awareness or comfort. Many clients, in effect, beg counselors to tell them how to live, what kinds of persons they should be, how they can meet the vicissitudes and seeming meaninglessness of life. Frequently, clients expect the counselor to relieve them of basic anxieties such as fear of nonbeing, or death.

We are not proposing that counselors set themselves up as authorities on such questions, nor that they should yield to client demands for answers to basic questions by giving their personal philosophies. What is being suggested, though, is that counselors be very much aware of this problem and be cognizant of temptations to pontificate on philosophical and religious questions.

It seems that one must recognize that religious and psychological concepts are not mutually exclusive. One must not assume that either religious concern or psychological interpretation is the total solution to, or explanation of, humanity's problems. Many people put this proposition into the form of an uncomfortable dichotomy. They feel inclined either to reject psychological interpretations and explanations of behavior or to reject their religious belief system. There seems to be a third position for clients to take, which we would like to explore. This view is that there is considerable overlap and congruence as well as conflict between the psychological and theological views of man. One should recognize these points of overlap and conflict and then look assiduously for areas where the meanings are congruent and seem to give greater combined insight into human existence and the solution of human problems.

We think that it is important to encourage colleagues to ponder questions on the relationships among scientific psychology, philosophy, and religion. If such an endeavor were successful, a "breakthrough" might be achieved that would be of great benefit to counselors and clients struggling with these interdisciplinary problems, many of which are presently outside the scope of scientific and professional psychology.

There are some compelling social reasons why such a breakthrough is needed. As we mentioned earlier in this chapter, the problem of improving the human condition is bound to questions of life philosophy or *Weltanschauung*. Mowrer (1957) thinks that we need a type of development program for twentieth-century man that will have genuine psychological survival value, something over and above the concern for mastery of the natural environment. Such an approach appears to be needed to prevent mass emotional disturbances. A means must be found, in addition to formal religion, to help clients with feelings of disillusionment, depersonalization, being unloved and abandoned, and of being a "thing" unscrupulously manipulated by other people. Development of such a philosophy may help clients to cope with gnawing free-floating anxiety, guilt over real or imagined misdeeds, and feelings of helplessness and resentment during periods of crisis. These are questions with which the average psychological counselor feels quite inadequate to cope, other than to use general techniques of psychological support and relatedness offered through a warm therapeutic relationship.

Several groups are searching for interrelationships between psychology and religion. The Academy of Religion and Mental Health is an example of such a group. The Society for the Scientific Study of Religion is another group designed to facilitate intercommunication between students of religion and social science.

Professional meetings of psychological and counseling groups have an increasing number of sections devoted to value concerns. There are special divisions within the American Psychological Association and the American Psychiatric Association devoted to this problem of relationship to values and formal religion. Educational agencies and growth centers sponsor popular value-clarification workshops and rap sessions. The pastoral-counseling movement has grown rapidly also, and is being accelerated through the clinical training of student clergymen.

Pastoral Psychology

Pastoral counselors are ordained clergymen trained in psychological counseling to deal with problems of belief, morals, guilt, and life crises. Such counselors assist parishioners with a wide range of human problems from marital conflicts through childrearing. Family clergy and family physicians have been the traditional helpers in most communities, and this special training in therapeutic psychology could expand their range of help. The average minister has had three years of general professional education leading to the B.D. degree. In pursuit of this degree, he is given general classes in personality and counseling theory, as well as supervised experience in a resident clinical setting for six weeks to a year.

To assist in establishing a frame of reference for pastoral counseling, various levels described by Oates (1951) are cited. Most of the pastoral functions listed below have some counseling aspects:

1. Level of friendship (rapport).
2. Level of comfort (support).
3. Level of confession (cathartic).
4. Level of teaching (informational).
5. Level of pastoral counseling (psychotherapeutic).
6. Level of referral.

The act of affirmation or loving, in the broad "agape" sense, is involved in pastoral counseling, too. Pastoral counselors generally subscribe to the view that humanity's love for humans is rooted in God's love for humans. The religious counselor ties in this client self-acceptance and love for his or her fellow humans with God's love as the principal source of attaining insight, freedom, security, and maturity.

The religious counselor, particularly one in the Christian tradition, often begins with a different set of assumptions about anthropology and psychology from that of the professional psychologist. The central values of the pastoral counselor reside in what is called divine law. It is difficult to generalize or be categorical about the teleological assumptions of theologians since they seem to hold many views depending on their unique perceptual vantage points and training. For example, some theologians do not see the traditional dichotomy between God and humankind since they view God and humankind in a common relationship. In any event, the view one holds about the nature, purpose, and origin of human beings influences his or her approach to counseling problems.

The psychologist, in contrast, generally operates on the more humanistic assumption that ultimate values are rationally determined and are found in humans themselves. Herein lies, in our opinion, the central issue between pastoral counseling and nontheologically oriented counseling. It is possible, however, to resolve this issue, somewhat, at the technique level, since both are concerned with helping suffering humanity. Psychologists can evaluate the techniques they use on the criterion of effectiveness in reaching limited goals quite apart from the basic philosophical assumptions and basic purposes involved.

For an extensive and fair analysis of the comparative assumptions underlying psychological science and Christianity the reader is referred to Meehl's early symposium *What, Then, Is Man?* (1958), on the unique and interrelated features of two basic ways of construing humankind.

There are many things the clergy can do to promote the same growth goals as psychologists. It must be recognized that the religious leader is concerned about many more aspects of parishioners' lives than their mental health, and that mental health is defined variously; but this is one area for which people look to him or her for leadership, albeit under a variety of guises. The pastoral counselor should recognize that the current surge of religious interest is probably more than a simple desire to renew the ties of childhood to a community institution, or to escape from tension. It may be viewed also as a search for a moral and spiritual framework for life, and a foundation on which to build a rich and satisfying life. It should be recognized that throughout history social crises have produced such great surges of religious interest.

So often a client's deep psychological problems come in the guise of moral or spiritual problems. The clergy must have the skill with which to distinguish a basically spiritual problem from one involving pathology in the personality. They must know, also, their own limitations in dealing with problems construed by the client as "spiritual," since one can put this type of interpretation on almost all human difficulties.

THE PASTORAL COUNSELOR'S ROLE IN RELATION TO OTHER SPECIAL-ISTS. The pastoral counselor's principal role, as far as psychological counseling is concerned, would seem to be to explore the client's initial problem to see where it touches upon areas of spiritual concern and value judgment, and where emotional conditions would warrant the services of a therapeutic psychologist, psychiatrist, or social worker. The principal techniques employed would be supportive and informational. Delving into history and motives could lead to a relationship fraught with deep transference and countertransference feelings, expectations of unrealistic accomplishments, or aggravation of a developing psychosis.

Personal problems may be approached from an interdisciplinary point of view in which the pastoral counselor and the psychologist or psychiatrist work together, and where cross-referral can be accomplished easily. Practically, however, this is difficult to achieve because remnants of mutual suspicion exist among practitioners, and clients often become confused when working with two similar types of specialists. This type of cross-referral among pastors and psychologists can work satisfactorily, but only under conditions where the primary responsibility is invested in one of the two specialists.

CONTRIBUTIONS OF THERAPEUTIC PSYCHOLOGY TO PASTORAL COUNSEL-
ING. The tools of therapeutic psychology are useful to the pastoral counselor in many ways. The application of relationship techniques, such as
listening, accepting, and reflecting, for example, can go far in overcoming
the traditional authoritarian advice-giving role into which the clergy have
so often been cast. The understanding of unconscious motivation in behavior and human culture can go a long way to gaining an understanding of
defensiveness and emotional problems as a type of ignorance, rather than
thinking of these behaviors in traditional moralistic terms so destructive
to a good counseling relationship. Greater knowledge of human motivation
should help the clergy deal with concepts of free will, moral responsibility,
guilt, and responsible action more understandingly.

POSSIBILITIES AND LIMITATIONS OF THE MINISTERIAL ROLE IN COUNSEL-
ING. The clergy can take advantage of a strategic helping relationship
with clients that is based on a traditional "pastor" perception of the clergy.
They have an advantage over other helping professionals in that they are
perceived by the family as helpers. They can deal with the whole family
as a casework problem, which is often as important as dealing with a selected
individual. However, they suffer from the clients' aforementioned perception of them as authoritarian figures, teachers, or as symbols of moralistic
judgment. Yet, in counseling it is imperative that the counselor be perceived
as an understanding person. The traditional exhortational or advice-giving
role is inimical to the general goals of present-day counseling.

Pastoral counselors are in a unique position to assist clients in confronting profound life problems, such as developing a philosophy of life.
They are in a strategic position to discuss moral problems also. Even here,
a cultural anthropology frame of reference is helpful in ascertaining more
clearly the areas of right, wrong, and neutral. When the religious dogma
is not clearly interpretable in a given case, it is useful to know the mores
of the culture and how these are distinguished from religious codes of
conduct. For example, a behavior which a client may regard as "sinful,"
and from which he or she suffers considerable anxiety and guilt, may be
more a deviation from the cultural norms than a violation of the moral
code of his or her religion or denomination.

The minister familiar with therapeutic psychology can utilize group
techniques to help create a climate of parish growth. These groups encourage mutual support and honest confrontation of personal problems.

ACTUALIZING CHURCHES. A church, synagogue, or temple traditionally has
been a community of people enhancing one another's growth, but critics
of current highly institutionalized churches feel that this *koinonia,* or fellow-
ship of persons, has been lost. The actualizing approach described in earlier
chapters is one way to recapture this spirit. Actualization groups conducted
by ministers and/or understanding therapeutic psychologists can provide
a vehicle for members to experience the rewards of peace, joy, and a renewed sense of community and commitment. Participants have possibilities
for reexamination of their values, rediscovery and enhancement of their

human dignity and worth, and respect for the "thou-ness" of others. Actualization groups in churches are more, therefore, than conventional encounter groups.

In a major study of the American Catholic priesthood, Greeley (1970) has reported a number of significant relationships between priests' levels of self-actualizing and amounts of perceived institutional support. In responding to questions concerning conflict between real and ideal distribution of power in the church, the more actualizing priests perceived a greater conflict and expressed a greater need to reform the church. Higher levels of actualizing, as defined by the Personal Orientation Inventory (POI), appeared to be negatively related to adherence to traditional values within the church, and positively associated with general dissatisfaction with the church. The correlation between self-actualizing, as measured by the POI Inner-Direction scale, and professed plans to stay in the priesthood was significant and negative.

Mowrer (1964) has shown that the original Christian church was a small-group movement. The faithful would meet secretly in caves to discuss their mutual concerns. The modern church must revitalize the spirit of the small-group sharing if it is to remain relevant for modern persons. It is our thesis that the actualizing process is a way to recapture this spirit. Efforts in this direction are the marriage enrichment programs of several denominations.

Introduction of the actualizing process through encounter group techniques has produced results in several church-affiliated studies. Reddy (1972) has reported the effects of a five-day residential human relations training program for forty interdenominational missionaries preparing for foreign service. He found significant increases in self-actualizing behaviors as defined by the POI. Knapp and Fitzgerald (1973) showed gains in actualizing behaviors with the Navy Chaplain Corps in an eclectic transgenerational workshop program with navy personnel. This program was established with the particular objective of building an increased sense of community among those persons whose feelings of alienation had led to such unsatisfactory behavioral expressions as drug abuse or alcohol addiction. Again, results from administration of the POI before and after the workshop demonstrate the positive effectiveness of programs of this type. Through such experiences, conducted by trained and sensitive clergy, participants had the opportunity to reexamine their personal values, to rediscover and enhance their dignity and worth, and to regain their respect for others.

VALUE PROBLEMS CONFRONTED BY THERAPEUTIC PSYCHOLOGISTS

The therapeutic psychologist must be aware of the dangers of becoming a spiritual counselor. The therapeutic psychologist, for example, generally does not give a client answers to direct questions on values. His or her principal role is to help clients to clarify their thinking and to discover feelings and thoughts regarding questions of values in their own personalities. When such values are lacking, are considered by clients to be inadequate, or are not discoverable with the usual therapeutic techniques, then the psychologist may present various cultural viewpoints and trends on the problem in question or refer clients to religious specialists for more detailed information. There they can obtain ideas in a type of setting characterized by teaching. These ideas can be discussed further in the psychotherapeutic interviews, where they can scrutinize their belief system and religious experiences. Finally, through counseling, clients can integrate their new discoveries smoothly into their personality core.

The therapeutic psychologist generally does not attempt consciously to influence a client's basic life values. Yet, it would be pure sophistry to presume that, in the deeply human relationship of counseling, the counselor does not influence the client's values. It is often quite apparent how the counselor feels about marriage and divorce, extramarital sex, the existence of God, and similar values without the counselor expressing himself or herself directly on the questions.

Perhaps the transmission of personal values is unavoidable in the close human relationship of psychotherapeutic counseling. Sullivan (1953) even went so far as to claim that therapists' personal values and attitudes toward life influence their professional work as much as their skills and training. If this statement is as valid as it seems on the surface, then there are many implications here for the selection and training of therapeutic psychologists and for referrals to psychological specialists.

However, there are counselors working in therapeutic psychology, or related areas, whose own personal problems are so well worked through in the value area that they are in a strategic position to help clients work through their value problems. Some therapists and counselors have particular interests and skills in working with basic value problems, just as they might have interests and abilities in marriage or career choice problems. For counselors with such interests, the following sections are included as samples of some counseling problems on value questions.

Our position on the question of transmitting counselor values is that if a counselor's own problems in the value areas are worked out to his or her satisfaction, if he or she is not aware of a need to "clear up" or "reform" the client's thinking, and if he or she is aware of tendencies to project his or her own needs and problems, then he or she could work with clients having basic value problems. If such help, however, involves information or interpretation of dogma, this should be done by a reliable minister on referral or through bibliotherapeutic references. If these conditions still do not allow a comfortable relationship, or they are doing violence to his or her own belief system, the counselor then must face the issue frankly and refer the client to another counselor.

Developing a Philosophy of Life

An assumption of this section is that each individual has a life philosophy, a life style, a set of religious beliefs, even though they may be implicit and not consciously known or felt by the person. A companion assumption is that behavior is an expression of a person's basic philosophy. When the behavior and the basic philosophy of life are at odds, the person usually is in trouble. A person's philosophy of life usually includes beliefs about the origin and nature of truth, the purpose and significance of his or her particular life, the nature of reality, including the possibility of a personal God. Further elements of a personal philosophy would include the nature and the hierarchy of values he or she holds, the origin and destiny of humanity, and the relative functions of reason and faith in the knowing process. The person's beliefs are sets of assumptions about these philosophical areas.

The process of learning, projecting, and incorporating values into a mature belief system or philosophy of life, as we see it, is diagrammed in Figure 26. The beliefs in the core level (a) are learned during the growing-up process from values held by parents and others close to the person. These internalized external values (b) are reperceived later as external to the person since they are projections of previously learned values.

During this projection process (c), the core and the rational processes of the actualizing level modify the projected values so that there is no one-to-one relationship between the core values and the projected values. For example, a person may project his or her security value system to external objects in such a way that he or she builds his or her security around a bank account, a family member, or an ideology.

The therapeutic task seems to consist of helping clients to examine

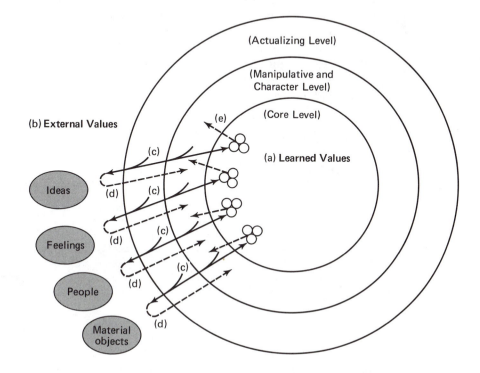

FIGURE 26. *The Process of Developing a Philosophy of Life*

their implicit beliefs, to know how they are projecting these core values, and then to see how they are perceiving external values. This phase of counseling leads them to reinvest these projected perceptions of external values into their core and character levels, as in (d) of Figure 26. Clients can see how their core values are influencing their character also. Armed with this rationally derived knowledge and insight, they can proceed to the development of a trustworthy and unified core value structure, which is no longer focused on external values. As a result, they should no longer be blind slaves to core needs and values, nor victims of an externally imposed value system. Clients need not, for example, depend as heavily upon the ideas, feelings, people, and objects about them since they now have a reconstituted, but cohesive and independent, value structure uniquely their own.

The role of the counselor in helping the client achieve a mature philosophy of life appears to us as diagrammed in Figure 27. At the beginning of counseling (a), the main task is to become aware of and to clarify the client's current value system. The second task (b) is to evaluate implicit values. Out of this effort often comes a more mature, expanded, unified, and effective world and life view. If steps (a) and (b) do not seem effective, it may be that the client either is not ready, or needs more specialized information which the counselor cannot provide. This condition may necessitate referral (c) for information and interpretation through resources such as bibliotherapy, pastoral counseling, or instruction in a belief system. Finally, if all goes well in the process, the client reaches a point (d) where he or she works out a tested personal philosophy adequate for his or her times and circumstances.

Though it is not the purpose of this section to set up a model philosophy of life, we consider it to be important to point out some of the problems clients face in developing or changing a philosophy of life. There seems to be evidence of a need for each person to work out a philosophy to fit

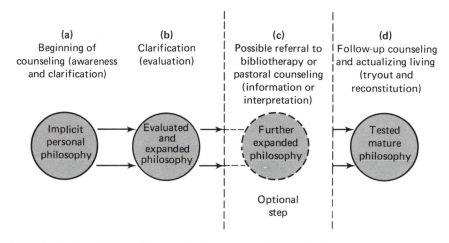

FIGURE 27. *The Role of Therapeutic Counseling in Value Problems*

times and circumstances. If he or she does not have such a philosophy, he or she generally suffers from feelings of drifting, pessimism, loneliness, disillusionment, and possibly even disintegration. Having a satisfying philosophy appears to build personal strength and to make more possible the goals of actualizing.

MEANING PROBLEMS.   It is common knowledge that an individual's beliefs about fundamental life questions are personal and vary widely according to cultural backgrounds and denominational dogma. As recommended earlier, this type of problem is considered from a therapeutic standpoint to be primarily one of instruction and clarification by a specialist in theological matters.

Belief conflicts, however, are at the root of many client anxieties. Most counselors, for example, are familiar with the typical late-adolescent problem of discovering that one's familial beliefs brought along from childhood suddenly seem to deteriorate into a morass of confusion and disillusionment. An example is the student who comes to college from the sheltered life of a small community with a cohesive theistic world view and is thrust suddenly into an intellectual atmosphere of naturalism, rationalism, scientism, humanism, and many other "isms" that pose threats to his or her neat childhood belief structure. This conflict and disillusionment may result in an even more rigid adherence to the childhood beliefs, or the conflicts may lead to a type of agnosticism where he or she refuses to take a position on the significant questions. As a third possibility, the person may reject his or her former beliefs as revealed by violent emotional and educational upheavals. Out of these upheavals often comes an allegiance to a different system offering similar satisfactions, such as political movements, social change, science, or philosophy.

If the client chooses one of the theistic views of life, he or she bases his or her search for meaning on faith in God and builds a world view about the central idea of God's existence. One way of viewing the so-called human quandary is humankind's perception of estrangement from God and later needs for reconciliation. A client with such a view would take the position that people have transcendental selves to be associated ultimately with God. He or she would feel that people are not alone in a universe that is not indifferent to their fate. The person believes he or she is a creature of God, responsible to God, and with the hope of reconciliation and reunion with God. A significant problem for this client would be how to be his or her true self within the tragic framework and disorder of society. The Christian view emphasizes this alienation from God, and humankind's realization of this estrangement results in much basic anxiety. Klann, in a symposium on psychology and Christianity, stated this view as follows:

> *Man's anxiety is the product of his sinfulness, that state of alienation or contradiction which exists between him and God, between man's will (taken as the expression of his being) and God's will. Because man's being is derived from God,*

as had been stated before, man in contradiction to God has good reason to feel himself threatened in his existence. It is the consequence of the threat upon his disobedience: "Thou shalt surely die" [Genesis 2:17]. (Meehl 1958, p. 55)

The redemption and conversion doctrines of Christianity provide the means whereby people are reconciled to God (Klann in Meehl, 1958).

Basic to a theistic view of life, then, is the existence of a personal God. Some clinicians, such as the Viennese neurologist Viktor Frankl, postulate a strong need for God, similar to the biologically based needs of hunger and thirst (1946). He postulates this need because of human striving to attach meaning to one's life. Frankl asserts that the human personality *(Das Geistige)* has laws that go beyond psychological laws and are concerned with humanity's ideals and responsible behaviors. He calls the methods of helping people to become more aware of their ideals and to focus on the awareness of their responsibilities "logotherapy." This is a form of therapy devoted to discovering the central purpose and meaning of life. The "existential analysis" methods of logotherapy do not determine which values clients will choose, but they impress on them the fact that they must make choices. The methods of logotherapy are especially suitable for conditions that an individual must accept, such as invalidism and suffering.

Mowrer is representative of a group of psychologists who are alarmed about the notion that neuroses and psychoses are illnesses. The sickness concept of emotional disorders, and the troubles of normal persons also, implies that the states of irresponsibility, narcissism, dependency, and extreme aggression, for example, are not one's own fault. The sickness view indicates that persons can hardly be "blamed" for their condition. They can place the blame conveniently on parental behaviors, environmental deprivation, or other factors outside their control or personal responsibility. Mowrer indicates that we need to examine this sickness explanation of emotional problems very carefully, even to the point of exploring the theological doctrine of sin as an explanatory concept for personality disorder. Emotional disorder, then, according to this latter view, is a type of moral problem emphasizing *personal responsibility* for behavior.

A second major philosophical choice, or focus of belief, is that position broadly described as humanism. The basic value of this view is a person's own existence. Two fundamental postulates are that people are alone in a morally neutral universe and that people are their own moral referents. Their troubles are believed to be of their own making. They are limited in their achievements only by their nature. People's quandaries are solved within themselves by a process of reason and the methods of self-discovery involved in psychotherapeutic or educational methods. There is a strong belief in people's powers of growth and positive motivation to solve their own and society's problems. Conditions like death, for example, must be accepted as human fact with no necessary implications for further life.

Erich Fromm is selected as an example of an "existential humanist" who attempts to bridge the chasm between these divergent views. The humanist position has its roots in the philosophical upheavals that took place during the enlightenment period of the seventeenth century. Fromm's view of human problems, which we trust is fair and typical of his ideas, is summarized in the following excerpts:

> *Humanistic religion . . . is centered around man and his strength. Man must develop his power of reason in order to understand himself, his relationship to his fellow men and his position in the universe. He must recognize the truth, both with regard to his limitations and his potentialities. He must develop his powers of love for others as well as for himself and experience the solidarity of all living beings. He must have principles and norms to guide him in this aim. Religious experience in this kind of religion is the experience of oneness with the All, based on one's relatedness to the world as it is grasped with thought and with love. Man's aim in humanistic religion is to achieve the greatest strength, not the greatest powerlessness; virtue is self-realization, not obedience. Faith is certainty of conviction based on one's experience of thought and feeling, not assent to propositions on credit of the proposer. The prevailing mood is that of joy, while the prevailing mood is that authoritarian religion is that of sorrow and guilt.*
>
> *Inasmuch as humanistic religions are theistic, God is a symbol of* man's own powers *which he tries to realize in his life, and is not a symbol of force and domination, having* power over man [*emphasis ours*]. (1950, p. 37)

Fromm indicates in another source that:

> *There is only one solution to his problem: to face the truth, to acknowledge his fundamental aloneness and solitude in a universe indifferent to his fate, to recognize that there is no power transcending him which can solve his problems for him. . . . If he faces the truth without panic he will recognize that there is no meaning to life except the meaning man gives his life by the unfolding of his powers, by living productively.* (1947, p. 44–45)

An essential point in the humanistic position is that people live in a confused human situation. They must face up to the incongruities in this human situation through their own powers. They must discover their own values within themselves and lean heavily on consensus and cultural norms. Their possibilities and troubles are largely of their own making.

There are many individuals who are trying to construct a "bridge" between these two basic views of people's situation in this universe. Clients often express anxieties about such problems, and it behooves the therapeutic psychologist to be aware of the basic philosophical assumptions underlying various belief systems. The counselor can aid clients to see discrepancies and contradictions in their system and can help them to a more clear definition of their life values. Lifton, for example, applies three criteria of counselor effectiveness in helping clients to more clear ideas in the area of religious belief:

> *(1) The client's feelings of achieving a satisfactory solution to his problem; (2) the counselor's feeling that the client is doing what the counselor believes is most appropriate; and (3) the degree to which the client's solution coincides with the approved answer in terms of mores of his society.* (1953, p. 367)

We agree most closely with criterion one. There is much potential danger in the counselor projecting too many of his or her own values into the discussion, as in criterion two. Criterion three in Lifton's list again is primarily the client's own concern, provided the implications of his or her religious beliefs do not threaten the welfare of others. The religious counselor probably would feel obligated to take a view different from these criteria because of his or her particular sectarian commitments.

Existentialist views are having an increasing influence on American counseling and psychotherapy. These views, imported from Europe, grew rather spontaneously and simultaneously in several centers. Existential views do not constitute a new school or new set of theories, but rather a fresh way of looking at human existence. The two basic problems in understanding the existential movement are the variety of ideas, some contradictory, which have come under its semantic cloak, and the difficulties in finding English language for the experiences and concepts developed within the existential framework.

Essentially, the existential approach seeks to avoid the usual subject-object approaches of studying human behavior, wherein people are broken into segmental "essences," by looking beneath these characteristics (May, Angel, and Ellenberger 1958). It is an effort to understand the essential nature of a particular person, in addition to the usual objective approaches of science. In psychotherapy, for example, attempts are made to help the client experience one's essential being, or humanness. Counseling and psychotherapy experiences are especially appropriate to this task because one finds this essential being in periods of crisis and distress that often characterize clients in the course of a therapeutic relationship. In fact, existentialism is a view of people as being in a perpetual process of becoming through continuous crises.

Since existentialism is not a philosophy or a way of life with palpable goals and identifiable axioms, but an effort to grasp reality, the reader is enjoined to investigate some of the original sources through writings of Kierkegaard, Jaspers, Heidegger, Tillich, Binswanger, and Buber, for example. May, Angel, and Ellenberger (1958) have written a summary and edited a collection of papers on existentialism and therapy that will serve the reader as an introduction.

Eastern views have had an impact on the thinking of many persons in the West. These include Zen forms of Buddhism, Kundalini Yoga, and Taoism. The central attractive features are their emphases upon viewing one's being as a part of nature, of grounding existence in the body through basic breathing exercises, and letting the meaning of life emerge naturally without strain. The life of meditation and quiet is especially attractive to Westerners tired of the pressures and dehumanizing effects of strong achievement drives. The growing popularity of Transcendental Meditation training and practice is an example.

THE COUNSELOR'S AND THERAPIST'S ROLE IN BELIEF PROBLEMS.   What can the counselor, *as a counselor,* do with client questions of religious belief? First, he or she can recognize the significance of religious sentiments and beliefs in personality development in general and in the life of this particular client. Secondly, counselors should know how to handle their own religious problems, which are precipitated by the client's problems. They should work them through to the point where they do not project them and where they do not interfere with an optimal relationship. Also, they should know their own faith well enough so that they can be accepting without jeopardizing that faith through the empathy process. Thirdly, they can regard problems of religious belief in much the same manner as they would treat any other affect-laden problem concerning marriage, job, children, or sex.

The counselor should have certain knowledge about clients, such as the origin of their beliefs. Were they derived from Sunday school, movies, life crisis, or family instruction? It would be well to note clients' social background, such as parental beliefs and church background, and their effects on their religious beliefs and practice. Finally, if the counselor finds his or her techniques and relationship are not meeting a client's needs, then something else, in the form of religious counseling by a specialist, or a human potential group experience, may be needed.

*Problems of
Relatedness*

To feel at home in the universe, to be valued as a person, and to feel close to someone are deep personal needs. Counselors are impressed by this overpowering need for relatedness, or more broadly speaking—love. The problems of giving and receiving love have been discussed at length elsewhere in this volume. The purpose of including the topic at this juncture, however, is to consider the gyroscopic effect of relatedness and love on a human life.

One of the appeals of membership in and identification with broad social, political, and religious movements is the feeling of close belonging and of being important to a significant cause. One's group affiliations, then, play a significant part in developing feelings of relatedness. It should be stressed that the relatedness must involve a high degree of intimacy— close friendships, comradeship, work organization, or marriage. Of these, marriage provides opportunity for the greatest satisfaction of the relatedness need because in marriage there is at least one other person who cares deeply about one's self.

Work provides further outlets for such feelings, but work is a paradox in several respects. Though work offers relatedness satisfaction, it often gives the individual the feeling that he or she is being manipulated and that he or she is regarded as a "marketable product." The specter of the "company person," for example, frightens many thoughtful people.

A second problem in connection with work relatedness is the common picture of the business executive or professional person who derives most of the satisfaction for his or her feelings of relatedness in work. Frequently, the person obtains little satisfaction from, or contributes little of himself or herself to, the family or community. Counselors and therapists often observe the phenomenon of the "vicious circle" of the individual gaining decreasing satisfactions from family life and increasing searches for satisfaction from work. This cycle can lead to other signs of personality deterioration such as alcoholism or infidelity. Shoben (1956) has analyzed the problem neatly in the less severe cases where the client's feelings of self-worth are sought increasingly in his or her occupational pursuits or in tangential social or sexual activities.

Many men and women feel they must choose between their intimate relationships and their work. The balance of these two features in a person's life is again a personal affair not to be dictated by a counselor. There seems to be an optimally proportionate emphasis on work and home, however, that leads to maximum satisfaction and productivity for all concerned. Freud is reputed to have answered the query on what a person must do to be mature with the reply, *"Lieben und arbeiten."* The mature, well-functioning person in our society must be able to both love and work in the proper balance.

Counselors must be ready for problems originating in underemployment. Satisfactions are so closely tied to work that the prospects of no work or being paid not to work have anxious implications. Counselors will have great service opportunities for actualizing counseling as people have increasing leisure and opportunity to look inward.

The main therapeutic implication here is that often client symptoms appear in the form of a basic management problem—such as finding the optimal balance among work, family, play, and civic participation. Such clients, furthermore, tend not to find their need satisfactions for relatedness and self-worth in the activities they currently employ. The counselor may be requested by the client to help him or her find some person or group to which he or she might relate. This bid needs to be assessed and interpreted in light of possible dependency reinforcement, and the extent to which counselors feel they can afford to be maneuvered into the role of "agent" for the client. The therapist definitely can help clients to understand their deep-seated needs for security and self-worth, which might be attainable through a more satisfying human relationship.

There are conditions where the counselor may need to help clients accept the limitations of their current situation through awareness and support. Examples of such situations would be the low probability of marriage for a chronic invalid, or the loneliness felt by new widows and divorcees, where such individuals may need to develop inner resources to cope with the lack of intimate relationships. Sometimes such clients can find compensations through small group relationships in their community.

Closely related to the relatedness-loneliness problem is that of depersonalization. We are not speaking so much of the type of detachment or splitting of affect and cognition that occurs in the psychotic, but of the normal person's feelings of being an "object" to be manipulated, bought and sold, traded, seduced, or used. Fromm (1957) warns of the damage that may result in personalities when they are led to feel like a "thing," a marketable commodity, rather than a person.

The counselor can help such clients through helping them to establish points of relatedness to people. The principal vehicle is the therapeutic relationship where clients can see their defenses more clearly, especially those that alienate them from other people. They will be less likely also to regard other people as "things" to be manipulated, used, or exploited when they discover the defensive distortions in their own personalities.

Meeting Life Crises

While the main discussion of crisis management was presented in Chapter 6, a more extended presentation on value choice crises is given here.

Medical and pastoral counselors generally confront clients in severe life crises more than psychological counselors. There are occasions, however, where problems associated with losing a job, death, divorce, disability, or financial disaster are brought to the psychologist for the purpose of working through the feelings associated with the crisis. Kunkel (1954) has developed a point of view on handling real or projected crises that is valuable for the therapeutic psychologist.

Often the crisis is due to a misperception of a situation, although the experience of anxiety or dread from the projected problem can be just as intense as the more objective kinds of crises. An example is the individual who had taken an examination for entry into a much-coveted position. A clerk made a remark to the candidate that was interpreted by the man to mean that he had failed. He brooded at length and finally moved into a mild depression and headaches for the next three days prior to receiving word of his standing. He heard that he had passed the examination and that he would very likely be appointed in the near future. The clerk's remark was then reperceived as being a warning that passing the examination did not necessarily mean employment in the desired position. The emotional effect, however, persisted for several days.

Kunkel's thesis is that people learn to face large crises later in life by a process of meeting minor life crises from early childhood on through development. He sees human life as one "unending chain of crises" (1954, p. 150). Old behavior patterns are disrupted and discarded for the new patterns required by the crises. Current life transition theory supports this idea that people can and do learn much from facing life crises (Brammer and Abrego 1981). The feelings of creativity and confidence that come out of a crisis solution constitute an important part of personality growth. Client experience of desperation and helplessness is the prelude to critical examination and transformation of their life style. Suffering is regarded as a facilitative force in their growth.

Crises require judgments and, usually, bring out strengths in judgment the person did not realize before the crisis. The process of making judgments that propel people forward in their mastery of life draws on many elements of personality and demands a high level of functioning. Each life crisis has a rich potentiality for building additional personal strength.

What can be said about the person who does not respond positively to crises and ends with feelings of inadequacy, failure, and incapacity to meet crises? The whole problem of the client's life style, creative potential, life philosophy, and religious outlook must be considered in a counseling relationship. Through counseling, clients may become more aware of their defenses and their problems of developing spiritual strength for meeting life crises. An example is the case where a client projected to God certain expectations of the help provided by his mother. When the crisis came and mother was not nearby to nurse his hurt, he blamed God, who had become equated psychologically with mother. He began to see that his inadequacies in meeting life demands and crises were rooted in his own immaturity and fear of psychological and spiritual creativity. The therapeutic psychologist, thus, utilizes the life crisis problem to help the client become more aware and to make changes in outlook and behavior.

A critical factor in achieving these growth objectives, as indicated so many times in this volume, is the growth relationship itself. The opportunity to face feelings of doubt, inadequacy, insecurity, and defeat in the presence of a warm and accepting counselor is what seems to us to be the primary factor in drawing from a client new powers to meet life's challenges. This discovery of feelings of confidence and creative power is what Kunkel has called the "miraculous center of every constructive crisis" (1954, p. 163). The alternatives to this creative experience are continued feelings of discouragement, defeat, and emptiness, often leading to personality deterioration.

Moral Problems

Moral problems are related to religious concerns in that formal religions incorporate an ethical and moral code and use the weight of religious authority to enforce the code. Moral problems, defined broadly as behavior contradictory to the established mores of the social order, can exist apart from problems of religious belief. The therapeutic psychologist's principal concern in the moral area is over the feeling of guilt associated with immoral behavior and the defensive function that immoral behavior performs for the personality. The psychologist is concerned also about the enhancing or damaging effects of moral and immoral behavior on clients and others affected by their behavior.

Kohlberg (1973) has formulated a developmental conception of moral behavior useful for counselors. People progress through stages from blind obedience to a moral authority to moral judgment based on the individual's own values. These stages are: (1) preconventional—responding to cultural rules and labels for good and bad, fearing punishment; (2) conventional—

maintaining family or social rules as valuable in their own right regardless of consequences, having personal loyalty to "law and order"; (3) autonomous—personally defining moral values in light of "social contracts" and universal ethics and moral principles. We emphasize the autonomous level in therapeutic psychology.

Some conceptions of morality are described briefly. One viewpoint stresses the dual and simultaneous presence of the "good" and the "bad" in people. For example, a person is said to be sinful and destructive, yet potentially virtuous and loving, too. The problem then becomes how to help the individual seek victory of the "good" over the "evil." This view may presuppose either an inherent knowledge of good and evil or a learned series of attitudes and behaviors. A contrary view is held also that "good" and "bad," used as nouns, are social artifacts and that people are neither by nature. When used as adjectives, they imply an arbitrary standard to be meaningful.

The view that people are by nature sinful beings (hence, by definition bad and reprehensible) is commonly held by the Hebraic-Christian world. This sinful-nature conception of humanity's moral condition is accompanied by a belief that there is potential good in humans expressed in such terms as humans' capacity to be kind, loving, and conscientious, for example. The "sinful nature" and "total depravity" concepts refer to the human condition from God's viewpoint. From a human standpoint, classical Judaism and Christianity both hold that people have great potential for either goodness or evil.

Certainly not all persons in the Hebraic-Christian moral framework subscribe strictly to this fundamental position; however, it is representative of the majority. To some extent, this view of innate evil is common to the Freudian group also. The main implication here is that this innate evil conception of moral behavior leads to the attitude that human nature cannot be trusted, must be restrained by external forces, or transformed by a mystical process.

That people basically have a heredity of socially constructive forces in their nature is a third view of moral nature. This is a belief in the basic "goodness" of people. The main implication is that our principal moral problem is to create conditions where the "good" can be brought out and the "bad" learnings extinguished. Horney holds such a growth and personal responsibility view of morality described briefly as follows:

> . . . the problem of morality is again different when we believe that inherent in man are evolutionary constructive forces, which urge him to realize his given potentialities. This belief does not mean that man is essentially good—which would presuppose a given knowledge of what is good or bad. It means that man, by his very nature and of his own accord, strives toward self-realization, and that his set of values evolves from such striving. Apparently he cannot, for example, develop his full human potentialities unless he is truthful to himself; unless he is active and productive; unless he relates himself to others in the spirit of mutuality. Apparently he cannot grow if he . . . consistently attributes

all his own shortcomings to the deficiencies of others. He can grow, in the true sense, only if he assumes responsibility for himself. (1950, pp. 14–15)

Kirkendall presents the hypothesis that immoral behavior is that which destroys self-respect and heightens difficulties in interpersonal relationships:

The obvious concern of students in classes in marriage and family life for values and principles of moral living has led me to the formulation of a concept useful in making decisions on right and wrong. The concept is that moral decision and conduct are those which result in improving the capacity of people to work together with trust and understanding. The outreach of individuals and groups toward others should be constantly furthered, and individual self-respect should be heightened by moral living. Immoral or wrong conduct is that which creates distrust and suspicion, produces withdrawal, and a decline in self-respect. (Unpublished, p. 5)

On college campuses particularly, there has been much talk about the "sex revolution." This appears to mean that a strong rational relative values point of view has guided student behavior. Visits to campuses by persons such as Nathaniel Branden (1965), who reflected views on "objectivist ethics" of Ayn Rand, have reinforced this position. Objectivist ethics emphasizes rational, responsible moral choices that consider human values, and human survival particularly, as the standard of value. Branden feels these views have strong implications for psychotherapy, because so much human misery and hypocrisy are due to irrational moral positions.

Disturbing the property and personal rights of others is another area of morals that involves the occasional client. Disturbing others' rights often creates guilt and anxiety when the acts are committed impulsively or under the influence of a narcotic.

There is another category of moral behavior surrounding the classification of psychopathic or inadequate personality. This group includes those persons classified under statute as delinquents, alcoholics, vagrants, truants, and drug addicts. Their acts of hostility, though directed against themselves sometimes, are mainly expressed against others.

Most of the problems of psychopaths involve some legal action against them. In this discussion we will not cover the legal, moralistic, or disciplinary implications of these behaviors but will attempt to suggest therapeutic roles and techniques for dealing with the feelings associated with problems that are judged by the client or society to be moral problems. Therapeutic psychologists are not concerned, then, with the concept of the "goodness"/ "badness" dichotomy so commonly thrust on human behavior. They are interested primarily in a rehabilitative approach, although they are interested also in the diagnostic problem of the meaning the immoral behavior has for the client and what some of the causes leading to this behavior might be. The therapeutic psychologist is interested also in the ethical problem of protecting the client and others who might be influenced by his or her behavior.

THE PROBLEM OF GUILT.   A striking characteristic of a client coming for help on a moral problem is the feeling described as guilt. The term *guilt* has two meanings in the present discussion. The first is a broad pervasive feeling of "wrongness." The client often feels a vague sense of "something is wrong with me; I'm not really doing what I should be doing; I should be something better." This feeling is closely related to feelings of inadequacy and fears of failure. Even persons successful by the usual social standards often have such feelings, which seem to come from early experiences and learned ways of handling hostile and dependent feelings, especially toward parents. The child experiences, very early, strong love and hostility feelings toward parents. Such ambivalent feelings may be distorted and experienced later as guilt. It seems that this type of normal guilt is an intimate condition of human life and may even perform protective functions for the individual and society. Therefore, it may not necessarily be a personal liability.

A second type of guilt feeling is that experienced as an acute emotional reaction to a specific behavior. For example, breaking rules against lying, cheating an associate, or stealing property may arouse strong subjective feelings of having done something reprehensible, which can be described as guilt. One is very much aware of having broken a social rule, a religious injunction, or a moral "law." These feelings seem to be characteristic of most cultures in the forms of awareness that one is being watched and will be held accountable for one's acts. Fromm summarizes the origin and consequences of the preceding type of guilt feeling as follows:

> The problem of guilt plays no less a role in psychoanalytic procedure than it does in religion. Sometimes it is presented by the patient as one of his main symptoms. He feels guilty for not loving his parents as he should, for failing to do his work satisfactorily, for having hurt somebody's feelings. The feeling of guilt has overpowered some patients' minds and they react with a sense of inferiority, of depravity, and often with a conscious or unconscious desire for punishment. It is usually not difficult to discover that this all-pervasive guilt reaction stems from an authoritarian orientation. They would give a more correct expression to their feeling if instead of saying that they feel guilty they said that they are afraid—afraid of punishment, or more often, of not being loved any more by those authorities whom they have disobeyed. In the analytic process such a patient will slowly recognize that behind his authoritarian sense of guilt is another feeling of guilt which stems from his own voice, from his conscience in the humanistic sense. Assume that a patient feels guilty for leading a promiscuous life. The first step in analyzing this guilt feeling will be to discover that he really feels afraid of being found out and criticized by his parents, by his wife, by public opinion, by the church—briefly, by anyone who represents authority to him. Only then will he be able to recognize that behind this authoritarian

feeling of guilt is another feeling. He will recognize that his "love" affairs are in reality expressions of his fear of love, of his inability to love anyone, to commit himself to any close and responsible relationship. He will recognize that his sin is against himself, the sin of letting his power to love go to waste. (1950, pp. 90–91)

It seems to us that Fromm, in the quotation, is pointing out the distinction between normal and neurotic guilt, which is developed later in this section.

Meehl and his symposium coworkers presented a distinction between valid and displaced guilt. Valid guilt is claimed to be present when people realize that their relationships with God are not proper. Their feeling is manifested by an awareness of anxiety, or even dread. The symposium described valid guilt as follows:

> . . . *we have been suggesting that man's objective sinful and alienated relation to God, with its attendant effects upon his relation to his fellows, gives rise to a psychological state of valid guilt.* (1958, p. 221)

Displaced guilt, however, is that feeling of guilt that is detached from the original idea (the alienation phenomenon described above) and appears in the individual's awareness as a different idea, such as remorse over some small act or a haunting fear that he or she has done something reprehensible like injuring someone with his or her automobile.

CONSCIENCE.   There is considerable difference of opinion concerning the validity and origin of the concept "conscience." In common usage, the term *conscience* connotes three quite different things: (1) involuntary submission to external authorities with the concomitant fear of discovery and punishment; (2) condemnatory self-accusations; and (3) discontent with self in a constructive sense (Horney 1937).

The classical religious conception of conscience from the Western Christian point of view is that people are born with a rudimentary, though very imperfect, knowledge of right and wrong. This rudimentary conscience is sharpened through religious training by means of the following rationale: God created people with a certain nature; people are obligated to live according to that nature; God revealed how people should behave; if they disobey, they have made an offense against God and, hence, are estranged from God. The result is that they feel guilty; this feeling of guilt creates a need for God's forgiveness and ultimately brings them back to God. This is an oversimplification, of course, but it points out the basic rationale for the development of conscience and guilt feelings from one religious point of view.

The Freudian view of the superego development, in contrast, is typical of psychological viewpoints on conscience. It is considered a learned concept arising largely out of internalization, or "introjection," as Freud called it, of parental prohibitions, threats, and values. These internalized values are picked up through the process of incidental learning during early childhood. Punishments rather than rewards seem to be the decisive determinants. Children learn to "hear" the parental voice of authority whenever they come against similar circumstances, and they suffer painful feelings when they transgress.

In the Freudian framework, personality problems are caused, to a great extent, by a severe superego overwhelming the ego and forcing it to repress the biologically based primitive impulses of the id. Mowrer (1951) thinks that a more correct view of the Freudian model would be that disturbances in personality are caused by the id and the ego joining forces against the superego. The latter is a type of guilt theory where the ego functions are immature and, under the influence of the id, have done things of which the superego disapproves. In this sense, the person with a diminutive superego and an immature ego would tend toward antisocial, criminal acts; whereas the person with the overdeveloped superego would tend toward oversocialization and rigidity which would place severe demands on the ego and restraint on the id. According to Mowrer, a dual task of the counselor is to help the client develop a stronger ego that is able to escape control by the id, and to develop a working relationship with the superego. This elaboration of Freudian superego or conscience theory, and its implications for counseling and psychotherapy, is an oversimplification of a very complex metaphorical system. We sketched it here because it is such a commonly held point of view in therapeutic psychology.

A humanistic view of conscience is popular among counselors. If children grow up feeling that this conscience is somehow absolute and synonymous with divine or cosmic law, they may go through life trying to live up to these expectations, justifying their actions, and forever feeling guilty that they should be doing something they aren't doing or not doing something they are doing. The psychological viewpoint (largely psychoanalytic in origin) is that the client must be helped to recognize the relativity of value systems and must be helped to develop a frame of value reference suited to his or her times, unique circumstances, and needs. This is a basic humanistic view that sees people as their own moral referents.

Allport (1955) asserts that the preceding explanation helps to account for childhood conscience, but it does not explain the adult conscience adequately. He postulates a shift from ad hoc habits of obedience built up through conditioning and punishments to broader permeation of the personality. The shift is from fear of punishment to feelings of obligation. In other words, the person has incorporated his or her former learnings into a value structure in the core and character levels of our system. The person changes his or her view from must to ought and from compulsion to obligation.

Normal or healthy guilt, in the mature adult, becomes a feeling of having violated the integrity of core values, a feeling of self-hostility for not achieving the ideal of the actualized person. Thus, a more voluntary and seemingly purposeful ethical act is substituted for the conditioned habit and fear of punishment. The habit of obedience in the adult, according to Allport, gives way to self-guidance based on a "broad schemata of values that confer direction upon conduct" (1955, p. 73). The child, in developing this mature schemata of values, sees that restraint and ideals have purposes other than merely pleasing one's parents. Horney emphasizes this approach to normal guilt or the mature conscience, too, in her term "constructive discontent with self" (1950). This view is the highest level of moral development in Kohlberg's (1973) hierarchy.

We believe that the preceding theory of conscience results in more permanence and flexibility than the views stressing internalization of parental authority or the theories of genetic origins. We feel also that conscience can be a positive creative force in interpersonal relationships, as well as an inhibiting, guilt-provoking force. According to May's (1953) view of conscience, learnings from past experience become blended with present experiences so that one's ethical sensitivity is sharpened and one's level of awareness is deepened. The actualizing conscience then becomes a device for tapping one's enlarged experience and for developing one's valuing center in the core level.

In Figure 28, we present our views on the development of a mature conscience, beginning with the rudimentary awareness of social values resulting from demands and punishments of parents. As the child grows, parental demands become internalized into feelings of "rightness" and "wrongness." Conditioning plays a significant part here also, since rewards and punishments are important. As the child grows into adolescence, he or she acquires a self-picture as a moral person, with the mores a part of his or her developing core value system. The value system is based on earlier learned values, a growing self-awareness, and a rationally determined view of the mores. Mature adults make more selective and rational responses to environmental demands. They still feel guilt, but it is *normal* guilt, which helps them to reduce the gap between actualizing self-values and inappropriate behavior.

Regardless of the position taken on the nature and origin of conscience, psychologists tend to agree that the phenomenon of conscience is a profound factor in the control of impulsive behavior and opportunism. They believe that it has a significant long-range influence on goals and values also. A key therapeutic implication here is that one of the roles of

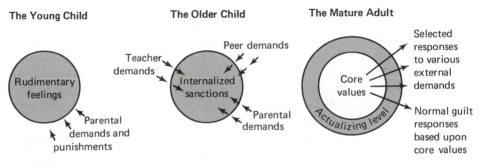

Figure 28. *The Development of a Mature Conscience*

counseling is facilitating the transformation of a blind, impulsive, infantile conscience into a mature moral structure. A second implication is the possibility of helping the client whose childhood coinscience is overly severe or fixated at a childhood level. The counselor may help to modify the compulsive demands and consequent neurotic guilt feelings of such conscience while the mature value system is developing.

Therapeutic Handling of Guilt and Conscience Problems

The handling of guilt in therapy is a most critical problem. A summary of methods for dealing with this significant problem in the therapeutic interview follows.

The counselor's first step is to release the client's tensions within a relationship characterized by acceptance on the counselor's part. A nonjudgmental attitude of a counselor is especially important to encourage free expression of guilt feelings. When the working-through phase of the process is reached, clients can be helped to see and understand the origins of their guilt and conscience problems.

According to May (May, Angel, and Ellenberger 1958) guilt is best understood if a differentiation is made between normal and neurotic guilt. Normal guilt is universal and is of three basic types: guilt against one's self for not fulfilling one's potentialities; guilt against one's fellow humans for not meeting their needs; and guilt against nature or God and a feeling of separateness or alienation therefrom. Neurotic guilt is defined as unaccepted and repressed normal guilt. Therapy, therefore, consists of assisting the client to accept and face his or her neurotic guilt and to turn it into normal guilt. This is in sharp contrast to the view that therapy should water down, expunge, or neutralize guilt entirely. The following steps are suggested for changing neurotic to normal guilt. The counselor should:

1. Help clients to *admit* what they have done to feel guilty.

2. Help them to become aware of the *motives* underlying their guilt feelings, especially those of destruction and hatred.

3. Cut through the *rationalizations*. This implies taking *responsibility* for what one does.

4. Transform neurotic (unfaced) guilt to *normal guilt* by assisting the client to see that it can be tolerated and constructive. When clients are able to express normal guilt, they can utilize the gap between their self-image and what they actually are for further growth.

Traumatic incidents can be desensitized so that the intense suffering associated with neurotic guilt can be minimized and understood. Neurotic suffering, for example, can be understood as a kind of atonement that the severe conscience is exacting for real or imagined misdeeds. Suffering from normal guilt can be used as a springboard to awareness, as indicated in the earlier discussion on crises.

Clients can be helped to understand the defenses they have used to handle guilt feelings. Sometimes this takes the form of physical symptoms and requires the collaboration of a physician. Often, the defense takes the form of projection where others are blamed for the very behaviors for which the client feels guilty. This development comes later in the working-through process, however, since it presupposes considerable ego strength to tolerate the loss of defensive strength. Another illustrative projective mechanism is that of the overdeveloped conscience, which expresses itself in a paranoid delusion. This type of client projects guilt feelings to others whom he or she accuses of criticizing or blaming. This projection may involve the belief that his or her deity is constantly condemning and punishing also.

A related defense often seen in guilt cases is the pharisaically self-righteous client who defends his or her guilt feelings stoutly by means of a superior demeanor and condemnation of others.

Counseling or therapy on guilt might involve referral. If the traditional rituals and methods of formal religious experiences are meaningful and acceptable to the client, perhaps referral to a church group or pastoral counselor would assist in both the emergency reduction and in the long-term resolution of his or her guilt feelings.

When it comes to the action phase of the process, the counselor frequently is in a dilemma. If the client has acquired some insight but his or her actualizing capabilities are still quite weak, he or she may not follow through with responsible behavior. Should the therapist assume a very authoritarian role and use shock techniques to assist clients to feel personally responsible for their behavior? An example is the case of a married man with a family, who is concerned about dating a young woman. Should the counselor depend on the relationship and the client's maturation potential to develop a conventional solution to the problem? The answers would depend greatly on the counselor's basic orientation to therapy as well as the degree of confidence he or she feels in his or her own value system. We feel that with some types of clients, direct methods can often effect drastic behavior changes. The limitations, however, are that without considerable awareness the changes will be temporary at best. In any case, it is very important for the counselor to assist the client to feel a sense of decision and responsibility for his or her own behavior. Therapy consists of assisting the client to make a decision even if it turns out to be a wrong decision.

The overall goal of counseling on moral problems is to help clients to develop greater feelings of responsibility to their core feelings, especially if their problem is one of too little anxiety about their behavior. The counselor also may suggest that clients having too much anxiety about their moral behavior develop a more stable and mature value structure, which consequently can lead to a greater degree of internal direction for their behavior. A positive self-regard manifested by strong actualizing capabilities appears to us to be the most dependable route to moral behavior.

In addition to individual counseling, the actualizing group provides a potent resource for the person to express and share his or her feelings of guilt with fellow humans. Ancient values of group "confession" are being rediscovered in the actualizing group experience.

As clients learn to trust their innermost feelings about themselves, they learn that such trust will help them to make more wise decisions. As they learn to listen to all these feelings, both positive and negative, their core feelings will be found to be trustworthy for aiding decisions that will be beneficial not only to themselves, but to society as well.

SUMMARY

In the science and profession of psychology, keen interest is being exhibited in problems of value. This chapter included some of the implications of value problems, such as developing an effective philosophy of life and working out feelings associated with moral problems. The therapeutic psychologist has a role to perform in each of these areas that is different from, but overlapping with, that of the pastoral counselor. The pastoral counselor has a unique role, yet in many ways it is similar to that of the therapeutic psychologist. A principal task of the therapeutic psychologist is helping the client to transform neurotic guilt into normal guilt and to help clients trust their core feelings.

References

ADAMS, D. K., et al. *Learning Theory, Personality Theory, and Clinical Research: The Kentucky Symposium.* New York: Wiley, 1954.

Ad Hoc Committee on Women. Principles concerning the counseling and therapy of women. *J. counsel. Psychol.,* 8 (1979):21.

AGUILERA, D. C. and MESSICK, J. M. *Crisis Intervention: Theory and Methodology,* 2d ed. St. Louis: C. V. Mosby, 1974.

ALAGNA, F.; WHICHTER, S.; FISHER, J.; and WICAS, E. Evaluative reaction to interpersonal touch in a counseling interview. *J. counsel. Psychol.* 26(1979):465–472.

ALEXANDER, F., and FRENCH, T. M. *Psychoanalytic Therapy.* New York: Ronald Press, 1946.

ALLEN, T., ed. Marriage and family counseling. *Counsel. Psychologist* 5(1975):1–136.

ALLMON, D. Verbal reexpression: its effects in social interaction. Ph.D. dissertation, University of Washington, 1981.

ALLPORT, G. W. *Becoming: Basic Considerations for a Psychology of Personality.* New Haven: Yale Univ. Press, 1955.

ALLPORT, G. W. *Personality: A Psychological Interpretation.* New York: Holt, 1937.

ALPERSON, B. L.; ALPERSON, E. D.; and LEVINE, R. Growth effects of high school marathons. *Experimental Publications System* 2(1971): Ms. No. 369–56.

ALSCHULER, R. H., and HATTWICK, L. W. *Painting and Personality: Study of Young Children.* Chicago: Univ. of Chicago Press, 1947.

American Personnel and Guidance Association. *Accreditation Procedures Manual for Counselor Education.* Washington, DC: American Personnel and Guidance Association, 1978.

American Personnel and Guidance Association. *Counseling Older Persons: A Training Manual for Paraprofessionals.* Washington, DC: American Personnel and Guidance Association, 1981.

American Personnel and Guidance Association. *Coun-*

seling the Aged: A Training Syllabus for Education. Washington, DC: American Personnel and Guidance Association, 1979.

American Personnel and Guidance Association. Ethical Standards (1981 Revision). *Guidepost* (April 1981).

American Psychiatric Association. *Diagnostic and Statistical Manual of Mental Disorders.* 3d ed. Washington, DC: American Psychiatric Association, 1980.

American Psychological Association. *Ethical Standards of Psychologists.* Rev. ed. Washington, DC: American Psychological Association, 1979.

American Psychological Association. *Psychology and Its Relations with Other Professions.* Washington, DC: American Psychological Association, 1954.

American Psychological Association. Standards for providers of counseling psychological services, Draft 6. July 1978. Mimeographed. Washington, DC: American Psychological Association.

American Psychological Association. Standards for providers of psychological services. *Amer. Psychologist* 30(1975):685–693.

American Psychological Association Committee on Counselor Training. Recommended standards for training counseling psychologists at the doctorate level. *Amer. Psychologist* 7(1952):175–181.

American Psychological Association Division 17 Committee on Definition. *Draft of Definition Statement.* Washington, DC: American Psychological Association, May 1980.

American Psychological Association Standards for Educational and Psychological Tests and Manuals. Washington, DC: American Psychological Association, 1966.

American School Counselors' Association. Tentative statement of policy for secondary school counselors. *Pers. and Guid. J.* 42(1963):194–198.

ANASTASI, A. *Psychological Testing.* 4th ed. New York: Macmillan, 1976.

ANDOLFI, M. *Family Therapy: An Interactional Approach.* New York: Plenum, 1979.

ANSBACHER, R., and ANSBACHER, H. *The Individual Psychology of Alfred Adler.* New York: Basic Books, 1956.

ASH, P. The reliability of psychiatric diagnosis. *J. abnorm. soc. Psychol.* 44(1949):272–276.

ASPY, D. N. Empathy. *The Counseling Psychologist* 5(1975):10–14.

ASSAGIOLI, R. *Psychosynthesis.* New York: Viking Press, 1965.

AXLINE, V. Mental deficiency: Symptom or disease. *J. consult. Psychol.* 13(1949):313–327.

AXLINE, V. *Play Therapy.* Boston: Houghton Mifflin, 1947.

BACH, G. R. *Intensive Group Psychotherapy.* New York: Ronald Press, 1954.

BACH, G. R. The marathon group: intensive practice of intimate interaction. *Psychological Reports* 18(1966):995–1002.

BANDLER, R., and GRINDER, J. *Frogs into Princes: Neurolinguistic Programming.* Moab, UT: Real People Press, 1979.

BANDLER, R., and GRINDER, J. *The Structure of Magic.* Palo Alto, CA: Science and Behavior Books, 1975.

BANDURA, A. *Principles of Behavior Modification.* New York: Holt, Rinehart & Winston, 1969.

BANDURA, A., and WALTERS, R. H. *Social Learning and Personality Development.* New York: Holt, Rinehart & Winston, 1963.

BANMEN, J., and CAPELLE, R. Human relations training in three rural Manitoba high schools. Paper presented at the Convention of the National Council on Human Relations. Winnipeg, Canada, April 1971.

BANMEN, J. and CAPELLE, R. Human relations training in three rural Manitoba high schools: A three-month follow-up. *Canadian Counsellor* 6(1972): 260–70.

BARAK, A., and LA CROSSE, M. Multidimensional perception of counselor behavior. *J. counsel. Psychol.* 22(1975):471–476.

BARBER, T.; SPANOS, H.; and CHAVES, J. *Hypnosis, Imagination, and Human Potentialities.* Elmsford, NY: Pergamon Press, 1976.

Barron's Educational Series. *Barron's Profiles of American Colleges.* Woodbury, NY: Barron's, 1980.

BARTEN, H. *Brief Therapies.* New York: Behavioral Publications, 1971.

BARTLETT, F. C. *Remembering.* Cambridge: Cambridge Univ. Press, 1932.

BARUCH, D. *How to Live with Your Teenager.* New York: McGraw-Hill, 1953.

BEBOUT, J., and GORDON, B. The value of encounter. In *New Perspectives on Encounter Groups,* ed. L. N. Solomon and B. Berzon. San Francisco: Jossey-Bass, 1972.

BECK, A. *Cognitive Therapy and Emotional Disorders.* New York: International Univ. Press, 1976.

BEERS, T., and FOREMAN, M. Intervention patterns in crisis interviews. *J. counsel Psychol.* 23(1976):87–91.

BEM, S. Fluffy women and chesty men. *Psychology Today* 9(1975):58–60.

BENSON, H. *The Relaxation Response.* New York: Avon, 1975.

BERDIE, R. F. An aid to student counselors. *Educ. psychol. Measmt.* 2(1952):281–290.

BERGER, M. The use of video tape with psychotherapy groups in a community mental health program.

Paper delivered at the American Group Psychotherapy Conference, January 1968.

BERGER, M. *Videotape Techniques in Psychiatric Training and Treatment.* New York: Brunner/Mazel, 1970.

BERGMAN, D. V. Counseling method and client responses. *J. Consult. Psychol.* 15(1951):216–224.

BERNE, E. *Transactional Analysis.* New York: Grove Press, 1961.

BERZON, B. Final narrative report: self-directed small group programs, NIMH Project RD 1748. Mimeographed. La Jolla, Cal.: Western Behavioral Science Institute, 1968.

BERZON, B.; REISEL, J.; and DAVIS, D. P. PEER: an auditape program for self-directed small groups. *J. humanistic Psychol.* 9(1969):71–86.

BERZON, B., and SOLOMON, L. The self directed therapeutic group: three studies. *J. counsel. Psychol.* 13(1966):491–497.

BETTLEHEIM, B. Self-interpretation of fantasy: the thematic apperception test as an educational and therapeutic device. *Amer. J. Orthopsychiat.* 17(1947):80–100.

BEVERLY, B. *In Defense of Children.* New York: Day, 1941.

BIXLER, R. H. Limits are Therapy. *J. consult. Psychol.* 13(1949):1–11.

BIXLER, R. H., and BIXLER, V. H. Test interpretation in vocational counseling. *Educ. psychol. Measmt.* 6(1946):145–155.

BLACK, J. D. Common factors of the patient-therapist relationship in diverse psychotherapies. *J. clin Psychol.* 8(1952):302–306.

BLANTON, S. *Love or Perish.* New York: Simon & Schuster, 1956.

BLOCHER, D. H. *Developmental Counseling.* New York: Ronald Press, 1966.

BLOCKSMA, D., and PORTER, E. A short-term training program in client-centered counseling. *J. consult. Psychol.* 11(1947):55–60.

BLOS, P. Psychological counseling of college students. *Amer. J. Orthopsychiat.* 6(1946):571–580.

BOILEAU, V. New techniques in brief psychotherapy. *Psychological Reports,* Monogr. Suppl. #7, 1958.

BOLLES, R. *The Three Boxes of Life.* Berkeley, CA: Ten Speed Press, 1978.

BOLLES, R. *What Color Is Your Parachute?* 4th ed. Berkeley, CA: Ten Speed Press, 1977.

BORDIN, E. S. Diagnosis in counseling and psychotherapy. *Educ. psychol. Measmt.* 6(1946):169–184.

BORDIN, E. S. *Psychological Counseling.* New York: Appleton-Century-Crofts, 1955.

BOROW, H., and LINDSEY, R. V. *Vocational Planning for College Students.* Englewood Cliffs, NJ: Prentice-Hall, 1959.

BRADFORD, L. P.; GIBB, J. R.; and BENNE, K. D. *T-group Theory and Laboratory Method: Innovation in Re-education.* New York: Wiley, 1964.

BRAMMER, L. M. *The Helping Relationship: Process and Skills* 2d ed. Englewood Cliffs, NJ: Prentice-Hall, 1979.

BRAMMER, L., and ABREGO, P. Intervention strategies for coping with transitions. *J. counsel. Psychol.* 9(1981):19–36.

BRANAN, J. M. Clients reaction to counselor's use of self-experience. *Pers. and Guid. J.* 45(1967):568–572.

BRANDEN, N. *The Psychology of Romantic Love.* Los Angeles: J. P. Tarcher, 1980.

BRANDEN, N. Psychotherapy and the objectivist ethics. Paper delivered before the Michigan Society of Consulting Psychologists, Nov. 24, 1965.

BRAUN, J. R., and LAFARO, D. A. Further study on the fakability of the Personal Orientation Inventory. *J. clin Psychol.* 25(1969):296–299.

BRAYFIELD, A. H. Counseling psychology: Some dilemmas of the graduate school. *J. counsel. Psychol.* 8(1961):17–19.

BRIM, O. Theories of the Male Midlife Crisis. In *Counseling Adults,* ed N. Schlossberg, and A. Entine. Monterey, CA: Brooks/Cole, 1977.

BRODSKY, A., and HARE-MUSTIN, R. *Women and Psychotherapy.* New York: Guilford, 1980.

BROWER, D. *Progress in Clinical Psychology,* Vol. 6. New York: Grune & Stratton, 1952.

BROWN, J. F. *Psychodynamics of Abnormal Behavior.* New York: McGraw-Hill, 1940.

BROWN, W. F., and HOLTZMAN, W. H. *Survey of Study Habits and Attitudes.* New York: Psychological Corp. 1955.

BUGENTAL, J. F. T. The person who is the psychotherapist. *J. consult. Psychol.* 28(1964):272–277.

BUGENTAL, J. F. T. A Phenomenological Hypothesis of Neurotic Determinants and Their Therapy. Unpublished paper. Los Angeles: Psychological Service Associates.

BUGENTAL, J. F. T. Psychological Interviewing. Unpublished manuscript, 1952.

BUGENTAL, J. F. T. *The Search for Authenticity; an Existential-Analytic Approach to Psychotherapy.* New York: Holt, Rinehart & Winston, 1965.

BUROS, O. K. *The Third Mental Measurements Yearbook,* 8th ed. New Brunswick, NJ: Rutgers Univ. Press, 1978.

BUTLER, R. *Why Survive? Being Old in America.* New York: Harper & Row, 1975.

BYRD, R. E. Training in a non-group *J. humanistic Psychol.* 25(1967):296–299.

BYRNE, R. H. Proposed revision of the Bordin-Pepinsky diagnostic constructs. *J. counsel. Psychol.* 5(1958):184–187.

CALLIS, R. A. Diagnostic classification as a research tool, *J. counsel. Psychol.* 12(1965):238–243.

440

CALLIS, R. A. Toward an integrated theory of counseling. *J. of College Student Pers.* 1(1960):2–9.

CAMPBELL, D. *The Results of Counseling: Twenty-Five Years Later.* Philadelphia: W. B. Saunders, 1965.

CAMPBELL, D. *Manual for the SVIB-SCII.* Stanford, CA: Stanford Univ. Press, 1977.

CANTRELL, D. Training the rehabilitation counselor. *Pers. and Guid. J.* 36(1958):382–387.

CARKHUFF, R. *Helping and Human Relations.* New York: Holt, Rinehart & Winston, 1969.

CARKHUFF, R., and TRUAX, C. Toward explaining success and failure in interpersonal learning experiences. *Pers. and Guid. J.* 44(1966):723–728.

CARNES, E. F. Counselor flexibility: Its extent, and its relationship to other factors in the interview. Unpublished doctoral dissertation, Ohio State University, 1949.

CARNES, E. F., and ROBINSON, F. P. The role of client talk in the counseling interview. *Educ. psychol. Measmt.* 8(1948):635–644.

CARTER, H. D. Vocational interests and job orientation. *Appl. Psychol. Monogr.* 2(1944).

CASAS, J.; FURLONG, M.; and CASTILLO, S. Stress and coping among university counselors: a minority perspective. *J. counsel. Psychol.* 27(1980):364–373.

CATTELL, R. B. *Personality.* New York: McGraw-Hill, 1950.

CHANCE, E. Measuring the anticipations of therapists about their patients. Unpublished paper, 1958.

CHESLER, P. *Women and Madness.* New York: Avon, 1972.

CLARK, C. Psychiatry with the resistant child. *Perspectives and Psychiatric Care* 15(1977):122–125.

COFFEY, H. S. Group Psychotherapy. In *An Introduction to Clinical Psychology,* ed. I. A. Berg, and L. A. Pennington. New York: Ronald Press, 1948.

COGSWELL, J. F., and ESTAVAN, D. P. Computer simulation of a counselor in student appraisal and in the educational planning interview. SDC document SP-1944. March 10, 1965.

COHEN, M. B. Countertransference and anxiety. *Psychiatry* 15(1952):231–243.

COHEN, R. C. Military group psychotherapy. *Mental Hygiene* 31(1947):94–103.

COLBY, K. M. *A Primer for Psychotherapists.* New York: Ronald Press, 1951.

COLLIER, R. M. A basis for integration rather than fragmentation in psychotherapy. *J. consult. Psychol.* 14(1950):199–205.

COLLINS, R. Counseling interventions and cognitive psychology: reactions to programs for social-cognitive growth. *Counsel. Psychologist* 6(1977):15–17.

COMBS, A. W. Counseling as a learning process. *J. clin. Psychol.* 1(1954):31–36.

COMBS, A. W. *Florida Studies in the Helping Professions.* Gainesville, FL: Univ. of Florida Press, 1969.

COREY, G. *Theory and Practice of Group Counseling.* Monterey, CA: Brooks/Cole, 1981.

COREY, G.; COREY, M.; and CALLAHAN, P. *Professional and Ethical Issues in Counseling and Psychotherapy.* Belmont, CA: Wadsworth, 1979.

COTTLE, W. C. Personal characteristics of counselors: I. *Pers. and Guid. J.* 31(1953):445–450.

COTTLE, W. C., and LEWIS, W. W. JR. Personality characteristics of counselors: II. Male counselor responses to the MMPI and GZTS. *J. counsel. Psychol.* 1(1954):27–30.

Counseling women (Special issue). *J. counsel. Psychol.* 4 (1973).

Counseling women II (Special issue). *J. counsel. Psychol.* 6 (1976).

Counseling women III (Special issue). *J. counsel. Psychol.* 8 (1979).

COUSINS, N. *Anatomy of an Illness.* New York: Norton, 1979.

COX, R. D. *Counselors and Their Work.* Philadelphia: Univ. of Pennsylvania Press, 1945.

CRAMPTON, W. How U.S. Men Can Live Longer. *This Week,* Feb. 20, 1955, 7–26. Also printed in C. Solomon and R. Brooks (eds.), *How to Enjoy Good Health.* New York: Random House, 1955.

CRIDER, B. The hostility pattern. *J. clin. Psychol.* 2(1946):267–273.

CRONBACH, L. J. Counselor's problems from the perspective of communication theory, in V. H. Hewer (ed.), New Perspectives in Counseling. *Minnesota Studies in Student Personnel Work, No. 7* Minneapolis: Univ. of Minnesota Press, 1955.

CRONBACH, L. *Essentials in Psychological Testing.* New York: Harper & Row, 1970.

CURRAN, C. A. Structuring the counseling relationship: A case report. *J. abnorm. soc. Psychol.* 39 (1944):189–216.

CUTLER, R. L. The relationship between the therapist's personality and certain aspects of psychotherapy. Ph.D. dissertation, University of Michigan, 1954.

DANSKIN, D. G. and BURNETT, C. W. Those superior students. *Pers. and Guid. J.* 31(1952):181–186.

DAULTON, J. A study of factors relating to resistance in the interview. M. A. thesis, Ohio State University, 1947.

DAVIS, S. E., and ROBINSON, F. P. A study of the use of certain techniques for reducing resistance during the counseling interview. *Educ. psychol. Measmt.* 9(1949):297–306.

DAY, R., and SPARACIO, R. Structuring the counseling process. *Pers. and Guid. J.* 59(1980):246–251.

DEABLER, H. L. The psychotherapeutic use of the

thematic apperception test. *J. clin. Psychol.* 8(1947):246–252.

DEL TORTO, J., and CORNYETZ, P. Psychodrama as an Expressive and Projection Technique. In: *Psychodrama Monograph #14,* ed. J. L. Moreno. Boston: Beacon Press, 1945.

DESPERT, J. L. *Children of Divorce.* New York: Doubleday, 1953.

DOLLARD, J., and MILLER, N. E. *Personality and Psychotherapy.* New York: McGraw-Hill, 1950.

DOLLARD, J., and MOWRER, O. H. A method of measuring tension in written documents. *J. abnorm. soc. Psychol.* 42(1947):3–33.

DREIKERS, R. *Challenge of Parenthood.* New York: Duell, Sloan, and Pearce, 1948.

DRESSEL, P. L., and MATTESON, R. W. The effect of client participation on test interpretation. *Educ. psychol. Measmt.* 10(1950):693–706.

DRIVER, H. I. *Multiple Counseling: A Small Group Discussion Method for Personal Growth.* Madison, WI: Monona, 1954.

D'ZURILLA, T., and GOLDFRIED, M. Problem solving and behavior modification. *J. abnorm. Soc. Psychol.,* 78(1971):107–126.

EASTON, H., and KRIPPNER, S. Disability, rehabilitation, and existentialism. *Pers. and Guid. J.* 43 (1964):230–234.

EDELWICH, J., and BRODSKY, A. *Burn-out.* New York: Research Press, 1980.

EHRLICH, R.; D'AUGELLI, A.; and DANISH, S. Comparative effectiveness of six counselor verbal responses. *J. counsel. Psychol.* 26(1979):390–398.

ELLIS, A. New approaches to psychotherapy. *J. clin. Psychol.,* Monograph Supplement. 11(1955).

ELLIS, A. A rational approach to interpretation. Paper delivered at a symposium for the American Psychological Association Convention, New York City, Sept. 1966.

ELLIS, A. Rational psychotherapy. *J. Gen. Psychol.* 59(1958):35–49.

ELLIS, A. *Reason and Emotion in Psychotherapy.* New York: Lyle Stuart, 1962.

ELLIS, A. Toward a more precise definition of emotional and intellectual insight. *Psychological Reports* 13(1963):125–126.

ELLIS, A. The treatment of a psychopath with rational psychotherapy, published in Italian, *Quaderni di Criminologia Clinica* 2(1949):1–11.

ENGLISH, H. B. The counseling situation as an obstacle to nondirective therapy. *J. consult. Psychol.,* 12(1948):217–222.

EPSTEIN, L. The therapeutic function of life in the countertransference. *Contemporary Psychoanalysis* 13(1977):442–461.

ERIKSON, E. H. *Identity and the Life Cycle.* New York: International Univ. Press, 1959.

EYSENCK, H. The effects of psychotherapy: an evaluation. *J. consult. Psychol.* 16(1952):319–324.

FARRELLY, F., and BRANDSMA J. *Provocative Therapy.* Cupertino, CA: Meta Publications, 1974.

FIEDLER, F. E. A comparison of psychoanalytic, nondirective, and Adlerian therapeutic relationships. *J. consult. Psychol.* 14(1950):436–445.

FIEDLER, F. E. The concept of an ideal therapeutic relationship, *J. consult. Psychol.* 14(1950):339–345.

FIEDLER, F. E. Method of objective quantification of certain countertransference attitudes. *J. clin. Psychol.* 7(1951):101–107.

FIEDLER, F. E., and SENIOR, K. An exploratory study of unconscious feeling reactions in fifteen patient-therapist pairs. *J. abnorm. soc. Psychol.* 47(1952):446–453.

FINE, S. A. A structure of worker function. *Pers. and Guid. J.* 34(1955):66–73.

FINNEY, B. C. Partnership psychotherapy: a new technique. Unpublished manuscript, San Jose State College, 1964.

FISCHER, J., and PAVEZA, G. The relationship between theoretical orientation and therapists' empathy, warmth, and genuineness. *J. counsel. Psychol.* 22(1975):399–403.

FIZDALE, R. A new look at fee charging. *Social Casework* 38(1957):60–65.

FORGY, E. W., and BLACK, J. D. A follow-up after three years of clients counseled by two methods. *J. counsel. Psychol.* 1(1954):1–8.

FORSTER, J. R. An investigation of the effects of two feedback methods when communicating psychological information. Ph.D. dissertation, University of Minnesota, 1966.

FOSTER, R. G. A point of view in marriage counseling. *J. counsel. Psychol.* 3(1956):210–216.

FRANCES, A. The DSM-III personality disorders section: a commentary. *Amer. J. Psychiat.* 9(1980):1050–1054.

FRANKL, V. E. *Ärtzliche Seelsorge.* Vienna: Franz Deuticke Verlog, 1946.

FRETZ, B. and MILLS, D. *Licensing and Certification of Psychologists and Counselors.* San Francisco: Jossey-Bass, 1980.

FRETZ, B., and WHITELEY, J. eds. *The Present and Future of Counseling Psychology.* Monterey, CA: Brooks/Cole, 1980.

FREUD, S. *A General Introduction to Psychoanalysis.* New York: Liveright, 1935.

FROMM, E. *The Art of Loving.* New York: Harper, 1956.

FROMM, E. *Escape from Freedom.* New York: Farrar and Rinehart, 1941.

FROMM, E. *Man for Himself.* New York: Farrar and Rinehart, 1947.

FROMM, E. Man is not a thing. *Saturday Review*, March 1957, pp. 9–11.

FROMM, E. *Psychoanalysis and Religion.* New Haven: Yale Univ. Press, 1950.

FROMM-REICHMANN, F. *Principles of Intensive Psychotherapy.* Chicago: Univ. of Chicago Press, 1950.

FRY, P., and CHARRON, P. Effects of cognitive style and counselor-client compatibility on client growth. *J. counsel. Psychol.* 27(1980):529–538.

FULLMER, D. *Counseling: Group Therapy and System.* Cranston, RI: Carroll Press, 1978.

GAMSKY, N. R., and FARWELL, G. F. Counselor verbal behavior as a function of client hostility. *J. counsel. Psychol.* 13(1966):184–190.

GARDNER, G. The psychotherapeutic relationship. *Psychol. Bull.* 61(1964):426–437.

GARDNER, J. *Self-Renewal.* New York: Harper & Row, 1965.

GARFIELD, S. *Psychotherapy: An Eclectic Approach.* New York: Wiley, 1979.

GARFIELD, S. Psychotherapy: a forty-year appraisal. *Amer. Psychologist* 36(1981):174–183.

GARFIELD, S. L., and KURTZ, R. Clinical psychologists: a survey of selected attitudes and views. *Clinical Psychologist* 28(1975):4–7.

GAZDA, G. *Group Counseling: A Developmental Approach.* New York: Allyn & Bacon, 1978.

GELATT, H. B. Decision-making: a conceptual frame of reference for counseling. *J. counsel. Psychol.* 9(1962):240–245.

GELATT, H., and BREW, S. *Teaching Personalized Decision-Making.* San Jose, CA: Santa Clara Superintendent of Schools, 1980.

GELSO, C. Gratification: a pivotal point in psychotherapy. *Psychotherapy, Research, and Practice* 16 (1979):276–281.

GENDLIN, E. *Experiencing and the Creation of Meaning.* New York: Free Press, 1962.

GENDLIN, E. *Focusing.* New York: Everest House, 1978.

GIBB, J. R. The effects of human relations training. In *Handbook of Psychotherapy and Behavior Change,* ed. A. E. Bergin and S. L. Garfield. New York: Wiley, 1970.

GIBB, J. R. Sensitivity training as a medium for personal growth and improved personal relationship. In *Encounter Groups: Basic Readings,* ed. G. Egan. Belmont, CA: Wadsworth, 1971.

GIBRAN, K. *The Prophet.* New York: Knopf, 1923.

GILBERT, W. M. and EWING, T. N. An investigation of the importance of the personal relationship and associated factors in teaching machine procedures. A study under Title VII of National Defense Education Act of 1958. Mimeographed. University of Illinois, 1965.

GILLAN, P., and RACHMAN, S. An experimental investigation of behavior therapy in phobic patients. *British Journal of Psychiatry* 124(1974):392.

GINZBERG, E. *Occupational Choice, an Approach to General Theory.* New York: Columbia Univ. Press, 1951.

GLADSTEIN, G. Empathy and counseling outcome: an empirical and conceptual review. *Counsel. Psychologist* 6(1977):70–77.

GLASSER, W. *Reality Therapy.* New York: Harper & Row, 1965.

GLATZER, H. The relative effectiveness of clinically homogeneous and heterogeneous psychotherapy groups. *Int. J. group Psychother.* 6(1956):258.

GLAZER, S. H. An open-ended questionnaire for pre-counseling orientation. *Vocational guid. Quart.* 5(1956):15–17.

GLOVER, E. *Freud or Jung.* New York: Norton, 1950.

GOLDFRIED, M. Toward the delineation of therapeutic change principles. *Amer. Psychologist* 35(1980): 991–999.

GOLDMAN, R. K., and MENDELSOHN, G. A. Psychotherapeutic change and social adjustment: a report of a national survey of psychotherapists. *J. abnorm. Psychol.* 74(1969):164–172.

GOLDSTEIN, K. *Human Nature in the Light of Psychopathology.* Cambridge: Harvard Univ. Press, 1940.

GONYEA, G. G. The ideal therapeutic relationship and counseling outcome. *J. clin Psychol.* 19(1963): 481–487.

GORDON, D. *Therapeutic Metaphors.* Cupertino, CA: Meta Publications, 1978.

GORDON, T. *Parent Effectiveness Training.* New York: Wiley, 1971.

GORHAM, D. R. Proverbs test. Missoula, MT: Psychological Test Specialists, 1954.

GOTTSEGAN, G., and GOTTSEGAN, M. Countertransference—the professional identity defense. *Psychotherapy: Theory, Research, and Practice.* 16 (1979).

GOUGH, H. *California Psychological Inventory.* Palo Alto, CA: Consulting Psychologist Press, 1952.

GRATER, H. A. Client preference for affective or cognitive counselor characteristics and first interview behavior. *J. counsel. Psychol.* 11(1964):248–250.

GRAVER, P. A. A study of counselors in selected industrial, education, and social service institutes. Ph.D. dissertation, Northwestern University, 1948.

GRAY, W. S. Gray oral reading paragraphs test. Bloomington, IL: Public School Publishing Co., 1923.

GREELEY, A. Personal communication, December 1970.

GREEN, A. W. Social values and psychotherapy. *J. Pers.* 14(1946):199–228.

GREENFIELD, S., ed. *National Directory of Addresses and Telephone Numbers.* New York: Nicholas, 1981.

GREENWALD, H. *Decision Therapy.* New York: Peter H. Wyden, 1973.

GROSSBERG, J. M. Behavior therapy. *Psychol. Bull.* 62(1964):73–88.

GROSSMAN, D. Ego-activating approaches to psychotherapy. *Psychoanalytic Rev.* 51(1964):65–88.

GRUMMON, D. L. Client-centered theory. In *Theories of Counseling*, ed. B. Stefflre. New York: McGraw-Hill, 1965.

GURMAN, A. Behavioral marriage therapy in the 1980s: the challenge of integration. *Amer. J. Family Therapy* 8(1980):86–96.

GUSTAD, J. W. The definition of counseling. In *Roles and Relationships in Counseling*, ed. R. F. Berdie. Minneapolis: Univ. of Minnesota Press, 1953.

GUSTAD, J. W. The evaluation interview in vocational counseling. *Pers. and Guid. J.* 36(1957):242–250.

HADLEY, S., and STRUPP, H. Contemporary views of negative side effects in psychotherapy. *Archives of General Psychiatry* 33(1976):1291–1302.

HAFNER, J., and MARKS, I. M. Exposure in vivo of agorophobics: the contributions of diazepam, group exposure, and anxiety evocation. *Psychological Medicine* 6(1976):71–88.

HAHN, M. E., and MCLEAN, M. S. *General Clinical Counseling.* New York: McGraw-Hill, 1950.

HAIGH, G. Defensive behavior in client-centered therapy. *J. consult. Psychol.* 13(1949):181–189.

HALEY, J. *Problem-solving Therapy.* San Francisco: Jossey-Bass, 1977.

HALEY, J. *Uncommon Therapy.* New York: Norton, 1973.

HALPERN, H. *Cutting Loose: An Adult Guide to Coming to Terms with Your Parents.* New York: Bantam, 1978.

HARLOW, H. F. Nature of love. *Amer. Psychologist,* 13(1958):673–685.

HATHAWAY, S. R., and MCKINLEY, J. C. *The Minnesota Multiphasic Personality Inventory.* New York: Psychological Corp., 1942.

HAVELOCK, R. G. *The Change Agent's Guide to Innovation in Education.* Englewood Cliffs, NJ: Educational Technology Publications, 1973.

HAVIGHURST, R. J. *Human Development and Education.* New York: Longmans, 1953.

HEINE, R. W. An investigation of the relationship between change in personality from psychotherapy as reported by patients and the factors seen by patients as producing change. Ph.D. dissertation, University of Chicago, 1950.

HELLER, K.; DAVIS, J. D.; and MYERS, R. A. The effects of interviewer style in a standardized interview. *J. consult. Psychol.* 30(1966):501–508.

HEPPNER, P. A review of the problem-solving literature and its relationship to the counseling process. *J. counsel. Psychol.* 25(1978):366–375.

HERZBERG, A. *Active Psychotherapy.* New York: Grune & Stratton, 1945.

HILL, C., and GORMALLY, J. Effects of reflection, restatement, probe, and nonverbal behaviors on client affect. *J. counsel. Psychol.* 24(1977):92–97.

HILL, C.; TANNEY, M.; LEONARD, M.; and REISS, J. Counselor reactions to female clients: type of problem, age of client, and sex of counselor. *J. counsel. Psychol.* 24(1977):60–65.

HILLS, D. A., and WILLIAMS, J. E. Effects of test information upon self-evaluation in brief educational-vocational counseling. *J. counsel. Psychol.* 12 (1965):275–281.

HINCKLEY, G., and HERMANN, L. *Group Treatment in Psychotherapy.* Minneapolis: Univ. of Minnesota Press, 1951.

HOBBS, N. Group-centered psychotherapy. In *Client-Centered Therapy*, ed. C. R. Rogers. Boston: Houghton Mifflin, 1951.

HOFF, L., and MILLER, W. *Marriage Enrichment: Philosophy, Process, and Program.* Bowie, MD: Charles Press, 1980.

HOLLAND, J. *A Counselor's Guide for the Self-Directed Search.* Palo Alto, CA: Consulting Psychologists Press, 1971.

HOLLAND, J. *Manual for the Vocational Preference Inventory.* 6th ed. Palo Alto, CA: Consulting Psychologists Press, 1965.

HOLLAND, J. *The Psychology of Vocational Choice.* Waltham, MA: Blaisdell Co., 1966.

HOLLAND, J. *The Self-Directed Search.* 3d ed. Palo Alto, CA: Consulting Psychologists Press, 1979.

HORNEY, K. *Neurosis and Human Growth.* New York: Norton, 1950.

HORNEY, K. *The Neurotic Personality of Our Time.* New York: Norton, 1937.

HORNEY, K. *Self-Analysis.* New York: Norton, 1942.

HOSFORD, R., and SORENSON, D. Participating in classroom discussions. Chap. 24 in J. Krumboltz, and C. Thoreson, eds. *Behavioral Counseling.* New York: Holt, Rinehart & Winston, 1969.

HOYT, D. P. College grades and adult achievement. *Ed. Rec.* 47(1966):70–75.

HUGHES, E. C. Psychology: science and/or profession. *Amer. Psychologist* 7(1952):441–443.

INGHAM, H. V., and LOVE, L. R. *The Process of Psychotherapy.* New York: McGraw-Hill, 1954.

IVEY, A. Cross-cultural counseling and psychotherapy: foundations, evaluation, and training. Paper delivered at University of Hawaii Conference on Cross-Cultural Counseling. Honolulu, Hawaii, June 1979.

IVEY, A. Cultural expertise: toward systematic outcome criteria in counseling and psychological education. *Pers. and Guid. J.* 55(1977):296–302.

444

IVEY, A., and AUTHIER, J. *Microcounseling*. 2d ed. Springfield, IL: Charles C Thomas, 1978.

IVEY, A., and GLUCKSTERN, N. *Basic Attending Skills: Participant Manual*. North Amherst, MA: Microtraining Associates, 1974.

IVEY, A., and GLUCKSTERN, N. *Basic Influencing Skills: Participant Manual*. North Amherst, MA: Microtraining Associates, 1976.

IVEY, A., and LEPPALUOTO, J. Changes ahead! Implications of the Vail Conference. *Pers. and Guid. J.* 53(1975):747–753.

IVEY, A., and SIMEK-DOWNING, L. *Counseling and Psychotherapy: Skills, Theories, and Practice*. Englewood Cliffs, NJ: Prentice-Hall, 1980.

JACOBSON, E. *Progressive Relaxation*. 2d ed. Chicago: Univ. of Chicago Press, 1938.

JACOBSON, N., and MARGOLIN, G. *Marital Therapy: Strategies Based upon Social Learning and Behavioral Exchange Principles*. New York: Brunner/Mazel, 1979.

JACQUES, E. The clinical use of the TAT with soldiers. *J. abnorm. soc. Psychol.* 4(1945):363–375.

JAHODA, M. *Current Concepts of Positive Mental Health*. New York: Basic Books, 1958.

JANOWITZ, M. Some obsrvations on the ideology of professional psychologists. *Amer. Psychologist* 9(1954):528–532.

JARVIK, L. *Aging into the 21st Century*. New York: Garden Press, 1978.

JOEL, W., and SHAPIRO, D. Some principles and procedures for group psychotherapy. *J. Psychol.* 29(1950):77–88.

JOHNSON, M., and RICHARDSON, M. *Models of Training Counselors of Women*. Mimeographed report of Division 17, Committee on Women Task Force on Training for Counseling Women (1981).

JOHNSON, W. *People in Quandaries*. New York: Harper, 1946.

JOSLIN, L. C. Knowledge and counseling competence. *Pers. and Guid. J.*, 43(1965):790–795.

JOURARD, S. M., and REMY, R. Perceived parental attitudes, the self and security. *J. consult. Psychol.* 19(1955):364–366.

JUNG, C. G. *Modern Man in Search of a Soul*. New York: Harcourt, Brace, 1933.

KAGAN, N. Issues in encounter. *Counsel. Psychologist* 2(1970): 43–50.

KAGAN, N. Presidential address to division of counseling psychology. *Counsel. Psychologist* 7(1977): 4–9.

KAPLAN, M. Uses of the group in gestalt therapy groups. *Psychotherapy: Theory, Research, and Practice* 15(1978):1.

KARPMAN, B. Objective psychotherapy. Clinical Psychology Monographs, *J. clin. Psychol.*, no. 6, 1960.

KATAHN, M., STRENGER S. and CHERRY, N. Group counseling and behavior therapy with test-anxious college students. *J. consult. Psychol.* 30 (1966):544–549.

KELLY, E. C. *Education for What is Real*. New York: Harper, 1947.

KELLY, G. A. *The Psychology of Personal Constructs*, vols. 1 and 2. New York: Norton, 1955.

KELLY, J. *Surviving the Break-Up: How Children and Parents Cope with Divorce*. (in press).

KIRKENDALL, L. A. Implications for college teaching of a concept of morality. Unpublished paper, Oregon State College.

KIRSH, C. The role of affect expression and defense in the character. Unpublished manuscript, 1973.

KLEIN, M. *The Psychoanalysis of Children*. New York: Hogarth, 1949.

KLOPFER, B. *Developments in the Rorschach Technique*, vol. 2. Yonkers, NY: World Book, 1956.

KNAPP, R. R., and FITZGERALD, O. R. Comparative validity for the Personal Orientation Inventory. *Educ. psychol. Measmt.* 33(1973):971–976.

KOESTER, G. A. A study of the diagnostic process. *Educ. psychol. Measmt.* 14(1954):473–486.

KOHLBERG, L. The contribution of developmental psychology to education; examples from moral education. *Educational Psychologist* 10(1973):2–14.

KOHLER, W. *The Mentality of Apes*. Translated by E. Winter. New York: Harcourt, 1925.

KORNER, I. N. Ego involvement and the process of disengagement. *J. consult. Psychol.* 14(1950): 206–209.

KRASNER, L., and ULLMANN, L. P. *Research in Behavior Modification*. New York: Holt, Rinehart & Winston, 1965.

KRUMBOLTZ, J. Behavioral goals for counseling. *J. counsel. Psychol.* 13(1966):153–159.

KRUMBOLTZ, J., and SHEPPARD, L. Vocational problem solving experiences. In *Behavioral Counseling*, eds. J. Krumboltz and C. Thoreson. New York: Holt, Rinehart & Winston, 1969.

KÜBLER-ROSS, E. *Death: The Final Stage of Growth*. Englewood Cliffs, NJ: Prentice-Hall, 1975.

KUNKEL, F. Growth through crises. In *Religion and Human Behavior*, ed. S. Doniger. New York: Association Press, 1954.

KUNKEL, F. *In Search of Maturity*. New York: Scribner, 1955.

LANGS, R. The adaptational-interactional dimensions of countertransference. *Contemporary Psychoanalysis* 14(1978):502–533.

LARSON, D. Therapeutic schools, styles, and schoolism: a national survey. *J. humanistic Psychol.* 20 (1980):3–20.

LAVELLE, J. A comparison of two interview styles in simulated crisis situations. *Counselor Education and Supervision* 18(1979):260–265.

LAYTON, W. L. Selection and counseling of students in engineering. *Minnesota Studies in Personnel Work, No. 4,* 1954.

LAZARUS, A. In support of technical eclecticism. *Psychological Reports* 21(1967):415–416.

LAZARUS, A. *Multi-Modal Behavior Therapy.* New York: Springer, 1976.

LAZARUS, R. Positive denial: the case for not facing reality. *Psychology Today* 17(1979):44–60.

LEARY, T. *Interpersonal Diagnosis of Personality.* New York: Ronald Press, 1957.

LEBO, D. The expressive value of toys recommended for nondirective play therapy. *J. clin. Psychol.* 11(1955):144–148.

LEE, A. M. Social pressures and the values of psychologists. *Amer. Psychologist* 9(1954):516–522.

LESSER, W. M. The relationship between counseling progress and empathic understanding. *J. counsel. Psychol.* 8(1961):330–336.

LEVINSON, D.; DARROW, C.; KLEIN, E.; LEVINSON, M.; and MC KEE, B. *The Seasons of a Man's Life.* New York: Knopf, 1978.

LEVITT, E. E. The inefficacy of therapeutic processes with children. *J. consult. Psychol.* 21(1957):189–196.

LEVY, L. H. *Psychological Interpretation.* New York: Holt, Rinehart & Winston, 1963.

LEWIN, K. *Principles of Topological Psychology.* New York: McGraw-Hill, 1936.

LEWIS, J., and LEWIS, M. *Community Counseling: A Human Services Approach.* New York: Wiley, 1976.

LIFTON, W. M. Counseling and the religious view of man. *Pers. and Guid. J.* 31(1953):366–367.

LIPKIN, S. Clients' feelings and attitudes in relation to the outcomes on client-centered therapy. *Psychol. Monogr.* 68(1954):372.

LIPSKY, M. M.; KASSINOVE, H.; and MILLER, N. Effects of rational-emotive therapy, rational role reversal, and rational-emotive imagery on the emotional adjustment of community mental health center patients. *J. consult. and clin. Psychol.* 3(1980):366–374.

LOESER, L. H. Some aspects of group dynamics. *Int. J. group Psychother.* 7(1957):5–19.

LONDON, P. *The Modes and Morals of Psychotherapy.* New York: Holt, Rinehart & Winston, 1964.

LOUGHARY, J.; FRIESEN, D.; and HURST, R. Autocoun: A computer-based automated counseling simulation system. *Pers. and Guid. J.* 45(1966):6–15.

LOUGHARY, J., and RIPLEY, T. *Helping Others Help Themselves.* New York: McGraw-Hill, 1979.

LOVEJOY, C. E. *Lovejoy's College Guide.* New York: Simon & Schuster, 1979.

LOWEN, A. *Betrayal of the Body.* New York: Macmillan, 1967.

LOWEN, A. *Training Manual in Bioenergetics.* Unpublished manuscript, 1972.

LUFT, J. Implicit hypotheses and clinical predictions. *J. abnorm. soc. Psychol.* 45(1950):756–759.

LURIA, A. *The Role of Speech in the Regulation of Normal and Abnormal Behavior.* New York: Liveright, 1961.

MCARTHUR, C. C. Analyzing the clinical process. *J. counsel. Psychol.* 1(1954):203–208.

MACE, D. Your marriage today. *Women's Home Companion,* April, 1956, pp. 29–33.

MACE, D., and MACE, V. Marriage enrichment—a preventive group approach for couples. In *Treating Relationships,* ed. D. Olson. Lake Miles, IA: Graphic Press, 1976.

MCGREGOR, R. Multiple impact therapy with families. *Family Process* 1(1962):15–29.

MCGREGOR, R.; RITCHIE, A. M.; SERRANO, A. C.; SHUSTER, F. P.; MCDONALD, E. C.; and GOOLISHIAN, H. A. *Multiple Impact Therapy With Families.* New York: McGraw-Hill, 1964.

MCHUGH, G. *The Sex Knowledge Inventory.* North Carolina: Duke Univ. Press, 1950.

Macmillan Information Division. *College Blue Book.* 17th ed. New York: Macmillan, 1979.

MADANES, C., and HALEY, J. Dimensions of family therapy. *J. of Nervous and Mental Disease* 165(1977):88–97.

MAGDEN, S., and SHOSTROM, E. Unpublished paper presented to annual meeting of American Psychological Association, New Orleans, 1974.

MAHLER, M., and RABINOVITCH, R. The effects of marital conflict on child development. In *Neurotic Interaction in Marriage,* ed. V. Eisenstein. New York: Basic Books, 1956.

MAHONEY, M. *Cognition and Behavior Modification.* Cambridge, MA: Ballinger, 1974.

MAHONEY, M. Cognitive and noncognitive views in behavior modification. In *Trends in Behavior Therapy,* eds. P. Sjoden and S. Bates. New York: Plenum Press, 1979.

MAHONEY, M. *Self-Change: Strategies for Solving Personal Problems.* New York: Norton, 1979.

MAHONEY, M., and THORESON, C. *Self-Control: Power to the Person.* Monterey: CA: Brooks/Cole, 1974.

MALAN, D. *The Frontier of Brief Psychotherapy.* New York: Plenum Press, 1976.

MANN, L. Persuasive doll play: a technique of directive psychotherapy for use with children. *J. clin. Psychol.* 13(1957):14–19.

MARKS, I. M. *Exposure Treatments: Behavior Modification* 2d ed. Boston: Little, Brown, 1978.

MASLACH, C. Burned out. *Human Behavior* 5(1976):74–78.

MASLACH, C. The client role in staff burnout. *J. of Social Issues* 34(1978):11–124.

MASLOW, A. H. *Motivation and Personality* 2d ed. New York: Harper & Row, 1970.

MASLOW, A. H. *The Psychology of Science*. New York: Harper & Row, 1966.

MASTERS, W. H., and JOHNSON, V. E. *The Pleasure Bond*. Boston: Little, Brown, 1974.

MAY, R. *The Art of Counseling*. New York: Abingdon-Cokesbury, 1939.

MAY, R. *Man's Search for Himself*. New York: Norton, 1953.

MAY, R. *Psychology and the Human Dilemma*. Princeton: Van Nostrand, 1967.

MAY, R. *Rollo May and Human Encounter*. Film. Santa Ana, CA: Psychological Films, 1969.

MAY, R.; ANGEL, F.; and ELLENBERGER, H. *Existence*. New York: Basic Books, 1958.

MEARA, N.; SHANNON, J.; and PEPINSKY, H. Comparison of the stylistic complexity of the language of counselor and client across three theoretical orientations. *J. counsel. Psychol.* 3(1979):181–189.

MEEHL, P. E. *Clinical Versus Statistical Prediction*. Minneapolis: Univ. of Minnesota, 1954.

MEEHL, P. E. The cognitive activity of the clinician. *Amer. Psychologist* 15(1960):19–27.

MEEHL, P. E. and others. *What, Then, is Man?* St. Louis: Concordia, 1958.

MEICHENBAUM, D. *Cognitive-Behavior Modifications: An Integrative Approach*. New York: Plenum Press, 1977.

MEICHENBAUM, D. Self-instructional training: a cognitive prosthesis for the ages. *Human Development* 17(1974):273–280.

MEICHENBAUM, D.; TURK, D.; and BURSTEIN, S. The nature of coping with stress. Paper presented at the NATO Conference on Stress and Anxiety, Korsor, Denmark, 1975.

MENDELSOHN, G. A. Effects of client personality and client-counselor similarity on the duration of counseling: a replication and extension. *J. counsel. Psychol.* 13(1966):228–234.

MENNINGER, K. *The Theory of Psychoanalytic Technique*, Menninger Clinical Monograph Series 12. New York: Basic Books, 1958.

MEYER, J.; STROWIG, W.; and HOSFORD, R. Behavioral reinforcement with rural high school youth. *J. counsel. Psychol.* 17(1970):127–132.

MICHAEL, J., and MEYERSON, L. A behavioral approach to counseling and guidance. *Harvard Educ. Rev.* 32(1962):382–402.

Michigan State University. *How to Make Referrals*. East Lansing, MI: Guidance and Counselor Training, College of Education, Michigan State University, 1956.

MICKELSON, D., and STEVIC, R. Differential effects of facilitative and nonfacilitative behavioral counselors. *J. counsel. Psychol.* 18(1971):127–132.

MILLER, D. The effects of immediate and delayed audio and videotaped feedback on group counseling. *Comparative Group Studies* 1(1970).

MINUCHIN, S. Conflict resolution in family therapy. In *Psychotherapy Research: Selected Readings*, ed. G. E. Stollak. Chicago: Rand McNally, 1966.

MINUCHIN, S. *Families and Family Therapy*. Cambridge, MA: Harvard Univ. Press, 1974.

MISCHEL, W. Toward a cognitive social learning reconceptualization of personality. *Psychol. Rev.* 80 (1973):252–283.

MITTELMANN, B. Analysis of reciprocal neurotic patterns in family relationships. In *Neurotic Interaction in Marriage*, ed. W. Eisenstein. New York: Basic Books, 1956.

MONTAGUE, A. *On Being Human*. New York: H. Schuman, 1950.

MONTAGUE, A. *Touching*. New York: Harper & Row, 1971.

MOONEY, R. L. *Mooney Problem Checklist*. New York: Psychological Corp., 1950.

MOORE, B. V., and BOUTHILET, L. The V. A. program for counseling psychologists. *Amer. Psychologist* 7(1952):684–685.

MORTON, R. B. A controlled experiment in psychotherapy based on Rotter's social learning theory of personality. Ph.D. dissertation, Ohio State University, 1949.

MORTON, R. B. An experiment in social psychotherapy. *Psychol. Monogr.* 69(1955):1–17.

MOUSTAKAS, C. E. *Children in Play Therapy*. New York: McGraw-Hill, 1953.

MOWRER, O. H. Anxiety theory as a basis for distinguishing between counseling and psychotherapy. In *Concepts and Programs of Counseling*, ed. R. Berdie. Minneapolis: Univ. of Minnesota Press, 1951.

MOWRER, O. H. *Learning Theory and Personality Dynamics*. New York: Ronald Press, 1950.

MOWRER, O. H. *The New Group Therapy*. Princeton, NJ: Van Nostrand, 1964.

MOWRER, O. H. Some philosophical problems in psychological counseling. *J. counsel. Psychol.* 4(1957):103–111.

MOWRER, O. H. Tension changes during psychotherapy with special reference to resistance. In *Psychotherapy: Theory and Research*, ed. O. Mowrer. New York: Ronald Press, 1953.

MUENCH, G. An investigation of the efficacy of time-limited psychotherapy. *J. counsel. Psychol.* 12(1965):294–298.

MURPHY, G. *Personality: A Biosocial Approach to Origins and Structure*. New York: Harper, 1947.

MUTHARD, J. E., and MILLER, L. A. *The criterion problem in rehabilitation counseling.* Iowa City: College of Education, 1966.

National Institute of Mental Health. Report of Research Task Force. "Research in the service of mental health." DHEW Pub. 75–236. Rockville, MD, 1975.

NYGREN, A. *Agape and Eros.* London: SPCK, 1953.

OATES, W. E. *The Christian Pastor.* Philadelphia: Westminster, 1951.

OPPENHEIMER, O. Some counseling theory: objectivity and subjectivity. *J. counsel. Psychol.* 1(1954):184–187.

OTTEN, J., and SHELLEY F. *When Your Parents Grow Old.* New York: New American Library, 1977.

OTTO, H., *Marriage and Family Enrichment: New Perspectives and Programs.* Nashville: Abingdon Press, 1976.

PACKER, J., and BAIN, J. Cognitive style. *J. educ. Psychol.* 70(1978):864–871.

PARHAM, W., and TINSLEY, H. What are friends for? Students' expectations of the friendship encounter. *J. counsel. Psychol.* 27(1980):524–527.

PATTERSON, C. H. Interest tests and the emotionally disturbed client. *Educ. psychol. Measmt.* 17(1957):264–280.

PEARSON, L., ed. *The Use of Written Communications in Psychotherapy.* Springfield, IL: Charles C Thomas, 1965.

PEPINSKY, H. B. Application of informal projective methods in the counseling interview. *Educ. psychol. Measmt.* 7(1947):135–140.

PEPINSKY, H. B. The selection and use of diagnostic categories in clinical counseling. *Appl. Psychol. Monogr.* 15(1948).

PEPINSKY, H. B., and PEPINSKY, P. N. *Counseling Theory and Practice.* New York: Ronald Press, 1954.

PERLS, F. *The Gestalt Approach and Eye Witness to Therapy.* Ben Lomand, CA: Science and Behavior Books, 1973.

PERLS, F. *Gestalt Therapy Verbatim.* Lafayette, CA: Real People Press, 1969.

PERLS, L. P.; GOODMAN, P.; and HEFFERLINE, H. *Gestalt Therapy—Excitement and Growth in Human Personality.* New York: Julian Press, 1951.

PETERSON, G., and BRADLEY, R. Counselor orientation and theoretical aptitudes toward counseling: historical perspective and new data. *J. counsel. Psychol.* 27(1980):554–560.

PETERSON, R., and DAVIS, G. *Education Directory: Colleges and Universities.* Washington, DC: National Center for Education Statistics, 1979–80.

PFEIFFER, J. W., and HESLIN, R. *Instrumentation in Human Relations Training.* San Diego: University Associates, 1973.

PHILLIPS, E. L. Attitudes toward self and others; a brief questionnaire report. *J. consult. Psychol.* 15(1951):79–81.

PHILLIPS, E. L. *Psychotherapy; a Modern Theory and Practice.* Englewood Cliffs, NJ: Prentice-Hall, 1956.

PHILLIPS, E. L., and AGNEW, J. W., JR. A study of Rogers' "reflection" hypothesis. *J. clin. Psychol.* 9(1953):281–284.

PICK, D. *Guidepak Workbook.* Palo Alto, CA: Behaviordyne, 1978.

PORTER, E. H., JR. *An Introduction to Therapeutic Counseling.* Boston: Houghton Mifflin, 1950.

PORTER, E. H., JR. Understanding Diagnostically and Understanding Therapeutically. In F. C. Williamson (ed), *Trends in Student Personnel Work.* Minneapolis: Univ. of Minnesota Press, (1949):113–19.

POSTMAN, L.; BRUNER, J. S.; and MCGINNIES, E. Personal values as selective factors in perception. *J. abnorm. soc. Psychol.* 43:(1948):142–154.

POWDERMAKER, F., and FRANK, J. *Group Psychotherapy.* Cambridge: Harvard Univ. Press, 1953.

PROGOFF, I. *At a Journal Workshop.* New York: Dialogue House Library, 1975.

RAIMY, V. *Misunderstanding of the Self.* San Francisco: Jossey-Bass, 1975.

RASKIN, A. Factors therapists associate with motivation to enter psychotherapy. *J. clin. Psychol.* 17(1961):62–65.

RASKIN, N. Studies on Psychotherapeutic Orientation. AAP Psychotherapy Research monograph. Orlando, FL: American Academy of Psychotherapy, 1974.

REDDY, W. B. On affection, group composition, and self-actualization in sensitivity training. *J. consult. and clin. Psychol.* 38(1972):211–214.

REDDY, W. B., and BEERS, T. Sensitivity training . . . and the healthy become self-actualized. *Small Group Behavior* 8(1977):525–531.

REID, D. K., and SNYDER, W. U. Experiment on "recognition of feeling" in non-directive psychotherapy. *J. clin. Psychol.* 3(1947):128–135.

REUSCH, J., and PRESTWOOD, A. R. Anxiety. *Arch. Neurol. Psychiat.* 62(1949):1–24.

RICHARDSON, H., and BOROW, H. Evaluation of technique of group orientation for vocational counseling. *Educ. psychol. Measmt.* 12(1952):587–597.

RIGGS, B. Resistance to transference—a general systems formulation. *J. of American Academy of Psychoanalysis* 5(1977):65–77.

RIPPEE, B. D.; HARVEY, W. E.; and PARKER, C. A. The influence of counseling on the perception of counselor role. *Pers. and Guid. J.* 43(1965):600–606.

ROBINSON, F. P. Modern approach to counseling diagnosis. *J. counsel. Psychol.* 10(1963):325–333.

ROBINSON, F. P. *Principles and Procedures in Student Counseling.* New York: Harper, 1950.

ROBINSON, M. A study of the effects of focused video-taped feedback in group counseling. *Comparative Group Studies* 1(1970):47–77.

ROE, A. *The Psychology of Occupations.* New York: Wiley, 1956.

ROGERS, C. R. *Becoming a Person.* Oberlin, OH: Board of Trustees, Oberlin College, 1954.

ROGERS, C. R. *Client-Centered Therapy.* Boston: Houghton Mifflin, 1951.

ROGERS, C. R. *Counseling and Psychotherapy.* Boston: Houghton Mifflin, 1942.

ROGERS, C. R. *Counseling with Returned Service Men.* New York: McGraw-Hill, 1946.

ROGERS, C. R. The fully functioning personality. Unpublished paper.

ROGERS, C. R. The increasing involvement of the psychologist in social problems. *California State Psychologist* 9(1968):29.

ROGERS, C. R. *On Becoming a Person.* Boston: Houghton Mifflin, 1961.

ROGERS, C. R. A personal view of some issues facing psychologists. *Amer. Psychologist* 10(1955):247–249.

ROGERS, C. R. Persons or science? A philosophical question. *Amer. Psychologist* 10(1955):267–278.

ROGERS, C. R. A process conception of psychotherapy. *Amer. Psychologist* 13(1958):142–149.

ROGERS, C. R. Some directions and end points in therapy. In *Psychotherapy: Theory and Research,* ed. O. H. Mowrer. New York: Ronald Press, 1953.

ROGERS, C. R. A therapist's view of the good life. *The Humanist* 5(1957):291–300, American Humanist Association, Yellow Springs, OH.

ROGERS, C. R., and DYMOND, R. F. *Psychotherapy and Personality Change.* Chicago: Univ. of Chicago Press, 1954.

ROTTER, J. B. *Social Learning and Clinical Psychology.* Englewood Cliffs, NJ: Prentice-Hall, 1954.

RUCH, F. L. *Psychology and Life.* Chicago: Scott, 1948.

RUSALEM, H. New insights on the role of occupational information in counseling. *J. counsel. Psychol.* 1(1954):84–88.

RUSH, A. J.; BECK, A. T.; KOVACS, M.; and HOLLON, S. Comparative efficacy of cognitive therapy and pharmacotherapy in the treatment of depressed outpatients. *Cognitive Therapy and Research* 1(1977):17–37.

RUSK, T. Opportunity and technique in crisis psychiatry. *Comprehensive Psychiatry* 12(1971):249–263.

RYAN, T. A., and KRUMBOLTZ, J. Effect of planned reinforcement counseling on client decision making behavior. *J. counsel. Psychol.* 11(1964):315–323.

SALTER, A. *Conditioned Reflex Therapy.* New York: Capricorn Books, 1961.

SANFORD, N. *Self and Society.* New York: Atherton, 1966.

SARASON, I. Verbal learning modeling and juvenile delinquency. *Amer. Psychologist* 23(1968):254–266.

SATIR, V. *Conjoint Family Therapy.* Palo Alto, CA: Science and Behavior Books, 1966.

SATIR, V. *Peoplemaking.* Palo Alto, CA: Science and Behavior Books, 1972.

SATIR, V. *Target Five.* 16mm. film. Santa Ana, CA: Psychological Films, 1967.

SAWIN, M. *Family Enrichment Through Family Clusters.* Valley Forge, PA: Judson Press, 1979.

SCHLOSSBERG, N.; TROLL, L.; and LEIBOWITZ, Z. *Perspectives on Counseling Adults: Issues and Skills.* Monterey, CA: Brooks/Cole, 1978.

SCHMIDT, H. O., and FONDA, C. P. The reliability of psychiatric diagnosis: a new look. *J. abnorm. soc. Psychol.* 52(1956):262–267.

SCHMIDT, L., and STRONG, S. Attractiveness and influence in counseling. *J. counsel. Psychol.* 18(1971):348–351.

SCHULDT, J. W. Psychotherapists' approach-avoidance responses and clients' expressions of dependency. *J. counsel. Psychol.* 13(1966):178–183.

SCHUTZ, W. C. *Elements of Encounter.* New York: Bantam, 1975.

SCHUTZ, W. C. *Here Comes Everybody.* New York: Harper & Row, 1971.

SCHWEBEL, M. Learning and the socially deprived. *Pers. and Guid. J.* 43(1965):646–653.

SCHWEBEL, M. Why unethical practice? *J. counsel. Psychol.* 2(1955):122–127.

SEEMAN, W.; NIDICH, S.; and BANTA, T. Influence of transcendental meditation on a measure of self-actualization. *J. counsel. Psychol.* 19(1972):184–187.

SEEMAN, J. A., and others. A coordinated research in psychotherapy. *J. consult. Psychol.* 13(1949):154–195.

SHAW, F. J. Some postulates concerning psychotherapy. *J. consult. Psychol.* 12(1939):426–432.

SHAW, R. *Finger Painting.* Boston: Little, Brown, 1934.

SHEEHY, G. *Passages: Predictable Crises of Adult Life.* New York: Dutton, 1976.

SHERMAN, D. An analysis of the dynamic relationships between counselor techniques and outcomes in larger units of the interview situation. Ph.D. dissertation, Ohio State University, 1945.

SHOBEN, E. J. Psychotherapy as a problem in learning theory. *Psychol. Bull.* 46(1949):366–392.

SHOBEN, E. J. Special review: Some recent books on counseling and adjustment. *Psychol. Bull.* 52(1955):251–262.

SHOBEN, E. J. Work, love and maturity. *Pers. and Guid. J.* 34(1956):326–332.

SHOSTROM, E. L. *Caring Relationship Inventory.* San Diego: EDITS, 1966.

SHOSTROM, E. L. *Man, the Manipulator.* New York: Bantam, 1968.

SHOSTROM, E. L. *Personal Orientation Inventory.* San Diego: EDITS, 1963.

SHOSTROM, E. L. *Three Approaches to Group Therapy.* 16 mm color films. Santa Ana, CA: Psychological Films, 1974.

SHOSTROM, E. L. *Three Approaches to Psychotherapy.* Films of Rogers, Perls, and Ellis. Santa Ana, CA: Psychological Films, 1966.

SHOSTROM, E. L. *Touching: Importance for Human Growth.* Film. Santa Ana, CA: Psychological Films, 1974.

SHOSTROM, E. L., and BRAMMER, L. M. *The Dynamics of the Counseling Process.* New York: McGraw-Hill, 1952.

SHOSTROM, E. L., and FERRY, N. W. *The Actualization Group.* Series of 16 mm films. Santa Ana, CA: Psychological Films, 1968.

SHOSTROM, E. L.; KNAPP, L.; and KNAPP, R. *Actualizing Therapy: Foundations for a Scientific Ethic.* San Diego: EDITS, 1976.

SHOSTROM, E. L., and LOCKWOOD, G. *Growth Process Inventory.* San Diego, CA: EDITS, 1980.

SHOSTROM, E. L., and MONTGOMERY, D. In *Innovative Psychotherapies,* ed. R. Corsini. New York: Wiley, 1981.

SHOSTROM, E. L., and RILEY, C. M. D. Parametric analysis of psychotherapy. *J. consult. and clin. Psychol.* 32(1968):628–632.

SHRODES, C., ed. *Psychology through Literature, an Anthology.* New York: Oxford, 1943.

SIFNEOS, P. *Short-term Psychotherapy and Emotional Crisis.* Cambridge, MA: Harvard Univ. Press, 1972.

SIMONTON, C., and SIMONTON, S. *Getting Well Again.* Los Angeles: J. P. Tarcher, 1978.

SINGER, J. *Imagery and Daydream Methods in Psychotherapy.* New York: Academic Press, 1974.

SKIDMORE, R. A., and others. *Marriage Consulting.* New York: Harper, 1956.

SKIDMORE, R. A., and GARRETT, H. Joint interview in marriage counseling. *Marriage and Family Living* 17(1955):320–324.

SKINNER, B. F. *Science and Human Behavior.* New York: Macmillan, 1953.

SLAVSON, S. R. *Analytic Group Psychotherapy with Children, Adolescents and Adults.* New York: Columbia Univ. Press, 1950.

SLAVSON, S. R. *The Practice of Group Psychotherapy.* New York: International Univ. Press, 1947.

SMALL, L. *The Briefer Psychotherapies.* New York: Brunner/Mazel, 1971.

SMITH, H. L. The value context of psychology. *Amer. Psychologist* 9(1954):532–535.

SNYGG, D., and COMBS, A. W. *Individual Behavior: A New Frame of Reference for Psychology.* New York: Harper, 1949.

SOROKIN, P. A. *Explorations in Altruistic Love and Behavior.* Boston: Beacon Press, 1950.

SPEER, G. S., and JASPER, L. The influence of occupational information on occupational goals. *Occupations* 28(1949):15–17.

SPITZ, R. A. Role of ecological factors in emotional development of infants. *Child Devel.* 76(1949):145–146.

STAMPFL, T. G. Implosive therapy: the theory, the subhuman analogue, the strategy, and the technique, Part I, the theory. In *Behavior Modification Techniques in the Treatment of Emotional Disorders,* ed. S. G. Armitage. Battle Creek, MI: Veterans Administration Publication, 1967.

STEIN, M., and STONE, G. Effects of conceptual level and structure on initial interview behavior. *J. counsel. Psychol.* 25(1978):96–102.

STENSRUD, R., and STENSRUD, K. Counseling may be hazardous to your health: how we teach people to be powerless. *Pers. and Guid. J.* 60(1981):71–79.

STEWART, N. Exploring and processing information. Chap. 26 in *Behavioral Counseling,* eds. J. Krumboltz and C. Thoreson. New York: Holt, Rinehart & Winston, 1969.

STEWART, N.; WONBORN, B.; JOHNSON, R.; BURKS, H.; and ENGELKES, J. *Systematic Counseling.* Englewood Cliffs, NJ: Prentice-Hall, 1978.

STONE, C. H. Are vocational orientation courses worth their salt? *Educ. psychol. Measmt.* 8(1948):161–181.

STRONG, E. K. *Vocational Interests Eighteen Years After College.* Minneapolis: Univ. of Minnesota Press, 1955.

STRONG, E. K. *Vocational Interests of Men and Women.* Stanford, CA: Stanford Univ. Press, 1943.

STRONG, E. K., and CAMPBELL, D. E. *Strong-Campbell Interest Inventory.* Palo Alto, CA: Consulting Psychologists Press, 1977.

STRONG, S., and SCHMIDT, L. Expertness and influence in counseling. *J. counsel. Psychol.* 17(1970):81–87.

STRUPP, H. H. The outcome problem in psychotherapy revisited. *Psychotherapy: Theory, Research, and Practice.* 1(1963):1–13.

SUE, D. Cross-cultural counseling competencies. A position paper presented to Division of Counseling Psychology, January, 1981. Mimeographed.

SUE, D., and SUE, S. Barriers to effective cross-cultural

counseling. *J. counsel. Psychol.* 24(1977):420–429.

SUE, S. Counseling the culturally different. *Pers. and Guid. J.* 55(1977):422–425.

SULLIVAN, H. S. *The Interpersonal Theory of Psychiatry.* New York: Norton, 1953.

SULLIVAN, H. S. *The Psychiatric Interview.* New York: Norton, 1954.

SUNDBERG, N. D., et al. *Clinical Psychology,* 2nd ed. Englewood Cliffs, NJ: Prentice-Hall, 1973.

SUNDLAND, D. Theoretical orientations of psychotherapists. In *The Therapist's Contribution to Effective Psychotherapy: An Empirical Assessment,* eds. A. Gurman and A. Kazin. Elmsford, NY: Pergamon Press, 1977.

SUPER, D. *Computer-Assisted Counseling.* New York: Teachers College Press, 1970.

SUPER, D. E. Career patterns as a basis for vocational counseling. *J. counsel. Psychol.* 1(1954):12–19.

SUPER, D. E. Transition from vocational guidance to counseling psychology. *J. counsel. Psychol.* 2(1955):3–9.

SUPER, D. E. Vocational adjustment: implementing a self concept. *Occupations* 30(1951):88–92.

SYMONDS, P. M. *Dynamics of Psychotherapy,* vol. 2. New York: Grune & Stratton, 1957.

SZASZ, T. S. The myth of mental illness. *Amer. Psychologist* 15(1960):113–118.

TART, C. *Transpersonal Psychologies.* New York: Harper & Row, 1975.

THOMPSON, A. S., and SUPER, D. E. *The Professional Preparation of Counseling Psychologists.* New York: Bureau of Publications, Columbia Univ., 1964.

THORESON, C. The counselor as an applied behavioral scientist. *Pers. and Guid. J.* 47(1969):841–848.

THORESON, C., and MAHONEY, M. *Behavioral Self-Control.* New York: Holt, Rinehart & Winston, 1974.

THORNE, F. C. Principles of personality counseling. Brandon, VT: Clinical Psychology Monograph, 1950.

THORNE, F. C. Principles of psychological examining. Clinical Psychology Monograph. *J. clin. Psychol.* (1955).

TINDALL, R. H., and ROBINSON, F. P. The use of silence as a technique in counseling. *J. clin. Psychol.* 3(1947):136–141.

TINSLEY, H., and HARRIS, D. Client expectations for counseling. *J. counsel. Psychol.* 23(1976):173–177.

TINSLEY, H.; WORKMAN, K.; and KASS, R. Factor analysis of the domain of client expectancies about counseling. *J. counsel. Psychol.* 27(1980):561–570.

TRUAX, C. B. Effective ingredients in psychotherapy. *J. counsel. Psychol.* 10(1963):256–263.

TRUAX, C. B., and CARKHUFF, R. R. The old and the new: theory and research in counseling and psychotherapy. *Pers. and Guid. J.* 42:(1964):860–866.

TYLER, L. E. *The Work of the Counselor.* 3d ed. Englewood Cliffs, NJ: Prentice-Hall, Inc., 1969.

U.S. Department of Education. *Annual Report.* Washington, DC: U.S. Government Printing Office, 1963.

U.S. Employment Service. *Dictionary of Occupational Titles.* 3d ed. Washington, DC: U.S. Government Printing Office, 1965.

U.S. Government Occupational Outlook Service. *Occupational Outlook Handbook.* Washington, DC: U.S. Government Printing Office, 1977.

U.S. Office of Education. *Computer-Based Vocational Guidance Systems.* OE 25053. Washington, DC: U.S. Government Printing Office, 1969.

VOLSKY, T.; MAGOON, T.; NORMAN, W.; and HOYT, D. *The Outcomes of Counseling and Psychotherapy.* Minneapolis: Univ. of Minnesota Press, 1965.

VYGOTSKY, L. *Thought and Language.* Cambridge, MA: MIT Press, 1962.

WAGMAN, M. Plato, DSC: An interactive computer system for personal counseling. *J. counsel. Psychol.* 27(1980):16–30.

WALKER, J. L. Four methods of interpreting test scores compared. *Pers. and Guid. J.* 44(1965):402–404.

WAREHEIM, R. G.; ROUTH, D. K.; and FOULDS, M. L. Knowledge about self-actualization and the presentation of self as self-actualized. *J. pers. and soc. Psychol.* 30(1974):155–162.

WARNER, W. L.; MEEKER, M.; and ELLS, K. *Social Class in America.* Chicago: Science Research Associates, 1949.

WATSON, R. I. *The Clinical Method in Psychology.* New York: Harper, 1951.

WATSON, R. I. *Psychology as a Profession.* New York: Random House, 1954.

WEINER, I. B. The role of diagnosis in a university counseling center. *J. counsel. Psychol.* 6(1959):110–115.

WEINRACH, S. *Career Counseling: Theoretical and Practical Perspectives.* New York: McGraw-Hill, 1979.

WHITE, R. W. *The Abnormal Personality.* 2d ed. New York: Ronald Press, 1956.

WHITE, V. *God and the Unconscious.* Chicago: Henry Regnery, 1953.

WICKES, F. *The Inner World of Childhood.* Englewood Cliffs, NJ: Prentice-Hall, 1978.

WILLIAMSON, E. G. Counseling and the Minnesota point of view. *Educ. psychol. Measmt.* 7(1947):141–156.

WILLIAMSON, E. G. *How to Counsel Students.* New York: McGraw-Hill, 1939.

WINDER, L. Group psychotherapy. In *Group Psychother-*

apy—A Symposium, ed. J. L. Moreno. New York: Beacon Press, 1945.

WINNICOTT, D. W. Hate in the countertransference. *Int. J. Psychoanal.* 30(1949):69–74.

WOLLERSHEIM, J.; MCFALL, M.; HAMILTON, S.; HICKEY, C; and BORDEWICK, M. Effects of treatment rationale and problem severity on perceptions of psychological problems and counseling approaches. *J. counsel. Psychol.* 27(1980):225–231.

WOLPE, J. *Psychotherapy by Reciprocal Inhibition.* Stanford, CA: Stanford Univ. Press, 1958.

WOOD, A. B. Transference in client-centered therapy and in psychoanalysis. *J. consult. Psychol.* 15(1951):72–75.

WRENN, C. G. Psychology, religion, and values for the counselor, Part III, in the symposium, the counselor and his religion. *Pers. and Guid. J.* 36(1958):326–334.

WULF, F. Uber die Veränderung von Vorstellangen. *Psychol. Forsch.* 1(1922):333–373.

WYSKOFF, H., ed. *Love Therapy and Politics.* New York: Grove Press, 1976.

YALOM, I. *The Theory and Practice of Group Psychotherapy.* 2d ed. New York: Basic Books, 1975.

YALOM, I. D.; LIEBERMAN, M. A.; and MILES, M. M. A study of encounter group casualties. *Archives of General Psychiatry* 25(1971):16–30.

YAMAMOTO, K. Counseling psychologists—who are they? *J. counsel. Psychol.* 10(1963):211–221.

ZARLE, T., and BOYD, R. An evaluation of modeling and experiential procedures for self-disclosure training. *J. counsel. Psychol.* 24(1977):118–124.

ZELEN, S. L. Acceptance and acceptability. *J. consult. Psychol.* 18(1954):316.

ZIMET, C. N. Developmental task and crisis groups: the application of group psychotherapy to maturational processes. *Psychotherapy: Theory, Research, and Practice* 14(1979):2–8.

ZWETSCHKE, C. T., and GRENFELL, J. E. Family group consultation: a description and a rationale. *Pers. and Guid. J.* 43(1965):974–980.

ZYTOWSKI, D. The study of therapy outcomes via experimental analogs: a review. *J. counsel. Psychol.* 13(1966):235–241.

For Further Help

The following films, produced or distributed by Dr. Everett L. Shostrom, are available from Psychological Films, Inc., 110 N. Wheeler Street, Orange, California 92669. (Catalogs with prices are available upon request.) To assist instructors, each film is keyed to the chapter to which it is most relevant.

CHAPTER 2: THEORETICAL FOUNDATIONS OF THERAPEUTIC PSYCHOLOGY

The Humanistic Revolution: Pioneers in Perspective. 16mm. Black and white. 32 minutes.
Interviews with the leaders of the "unnoticed revolution" in psychology, including Abraham Maslow, Gardner Murphy, Carl Rogers, Rollo May, Paul Tillich, Frederick Perls, Viktor Frankl, and Alan Watts.

Search and Research: Psychology in Perspective. 16mm. Black and white. 30 minutes.
Through the medium of a story of a young lady seeking psychotherapy, this film attempts to describe the three forces in psychology: experimental, psychoanalytic, and existential (or humanistic). Intimate visits are provided with three prominent psychologists: Harry Harlow, Rollo May, and Carl Rogers.

Actualizing Therapy: An Integration of Rogers, Perls, and Ellis. 16mm. Color. 30 minutes.
Sequences from the film series *Three Approaches to Psychotherapy* illustrate the work of Carl Rogers, Frederick Perls, and Albert Ellis. Following the sequences, Everett L. Shostrom analyzes the three styles and describes his integration of these approaches into a working unity.

Defensive and Supportive Climates. 16mm. Color. 30 minutes.
An interview with Dr. Jack Gibb, industrial psychologist, by Dr. William Banks, University of Louisville. Dramatizations show contrast between defensive versus supportive counseling.

Reflections. 16mm. Color. Two films. 30 minutes each.
Warren Bennis interviews Carl Rogers. Rogers describes his theories and how they were formed.

Maslow and Self-Actualization, Film no. 1. 16mm. Color. 30 minutes.
Abraham Maslow discusses honesty and awareness as dimensions of self-actualization and elaborates on recent research and theory related to each.

Maslow and Self-Actualization, Film no. 2. 16 mm. Color. 30 minutes.
A continuation of the previous film. Maslow discusses self-actualization in terms of the dimensions of freedom and trust, and examines recent research and theory related to them.

Transactional Analysis: Group Therapy. 16 mm. Color. 32 minutes.
A demonstration of Transactional Analysis group therapy by internationally known Dr. Murial James.

CHAPTER 3: ACTUALIZING COUNSELING AND PSYCHOTHERAPY: A MULTIDIMENSIONAL VIEW

Childhood. The Enchanted Years. 16 mm. Color. 52 minutes.
The studies of Jerome Bruner, Burton White, Jerome Kagan, Wanda Bronson, Jean Block, and others are highlighted as the growing process is shown from a child's eye view. In candid detail, the film shows how children—from infancy to age four—learn to reach, perceive, walk, and talk.

Rollo May and Human Encounter: Self-Self Encounter and Self-Other Encounter. 16 mm. Color. 30 minutes.
May describes the human dilemma as having to see ourselves as both subject and object in life, and discusses the four elements of human encounter: empathy, eros, friendship, and agape.

Rollo May and Human Encounter: Manipulation and Human Encounter—Exploitation of Sex. 16 mm. Color. 30 minutes.
May discusses how the individual is manipulated when any of the four elements of human encounter is missing, the problem of transference in psychotherapy as a distortion of human encounter, and the modern human being's fixation on sexuality as related to fear of death.

Touching: Importance for Human Growth. 16 mm. Color. 29 minutes.
A conversation with Ashley Montagu on the key concepts of his recent work, *Touching*. Utilizing psychological research and medical opinion, Montagu develops the case that touching is necessary for human life.

A Time for Every Season. 16 mm. Color. 36 minutes.
Dr. Everett Shostrom explains that the four polarities of actualizing therapy strongly resemble winter, summer, spring, and fall. From our macrocosmic mirror in nature, we can gain a sense of our own microcosmic rhythm.

CHAPTER 4: THE PROCESS OF COUNSELING AND PSYCHOTHERAPY

Target Five, Film no. 1. 16 mm. Color. 26 minutes.
Virginia Satir and Everett L. Shostrom discuss the four manipulative response forms, which are then demonstrated by simulated family situations.

Target Five, Film no. 2. 16 mm. Color. 22 minutes.
Satir and Shostrom describe the three essential qualities of an actualizing relationship, which are then demonstrated.

Three Approaches to Psychotherapy I: Part One—Dr. Carl Rogers. 16 mm. Color and black and white. 48 minutes.
Following a general introduction to this film series and a description of Client-Centered Therapy, Rogers conducts a therapy session with the patient, "Gloria."

Three Approaches to Psychotherapy I: Part Two—Dr. Frederick Perls. 16 mm. Color and black and white. 32 minutes.
After a description of Gestalt Therapy, Perls interviews "Gloria" and presents a summation of the interview.

Three Approaches to Psychotherapy I: Part Three—Dr. Albert Ellis. 16 mm. Color and black and white. 38 minutes.
This film presents a description of Rational-Emotive Psychotherapy as well as Ellis's interview with "Gloria" and his summation. "Gloria" is also seen giving an evaluation of her experiences with the three therapists.

Three Approaches to Psychotherapy II: Part One—Dr. Carl Rogers. 16 mm. Color. 48 minutes.
Technique: Client-Centered Therapy. Second of a series—preceded by the famous "Gloria" films.
Dr. Rogers with Kathy. She experiences Dr. Rogers as fatherly and comfortable and is enabled by her work with him to open up and freely have a catharsis.

Three Approaches to Psychotherapy II: Part Two—Dr. Everett Shostrom. 16 mm. Color. 48 minutes.
Technique: Actualizing Therapy.
Kathy felt challenged through Shostrom's work with thinking, feeling, and bioenergetic techniques and sees this as a "working session."

Three Approaches to Psychotherapy II: Part Three—Dr. Arnold Lazarus. 16 mm. Color. 48 minutes. Technique: Multimodal Behavior Therapy.

When going through the "BASIC ID," Kathy experiences Lazarus as employing a "doing" approach to therapy.

Lowen and Bioenergetic Therapy. 16 mm. Color. 48 minutes.

Alexander Lowen describes the key ideas of bioenergetic therapy and demonstrates them in his work with a young female patient.

Manipulation and Actualization. 16 mm. Color. 30 minutes.

A description of manipulation and actualization through dramatization. Produced by Dr. William Banks, University of Louisville. Interview with Dr. Shostrom.

Frederick Perls and Gestalt Therapy. Two-film series. 16 mm. Black and white. Film no. 1: 39 minutes; film no. 2: 36 minutes.

Comprehensive overview films on Gestalt Therapy, representing the latest and best summary of Frederick Perls's theories.

In the Now. 16 mm. Black and white. 45 minutes.

Three segments from a ten-hour workshop conducted by James S. Simkin, demonstrating the individual application of Gestalt Therapy techniques with three different persons. Subject matter includes work with a dream, an incident of the recent past, and a current interaction—all in the "here and now."

CHAPTER 11: GROUP PRINCIPLES AND METHODS

Encounter: To Make a Start. 16 mm or videocassette. Black and white. 31 minutes.

Documentation of a day-long workshop-encounter session, conducted by Joel Fort and Sara Miller, between seven policemen and seven young people, most of whom described themselves as revolutionaries.

A Conversation with Carl Rogers. 16 mm. Black and white. 30 minutes.

In conversation with Keith Berwick, Rogers comments on his own Client-Centered Therapy, humanistic psychology, his own affinity for a phenomenological approach to human beings, the worth of encounter or sensitivity groups, and many other topics.

The Actualization Group. Seven-film series. 16 mm. Black and white. Approximately 45 minutes each.

This series follows one group through seven sequential sessions of therapy with Everett L. Shostrom and Nancy W. Ferry. Each session focuses on a different general theme: "Risking Being Ourselves," "Freedom and Actualiza-

tion," "Aggression and Actualization," "Manipulation and Actualization," "The Divorce from Parents," "Self-Disclosure of the Therapist," and "From Deadness to Aliveness."

Gestalt Dream Interpretation (Formerly *A Session with College Students*). 16 mm. Black and white. 60 minutes.

Frederick Perls demonstrates his method for discovering and expressing the meaning of dreams.

Three Approaches to Group Therapy. Three-film series. 16 mm. Color. Film no. 1: 38 minutes; film no. 2: 40 minutes; film no. 3: 38 minutes.

In these films, Everett Shostrom (film no. 1), Albert Ellis (film no. 2), and Harold Greenwald (film no. 3) use a group setting to demonstrate Actualizing Therapy approaches, Rational-Emotive Therapy approaches, and Decision Therapy approaches, respectively.

Two Faces of Group Leadership. 16 mm. Color. 30 minutes.

Skilled counselors, under the direction of Dr. Marilyn Bates, apply group leadership under real conditions. Two basic functions are demonstrated: mobilizing and managing.

Focusing: 16 mm. Color. 30 minutes.

A demonstration of the principles of focusing in counseling and therapy by the originator, Dr. Eugene Gendlin.

CHAPTER 12: COUNSELING AND PSYCHOTHERAPY WITH COUPLES AND FAMILIES

Between Man and Woman. 16 mm. Color. 33 minutes.

In conversation with Howard Miller, Everett L. Shostrom discusses various marital roles people play. Professional actors demonstrate modes of reacting.

CHAPTER 14: COUNSELING AND HUMAN VALUES

Frankl and the Search for Meaning. 16 mm. Color. 30 minutes.

Viktor Frankl describes the search for meaning as a form of "height" psychology, as opposed to Freudian theory, which he describes as "depth" psychology. Frankl says that, in the continuous growth toward self-actualization, we discover new meanings for ourselves. He describes meaning as a form of personalized valuing that each of us must have in order to make life meaningful.

Index